Patterns of Sexual Arousal

Patterns of Sexual Arousal

Psychophysiological Processes and Clinical Applications

RAYMOND C. ROSEN
University of Medicine and Dentistry of New Jersey
Robert Wood Johnson Medical School

and

J. GAYLE BECK
University of Houston

FOREWORD BY JAMES H. GEER

THE GUILFORD PRESS
New York   London

To my boys, Joshua and Michael.—R. C. R.

To my grandmother, Mary Ellen Gayle.—J. G. B.

© 1988 The Guilford Press
A Division of Guilford Publications, Inc.
72 Spring Street, New York, NY 10012

Printed in the United States of America

Last digit is print number: 9 8 7 6 5 4 3 2 1

Library of Congress Cataloging-in-Publication Data

Rosen, Raymond, 1946–
   Patterns of sexual arousal.

   Includes bibliographies and index.
   1. Sex (Psychology)   2. Psychology, Physiological.
I. Beck, J. Gayle.   II. Title.   [DNLM: 1. Psycho-
physiology.   2. Sex.   3. Sex Behavior.   BF 692 R8125p]
QP251.R626   1988   155.3   87-19726
ISBN 0-89862-712-5

Foreword

When I was first asked to serve as a reviewer of a textbook on sexual psychophysiology, I had some reservations as to whether or not the field was ready for such a book. It seemed to me that the study of human sexuality using the methodologies of the psychophysiologist was too new to have provided sufficient material for a text. I am pleased to report that I was in serious error. The field has grown so rapidly that the problem is one of appropriate selectivity rather than paucity of content. Rosen and Beck have written a text that not only is comprehensive in content but also pulls together in a cohesive manner what has become, in a surprisingly short time, a field of considerable breadth.

As I read the book the first thing that struck me was the scholarship it demonstrated. A great deal of time and effort have gone into a detailed examination and evaluation of the germane literature, including the identification and incorporation into the work of studies which, although not well known, are directly relevant. In writing what will be the first comprehensive collection of work on the psychophysiology of sexuality, the authors provide us with cogent evaluations and thoughtful insights into where the field is moving and where problems still exist. I predict that the study of the psychophysiology of human sexuality will be significantly advanced as others are encouraged and stimulated by this book.

I am pleased to have played a very minor role in the production of this book and trust that practitioners who face the real problems so often surrounding human sexuality will read it. They will gain much from having a more complete understanding of the phenomena being addressed. In the natural desire to help, there is a tendency to grasp at what may be "will-o'-the-wisps." Having an authoritative text that can point to both strengths and weaknesses that the field of psychophysiology can offer will be of great value both in applied matters and in the conceptualization of sexuality.

James H. Geer
Professor and Chairman
Department of Psychology
Louisiana State University

v

Preface

For much of the present century sexual science has been preoccupied with two central issues. First is the perennial problem of defining sexual normality—that is, which behaviors, relationships, and sexual needs are to be accepted as normal or healthy. Despite the lifelong efforts of Havelock Ellis, Kinsey, Gagnon, and other sexual modernists to challenge our traditional concepts of sexual normality, the issue continues to dominate sexual thinking on many topics.

Equally engrossing is the question of sexual determinism—that is, what are the relative impacts of biological factors, life events, and social circumstances in shaping our sexual identities and desires? Discussions of homosexuality and sexual dysfunction, in particular, remain a major battleground for both sides in the nature–nurture controversy. An important corollary question is the extent to which sexual choices or preferences can be modified. Certainly, the meteoric rise of sex therapy in the past two decades reflects our current optimism regarding sexual change.

With the dawn of the laboratory era in sex research, due largely to the pioneering contributions of Masters and Johnson, we have seen significant changes in the form, if not the substance, of these underlying questions. Along with the current emphasis on multidimensional models of sexual arousal and the interaction of response systems, attention has been directed to the complexity and subtlety of psychophysiological mechanisms in sexual response. The growth of research in this area may also be attributed to innovative developments in laboratory measurement techniques during the past two decades, along with a generally tolerant academic climate in which empirical research on sexual behavior is possible.

Our goal in this book is to provide the first comprehensive review of theory and data in the emerging field of sexual psychophysiology. Drawing upon general principles of psychophysiology, we have attempted to develop the concept of response patterning as a primary source of individual variation in sexual response. We believe that the processes involved in sexual arousal, particularly the relationship between physiological and subjective dimensions of arousal, are especially amenable to laboratory psychophysiological research. Recognizing the importance of applied and clinical issues in the field, the second part of the book is devoted entirely to current areas of application, such as the effects of violent pornography, drugs, and alcohol on patterns of sexual response. The complex issues of sexual deviation and dysfunction are also addressed in depth. Finally, we hope this book will serve as a guide and stimulus for future research in a uniquely challenging field of investigation.

Although we critique their concepts and findings in several places, we freely acknowledge our enormous debt, and that of the entire field, to Masters and Johnson. It is not an exaggeration to say that without their landmark studies of human sexual response, none of this work would have been possible! Aside from the scientific impact of their work, their presence and ideas have contributed immeasurably to public and professional acceptance of sexuality as a legitimate field of study.

Numerous debts are also owed to friends and colleagues who have made significant contributions to the field, and who have guided or assisted us in various aspects of the book. We especially acknowledge the contributions of Gene Abel, Paul Abramson, John Bancroft, David Barlow, Judith Becker, Joseph Bohlen, Donn Byrne, Harvey Cohen, Walter Everaerd, Charles Fisher, Kurt Freund, Julia Heiman, Peter Hoon, Richard Laws, William Marshall, Patricia Morokoff, Vernon Quinsey, Raul Schiavi, Patricia Schreiner-Engel, and John Wincze. Much of the credit for the strengths of this book is owed to them, whereas the authors accept full responsibility for its weaknesses and limitations.

We are also much indebted to James Geer for his thoughtful critique of the entire manuscript, and to Bob Edelberg for reviewing selected chapters. Julian Davidson and Lin Meyers have greatly enhanced the scope of the book with their critical chapter on endocrine factors in sexual psychophysiology. Other colleagues provided assistance and encouragement in numerous ways, and we are especially grateful for the support of Sandra Leiblum, John Kostis, Katherine Hall, Terry Wilson, Linda Rosen, Ed Willems, Ed Blanchard, Marco Mariotto, Dale Johnson, and John Vincent. Finally, we thank the editorial staff of The Guilford Press, in particular Seymour Weingarten, Sharon Panulla, and Judith Grauman, for their commitment to excellence throughout the project.

Raymond C. Rosen
J. Gayle Beck

Contents

I. CONCEPTUAL FOUNDATIONS AND HISTORICAL OVERVIEW   1

1. Historical Antecedents of Contemporary Sex Research   3
Contributions from the Case Study Method, 5
Contributions from Normative Survey Research, 7
Contributions from the Laboratory Physiological Approach, 10
Contributions from Behavioral Psychology, 14
Current Aspects of the Field and Plan of the Book, 16

2. Patterns of Sexual Response   23
Defining the Sexual Response, 24
The Role of Cognitive Labeling and Subjective Experience, 26
Response Patterns in Sexual Arousal, 29
Interactive Mechanisms and the Components of Sexual
     Response, 33
Models of the Sexual Response Cycle, 38
Patterns of Response in Sexually Dysfunctional Individuals, 44
Response Patterning: A Reconsideration, 46
Summary, 50

3. Genital Blood Flow Measurement in the Male:
Psychophysiological Techniques   53
Male Genital Anatomy, 54
Physiological Mechanisms of Erection, 57
Measures of Penile Tumescence, 61
Correspondence between Physiological Measures of Erection
     and Subjective Arousal, 72
Summary, 75

4. Genital Blood Flow Measurement in the Female:
Psychophysiological Techniques   78
Female Genital Anatomy, 79

New Horizons in Female Sexual Anatomy?: The Grafenberg
    Spot, 83
The Physiology of Sexual Response in Women, 84
Measures of Vaginal Vasocongestion, 87
Correspondence between Genital Blood Flow Measures and
    Subjective Arousal, 103
Summary, 106

5. **Extragenital Components of Sexual Arousal**   108
Extragenital Response Patterning: The Role of Stereotypy, 109
Measures of Extragenital Arousal, 110
Summary, 131

6. **The Psychophysiology of Orgasm**   134
Central versus Peripheral Models of Orgasm, 135
Male–Female Patterns of Orgasm, 137
Types of Female Orgasm, 139
Male Orgasm and Ejaculation, 144
Orgasm "Triggers" and the Role of Pelvic Muscle Contractions,
    148
Cardiovascular and Respiratory Changes during Orgasm, 151
CNS and Subjective Changes during Orgasm, 152
Summary and Conclusion, 156

7. **Endocrine Factors in Sexual Psychophysiology**   158
JULIAN M. DAVIDSON AND LIN S. MYERS
Introduction, 158
Hormone Replacement Therapy as an Experimental Method,
    160
Actions of Testosterone on Male Sexuality, 162
Differential Diagnosis of Hormone-Related Conditions in the
    Male, 168
Role of Hormones in Female Sexual Psychophysiology, 174
The Hormonal Sexual Response, 183
Summary and Conclusion, 186
Acknowledgments, 186

II. **CURRENT APPLICATIONS OF SEXUAL PSYCHOPHYSIOLOGY**   187

8. **Laboratory Responses to Erotica and Pornography**   189
Laboratory Studies of Erotica, 190
Male–Female Patterns of Arousal to Erotica, 192

Personality Factors and Individual Differences in Response to
    Erotica, 199
Effects of Repeated Exposure to Erotica, 200
Exposure to Violent Pornography, 204
Summary, 210

9. Assessment and Treatment of Sexual Deviation (Paraphilias)   **212**
Background, 212
Defining Sexual Deviance, 213
Causal Factors in the Etiology of Sexual Deviation, 217
Laboratory Methods in the Assessment of Deviant Arousal, 221
Psychophysiological Measures in the Treatment of Sexual
    Deviation, 233
The Use of Antiandrogens in the Treatment of Sexual
    Deviation, 241
Summary and Conclusion, 242

10. Male Sexual Dysfunction   **244**
Classification, Nosology, and Diagnosis, 244
Laboratory Analogue Studies of Male Sexual Dysfunction, 260
Treatment Concerns: Psychophysiology in Application, 269
Summary, 271

11. Female Sexual Dysfunction   **274**
Classification, Definitions, and Diagnosis, 275
Laboratory Analogue Studies of Female Sexual Dysfunction,
    286
Applications of Psychophysiology to Sex Therapy, 293
Summary, 298

12. Alcohol and Other Drug Effects on Sexual Response   **299**
Alcohol Effects on Sexual Function, 301
Marihuana Effects on Sexual Function, 312
Effects of Cocaine and Other Illicit Drugs on Sexual Function,
    315
Effects of Prescription Drugs on Sexual Response, 318
Summary, 327

III. CONCLUSION   **329**

13. Future Directions in Sexual Psychophysiology   **331**
Response Patterns in Sexual Arousal, 334
Models of the Sexual Response Cycle, 337

Measurement Issues in Sexual Psychophysiology, 339
Applied and Clinical Issues in Sexual Psychophysiology, 341
Social and Ethical Concerns in Sexual Psychophysiology, 343

**Appendix. Concerns Involving Human Subjects in Sexual
Psychophysiology**   345
Laboratory Construction, 345
Protection of Subjects, 347
Procedural Concerns, 349
A Final Note, 354

References   357

Index   396

Conceptual Foundations and Historical Overview

Sexual science, or "sexology," is a broad and multifaceted field of study that has gained increasing social and scientific respectability in the past two decades. Although the origins of modern sexology can be traced to the early writings of Krafft-Ebing, Havelock Ellis, and others, the current era of laboratory sex research was clearly initiated by the landmark studies of Masters and Johnson in the late 1960s. Since that time, we have seen the emergence of *sexual psychophysiology* as a relatively independent branch of sexology, in which a particular conceptual and methodological focus has been applied to a broad range of sexual arousal phenomena in human subjects. This approach has benefited, in part, from the development of a wide array of measurement devices for assessing genital responding in both sexes, as well as from a growing interest in the interplay between physiological and psychological dimensions of sexual behavior.

Two central theoretical issues are addressed in Section I. First, factors contributing to response specificity, or the *patterning* of sexual arousal responses from one individual or situation to another, are considered. Second, the underlying *processes* determining the occurrence of sexual arousal to a specific stimulus are explicated. In dealing with these issues our major emphasis in Chapter 2 is on the development of linkages with concepts and findings from other areas of psychophysiology. Thus, a "cognitive arousal" model of sexual response is presented to account for physiological–subjective interactions, and to address the role of cognitive factors in sexual arousal.

Measurement issues have featured equally prominently in the development of laboratory sex research. In Chapters 3 and 4 we therefore review in detail current approaches to assessment of genital responding in males and females, while Chapter 5 discusses the role of extragenital measures of sexual arousal. Included in these chapters is a consideration of the underlying neurophysiological processes, as well as the complex relationship between physiological and subjective measures of arousal. Laboratory

1

studies of orgasm are presented in Chapter 6, as this elusive and perplexing aspect of sexual behavior is considered from a psychophysiological perspective. The section concludes with a provocative discussion by Davidson and Myers of endocrine factors in sexual psychophysiology.

CHAPTER ONE

Historical Antecedents
of Contemporary Sex Research

Throughout most of European and American history sexual "thinking"
has amounted to little more than an assortment of popular prejudices,
sometimes codified by medical authorities or exploited by pornogra-
phers, but rarely achieving the coherence and dignity that one associates with the word "thought."—Robinson (1976, p. vii)

As W. C. Fields once said, "Sex isn't the best thing in the world, or the
worst thing in the world—but there's nothing else quite like it." Despite
the unique and special place that sexuality occupies in most of our lives,
the intellectual tradition of sexology as we know it today has evolved in
fits and starts, and has depended heavily on the guidance and direction of
sister disciplines, such as psychology, anthropology, and sociology.

The first systematic attempts at establishing a scientific understanding
of human sexuality, beginning in the late 19th century, originated with the
writings of Krafft-Ebing, Freud, and Havelock Ellis. Each of these scholars
viewed sexuality as a legitimate and viable topic for study, and attempted
individually to integrate sexual theorizing into their respective disciplines.
Despite the moralistic and restrictive norms of the Victorian era, these
three writers explicitly addressed the diversity of sexual behavior and motivation, often in the face of considerable social and professional resistance.
It is interesting to note, for example, that key parts of Krafft-Ebing's
Psychopathia Sexualis (1886/1965) were written in Latin, as he felt obligated
to protect the lay reader from graphic details of sexual variation. Similarly,
Havelock Ellis's *Studies in the Psychology of Sex* (1906) could not be
published in his native England for several decades and created considerable controversy both at home and abroad. As these examples indicate,
the birth of modern sexology was not without a protracted and difficult
labor.

Fortunately, the field has grown and developed considerably since these times, following its multidisciplinary origins. At present, it is not uncommon for sexologists to study topics as diverse as sexual medicine, sexual dysfunction, sexual anatomy and physiology, sexual abuse, sex and aging, gender-role socialization, interpersonal attraction and intimacy, and a host of loosely related subjects (cf. Money & Musaph, 1977).

This book is intended to detail and synthesize a growing body of conceptual and empirical work in the area of sexual psychophysiology. While this approach has recently been applied to various related topics, such as the influences of pornography, drugs and alcohol, and hormonal factors on sexual response in men and women, the major objective of this book is to develop a cohesive framework for understanding the interaction of physiological and psychological processes in human sexuality.

Sexual psychophysiology is distinguished from other branches of sexology by several key features. First, systematic exploration of the interdependence among cognitive, affective, and behavioral processes in association with physiological activation of sexual arousal is the primary topic. A focus on sexual responding in individual human subjects—separate from dyadic and interpersonal determinants, or comparative studies of sexual behavior—is another distinguishing feature. This focus encompasses clinical applications of psychophysiological methods, as well as studies of applied questions concerning male and female arousal processes. The use of a methodology that emphasizes empirical assessment of subjective and objective concomitants of sexual response—in particular, surface electrophysiological measures of genital and nongenital arousal—further demarcates sexual psychophysiology from related fields. A final salient feature is the overall objective of providing controlled laboratory demonstrations of key measures and constructs, with special attention to validity and reliability.

Sexual psychophysiology thus shares with sexology a focus on sexual arousal and behavior processes, while distinguishing itself in its reliance on a particular conceptual and methodological approach. "Sexual psychophysiology" can be defined as the application of psychophysiological methods to the study of sexual arousal processes in individual human participants, with special emphasis on the interplay between subjective and physiological determinants of arousal.

Historically, this approach has evolved from at least four separate traditions within the larger field of sexology: specifically, the case study method; the use of normative survey research; the laboratory physiological approach; and behavioral assessment and treatment studies. This heterogeneity of sources has resulted in a wide variety of experimental methods and, not surprisingly, a lack of consistency in the findings obtained. A task for the present book is to integrate concepts and findings from these four loosely related areas into a unified body of thought.

CONTRIBUTIONS FROM THE CASE STUDY METHOD

The case study method rests upon careful and in-depth description of disturbed individuals, with their particular behavior patterns and psychological motivations. The earliest sexologist to be identified with this tradition was Richard von Krafft-Ebing (1840–1902), whose expertise in neurology and psychiatry was reflected in the detailed clinical observation of sexual deviations, referred to at that time as "perversions," that he included in his writing. On the basis of his clinical analysis, Krafft-Ebing postulated that sexual perversions were due to disease or "degeneration" of the nervous system, resulting either from genetic factors ("hereditary taint") or from traumatic experiences.

Noting the prevalence of autoeroticism among his patients, Krafft-Ebing further theorized that masturbation is the source from which all of the sexual variations spring (Brecher, 1969). Many of his case studies emphasized the more bizarre and horrifying practices of his patients, in support of his view that even apparently harmless aspects of sexual attraction contain aberrant elements. The following case study typifies many of Krafft-Ebing's characteristic ideas about the etiology of sexual deviation:

Case 15. A four year-old girl was missing from her parents' home. . . . Menesclou, one of the occupants of the house, was arrested. The forearm of the child was found in his pocket, and the head and entrails, in a half-charred condition, were taken from the stove. . . . The circumstances, as well as an obscene poem found on his person, left no doubt that he had violated the child and then murdered her. M. expressed no remorse, asserting that his deed was an unhappy accident.

Convulsions at the age of nine months. Later he suffered from disturbed sleep; was nervous and developed tardily and imperfectly. . . . He did not run after women, but gave himself up passionately to masturbation, and occasionally indulged in sodomy with dogs. His mother suffered from *mania menstrualis periodica*. An uncle was insane, and another a drunkard. The examination of M.'s brain (after his execution) showed morbid changes of the frontal lobes, of the first and second temporal convolutions, and of a part of the occipital convolutions. (Krafft-Ebing, 1886/1965, p. 118)

As exemplified in this case study, a notable feature of Krafft-Ebing's work was his willingness to address sexual behavior with explicit, detailed case descriptions. Given the historical context of the times, the use of this approach in the study of sexual variation was daring and innovative, placing sexuality in the mainstream of academic psychiatry. However, the focus on highly disturbed individuals, along with an exclusive reliance on idiographic case study material, strongly influenced his conclusions. For example, had Krafft-Ebing included a sample of matched control cases, as Havelock Ellis did some years later, his conclusions regarding masturbation and other etiological factors would certainly have been different.

Following the same case study tradition is the work of Sigmund Freud (1856–1939). Although best known for his theories of personality and psychosexual development, Freud also deserves recognition as a sexologist, particularly for his contributions to the understanding of childhood sexuality and the role of sexual conflict in adult "neuroses." Like Krafft-Ebing, he also made innovative use of the case study method, as exemplified by the classic discussion of hysterical neurosis in the case of Dora (Freud, 1905/1963). In his later work, Freud emphasized the important role of erotic drives and motives in childhood, and in particular the functions of the erogenous zones in psychosexual development. It is noteworthy that a recent re-examination of Freud's personal papers (Masson, 1984) suggests that he was aware of, but chose to discount the validity of, certain patients' recollections of sexual seduction during childhood. Current accounts of childhood influences on adult sexuality have reintroduced this issue, stimulated by considerable public attention to the prevalence of child molestation as a social problem; this matter is discussed in Chapters 9 and 11.

Freud's views on female sexuality have been equally controversial and influential with respect to the conceptualization of sexual response in women. Much has been written concerning the vaginal–clitoral orgasm distinction (e.g., Hite, 1976; Jayne, 1981), for example; while Freud's ideas on this issue generally have been discredited, the notion of differentiating between various types of female orgasm continues to influence research in this area (e.g., Singer & Singer, 1978; Perry & Whipple, 1981). Regardless of the validity of his theory, Freud's explicit discussion of female sexuality represented a bold step away from the Victorian caricature of the "ideal" woman as an asexual and chaste individual.

While the influence of Freud's concepts has been profound in all aspects of contemporary culture, his work has had a greater impact on developmental psychology and clinical psychiatry, in contrast to modern sexology. A notable exception to this is the influence of psychoanalytic concepts in the theories of Helen Singer Kaplan (1929–   ), whose recent account of the etiology and treatment of sexual dysfunction has included an emphasis on the contribution of unconscious factors in disorders of sexual function. Like Freud, Kaplan has employed the case study approach to illustrate key concepts, although, unlike her predecessor, she places equal importance on the role of behavioral and interpersonal aspects of sexual dysfunction, as illustrated in the following case vignette:

The immediate cause of Britt's lack of desire and avoidance was the angry feelings she experienced whenever Benjamin approached her. Sexual avoidance was the only means she had of asserting herself. But she was not aware of this. Her rigid conscience would not allow her to "rebel" or to consciously withhold anything from her husband. . . .

On a deeper level, Britt was extremely angry at Benjamin. She felt helpless and overwhelmed by his strong personality and was unconsciously taking vengeance on him. Her intense anger was partially due to his controlling style and her real feelings of weakness vis-a-vis him. On a deeper level, their relationship evoked old angers at her father and at other men who had rejected her. (Kaplan, 1979, p. 138)

As this case illustrates, Kaplan has attempted to integrate notions from classical psychoanalytic theory with more contemporary conceptions of behavioral and systemic influences on sexual functioning.

Overall, the case study tradition in sexology stands as the first major approach to understanding sexual behavior, with particular emphasis on sexual dysfunction and deviation. The serious methodological limitations of this tradition notwithstanding, it has served to generate important ideas and hypotheses regarding sexual function, and has provided a rich source of descriptive observations illustrative of the complexity and diversity of human sexuality. Although there has been less reliance on idiographic material as a source of sexological theory development in recent years, case descriptions continue to play an important role in the demonstration and application of key concepts.

CONTRIBUTIONS FROM NORMATIVE SURVEY RESEARCH

The second major tradition in sexology, normative survey research, originated as a reaction against the shortcomings of the idiographic approach in general, and in particular the selective focus on clinical patients as the sole source of reference. The forerunner of this approach undoubtedly was Havelock Ellis (1859–1939), who emphasized individual and cultural relativism in sexual behavior. While Ellis also collected innumerable case histories, he was principally concerned with documenting the wide range of individual variation in ordinary sexual behavior. In the words of Bullough (1976), "Ellis was a naturalist, observing and collecting information about human sexuality instead of judging it" (p. 643).

Despite the far-reaching effects of his work on contemporary sexual thought, Ellis ironically never received the degree of public or professional recognition accorded to Krafft-Ebing and Freud. His seven-volume *Studies in the Psychology of Sex* (1906) remains today a monumental panorama of the enormous diversity of human sexual behavior. Among his many contributions, Ellis deserves particular recognition for his observations on masturbation as a common sexual outlet, which he subsumed under the broader category of "autoeroticism," including sexual fantasy and erotic dreams.

On the topic of female sexuality, Ellis included a full discussion of the sexual capacity of women, and placed the female sexual response on a par with that of men. He proposed that masturbation was as frequent among women as among men, if not more so—a truly shocking notion in the context of the times. Multiple orgasm, according to Ellis, was also prevalent among women—an observation that anticipated Masters and Johnson's later findings.

Concerning homosexuality, Ellis argued strongly for a nonpathological but genetically determined view of preference for same-sex partners, and presented many detailed case descriptions of accomplished and productive homosexuals. In addition to these contributions, he presented one of the first psychophysiological models of the sexual arousal process, introducing the concepts of "tumescence" and "detumescence"; this model is reviewed in depth in Chapter 2.

Even among contemporary sex researchers, there has been insufficient attention paid to the breadth and scope of Ellis's ideas. Beyond the specifics of his observations, his search for a *normative* perspective on human sexual behavior set the stage for the prevailing 20th-century *Zeitgeist*, as exemplified by the large-scale survey research of Bromley and Britten, Hamilton, Hohman and Schaffner, and Kinsey and colleagues. In this regard, Robinson (1976) has commented, "Havelock Ellis stands in the same relation to modern sexual theory as Max Weber to modern sociology, or Albert Einstein to modern physics" (p. 3).

Following in this tradition, Alfred Kinsey (1894–1956) and his collaborators (Pomeroy, Gebhard, and Martin) advanced normative survey research by accumulating a large quantitative data base, detailing sexual behaviors of men and women across the life span. Their systematic tabulations and descriptive statistics concerned a wide range of sexual activities and did much to legitimize the conduct and content of sex research. As one reviewer has observed, "Putting a percentage in front of the topic made it speakable" (Gagnon, 1978, p. 93). Given his background as a zoologist, Kinsey naturally approached human sexuality in much the same way that a biologist might study the sexual behavior of any other species—by categorizing behavior in an objective and taxonomic fashion. Furthermore, he sought to dispel the notion of sexual "normality" and to foster an attitude of tolerance by documenting the enormous variability of human sexual behavior.

The method employed by Kinsey and his group was the standardized sex history interview, which was used to obtain detailed information in nine specific content areas, including nocturnal sex dreams, masturbation, homosexual and heterosexual histories, and animal contacts. Much attention was paid to the style as well as the content of these interviews, each of which lasted from 2 to 4 hours. The Kinsey interview technique remains a model of scientific survey research. All in all, the Kinsey group collected some 18,000 interviews, of which Kinsey personally conducted about 8,000.

Survey responses of both sexes in the Kinsey studies indicated that homosexual experience leading to orgasm, premarital and extramarital intercourse, and child–adult sexual contacts were surprisingly high. Kinsey also reported that women masturbated less frequently, were less influenced by sexual fantasy, and reported fewer nocturnal sex dreams than men; from these data, he drew the conclusion that females are generally less sexually responsive to psychological stimulation. He further suggested that these sex differences were a probable result of central (i.e., brain structure) differences between men and women. Thus, while in the same tradition as his predecessors, Kinsey's careful interview methodology produced more detailed information regarding sexual patterns among men and women that had been collected previously, and often revealed surprising results.

Despite the gargantuan efforts of the Kinsey studies, the overall initial response of the academic and professional communities was highly critical. Not only had Kinsey displayed unprecedented audacity by asking such frank and direct questions of middle-class Americans; he had gone even further in publishing the detailed findings in two accessible and clearly written volumes. According to Christenson (1971), a close collaborator at the time, criticism of the volume on female sexuality in particular led to termination of all of Kinsey's financial support, leaving him an embittered man until his death in 1956.

More substantive criticisms have been raised against Kinsey's expression of tolerance for all forms of sexual expression, based solely upon the evidence of statistical prevalence. For example, in his discussion of child–adult sexual contacts, Kinsey downplayed the potential psychological harm to the child and argued for greater acceptance of the normality and potential benefits of such interactions, based upon the high prevalence observed in his sample. In addition, a major methodological weakness of the studies was the reliance on sexual "outlets," defined exclusively as sexual activity leading to orgasm, as the sole quantitative measure of sexual behavior. As a result of this focus, there is a relative neglect in Kinsey's work of the role of cognitive, interpersonal, and other nonbehavioral dimensions of sexuality.

In the 30 years since Kinsey's death, the Kinsey Institute at the University of Indiana has continued to coordinate large-scale normative studies of specific topics, including sexual deviation (Gebhard, Gagnon, Pomeroy, & Christenson, 1965) and homosexuality (Bell & Weinberg, 1978; Bell, Weinberg, & Hammersmith, 1981). The normative survey tradition has also led to several major studies of female sexuality in the past decade (e.g., Hite, 1976; Wolfe, 1981), and more recently has been expanded to investigation of sexual relationship styles in couples (Blumstein & Schwartz, 1983). In contrast to the case study tradition, with its detailed attention to individual processes, the principal contribution of the normative survey approach has been to provide a macroscopic perspective on human sexual behavior. This has served a major hypothesis-generating function, from which laboratory investigations have blossomed, as well as providing a frame of reference for validation of experimental findings.

CONTRIBUTIONS FROM THE LABORATORY PHYSIOLOGICAL APPROACH

The third major tradition in sex research, and the most relevant to sexual psychophysiology, is the laboratory physiological approach. In contrast with the case study and survey methods, the hallmark of this approach is use of techniques for direct observation and measurement of bodily responses during the process of actual sexual arousal. The first systematic observations of this type were reported by Robert Latou Dickinson (1861–1950), an early post-Victorian sexologist in the United States. In many respects Dickinson's contributions were made possible by the enormous changes in cultural attitudes following World War I, most particularly the newfound sexual freedom of the 1920s.

As a practicing gynecologist, Dickinson examined and treated thousands of women in his New York offices; based on his extensive clinical experience, he made numerous observations concerning female anatomy and physiology. In addition to his skill as a physician, Dickinson was a highly gifted illustrator, and is best known for *Human Sex Anatomy* (1933), an impressive collection of illustrations of all aspects of male and female sexual anatomy (see Figure 1.1). In order to observe female internal anatomy directly, Dickinson pioneered the use of a glass observation tube, later adapted by Masters and Johnson for use in the St. Louis studies. When a light was passed through the device, it was possible to observe changes in the cervix and in the vaginal lining during sexual response. Given his considerable interest in the causes of infertility in women, Dickinson employed this device principally for studying intravaginal physiology associated with conception.

Dickinson's studies also included a focus on the sources of female sexual development, and specifically on the acquisition of the orgasmic response in women. In this respect he anticipated the work of Kinsey and others by postulating the central role of experiential learning, particularly masturbation, in the development of adequate sexual responsivity. His interest in this topic led to the introduction of the vibrator as a therapeutic tool for anorgasmic women—an innovation that again foreshadowed contemporary sex therapy practices.

In retrospect, Dickinson's accomplishments have been largely overlooked, particularly with respect to his influence on later sexual psychophysiology research (Brecher, 1969). Perhaps this is due to the absence of a comprehensive account of the sexual response in his writing; his strengths were clearly in documenting sexual anatomy and in the practice of clinical

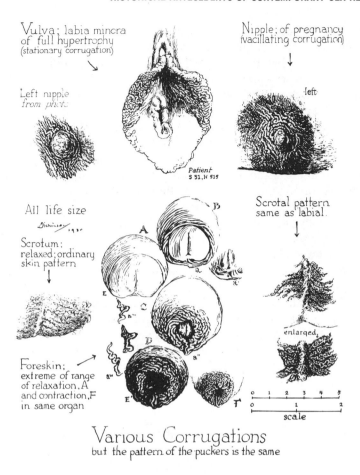

Figure 1.1. One of Dickinson's illustrations for *Human Sex Anatomy*. From *Human Sex Anatomy* (p. 172) by R. L. Dickinson, 1933, Baltimore: Williams & Wilkins. Copyright 1933 by Williams & Wilkins, Inc. Reprinted by permission.

sexology. However, Dickinson clearly deserves credit for his pioneering use of direct observation techniques for studying sexual arousal, and his work has served as a methodological model for future researchers in this tradition.

In the decades following Dickinson's *Human Sex Anatomy*, a small number of unrelated observational studies appeared. For example, Theodoor Van de Velde (1873–1937), the Dutch gynecologist who is best known for his highly successful marriage manual, *Ideal Marriage* (1926), also made observations of female orgasm during masturbation. Cardiovascular researchers at New York's Mount Sinai Hospital, Boas and Goldschmidt

11

(1932), recorded heart rate simultaneously from a husband and wife during sexual intercourse and plotted patterns of heart rate activity during orgasm in both sexes (see Figure 1.2). Further cardiovascular studies on male and female orgasm were conducted by Klumbies and Kleinsorge (1950), who recorded a wide range of autonomic measures from a female subject capable of achieving orgasm solely through fantasy. At about the same time, a pair of Argentinian researchers, Mosovich and Tallafero (1954), presented electroencephalographic (EEG) data during orgasm from volunteers of both sexes. This collection of geographically and conceptually disparate findings, although interesting and important in some respects, was not integrated until Kinsey and colleagues' review of the field (Kinsey, Pomeroy, Martin, & Gebhard, 1953).

Historically, Kinsey is associated primarily with the survey research tradition, as discussed above. An important, but virtually unknown aspect of his work was the use of direct observational techniques for the study of physiological processes in sexual response. The sole mention of these observations is found in a footnote to the concluding chapter of the volume on female sexuality: "We have had access to a considerable body of observed data on the involvement of the entire body in the spasms following orgasm . . ." (Kinsey *et al.*, 1953, p. 631).

In discussing the possible reasons for Kinsey's failure to elaborate this aspect of his research more fully, Brecher (1969) speculates, "No doubt Dr. Kinsey expected his report to stir up enough of a fuss without his giving

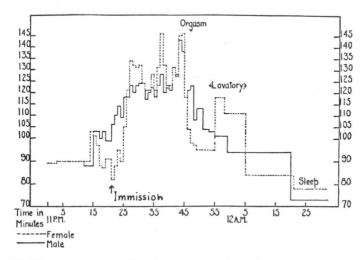

Figure 1.2. Heart rate from a human female and male during sexual intercourse. From *The Heart Rate* (p. 99) by E. P. Boas and E. F. Goldschmidt, 1932, Springfield, IL: Charles C Thomas. Copyright 1932 by Charles C Thomas, Inc. Reprinted by permission.

his critics added ammunition by confessing that sexual intercourse had actually been observed at Indiana University during the 1940s" (p. 291). Without revealing details of the methods or findings of his own physiological research, Kinsey did provide a comprehensive presentation of prior studies of sexual physiology.

It was not until the pioneering studies of William Masters (1915–   ) and Virginia Johnson (1925–   ) that the laboratory physiological approach finally came of age. The publication of their first book, *Human Sexual Response*, in 1966 was a landmark in the history of modern sexology. The impact of their work has been enormous, and they are generally regarded as among the foremost sex researchers of the present era. Several of the factors that enabled them to conduct direct observational studies were the changing cultural attitudes toward sexuality, the influence of Kinsey's earlier survey research, and William Masters's established reputation as a researcher in reproductive biology.

In contrast to the limited observations of their predecessors, Masters and Johnson recruited a total of 694 male and female volunteers of all ages for laboratory study. On the whole, this was a well-educated sample of married couples; however, Masters and Johnson were careful to include a group of older subjects (aged 50 and upward), so that they could examine postmenopausal and other effects of aging on the sexual response. Many of these participants were paid to perform acts of masturbation or sexual intercourse while being filmed or wearing physiological recording devices. Among the instruments used was an updated version of Dickinson's glass observation tube, improved by the addition of a camera and an optical light source.

Many noteworthy findings emerged from these observations, including the remarkable similarities in male and female sexual physiology, the role of vaginal lubrication in female sexual arousal, and the physiology of multiple orgasms. These findings, as well as the resulting conceptual model of the sexual response cycle that developed from their observations, are discussed in detail in Chapters 2 through 6. The Masters and Johnson sexual response cycle also served as the basis for their classification of sexual dysfunction and subsequent treatment approach, which are presented in detail in Chapters 10 and 11.

Despite the enormous impact of their work on modern sexology, the contribution of Masters and Johnson has received criticism on several counts. In particular, the generalizability of their findings to nonlaboratory settings (external validity) has been questioned in two major respects. First, the representativeness of individuals who are able and willing to perform sexually under laboratory conditions has been raised. Second, the potential reactivity of their physiological measurement procedures might well have produced atypical response patterns in some of their subjects. Other objections to the research methods have included their initial choice of prostitutes as subjects, and their use of the "artificial coition machine"—a mechanically driven, penis-shaped device for observing the interior of the vagina during sexual stimulation. The use of this device, in particular, led to the objection that their approach was overly mechanistic and essentially dehumanizing. In response to such criticisms, Masters and Johnson have recently written, "Relatively few people recognized that the physiological information was not an endpoint but was instead a foundation. . . . It is noteworthy that all of medical science is based on understanding normal anatomy and physiology before meaningful advances can be made in treating abnormalities" (Masters, Johnson, & Kolodny, 1982, p. 16).

Perhaps even more important than the specific findings of Masters and Johnson's research was the resulting change in public attitudes toward sex research. Largely as a result of their contribution, laboratory studies of sexual arousal have achieved a degree of respectability and acceptance in the scientific community. Furthermore, due to the application of their findings to the treatment of sexual problems, Masters and Johnson revitalized sex therapy by introducing direct, problem-focused interventions and increasing public acceptance of the directive approach to sexual dysfunction.

CONTRIBUTIONS FROM BEHAVIORAL PSYCHOLOGY

The fourth and final perspective that has played a significant role in shaping the concepts and methods of sexual psychophysiology is behavioral psychology. This tradition, first introduced to the United States by John B. Watson (1878–1958), is best known for its use of observable methods in the study of human behavior and for a focus on environmental determinants of behavior. A consistent albeit less widely researched topic throughout the recent history of behaviorism has been sexual responding in humans. This approach has contributed in important ways to the conceptual framework of sexual psychophysiology, to the development of specific assessment procedures, and more recently to the application of intervention methods for problems of sexual deviation and dysfunction.

A curious and little-known episode in the history of modern psychology is the early sex research of John B. Watson. According to Magoun (1981), Watson was initiated into the field of sexology along with Karl Lashley, through his work for the military in World War I on attitudes toward sex hygiene and the prevention of venereal disease. Subsequently, Watson returned to his laboratory at Johns Hopkins and privately began observational studies of sexual behavior, using as subjects himself and his female research assistant. During the brief course of his studies, Watson is said to have accumulated an impressive collection of sexual response data. Upon the discovery of these activities by his wife, his research records were confiscated and introduced in court as evidence in divorce proceedings. Watson's academic career was ended, and he resigned his professorship soon thereafter. His own subsequent comments are noteworthy:

The study of sex is still fraught with danger. It can be openly studied only by individuals who are not connected with universities. What a confession to make! It is admittedly the most important subject in life. It is admittedly the thing that causes the most shipwrecks in the happiness of men and women. And yet our scientific information is so meager. Even the few facts that we have must be looked upon as more or less bootlegged stuff. (Watson, 1929, p. xiv)

In the following decades, a number of attempts were made to modify sexual behavior by means of conditioning techniques, thus providing an additional impetus to the study of sexual response. For example, application of the "conditioned reaction technique" in the treatment of a homosexual was reported by Max (1935). This procedure involved the pairing of electric shock and homosexual stimuli until the "emotional aura" of the stimulus was diminished. Similarly, Raymond (1956) reported the use of a form of aversion therapy, which had been used previously in the treatment of alcoholism, to a case of fetishism. Further studies of conditioning in the treatment of homosexuality were reported by Freund (1960). Although Freund's results in modifying sexual preference were unimpressive, his interest in assessing sexual arousal in a reliable and quantifiable fashion led to the development of the first laboratory penile plethysmograph (Freund, 1963). A detailed critique of this methodology is provided in Chapter 3.

Behavioral studies of sexual deviance have continued to stimulate research on laboratory methods for assessment and treatment of sexual behavior. For example, Bancroft, Gwynne Jones, and Pullan (1966) described the construction of the first mercury-in-rubber penile circumference gauge, which was subsequently used in a number of treatment studies (e.g., Bancroft, 1974). Experimental studies of deviant arousal similarly have been conducted by Abel and his associates (e.g., Abel, Blanchard, Barlow, & Mavissakalian, 1975), making use of the Barlow electromechanical strain gauge (Barlow, Becker, Leitenberg, & Agras, 1970). Each of these applications has led to further refinements of measures of male genital responding, as well as to the development of highly specific treatment interventions.

A concurrent interest of the behavioral tradition has been the assessment and treatment of sexual dysfunction. As part of his formulation of "reciprocal inhibition," Wolpe (1958) postulated that anxiety and sexual arousal are mutually exclusive states of autonomic arousal. In particular, he outlined the role of conditioned anxiety in the etiology of sexual dysfunction. In 1960 Wolpe anticipated many of the treatment interventions later elaborated by Masters and Johnson. The following case example illustrates both the behavioral formulation and the resulting therapy approach to the treatment of erectile dysfunction:

Mr. S, a 40 year old accountant, was sent to me (JW) for the treatment of impotence. . . . At puberty the patient had masturbated a good deal, and at some stage had been told that among other ill effects this might lead to impotence. At 22 he had a regular girlfriend with whom he indulged in frequent petting which usually culminated in non-copulatory orgasms for both of them. After a time he noticed with perturbation that he was ejaculating increasingly quickly. . . .

About a year before coming for treatment he had fallen progressively more deeply in love with a girl of 24, called May, who worked in his office. She was responsive to him and one day, despite ejaculating prematurely he managed to deflorate her. Finding that he had made a good impression in this act he used all sorts of excuses to avoid further intercourse. After six months, when May was about to go on holiday, he felt obliged to make another attempt but ejaculated before entry. May began to show signs of coolness towards Mr. S when later coital attempts were also unsuccessful.

. . . The reciprocal inhibition principle was explained to Mr. S and he was given lessons in progressive relaxation and instructed to adopt a relaxed attitude in the sexual situation. He was not to attempt coitus unless he had a strong erection beforehand and after intromission was not to aim at any set level of performance but just to let himself go. (Wolpe, 1960, pp. 110–111)

Following the early descriptions of Wolpe (1960) and Lazarus (1964) of behavioral sex therapy for impotence, other authors developed related methods for treating sexual difficulties in women. For example, Lobitz and LoPiccolo (1972) originated a multicomponent treatment program for anorgasmic women. Similarly, Leiblum, Pervin, and Campbell (1980) and others have reported on the use of behavioral methods for overcoming vaginismus. In addition to the effect of these approaches on the current practice of sex therapy, an additional impetus has been given to psychophysiological studies of sexual dysfunction. In particular, the effects of anxiety on both normal and dysfunctional patterns of arousal continue to constitute an important focus of laboratory psychophysiological studies in this area (e.g., Wolchik et al., 1980; Barlow, Sakheim, & Beck, 1983). Overall, the concepts and methods from behavioral psychology have had a major impact on current formulations and treatment of sexual dysfunction, as discussed in Chapters 9 and 10.

CURRENT ASPECTS OF THE FIELD AND PLAN OF THE BOOK

Having briefly discussed the separate influences of these four major approaches in the evolution of sexual psychophysiology, we should note that there has been little if any synthesis or cross-fertilization to date. Until recently, it has been an unfortunate characteristic of the field of sexology in general that individual contributors have tended to pursue their research endeavors in relative isolation. Fortunately, a newer trend appears to be emerging with the current emphasis on multidisciplinary models and methods in sex research (e.g., Byrne & Kelley, 1986; Geer, 1980), in conjunction with the newfound academic respectability of the field (Reinisch & Rosen, 1981).

Psychophysiological approaches to sexual behavior, in particular, have attempted to bridge the gap between these different research traditions through empirical study of the complex phenomena of sexual arousal. The advances that have been made are attributable in part to improved measurement technology and a social climate that is favorable with respect to the laboratory conduct of sex research. As sexual psychophysiology continues to mature, greater synthesis of conceptual and methodological contributions from numerous fields is likely to occur.

The Role of Measurement Technology

Like all empirical endeavors, the laboratory study of sexual response has depended heavily on a suitable measurement technology for precise and reliable recording. Perhaps more so than in other areas of biobehavioral science, sex research has been especially reliant on the availability of a measurement technology that is both functional and acceptable for use in monitoring this sensitive aspect of human behavior. In some instances, the instrumentation used has been adapted from related areas, as with the development of photoelectric transducers for the measurement of vaginal blood flow. In other areas, devices have been developed for the specific purpose of measuring particular aspects of sexual response (e.g., volumetric penile plethysmography).

From a historical perspective, it is interesting to note that several early measurement devices were adapted from unusual techniques used with other species, as illustrated by the history of penile erection monitors in horse breeding (Mountjoy, 1974). According to this author, the first devices for detecting erection in mammals were developed in the late 19th century by horse breeders for the purpose of preventing masturbation in stud horses. Breeders were concerned with the possibility of lowered sperm count in their stallions as a result of ejaculation through self-stimulation. Altogether, 35 patents were granted prior to 1919 for equine antimasturbatory devices, as shown in Figure 1.3 (Mountjoy, 1974, p. 292). (It is worth noting that 14 patents were developed during the same time period for the prevention of masturbation in young boys.)

As research on tumescence in stallions contributed to measures of erection in human males, studies of vasocongestion in sheep likewise have influenced the recording of vaginal blood flow in human females. For

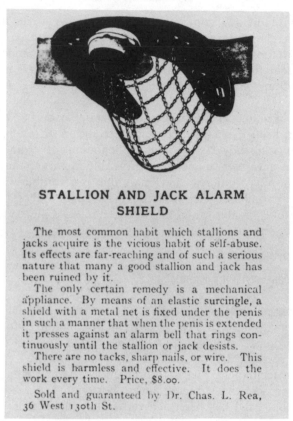

**STALLION AND JACK ALARM
SHIELD**

The most common habit which stallions and
jacks acquire is the vicious habit of self-abuse.
Its effects are far-reaching and of such a serious
nature that many a good stallion and jack has
been ruined by it.

The only certain remedy is a mechanical
appliance. By means of an elastic surcingle, a
shield with a metal net is fixed under the penis
in such a manner that when the penis is extended
it presses against an alarm bell that rings continuously until the stallion or jack desists.

There are no tacks, sharp nails, or wire. This
shield is harmless and effective. It does the
work every time. Price, $8.oo.

Sold and guaranteed by Dr. Chas. L. Rea,
36 West 130th St.

Figure 1.3. The stallion and jack (i.e., male donkey) alarm shield (a device for
ringing an alarm bell when the penis is extended). From "Some Early Attempts
to Modify Penile Erection in Horse and Human: An Historical Analysis" by P. T.
Mountjoy, 1974, *The Psychological Record, 24,* 291–308. Copyright 1974 by *The
Psychological Record.* Reprinted by permission.

example, an elaborate but highly sensitive vaginal probe was devised for
use in ewes, in order to investigate estrogen effects on vaginal blood flow
in ovariectomized females (Abrams & Stolwijk, 1972). However, in view
of the fact that this device was constructed of four independent heat flow
discs, which were encased in a cylindrical probe and cooled by circulating
fluid, it appeared too cumbersome and invasive for measurement of human
female responses. The construction of suitable transducers for assessing
vaginal engorgement in females has lagged behind the development of
comparable male tumescence measures, in part as a result of the Victorian
legacy of attitudes toward female sexuality. In recent years, however, a

number of devices have been developed for the express purpose of measuring sexual responsivity in women; these are reviewed in Chapter 4.

Although the bulk of research in this area has been directed toward the construction of measurement devices for assessing genital blood flow responses, some attention has also been directed toward monitoring nongenital response systems during sexual arousal. Early studies of this type included assessment of skin conductance, pupil dilation, cardiovascular changes, and other autonomic measures, as reviewed by Zuckerman (1971). Despite the inconclusive status of these studies, recent developments have focused on a broader description of response patterning during both arousal and orgasm. Thus, Cohen, Rosen, and Goldstein (1976) and Tucker (1983), for example, have documented shifts in EEG hemispheric laterality associated with sexual stimulation, which appear to differentiate response patterns in sexually functional and dysfunctional men (Cohen, Rosen, & Goldstein, 1985). Similarly, Abramson, Perry, Seeley, Seeley, and Rothblatt (1981) have described thermographic assessment of body heat transfer patterns at all stages of the sexual response cycle.

Considering the degree of sophistication achieved in the measurement technology and approaches to data analysis to date, the field of sexual psychophysiology may be viewed as barely in its infancy. Reliability and validity studies, for example, are urgently needed. Whereas most studies in the past have focused on the analysis of single response measures, there is also a pressing need for methods to integrate multiple measure of sexual responding. Future studies in this area will no doubt employ more refined and precise measurement approaches, as well as making use of multivariate and other multidimensional statistical tools.

The Social Context and Implications for Contemporary Sex Research

Even though social life, which includes the study of social life, has been secularized, sexuality still manages to retain for many people its exemplary status as the observable margin between the sacred and the profane.—Gagnon, (1978, p. 95)

There is no doubt that a considerable price was paid by each of the early sexologists for their involvement in the field of sex research. As we have already noted, the major figures in the "modernization of sex" (Robinson, 1976) all experienced varying degrees of social and professional approbation for their sexological investigations. Watson and Kinsey, in particular, both suffered traumatic personal consequences as a result of their research activities. Although the conduct of sex research has become increasingly accepted (and acceptable) in recent years, sexologists continue to face a degree of professional prejudice and social disapproval. Currently, the social pressures exerted against investigators in this area tend to be less obvious and, perhaps, less extreme.

A notable exception to this more relaxed attitude in recent years can be found in the events surrounding the sexual psychophysiology studies of Harris Rubin at Southern Illinois University (Holden, 1976). Having published a number of reports on voluntary control of penile tumescence in normal males (Laws & Rubin, 1969; Henson & Rubin, 1971), Rubin proposed to conduct a laboratory investigation of the effects of marihuana on sexual responsivity in males. In 1973, Rubin and his colleagues submitted a grant proposal to the National Institute on Drug Abuse (NIDA); although this grant initially was approved on its scientific merits, intense reactions in Congress to news stories of the proposed research resulted in an administrative veto in the form of a supplemental appropriations bill (Holden, 1976). In addition, an Illinois congressman mounted a public campaign to withhold federal funding from Southern Illinois University if the project was funded and to remove Rubin from his post at the university. Although he managed to maintain his academic position, Rubin was forced to curtail this line of research and experienced considerable personal harassment.

One positive consequence of the increasing sensitivity to social reactions has been the evolution of far-reaching ethical safeguards for the conduct of sex research with human subjects (Masters, Johnson, & Kolodny, 1977; Bohlen, 1980). For example, detailed procedures have been developed for orienting subjects to the laboratory setting, obtaining complete informed consent, and debriefing subjects following participation in experimental studies (see the Appendix). Furthermore, this ethical concern has been applied in the development of genital measures that are as unobtrusive and free of risk to the subject as possible.

The social context has influenced the scientific study of sexuality through less direct means as well. Historically, sex research has been anchored in the study of clinical and applied concerns, a review of which is included in Section II. Thus, for example, public concerns about the impact of sexual abuse have led to a new urgency in research on the biological and behavioral determinants of rape and child molestation (e.g., Greer & Stuart, 1983). Similarly, a growing awareness of the sexual correlates of aging and physical illness has led to a mushrooming of research in these areas (e.g., Schover & Jensen, in press). Related to this association with applied and clinical concerns is a growing empirical focus on the mechanisms and efficacy of sex therapy, as well as more thorough understanding of the nature of various sexual disorders. Increasingly refined assessment and diagnostic procedures have resulted from this association as well.

An unintended and unfortunate consequence, however, of the continuing link between clinical applications and basic methodology in sex research has been a degree of neglect of conceptual integration. In the midst of rapid refinements of the measurement technology and a growing accumulation of empirical findings, insufficient attention has been paid to the task of theoretical synthesis. Moreover, assumptions about the internal and external validity of the methods of sexual psychophysiology have been accepted uncritically, as has the lack of replicability in the case of many findings. A major purpose of this book is to explore the multifaceted nature of the sexual response, with attention to the correspondence between objective and subjective measures of arousal, and to develop theoretical models to guide future research on this topic.

Rationale for the Book

A major consequence of the so-called "sexual revolution" of the last two decades has been the appearance of a plethora of popular and professional books on all aspects of sexuality. In fact, the public has been veritably bombarded with all manner of sexual information and exhortation on everything from creating an androgynous society to locating the "G spot"! In scientific and academic circles, journals, professional societies, and training programs devoted to human sexuality have also blossomed in recent years (Reinisch & Rosen, 1981). So the reader may well ask, "Why another book on sexuality?"

This book, unlike many others that have appeared in the past several years, is not intended to improve the reader's sexual performance or to advance any particular sexual "cause." On the contrary, it is our intent to provide a thoughtful and scholarly examination of the current state of the field of sexual psychophysiology. Toward this end, we critically review the extant literature on methods and measures of laboratory sex research, with detailed consideration of the many applications of this approach. Ultimately, we aim to provide a conceptual integration of existing data and theories concerning sexual arousal. Drawing upon the general principles of psychophysiology, we develop the concept of response patterning as the primary source of individual variation in sexual response.

This book is organized into three major parts. The first section reviews relevant models of sexual arousal in some detail, with particular attention to the role of individual differences. Emphasis is given to the reconciliation of theoretical and empirical perspectives on the sexual response cycle. Section I also includes a critical evaluation of the methodology for laboratory sex research with males and females. Some of the assessment approaches evaluated are vaginal and penile blood flow measures, thermographic assessment of sexual arousal, monitoring of vaginal and anal electromyographic (EMG) activities, and a range of extragenital measurement techniques. Section II considers the various applications of sexual psychophysiology to a broad range of topics, including the effects of pornography on sexual behavior, the evaluation of deviant sexual preferences, the use of psychophysiological methods in the assessment and treatment of sexual dysfunctions, and drug and alcohol effects. In the final section, future directions for research in this field are discussed, and an overall assessment of the current status of the field is provided.

Following the sentiment expressed by Robinson (1976) in the opening quotation, it is our overriding goal to dignify laboratory research in sexuality by striving for sexual "thinking" that is unbiased and coherent. In this way, we also seek to stimulate further research into this fundamental, yet complex and challenging facet of human behavior.

CHAPTER TWO

Patterns of Sexual Response

In view of the pervicacious gonadal urge in human beings, it is not a
little curious that science develops its sole timidity about the pivotal
point of the physiology of sex. . . . Perhaps this shyness is begotten by
the certainty that such study cannot be freed from the warp of personal
experience, the bias of individual prejudice, and, above all, from the
implication of prurience.—Dickinson (1925, p. 1115)

The sexual response, like other emotional reactions, is experienced intu-
itively, and is elusively difficult for the scholar or scientist to define. While
the average sixth-grader knows with some certainty what "it" is, scientific
definitions of "sexual arousal" can rarely encompass the complexity and
subtlety of this fundamental emotional experience. Even the most sophisticated conceptualizations tend to describe the components involved, such
as sexual appetite, central arousal, and genital responses (Bancroft, 1983),
but fail to specify the necessary and sufficient conditions for labeling a
response as "sexual." For example, would "feeling sexy" in the absence
of erection or vaginal lubrication qualify as a sexual response? Conversely,
examples abound of genital responding in the context of nonsexual situations, such as during heightened emotional arousal (Zillmann, 1986) and
erections accompanying rapid eye movement (REM) sleep (Karacan, 1978).
This definitional issue is not unique to the topic of sexual responding, as
the study of human emotion has traditionally faced complex problems in
formulating definitions of feeling states, including anger, fear, and curiosity.

Through the brief history of sexology, as reviewed in Chapter 1, few
contributors have directly addressed the need for an adequate definition
of sexual arousal. This chapter therefore critically examines definitions of
sexual arousal in light of current psychophysiological theories of emotion.
In this context, we place special emphasis on the concept of "response
patterning," with particular reference to the salient role of cognitive and
affective processes in sexual arousal. This chapter also critiques available
models of the sexual response cycle, highlighting the assumption of a spe-

cific and predictable cycle of arousal believed to be associated with sexual response. This notion of the sexual response cycle is described succinctly by Bancroft (1983) as "an inevitable sequence of physiological events; a unitary concept of sexual arousal of both an incremental and sequential kind" (p. 48). Finally, we review the evidence for psychophysiological processes, such as habituation, conditioning, and autonomic balance, as additional determinants of response patterning in sexual arousal.

DEFINING THE SEXUAL RESPONSE

Historically, attempts to define the nature of human emotion have included a focus on both physiological and subjective processes. From the earliest times, it was recognized that perceptual processes were relevant in the experience of emotion. Aristotle included sense perception and emotional feelings as key functions of the "sensitive soul," which was postulated to differentiate animals from plants (Tyrer, 1976). Descartes, in keeping with his philosophy of dualism, separated physiological concomitants from the mental experience of emotion, which were believed to occur as parallel but noninteractive processes. It was not until the late 19th century, however, and the theories of William James (1884) and C. Lange (1885), that our current conceptualizations of human emotion began to emerge.

Influenced by the belief of 19th-century physiology that emotions arise from the activities of the internal (visceral) organs—in contrast to memory, judgment, and intelligence, which were attributed to the functions of the brain (Boring, 1950)—the James–Lange theory proposed that the experience of emotion results directly from the perception of somatic or peripheral physiological signs of arousal (e.g., increased heart rate, hyperventilation, tremors, and sweating). Lange, a Danish physician, drew particular attention to the role of peripheral physiological determinants by specifying that the vasomotor system functions as the coordinating center for the expression of all human emotions.

Subsequent theorizing (e.g., Dana, 1921; Cannon, 1927) focused greater attention to the role of central mechanisms in the mediation of emotional arousal. For example, according to Cannon's thalamic theory of emotion, the neurons of the thalamus "not only innervate muscles and viscera but also excite afferent paths to the cortex by direct connection or by irradiation" (Cannon, 1927, p. 58). The role of brain mechanisms in the specific control of sexual behavior was demonstrated first by Kluver and Bucy (1939), and was expanded upon greatly through studies of the psychosexual function of the limbic system by MacLean (1965) and others.

Primarily on the basis of brain stimulation studies in male squirrel monkeys, MacLean suggested that the central neural circuitry mediating sexual arousal in mammals is made up of specific components of the limbic system and median forebrain bundle, including the septum, mammillary bodies, mammillo-thalamic tract, anterior thalamic nuclei, and the anterior cingulate gyrus. In particular, the medial dorsal nucleus and medial septo-preoptic region were indicated as the nodal points for erection. Other studies have shown the importance of neural subsystems at the level of the spinal cord, leading one reviewer to the conclusion that "there is no [single] sex center; there are, rather, interacting neuronal subsystems that mediate different facets of the sexual process" (Whalen, 1976, p. 244).

In evaluating developments in laboratory sex research in recent years, it is apparent that the original Jamesian emphasis on peripheral physiological signs has probably been more influential, overall, in guiding current definitions of sexual response. Certainly, this approach is at the heart of the Masters and Johnson (1966) studies, which focused exclusively on the role of peripheral (autonomic) changes in their description of sexual arousal. In addition, the emphasis on peripheral physiology, particularly the genital vasocongestive processes associated with sexual response, may reflect the influence of primarily male-dominated theorizing and research in sexology, with its inevitable emphasis on penile–vaginal sexual contact—or as Zilbergeld has humorously described it, the "it's two feet long, hard as steel, and can go all night . . . model of sex" (Zilbergeld, 1978, p. 21).

The occurrence of relatively intense physiological arousal as a frequent concomitant of sexual response naturally focuses attention on the autonomic and somatic manifestations of this emotional state. Thus, in the tradition of Masters and Johnson, it is not unusual for accounts of sexual arousal to enumerate, extensive changes in cardiovascular, respiratory, vasocongestive, muscular, and other physiological activities occurring in response to sexual stimulation. While this approach has been useful in describing the widespread physiological reactions occurring during sexual arousal, the result has been a relative neg'ect of cognitive–affective processes and the potential interaction of these response dimensions. This issue is especially highlighted in this and subsequent chapters.

The emphasis on peripheral physiology has also included a focus on the importance of orgasm as a pivotal component and the culmination of the sexual arousal process. In fact, sex researchers since Kinsey have frequently viewed the occurrence of orgasm as a necessary condition in the definition of sexual response. For Kinsey, this emphasis was guided, in large part, by the practical considerations involved in choosing a quantifiable unit of sexual behavior for study as a "sexual outlet":

Since practically all sexual contacts . . . involve emotional changes, all adult contacts might be considered means of outlet, even though they do not lead to orgasm. These emotional situations are, however, of such variable intensity that they are difficult to assess and compare; and, for the sake of achieving some precision in analysis, the present discussion of outlets is confined to those instances of sexual activity which culminate in orgasm. (Kinsey, Pomeroy, & Martin, 1948, p. 193)

Despite the empirical advantages of excluding nonorgasmic sexual expe-

riences and feelings from the definition of a sexual outlet, this approach inevitably resulted in certain biases and limitations in the Kinsey *et al.* data (Robinson, 1976). In the models of sexual response described by Masters and Johnson (1966) and Kaplan (1979), the occurrence of orgasm similarly occupies a central role. Recent writers on the topic (e.g., Ladas, Whipple, & Perry, 1982) have placed even greater emphasis on the peripheral physiological concomitants of orgasm. While unarguably an important aspect of most sexual interactions, the prevailing emphasis on orgasm is problematic in several respects.

Most authors acknowledge the prevalence of sexual arousal phenomena that do not culminate in orgasm (e.g., sexual fantasy, sexual dreams, viewing erotica). While such experiences may be judged as less intense than sexual stimulation to the point of orgasm, inclusion of these phenomena in the definition of sexual response is clearly important. In addition, instances of orgasm occurring in nonsexual situations are well known in the literature (e.g., Ramsey, 1943; Redmond, Kosten, & Reiser, 1982; Flor-Henry, 1978) and are frequently accompanied by nonspecific sympathetic arousal. Lastly, despite the pivotal role of orgasm in psychophysiological formulations of sexual response, much of the available laboratory research to date has focused on the early stages of sexual arousal, usually reporting relatively low to moderate levels of arousal. In fact, much of the experimental research to be reviewed in subsequent chapters has been conducted on sexual arousal in the absence of orgasm. Thus, while orgasm is an important component of the sexual response, it has overshadowed other aspects of the response process in most models of sexual arousal.

THE ROLE OF COGNITIVE LABELING AND SUBJECTIVE EXPERIENCE

Despite an emphasis in the literature on peripheral physiological concomitants of sexual arousal, a key thesis to be advanced in this book is that physiological changes *alone* are not sufficient to account for the range of experiences involved in sexual arousal. The interrelationships between subjective and physiological dimensions of arousal have only recently begun to be explored in sexual psychophysiology, in contrast to extensive research on this topic in other areas of emotion. In particular, since the early studies of Schachter and Singer (1962), and their proposal of the "cognitive arousal" theory of emotion, two decades of concentrated research have been devoted to the interaction between physiological and cognitive processes in emotion (see reviews by Leventhal, 1980; Reisenzein, 1983; Zillmann, 1978).

The theory of cognitive arousal generally holds that the experience of emotion is predicated on the occurrence of both physiological arousal and a state of "emotional" cognition, as illustrated in Figure 2.1. In the case

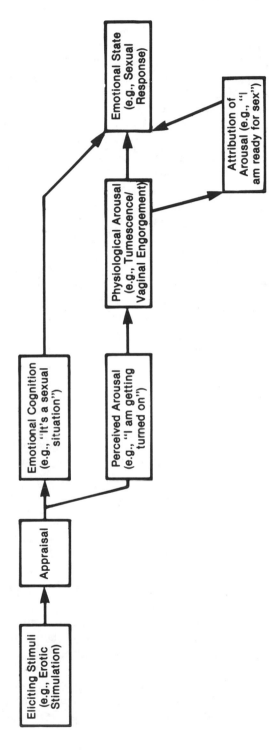

Figure 2.1. A cognitive arousal model for sexual response. This model illustrates the interaction between physiological and cognitive aspects of sexual arousal. Adapted from Reisenzein (1983).

of sexual feelings, it can be hypothesized that following the initial appraisal of a situation as "sexual," erotic cues function both to arouse physiological reactions and the perceptions thereof, as well as initiating a concomitant cognitive labeling process. After the initial response to stimulation, the individual's perception of his or her state of autonomic arousal (e.g., erection, vaginal lubrication) might be expected to contribute further to the subjective awareness of feeling aroused. An important implication of the cognitive arousal theory is that a given situation will not be experienced as sexual, despite the presence of genital arousal, without the occurrence of the appropriate emotional attribution.

It should be noted that experimental support for the cognitive arousal approach, as a general theory of emotion, is mixed. Schachter and Singer's original emphasis on "a general pattern of sympathetic excitation" (1962, p. 380) as the energizing force for most or all emotional experiences has not been strongly supported (Marshall & Zimbardo, 1979; Maslach, 1979). However, the hypothesis that arousal from an extraneous source can intensify emotional experiences in some situations has led to some interesting findings. For example, Cantor, Zillmann, and Bryant (1975) examined this "excitation transfer" hypothesis in the context of a study of the effects of prior physical exercise on subsequent exposure to erotic films. Specifically, these authors were able to demonstrate that residual autonomic arousal following exercise enhanced self-ratings of sexual arousal, but only under circumstances in which the residual arousal was not likely to be attributed to the effects of the exercise. An interesting clinical application of the "excitation transfer" concept can be found in a case presentation of treatment for low sex drive by Zilbergeld and Ellison (1980), in which the authors successfully recommended the use of prior physical exercise (tennis) to heighten the patient's interest and arousal during subsequent sex with her partner.

In the tradition of the cognitive arousal theory of emotion, we would assert that the interactions among several dimensions of arousal, including the physiological, cognitive, affective, and motivational components, are crucial for defining a response as sexual. In contrast to the original formulations of Schachter and Singer (1962), however, we would emphasize that sexual arousal cannot be viewed as arising out of a state of diffuse or nonspecific (sympathetic) activation, given the stimulus–response specificity of genital vasocongestion. With reference to the salience of cognitive attributional processes in defining emotional experiences generally (e.g., Reisenzein, 1983), however, we find that much of the theory and research on sexual response has neglected this all-important dimension. From our perspective, sexual arousal cannot be defined adequately without highlighting the critical role of cognitive labeling and subjective experience in determining the response to a given stimulus *as sexual*. Ultimately, we would hold that an individual's awareness or self-report of internally experienced arousal is primary in defining a response as sexual, irrespective of the nature or extent of his or her physiological reactions.

Recognizing that this position represents a departure from the peripheral and physiological emphasis seen in most conventional definitions of sexual response, we nevertheless maintain that the inclusion of a cognitive–subjective criterion for defining sexual response is essential. In most instances, a relatively high degree of concordance between physiological and subjective dimensions of response is to be expected. In fact, the perception of physiological arousal may function as a primary cue for subjective experience in most sexual situations (e.g., Sakheim, Barlow, Beck, & Abrahamson, 1984). However, for the purposes of understanding the underlying causal relationships, and of defining systematically the necessary components of sexual response, this concordance should not be taken for granted.

Instances of discordance between these response components serve to highlight the potential complexity of sexual arousal phenomena, and the resulting need for a multidimensional methodology in sexual psychophysiology. Of particular note are examples in which sexual arousal may be experienced in the relative absence of physical stimulation or genital arousal, such as sometimes occurs during visual stimulation or sexual fantasy. These examples underscore the necessity for placing subjective experience in a central role in our definition and account of sexual response, as is humorously illustrated in Erica Jong's fictional observations on the experience of sexual arousal without subjective involvement:

She feels as if he has outlined the erogenous zones of her body with eyebrow pencil, so that he can find them more easily. First he stimulates her nipples with his fingertips, then he proceeds to her thighs. . . . She responds (she nearly always responds) but her overwhelming impulse is to giggle. She thinks of that early Brian dePalma movie, *Greetings*, in which a Kennedy-assassination nut of the late sixties is drawing entry and exit wounds on his girl friend's naked body. Roland's lovemaking seems oddly cerebral. . . . What is sex when feeling is removed? (Jong, 1985, p. 106)

RESPONSE PATTERNS IN SEXUAL AROUSAL

Much of traditional psychophysiological research on emotion has focused on the interrelationships between response systems in differentiating patterns of activation to specific stimuli or to specific affective states (e.g., Ax, 1953; Davis, 1957; Schwartz, 1978). In the first approach, different classes of physical and psychological conditions that evoke characteristic response patterns are identified, the objective being to assess "stimulus-specific response" (SSR) patterning. For example, Farkas and Rosen (1976) presented erotic films to normal male volunteers under conditions of alcohol and placebo administration. In this study, distinct patterns of penile tumescence and heart rate were observed in association with each of the alcohol dosage levels and conditions of erotic stimulation. Further details of the study are discussed in Chapter 12.

Recognizing that response patterning to specific stimuli may vary greatly, according to the affective state of the individual and cognitive appraisal of the experimental situation, Ax (1964) and others have described the role of "motivation-specific response" (MSR) patterning. According to Fahrenberg (1986), MSR patterning is distinguished from SSR patterning in the focus on response correlates of a given *emotional state*, as opposed to activation patterns attributable to a *specific stimulus*. For example, Tucker and Dawson (1984) examined a range of EEG variables in Method actors during self-induced states of depression and sexual arousal, demonstrating distinctive MSR patterning in association with each emotional state. In applying these concepts to studies of sexual response generally, the key question to be addressed is our ability to differentiate sexual arousal from other emotional states—or, as Zuckerman (1971) has asked, "Are there any autonomic [or other physiological] reactions that can distinguish sexual arousal from other states of arousal such as fear and anger?" (p. 301).

In the earliest laboratory study of this issue, Wenger, Averill, and Smith (1968) compared patterns of change in blood pressure, skin conductance, respiration, finger pulse volume, skin temperature, and heart rate as male volunteers read sexually stimulating or control (travelogue) materials. Each of the experimental and control conditions were separated by a 6-minute rest period, during which subjects were instructed to relax prior to the next stimulus presentation. As shown in Figure 2.2, results indicated significant increases in systolic and diastolic blood pressure, as well as elevations in palmar skin conductance, during sexual stimulation. In contrast, heart rate and respiration rates remained relatively constant throughout the experimental procedure. A biphasic pattern of response was observed in finger pulse volume and skin temperature measures. Although no independent measures of genital response were employed, self-report data from the subjects indicated that the erotic materials had induced moderate levels of sexual arousal in most subjects. The authors recommended a cautious interpretation of these findings, however, suggesting that autonomic response patterns may change qualitatively as well as quantitatively with higher levels of arousal. We return to this issue in our discussion of the sexual response cycle.

While much of the basic psychophysiological research on emotion has focused on response patterning associated with fear and anger (e.g., Ax, 1953; Davis, 1957), this concept has clear relevance for investigations of sexual response. In fact, the patterning of peripheral physiological changes during sexual arousal has been explored extensively, most notably in the work of Masters and Johnson (1966). Although these studies have been

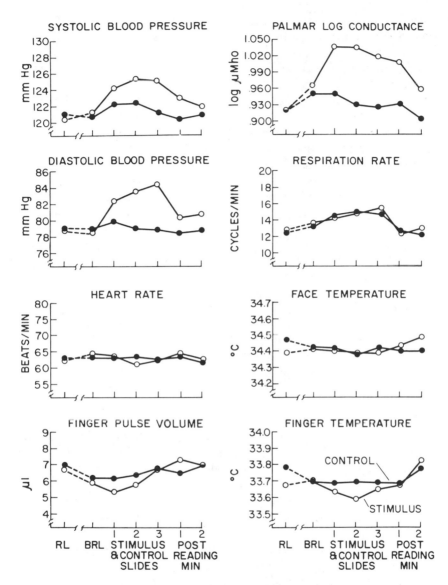

Figure 2.2. Mean activity of eight autonomic variables during the reading of sexually stimulating and innocuous material (stimulus and control reading series). The abscissa of each graph represents the following data points: the prereading or resting level (RL), the basal reading level (BRL), the three stimulus and control slides, and the first and second postreading minutes. Control series data are shown by closed circles; stimulus series data are shown by open circles. From "Autonomic Activity during Sexual Arousal" by M. A. Wenger, J. R. Averill, and D. D. Smith, 1968, *Psychophysiology, 4,* p. 473. Copyright 1968 by the Society for Psychophysiological Research. Reprinted by permission.

criticized for paying little attention to the interaction of physiological and subjective dimensions of arousal, more recently, a number of investigators (e.g., Heiman, 1980; Farkas, Sine, & Evans, 1979; Stock & Geer, 1982) have included a focus on subjective arousal variables in describing sexual response patterns. Mosher (1980), in particular, has developed an elaborate framework for understanding subjective involvement in sexual arousal, modeled after the shifts in consciousness believed to occur during hypnotic trance states. Similarly, Cohen *et al.* (1976) and Tucker (1983) have described characteristic patterns of central (EEG) arousal associated with sexual arousal in both sexes.

An alternative approach to the study of response patterning can be found in the concept of "individual-specific response" (ISR) patterning, or the consistency of individual reactions across stimulus situations (Fahrenberg, 1986). This approach arises from the observation that while most individuals will respond to a given stimulus with a characteristic response pattern (SSR), some subjects will display idiosyncratic or stereotypical aspects of response patterning (ISR). With respect to sexual responding, the ISR concept implies that individual or subject variables may play an important role in determining the overall pattern of sexual arousal. For example, Bancroft and Bell (1985) have recently described various patterns of penile tumescence and pulse amplitude responses to sexual stimulation in normal males. Many of the subjects in this study showed a distinctive pattern of association between these two variables, which did not appear to be related to the type of stimulus presented or the extent of arousal achieved.

This concept also draws our attention to the importance of individual differences in the experience of sexual arousal, and the need to recognize diversity in styles of sexual expression. Perhaps more so than with other emotional states, concerns about sexual "normality" are pervasive in our society, and are readily translated into idealized standards for performance. An emphasis on ISR patterning, on the other hand, serves as a reminder of the dangers inherent in attempting to establish societal norms for sexual conduct.

Certain issues within sexual psychophysiology have been approached predominantly from one or another of these perspectives. For example, measurement concerns usually are studied with SSR patterning in mind (e.g., Rosen & Keefe, 1978; Hatch, 1979), while clinical investigations often are organized around ISR paradigms (e.g., Beck & Barlow, 1984; Heiman & Rowland, 1981). Despite the differences in emphasis, however, these major approaches to the study of response patterning should not be viewed as antithetical or mutually exclusive. Rather, as suggested by Fahrenberg (1986), ISR patterning can be conceptualized as being "superimposed" on the psychophysiological arousal patterns generated by specific stimuli or emotional states.[1] While this emphasis has been applied mainly to research on personality factors in psychosomatic disorders, the concepts and methodology for analysis of response patterning may be particularly applicable in future studies of sexual arousal.

INTERACTIVE MECHANISMS AND THE COMPONENTS OF SEXUAL RESPONSE

In contrast to the growing body of research on stimulus and individual factors as determinants of response patterning in sexual arousal, little systematic attention has been given to specifying the relevant components of sexual arousal or to investigating the interactive mechanisms involved. The key question to be addressed here is "What are the essential components of sexual response, and how do they interact to produce arousal?" While most studies have focused on genital vasocongestion and subjective arousal as the two primary response components, inclusion of other important response dimensions has been suggested, and investigation of the potential interrelationships between and among components is an issue of growing concern. In Chapters 3 and 4, for example, we consider in detail the interactive mechanisms affecting genital and subjective measures of arousal in both males and females.

Among the current theorists to identify specific dimensions of sexual response, Bancroft (1983) has described four essential features of sexual arousal: (1) sexual appetite or drive; (2) central arousal; (3) genital responses; and (4) peripheral arousal. Included in the category of sexual appetite or drive, according to Bancroft, are both motivational factors (e.g., "libido") and sexual arousability. Other authors (e.g., Whalen, 1966) have viewed sexual arousability as a dimension separate from desire, and have defined it as the individual's propensity for arousal given an adequate source of sexual stimulation. Central arousal, Bancroft's second component of sexual response, refers to central nervous system (CNS) activation and attentional factors that underlie psychological processing of sexual stimuli. This component of sexual response is one of the most recent to be studied empirically, as we describe below. In contrast, the third and fourth components described by Bancroft, genital responses and peripheral arousal, have received the most extensive discussion to date (e.g., Masters & Johnson, 1966) and are generally the least controversial.

---

1. In this regard, Fahrenberg has described the use of a particularly innovative approach to pattern analysis, in which the basic concepts of concordance analysis developed by Engel and his colleagues (Engel, 1960; Engel & Bickford, 1961) are used to superimpose individual data from multiple subjects across different task conditions.

While this approach to identifying specific components of arousal is noteworthy, Bancroft, like most other contributors in the field, is able to offer few specific predictions concerning the interrelationships between and among components. Recognizing the inherent complexity of interactional mechanisms, he introduces the possibility of reciprocal influences between at least two of the key response elements, central and peripheral arousal:

We should not assume . . . that central arousal and peripheral arousal are linked manifestations of the same process. They are clearly related, but in a potentially complex way. One individual may respond to awareness of peripheral changes with increased excitement, another may interpret changes inappropriately and react with fear. The two processes whilst interrelated are potentially independent of one another. (Bancroft, 1983, p. 52)

Beyond acknowledging the importance of interactive processes in relating the effects of central and peripheral components of arousal, Bancroft resists further speculation about these interrelationships. Other authors, however, have begun to explore systematically certain aspects of the cognitive–physiological interaction. For example, Geer and Fuhr (1976), in the first study of this type, employed a dichotic listening paradigm to examine the influence of cognitive distraction on peripheral arousal (penile tumescence) in college-aged males. Specifically, these authors presented arithmetic tasks of increasing complexity simultaneously with erotic audiotapes. The results indicated that as the cognitive tasks became more demanding, tumescence diminished in direct proportion to the level of distraction. At the most extreme level of distraction, which consisted of a complex counting and labeling task, some subjects reported "not hearing" the erotic stimulus; this finding suggests overloading of the cognitive processing that is necessary for sexual arousal to occur.

In the course of replicating the results of this study, Farkas et al. (1979) examined the interactive effects of distraction and performance demand on tumescence. Related areas of investigation have included studies of the effects of attentional focus on sexual dysfunction (Beck, Barlow, & Sakheim, 1983b), alcohol expectancy effects on male sexual arousal (G. T. Wilson & Lawson, 1976b), and exploration of the effect of anxiety on sexual responding (Wincze, Hoon, & Hoon, 1976). These studies have begun to delineate key aspects of the interaction between cognitive and physiological processes involved in the experience of sexual arousal, while also highlighting the methodological difficulties inherent in studying such interactive mechanisms.

Perhaps the most comprehensive model to date of interaction between response components in sexual arousal has been proposed by Byrne (1977, 1986). According to Byrne, the sexual behavior sequence is multidetermined and comprised of several reciprocally influencing processes (see Figure 2.3). Included in this model is a description of (1) external events,

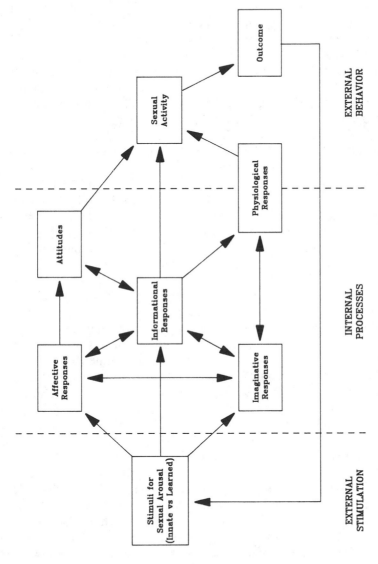

Figure 2.3. Byrne's model of the sexual behavior sequence. Adapted from Byrne and Fisher (1983).

such as erotic stimuli and specific partner behaviors; (2) internal mediational variables, which subsume transitory emotional responses; and (3) more enduring cognitive–affective reactions, and the full range of behavioral outcomes.

Three cognitive–affective dimensions, in particular, are hypothesized to mediate the effects of erotic stimulation on physiological arousal. These include imagery processes, such as memories, fantasies, and other imaginal representations; informational responses, encompassing beliefs, knowledge, and expectations concerning sexuality; and affective responses, such as judgments, feelings, and other subjective perceptions. In regard to this latter component, Byrne (1983) has further described a dimension of affective reaction, termed "erotophobia–erotophilia," which is viewed as a key mediating variable. This constellation of attitudes refers to a generalized evaluative–emotional response to sexuality, which has a positive (erotophilia) or negative (erotophobia) valence. This affective response has been shown to influence individuals' willingness to experience erotic stimulation (Byrne, Jazwinski, DeNinno, & Fisher, 1977); the duration and intensity of erotic fantasies (Moreault & Follingstad, 1978); and the degree of subjective arousal and perception of genital sensation in response to erotic stimulation (Mosher & O'Grady, 1979). While much of Byrne's research has explored the influence of erotophobia–erotophilia upon other components of the sexual behavior sequence, this model represents the most comprehensive attempt to date to explain relevant interactive mechanisms of sexual arousal. However, as can be seen in Figure 2.3, the model is highly complex, with little potential for clear predictive statements in view of the complex network of feedback loops throughout.

The most recent model of interactive mechanisms in sexual arousal has been proposed by Barlow (1986). Focusing primarily on factors involved in the development of sexual dysfunction, Barlow describes a postulated sequencing of interactive processes as follows (see Figure 2.4). Beginning with the perception of external expectations for sexual arousal, the individual responds emotionally to these perceptions with a positive or negative affective evaluation. This affective response, in turn, influences those features of the erotic situation that are most salient for attention. The affective response also triggers autonomic arousal, which further sharpens attentional focus. Continued processing of erotic cues produces further synergistic effects on genital arousal, which ultimately lead to sexual approach behavior. Sexual avoidance behavior, which is characteristic of dysfunctional arousal patterns, is hypothesized to result from disturbances in the mediating attentional processes. As reviewed by Barlow (1986), preliminary laboratory support for this model has been obtained from a number of studies.

A common element in both Byrne's and Barlow's models is a focus on cognitive–affective processes in the mediation of sexual arousal, with

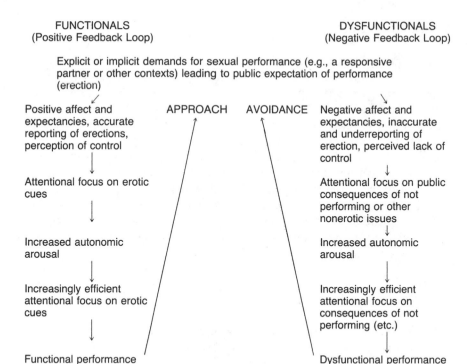

FUNCTIONALS
(Positive Feedback Loop)

DYSFUNCTIONALS
(Negative Feedback Loop)

Explicit or implicit demands for sexual performance (e.g., a responsive
partner or other contexts) leading to public expectation of performance
(erection)

APPROACH   AVOIDANCE

Positive affect and
expectancies, accurate
reporting of erections,
perception of control

Negative affect and
expectancies, inaccurate
and underreporting of
erection, perceived lack of
control

Attentional focus on erotic
cues

Attentional focus on public
consequences of not
performing or other
nonerotic issues

Increased autonomic
arousal

Increased autonomic
arousal

Increasingly efficient
attentional focus on erotic
cues

Increasingly efficient
attentional focus on
consequences of not
performing (etc.)

Functional performance

Dysfunctional performance

Figure 2.4. Barlow's model of the psychophysiological processes involved in sexual
function and dysfunction. From "Causes of Sexual Dysfunction: The Role of Anxiety and Cognitive Interference" by D. H. Barlow, 1986, *Journal of Consulting
and Clinical Psychology, 54,* p. 146. Copyright 1986 by the American Psychological
Association. Reprinted by permission.

particular emphasis on the perception of physiological activation and the
processing of erotic cues. Both models have served as useful heuristics for
exploring the interactive mechanisms involved in sexual response. However, neither model specifies with adequate precision the necessary or
sufficient conditions for the occurrence of sexual arousal, nor does either
approach pay detailed attention to factors responsible for response patterning from one individual to another. In addition, both of these models
tend to view physiological arousal as a simple, unitary construct. Nonetheless, these models represent an important first step toward a conceptualization of interactive mechanisms and a specification of key components
of sexual response. Just as we have emphasized that the subjective experience of arousal should be viewed as the *sine qua non* for defining a sexual
response, we would similarly contend that interactive mechanisms function
as the key to mediation of sexual arousal. This perspective is elaborated
further in our discussion of the sexual response cycle.

MODELS OF THE SEXUAL RESPONSE CYCLE

A fundamental assumption underlying most conceptualizations of sexual response is that sexual arousal processes are likely to follow a predictable sequence of events, and that a cyclical pattern of physiological responding can be identified. This key concept has guided much of the theorizing on sexual response since the earliest writings of Havelock Ellis (1906). Despite the general acceptance and common-sense appeal of this concept, it is important to note that there is a lack of consensus among researchers in the field concerning the number of phases to be included in the sexual response cycle, as well as the order and sequencing of such phases. However useful and appealing, the concept of a sexual response cycle ought to be viewed as little more than a convenient abstraction, which may mask important variations in response patterns and sequencing from one individual or instance to another.

Two-Stage Models

Historically, the first explicit depiction of a sexual response cycle was the two-stage model of Havelock Ellis (1906), which was based on the processes of "tumescence" ("the piling on of the fuel") and "detumescence" ("the leaping out of the devouring flame"). In Ellis's description: "In tumescence the organism is slowly wound up and force accumulated; in the act of detumescence the accumulated force is let go, and by its liberation the sperm-bearing instrument is driven home" (1906, Vol. 1, p. 142). For Ellis the terms "tumescence" and "detumescence" were synonymous with the buildup and release of sexual energy, and were applied to the cycle of sexual arousal in both males and females. While these terms continue to be widely used, their meaning has become restricted to genital vaso-congestion, principally in the male.

In addition, Ellis recognized the importance of psychological processes, despite the apparent emphasis of his model on autonomic changes: "Yet detumescence is the end and climax of the whole drama; it is an anatomic–physiological process, certainly, but one that inevitably touches psychology at every point (1906, Vol. 1, p. 142).

As in other areas, Ellis's two-stage model of sexual response has been highly influential in guiding contemporary sexual thought. His basic differentiation of sexual arousal into a process of building excitement ("tumescence"), to be followed by a climactic release ("detumescence"), has served as a cornerstone for more elaborate models of sexual response.

Based on experimental studies of copulatory behavior in rats, Beach (1956) has proposed an alternative two-stage model of male sexual arousal, in which the initial stages of excitement are attributed to the "sexual arousal mechanism" (SAM). Once the male animal has become sufficiently aroused to mount the female and to achieve intromission, the second stage of the process, described as the "intromission and ejaculatory mechanism" (IEM), is said to occur. After copulation has been achieved, excitement is typically maintained through the action of this mechanism until ejaculation occurs. Male rats experience a postejaculatory refractory period lasting for several minutes, following which "the SAM is reactivated and mating is resumed" (Beach, 1956, p. 23). In reviewing the evidence for such mechanisms in human sexual behavior, Zuckerman (1971) has suggested that the SAM is primarily stimulated by parasympathetic activity, whereas the IEM is associated with the sympathetic components of sexual arousal. Subsequent evidence suggests that penile erection can be due either to parasympathetic or to sympathetic activity, with a delicate homeostasis maintained between the two systems (e.g., McConnel, Benson, & Wood, 1979; Weiss, 1972). Much of the impetus for this later research was derived from Beach's original formulations of the SAM–IEM model of sexual arousal.

The Four-Stage Model of Masters and Johnson

The four-stage model of Masters and Johnson (1966) has served as the central organizing schema for their observations of sexual physiology in both sexes (see Figure 2.5), as well as for their subsequent classification of sexual dysfunction (Masters & Johnson, 1970). The model includes the well-known phases of excitement, plateau, orgasm, and resolution, each of which has associated genital and extragenital changes.[2] As has already been noted, this model focuses exclusively on peripheral physiological changes that occur in response to "effective sexual stimulation." Whereas Ellis emphasized the interaction between the physiological and cognitive–subjective aspects of sexual response, Masters and Johnson have constructed their four-stage model entirely on the basis of bodily responses to sexual arousal. Moreover, they have emphasized that their model should be viewed as little more than an arbitrary construct, or a "framework of reference," in the sense that numerous alternatives and variations in the particulars of sexual response have been recognized.

The assumption of male–female similarities in sexual response is a major hallmark of the Masters and Johnson model. In seeking to highlight the capacity of women for sexual responding, and to dispel popular myths concerning the "sexual inferiority" of the female, they have attempted to draw parallels on multiple dimensions between male and female arousal

---

2. According to Money (1980), the earliest four-stage model can be found in the writings of Albert Moll at about the turn of the century, which antedated the four phases of Masters and Johnson.

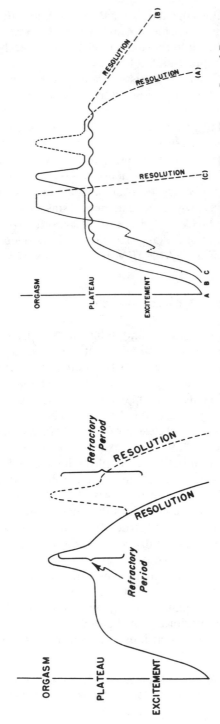

Figure 2.5. The male (left) and female (right) sexual response cycle according to Masters and Johnson. From *Human Sexual Response* (p. 5) by W. H. Masters and V. E. Johnson, 1966, Boston: Little, Brown. Reprinted by permission.

processes. For example, during the excitement phase, vaginal lubrication in the female is compared directly to penile erection in the male, particularly in respect to such parameters as "reactive intensity," the timing of the response, and age-related changes. However, this tendency to equate male and female sexual response may unintentionally have obscured possible sex differences in excitement and orgasm. In their observations on the vaginal–clitoral orgasm distinction, Masters and Johnson have again emphasized the relative uniformity of orgasmic processes between the sexes.

In recent years, this model has been the target of criticism on both conceptual and empirical grounds. These criticisms are not intended to detract from the profound impact of the Masters and Johnson studies of sexual response, or from their ongoing contribution to contemporary sexology. Indeed, their initial studies provided, in large part, the major paradigm for subsequent laboratory sex research, despite the oversimplification and limitations of the four-stage model of sexual response.

In examining the Masters and Johnson four-stage model, Robinson (1976), for example, has drawn attention to the largely contrived separation of sexual response into four discrete stages, especially the distinction between the excitement and the plateau phases, which Robinson refers to as "a groundless differentiation." He emphasizes that most of the phenomena identified with the excitement phase are also observed in the plateau phase, and that the process of arousal is better conceptualized as a continuous progression of events: "Clearly what is being described here . . . is not a two-stage process (excitement/plateau), but a continuous progression, or, if you prefer a musical metaphor, a gradual crescendo" (Robinson, 1976, p. 129).

Another criticism of the Masters and Johnson model is the relative lack of synthesis of cognitive–affective states with the physiological processes of sexual arousal. Subjective arousal factors are generally overlooked in their model. Moreover, even when discussing changes in physiological activity, they fail to provide an explanation for the observed patterning of autonomic, somatic, and central concomitants of sexual response. While Masters and Johnson have enumerated in considerable detail the specifics of physiological response, explanatory concepts for integrating these separate response dimensions are lacking. Overall, one is left with an impressive but essentially disjointed description of physiological events.

The Kaplan Three-Stage Model

Noting the relative neglect of motivational and psychological factors in the Masters and Johnson model, Kaplan (1977, 1979) has served as another critic of the field of sex therapy for failing to address the importance of sexual desire deficits in clinical disorders of sexual function. Accordingly, she has recommended that the sexual response cycle be reconceptualized as consisting of three phases: desire, excitement, and orgasm. The Kaplan triphasic model has had its greatest impact on the current clinical classification system (the *Diagnostic and Statistical Manual of Mental Disorders*, third edition [DSM-III]), in which Inhibited Sexual Desire and Inhibited Sexual Excitement have recently been included as separate diagnostic categories (American Psychiatric Association, 1980).

Kaplan's proposed first stage, desire, is comparable to the traditional concept of "libido," and is described as the experience of specific sensations that motivate the individual to initiate or become responsive to sexual stimulation. In addition to specifying the manner in which desire is experienced, Kaplan identifies the source of libido as originating from activation of certain centers in the limbic system:

These sensations are produced by the physical activation of a specific neural system in the brain. When this system is active, a person is "horny," he may feel genital sensations, or he may feel vaguely sexy, interested in sex, open to sex, or even just restless. These sensations cease after sexual gratification, i.e., orgasm. (Kaplan, 1979, p. 10)

According to the Kaplan model, the second stage, excitement, is identified with reflex genital vasocongestion in both sexes. Little additional information is provided about this phase, beyond Masters and Johnson's description of the physiology of excitement and plateau. Orgasm, the third stage of Kaplan's model, consists of reflex pelvic muscle contractions. A key postulate of this model is that these three phases are mediated by separate and interrelated neurophysiological mechanisms. While the first phase, desire, is said to be generated by central mechanisms (i.e., limbic activation), excitement and orgasm are associated with the stimulation of peripheral reflex pathways in the lower spinal cord. This distinction is novel and appealing in certain respects, but specification of anatomical sites and physiological mechanisms is lacking, as are data in support of the differentiation of drive as centrally mediated versus excitement and orgasm as peripherally based processes.

By introducing a motivational component to her model of the sexual response cycle, Kaplan has taken an innovative and important step toward a broader conceptualization of sexual arousal. Certainly, in regard to the current nosology and classification of sexual dysfunction (e.g., DSM-III; American Psychiatric Association, 1980), this approach has had a major effect on clinical theory and practice. However, Kaplan's concept of desire appears to be derived largely from her psychodynamic perspective of motivational processes. As a result, this phase of sexual response is lacking in operational definition and is linked inadequately to the other two phases of sexual response (i.e., excitement and orgasm).

More specifically, the hypothesis that desire is a necessary precondition for the occurrence of excitement and orgasm is contradicted by evidence from multiple sources. For example, Garde and Lunde (1980) have reported that approximately 33% of a representative sample of 40-year-old Danish women never experience spontaneous desire, despite adequate arousal and orgasm. It is noteworthy that these women were not selected on the basis of sexual dysfunction, and that almost all (96%) of the sample were able to achieve orgasm. In addition, examples from clinical case studies indicate the complex and often subtle interplay between desire and arousal difficulties in both men and women (Leiblum, & Rosen, in press).

Another criticism of Kaplan's triphasic model is the lack of elaboration of the excitement and orgasm phases. To an even greater extent than Masters and Johnson, Kaplan describes these phases of sexual response in purely reflexive terms, and focuses exclusively on peripheral physiological changes in defining excitement and orgasm. Like her predecessors, Kaplan also has strongly emphasized the similarities between male and female physiological responses during excitement and orgasm, although she overlooks the role of extragenital or subjective changes during the latter phases of the response cycle. While the addition of a desire phase in her triphasic model is clearly an original and significant contribution, the model is disappointing in the lack of information provided concerning the processes of sexual excitement and orgasm.

Comment

In reviewing these models of the sexual response cycle, one can draw a number of key generalizations concerning the need for such models and the particular emphases of each. In general, attempts to characterize sexual arousal as an orderly sequence or progression of psychophysiological events are defensible on both logical and empirical grounds. Emotional states are generally viewed as incorporating patterns of activation, in which the individual progresses from a neutral state through a process of increasing arousal, terminating with a return to the unaroused condition (e.g., Cannon, 1939; Davis, 1958). Certainly, everyday experience attests to the progressive nature and "buildup" of sexual response, with the process of resolution being as intricate and remarkable as the experience of arousal.

Thus, while we would concur with the need for a formulation of sexual arousal in these terms, existing attempts to delineate multiple, specific stages of sexual response have presented an incomplete and potentially biased view of the process. Ellis's (1906) original two-stage model, or the similar two-stage model presented by Beach (1956), perhaps are the most viable in this respect; they are the most parsimonious, while posing the fewest artificial constraints on the phenomena of arousal. In fact, the bulk of the research to be reviewed in subsequent chapters is focused on the two fundamental phases of excitement and orgasm. The four-stage and three-stage models can be viewed as little more than elaborations of this biphasic concept, with questionable justification for categorization of additional phases.

Despite the overall emphasis on physiological processes in each of the models described, it is somewhat surprising that scant attention has been paid to key psychophysiological concepts such as autonomic balance and adaptation–rebound in this regard. "Autonomic balance" refers to the relative state of activation of the sympathetic and parasympathetic branches of the autonomic nervous system, and the tendency for a homeostatic return to stability between these two neurophysiological systems following emotional activation (e.g., Gellhorn, 1957; Wenger, 1966, 1972). Whereas this concept has been applied extensively to the explanation of cardiovascular activation processes (e.g., Obrist, 1981), and while the interaction between parasympathetic and sympathetic processes in cardiac regulation has been extensively studied, the sexual response has yet to be examined from this perspective. As an example, this concept might be of value in clarifying mechanisms involved in the resolution phase, or as a framework for understanding the sequence of responses subsequent to orgasm.

Similarly, the concepts of "adaptation" and "rebound" refer to changes in the strength of physiological responding with continuous stimulation over time. In particular, the phenomenon of rebound has been defined as an "overshooting" of resting physiological levels following an intense period of stimulation (Gellhorn, 1957). Possibly, the "refractory phase," which Masters and Johnson (1966) have identified as occurring during the postorgasmic interval, and in which "effective restimulation" will not result in sexual tension, can be conceptualized as a specific instance of the rebound phenomenon. A similar process has been identified in the opponent process theory of motivation (Solomon & Corbit, 1974), suggesting that the rebound concept might be usefully applied to the study of sexual interest and desire. Overall, definitions of sexual response would benefit greatly from increased attention to key psychophysiological concepts.

PATTERNS OF RESPONSE IN SEXUALLY DYSFUNCTIONAL INDIVIDUALS

Historically, concepts of sexual response have been anchored in the study of clinical and applied concerns. The models of Masters and Johnson and of Kaplan were clearly conceived as frameworks for classifying types of sexual dysfunction, and have served to guide etiological and treatment formulations for the field of sex therapy generally. In particular, Kaplan's introduction of a desire phase in her model of the sexual response cycle was instigated largely by her disillusionment with the outcome of conventional sex therapy interventions for individuals with diminished sexual interest. One positive outcome of this clinical emphasis has been a growing empirical focus on the mechanisms and efficacy of sex therapy, as well as a more thorough understanding of the nature of the various sexual disorders. As we discuss in Chapters 10 and 11, increasingly refined assessment and diagnostic procedures for sexual dysfunction have resulted from this association as well. In this section, we review several key areas of application of models of the sexual response in the study of sexual dysfunction. As will be noted, clinical research has provided a rich source of data for examination of theoretical formulations of sexual arousal.

Current interest in clinical applications has fostered a strong research emphasis of comparisons between patterns of response in functional and dysfunctional individuals. For example, Kockott, Feil, Ferstl, Aldenhoof, and Besinger (1980) have described patterns of autonomic and somatic arousal during sexual stimulation in matched samples of men with primary and secondary erectile dysfunction, premature ejaculation of two types, diabetes-related erectile failure, and normal controls. Similarly, Morokoff and Heiman (1980) have compared patterns of genital vasocongestion and subjective arousal in functional and dysfunctional women, with the goal of establishing clinical profiles for orgasmic dysfunction. Based upon the findings of a number of studies such as these, Barlow (1986) has proposed a psychophysiological theory of sexual arousal (described above), which contrasts the response patterns of dysfunctional and normal samples. Clearly, there is a growing accumulation of clinical comparison studies describing the range of functional and dysfunctional reactions to sexual stimulation. This research paradigm has evolved rapidly, despite the relative lack of information concerning response patterning in normals.

Perhaps the most striking example of this trend can be found in the recent literature on nocturnal penile tumescence (NPT). As reviewed in Chapter 10, the last decade has witnessed a plethora of studies on NPT, most of which have attempted to delineate patterns of arousal in various clinical subgroups (e.g., Karacan, 1978; Marshall, Surridge, & Delva, 1981; Fisher *et al.*, 1979). Again, these studies have placed considerable emphasis on differentiating functional and dysfunctional patterns, without adequate explanation of the basic processes involved in NPT per se (Rosen, Goldstein, Scoles, & Lazarus, 1986).

The influence of clinical concerns in sexual psychophysiology has extended beyond assessment issues as well. Current clinical formulations of sexual response have been pervasive in shaping our working definitions of the arousal process. For instance, sexual arousal without orgasm in women is commonly termed "anorgasmia" in the clinical literature, and is viewed as a dysfunctional condition; yet researchers since Masters and Johnson (1966) have documented the prevalence of this pattern in the general population (e.g., Hite, 1976; Frank, Anderson, & Rubenstein, 1978). The risk in formulating definitions of normal arousal on the basis of comparisons between clinical and nonclinical samples is clear. In this instance, prescriptive notions of normal or adequate sexual function are all too easily derived from clinically based definitions of sexual response.

Treatment studies on the outcome of sex therapy similarly have influenced psychophysiological formulations of sexual response. Recent outcome studies that have investigated psychophysiological response patterning before and after treatment have been reported by DeAmicis, Goldberg, LoPiccolo, Friedman, and Davies (1985), Levine and Agle (1978), and Heiman and LoPiccolo (1983). A major conclusion from each of these studies is that participants in sex therapy tend to report generalized, nonspecific changes in sexual and relationship satisfaction, while improvement of specific (physiological) aspects of sexual function is more variable. Assessment of sexual function in each of these studies has been based upon a three- or four-stage model, which implicitly may have biased the results obtained. It is possible, for example, that greater emphasis on measures of cognitive–subjective arousal could provide a different perspective on the processes of change resulting from sex therapy.

In considering the influence of clinical and applied issues upon theoretical conceptualizations of the sexual arousal process, it becomes apparent that the applied research has provided a rich source of information concerning human sexual responding and has stimulated the development of more sophisticated models of the arousal process (e.g., Levine, 1980; Barlow, 1986). The nature of this association has not been without difficulties, however, as clinical practice needs frequently require development of certain assessment and treatment procedures (e.g., NPT) before adequate experimental investigation of the underlying psychophysiological processes has occurred. Given the relative immaturity of the field of sexology, this somewhat disjointed relationship between basic and applied research is to be expected, and the need remains for an integrated formulation of sexual arousal, in which both basic psychophysiological processes and clinical observations are considered.

RESPONSE PATTERNING: A RECONSIDERATION

The story is often told of the campaign visit once made by President Calvin Coolidge and his wife to a chicken farm. One author has described the incident as follows:

One day President and Mrs. Coolidge were visiting a government farm. Soon after their arrival they were taken off on separate tours. When Mrs. Coolidge passed the chicken pens, she paused to ask the man in charge if the rooster copulates more than once each day. "Dozens of times," was the reply. "Please tell that to the President," Mrs. Coolidge requested. When the President passed the pens and was told about the rooster, he asked, "Same hen every time?" "Oh no, Mr. President, a different one each time." The President nodded slowly, then said, "Tell that to Mrs. Coolidge." (Bermant, 1976, pp. 76–77)

Based upon this well-known anecdote, the so-called "Coolidge effect" has become synonymous with the phenomenon of dishabituation, or the association between novelty and arousability in the sexually gratified male. This effect is one of several examples of adaptation and the role of learning factors in shaping patterns of response in sexual arousal. Findings from several current areas of research, including the effects of habituation on sexual arousal, the use of classical and instrumental conditioning and autonomic feedback, and studies of voluntary control of sexual response, have served to highlight the variability and plasticity of response patterns in sexual arousal.

"Habituation," traditionally viewed as a primary form of nonassociative learning, is defined as a decrease in the strength of a response due to repeated presentation of a non-noxious stimulus (Marx, 1969). The phenomenon of habituation is of special interest to sexual psychophysiological research for three reasons. First, as noted by Schaefer and Colgan (1977), habituation poses a potential confound for most laboratory studies that employ repeated erotic presentations. Second, the topic of exposure to pornography is an increasing source of societal and professional concern, as discussed in Chapter 8. The possible role of habituation or sensitization effects in this context has guided much of the available laboratory research on the effects of pornography. Finally, the phenomenon of habituation of arousal is important intrinsically, as a specific instance of nonassociative learning in determining patterns of sexual response.

Several studies have examined directly the effects of habituation in volunteer male subjects exposed to visual and auditory erotica. The first and most extensive study of this type was reported by Howard, Reifler, and Liptzin (1971), who exposed male college students to daily viewing of pornographic films and texts over a 3-week period. Despite considerable variability across measures in the decline of arousal, clear evidence of habituation was observed in self-report, physiological, and behavioral indices of arousal. This study has been criticized by Bancroft (1976) and others on methodological grounds, such as the failure to define and calibrate the measures of genital response. Furthermore, O'Donohue and Geer (1985) have noted that physiological fatigue was not controlled in this study, so that intrasession comparisons of stimulus arousability were confounded by fatigue effects. A subsequent study by Julien and Over (1984) presented relatively brief (12-minute) segments of erotic stimuli, in a range of modalities (e.g., films, slides, audiotapes, written material), to normal men. In contrast with the earlier results, this study found little or no evidence of habituation, perhaps due to variations in stimulus modality across presentations.

Recently, O'Donohue and Geer (1985) have examined the effects of specific stimulus characteristics on habituation. Two levels of erotic intensity (medium and high) and variability of content (constant or varied) were presented to normal male volunteers in a single laboratory session. The results of this study indicated that variations in the content of the erotic stimuli attenuated the rate of habituation, as compared to the presentation of stimuli of homogeneous content (see Figure 2.6)—a finding that suggests a process much like the Coolidge effect. Overall, this study represents one of the few methodologically sound investigations of habituation effects to date, particularly with respect to the possible confounding effects of fatigue. An unexplained finding, however, was the relatively low correlation observed between self-reported arousal and penile tumescence ($r = .45$), suggesting alterations in the patterning of cognitive–physiological aspects of arousal during the course of habituation, as can be seen by the contrasting patterns in Figure 2.6.

Just as habituation has been shown to affect patterns of sexual arousal to repeated presentations of erotic stimuli, a number of studies have examined the roles of classical and instrumental conditioning in shaping arousal responses to neutral or unconditioned stimuli. In one of the first experiments of this type, Rachman (1966) conducted an experimental analogue study of conditioned fetishism in normal males. For this purpose, a classical conditioning paradigm was employed, in which a conditioned stimulus (CS; a photograph of women's boots) was paired with an unconditioned stimulus (UCS; slides of attractive nude females). After 20 or more such pairings, each of the subjects showed a conditioned response (CR) to the CS. The author was also able to demonstrate the effects of extinction and spontaneous recovery, two other important dimensions of conditioning. Subsequently, Rachman and Hodgson (1968) replicated the original findings and controlled for the possible confounding effects of sensitization or pseudoconditioning through the application of a "backward conditioning" paradigm. These studies are noteworthy as the first to make use of a circumference strain gauge method for the measurement of penile tumescence. Originating with these early studies, a large body of experimental literature has developed around the application of classical conditioning approaches to the modification of deviant sexual arousal, as we discuss in Chapter 9.

Instrumental conditioning of patterns of sexual response has also been demonstrated in a number of studies (e.g., Rosen, 1973; Rosen, Shapiro, & Schwartz, 1975; Quinn, Harbison, & McAllister, 1970). For example, Rosen (1973) examined the effects of contingent feedback on conditioned suppression of arousal during erotic audiotapes presented to normal male volunteers. Significant instrumental conditioning of penile tumescence was demonstrated relative to the control conditions (in this case, noncontingent feedback and instructions alone). These results were interpreted as consistent with findings from other areas of psychophysiology in which spec-

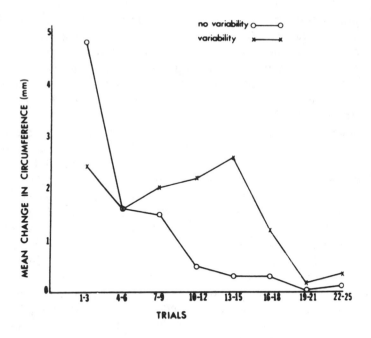

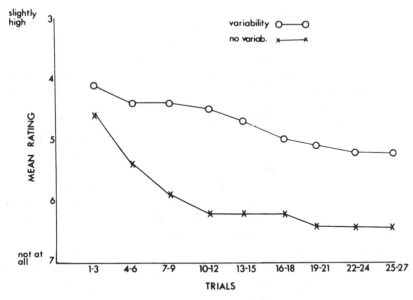

Figure 2.6. Habituation of penile response (above) and subjective arousal (below) over successive stimulus presentations, with and without stimulus variability. From "The Habituation of Sexual Arousal" by W. T. O'Donohue and J. H. Geer, 1985, *Archives of Sexual Behavior, 14,* pp. 240 and 242. Copyright 1985 by Plenum Publishing Corporation. Reprinted by permission.

ificity of autonomic functioning has been shown to be associated with instrumental conditioning. Similarly, Rosen *et al.* (1975) and Quinn *et al.* (1970) used feedback and reward procedures to increase tumescence in laboratory studies of operant conditioning. Other authors (e.g., McGuire, Carlisle, & Young, 1965) have commented extensively on the significance of conditioning processes in the acquisition of deviant arousal patterns in more naturalistic settings.

A related area of research with important implications for the psychophysiology of response patterning is the study of voluntary control of sexual arousal in males and females. In keeping with their peripheralistic and reflexive view of sexual response, Masters and Johnson (1970) originally stated the impossibility of voluntary control: "Erections develop just as involuntarily and with just as little effort as breathing" (1970, p. 196). On the other hand, a growing number of experimental studies have demonstrated that voluntary control of sexual arousal is readily accomplished by both male and female subjects (e.g., Laws & Rubin, 1969; Henson & Rubin, 1971; Hoon, Wincze, & Hoon, 1977a; Zingheim & Sandman, 1978). Although some attempts have been made to further strengthen voluntary control through the application of biofeedback techniques (e.g., Hoon, 1980; Csillag, 1976), the clinical applicability of these techniques in the treatment of sexual dysfunction has been limited. However, findings from studies of voluntary control of sexual arousal, as well as the classical and instrumental conditioning studies described above, strongly support the postulated role of learning factors in the etiology of sexual dysfunction (Hatch, 1981).

Research on the factors involved in the mediation of sexual response patterning should be viewed as in the early stages of development. The studies presented in this section clearly highlight the need for inclusion of basic psychophysiological mechanisms, such as habituation and conditioning, in our present account of sexual arousal. However, these factors are hardly the only, or necessarily the most important, mechanisms involved in the mediation of response patterning. While this area of research represents a first step toward the ultimate description of mediating mechanisms in sexual response, it is hoped that future studies will include greater emphasis on more subtle and complex forms of mediation, such as the role of imagery, memory, and attentional states. Only with the incorporation of cognitive–subjective factors such as these will our models of response patterning adequately reflect the intricacy of psychophysiological interactions involved in sexual arousal.

SUMMARY

Several key concepts and hypotheses have been proposed in this chapter concerning the definition of sexual response; theoretical frameworks for understanding patterning of sexual arousal processes; the interaction of physiological and subjective dimensions of arousal; and the development of models of the sexual response cycle. In particular, we have focused on the need for a broadening of available definitions of sexual response to include a criterion of subjective experience. Instances of subjective arousal in the absence of genital response (e.g., sexual fantasy) are perhaps the most compelling in this regard.

Is there a unique pattern of physiological–subjective concomitants that can be used to differentiate sexual arousal from other emotional states? How much individual variation exists in this pattern from one situation to another? These questions have been addressed in the context of basic psychophysiological concepts, such as SSR and ISR patterning. Issues such as the comparison of male and female patterns of sexual arousal have been examined in this regard. Clearly, these concepts have much to offer as organizing principles for the understanding of sexual response patterns.

Another major emphasis of the present chapter has been on the interaction of physiological and subjective dimensions of sexual arousal. This issue has been explored from the perspective of cognitive attributional mechanisms in the experience of emotional states generally. Specifically, we have attempted to integrate key formulations of affective processing (e.g., Schachter & Singer, 1962) into a broader framework for understanding sexual arousal. Implications for identifying specific components of sexual response are discussed, and the specific models of Bancroft (1983), Byrne (1977), and Barlow (1986) are reviewed. Overall, this integration represents a valuable first step toward applying cognitive–affective arousal theory to sexual responses. Empirical research, however, has yet to examine these issues adequately.

Models of the sexual response cycle are reviewed in historical sequence. We have critiqued the Ellis and Beach two-stage models, the Masters and Johnson four-stage model, and the subsequent triphasic model of Helen Kaplan. Each of these models has attempted to conceptualize the underlying progression of physiological and subjective events that make up the sexual response cycle. However, we have emphasized that attempts to distinguish specific stages of arousal have generally produced an incomplete and potentially biased account of sexual response. Current models of the response cycle have also neglected to consider basic psychophysiological concepts, such as autonomic balance and adaptation–rebound. In this vein, we have proposed further application of these concepts to the explanation of phenomena such as the refractory period.

Clinical processes have been influential in shaping formulations of response patterning in men and women, as well. For example, selected studies that have contrasted clinical and nonclinical groups in their arousal patterns to erotic stimuli have been reviewed, especially as these have contributed to present definitions of sexual response. Treatment outcome studies of sex therapy have also offered a perspective for differentiating functional and dysfunctional arousal patterns. Drawing inferences from such clinical comparisons, however, is potentially misleading in making generalizations to nonclinical aspects of sexual response.

Finally, we have mentioned research in three key areas on the effects of psychophysiological processes in mediating patterns of sexual response. These areas include habituation, the role of classical and instrumental conditioning in autonomic learning, and mechanisms of voluntary control in sexual response. Research on the mediating processes of sexual arousal should be viewed as in the early stages of development, with the inclusion of more complex and subtle cognitive–subjective processes awaiting further study.

CHAPTER THREE

Genital Blood Flow Measurement in the Male: Psychophysiological Techniques

Culturally, sexual aggression [responsiveness] has been accepted as a mode of expression for the human male, an integral part of the "plumage" of his dominant role. . . . It is presumed that only physical defect or the depletions of the aging process will interfere with the male's innate erotic interests and his ability to respond to sexual stimuli.—Masters and Johnson (1966, p. 301)

The predominant focus of sexual psychophysiology in the last two decades has been on genital measures of tumescence in the male, resulting in the development of a variety of transducers and measurement approaches. This emphasis on penile tumescence in laboratory studies of male sexual arousal can be traced to a number of sources. First, the Masters and Johnson (1966) studies highlighted the role of penile erection as the earliest and most easily identified index of sexual arousal in the male. Second, because penile tumescence is readily assessed by means of various circumferential, volumetric, and temperature-sensitive devices, laboratory measurement approaches have proliferated in recent years (Rosen & Keefe, 1978; Earls & Marshall, 1982). Finally, considerable impetus has been provided by the increasing clinical use of penile erection measures in the laboratory diagnosis of male erectile dysfunction (Karacan, Salis, & Williams, 1978; Fracher, Leiblum, & Rosen, 1981), along with the investigation of penile tumescence responses in the assessment of deviant arousal patterns (Quinsey & Marshall, 1983).

Before we review the development of current measurement approaches, we consider the role of underlying anatomical and physiological determinants of erection, particularly the present understanding of penile hemodynamics. For example, recent research on the neurovascular basis of erection has called into question a number of basic assumptions about the relevant physiological mechanisms (Newman & Tchertkoff, 1980; Benson, McConnell, & Schmidt, 1981). Similarly, recent studies of the neural

53

mediation of tumescence have led to a re-evaluation of the traditional view of parasympathetic control of erection (Krane & Siroky, 1981; Van Arsdalen, Malloy, & Wein, 1983). These neurophysiological considerations are clearly important in evaluating current laboratory transducers, as well as in the future development of alternative measurement approaches. Current understanding of vascular physiology may also lead to the conclusion that certain existing measures—specifically, devices that detect tumescence via changes in circumference of the penis—may not adequately assess key aspects of erection (Metz & Wagner, 1981).

MALE GENITAL ANATOMY

The male sexual system is made up of the external organs (the penis, scrotum, and testes) and the internal organs (the vas deferens, prostate, seminal vesicles, and Cowper glands). The external genitals of the male are clearly visible, and their prominence may account in part for the fact that complete female nudity tends to be more acceptable in Western cultures than complete male nudity (Rosen & Hall, 1984). Unlike the clitoris or vagina, the penis also plays a role in urination, thus insuring that boys develop familiarity with touching and handling the penis from an early age. Similarly, masturbation begins at an earlier age for males than females (Kinsey *et al.*, 1953; Hunt, 1974), is more likely to involve direct manual stimulation of the genitals, and therefore contributes further to males' familiarity with the penis and its functions. Although most studies of male sexual response have focused on measurement of penile erection, Masters and Johnson (1966) have described important changes occurring in the scrotum and testes, as well as in the internal organs, during the process of sexual arousal. Finally, the male sexual system, like its female counterpart, is designed to fulfill both sexual and reproductive functions.

The Penis

It is not much of an exaggeration to say that the penises in fantasyland come in only three sizes—large, gigantic, and so big you can barely get them through the doorway.—Zilbergeld (1978, p. 23)

No organ of the body has been assigned as many symbolic and emotional meanings as the penis. Among both ancient and modern civilizations, the penis has been used to symbolize fertility, power, male domination, aggression, and even life itself. In D.H. Lawrence's novel *Lady Chatterley's Lover* (1928/1959), for example, the hero's penis is described as proud, lordly, terrifying, and lovely; it even has a name of its own—"John Thomas." In spite of changing sexual norms in recent years, men continue to be preoccupied with the size, appearance, and performance of the penis (Zilbergeld,

1978; Nowinski, 1980). From a reproductive view, the simple but important function of the penis is the delivery of male ejaculate into the vagina. However, the penis also functions as the primary organ of male sensory stimulation, as well as serving to pass urine from the body.

The anatomical structure of the penis is generally divided into two major parts: the proximal anchored portion, or root (radix); and the distal shaft, or body (corpus), which terminates in an acorn-like enlargement, the glans penis. Erectile tissue is contained within two dorsally located cylindrical bodies, the corpora cavernosa, and a single ventral body, the corpus spongiosum, which also contains the urethra. These bodies are enclosed by the penile fascias and the fusion of their capsules (tunica albuginea) (see Figure 3.1). Separating the corpora cavernosa is a narrow septum, which is incomplete in many places. This allows blood to flow freely from one side to the other, causing the two cavernosal bodies to function largely as a single unit (Van Arsdalen *et al.*, 1983).

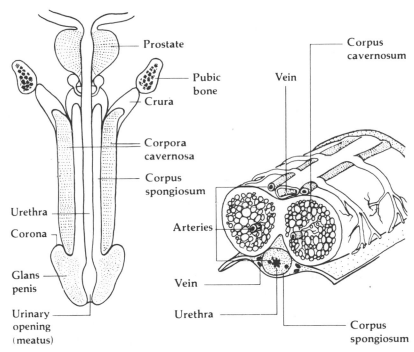

Figure 3.1. Two schematic cross-sections of the penis. Left: Longitudinal section. Note how the corpora cavernosa (upper bodies) form the crura, which attach to the pubic bone. Right: Cross-section through the shaft indicating the major blood vessels of the penis. Erection is caused when the spongy bodies (corpora), which are composed of erectile tissue, fill with blood. From *Sexuality* (p. 106) by R. C. Rosen and E. Hall, 1984, New York: Random House. Copyright 1984 by Random House, Inc. Reprinted by permission.

At the root of the penis the corpora cavernosa diverge to form the crura, which are firmly attached to the pelvic bone (ischiopubic rami). Each crus is surrounded by the ischiocavernosus muscle. The corpus spongiosum attaches at the penile bulb to the urogenital diaphragm, and is covered by the bulbocavernosus muscle. Contraction of these muscles facilitates the expulsion of semen or urine through the urethra. At its anterior end the corpus spongiosum expands to form the glans, or head of the penis. Dickinson (1933) observed that the tissue of the glans is especially soft and yielding, perhaps adapted through evolution to avoid injury to the internal organs of the female during intercourse.

Each of the penile bodies (corpora) are composed of many small compartments separated by bands of smooth muscle tissue, the trabeculae. In the spaces between this loose trabecular network are vascular sinuses, or cavernae. The arterioles supplying blood to these bodies are derived from the internal pudendal arteries, which divide, in turn, into the deep and dorsal arteries of the penis. Multiple anastomotic channels further connect the penile arteries throughout the length of the penis. The main branches of the deep or profunda artery of the penis terminate in the helicine arteries, or spiral-shaped vessels that pour arterial blood into the cavernous spaces, and thereby play a major role in the physiology of erection.

The Scrotum and Testes

The scrotum is a loose sac or pouch within which the testes are suspended by the spermatic cord. The surface of the scrotum has a distinctive, wrinkled appearance, is sparsely covered with hair, and contains numerous sweat glands. Beneath the skin a layer of smooth muscle fibers, the dartos muscle, surrounds the testes. Due to the action of this muscle, in conjunction with the cremaster muscle, testicular elevation is achieved in response to sexual stimulation or cold.

The word "testis" is derived from the Latin word for "witness," implying that in ancient Rome a man's word was literally as good as his testes. Like the penis, the male testes are frequently viewed as possessing important symbolic or emotional connotations. From a physiological perspective, the principal functions of the testes are the production of spermatozoa and the "male hormone," testosterone. Sperm production occurs in the seminiferous tubules, while testosterone is produced in the interstitial (Leydig) cells. From the seminiferous tubules the developing sperm cells pass into a convoluted duct system, the epididymis, and finally are transported from the testes by means of the vas deferens.

During sexual arousal, the scrotal sac and testes respond with vasocongestion and increased muscle tension. Thickening and tightening of the scrotum occur, and the testes are elevated by contraction of the cremasteric and dartos muscles, and a corresponding shortening of the spermatic cords. In response to increased vasocongestion, the testes also show an increase in size of about half during the latter part of the sexual arousal process (Masters & Johnson, 1966). Despite general acceptance of the importance of these phenomena, scant attention has been paid in psychophysiological research to the measurement of scrotal or testicular changes during sexual response.

The Internal Organs

The internal sexual organs of the male function primarily as a system of sperm delivery. In the course of transport from the testes to the urethra, sperm is mixed with fluids from several accessory reproductive glands: the prostate, the seminal vesicles, and the Cowper glands. The prostate is a chestnut-sized organ that surrounds the urethra and is located beneath the bladder. Approximately 30% of the seminal fluid originates from the prostate, with most of the remaining fluid being produced by the seminal vesicles. These are two coiled sacs that lie behind the prostate and bladder and join with the vas deferens before entering the prostate. A few drops of additional fluid are contributed by the bulbourethral (Cowper) glands. Discharge of fluid from these glands may occur well before ejaculation, leading not only to embarrassment on the part of many men, but also to a risk of conception if sperm are present in the urethra (Bancroft, 1983).

The prostate may be palpated or sexually stimulated through the rectum. Among homosexual males it is not uncommon for stimulation of the prostate during the course of anal intercourse to result in ejaculation (Rosen & Hall, 1984). For most males, however, the role of the internal organs in sexual arousal is limited to a brief series of reflexive contractions during the emission phase of ejaculation. Again, little attention has been focused on changes in these internal organs in laboratory studies of sexual arousal to date.

PHYSIOLOGICAL MECHANISMS OF ERECTION

Penile tumescence is achieved through the engorgement of erectile tissue in the cavernous and spongy corpora of the penis. Although it is clear that increased arterial inflow is the primary hemodynamic event leading to erection (Benson, 1981), some controversy exists over the specific vascular mechanisms involved. The traditional view has been to emphasize the role of polsters, or von Ebner pads, which are described as smooth muscle structures in the lumen of the vessels. According to the theory of erection

57

first proposed by Conti (1952), active contraction or relaxation of these pads is the principal means by which blood flow distribution to the penile corpora is controlled. This theory has been refuted, however, by recent evidence showing that polsters are nothing more than early manifestations of atherosclerotic disease (Benson *et al.*, 1981; Newman & Northup, 1981).

Also controversial is the role of venous mechanisms in the control of erection. In addition to emphasizing the importance of polsters, Conti (1952) hypothesized that a unique system of arteriovenous shunting is responsible for the maintenance of adequate intracorporeal pressure. In particular, it was proposed that these shunt vessels are open in the flaccid state, allowing blood to bypass the corpora, and closed during erection, in order to divert blood flow from the helicine arteries to the cavernous spaces. Other authors (e.g., Wagner, 1981a,; Bancroft, 1983) have speculated further that the active closure of venous "bleed valves" may be necessary to prevent drainage from the arterial system during erection. However, on the basis of radiographic studies of erection using direct infusion of xenon dye into the penile corpora, Shirai and Ishii (1981) have reported that efferent venous closure plays a relatively insignificant role in the normal physiology of erection.

Although little attention has been paid to the potential role of the perineal muscles in controlling blood flow to the penis, Karacan, Aslan, and Hirshkowitz (1983) have shown that contractions of the bulbocavernosus and ischiocavernosus muscles are associated with the initiation and maintenance of sleep erections. These observations await replication, however, and it is unclear whether the action of these muscles is involved to any significant extent in the mediation of waking erections (Bancroft, 1983).

Regarding the neurophysiology of erection, Weiss (1972) has presented a dual-innervation model (see Figure 3.2), in which separate pathways are proposed for the psychogenic and reflexogenic control of erection. According to this model the reflexogenic component consists of a sacral parasympathetic pathway, mediated via the nervi erigentes, while the psychogenic pathway is sympathetic in origin, with efferent innervation descending from the thoracic–lumbar portion of the cord. The interaction between these two sources of neural innervation is described as follows:

Psychic and reflexogenic stimuli often act synergistically in producing erections. For example, in a normal male the degree of tactile genital stimulation required to produce erection is diminished in the presence of concomitant erotic psychic stimulation. . . . Also, psychogenic stimuli such as guilt or hostility, often acting at a subconscious level, can inhibit the erection reflex. (Weiss, 1972, p. 794)

Numerous exceptions to the general principle of synergistic innervation of tumescence have, however, been noted. In men with severe spinal cord injuries, for instance, in whom suprasegmental connections are severed, reflexogenic erections can occur on the basis of sacral innervation alone

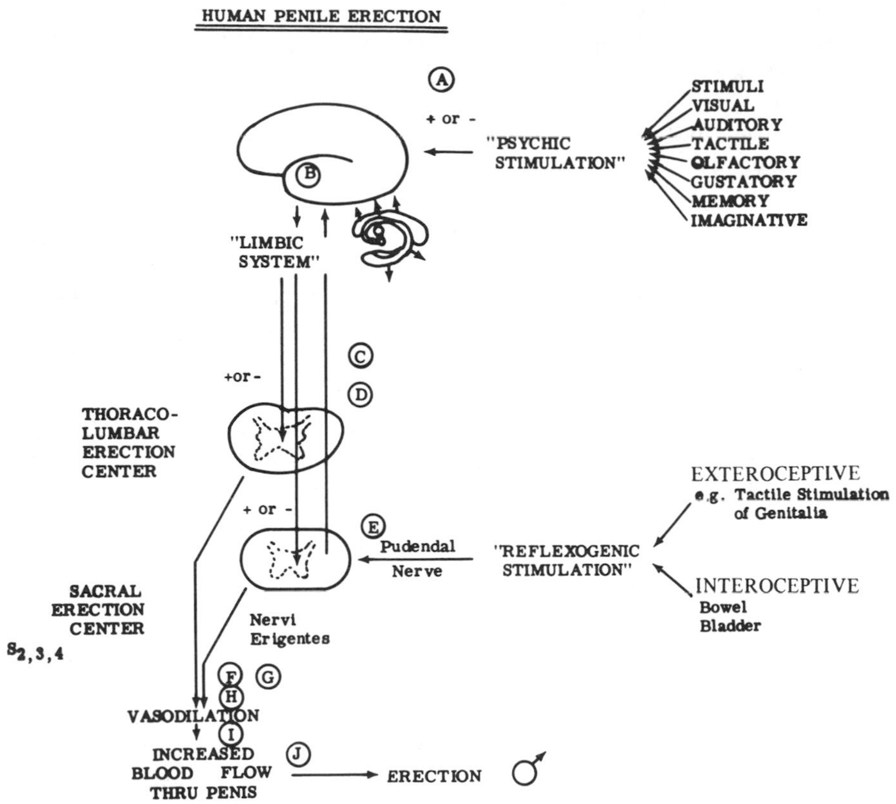

HUMAN PENILE ERECTION

Figure 3.2. A schematic diagram of the pathways involved in human penile erection, according to Weiss (1972). The letters (A to J) represent potential sites of lesions that could cause erectile dysfunction. From "The Physiology of Human Erection" by H. D. Weiss, 1972, *Annals of Internal Medicine, 76,* 793–799. Copyright 1972 by the American College of Physicians. Reprinted by permission.

(Munro, Horne, & Paul, 1948). Commenting on this phenomenon, Money (1980) has observed, "The genitalia can function in a partial and disjunctive way on a reflex basis, without connections back and forth to the brain" (p. 96). Sleep erections may provide another exception, as these appear to occur with relative independence of reflexogenic stimulation (Bancroft, 1983). As noted in Chapter 2, there are also numerous instances in which erections have been noted to occur in nonsexual waking situations.

The role of neurotransmitters in the mediation of erection has also begun to be explored in more detail in recent years. For example, despite the long-standing acceptance of a reflexive, parasympathetic component of erection, Wagner and Brindley (1980) have reported little effect of atropine blockade on tumescence, thereby raising doubts about the role

59

of cholinergic mediation. Similarly, adrenergic mechanisms in the control of erection are poorly understood, although histological examination has revealed that the penile corpora are richly endowed with alpha-adrenergic receptors (Levin & Wein, 1980). In addition, Brindley (1983) has demonstrated that alpha-adrenoceptor blockers (phenoxybenzamine, phentolamine) produce reflex erections when locally administered, as does injection of papaverine, a smooth muscle relaxant (Virag & Virag, 1983; Zorgniotti & Lefleur, 1985). Recent studies have also highlighted the role of a vasoactive intestinal polypeptide (VIP) in the mediation of erection (Ottesen, Wagner, Virag, & Fahrenkrug, 1984; Polak & Bloom, 1984). Specifically, it appears that VIP release is associated with relaxation of the smooth muscle tissues, decreased peripheral resistance, and increased arterial inflow.

Detumescence is generally thought of as a reversal of the physiological processes responsible for the initiation and maintenance of erection. Although "detumescence" was first used by Ellis (see Chapter 2) to refer to the physiological concomitants of orgasm and resolution, more recently the term has been applied to the loss of erection, occurring either before or after orgasm. In regard to the neurovascular control of detumescence, it has been suggested that an active arteriolar constriction may play an important part in this process, in addition to an increase in venous outflow (Bancroft, 1983). Wagner (1980) has also distinguished between an initial period of rapid detumescence, characterized by high venous outflow (up to 50 ml/min), which is followed by a period of slower outflow that gradually approaches basal values. This author further postulates that the latter phase of the detumescence cycle may be controlled by contraction of the smooth muscle of the cavernous tissue. Failure of detumescence is typically associated with "priapism," or prolonged erection in the absence of stimulation. This is a potentially harmful condition, usually requiring medical or surgical intervention.

In general, it is accepted that erection is caused by engorgement of the penile corpora, and the resulting pressure against the surrounding sheath. Newman and Northup (1981) describe the ultimate hemodynamic effect as "similar to the straightening of a coiled garden hose when water under pressure is turned on" (p. 399). However, serious questions have been raised in recent years concerning the understanding of basic neurovascular mechanisms involved. The traditional polster theory of erection has been largely abandoned, and it is unclear whether specialized vascular mechanisms are necessary for adequate engorgement of the corpora. Similarly, there is little agreement at present concerning the importance of venous mechanisms and the role of arteriovenous shunts in the control of tumescence. Finally, key questions have been raised concerning the neural mediation of erection, particularly the role of sympathetic and parasympathetic pathways. In this regard, research appears to have focused increasingly on the effects of adrenergic mechanisms and the specific function of VIP in the neurochemistry of erection.

MEASURES OF PENILE TUMESCENCE

As described in Chapter 1, the first devices for monitoring erection responses in animal and human males were developed primarily in order to detect and prevent masturbation (Mountjoy, 1974). However, these early transducers had little impact on the laboratory study of sexual arousal, until the first report of a simple electromechanical transducer for objective measurement of erections (Ohlmeyer, Brilmayer, & Hullstrung, 1944). This was a circular contact ring that could be fitted around the subject's penis, and was used to provide a simple binary signal of the presence or absence of erection. The authors initially used this method for monitoring sleep erections in their subjects. In a second study (Ohlmeyer & Brilmayer, 1947) the device was used to record erections during waking hours. Current research in sexual psychophysiology, however, awaited the development of the mercury-in-rubber strain gauge and volumetric approaches to measurement as described below.

Volumetric Plethysmography

Laboratory techniques for volumetric measurement of erection were developed independently by Freund (1963) in Czechoslovakia; by Fisher, Gross, and Zuch (1965) in the United States; and by McConaghy (1967) in Australia. These techniques are all derived from the general principles of volumetric plethysmography (Hyman & Winsor, 1961), in which a limb or body part is enclosed in a sealed container of known volume with fluid displacement capacity. Changes in the size of a body part result in displacement of fluid into an attached reservoir. The plethysmograph described by Fisher et al. (1965) made use of water displacement for this purpose, resulting in a transducer that was excessively bulky and awkward to use and has not been used in subsequent research for this reason.

The most widely used volumetric transducer to date is the penile plethysmograph developed by Freund and his colleagues (Freund, 1963; Freund, Sedlacek, & Knob, 1965). This apparatus consists of several parts (see Figure 3.3) and is positioned on the subject as follows. First, the penis is inserted through a soft sponge-rubber ring into an inflatable tube made from a condom. Next, a glass cylinder with a funnel at the top is fitted over the sponge-rubber pad and strapped to the subject's body. The cuff is then inflated with air, and changes in penile volume result in displacement of air from the cylinder to an attached volumetric strain gauge. Additional

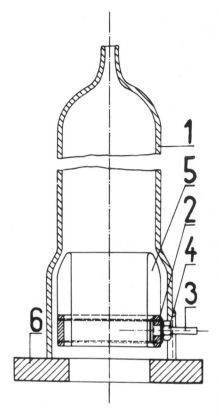

Figure 3.3. The Freund volumetric plethysmograph: (1) glass cylinder; (2) plastic ring; (3) metal tube with threads; (4) locknut; (5) rubber cuff; (6) flat, soft sponge-rubber ring. From "A Simple Transducer for Mechanical Plethysmography of the Male Genital" by K. Freund, F. Sedlacek, and K. Knob, 1965, *Journal of the Experimental Analysis of Behavior, 8,* 169–170. Copyright 1965 by the Society for the Experimental Analysis of Behavior, Inc. Reprinted by permission.

displacement containers can be added to increase the potential range of sensitivity of the device (Langevin & Martin, 1975). Early uses of this device primarily involved assessment of sexual preference in homosexual and heterosexual subjects (Freund, 1963; Freund, 1967a). It has subsequently been used in the evaluation of deviant arousal patterns in the diagnosis and treatment of paraphilias (Freund, 1965, 1967b; Freund & Langevin, 1976; Freund, Scher, & Hucker, 1983).

A variation of the air-filled penile plethysmograph has been described by McConaghy (1967). This device consists of a cylindrical tin about 2 inches in diameter and 3 inches in length, and a rubber "finger stall." The penis is inserted into the finger stall, which maintains an airtight seal, and the open end of the tin is positioned directly above it. A nipple is soldered into the closed end of the tin and connected by means of a plastic tube to a pressure transducer. Although this transducer appears to be simpler and more easily assembled than the Freund plethysmograph, the details of the apparatus and the means for attachment (i.e., how the tin is secured to the subject's body) have not been adequately described.

The device has been used by McConaghy and his colleagues in a number of basic and applied studies of sexual arousal patterns in males. For example, in one of the earliest laboratory studies of sexual arousal, McConaghy (1967) demonstrated that penile volume changes assessed by this means could be used to discriminate between the responses of heterosexual and homosexual subjects. Barr and McConaghy (1971) used the volumetric plethysmograph to assess changes in aversive conditioning of homosexual subjects, and Buhrich and McConaghy (1979) have similarly used the device for investigating patterns of arousal in different categories of transvestites. Despite the novel and interesting applications reported by these authors, the McConaghy transducer has not been used in other laboratories to date.

In addition to being the first major approach to the laboratory measurement of penile tumescence, volumetric plethysmography offers the advantage of maximum sensitivity and precision in the recording of penile blood flow. This may not be of particular importance in detecting tumescence at relatively low levels of arousal, where circumference measures may not be adequate (Earls & Marshall, 1982). However, certain clear disadvantages are also apparent. Volumetric devices require the use of relatively complex and cumbersome apparatus and involve numerous possible sources of measurement artifact, such as temperature or movement. Perhaps the most serious problem facing use of volumetric plethysmography is the potential obtrusiveness and restricted range of situations in which these transducers may be used. Clearly, this apparatus would not be appropriate for studies involving masturbation or nocturnal erection, for example, where subject movements would greatly interfere with recording.

Circumference Measures

In contrast to the problems encountered with volumetric transducers, measures of penile circumference have been found to be both reliable and highly adaptable (Rosen & Keefe, 1978), and are generally preferred for the laboratory study of male arousal. Because of the increasing popularity of the circumferential approach to penile tumescence measurement, a number of alternative transducers have been described. Among these, the mercury-in-rubber and electromechanical strain gauges are the most widely used. Despite the clear advantages of these devices compared to the more bulky and obtrusive volumetric measures, a number of disadvantages have also been noted, and these are discussed below. It should also be noted that each of these devices is intended to measure changes in penile tumescence via an increase in circumference, and no information is provided regarding the firmness or rigidity of erection.

The first application of the mercury-in-rubber strain gauge for measurement of nocturnal erections was described by Fisher *et al.* (1965). After noting the problems with their water-filled plethysmograph described above, these authors investigated the use of a circumference gauge consisting of a fine-bore rubber tube filled with mercury, which was sealed at both ends with platinum electrodes and attached to a Wheatstone bridge (a device for balancing the resistances). This gauge was adapted from similar transducers previously used in the study of respiration (Shapiro & Cohen, 1965). The authors were successful in using this method for the assessment of nocturnal tumescence, demonstrating that 95% of REM periods in healthy male subjects were associated with full erection (Fisher *et al.*, 1965). This study therefore was important in demonstrating the utility of the circumference approach for the measurement of penile blood flow, as well as in documenting the association between REM sleep and erection in normal males.

A variation of the mercury-in-rubber circumference gauge was independently developed by Bancroft *et al.* (1966) for use in laboratory studies of normal and deviant arousal (Rachman, 1966; Marks & Gelder, 1967; Rachman & Hodgson, 1968). Based on the same principle as the Fisher *et al.* (1965) device, the Bancroft *et al.* gauge was mounted onto a moveable plastic carriage, thus allowing for individual fitting of the gauge prior to use. By making the length of the gauge adjustable in this way, a greater variation in penis size could be accommodated. On the other hand, as commercially manufactured mercury-in-rubber gauges have become available in a full range of sizes (see Figure 3.4), this apparent advantage of the Bancroft *et al.* gauge has been largely negated. Presently, mercury circumference gauges are available from several sources (e.g., Parks Electronics, D. M. Davis), and have been found to be generally reliable and robust with regard to a wide variety of laboratory applications (Rosen & Keefe, 1978).

The operating principle of the capillary strain gauge can be explained as follows. During erection, the rubber tube is stretched and the mercury column narrows, causing an increase in resistance to be displayed on the polygraph. These resistance changes are directly proportional to changes in the circumference of the penis (Geer, 1976). The strain gauge typically is calibrated against a graduated cylinder with known diameters before and after each recording, allowing polygraph tracings to be converted to an absolute scale of circumference change.

An alternative, albeit highly invasive, approach to the calibration of penile tumescence for NPT studies has been described by Dhabuwala, Ghayad, Smith, and Pierce (1983). These authors recommend initial injection of heparinized saline solution into the corpora cavernosa in order to produce an "artificial erection" prior to testing. Circumference changes produced by this means are then compared to subsequent changes observed during REM sleep.

Figure 3.4. Left: A mercury-in-rubber strain gauge attached to a variable resistance bridge, which, in turn, is connected to a polygraph. Right: A cone device (D. M. Davis) for calibration of the strain gauge over a range of standard circumferences.

Although most circumference gauges have made use of mercury as the conductive medium, Jovanovic (1967) developed a transducer consisting of a highly elastic, narrow-bore rubber tube filled with graphite dust. Electrodes placed at both ends of the tube are sensitive to changes in the resistance of the graphite column, as with the other circumference gauges. Prior to use the tube is looped around the penis and secured by means of a Velcro collar. Despite its demonstrated usefulness in studies of nocturnal tumescence (Jovanovic, 1967) and the differential diagnosis of organic impotence (Jovanovic, 1972), the major limitation of this transducer is the tendency of the graphite dust to separate with stretching of the gauge.

At present, the major alternative to mercury-in-rubber measures of penile circumference is the electromechanical strain gauge developed by Barlow and his associates (Barlow *et al.*, 1970). This device consists of two arcs of surgical spring material with a pair of mechanical strain gauges at the junction (see Figure 3.5). Increases in penile circumference result in a flexing of the gauges and a corresponding change in resistance. As with the mercury gauge, resistance changes are displayed on the polygraph, and the device is calibrated over a cylinder with known circumferences. The gauge has been widely used in applied research, particularly in studies of deviant arousal (e.g., Barlow & Agras, 1973; Abel, Blanchard, *et al.*, 1975). While potentially more rugged and long-lasting than the mercury-in-rubber

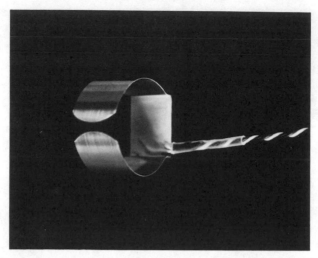

Figure 3.5. The electromechanical strain gauge developed by Barlow and his associates.

gauges, the Barlow *et al.* gauge appears to be more susceptible to movement and positioning artifacts (Geer, 1980).

Penile circumference gauges offer a number of important research advantages, which account for their growing popularity in recent years. Generally speaking, these devices are simple to use, reliable, and relatively unobtrusive. The mercury-in-rubber gauge has been shown to respond in a linear fashion over a wide range of circumference values (Davidson, Malcolm, Lanthier, Barbaree, & Ho, 1981) and is reliable over repeated testing (Farkas *et al.*, (1979). It is also relatively unaffected by transient temperature changes (Earls & Jackson, 1981). Movement artifacts are easily detected (Laws & Holmen, 1978), and these gauges therefore are well suited for overnight recording. Finally, a number of alternative approaches to response quantification are available, including high- and low-gain direct current (DC) recording (Rosen, 1973), alternating current (AC) pulse amplitude recording (Jovanovic, 1967), percentile erection scales (Barlow *et al.*, 1970), and measures of integrated amplitude change (Abel, Blanchard, Murphy, Becker, & Djenderedjian, 1981; Rosen *et al.*, 1986). Despite the convenience and widespread use of these measures in laboratory studies of sexual arousal, several important limitations have been identified.

First, as noted by a number of investigators, penile circumference frequently shows a slight *decrease* at the onset of stimulation (Abel, Blanchard, *et al.*, 1975; Laws & Bow, 1976; Earls & Marshall, 1982). This brief reduction in circumference is problematic, in that the onset of tumescence may appear as a decrease in responding below basal values. In accounting for this difficulty, Earls and Marshall (1982) have demonstrated that during the early stages of erection the penis undergoes a substantial increase in length, which typically is associated with a simultaneous decrease in circumference. Evidence for the effect of initial lengthening of the penis while circumference decreases was provided by means of both videotaped recordings of erection, as well as data obtained from the use of a combined array of open-ended and closed mercury gauges, as shown in Figure 3.6. From these studies it appears that the penis may undergo an increase in length up to 30% before diameter begins to increase.

In addition, several authors have noted that circumference gauges may be unreliable at the upper end of the tumescence curve. For example, Earls and Marshall (1982) have reported that circumference recordings in their laboratory frequently reach a maximum value some time before subjects report feeling that full erection has occurred. Similarly, Metz and Wagner (1981) found in postmortem studies of artificial erection that maximum circumference was recorded well before full intracavernosal pressure and firm erection was achieved. Studies of nocturnal erection have also noted frequent occurrences of maximum circumference change in the absence of full penile rigidity (Wein, Fishkin, Carpiniello, & Malloy, 1981).

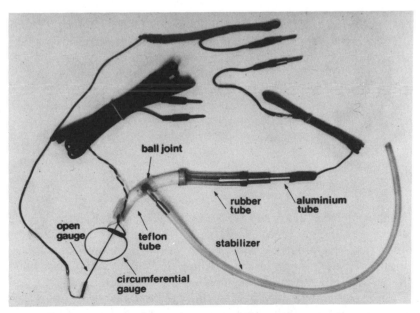

Figure 3.6. The Marshall strain gauge for simultaneous measurement of penile length and circumference changes. From "The Simultaneous and Independent Measurement of Penile Circumference and Length" by C. M. Earls and W. L. Marshall, 1982, *Behavior Research Methods and Instrumentation, 14,* p. 449. Copyright 1982 by the Psychonomic Society. Reprinted by permission.

For this reason, Karacan *et al.* (1978) have recommended that penile rigidity be separately assessed during NPT evaluations by means of a specially designed "buckling pressure" device. This device is described as "essentially a large syringe with a rubber cap on one end and a sphygmomanometer on the other, which is pressed against the glans of the penis towards the base" (p. 365). The pressure being applied at the time that the penis first buckles is noted as the "buckling pressure." More recently, Hahn and Leder (1980) have described a device known as a "buckling tonometer," which is a hand-held beam, fitted with strain gauges to measure bending of the penile shaft at several precalibrated pressure levels. This system also provided an analog signal to be displayed on the polygraph by means of a standard Grass amplifier.

Overall, observations from both laboratory and clinical studies have consistently pointed toward the presence of a nonlinear relationship between tumescence (or penile rigidity) and circumference changes at the upper, as well as the lower, end of the response curve. These are serious limitations if the measures are being used for determining the full range of individual erectile capacity, as in NPT assessment, or in studies requiring precise measurement of initial arousal states.

A final criticism of circumference measures in regard to NPT assessment concerns the need for a polygraph and sleep laboratory, and the resulting cost and inconvenience to the patient. In recent years a number of alternative methods have been described for the measuring of nocturnal erection, either by means of portable electrophysiological monitors (e.g., Leyson & Powell, 1982) or the so-called "stamp ring" method (Barry, Blank, & Boileau, 1980). These methods have been shown to have serious limitations (Marshall, Morales, Phillips, & Fenemore, 1983), and are discussed in further detail in Chapter 10.

Comparison Studies of Volumetric and Circumference Methods

Although volumetric and circumference methods have been the most widely used measures of tumescence to date, only two studies to date have directly compared these approaches. McConaghy (1974) compared simultaneous tracings obtained from an air-filled volumetric plethysmograph with the output from a Bancroft *et al.*-type mercury-in-rubber strain gauge. Results were quite inconsistent overall, with the volumetric device at times indicating much greater sensitivity at the lower end of the scale. However, these results should be cautiously interpreted, in view of the small number of subjects ($n = 4$) and the absence of statistical analyses.

A similar study by Freund, Langevin, and Barlow (1974) compared the Freund plethysmograph with the Barlow *et al.* electromechanical strain gauge. Again, the volumetric device was found to be the more sensitive transducer. In this study, however, the attempt to record simultaneously from both transducers caused frequent difficulties due to equipment malfunction; as a result, most of the data had to be discarded. Despite these technical difficulties, it has been generally accepted in the literature that volumetric transducers provide a more sensitive, albeit more intrusive and cumbersome, approach to measurement (Rosen & Keefe, 1978; Earls & Marshall, 1982).

In comparing the Barlow *et al.* gauge with a standard mercury-in-rubber gauge, Laws (1977) found that the two circumference measures produced similar polygraph records, but that the Barlow *et al.* gauge tended to become displaced if initial detumescence occurred. Output from the gauges was most clearly correlated at the upper and lower ends of the range of measurement. This result should be viewed cautiously, however, as data were obtained from only one subject during a single session of recording.

In view of the surprisingly limited research to date directly comparing the principal measures of penile tumescence in the male, it is difficult to draw firm conclusions regarding the sensitivity, reliability, or utility of these approaches. Clearly, further comparison studies are needed at this time.[1]

Thermistor Measures

Following their initial unsuccessful attempt to develop a water-filled volumetric plethysmograph, Fisher *et al.* (1965) investigated the measurement of nocturnal tumescence by means of a small thermistor attached to the dorsal surface of the penis. Although temperature changes did appear to be related to the onset of REM periods, major difficulties were encountered with the attachment of the thermistor, resulting in successful recording in only 2 out of 17 attempts.

More recent attempts to compare thermistor measures of tumescence with circumference plethysmography have been described by Solnick and Birren (1977) and Webster and Hammer (1983). In a study comparing the erectile responsiveness of younger (aged 19–30) and older (aged 48–65) males, Solnick and Birren (1977) obtained measures of both penile circumference and shaft temperature in response to presentation of erotic films. Penile temperature was assessed by means of a thermistor probe, which was crudely attached to the dorsal surface of the penis by means of two rubber bands approximately 1 inch apart. A strip of plastic foam was

1. Since this book was sent to the typesetter, Wheeler and Rubin (1987) have reported the results of an additional comparison of volumetric and strain gauge plethysmography. Overall, the measures were significantly correlated ($r = .68$), although the volumetric device produced more artifacts.

used to insulate the transducer from ambient temperature changes during the experiment. Penile circumference was assessed by means of a mercury-in-rubber strain gauge, placed just above the thermistor probe.

Although the authors failed to provide a detailed analysis of the thermistor findings, the overall results indicated a relatively high correlation between temperature change scores and penile circumference ($r = .75$). Furthermore, both measures were related significantly to the age of the subjects, with younger subjects showing greater circumference and temperature changes than older subjects. Increased responsivity in both measures of tumescence were also noted for the younger subjects.

The only other study to date to investigate thermistor measurement of male sexual arousal has been reported by Webster and Hammer (1983). These authors assessed penile temperature changes in eight male subjects using a Fenwal epoxy-coated thermistor, secured on the dorsal surface of the penis with surgical tape. Sexual arousal was elicited by a series of brief erotic videotapes, and penile circumference was measured concurrently by means of a Barlow *et al.* strain gauge. Although the thermistor provided a sensitive and reliable measure of temperature change during sexual arousal, a major drawback noted was the relatively slow time constant (10 seconds) due to the epoxy coating on the transducer, which appeared to cause a slower response to maximum tumescence and the onset of detumescence. Overall correlations between the thermistor and strain gauge were relatively high, however, with seven of the eight subjects showing strain gauge–thermistor correlations of .70 or better. Possible advantages of the thermistor are the lightness and durability of the transducer, and the potential comparability of results obtained from male and female studies of vasocongestion during sexual arousal. Perhaps the use of a thermistor with a faster time constant (e.g., 1 second) would eliminate the major limitation observed in this study—the relatively slow response to detumescence.

Photoplethysmography

Noting the need for more comprehensive assessment of the neurovascular processes associated with erection, Bancroft and Bell (1985) have developed a reflectance photoplethysmograph for noninvasive measurement of penile arterial pulse amplitude. This device consists of a cadmium selenide (CdSe) photoconductive cell and a light-emitting diode (LED) probe enclosed in a perspex case, which is mounted on the dorsal midline of the penis by means of adhesive chiropodist's felt. The adhesive felt has been found to provide adequate contact with the skin, as well as shielding the transducer from ambient light. For optimal positioning of the photometer, the authors recommend first locating the dorsal artery by means of a Doppler probe. It is noteworthy that the essential components of the Bancroft and Bell penile photometer are identical to those used in the vaginal photoplethysmograph devices for assessment of female sexual arousal (see Chapter 4). Despite the increasing use of photoplethysmography for the assessment of female sexual arousal, these studies represent the first attempt to date to utilize such a device for measuring genital arousal in the male.

In this study, as well as in a subsequent clinical report (Bancroft *et al.*, 1985), the authors compared the output from the photometer to simultaneous recordings from a mercury-in-rubber strain gauge. As can be seen in Figure 3.7, the two measures were imperfectly correlated, with maximum pulse amplitude occurring approximately 15 seconds after maximum diameter was achieved. In addition to the pattern of results illustrated in the figure, several other distinctive patterns of association between the measures were observed. Typically, pulse amplitude lagged behind changes in circumference, and it was not uncommon for a transient decline in pulse amplitude to be observed in the early stages of erection, with or without a parallel decrease in circumference. The authors also noted that the latency to full erection was increased when pulse amplitude and circumference were most clearly dissociated.

Considering the variable association observed between these two response measures, Bancroft and Bell (1985) speculate that separate proc-

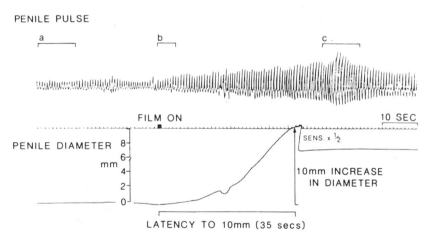

Figure 3.7. A typical normal tumescence response showing the variables measured: change in maximum penile diameter; latency of erectile response to 10-mm diameter (in this case 35 seconds); penile pulse amplitude—(a) baseline pulse amplitude, (b) minimum pulse amplitude during stimulation, (c) maximum amplitude during stimulation. From "Simultaneous Recording of Penile Diameter and Penile Arterial Pulse during Laboratory-Based Erotic Stimulation in Normal Subjects" by J. H. Bancroft and C. Bell, 1985, *Journal of Psychosomatic Research, 29,* p. 306. Copyright 1985 by Pergamon Journals, Ltd. Reprinted by permission.

esses involved in erection are probably being monitored. Specifically, it is postulated that penile pulse amplitude may provide an index of arterial inflow, which is related to generalized penile tumescence, but is independent of the extent of engorgement of the corpora cavernosa. According to the authors, "this implies the existence of independent control mechanisms for the arterial and engorgement components of erection, with the corollary that the two components may be separately interfered with by various psychological or pathological factors" (Bancroft & Bell, 1985, p. 312). Clinical findings with the photometer (Bancroft *et al.*, 1985) have partially substantiated this claim by demonstrating that men with diabetic (organic) erectile dysfunction have relatively greater impairment of penile pulse amplitude in response to erotic films, compared to nondiabetic dysfunctionals or normal controls.

Comment

Although strain gauge (circumference) measures of penile tumescence remain the index of choice in psychophysiological studies of male sexual arousal, further investigations of temperature and pulse amplitude changes are clearly warranted. From the studies reviewed, it appears that these approaches provide correlated, albeit independent, measures of penile tumescence, and may reflect the influence of different underlying vascular processes. While Bancroft *et al.* (1985) have suggested that the differential reactivity of these measures may have diagnostic significance in the evaluation of erectile dysfunction, this finding awaits replication. Thermistor and pulse amplitude measures are also of interest as providing indices of vasocongestion in the male that may prove comparable to similar measures of sexual arousal in the female, to be discussed in Chapter 4.

CORRESPONDENCE BETWEEN PHYSIOLOGICAL MEASURES OF ERECTION AND SUBJECTIVE AROUSAL

A major concern in assessing the validity of penile tumescence measurement is the correlation between measures of erection and self-reports of subjective arousal. Given the prevailing view that penile erection is the most valid and reliable index of sexual arousal in the male (Masters & Johnson, 1966; Zuckerman, 1971), a high degree of concordance with subjective excitement is generally to be expected. On the other hand, several models of sexual arousal have been presented in which multiple response components are viewed as interacting in variable and complex ways (e.g., Bancroft, 1983; Barlow, 1986). We have also noted a number of instances in which genital response may not be accompanied by the subjective experience of arousal, and vice versa. In addition, studies of voluntary control of sexual arousal have highlighted the potential for dissociation between measures of tumescence and subjective arousal (e.g., Laws & Rubin, 1969; Rosen *et al.*, 1975). Finally, in some instances, the lack of correspondence between measures can be attributed to limitations of the procedures used for assessment of self-report.

Several early studies of sexual arousability to deviant and nondeviant erotic stimuli reported a high degree of concordance between penile circumference and self-report measures of arousal (Bancroft, 1971a; Mavissakalian, Blanchard, Abel, & Barlow, 1975; Abel, Barlow, Blanchard, & Guild, 1977). Similarly, studies of the effects of alcohol and alcohol expectations on sexual arousal in normal males (e.g., Farkas & Rosen, 1976; Briddell & Wilson, 1976) have generally found a high degree of correspondence between tumescence and subjective arousal, with correlations typically in the .70–.90 range. It is important to note, however, that in each of these studies subjective arousal was measured by means of a single retrospective posttest questionnaire, in terms of which sexual arousal was assessed in global terms. It could be argued that this methodology has provided an inflated estimate of subjective–physiological correspondence.

The first study to compare penile tumescence with a *continuous* measure of subjective arousal was reported by Farkas *et al.* (1979). For this purpose, these authors developed a variable-resistance potentiometer dial, which could be rotated by subjects to indicate varying levels of sexual arousal. The experimental design for the study included viewing of explicit and nonexplicit erotic films under conditions of high and low performance demand, during which continuous objective (strain gauge) and subjective measures of arousal were obtained. Cognitive distraction effects were also assessed through the inclusion of a concurrent mental arithmetic task. Although the results for the distraction manipulation are discussed in further detail in Chapter 10, overall there was considerable variation in the within-subject correlations between physiological and subjective arousal, which tended to be higher with increasing levels of arousal. Interestingly, the cognitive distraction task was found to have a significant negative effect on tumescence, but not on subjective arousal, whereas the degree of explicitness of the stimuli was found to affect subjective but not physiological arousal.

Wincze, Venditti, Barlow, and Mavissakalian (1980) similarly compared strain gauge measures of penile circumference with continuous assessment of subjective arousal by means of a lever-driven potentiometer. The use of the so-called "cognitive lever" in this study appeared to result in a slight diminution of physiological arousal, probably due to distraction effects. Despite the potential obtrusiveness of the measure, however, the overall correlation between tumescence and subjective arousal was found to be relatively high ($r = .69$). As in the Farkas *et al.* study, correlations tended to be higher with increasing levels of arousal.

Given that male subjects tend to estimate subjective arousal as consistent with changes in penile tumescence, it is possible that the concordance between response measures is dependent upon the subjects' receiving visual feedback of erections. This issue was addressed experimentally in a study by Sakheim et al. (1984), in which visual feedback of tumescence was screened by means of a sheet placed across each subject's lap. Physiological responses were assessed with a circumference strain gauge, and the continuous measure of subjective arousal (cognitive lever) was again used for monitoring of subjective arousal. Results indicated that at low levels of arousal, the availability of visual feedback appeared to inhibit erections, while the opposite result (increased responding) was obtained at higher levels of arousal. Visual feedback did not, however, increase the overall concordance between physiological and subjective measures of arousal.

This study is also noteworthy for the inclusion of two different measures of response concordance—namely, the relative agreement between the *direction* and *intensity* of response systems. As predicted, the degree of directional concordance was found to increase at higher levels of arousal. In contrast, the intensity comparison produced the lowest level of response concordance at high levels of arousal. A possible explanation for this finding is that the subjects continued to experience greater subjective intensity of arousal beyond the point of maximum circumference change. These results are consistent with the report by Earls and Marshall (1982) of a discontinuity between physiological arousal and self-report at the upper end of the arousal scale. As indicated above, changes in length or rigidity of the penis may continue beyond the point of maximum circumference.

A final study in this series has recently been reported by Hall, Binik, and DiTomasso (1985). In addition to assessing the relationship between continuous measures of subjective and physiological arousal to erotic audiotapes in normal male volunteers, this study controlled for the type of stimulus (male vs. female narrator) and degree of arousal experienced by the subject. As in previous studies, a significant positive correlation ($r = .66$) was found between physiological and subjective arousal across all subjects and between both conditions. Also as in previous studies, correlations were found to be higher in those subject with the greatest degree of physiological arousal. However, in examining the correlations within each of the stimulus conditions, it appeared that subjective arousal and physiological–subjective correlations were higher in the female-narrator condition. Although physiological arousal was relatively unaffected by the sex of the narrator, both subjective arousal and physiological–subjective correlations were lower in the male-narrator condition.

Another interesting feature of this study was the investigation of individual demographic and sexual experience variables on measures of concordance. Specifically, it was found that correlations were highest for those subjects who reported using fantasy more often when masturbating, and for those who reported greater satisfaction with their current level of sexual responding. In explaining these findings, the authors speculate that "Comfort with one's sexuality combined with greater experience using fantasy to enhance sexual arousal may allow one to be more responsive to feelings of sexual arousal (especially in research settings) and may result not only in synchrony among measures of arousal but also in higher levels of arousal" (Hall *et al.*, 1985, p. 302). Higher correlations in this study were not simply attributable to higher levels of arousal, however, as these subjects showed high correlations between subjective and physiological arousal even at relatively low levels of arousal.

In conclusion, studies that have investigated the correspondence between physiological arousal and self-report in males have produced a complex and somewhat inconsistent series of findings. Response concordance has been found to be higher using the more global, Likert-type measures of self-report, although recent research has tended to favor the continuous-assessment approach to subjective arousal (Wincze *et al.*, 1980; Sakheim *et al.*, 1984; Hall *et al.*, 1985). In this regard, however, Earls and Marshall (1982) have questioned whether it is feasible for subjects to maintain a precise tracking of moment-to-moment changes in perceived arousal. It has also been noted that continuous measures of self-report tend to be mildly obtrusive. Overall, the correlations between physiological and subjective arousal appear to be higher with increasing levels of arousal, although this relationship appears to depend upon which subjects are studied (Hall *et al.*, 1985) or which particular measures of concordance are utilized (Sakheim *et al.*, 1984). Finally, it has been shown that response concordance may vary as a function of the methodology used for determining subjective–physiological correlations, as well as the experimental set and degree of cognitive distraction available to subjects (Farkas *et al.*, 1979).

SUMMARY

Based upon the existing research in sexual psychophysiology at the time, Zuckerman (1971) concluded that volumetric and circumferential measures of penile tumescence were the most logically sound and empirically promising measures for the laboratory study of sexual arousal in the male. Over 15 years later, these conclusions, while still largely valid, are facing new challenges on both conceptual and methodological grounds. For purposes of conducting research on basic processes in sexual psychophysiology (e.g., learning and habituation, effects of drugs and alcohol, cognitive mechanisms in sexual arousal), circumferential measures continue to be widely used. Clinically, the assessment of penile erection during sleep has relied heavily on circumference measurement, as Karacan (1970) and others have particularly recommended the mercury-in-rubber strain gauge for this purpose.

Volumetric measures, on the other hand, have been used primarily in studies of basic learning processes and the assessment and treatment of sexual deviation, as we discuss in Chapter 9. Despite the opportunity for increased precision in quantification of tumescence, the bulkiness and obtrusiveness of these measures have limited their application in other contexts.

Zuckerman's (1971) second major conclusion—that psychophysiological research had paid scan attention to the changes in other internal or external genital organs—is also largely true today. Although Masters and Johnson (1966) have documented the dramatic changes in scrotal temperature and size during sexual arousal, for example, psychophysiological research on these phenomena has not been attempted as yet.

Genital blood flow measures in both men and women are based on the assumption that sexual arousal is characterized by increasing vasoengorgement of the genital organs. The specific vascular processes that underlie penile erection have been the subject of recent controversy, however, as the traditional theory of erection as controlled by polsters has been challenged. Equally controversial is the role of the venous system—particularly of the arteriovenous shunts, which are regarded by some researchers as playing an active part in the maintenance of adequate intracorporeal pressure (Wagner, 1981a). In addition, contractions of the bulbocavernosus and ischiocavernosus muscles have been implicated in the control of erections during sleep (Karacan et al., 1983). In reviewing each of these areas of current physiological research, it would appear that a major re-evaluation of the role of specific hemodynamic factors is taking place, and that a new understanding of the vascular mechanisms in erection will have important implications for laboratory studies of tumescence in the future.

Regarding the neural mediation of erection, the dual-innervation model proposed by Weiss (1972) has guided much of the theory and research in the field. According to this model, reflexogenic erections are controlled by sacral parasympathetic innervation, whereas psychogenic erections are mediated by sympathetic pathways from the thoracic–lumbar portion of the cord. Although these pathways are postulated to interact in a synergistic fashion, important exceptions have been discussed. Despite the traditional view of erection as parasympathetically mediated, recent studies have challenged the role of acetylcholine as a neurotransmitter (Wagner & Brindley, 1980). In contrast, several studies have indicated the importance of VIP in the mediation of erection.

Among the various approaches to the measurement of penile tumescence reviewed in this chapter, the volumetric devices developed by Freund (1963) and McConaghy (1967), and the circumferential strain gauges developed by Fisher *et al.* (1965), Bancroft *et al.* (1966), and Barlow *et al.* (1970), have clearly had the greatest impact on the field. While volumetric devices offer the potential for greater precision of measurement, circumference gauges have been shown to be simple to use, inexpensive, and readily applicable to a wide range of laboratory paradigms (Rosen & Keefe, 1978). On the other hand, despite the current popularity of these transducers in sexual psychophysiology research, Earls and Marshall (1982) have cautioned that changes in circumference may be unreliable indicators of sexual arousal at the upper and lower ends of the range. Other investigators have demonstrated the dissociation between penile circumference and rigidity in some instances, leading to the use in certain sleep laboratories of independent measures of rigidity (Wein *et al.*, 1981).

Insufficient attention has been paid to date to the use of thermistor or penile pulse amplitude measures of erection. Recent studies suggest that these measures may provide an important alternative to circumference measures, and may reflect the influence of other aspects of the vascular process (Bancroft & Bell, 1985). In addition, the use of these devices offers the potential for comparing measures of arousal in males and females.

In evaluating laboratory measures of genital blood flow, it is also important to consider the degree of concordance with subjective reports of arousal. Although most studies have reported a relatively high degree of correspondence between physiological measures of tumescence and retrospective self-reports of arousal, the use of techniques for continuous assessment of subjective arousal (e.g., the "cognitive lever") has raised the possibility of more complex relationships under certain circumstances. For example, Sakheim *et al.* (1984) have observed that response concordance is considerably greater between measures of response direction than between measures of response intensity. Furthermore, Hall *et al.* (1985) have demonstrated that individual differences and the nature of the erotic stimulus presented are likely to affect the degree of synchrony between response components.

Overall, it appears likely that current measures of penile tumescence, particularly the mercury-in-rubber and Barlow *et al.*-type gauges, will continue to play a major role in psychophysiological studies of male sexual arousal. Certainly, these measures have contributed substantially to both basic and applied research in a variety of areas, each of which is reviewed in later chapters. However, with increased understanding of the underlying physiological mechanisms involved, and in view of the recent evidence concerning methodological limitations of current transducers, increased impetus has been given to the development of alternative measurement approaches.

CHAPTER FOUR

Genital Blood Flow Measurement in the Female: Psychophysiological Techniques

Feminine sex desire is the soft throbbing of a mollusk.—Simone de Beauvoir (1949/1961, p. 362)

The existence of psychophysiological measures for the assessment of genital blood flow in women has a relatively short history in sexology, originating with a light reflectance device constructed by two American gynecologists to determine vaginal capillary changes during the course of the menstrual cycle (Palti & Bercovici, 1967). Other approaches available during this period were developed principally for animal studies of genital blood flow, such as a device constructed by Abrams and Stolwijk (1972) for use in determining vaginal changes resulting from ovulation in ewes. The technology derived from these early genital blood flow measures has contributed substantially to our current assessment approaches. However, the primary concerns of these early developments were reproductive issues, such as the detection of ovulation and biological markers of fertility and sterility. With greater awareness and acceptance of the diverse physiological and affective processes involved in female sexuality, available technology has blossomed, resulting in the gradual introduction of other types of measurement devices.

In reviewing the productive, albeit brief, history of the development of a technology for assessment of female genital blood flow, this chapter begins with an overview of female genital anatomy and physiology of the sexual response. This review provides a background for examining the full range of available genital measurement devices for women, as well as highlighting possibilities for future developments. In the final section of this chapter, the focus is on topics of current concern for understanding the female sexual response, including the concordance between physiological and subjective indices of arousal and the possible significance of "female ejaculation."

FEMALE GENITAL ANATOMY

The External Organs

Unlike the male, the female is not confronted with obvious external manifestations of her sexual responding. Thus, female genital anatomy can be most easily described by distinguishing between external and internal organs, with considerable individual variation existing among women. The external sex organs of the female are termed the vulva (meaning "covering" in Latin) and consist of the mons, the labia, the clitoris, and the perineum (see Figure 4.1). The external opening of the vagina, termed the introitus, is principally an internal organ, and thus is not included in this section.

THE MONS

The mons veneris is the area at the base of the abdomen where a layer of fatty tissue and hair cover the pubic bone. The name of this region translates from the Latin as "the mount of Venus," deriving its name from the goddess of love. This region is richly innervated and is sensitive to both pressure and touch. For some women, stimulation of the mons can be as arousing as direct clitoral contact.

THE LABIA

Extending from the bottom of the mons are two skin folds called the labia majora; these structures are comprised of fatty tissue and a thin layer of smooth muscle. Pubic hair covers the outer surfaces of the labia majora, which contain numerous sweat glands, sebaceous glands, and nerve endings. The inner surfaces of the labia majora are smooth and hairless and are thicker toward the front of the body. In the sexually unstimulated state, the labia majora are often folded together to provide covering and protection for the urethral opening and the introitus. The labia majora merge into the perineum, the area between the most posterior portion of the genitals and the anus. In parous women, the vascular engorgement of the labia majora that accompanies pregnancy and childbirth leads to permanent enlargement of these structures, owing to varicosity. This accounts for some of the individual variation in the appearance of the vulva across women.

Within the labia majora are the labia minora, a smaller, thinner set of skin folds comprised of spongy tissue rich in small blood vessels. The inner lips enclose an area termed the vestibule, which contains the clitoris, the urethral opening, and the introitus. The labia minora converge anteriorly and bifurcate into two smaller sets of folds, the inner of which merge to form the frenulum of the clitoral glans. The outer folds form a skin flap over the tip of the clitoris. The labia minora are joined posteriorly by the fourchette, a fold of skin that demarcates the posterior boundary of the vestibule.

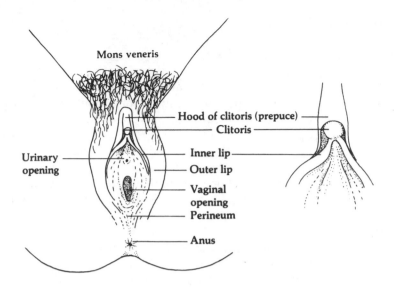

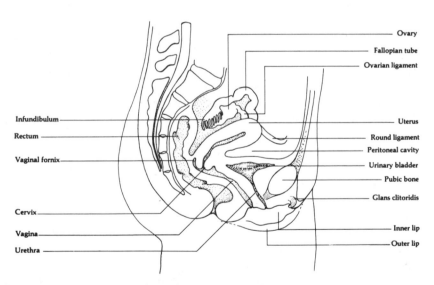

Figure 4.1. The external (above) and internal (below) genital structures of the human female. From *Sexuality* (pp. 66 and 71) by R. C. Rosen and E. Hall, 1984, New York: Random House. Copyright 1984 by Random House, Inc. Reprinted by permission.

The vestibule contains mucuous glands that secrete fluid; in addition, both the vagina and the urethra open into the vestibule. On either side of the introitus lie the vestibular bulbs, which are composed of erectile tissue and thus engorge during sexual arousal. The vestibular bulbs are surrounded by the pubococcygeus (PC) muscle, which contracts involuntarily during orgasm, leading some researchers to emphasize its importance in the experience of arousal and orgasm.

Behind the vestibular bulbs are Bartholin glands, small, rounded vestibular glands that are homologues to Cowper glands in the male. These glands discharge mucoid secretion late in the process of sexual arousal through a small duct that opens at the introitus. At one time, it was believed that Bartholin glands were responsible for producing vaginal lubrication. However, the careful research of Masters and Johnson (1966) revealed that these glands secrete only a few drops of fluid, and that this occurs too late in the sexual response to contribute noticeably to vaginal moistening.

THE CLITORIS

The clitoris is made up of several component structures. While the primary function of this organ is sensory, the clitoris's deeper structures serve other, additional functions, such as providing a cushion during sexual intercourse. The only part of the clitoris that is directly visible is the glans, which is protected by the clitoral hood. The average diameter of the glans is 4–5 mm, although Masters and Johnson (1966) report the normal range of this diameter to be from 1 mm to 1 cm. One prevailing myth holds that the size of the clitoral glans is reflective of the intensity of a woman's sexual response—a relationship that has not been supported by research (Masters & Johnson, 1966). In fact, the intensity of a woman's sexual response may be more reflective of the state of the internal sexual organs.

The body of the clitoris, referred to as the clitoral shaft, is the homologue of the male penis and is a richly innervated structure that is approximately 1 inch long by 1/4 inch in width. The clitoral shaft is comprised of two córpora cavernosa and the corpus spongiosum. The base of the clitoral shaft bifurcates to form the crura, which are attached to the pelvic bone; the crura are the roots of the corpora cavernosa and demonstrate engorgement during sexual arousal. The crura also serve to provide a cushion during sexual intercourse, as well as providing stimulation to the deeper structures of the clitoris.

THE PERINEUM

The perineum is the hairless area between the posterior boundary of the labia and the anus. This region also is innervated with sensory nerve endings, and, as such, can be an additional source of sexual stimulation.

The Internal Organs

The internal genital structures of the female have been described in considerable detail by reproductive physiologists (e.g., Nalbandov, 1976) and gynecologists (e.g., Dickinson, 1933). These organs are encased within the pelvic bones and secured by the muscles of the pelvic diaphragm. The internal genital organs of the female consist of the vagina, the cervix, the uterus, the ovaries, and the fallopian tubes (see Figure 4.1).

THE VAGINA

In the unaroused state, the vagina is a collapsed tube that is shaped like the letter S. In nulliparous women, the length of the vagina averages 8–10 cm; it is shorter in prepubertal girls and decreases in length once a woman has reached menopause. During the sexual arousal process, the vagina increases up to 50% in length and diameter. In most respects, the vagina functions as "potential space," able to contract and expand to accommodate, for example, the head and shoulders of a baby during childbirth. The vagina tilts upward at a 45° angle toward the lower vertebrae of the back, with the muscles of the lower third of the canal closely integrated with the surrounding muscles of the pelvic floor.

The inner surface of the vagina is comprised of tissue folds called rugae. During intercourse, these smooth out, permitting vaginal expansion. The vagina itself is composed of smooth muscle, the strongest of which is the levator ani, which forms a U-shaped sling around the posterior and lateral vaginal wall. The PC muscle surrounds the outer one-third to one-half of the vagina and is subject to voluntary control. This part of the vagina is quite sensitive to stimulation, reflecting the rich vascularization of this area. In contrast, the inner two-thirds contain few tactile receptors and are sensitive primarily to pressure. The entire vagina is lined with squamous epithelium cells, which are the source of vaginal lubricant. While there are no secretory cells in this structure, the vagina is supplied by an extensive network of arterial blood vessels. Prior to puberty, the vaginal epithelium is delicate and fragile. The onset of menstruation produces a thickening of these membranes, owing to changes in the hormonal environment. Throughout the various phases of the menstrual cycle, the cells of the vaginal lining are shed and converted into lactic acid and other by-products, which provide increased immunity from topical infections.

THE CERVIX

At the base of the uterus is the cervix, which serves as the passageway between the vagina and the uterus. The mouth of the cervix, termed the cervical os, varies in mucosal quality depending on the phase of the menstrual cycle. At points, the mucosa at the os becomes extremely thick and can act as a barrier to sperm passage. The cervical canal varies in diameter, depending on the menstrual phase, and also contains many secretory cells that produce mucus.

THE UTERUS

The uterus is a hollow, muscular structure, approximately 3 inches long and 2 inches wide, secured in the pelvic cavity by six muscles. The actual position of the uterus changes slightly, depending on whether the bladder or rectum is full. In most women, the uterus is perpendicular to the vaginal canal, although considerable individual variation exists.

Three layers comprise the uterus: the outer covering, which serves as protection from infection during pregnancy; the inner mucosal lining, called the endometrium; and a dense bulk of well-integrated muscle, called the myometrium, which constitutes the majority of the uterus. During pregnancy, hormonal changes foster the development of new muscle tissue and prepare for the powerful muscle contractions that are necessary for delivery of the child.

THE OVARIES AND FALLOPIAN TUBES

The ovaries are a pair of almond-shaped structures located one on either side of the uterus; they secrete hormones, notably estrogen and progesterone, and release the ovum necessary for conception and childbirth. During the course of normal adulthood, the average woman releases approximately 400 mature ova, each of which is transported by the fimbria of the fallopian tube into the uterine cavity. The mechanism by which ova are transported from ovary to tube is not well understood at present.

In understanding the anatomy of the female sexual response, it is important to emphasize the delicate interplay between sexual and reproductive functions of these structures. For example, changes in the hormonal environment created by menopause affect the process of lubrication during sexual arousal in older women. Similarly, variations in the sensitivity of the vulva appear to accompany the phases of the menstrual cycle, although this topic has produced inconsistent findings in the research literature (e.g., McCauley & Ehrhardt, 1976; Hoon, Bruce, & Kinchloe, 1982). Greater understanding of this anatomic interplay of structure and function would be useful for constructing additional measures of genital responsivity for women, particularly given the need to expand upon available approaches.

NEW HORIZONS IN FEMALE SEXUAL ANATOMY?:
THE GRAFENBERG SPOT

Among current issues involving female sexuality are the recent revisions in explanations of orgasm in women (e.g., Ladas *et al.*, 1982; Belzer, 1981; Bohlen, 1982; Sevely & Bennett, 1978). Drawing upon earlier physiological studies of the paraurethral ducts (e.g., Skene, 1880, 1898; Korenchevsky, 1937; Huffman, 1947), Perry, Whipple, and their colleagues have proposed several changes in current accounts of female anatomy and sexual physiology. First, these authors have described a small, sensitive glandular structure located on the anterior wall of the vagina, which they term "the Grafenberg spot" (or "the G spot" for short) after the German physician who first described this site. According to the original account, stimulation of this nickel-sized spot could result in orgasm without accompanying clitoral stimulation. Second, Perry and Whipple have reported that some women emit a fluid during orgasm, which is distinct from urine and is not symptomatic of a genital or urinary tract disorder, such as urinary stress incontinence. Finally, an examination of women who "ejaculated" during orgasm revealed that these women had stronger PC muscle tonus than did "nonejaculators" (Perry & Whipple, 1981).

Needless to say, these proposed revisions in accounts of female genital anatomy and sexual physiology have elicited considerable controversy among sex researchers, particularly given the recent "liberation" from Freudian accounts of female orgasm and greater emphasis upon the multidimensional nature of arousal. For example, the preliminary studies describing female ejaculation have been challenged on the basis of numerous methodological problems, such as reliance on data from a small number of individual cases (e.g., Addiego *et al.,* 1981) and the use of unstandardized assessment procedures (e.g., Perry & Whipple, 1981). In addition, while continued study of physiological processes of the sexual response in women is warranted and sorely needed, most reports of the G spot have been colored by a prescriptive tone (Szasz, 1980).

To date, one investigation has appeared that has systematically examined the original hypotheses of Perry and Whipple. Goldberg *et al.* (1983) reported the findings of controlled gynecological examinations with 11 women, 6 of whom claimed to experience ejaculation at orgasm. Four of these subjects were found to have a sensitive site, 2–4 cm in diameter, located on the anterior surface of the vagina, which swelled when continuously palpated. Only half of this small subsample (two subjects) reported ejaculation at orgasm. In addition, biochemical assays of "ejaculate" from six women failed to detect elevated levels of prostatic acid phosphatase; in fact, the substance closely resembled urine in its chemical contents. The authors offer a number of explanations for their findings, including the possibility that the G spot may actually be a form of irregularity in the soft tissue. The linking of the G spot and female ejaculation appears to have been premature, based on these data, and the findings suggest that more careful evaluation of female genital anatomy and tissue composition is necessary prior to postulating the existence of a "new" source of orgasm.

THE PHYSIOLOGY OF SEXUAL RESPONSE IN WOMEN

In addition to a knowledge of female genital anatomy, an understanding of the physiological processes that occur during sexual arousal is critical for evaluating the role of assessment devices.

As outlined by Masters and Johnson (1966), the first observable physiological index of sexual arousal in the female is vaginal lubrication, which appears approximately 20 seconds after stimulation begins. Vaginal lubricant is thought to originate from the vaginal epithelium and appears simultaneously with increased blood flow to the internal and external genitals. Observational reports describe the process of vaginal lubrication as "sweating," with individual droplets of the lubricant scattered over the rugae. Content analyses of vaginal lubricant suggests that it is a modified plasma transudate (Levin, 1981), with an average pH of 4.7 to 4.9 (Lang, 1955). *In vivo* measurement of vaginal pH during sexual arousal suggests that orgasm results in large, increasing shifts in acidity (Wagner & Levin, 1978b). Additional research is needed on this issue, however, as other authors (e.g., Masters, 1959; Fox, Meldrum, & Watson, 1973) have reported insignificant or nonexistent pH shifts during lower levels of arousal.

The relationship between the process of vasocongestion and the appearance of vaginal lubrication is not well understood, although a hydrostatic mechanism is generally believed to cause increased pressure in the tissue walls, which results in gradual transudation (Masters & Johnson, 1966). A more detailed model of this process has been presented by Wagner and Levin (1978b), involving fluctuations in the regulation of the sodium–potassium balance of the vaginal tissue as a relevant mechanism mediating the production of vaginal lubricant. Preliminary studies of the organic constituents of vaginal transudate indicate that during sexual arousal, increases in the concentration of lactic acid, glycerol, and higher-molecular-weight lipids occur (Huggins & Preti, 1976); to date, most of the existing studies of vaginal lubrication have involved biochemical assays in extremely small samples. An exception is the recent report of Levin and Wagner (1976): These authors blocked the cervixes of female volunteers, in order to collect vaginal fluid using preweighed filter paper. Each volunteer was asked to masturbate to orgasm, and the resulting vaginal transudate was analyzed for its biochemical components. Potassium levels following orgasm approximated blood plasma levels, thus validating Masters and Johnson's contention that the source of lubrication is the vaginal wall, not the uterus. This would appear to be a fruitful topic for further study, particularly given the absence of adequate laboratory measures of lubrication.

During the beginning phases of the arousal process, local vasocongestion in the genital region produces engorgement of the erectile tissue of the vestibule and the venus plexus, which surrounds the lower portion of the vagina. A result of increased blood flow is swelling of the outer third of the vagina, which forms, in Bancroft's (1983) terms, a "turgid cuff" through narrowing and elongation. The vaginal walls also change hue, becoming dark purple as a consequence of engorgement. Physiological tracking of blood flow, using a xenon washout procedure, has indicated that average vaginal blood flow in an unaroused state ranges from 5.5 to

19.6 ml/min. Sexual stimulation results in increased blood flow, ranging from 21.5 to 45.0 ml/min (Wagner & Ottesen, 1980). As vasocongestion proceeds, the labia majora move somewhat away from the midline, where they normally meet in the unaroused state. In addition, the labia minora change color as a result of vasocongestion, becoming deeper red. During early parts of the arousal process, the clitoris shows increases in size and diameter, the magnitude of which varies considerably across individual women.

As the arousal process continues, the clitoris retracts under the clitoral hood, without a significant reduction in size. At the same time, uterine elevation occurs, accompanied by vasoengorgement and expansion. Some women report involuntary vaginal contractions accompanying uterine elevation. At high levels of arousal, the uterus creates a "tenting," or open area at the inner third of the vagina. It is currently held that uterine elevation is the result of contraction of the parametrial muscle fibers surrounding the vagina and uterus. Another physiological change that occurs during elevated levels of arousal is the formation of the "orgasmic platform" in the outer third of the vagina, which indicates that complete vasocongestion has occurred. At this point, the Bartholin glands may secrete several drops of fluid via ducts located at the introitus.

The specific hemodynamic factors that control vasocongestion, including underlying arterial and venous vasomotor responses, have been the focus of study for some time (e.g., Dickinson, 1933; Danesino & Martello, 1976), with the current emphasis given to key physiological processes. For example, Levin (1981) has recently described a model of hemodynamic function to explain genital vasocongestion. In this account, arterial inflow to the genitals occurs because of greater heart stroke volume and dilation of polsters (columns of smooth muscle cells) in the major arteries supplying this tissue in both males and females. In women, preliminary data suggest that precapillary arterial dilation accompanies the early phases of vasocongestion, and that this gradually shifts to arterialized blood flow and increased venous output as arousal proceeds (Wagner & Ottesen, 1980). Accompanying this, polsters in surrounding larger veins constrict, directing blood flow to the genital tissue. A third component of this model is relaxation of the smooth muscle surrounding the vascular bed, which contributes further to increased congestion. At present, this model is beginning to receive empirical attention in both men and women (e.g., Benson et al., 1981; Ruzbarsky & Michal, 1977).

Another issue of current interest involving the physiological mechanisms of arousal and orgasm in women concerns the role of pelvic musculature. In particular, this issue concerns normative variations in the female orgasmic response, as well as the determining processes of sexual arousal that culminate in orgasm. On the basis of his clinical observations of postpartum urinary stress incontinence, Kegel (1948a, 1948b, 1952) noted that tonus of the circumvaginal muscles (particularly the PC and levator ani muscles) seemed to be important in the control of bladder function, as well as in maintenance of adequate intravaginal tension during intercourse. In response to this observation, Kegel (1950) developed a set of exercises for strengthening the PC muscles, which have been adapted by sex therapists for use in the treatment of orgasmic dysfunction (e.g., Barbach, 1975; Kline-Graber & Graber, 1978).

Despite the enthusiasm with which PC muscle training has been embraced by many sex therapists, research evidence is mixed concerning the role of circumvaginal musculature in female sexual function. As reviewed by Graber (1981), much of the information concerning muscle physiology is still in the investigative stage. It appears, for example, that individual muscle groups tend toward either tonic or phasic activity, and that these actions operate in a homeostatic fashion during sexual arousal and orgasm (e.g., Eyzaguirre & Fidone, 1975).

In sum, many questions remain concerning the relevant physiological processes in female genital responding. At present, existing measures of female sexual arousal reflect our current understanding of sexual physiology in women, with most devices relying on assessment of correlated physiological changes, such as surface vaginal blood flow and fluctuations in skin temperature. Certain changes that occur during the sexual response appear salient in considering potential new assessment strategies, including lubrication and the "tenting" that occurs in the upper portion of the vagina, and may offer new insights into underlying physiological mechanisms during the arousal process. The prospects for new assessment approaches thus appear promising.

MEASURES OF VAGINAL VASOCONGESTION

Whereas physiological measures of sexual arousal in males have focused primarily on penile tumescence, vasocongestion in women effects a variety of changes in both the internal and the external genital organs. As a result, a number of different devices have become available for the measurement of genital blood flow in women. Consideration of each of these alternatives is complicated by the issues of transducer design, safety to subjects, and response interpretation. To date, these various measures can be categorized into three general types: (1) mechanical means of monitoring tissue changes resulting from genital tumescence; (2) indirect measurement of blood flow changes using techniques of photometry and heat dissipation; and (3) assessment of other changes in the genitalia that correspond to vasocongestion. Each of these assessment approaches relies on an indirect measure of vasoengorgement, as the technology necessary for direct assessment of vasocongestion would be too invasive for use with human subjects.

History and Background

One of the earliest attempts to assess vaginal vasocongestion by indirect measurement techniques was described by Palti and Bercovici in 1967. These investigators mounted a photoelectric cell and a miniature light source on a speculum and configured this device to assess changes in vaginal pulse amplitude using AC. Despite clear differentiation of pulse amplitude at different stages of the menstrual cycle in 47 women, this type of transducer has not been adopted, due to its obtrusiveness and the restrictions it imposes on subject positioning. Apparently Palti and Bercovici were unaware that their device could detect vasoengorgement during sexual arousal, as no mention of this application was made in their original report.

At about the same time, Shapiro, Cohen, DiBianco, and Rosen (1968) described a method for assessing differences in the temperature of the vaginal wall and core body temperature, as an indirect measure of internal vasocongestion. This device consisted of two thermistors mounted on a cervical diaphragm; one of the thermistors was heated slightly by current flow, in order to maintain a constant temperature differential between the two thermistors. When the amount of current necessary to maintain this constant differential was determined, a measure of heat dissipation in the vagina was obtained, reflecting the degree of vaginal capillary engorgement. In this initial report, data from a pilot subject were presented, based upon three nights of monitored sleep. Of the seven REM episodes observed, three were accompanied by at least one interval of vasocongestion. A subsequent investigation (Cohen & Shapiro, 1970) provided further validation for this device, as correspondence was noted between a subject's reports of subjective sexual arousal and increased vaginal blood flow. More recent adaptations of this technology have appeared and seem promising.

Other early attempts to measure genital blood flow in women were largely unsuccessful. For example, in addition to their measure of vasocongestion, Shapiro *et al.* (1968) also attempted to measure vaginal pH as an indicator of lubrication, with mixed results. Tart (cited in Zuckerman, 1971) created a device to assess blood flow in the clitoris, using photoplethysmographic techniques; no results are reported for this device, and it has not been utilized in subsequent studies. An adaptation of this measurement approach was made by Fisher and Davis (cited in Zuckerman, 1971), who devised an instrument to assess vaginal blood flow, vaginal temperature, and intravaginal movements; this probe was not sensitive to genital responding during REM sleep and has not received further attention from researchers concerned with female genital responding.

One of the more innovative devices to appear during this time was described by Karacan, Rosenbloom, and Williams (1970). These authors employed a mechanical strain gauge to detect clitoral engorgement in seven women with congenital clitoral enlargement; their results indicated that clitoral erection occurred during sleep at the same frequency as penile tumescence in healthy males. Because this measure was not applicable to the general female population, it has not been adopted for use in related studies of vasocongestion in women. To date, this is the only measure based on mechanical detection of tissue changes to be reported for use with females.

Of interest also is the early device developed by Bardwick and Behrman (1967) for the measurement of uterine contractions. The transducer consisted of a thick-walled polyethylene tube connected to the tip of a rubber balloon, which was inserted through the cervix into the uterus and inflated with water. The water pressure was matched to atmospheric pressure, and measures of uterine contractile amplitude, duration, and frequency were derived. Problems developed in the use of this approach, as highly anxious women tended to extrude the balloon. In addition, the placement of this device was quite painful, thus prohibiting its routine application.

In certain respects, none of these early devices were particularly successful for determination of vaginal lubrication and engorgement; yet several of these devices were important in paving the way for later developments. Prior to the introduction of the vaginal photoplethysmograph in 1975, this technology had received sporadic attention, as a unified approach to the study of female genital responses had yet to emerge.

The Vaginal Photoplethysmograph

The first practical and reliable method for the laboratory measurement of genital blood flow in women was introduced by Sintchak and Geer in 1975. These authors described the use of a light reflectance method (Brown, 1972; Weinman, 1967) involving an incandescent light source and a CdSe photodetector, encased in an acrylic probe measuring 2 cm × 5 cm (see Figure 4.2). The probe signal reflects changes in the amount of light backscattered to the photocell—an indirect measure of vasoengorgement, owing to differences in transparency of engorged and unengorged tissue. Two components of the signal can be derived. When the signal is AC-coupled, a measure of vaginal pulse amplitude (VPA) is obtained, reflecting short-term changes in engorgement. Fluctuations in VPA reflect the arrival of the pulse wave in the cardiac cycle, with larger amplitudes believed to reflect greater levels of vasoengorgement (e.g., Geer, Morokoff, & Greenwood, 1974). When the signal is DC-coupled, a measure of vaginal blood volume (VBV) is obtained, reflecting slow changes in the pooling of blood in the vaginal tissue (Hatch, 1979).

A subsequent modification of this instrument was introduced by P. W. Hoon, Wincze, and Hoon (1976), which included replacement of

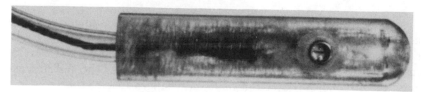

Figure 4.2. Vaginal photoplethysmograph.

the incandescent light source with a more electrically efficient and reliable LED and substitution of a phototransistor detector for the CdSe photocell. These improvements have minimized the influence of recording artifacts, such as blood oxygenation effects (e.g., Weinman, 1967). To date, no absolute calibration methods related to physiological events have been devised for these probes. Thus, most investigators report data from both the AC and DC signals as relative units, such as millimeters of polygraph pen deflection or number of pulses per unit of time.

One of the earliest issues to arise in application of the photoplethys-mograph is the choice of signal type—that is, whether to employ the AC or the DC signal for detection of vasocongestion. Uncertainty exists concerning the exact nature and source of each signal; this stems in part from an incomplete understanding of the physiological mechanisms of vaginal engorgement. For example, while the AC signal clearly represents changes in pulse rate and other cardiac fluctuations, the significance of VPA is not well understood in the complex process of engorgement. One interpretation of increases in VPA involves peripheral vascular dilation, for example (Palti & Bercovici, 1967), while other authors have emphasized the role of cardiac stroke volume (e.g., Cook, 1974) in determining VPA.

Most investigators have resolved this issue by including both the VPA and VBV signals within standard laboratory paradigms. In this type of comparison, the VPA signal has been found by some investigators to be the more sensitive index (Geer *et al.*, 1974; Heiman, 1977; Osborn & Pollack, 1977) and to show a more rapid return to baseline after presentation of the stimulus has ended (C. Henson, Rubin, & Henson, 1979). In contrast, P. W. Hoon *et al.* (1976) have argued that VBV should be the more relevant measure, as changes in VPA account for only a small percentage of the total blood volume during engorgement. In practice, most investigators currently utilize the VPA signal, owing to its greater ability to discriminate between responding during erotic and nonerotic presentations, in comparison with the VBV signal. Furthermore, the use of VBV is complicated by variability in the resting DC signal both between and within subjects (e.g., Beck, Sakheim, & Barlow, 1983; C. Henson *et al.*, 1979). Despite this preference in application of these two signals, both VPA and VBV need to be viewed as *relative* measures of response, given

90

the absence of a means for calibration and the ambiguity concerning the physiological processes of vasoengorgement.

A related question concerns the degree of correspondence between these two signals. Traditionally, correlations between the VPA and VBV measures have been low in the psychophysiological literature on cardiovascular reactivity (e.g., Cook, 1974). VPA has been described as an index of peripheral blood flow, whereas VBV appears to reflect the difference between rates of blood inflow and outflow to a specified site. Heiman (1976) has reported significant positive correlations between VBV and VPA in a large group of volunteer subjects, tested on two occasions. Because the relative levels of both signals, as well as their intercorrelation, were lower on the second day of testing, Heiman has suggested that the magnitude of correspondence between the two signals may depend on the level of arousal achieved. A second study that directly compared the VBV and VPA signals reported low correlations between the two signals in female subjects who were not highly aroused (Zingheim & Sandman, 1978). From these reports, it would appear that the two signals assess separate features of vasocongestion and may need to be used together in order to provide complete data on the engorgement process.

The issue of which signal to use as a measure of arousal in women is related to validity concerns as well. One approach to the establishment of validity is to examine correlations between vaginal blood flow measures and reports of subjective arousal. For example, Heiman (1977) reported that the correlations between VPA and poststimulus ratings of subjective arousal were higher than the correlations between VBV and self-ratings. In contrast, Cerny (1978) reported significant correlations between self-reported arousal and VBV only; there was no observed statistical relationship between VPA and subjective arousal in this study. Generally, most authors (e.g., Geer et al., 1974; P. W. Hoon et al., 1976; Osborn & Pollack, 1977; Wincze et al., 1977; Wilson & Lawson, 1976a, 1978) report either low or insignificant correlations between measures of physiological arousal using the vaginal photoplethysmograph and measures of subjective arousal—a finding that is subject to several interpretations. This issue receives more detailed discussion in the last section of this chapter.

Another approach to determining the validity of this device is the assessment of differential responsivity to erotic and nonerotic stimuli. For example, one of the earliest studies of this type was reported by Geer et al. (1974), in which female volunteers were shown films of heterosexual foreplay and scenes of battles and court life during the Middle Ages. Both VPA and VBV showed increases only during the erotic films, relative to resting baseline conditions. Similar studies have been reported by Heiman (1977), P. W. Hoon et al. (1976), and Osborn and Pollack (1977), and provide a good index of the validity of the vaginal photometer. In reviewing these studies, it is notable that only the issue of detection of the sexual

response is raised; related concerns, such as sensitivity of the vaginal photoplethysmograph to varying levels of arousal, have not yet been evaluated
in laboratory studies of validity. Central questions for further study also
include the influence of changes in probe positioning and the role of movement artifacts in recording the vasocongestive response (Heiman & Rowland, 1981). To date, unpublished findings suggest that probe positioning
does not influence the VPA signal (J. H. Geer, personal communication,
January 1987).

A related psychometric issue involves the reliability of measurement.
Several studies have addressed the consistency of responses between and
within sessions (Heiman, 1977; C. Henson *et al.*, 1979). In the latter study,
although neither VPA nor VBV showed adequate cross-session reliability,
qualitative assessment of the data records indicated consistent patterning
in individual subjects' responses to particular stimuli. Although not an
adequate measure of reliability, this finding does suggest that some degree
of consistency in measurement may be expected when this device is used.
In an attempt to explore possible causes for lowered reliability of measurement with the DC signal, Beck, Sakheim, and Barlow (1983) examined
stability of the VBV signal when the probe was placed in a light- and
temperature-controlled environment. These authors reported a distressing
lack of stability in this measure over intervals as long as 10 hours and
between repeated trials, suggesting that one possible source of artifact
affecting reliability of measurement may be instability of the electronic
components when operated in the DC mode. This potentially serious problem does not appear to affect the VPA signal, given the use of AC coupling,
but this assumption warrants further study.

A number of other factors are relevant in considering the validity and
reliability of the vaginal photoplethysmograph. For example, movement
artifacts have been shown to interfere markedly with signal recording. Geer
and Quartararo (1976), in recording both VPA and VBV during masturbation to orgasm, found that these measures were confounded by movement artifacts (see Figure 4.3). As can be seen, movement artifact was
marked, and it disrupted measurement of both VBV and VPA, despite
the use of highly experienced subjects in this study. A similar problem is
the potential confounding effect of probe positioning. While Gillan (1976)
has reported marked differences in responsivity from various locations in

---

Figure 4.3. Three subjects' responses during orgasm arranged in approximate order
of clarity of response (top line on each record is pooled blood volume and bottom
line is pressure pulse). From "Vaginal Blood Volume Responses during Masturbation" by J. H. Geer and J. Quartararo, 1976, *Archives of Sexual Behavior, 5,*
p. 409. Copyright 1976 by Plenum Publishing Corporation. Reprinted by permission.

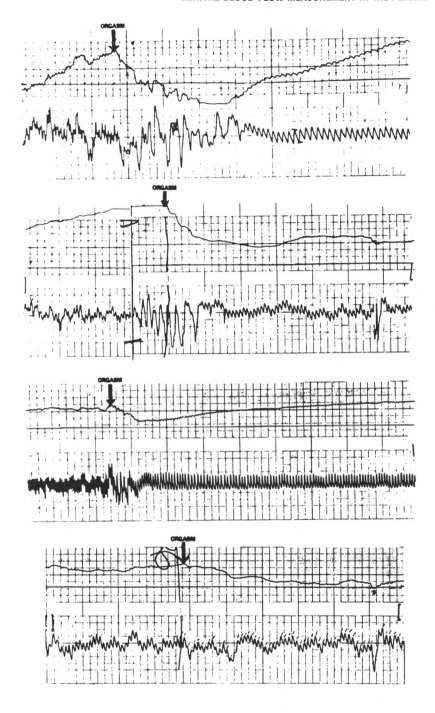

the vagina, Hoon, Murphy, Laughter, and Abel (1984) and Geer (personal communication, January 1987) have failed to find a significant effect of probe placement. Since the typical laboratory paradigm involves insertion of the device by the subject herself in the privacy of the experimental chamber, determination of relative positioning of the probe across subjects and trials is difficult. Some investigators (e.g., Heiman, 1980) have attempted to reduce the influence of placement factors by providing subjects with a diagram detailing the proper location of the device. Another approach to standardization of probe placement has been to attach a plastic shield to the probe cabling at a predetermined distance, with a mark to insure proper orientation of the photocell (J. H. Geer, personal communication, January 1987). The adequacy of these procedures for reducing position effects appears promising.

Other potential sources of bias include menstrual cycle effects on vasocongestion and related temperature fluctuations. With respect to menstrual cycle effects, Wincze, Hoon, and Hoon (1976) have reported a significant overall correlation ($r = .64$) between VBV responsivity and day of the menstrual cycle. These data could reveal a potential confound, or, alternatively, could reflect changes in vasocongestive reactivity during the course of the menstrual cycle (see Chapter 7). Sensitivity to temperature fluctuations also appears to pose a potentially serious confound for the DC signal, as reported by Beck, Sakheim, and Barlow (1983). Despite these findings, few studies have assessed or controlled for the potential influences of menstrual phase variations in vasocongestion or for shifts in body temperature, such as occur during the initial positioning of the device and during menstrual phases (Turner & Bagnara, 1971).

Gillan and Brindley (1979) have reported a controlled comparison study of the vaginal photoplethysmograph and related measures of vasocongestion. Using a probe that contained two photocells and four CdSe photodetectors to measure VPA, these authors also obtained relative measures of hemoglobin and red blood cell count during resting and sexual arousal. VPA and hemoglobin count were well correlated with each other, supporting the use of the vaginal photoplethysmograph as an indirect measure of the degree of vasocongestion. In addition, a vaginal thermistor was included in this study, to determine the concordance with light reflectance measures; the data suggest that vaginal temperature changes closely parallel increases in VPA, although temperature changes lagged somewhat behind blood flow, owing to the slow-changing response of the thermistor.

The most recent advance in photoplethysmography has been introduced by Hoon *et al.* (1984). These authors describe a probe constructed with an infrared LED and a phototransistor, including design alterations to insure an even distribution of light onto the vaginal wall. This transducer is designed to allow measurement of blood volume from a larger portion of the vaginal barrel and to be less sensitive to movement artifacts. Preliminary data indicate that the probe is not sensitive to respiration artifacts, although intravaginal placement appears to affect recording, as do movement and contraction of the vaginal musculature. Perhaps the major advantage of this device is that it can be calibrated in the DC mode, using two chambers covered with reflectance paper of known values. P. W. Hoon and colleagues caution that "use of this box permits calibration of probe response into units of reflectance, [but] . . . relative units as the calibration box is only an analog to vaginal tissue" (1984 p. 145). To date, applications of this device appear promising, particularly with respect to determination of vasocongestion during sleep in women (Hayashi, Hoon, & Amberson, 1983).

Overall, the vaginal photoplethysmograph is currently the most widely used device for the assessment of vaginal vasocongestion. Although reliability and validity of this device have not been satisfactorily established, the vaginal photometer remains the most accurate means to date for the study of female genital responding. The majority of investigations concerning sexual arousal patterns in women have relied upon this measurement approach, as have available applied investigations, including studies of sexual dysfunction, the influence of alcohol on sexual arousal, and hormone effects. Despite this growing body of research, exclusive reliance upon the vaginal photoplethysmograph for studies of vasoengorgement appears ill advised, particularly given the large number of unanswered questions concerning the mechanisms of vaginal lubrication and engorgement.

Indirect Measures of Heat Dissipation

THE LABIAL THERMISTOR

The first measure of external temperature change associated with sexual arousal in women was described by Jovanovic in 1971. This author devised a thermistor for the measurement of clitoral temperature changes during arousal (termed a "clitorograph"). More recently, Henson, Rubin, Henson, and Williams (1977) have described a system for detecting temperature changes of the labia minora. This method consists of a thermistor that is attached to the labia with a three-conductor wire clip (see Figure 4.4). In addition, reference thermistors are placed on the subject's chest and on the wall of the experimental chamber, in order to control for fluctuations in body and atmospheric temperature. In the initial presentation, changes in labial temperature ranging from 0.10° to 1.38°C were found to accompany exposure to erotic films. Furthermore, significant correlations (average $r = .53$) were obtained between labial temperature changes and estimates of subjective arousal, sampled immediately after the end of the films.

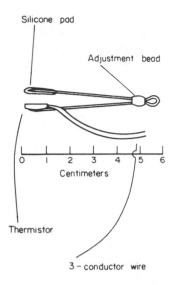

Silicone pad

Adjustment bead

0 1 2 3 4 5 6
Centimeters

Thermistor

3 – conductor wire

Figure 4.4. A scale drawing of the labial thermistor clip. From "Temperature Changes of the Labia Minora as an Objective Measure of Human Female Eroticism" by D. E. Henson, H. B. Rubin, C. Henson, and J. R. Williams, 1977, *Journal of Behavior Therapy and Experimental Psychiatry, 8,* p. 403. Copyright 1977 by Pergamon Journals, Ltd. Reprinted by permission.

Subsequent investigations of this device have demonstrated consistency in labial temperature response patterns between sessions (C. Henson *et al.,* 1979; Henson & Rubin, 1978; D. E. Henson, Rubin, & Henson, 1979). In particular, consistency was noted across two sessions with regard to the rate at which a subject's labial temperature subsided to basal levels following exposure to erotic stimulation. These authors have also compared the responses of the labial thermistor to both VBV and VPA, obtained by means of the vaginal photoplethysmograph (C. Henson *et al.,* 1979; D. E. Henson *et al.,* 1979; Henson, Rubin, & Henson, 1982), with positive correlations reported among these three indices of vasocongestion. In all of these reports, labial temperature showed a slower return to prestimulus baseline levels following cessation of the erotic presentation than did VBV or VPA. In the most recent report (Henson *et al.,* 1982), a comparison of VBV and labial temperature during and subsequent to orgasm revealed striking differences in response patterning. VBV decreased dramatically during orgasm, sometimes below basal levels, and then increased to prestimulation values. In contrast, labial temperature did not change during orgasm, but showed a rapid decline soon after. The authors speculate that the considerable reactivity noted in VBV may be the result of a movement artifact produced by the vaginal contractions that accompany orgasm—a finding that has been noted in other investigations of this type (e.g., Gillan & Brindley, 1979; Geer & Quartararo, 1976). In contrast, labial temperature did not show this artifact; rather, it followed a slowly diminishing course following orgasm, as predicted from Masters and Johnson's observations.

To date, the labial thermistor has not been accepted generally for use in the assessment of female genital responding, despite considerable support for its validity and reliability. One of the primary drawbacks of this approach is the long latency required for return to basal levels following stimulation. This feature precludes its use in most daytime assessment studies, where multiple erotic presentations are included in a single session. However, the use of the labial thermistor in studies of nocturnal genital responding would seem to be an interesting possibility. Recording labial blood flow by means of this device could conceivably expand our understanding of the mechanisms of peripheral vasocongestion, given the opportunities offered for comparison with measures of internal blood flow. Further studies of the labial thermistor are clearly warranted, on the basis of the available data.

VAGINAL THERMISTOR DEVICES

Another temperature measure is the vaginal thermoconductive device of Cohen, Shapiro, and colleagues (Shapiro *et al.*, 1968; Cohen & Shapiro, 1970), described earlier and shown in Figure 4.5. The early reports of this device appeared promising, yet did not involve the necessary experimental controls needed to validate this measurement approach. More recently, Fisher and colleagues (Fisher *et al.*, 1983) have presented extensive data from 10 female volunteers on patterns of female sexual arousal during sleep and waking using the vaginal thermistor probe. Among its advantages is the relative absence of movement artifacts, as the device yields a measure of the temperature differential between an electrically active and an inactive thermistor. Nocturnal patterns indicated a pattern of cyclical blood flow changes during sleep in these female volunteers. Unlike studies of NPT in males, vaginal engorgement appeared to be less closely linked to REM sleep and of shorter duration. Waking assessment indicated that the device was sensitive to the effects of erotic stimulation, including masturbation to orgasm, although further study is needed to determine whether varying levels of arousal in the waking state can be differentiated. A more elaborate thermoconductive probe has been developed by Abrams and

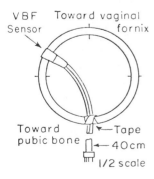

Figure 4.5. Diagram of vaginal blood flow sensor clipped to diaphragm ring. From "Patterns of Female Sexual Arousal during Sleep and Waking: Vaginal Thermo-Conductance Studies" by C. Fisher, H. D. Cohen, R. C. Schiavi, D. Davis, B. Furman, K. Ward, P. Edwards, and J. Cunningham, 1983, *Archives of Sexual Behavior, 12,* p. 101. Copyright 1983 by Plenum Publishing Corporation. Reprinted by permission.

colleagues (Abrams & Stolwijk, 1972; Abrams, Kalna, & Wilcox, 1978; Frisinger, Abrams, Graichen, & Cassin, 1981), although its use has been marked by numerous measurement artifacts.

A similar transducer has been reported recently by Fugl-Meyer, Sjogren, and Johansson (1984). These authors describe a radiotelemetric method for measuring vaginal temperature, using a battery-powered transducer mounted on a diaphragm ring. The device is constructed using a radio-frequency (RF) oscillator, which is controlled by four miniature, temperature-dependent thermistors; a receiver that is interfaced with an AC–DC converter; and a recorder for permanent storage of the signal output. Preliminary data obtained from two subjects in their home environments revealed significant decreases in vaginal temperature immediately upon retiring. Any form of sexual activity, including fantasy, masturbation, and intercourse, resulted in an additional drop in vaginal temperature, reaching a nadir at orgasm. Fugl-Meyer *et al.* speculate that this consistent decrease in vaginal temperature may be due to vaginal wall edema during sexual arousal (Wagner & Levin, 1978a, 1978b).

One advantage of this radiotelemetric device is the absence of movement artifacts, which permits accurate assessment during sexual activity. In addition, Fugl-Meyer *et al.* stress the importance of the more naturalistic assessment that radiotelemetry offers. This device appears to represent the first application of highly sophisticated technology for the study of female genital responding and ultimately may replace current transducers such as the vaginal photoplethysmograph. Greater knowledge concerning the physiological sources of vaginal temperature changes is needed in order for this measurement approach to be fully understood and used in applications relevant for further understanding of female sexuality.

While measures of vaginal temperature changes offer a promising alternative to the use of the vaginal photoplethysmograph, more detailed comparison of these two approaches to measurement devices is needed. To date, the only report of this type is Gillan and Brindley's (1979) study— a comparison that is clouded by the use of an atypical photometer with twice the number of photocells. In addition, there is a need for controlled investigations of the reliability and validity of measures of vaginal temperature changes. Other constraints of this approach include the requirement that subjects be fitted individually for devices employing the vaginal diaphragm ring (Geer, 1976) and potential confounds resulting from slight repositioning of the diaphragm during muscle contraction at higher levels of arousal (Semmlow & Lubowsky, 1983).

OXYGENATION–TEMPERATURE MEASURES

Recently, Levin and Wagner (1977) have introduced an intravaginal measure of transcutaneous oxygen partial pressure (pO_2), in conjunction with thermistor assessment of heat dissipation. The device is constructed to assess oxygen diffusion, which is correlated closely with arterial oxygenation levels, in a noninvasive fashion (Baumberger & Goodfriend, 1951; Rooth, Sjöstedt, & Caligara, 1957) (see Figure 4.6). An oxygen electrode, constructed of a combined platinum cathode and silver anode and covered with an oxygen-permeable hydrophobic membrane, is utilized. A polarizing voltage is applied to the cathode, and the resulting pO_2 values reflect the current generated by the reduction of oxygen taking place at the cathode. The electrode is held against the vaginal wall by means of a suction device and produces two possible measures of vasocongestion. First, the power necessary to maintain the electrode at 43°C, derived in milliwatts, has been reported in several investigations (e.g., Semmens & Wagner, 1982; Levin & Wagner, 1977). Second, the device can be calibrated to yield a measure of pO_2 in mm Hg (e.g., Wagner & Levin, 1978a). To date, use of this instrumentation has been limited because of the novelty of this application, the expense of the instrumentation, and the need to limit measurement sessions to $1-1\frac{1}{2}$ hours.

In the first report (Levin & Wagner, 1977), sexual arousal and orgasm resulted in increased heat dissipation and surface oxygenation. The two measures appeared to covary, although no statistical analyses were pre-

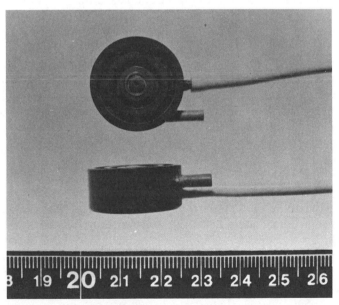

Figure 4.6. The oxygen electrode placed inside the suction device attachable to the vaginal wall. The scale beneath is in centimeters. From "Oxygen Tension of the Vaginal Surface during Sexual Stimulation in the Human" by G. Wagner and R. J. Levin, 1978, *Fertility and Sterility, 30,* p. 51. Copyright 1978 by The American Fertility Society. Reprinted by permission.

sented. Return to prestimulation levels required 10–30 minutes following orgasm, suggesting a protracted resolution of the vasocongestive process. A subsequent report presented more extensive data on pO_2 levels during resting states, as well as during arousal processes (Wagner & Levin, 1978a). In the unstimulated state, low levels of vaginal pO_2 were noted, suggesting either that arterial flow is modest in the absence of sexual stimulation, or that the vaginal epithelium serves to prevent the free diffusion of oxygen. The values obtained during resting phases were comparable to oxygenation levels from external tissue sites, such as the arm. Sexual stimulation resulted in increased oxygenation of the vaginal tissue, which the authors suggest may have been due to greater inflow of oxygenated blood to the capillaries underlying the epithelium. These findings appear relevant to fertility and the impact of thermodynamic factors on sperm motility.

A subsequent investigation examined in greater detail the regulatory mechanisms involved in vaginal blood flow, using the oxygenation probe (Wagner & Levin, 1980). In this report, six sexually functional women were administered atropine intravenously, following which each subject was asked to stimulate herself to orgasm. While atropine produced the expected blockade of the muscarinic innervation of the heart and salivary glands, no significant effect of the drug was observed on vaginal blood flow. Atropine did not appear to suppress sexual arousability or to decrease the intensity of orgasm experienced. A second sample of five women was administered methylatropine, an anticholinergic compound that produces stronger blocking of muscarinic activity prior to stimulation to orgasm. Despite the stronger pharmacological effect produced by methylatropine, no effect was noted on vaginal blood flow. Wagner and Levin (1980) conclude that current formulations concerning the role of acetylcholine in mediating vaginal blood flow during the sexual response deserve reconsideration, in light of these data.

Semmens and Wagner (1982) have utilized the oxygenation probe to assess vaginal blood flow in postmenopausal women. In this study, measures from the probe were compared with indices of vaginal lubrication (pH, as well as quantity of lubricant) and transvaginal potential difference, in order to examine the influence of aging on vaginal physiology. Results indicated that immediately upon the administration of estrogen replacement to the postmenopausal sample, vaginal blood flow during resting conditions approximated levels seen in a younger sample of sexually functional, premenopausal women. After 6 months of hormone therapy, vasoengorgement in the postmenopausal sample had declined somewhat, although it continued at a higher level than prior to hormone administration.

A recent application of the oxygenation probe has been reported by Amberson and Hoon (1985), in a study of the hemodynamics of sequential orgasm in 17 normal women. Subjects were asked to masturbate to orgasm repeatedly, while measures of vaginal blood flow, subjective arousal, and vaginal oxygenation were taken. No evidence for the speculation that successive orgasms are either physiologically or subjectively stronger was found, although substantial vasoengorgement was observed after orgasm. In addition, these authors note that considerable variation in oxygen levels was found across subjects. Further applications of this type will be important for validating the oxygenation probe as a measure of genital blood flow in women. This device appears to offer a promising approach for understanding the arousal process in women, particularly with respect to the exploration of underlying mechanisms.

Other Measures of Female Genital Responding

Other procedures have been reported for the measurement of female genital responding. One such approach has been reported by Gillan and Brindley (1979). These authors describe the use of a pneumatic stimulator that was affixed to the glans of the clitoris with nonirritating glue (eyelash adhesive), in order to provide vibratory stimulation of 80 Hz. Concomitantly, pelvic floor EMG was recorded from the lower vagina via electrodes held in place with suction. In this report, sustained reflex contractions of the pelvic floor were noted during clitoral stimulation. The magnitude of contractions observed from the pelvic floor was greater than that of contractions observed from other vaginal placements during stimulation. The authors speculate that this reflex may be regarded as a tonic counterpart of the phasic bulbocavernosus reflex, as muscle activity remained enhanced for at least 2 minutes following orgasm. While this approach has limitations, owing to the instrumentation involved, the technology described by Gillan and Brindley appears to extend the observations of Masters and Johnson by providing a quantifiable index of vaginal contractile responses. Information concerning the reliability and validity of this approach await further reports.

A final measure of female genital responsivity is the vaginal perineometer, a device originally introduced by Kegel (1948a, 1948b, 1952) in his studies of the role of the PC muscle in urinary stress incontinence and sexual function. This device is pressure-sensitive to muscle contraction and has been used to determine resting levels of PC muscle tone, as well as sustained contractile strength, measured in mm Hg (e.g., Graber & Kline-Graber, 1979; Freese & Levitt, 1984; Logan, 1975). While the importance of the PC muscle in the female sexual response is controversial, this device has proven useful in empirical examinations of the role of Kegel exercises in improving orgasmic function (e.g., Chambless et al., 1984).

Preliminary studies of vaginal musculature in normal women have focused on the distinction between "vulval" and "uterine" orgasms, following from Freud's (1931/1959) formulations concerning psychosexual development and the types of orgasm experienced by a woman. For example, Fox (Fox & Fox, 1971; Fox, Wolff, & Baker, 1970), using radiotelemetry with normal women, demonstrated differences in intrauterine pressure between "uterine" and clitorally induced orgasms. Similarly, Perry and Whipple (1981) found greater PC muscle strength in women who reported more intense orgasms using the perineometer. Missing from these accounts, however, are direct measures of muscle activity (EMG) and comparisons of the relative actions of specific muscle groups. To date, much of the research conducted with women on this topic has been guided exclusively by controversial conceptual schemes, which have not provided the type of carefully controlled investigations necessary for further understanding of the role of circumvaginal musculature in female sexual function.

One exception to this trend is a recent study reported by Messé and Geer (1985). These authors examined the effects of training and practice with Kegel exercises on vaginal vasocongestion and subjective arousal in normal women. Vaginal contractions enhanced both subjective arousal and VPA in the experimental subjects, relative to control subjects who did not receive Kegel training. Additional practice did not appear to augment these effects, although the authors note that Kegel's original recommendations included an extensive 6- to 8-week course of vaginal exercise in order to produce healthy muscle tonus. While this study does not identify the mechanisms through which Kegel exercises operate, it does appear that circumvaginal musculature plays an important role in the arousal process.

Unfortunately, a number of methodological problems have surfaced in studies that have utilized the perineometer. For example, Levitt, Konovsky, Freese, and Thompson (1979) reported that perineometer readings were highly influenced by the posture of the subjects, particularly the positioning of the legs and torso. In addition, both resting and contractile pressure levels were affected by the use of nonpelvic (gluteal and abdominal) muscles in this study. Chambless et al. (1984) found that test–retest reliability of the device was extremely poor, despite the use of procedural safeguards to insure standardization across sessions. In response to these concerns, Perry (1980) has recommended the use of an improved electronic perineometer, termed a "vaginal myograph," although the problem of reliability of measurement does not appear to have been resolved by this refinement (Perry & Whipple, 1981). In view of the inconsistency of data concerning the role of PC muscle tonus and sexual response, however, the value of further methodological improvements of this device is questionable.

Comment

In reviewing the full range of devices available for the assessment of genital responses in women, it becomes apparent that the majority of these are constructed to detect internal physiological changes resulting from vasoengorgement. The most widely adapted measure is the vaginal photoplethysmograph, which has served as an indirect index of blood flow. Similarly, a number of approaches for the measurement of vaginal heat dissipation and internal temperature changes have been described, and these also provide indirect measures of engorgement. There is a notable paucity of reliable measures assessing the lubrication process, and those that do exist are cumbersome to use. Thus, most of what has been learned about female genital response in the past two decades has involved internal vasocongestive processes.

Despite this narrow focus in current measurement approaches to the female sexual response, the existence of other measures, particularly the labial thermistor and the vaginal oxygenation measure, provides an excellent opportunity to expand current knowledge of the female genital response. The need for measures of external physiological changes resulting from vasoengorgement is clear, particularly in view of concerns about the correspondence between vaginal blood flow measures and subjective arousal. To date, thermographic assessment is the only measurement approach for recording external vascular changes (although, as discussed in Chapter 5, thermography suffers from several drawbacks that limit its usefulness). Furthermore, direct indices of blood flow, such as Wagner and Levin's device, are important for establishing the validity of available models of vasocongestion. The rapid developments that have occurred since Sintchak and Geer's introduction of the vaginal photoplethysmograph in 1975 provide direction for continued refinements of this technology.

CORRESPONDENCE BETWEEN GENITAL BLOOD FLOW MEASURES AND SUBJECTIVE AROUSAL

One of the more pervasive issues in the laboratory study of female sexual response is the relationship between physiological and subjective indices of arousal. As with similar studies of male subjects, reviewed in Chapter 3, the growing literature on correspondence between objective and subjective measures in females is complicated by a number of concerns. Across studies, correlations have varied widely, depending on the methodology and procedures employed, with a number of explanations being proposed to account for this variability. Moreover, the discordance between measures raises important conceptual issues in the definition of "sexual arousal" and is particularly salient in research with females.

In one of the first studies of this issue, Geer *et al.* (1974) presented erotic and neutral films to 20 normal female volunteers, while measuring VPA, VBV, and global subjective ratings of arousal following the films' conclusions. While both signals of the vaginal photoplethysmograph differentiated the effects of the erotic and neutral films, neither was correlated significantly with subjective arousal. This lack of correspondence was attributed by the authors to the approach used to assess subjective arousal, although this finding has been replicated in subsequent studies. For example, Heiman (1977) has reported correlations between VPA and estimates of subjective arousal ranging from .44 to .68 with a nonclinical sample of women. D. E. Henson *et al.* (1979) reported average correlations between subjective ratings and VPA of .76, but average correlations between VBV and subjective arousal of only .42. In general, correlations with subjective arousal have been higher for VPA than for VBV in these studies; however, the lack of significant correlations originally reported by Geer *et al.* has been found consistently by other investigators as well.

Studies that have employed continuous assessment of subjective arousal have revealed similar results (Wincze *et al.*, 1977, 1980). Using a lever that could be moved continuously throughout stimulus presentation to indicate subjective arousal, Wincze *et al.* (1977) presented a hierarchy of visual erotic stimuli to six normal subjects. Even though the use of the continuous lever did not disrupt physiological responding, correlations between engorgement and subjective arousal showed considerable variability, ranging from .12 to .78. In a second study, which experimentally examined the influence of continuous measurement (Wincze *et al.*, 1980), use of the lever by women did not influence physiological reactivity; yet this device did not promote higher correlations between subjective arousal and vasocongestion.

Among the explanations that have been offered for the generally low concordance between measures of sexual arousal in women is Heiman's (1976) suggestion that at lower levels of arousal, women may display differential abilities to identify VBV changes. Across studies involving measures of both subjective and physiological arousal, higher levels of arousal infrequently result in improved response concordance. A related explanation for lowered concordance involves measurement error resulting from the vaginal photoplethysmograph (e.g., Hatch, 1979; Beck, Sakheim, & Barlow, 1983), the device that has been used for the majority of these studies.

A recent study (Korff & Geer, 1983) provides support for a third explanation—that is, that women may be estimating their degree of subjective arousal according to other standards besides physiological arousal. These authors experimentally manipulated attentional cues for gauging arousal: One group was instructed to focus on specific genital changes; a second was told to focus on overall somatic arousal (e.g., increased heart rate); and a third was given no specific attentional cues. Both forms of attentional instructions resulted in substantially higher correlations between vasocongestion and subjective arousal than did the no-instruction control condition. There were no differences in correlations observed between the two instructional sets. Another aspect of this investigation was that it included stimuli that produced moderate levels of sexual arousal; this can also account for the increased correlations observed between vasocongestion and subjective arousal measures as suggested by Heiman (1976). These data suggest that in previous studies subjective arousal ratings may not have been based upon specific physiological cues of arousal, and that this may have contributed to both the variability observed between subjects and the overall low correlations obtained between vasocongestion and subjective arousal. It is possible that individual subjects intrinsically employ different criteria for estimating their degree of sexual arousal, ranging from various physiological indicators to the detection of subjective affective states. The use of experimental instructions thus may result in all subjects' using the same cues to estimate sexual arousal. Korff and Geer's study unfortunately does not clarify which physiological indices may be most important for gauging arousal in the laboratory, suggesting the need for further research in this area. This investigation also highlights the need to include stimuli that produce varying degrees of sexual arousal, in order for correlational analyses to be meaningful.

Several related issues deserve mention in this context. Both Heiman (1980) and Morokoff and Heiman (1980) have discussed the importance of setting and practice effects in determining subjective arousal states. For example, one study (Stock & Geer, 1982) demonstrated that female subjects who used fantasy during masturbation outside of the laboratory showed higher arousal (both physiological *and* subjective) during fantasy in the laboratory. In addition, response concordance appears to be mediated by affective states; Heiman (1980) has demonstrated a strong correlation between positive emotional states and increased ratings of subjective arousal in normal female volunteers. These issues are particularly salient in comparisons of clinical and nonclinical subjects, in view of the fact that formulations of sexual dysfunction in women have emphasized lack of awareness of physiological arousal as an etiological factor (e.g., Barbach, 1975). Given the wide range of available alternative explanations for lowered response concordance, this speculation deserves closer experimental evaluation.

It appears, for example, that negative sexual attitudes may play a minor but important role in influencing patterns of response covariation, based on the findings of Rogers, Van de Castle, Evans, and Critelli (1985) and Morokoff (1985a). In the Rogers *et al.* report, women who showed high correlations between genital and subjective measures of arousal were contrasted with women who showed low response concordance on attitudinal measures. There were no significant differences between groups on several sexual attitude scales. Morokoff (1985a) has examined this issue more directly. In this investigation, female subjects were shown either an erotic or a nonerotic film, and then were asked to engage in sexual fantasy. Sex guilt, sexual experience, and self-reported "arousability" were assessed for all subjects. Results indicated that women high in sex guilt reported less subjective arousal but showed significantly greater VPA during the erotic film than did women low in sex guilt. For the high-guilt women, the erotic stimulus facilitated physiological arousal during fantasy. The issue of the correspondence between genital blood flow measures and subjective arousal clearly deserves continued attention, particularly in view of the salient role of subjective states and attitudinal factors in determining emotional experience in general.

SUMMARY

In certain respects, the state of genital blood flow measurement in the female represents one of the forefronts of the field of sexual psychophysiology. In the past two decades, considerable knowledge has accumulated concerning the anatomic sites and physiological mechanisms of arousal in women, including refinements in the conceptualization of underlying physiological processes. In this chapter, a review of internal and external genital anatomy has highlighted the full range of structures involved in the sexual response, and has illustrated the intricate overlap between sexual and reproductive functions. For example, uterine contractile strength appears to be important both in the experience of orgasm and during childbirth. At present, questions remain concerning specific aspects of female genital anatomy, including (1) menstrual cycle effects on sensitivity to sexual stimulation; (2) the role of circumvaginal musculature in arousal and orgasm; (3) the relevant mechanisms responsible for vaginal lubrication; and (4) details concerning the processes of vasocongestion. The presence of working models, such as Levin's account of hemodynamic processes in engorgement, should serve as heuristics for continued study of these issues.

The available technology for assessment of female genital response appears to have developed directly from present understanding of physiological processes. Current assessment approaches have developed from a colorful history, including the use of a water-filled balloon to detect uterine contractions. To date, the vaginal photoplethysmograph is the most widely used measure of this sort, with most studies finding that VPA, the AC signal, appears to be maximally sensitive to erotic presentations, while VBV, the DC signal, may be more reflective of blood pooling. This device has been refined several times in attempts to minimize various measurement artifacts and improve reliability. Other indirect measures of blood flow have been reported as well, including the labial thermistor for detection of temperature changes of the external genitalia. This device appears to warrant greater attention in research and applied settings, as it seems to be less influenced by a number of artifacts than is the vaginal photoplethysmograph. A potential drawback of the labial thermistor, however, is the protracted time course required for return to basal values following stimulation.

More recent devices include vaginal thermistors and the intravaginal measure of transcutaneous pO_2, which have been used in basic laboratory investigations of physiological processes of genital arousal. These approaches appear to offer considerable promise, although adaptations are required for greater ease in applied uses, such as clinical assessment.

A recurrent issue throughout the history of measurement of female genital blood flow is the correspondence between physiological and subjective measures of arousal. Despite speculation concerning the role of poor concordance in creating and maintaining sexual dysfunction in women, it appears from the recent data of Korff and Geer (1983) that response concordance can be improved by attentional instructions; this finding suggests that women may naturally use criteria other than genital responsivity in labeling their emotional arousal as "sexual." This is consistent with a multidimensional account of sexual arousal, and would be predicted from contemporary theories of affect, as discussed in Chapter 2. Future studies examining the specific cues involved in the detection and labeling of an autonomic state as "sexual" would be extremely useful in unraveling the complex issue of response covariation in sexual responding in women.

Finally, in this chapter, we have briefly reviewed the current controversy concerning the "G spot" and the possibility of female ejaculation. While the issue of female ejaculation has surfaced repeatedly in erotic literature in the past, there does not appear to be strong support at present for this phenomenon. More refined examination of vaginal tissue composition, including normative data, are called for in substantiating the existence of the G spot. The presumed relation between this site and female ejaculation appears to have been drawn rather hastily, and greater knowledge could be gained from exploration of the relevant anatomic features at this juncture. In general, female sexuality has become a legitimate focus of study through the development of genital blood flow measures. The ability to validate (or disconfirm) cultural myths concerning women's sexual functions through laboratory research appears to be well established, and a foundation of scientific knowledge has begun to be developed.

CHAPTER FIVE

Extragenital Components of Sexual Arousal

> Whatever the poetry and romance of sex, and whatever the moral and social significance of human sexual behavior, sexual responses involve real and material changes in . . . physiologic functioning.—Kinsey *et al.* (1953, p. 594)

In certain respects, the study of extragenital components of the sexual response predates research on genital vasocongestion. For example, some of the earliest animal studies examined nongenital sexual responses in an effort to identify sympathetic and parasympathetic concomitants of arousal (e.g., Semans & Langworthy, 1938; Beach, 1956). Since that time, considerable knowledge has accumulated concerning the autonomic, somatic, and CNS processes associated with the sexual response in humans. Unfortunately, many findings concerning extragenital arousal processes have been reported in isolation, and attempts at integration of research on genital and extragenital response patterns have been rare. One consequence of this lack of theoretical integration has been the tendency for investigators either to understate the role of nonspecific arousal processes or to focus exclusively on peripheral physiological changes, with limited discussion of the interaction between genital and nongenital aspects of arousal.

Thus, studies of extragenital components of sexual arousal, although important in many ways to a broader understanding of the psychophysiology of sexual response, have received relatively less attention than has research on genital arousal processes, as reviewed in Chapters 3 and 4. Examination of this literature suggests several reasons for this state of benign neglect. First, although early investigators such as Bartlett and Wenger indicated the possible role of autonomic and somatic correlates of sexual arousal, these investigators were unable to demonstrate *specificity* of these responses during sexual stimulation, as has been shown with genital blood flow measures. Second, throughout its development, the field has been lacking in appropriate psychophysiological models for integrating patterns of autonomic, somatic, and CNS activation. As a result, much of the research on extragenital processes has emerged piecemeal, with arbitrary choices of response variables, experimental subjects, and laboratory paradigms. Overall, investigators have tended to underemphasize extragenital components of the sexual response, drawing upon Zuckerman's (1971) early and influential conclusions concerning the lack of utility of extragenital measures as specific indicators of sexual arousal.

While acknowledging the need to view sexual arousal as a "whole-body" phenomenon, psychophysiological studies have tended to focus on genital and subjective measures of the sexual response, with certain notable exceptions. This emphasis on genital arousal processes is in contrast to Masters and Johnson's (1966) observations on the important role of extragenital processes: "Physical evidence of sexual tension develops throughout the entire body. . . . [P]hysical reactions other than those involving the organs of reproduction are of sufficient magnitude to merit separate consideration" (p. 171). At the risk of perpetuating a "sexual dualism" between genital and nongenital aspects of sexual arousal (cf. Davidson, 1980), this chapter reviews current knowledge of extragenital correlates of sexual arousal, including electrodermal, cardiovascular, thermographic, muscular, and EEG indices of arousal.

EXTRAGENITAL RESPONSE PATTERNING: THE ROLE OF STEREOTYPY

In their laboratory observations of sexual responses in the male and female, Masters and Johnson (1966) have provided the most complete picture to date of nongenital physiological processes during sexual arousal. This account includes a comprehensive (albeit qualitative) description of nongenital physiological events that occur in response to "effective sexual stimulation," and it serves as a clear model of response patterning during sexual arousal. In the Masters and Johnson scheme, the presence of nongenital arousal appears to contribute in an important fashion to establishing a response as "sexual," as extragenital activation is postulated to heighten the subjective experience of arousal. At present, however, the role of extragenital activation in the experience of sexual arousal is poorly defined, given a lack of specificity in patterns of central and peripheral activation in discriminating sexual arousal from other emotional states such as fear, anger, or disgust (e.g., Bancroft, 1983; Zuckerman, 1971). While the Masters and Johnson account is inadequate in some respects, particularly concerning individual response stereotypy in peripheral and CNS functions, this framework has served to guide much of the research on extragenital arousal.

A recurrent theme of this book is the centrality of cognitive–subjective phenomena in defining a response as "sexual." In light of the lack of specificity of extragenital measures in differentiating sexual arousal from other emotional states, the role of cognitive attributions appears especially important in understanding the interaction between genital and nongenital aspects of arousal. Converging evidence from multiple perspectives suggests that these two dimensions of arousal affect each other in a synergistic or reciprocal fashion; that is, genital response appears to be heightened by extragenital activation, and vice versa. A task for subsequent research is to unravel this interactive sequence of psychophysiological events and to examine the respective contributions of genital and nongenital processes to cognitive–subjective arousal. Given the wide range of individual variation in response patterning to erotic stimuli, this would appear to be a particularly fruitful area for future studies. For example, are there forms of individual response stereotypy in which extragenital arousal in the presence of erotic cues precedes genital arousal, perhaps also serving as the basis for cognitive–emotional labeling of sexual arousal? Such a response pattern could occur, for example, in individuals with spinal cord injuries, as illustrated by Money (1960) in his description of "phantom" orgasm in male and female paraplegics. Closer examination of individual response patterning of extragenital arousal could conceivably contribute to our understanding of the interplay among physiological, cognitive, and affective indices of the sexual response.

In addition, current accounts of sexual dysfunction—notably the models of Barlow (1986) and Kaplan (1977, 1979)—have emphasized the importance of generalized autonomic arousal both in enhancing cognitive attributions of sexual arousal and as a potential source of distraction from sensations of genital responding. The mechanisms through which nongenital peripheral arousal states facilitate or diminish genital arousal constitute an additional area for study. Investigations of the autonomic and central effects of anxiety on sexual responding, for example, are reviewed in Chapter 10. Furthermore, it is conceivable, on the basis of preliminary data, that physiological indices of somatic and central arousal (e.g., facial EMG and EEG) may add to our understanding of the mechanisms through which extragenital activation influences the subjective experience of arousal, as we discuss below.

MEASURES OF EXTRAGENITAL AROUSAL

The earliest use of extragenital measures in laboratory studies of sexual arousal was characterized by an attempt to establish SSR patterning (see Chapter 2) to erotic stimuli. In his review of early research in this area, Zuckerman (1971) concluded that most studies failed to demonstrate a consistent pattern of activation in somatic, autonomic, and CNS response systems that could differentiate sexual arousal from other emotional states. However, it should be noted that these studies focused exclusively on extragenital activation and neglected measures of genital or subjective arousal. While more recent studies have included indices of both objective and subjective sexual responding, there has been continuing concern with the lack of SSR patterning of extragenital measures in detecting sexual arousal. Relevant questions concerning ISR and MSR patterning have not as yet been adequately explored, although several recent studies have begun to address these issues. In this part of the chapter, a number of measures of extragenital sexual arousal are reviewed; these are grouped into electrodermal measures, indices of pupillary responding, cardiovascular changes, thermal measures, respiration, muscle activity, and central (EEG) correlates.

Electrodermal Measures

According to Masters and Johnson's laboratory observations, one component of sexual responding is perspiration, which is most pronounced immediately preceding and following orgasm. The mechanisms of the eccrine system, however, are considerably more intricate than indicated by visual observation of surface sweating, and are best approached using measures of electrodermal activity, such as skin resistance, skin conductance, and skin potential (Fowles, 1986). In particular, a two-stage process occurs during the sweating response, involving (1) secretion of primary or precursor perspiration in the secretory coil of the gland, and (2) modification of this perspiration as it passes through the duct to the skin, forming surface sweat (Prince, 1977). Electrodermal measures appear to assess both phases of this process, depending upon which type of measure is used (e.g., Edelberg, 1972; Fowles, 1974).

Historically, electrodermal measures were the earliest nongenital measures to be employed in laboratory studies of sexual arousal. Wilhelm Reich (1937/1967) experimented with skin conductance measurement in an effort to provide empirical support for his bioelectric theory of the sexual response. In his investigations, Reich applied electrodes to various bodily organs, including the genitals, in an effort to demonstrate that the erogenous zones maintain higher electrical potential than the nonerogenous zones, and that fluctuations in skin conductance reflect changes in subjective pleasure and displeasure. A number of methodological confounds (e.g., the use of measurement electrodes both to stimulate and to assess skin potential, and the crudeness of the assessment apparatus) clouded the conclusions of this study.

Subsequent research examined indices of electrodermal activity during

111

slide presentations, including neutral scenes, nudes, fear-inducing photos, and geometric shapes (e.g., Davis & Buchwald, 1957; Martin, 1964; Koegler & Kline, 1965). Typical is the study by Wenger *et al.* (1968), who assessed electrodermal level (EDL) and skin potential responses (SPRs), as well as other autonomic measures, in normal males during the reading of erotic and neutral texts. Palmar EDL proved to be sensitive in differentiating the erotic from the neutral condition, although no difference in the number of SPRs was noted between conditions. Across studies, electrodermal responses have appeared sensitive to autonomic activity during erotic presentations in a number of modalities, including text, fantasy, still slides, and films. However, when attempts have been made to differentiate between the content of erotic stimuli, such as male versus female nudes (e.g., Loisselle & Mollenauer, 1965), results have been inconsistent. Similarly, in studies of individuals with deviant arousal patterns (e.g., fetishists and pedophiles), a lack of consistent differences in patterns of electrodermal responding between preferred (deviant) and heterosexual slides has been reported. As we elaborate in Chapter 9, several studies have reported differential patterns of electrodermal responding in deviant and control subjects (e.g., Kercher & Walker, 1973; Barr & Blaszczynski, 1976), while others (e.g., Solyom & Beck, 1967; Barlow, Leitenberg, & Agras, 1969) have failed to replicate these results.

More recent studies including electrodermal measures of sexual arousal have produced similarly inconsistent results. To date, one of the more ambitious investigations of extragenital processes, including a measure of the number of spontaneous electrodermal fluctuations, has been reported by Kockott *et al.* (1980) in their examination of three types of male sexual dysfunction. These authors compared five groups of sexually dysfunctional males (men with primary and secondary erectile dysfunction of psychogenic origin, men with premature ejaculation of two types, and men with diabetes-related erectile failure) with two groups of age-matched normal volunteers in two sessions involving presentation of erotic films. Measures included systolic and diastolic blood pressure, skin resistance, and tumescence. As can be seen in Table 5.1, small and statistically nonsignificant differences in systolic blood pressure and skin resistance were found between the patient and control samples, although the authors note that the start of a film resulted in significant increases in spontaneous fluctuations for subjects in all groups. Similarly, Wincze *et al.* (1976) contrasted sexually functional and dysfunctional women on a measure of skin conductance response during erotic films. No differences between the clinical and control samples were observed in this study.

In considering these data, it is important to note that electrodermal responses have been shown to be reactive to a wide range of affective states, both negative and positive (e.g., Venables & Christie, 1980), as well as being sensitive to initial orienting effects at stimulus onset. Thus,

Table 5.1. Mean Amount of Change in Extragenital Response Parameters Due to the Erotic Film, by Subject Group

		Diabetes-related impotence (n = 10)	Primary erectile dysfunction (n = 8)	Secondary erectile dysfunction (n = 8)	Premature ejaculation (all sexual encounters) (n = 7)	Premature ejaculation (intercourse only) (n = 9)	Young normals (n = 16)	Old normals (n = 8)
Increase in systolic blood pressure (mm Hg)	Session 1	19.0	15.8	19.4	19.2	17.2	18.6	16.2
	Session 2	21.0	15.7	23.4	24.8	16.6	16.0	17.3
Change in no. of spontaneous fluctuations in skin resistance	Session 1	1.7	0.1	2.8	1.7	2.4	3.1	2.6
	Session 2	3.3	−0.2	3.7	3.0	1.3	2.3	1.9

Note. From "Psychophysiological Aspects of Male Sexual Inadequacy: Results of an Experimental Study" by G. Kockott, W. Feil, R. Ferstl, J. Aldenhoff, and U. Besinger, 1980, *Archives of Sexual Behavior, 9*, p. 487. Copyright 1980 by Plenum Publishing Corporation. Reprinted by permission.

specificity of SPRs or skin resistance changes to sexual arousal processes would not necessarily be expected. Conceivably, it would be possible to employ a measure of spontaneous electrodermal fluctuations to examine the intensity of affective responding during sexual arousal, although this use of electrodermal measures has not as yet been attempted.

A further extension of electrodermal measures in sexual psychophysiology has been reported by Ware, Karacan, Salis, Thornby, and Hirshkowitz (1984). On the basis of the observation that spontaneous electrodermal fluctuations occur predominantly in non-REM sleep, with the highest frequency in Stage 4 sleep and the lowest in REM sleep (e.g., McDonald, Shallenberger, Keosko, & Kinney, 1976; Johnson & Lubin, 1966), Ware *et al.* examined electrodermal patterns during assessment of NPT in 60 men with organically based erectile dysfunction. Dysfunctional patients with impaired NPT ($n = 42$) showed less electrodermal activity during Stage 2 sleep and greater activity during REM sleep, relative to patients with normal NPT results ($n = 18$). The authors discuss the possibility that changes in the distribution of electrodermal activity during sleep stages may reflect increasing development of central nervous system control; this hypothesis is based on findings from studies of electrodermal activity and nocturnal tumescence in neonates (e.g., Korner, 1968). Furthermore, Ware *et al.* suggest that subtle changes in the CNS, possibly involving disturbed limbic system function, may be operative in certain cases of erectile dysfunction. In the absence of similar data from sexually functional men, however, these findings raise a number of interesting questions concerning the mechanisms by which nocturnal erections are controlled and the role of generalized autonomic activity in this process.

In considering the use of electrodermal measures in studies of sexual psychophysiology, it appears that the lack of SSR patterning has overshadowed other potentially fruitful avenues of study. Examples of possible areas for future investigation include study of the underlying mechanisms of tumescence and vaginal engorgement, as illustrated by the Ware *et al.* (1984) study, as well as studies of the role of hormonal variation in sexual responding. It is well established, for example, that the eccrine system is mediated by specific hormonal processes, including aldosterone and antidiuretic hormone (Fowles, 1986; Venables & Christie, 1980). Future studies may consider the effects on sexual responding of electrodermal and other autonomic correlates associated with menopause and other hormonal changes.

Measures of the Pupillary Response

Just as the use of electrodermal measures has diminished, owing to a lack of studies demonstrating specificity in the detection of sexual arousal, the use of pupillometry measures has followed a similar course. Within neurology, it is well established that pupillary dilations, known as "task-evoked pupillary responses," reliably accompany mental events. In the tradition of assessing pupillary reactions, task-evoked responses have been shown to vary with the complexity of the cognitive task presented to the subject and with the degree of attention devoted to the task (Beatty, 1982). Thus, a natural application of pupillometry measures to sexual psychophysiology is the investigation of attention to specific sexual stimuli, or, more generally, sexual interest.

The first application of this approach began with the observations of Hess (Hess & Polt, 1960; Hess, Seltzer, & Shlien, 1965). In the initial report, Hess and Polt (1960) presented pilot data from six subjects (two females and four males), using a measure of pupil dilation. Subjects were presented with slides of a baby, a mother and a baby, a nude male, a nude female, and a landscape. The female subjects showed greater pupil dilation to the baby, the mother and baby, and the nude male stimuli, while the males showed greater dilation during the slides of nude females. A subsequent report (Hess et al., 1965) examined heterosexual and homosexual subjects' responses to nude male and female slides and to neutral art slides, with somewhat less consistent findings. On the basis of these two early studies, Hess (1968) postulated that the pupillary response may be a more sensitive physiological index of sexual attitudes than either electrodermal or cardiovascular responses. A further aspect of this theory held that pupil dilation is an indication of positive arousal, while pupil contraction reflects negative affect.

In considering this hypothesis, Zuckerman (1971) has outlined a number of response characteristics of the pupillary response that may moderate Hess's conclusions, including the necessity for controlling visual gaze in paradigms involving complex stimuli that have shading variations, as the pupil may contract by 1–5% when a subject's gaze shifts from a dark region to a relatively bright area of the slide. In addition, like the electrodermal response, pupillary dilation evidences an orienting response, with transient fluctuations in diameter occurring during initial stimulus presentation. Low reliability is also common in laboratory assessment of pupil responses, further confounding the use of this measure. Despite these cautions, other investigators have examined pupil dilation during sexual stimuli with normal male and female subjects. For example, Scott, Wells, Wood, and Morgan (1967) attempted to replicate Hess's original studies, with negative results. In this investigation, no sex differences were noted in dilation to slides of partially clothed and nude males and females. Moreover, no between-group differences were found for heterosexual and homosexual male subjects using slides that depicted preferred and nonpreferred stimuli.

The most recent use of pupillometry has been reported by Lucas, Abel, Mittelman, and Becker (1983), in a study designed to detect sexual preferences of paraphiliacs. This investigation examined pupil dilation in 13 exclusively homosexual and 13 exclusively heterosexual pedophiles. Subjects were presented with slides of nude male and female children, adolescents, and adults, along with neutral slides. Penile tumescence data were collected simultaneously with the assessment of pupil dilation. Results indicated that homosexual pedophiles had significantly greater dilation to slides of male children and adolescents than to slides of young females. No stimulus effects were found for heterosexual pedophiles, and the authors did not report correlations between pupil dilation and genital arousal.

In many respects, applications of pupillometry have yielded disappointing results in studies of sexual response. The cost of the apparatus required for reliable assessment of slight changes in pupil dilation appears prohibitive for most investigators, particularly those in clinical settings; also, without sufficient methodological controls, the resulting data are difficult to interpret. Furthermore, the outcome of research employing pupillometry has been meager to date, with only a handful of studies showing positive correlations between pupil dilation and the presentation of sexual stimuli. Subsequent attempts to replicate these findings have generally failed, suggesting that further use of pupillometry may be of limited value.

Cardiovascular Measures

Relative to electrodermal and pupillometric measures of autonomic activation, measures of cardiovascular arousal have traditionally maintained a more central role in laboratory studies of extragenital arousal. Recent studies in this area have frequently included one or more indices of the cardiac cycle, often in conjunction with genital measures, with the aim of differentiating subject groups or experimental conditions. In considering these investigations, it is clear that studies including cardiovascular measures have contributed significantly to our understanding of the overall patterning of extragenital arousal during the sexual response.

As observed by Masters and Johnson (1966), a variety of cardiovascular changes occur during sexual arousal, ranging from peripheral vasocongestive responses to direct effects on heart rate and blood pressure. Cardiovascular changes are influenced, in turn, by a variety of related physiological determinants, including changes in respiration, posture, and somatic muscle tension (e.g., Larsen, Schneiderman, & Pasin, 1986). Overall, direct cardiovascular effects, such as heart rate, pulse amplitude, and blood pressure, have been the most widely studied, although recent advances in temperature measurement, particularly thermography, have produced a growing number of studies concerning generalized vascular responses during sexual arousal. (Thermal measures are discussed in more detail in a later section.) With the increased availability of devices for measurement of ambulatory heart rate and blood pressure, the possibility has arisen for direct investigation of cardiovascular activity during actual sexual encounters—an advance that would add to the external validity of research in this area. An additional advantage of utilizing *in vivo* assessment approaches is the possibility for refining our understanding of cardiovascular changes during varying levels of subjective sexual arousal.

HEART RATE CHANGES

In an early *in vivo* study, Bartlett (1956) reported marked fluctuations in heart rate in both men and women during foreplay—a finding that may have been confounded by increased activity levels. However, consistent accelerations in heart rate were noted following intromission, with rates approaching 170 beats per minute in some individuals at the point of orgasm. These data are consistent with the subsequent findings of Masters and Johnson.

Another early application of cardiovascular psychophysiology was reported by Wood and Obrist (1968), who employed heart rate measures to investigate conditioning of the sexual response. In two related studies, these authors employed photos of nude centerfolds as UCSs in a classical conditioning paradigm. A red light was used as the CS, and each presentation of the light was followed by an 8-second presentation of an erotic slide (the UCS). Heart rate served as the CR in both experiments. The first study revealed no significant conditioning effects; this finding was attributed to subjects' reduced motivation to attend visually to the CSs after repeated trials. A second study included monetary incentives to remedy this potential confound, using the same experimental paradigm. With this addition, a significant conditioning effect was obtained on reinforced stimulus trials. Heart rate deceleration was noted in the second prior to CS presentation and during the first second of UCS exposure. In the following 3 seconds of UCS exposure, heart rate acceleration was noted, followed by a deceleratory pattern in the final 4 seconds of stimulus presentation. The authors commented that the heart rate response during sexual presentations appears to be brief and biphasic in nature—an observation that has been echoed by Bancroft (1983), and may be reflective of the process described by Lacey and colleagues as "environmental intake," or enhanced attention to external events (Lacey, Kagan, Lacey, & Moss, 1963).

More recent observations of heart rate changes during sexual arousal have been obtained in the context of studies of instrumental conditioning (Rosen, 1973; Rosen *et al.*, 1975), in which the inclusion of cardiovascular measures has assisted in delineating individual response patterns. For example, Rosen *et al.* (1975) utilized measures of heart rate and respiration in a study of voluntary control of tumescence in normal males. In this report, two response patterns were noted, as shown in Figure 5.1. Some

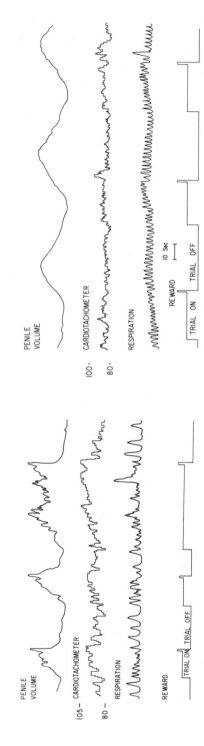

Figure 5.1. Sample polygraph records illustrating the "tension" (left) and "relaxation" (right) responses (see text for details). From "Voluntary Control of Penile Tumescence," by R. C. Rosen, D. Shapiro, and G. Schwartz, 1975, *Psychosomatic Medicine, 37,* p. 481. Copyright 1975 by The American Psychosomatic Society, Inc. Reprinted by permission.

subjects demonstrated a pattern of accelerated heart rate, irregular respiration, and variable tumescence responses; this was characterized as a "tension" pattern. Other subjects showed a more constant pattern of heart rate and respiration, accompanied by smooth, regular tumescence curves; this was characterized as a "relaxation" pattern. The authors discuss the possible role of experimental demand, produced by the use of feedback and monetary rewards to facilitate voluntary control of erection, in creating the tension-like patterns observed in some of their subjects. To date, this is one of the few available studies of ISR patterning to utilize a measure of tumescence in conjunction with assessment of extragenital concomitants of arousal.

Similarly, investigations of alcohol effects on male sexual arousal have included assessment of heart rate (e.g., Farkas & Rosen, 1976; Briddell *et al.*, 1978), as described further in Chapter 12. In each case, these studies consistently revealed a negative correlation between tumescence and heart rate activation. For example, Briddell *et al.* (1978) reported a correlation of $-.25$ between tumescence and heart rate changes—a finding that is suggestive of the decelerating component of the biphasic response pattern noted above.

Clinical investigations have also assessed cardiovascular functioning in sexually dysfunctional men and women. For example, Wincze *et al.* (1976) compared resting heart rate of women with low sexual arousal to that of normal controls; results indicated that the clinical sample had higher heart rates ($\bar{x} = 90.5$) than did the normal sample ($\bar{x} = 73.6$). These subjects were reassessed 2–7 months later, after the clinical sample had participated in sex therapy (Wincze, Hoon, & Hoon, 1978); no significant changes in heart rate or blood pulse amplitude were reported following treatment. Similar data have been presented by Morokoff and Heiman (1980). A comparable study with sexually functional and dysfunctional men (Heiman & Rowland, 1983) also failed to reveal significant differences in heart rate during sexual responding to erotic audiotapes.

The future role of cardiovascular measures in laboratory psychophysiology may be best illustrated by two recent reports of the physiological concomitants of genital arousal in males. As discussed in Chapter 3, Bancroft and his colleagues (Bancroft *et al.*, 1985) have reported the use of penile arterial pulse amplitude as an additional measure of neurovascular control of erection in men. As part of these investigations, peripheral pulse rate and blood pressure measures were included, primarily to ascertain whether the observed pattern of genital changes were attributable to local or to generalized vasodilation effects. As in prior investigations, a biphasic heart rate response was observed during sexual arousal, and graded increases in systolic and diastolic blood pressure occurred during erotic fantasy and films, both for sexually functional men and for men with erectile failure. This pattern of findings indicates that penile pulse amplitude changes are mediated locally, as opposed to being influenced by more generalized cardiovascular changes. The use of peripheral pulse amplitude measures in this instance permitted the exclusion of one hypothesis concerning mediating processes in penile tumescence. To date, this appears to be a highly promising use of these measures.

BLOOD PRESSURE

In certain respects, the assessment of blood pressure responsivity during sexual arousal has proven to be a particularly sensitive index of cardiovascular activation, especially at lower levels of arousal. In summarizing research findings prior to 1970, Zuckerman (1971) concluded that changes in blood pressure appeared to be one of the few extragenital measures to show gradations in response proportional to the strength of the sexual stimulus employed. For example, Wenger et al. (1968) reported maximal average increases of 4 mm Hg for systolic pressure and 5 mm Hg for diastolic pressure while male subjects silently read erotic prose. Similarly, Corman (1968) reported blood pressure changes averaging 11 mm Hg (systolic) and 6 mm Hg (diastolic) in males viewing explicit erotic films, a stimulus modality that typically results in higher levels of sexual arousal (e.g., Heiman, 1980). More recent studies (e.g., Wincze et al., 1976) have supported Zuckerman's original conclusion, reporting differences between clinical and nonclinical samples in diastolic pressure of 13.7 mm Hg during erotic film presentations ($\bar{x} = 76.42$ for clinical subjects, $\bar{x} = 62.75$ for nonclinical subjects). In addition, blood pressure changes appear to be a sensitive index of treatment effects following sex therapy. For example, Wincze et al. (1978) reported significant reductions in systolic and diastolic pressures in posttreatment response to erotic film presentations for a group of sexually dysfunctional women.

Kockott et al. (1980) included measures of systolic and diastolic blood pressure in their examination of three forms of male sexual dysfunction. As seen in Table 5.1, subjects in each of the seven groups demonstrated elevations in both systolic and diastolic pressures during the erotic film, relative to resting levels, and the observed changes were consistent across two measurement sessions. While the original intent of this study was to establish psychophysiological "profiles" that might distinguish the clinical samples, the results of this study revealed surprising similarities in autonomic arousal patterns across groups. Differential tumescence responses were noted, however; these are described further in Chapter 10.

COMMENT ON CARDIOVASCULAR MEASURES

In certain respects, the state of research on cardiovascular measures as an index of sexual arousal is encouraging. Recent studies have elaborated specific response patterns, such as the biphasic heart rate response and gradation of blood pressure changes during presentation of sexual stimuli.

These studies, however, have paid insufficient attention to the issue of response specificity; it is unknown, for example, whether similar patterns of response are observed consistently during other emotional states. Furthermore, there is little information concerning the contribution of cardiovascular changes to the subjective experience of arousal, particularly during the early stages of the arousal response. For example, we would wonder whether biphasic heart rate changes can be detected and labeled as "arousal" during sexual interactions. Similarly, the role of gradual increases in blood pressure in the cognitive labeling of a response as "sexual" warrants further exploration, particularly given recent data concerning voluntary control of peripheral vascular changes (e.g., Patel, Marmot, & Terry, 1981).

Thermal Measures

Thermal changes in the skin surface of various extragenital sites have also served as indicators of generalized vascular and circulatory processes. As originally noted by Masters and Johnson (1966), widespread increases in peripheral blood flow—termed by these authors the "sex flush"—have been noted as sexual arousal occurs. By this account, vasocongestive skin flushing is noted in 75% of females and 25% of males; it originates in the epigastrium and spreads to other areas of the body as sexual stimulation continues. The sex flush is characterized by a reddish measle-like rash, which can spread to the neck, lower abdomen, shoulders, thighs, and back. While Masters and Johnson were careful to note that the flushing observed in their highly responsive subject sample may overrepresent the occurrence of this response in the population at large, flushing appears to be indicative of generalized changes in surface blood flow. This vasocongestive reaction is accompanied by increased skin temperature, as documented by Kinsey *et al.* (1953) and others (e.g., Gardner, 1950).

One of the earliest studies to assess skin temperature from the face and forefinger was reported by Wenger *et al.* (1968). These authors reported a significant decrease in finger temperature during the reading of erotic prose, relative to neutral text, while facial temperature changes were not observed in response to presentation of erotic stimuli. Corman (1968) has reported similar results.

Since these early studies, considerable progress has been made in the measurement technology of thermography. Based on the observation that all heat-emitting objects emit infrared energy, thermography was designed to detect and photograph individual patterns of heat generation using non-invasive instrumentation (Bacon, 1976). The resulting photograph is in the form of a temperature "map," which delineates hot and cold areas, as well as indicating underlying vascular patterns. Seeley, Abramson, Perry, Rothblatt, and Seeley (1980) have pioneered the application of this approach to sexual psychophysiology. In the initial report, a male and female volunteer were asked to disrobe and masturbate to orgasm while thermographic measures of the lower abdomen were taken. Results supported Masters and Johnson's original observations of generalized pelvic vasocongestion during the arousal and orgasm process.

A subsequent study (Abramson *et al.*, 1981) extended these preliminary findings. A total of 37 women and 32 men participated in one of three conditions: reading erotic text, reading a description of the massacre of animals (pretested to evoke negative affect), or no stimulus. Thermographic photographs were taken before and after stimulus presentation, and subjects rated their degree of subjective sexual arousal at the completion of participation. Adequate discriminant validity was demonstrated in this study, as significant increases in pelvic and genital vasocongestion were observed only in the sexual arousal condition. In addition, temperature changes were correlated significantly with ratings of subjective sexual arousal. The authors discuss the relative comparability of heat transfer patterns in women and men; both sexes showed surface cooling of the lower abdomen, corresponding with venous drainage from the genital region. Simultaneously, the thermographic photographs indicated that veins in the abdomen constricted to sustain blood pooling in the genitals.

While thermography offers a considerable advance in the measurement of thermal changes during the arousal response, it has the unfortunate drawbacks of only providing discrete recordings at a given instant in time, and of requiring the subject to stand or to lie supine during measurement. Furthermore, the procedure involved is highly invasive, as subjects must undress completely during thermographic assessment and face the device, which resembles a television camera. However, based on the patterns of heat distribution observed during thermographic recording, several investigators have recorded changes in skin temperatures from the abdomen and groin during sexual arousal. Beck, Barlow, and Sakheim (1983a) assessed penile tumescence, subjective arousal, and abdominal temperature changes during erotic presentations to normal males. Although some evidence was found for skin temperature decreases during sexual arousal, corresponding with the results obtained using thermography, the thermistor results did not correlate well with either tumescence or subjective arousal. Similar data have been reported by Webster and Hammer (1983), using a penile skin temperature probe simultaneously with the assessment of tumescence in normal males. In this study, tumescence was accompanied by increases in penile temperature, although detumescence occurred more rapidly than temperature return to resting levels following sexual arousal. As discussed in Chapter 3, the use of a slow time-constant setting with the temperature measure may have contributed to this difficulty.

Several studies have examined groin temperature, making simultaneous use of a thermistor located on the pubis symphysis and measurement of genital blood flow in male and female volunteers. In a recent study by Rubinsky, Hoon, Eckerman, and Amberson (1985), male and female subjects were presented with films that evoked sexual arousal, anxiety, and neutral states, in a repeated-measures design. Unlike abdominal temperature, groin skin temperature correlated highly with genital responding (vaginal vasocongestion and penile tumescence) for 16 of the 20 subjects. Groin temperature yielded a more variable pattern of results, however, relative to genital measures; it showed changes during some of the nonerotic stimuli, as well as during rest intervals. The order of stimulus presentation appeared to be important in this pattern of findings: When nonerotic films were presented first, temperature increases were noted during stimulus presentations, despite stabilization of the thermistor during a prestimulus habituation interval. A similar pattern of results with groin skin temperature measurement has been reported by Wincze et al. (1977), with positive correlations between groin skin temperature and VBV changes noted for five of six normal females.

An unusual application of thermography has been reported recently by Abramson and Pearsall (1983). Drawing on Masters and Johnson's observation of changes in vasocongestion of the breast in both males and females, these authors examined pectoral temperature changes during masturbation to orgasm and a condition designed to control for muscle movements (rubbing the kneecaps) in three heterosexual couples. An asymmetrical pattern of vasocongestion was reported, with increased blood flow to the right pectoral region and axilla noted for both sexes during sexual arousal. In discussing this finding, the authors raise the possibility of lymphatic involvement in sexually created vasocongestion. As the results of this study indicate, thermography offers the possibility for extending the earlier work of Masters and Johnson in examining the physiology of the sexual response.

In many respects, the use of surface temperature measures in sexual psychophysiology is in its infancy, particularly given recent advances in assessment, such as thermography. A related aspect of extragenital temperature changes is skin coloration, which has not been examined directly since Masters and Johnson's original observation of skin flushing. The development of a measurement approach for detection and quantification of skin flushing would be particularly valuable in this regard, and would have ready application to related areas of sexology, such as the study of rapid thermal changes during menopause (e.g., Swartzman, 1986). In addition, greater knowledge of the relationship during sexual arousal between peripheral vascular changes, as indicated by thermal measures, and specific cardiovascular indices, such as heart rate and blood pressure changes, would further refine our understanding of extragenital response patterns.

Respiration Measures

Other extragenital indices, such as respiration rate and volume, have not been extensively reported in recent studies of sexual psychophysiology, although earlier reports included several of these measures. The earliest of these studies was conducted by Bartlett (1956), who measured respiratory rate, minute volume, and tidal volume in couples during coitus. The instrumentation for this study involved a mouthpiece, valved to direct expired air into a dry-gas meter, which was attached to a smoked drum to record pressure changes. The subject's nose was "lightly clamped" to prevent measurement error during this procedure. The results indicated fluctuations in both respiratory rate and volume before intromission, with steady increases in both measures following penetration. At orgasm, marked peaks in breathing rates were observed, ranging from 20 to 70 breaths per minute. Male and female respiratory patterns were closely parallel during the entire arousal process. As one commentator has noted, "one must admire the heroic performance of Bartlett's subjects" (Zuckerman, 1971, p. 309).

Masters and Johnson (1966) also included observations of breathing patterns in their study, noting that increased respiration occurs at moderate levels of arousal and reaches a peak at orgasm. These authors observed respiratory rates as high as 40 breaths per minute at orgasm in both males and females. The role of hyperventilation in the experience of orgasm is unknown at present, but related research (e.g., Hardonk & Beumer, 1979) suggests that acute increases in breathing rate can produce heightened muscular and cardiovascular activation, as we discuss further in Chapter 6. Related research by Koegler and Kline (1965) reported no effect on respiration rate during exposure to erotic films with young male and female volunteers—a finding that is similar to data reported by Wenger et al. and Smith (1968).

Other applications of respiratory psychophysiology during sexual arousal have included investigations of deviant arousal patterns, discussed in Chapter 9. In addition, a recent study involving respiration measures during sexual arousal has been reported by Rosen et al. (1975), described above. The identification of two respiratory patterns, characterized as "steady and regular" and "shallow and irregular," is most interesting in this study, particularly in light of differences in penile tumescence for subjects showing the "tension" and "relaxation" patterns (see Figure 5.1). Despite the intriguing implications of this particular study, respiration measures have generally been seldom used in studies of sexual psychophysiology, owing to inconsistent findings and the need for relatively cumbersome assessment devices. The interaction of respiratory and cardiovascular changes during sexual arousal (e.g., Porges, McCabe, & Yongue, 1982) remains an unexplored area, despite its potential significance for our understanding of the complex process of sexual response.

124

Measures of Muscle Tension

In addition to the extragenital measures outlined above, several investigators have reported the use of surface EMG recording during sexual arousal. In reviewing these studies, it is important to mention that Masters and Johnson (1966) noted that heightened somatic activation, characterized by an overall pattern of muscle tension, occurs at high levels of sexual arousal and as such may not be apparent in typical laboratory paradigms, which generally involve low to moderate levels of responding. However, several studies to date have included at least one measure of surface EMG activity during sexual arousal.

Briddell and Wilson (1976), for example, included assessment of frontalis EMG in their investigation of alcohol expectancy effects on male sexual arousal. While alcohol significantly reduced the observed level of penile tumescence in response to erotic films in this study, muscle tension levels were not affected by either alcohol or the expectancy set. Furthermore, muscle tension was not correlated with tumescence and did not appear to be a sensitive measure of fluctuations in somatic arousal in this context. It is possible that the frontalis muscle may not be a sensitive site for assessing myotonia during sexual arousal, although this finding illustrates the difficulty in demonstrating response specificity with the use of extragenital measures in laboratory studies.

A recent study illustrates an innovative use of EMG in investigating the influence of pelvic muscle tension and expectancy on both genital and extragenital indicators of sexual arousal (Oswald & Cleary, 1986). Forty normal males were presented with erotic and neutral slides during both tension and relaxation of pelvic muscles (the rectus abdominis muscle and the adductor muscles of the left leg). Prior to participation, subjects were trained to criterion on EMG levels for each of these two conditions. Half of the sample was instructed that relaxation would facilitate arousal and erection, while the remaining subjects were told that tension would create higher levels of sexual responding. Penile volume was monitored using the air-filled plethysmograph designed by McConaghy (1967); in addition, heart rate and respiration amplitude and frequency were assessed.

Results indicated that relaxation of pelvic musculature was accompanied by lower levels of tumescence, relative to tension of these muscle groups, but only under instructions that relaxation would facilitate sexual arousal. A similar pattern of activation was found for heart rate and respiration parameters, although, as would be expected, a principal-components analysis found little correspondence between penile responding and extragenital arousal. The authors discuss the independent and interactive contributions of autonomic arousal and cognitive labeling in voluntary control of tumescence, drawing upon the earlier findings of Rosen *et al.* (1975). To date, this is the first investigation to explore systematically the role of pelvic tension and expectancies for arousal in men. The findings

125

illustrate the usefulness of including EMG measures in conjunction with genital assessment in studies of underlying mechanisms.

Research in related fields has shown facial EMG to differentiate between positive and negative affective states. This research includes studies utilizing recollection imagery (Schwartz, Ahern, & Brown, 1979), music (Cohen & Thayer, 1982), emotional self-statements (Sirota & Schwartz, 1982), and counterattitudinal messages (Cacioppo & Petty, 1981). Across studies, increases in corrugator site muscle activity have been correlated with negative affect, while increased zygomatic activity appears to vary as a function of pleasant affect (e.g., Cacioppo, Petty, Losch, & Kim, 1986). Recently, Sullivan and Brender (1986) examined facial (corrugator and zygomatic) EMG during sexual arousal, in an attempt to determine whether similar patterns of facial muscle activity could differentiate between emotional states during sexual arousal. In this report, 40 female volunteers were presented with audiotape narratives in a between-subjects design. Participants listened to a tape describing one of four situations: (1) pleasant affect/sexual interaction (mutually consenting sexual partners); (2) unpleasant affect/sexual interaction (a nonconsenting sexual interaction); (3) pleasant affect/nonsexual interaction (description of a couple on a sailing expedition); and (4) unpleasant affect/nonsexual interaction (description of a brutal robbery of a woman). Bilateral EMG (taken from the corrugator and zygomatic sites) and subjective ratings of sexual arousal were included, although, unfortunately, no measure of vaginal vasocongestion was included in this study.

The results of this study revealed increases in corrugator muscle activity during the unpleasant narratives, relative to activity at this site during the pleasant audiotapes. During sexual arousal, corrugator activity on the left side of the face was significantly higher than activity on the right side of the face. For the zygomatic muscle, activity was greater during the two sexual audiotapes than during the nonsexual tapes, with no significant effects noted as a function of affect (see Table 5.2).

Sullivan and Brender (1986) discuss the implications of these findings for delineating hemispheric mediation of emotional states; they draw on prior research that implicates the role of right-hemisphere control in the regulation of affect. For example, related studies by Ekman, Hager, and Friesen (1981) and Sackeim, Gur, and Saucy (1978) have examined lateralization of facial muscle activity during emotional states, revealing asymmetrical activity on the right side of the body. A recent review of facial muscle neurophysiology (Rinn, 1984), however, aptly cautions against overgeneralization of these results, given our limited knowledge of the interaction between cortical and limbic structures in mediating facial muscle display. As discussed further in Chapter 6, studies of CNS activity during sexual arousal and orgasm indicate greater activation of the right (nondominant) hemisphere during both NPT and waking arousal (Hirshkowitz,

Table 5.2. Adjusted Cell Means for Corrugator and Zygomatic EMG Activity during Narratives of Different Affect and Sexual Content

	Left		Right	
Narrative affect	Sexual	Nonsexual	Sexual	Nonsexual
	Corrugator amplitudes			
Pleasant	131.34	110.02	131.18	126.74
Unpleasant	163.14	141.25	125.12	141.64
	Zygomatic amplitudes			
Pleasant	139.89	135.77	140.62	115.01
Unpleasant	166.87	122.65	124.91	117.99

Note. Adapted from "Facial Electromyography: A Measure of Affective Processes during Sexual Arousal" by M. J. L. Sullivan and W. Brender, 1986, *Psychophysiology, 23*, p. 185. Copyright 1986 by the Society for Psychophysiological Research. Adapted by permission.

Warc, Turner, & Karacan, 1979; H. D. Cohen *et al.*, 1976; A. S. Cohen *et al.*, 1985); this suggests that future studies could benefit from inclusion of both EEG and EMG measures of laterality in exploring physiological concomitants of emotional states during sexual arousal. Furthermore, the implications of this pattern of EMG activation suggest that specific muscle activation patterns may differentiate complex emotional concomitants of sexual arousal, thus contributing to our understanding of response patterns that encompass physiological, cognitive, and affective dimensions of sexual response.

Measures of Central (EEG) Activation

Considering the well-worn cliche of sex education that "the primary sexual organ is the one between the ears," it is somewhat surprising that little systematic research has been directed at central (EEG) correlates of sexual arousal. Central arousal states clearly are given major importance in the sexual arousal models proposed by Bancroft (1983), Davidson (1980), and others, and the development of electrocortical measures for assessing subjective arousal would contribute greatly to the scope of sexual psychophysiological research. Moreover, as recent research has indicated the potential sensitivity of EEG measures to both cognitive and emotional states (e.g., R. J. Davidson, Schwartz, Saron, Bennett, & Goleman, 1979; Tucker, Stenslie, Roth, & Shearer, 1981), we would anticipate that such measures could be used to differentiate sexual arousal from other emotional or nonemotional states of arousal.

Among the few available studies to date in which EEG measures of arousal have been reported, the primary focus has been on electrophysiological correlates of orgasm, with little attention paid to earlier phases of arousal. Thus, the first study of this type (Mosovich & Tallafero, 1954) focused on EEG frequency and amplitude changes during orgasm in six male and female subjects. Subsequently, Cohen *et al.* (1976) and Sarrel, Foddy, and McKinnon (1977) have reported significant EEG correlates of orgasm in normal males and females. Other authors, however, have questioned the replicability of these results (Graber, Rohrbaugh, Newlin, Varner, & Ellingson, 1985). The controversial issue of CNS changes during orgasm is discussed in greater detail in Chapter 6.

Two early studies described specific electrocortical responses to sexual arousal prior to orgasm in normal subjects. In the first of these studies, Lifshitz (1966) found qualitative differences, such as a more pronounced waveform, in the average evoked responses (AERs) of 10 male subjects as they viewed slides of female nudes, as opposed to neutral or repulsive (ulcerated body parts) images. It was noted, however, that some subjects failed to show differential responsivity between conditions, and it is also unclear whether the AER is specifically responsive to sexual stimuli as opposed to emotionally positive stimuli in general.

Similarly, Costell, Lunde, Koppell, and Wittner (1972) reported increased contingent negative variation (CNV) activity when male and female subjects were shown pictures of opposite-sex nudes, as compared to same-sex nudes and neutral stimuli. The CNV, which has also been referred to as the "expectancy wave," is described by the authors as "a relatively slow surface-negative shift in the baseline of the scalp-recorded EEG" (p. 718), and is typically recorded in the period immediately prior to presentation of a specific stimulus. In this study CNV amplitude was found to be greater for opposite-sex stimuli in both male and female subjects (see Figure 5.2), despite the fact that subjects were not screened for sexual orientation prior to participation. An unexplained finding was that significant responses to same-sex stimuli were observed for female but not male subjects in the study. Although the authors suggested that the CNV methodology described could be of potential value in assessing deviant as well as normal arousal patterns, this hypothesis regrettably has not been tested to date.

Noting the growing evidence of interhemispheric EEG differences as an index of emotional activation, Tucker and Dawson (1984) recorded left and right EEG from a number of cortical sites under conditions of sexual arousal and depression. The subjects were nine experienced Method actors (four males and five females) who were able to generate intense feelings of sexual excitement through imagery alone. Based on a spectral analysis of the EEG and coherence analyses of both intra- and interhemispheric amplitude patterns, the authors were able to demonstrate that sexual arousal in these right-handed subjects was associated with greater involvement of the right (nondominant) hemisphere. Specifically, significantly higher coherence ratios (a measure of association between EEG sites) were reported for the right central and posterior recording sites during sexual arousal

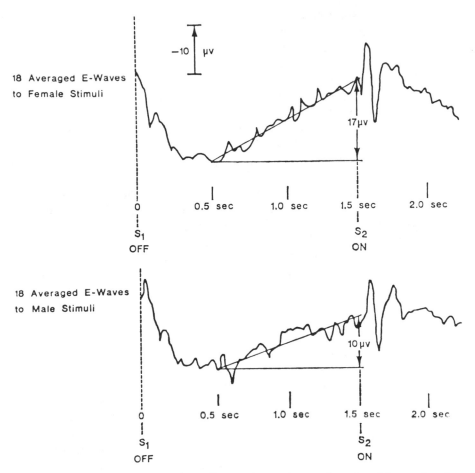

Figure 5.2. Typical averaged CNV (E-wave) waveforms of a male subject to female and male stimuli. From "Contingent Negative Variation as an Indicator of Sexual Object Preference" by R. M. Costell, D. J. Lunde, B. S. Kopell, and W. K. Wittner, 1972, *Science, 177,* 718–720. Copyright 1972 by the American Association for the Advancement of Science. Reprinted by permission.

than during depression. In interpreting these results, Tucker and Dawson speculate that "sexual arousal draws upon the imaginal, analogical perceptual skills of the right hemisphere, whereas right hemisphere conceptual processes are specifically impaired in depression" (1984, p. 72).

In the most recent study of this type, Cohen *et al.* (1985) investigated patterns of EEG hemispheric asymmetry and penile tumescence in sexually functional and dysfunctional males. In addition to replicating the above-described findings of greater right-hemisphere activation during sexual arousal

129

in normals, this study further demonstrated a strong association between right-hemisphere temporal activation and maximum tumescence responses, as measured by a mercury-in-rubber strain gauge. Significant differences were found as well in the EEG responses to visual versus auditory erotic stimuli, although this effect was confounded by the presentation of visual stimuli with eyes open and auditory stimuli with eyes closed. It is note-worthy that this study also represents the first attempt to provide inde-pendent validation of EEG correlates of sexual arousal through concom-itant assessment of penile blood flow. The differences observed between normals and dysfunctional males also were found to be significant; these are discussed in greater detail in Chapter 10.

Finally, it is interesting to note that at least two studies to date have demonstrated an association between sleep erections (NPT) and specific patterns of interhemispheric EEG activity in normal subjects. In the first study of this type, Hirshkowitz et al. (1979) reported a pattern of marked cortical asymmetry during REM sleep in 12 male subjects, the onset of which was correlated with the appearance of NPT in all subjects. This finding recently has been replicated by Rosen et al. (1986), with the inclu-sion of additional measures of sleep physiology and daytime sexual activity. Results indicated a strong association between the occurrence of NPT and nondominant-hemisphere activation, which appeared to strengthen with successive REM periods over the course of the night. On the other hand, no significant correlations were found between daytime sexual activity and NPT or sleep EEG. Although it is tempting to conclude that right-hemi-sphere activation is a key element in the central processing of sexual arousal in both sleep and waking states, we are reminded that different neuro-physiological processes may be involved in mediating NPT and waking erections (Bancroft, 1983). Whether the associated increase in right-hemi-sphere activity is coincidental or not remains to be determined.

Comment

In many respects, the evolution of extragenital measures in sexual psy-chophysiology has continued steadily, despite the early skepticism of Zuck-erman's (1971) influential review. Since this time, researchers have con-tinued to examine somatic, autonomic, and central processes associated with sexual arousal, albeit with a different aim from that of earlier research. As we have noted, attempts to identify SSR patterning for sexual arousal have yielded inconsistent and generally disappointing results. However, given that genital measures have been established as the preferred approach for detection of sexual arousal, recent studies have begun to emphasize the role of response stereotypy. In this regard, a number of innovative studies have examined the relationships between genital and extragenital patterns of arousal, often with surprising results.

In considering the available approaches to the study of extragenital arousal processes, it is notable that most investigations have employed simple regression and analysis of variance (ANOVA) methodologies for examination of sexual response patterns. As discussed in Chapter 2, alternative approaches to pattern analysis, such as the one described by Fahrenberg (1986), appear ideally suited for examination of concordance patterns across physiological response systems. Future studies of sexual arousal could benefit greatly from application of these statistical approaches.

To illustrate this point, several studies reviewed in this chapter have reported asymmetrical patterns of activation in extragenital processes. For example, Abramson and Pearsall (1983) reported increased blood flow to the right pectoral region and axilla in both males and females during sexual arousal, using thermography. Similarly, Sullivan and Brender (1986) have shown increased EMG activity of the corrugator muscles on the left side of the face during sexual stimuli. In studies of central (EEG) arousal processes, several authors have reported greater involvement of the right (nondominant) hemisphere during sexual responding in normal subjects during both waking and sleep states (Tucker & Dawson, 1984; Cohen *et al.*, 1985; Hirshkowitz *et al.*, 1979; Rosen *et al.*, 1986). Further investigations of the patterning of asymmetrical lateralization of extragenital responding in central and peripheral systems would be most interesting. The approach described by Fahrenberg (1986) may well prove useful in drawing comparisons of patterns of activation across response systems and individuals. Furthermore, through the use of this approach, it is conceivable that patterns of lateralization may be detected that will illuminate relevant processes in sexual deviance and dysfunction.

SUMMARY

Considerable progress has occurred in the use of extragenital measures of sexual arousal in the past two decades; this progress reflects advances in our understanding of the mechanisms of sexual responding, as well as creativity in the application of peripheral and central measures of arousal. While recognizing that these measures have limited value in differentiating SSR patterns, investigators have begun to explore concomitants to genital responding, with the aim of delineating autonomic, somatic, and central dimensions of the arousal response.

Studies of electrodermal responding, while among the earliest to emerge in the history of sexual psychophysiology, have tended to focus on group differences in skin conductance responses between sexually functional and dysfunctional individuals. Included in this collection of studies are investigations of EDL and SPR in the full range of male sexual dysfunctions during erotic presentations, as well as during sleep states. Electrodermal measures have been less often used with female subjects, although the available research parallels findings with males. Areas for future research include the use of electrodermal measures as an indicator of the intensity of affective involvement during sexual arousal, as well as possible examination of the role of hormonal mediation in extragenital arousal processes.

Pupillary reactions, although one of the more difficult response systems to assess reliably in the laboratory, have also played a role in investigations of sexual psychophysiology. To date, however, findings of pupil dilation as an index of sexual preference or interest have been inconsistent, based on studies with male and female heterosexuals, homosexuals, and pedophiles. Other limitations of pupillography include the elaborate experimental controls necessary for accurate and valid measurement of pupillary responses and the prohibitive expense of appropriate recording devices.

In contrast, studies of cardiovascular arousal—specifically, changes in heart rate, pulse amplitude, and blood pressure—have yielded valuable information concerning extragenital arousal processes. Differential forms of responding, as illustrated by Rosen et al. (1975), have been demonstrated with heart rate measures and appear to correspond to particular patterns of penile tumescence. In addition, comparisons of clinical and normal samples have indicated differences in heart rate reactivity during erotic presentations, although these findings have not been consistent across studies. Recent studies by Bancroft and his colleagues have illustrated the potential value of penile arterial pulse amplitude as an additional measure of tumescence in normal and dysfunctional men. These studies have suggested that the process of penile vasodilation appears to be mediated locally—a finding that has implications for current conceptualizations of neurovascular influences on tumescence.

Among recent advances in the study of extragenital arousal processes is the application of thermography for the study of heat generation patterns during sexual responding (Seeley et al., 1980). While the complex technology involved in this type of measurement prohibits studies involving a large number of subjects, studies using thermography have revealed interesting and important results concerning the underlying vascular processes of genital engorgement, and have also provided quantifiable data in support of Masters and Johnson's original observations. In addition, continuous temperature measures have suggested the possibility for comparison of vascular processes in males and females (Rubinsky et al., 1985). The use of thermal measures in studies of sexual psychophysiology would appear to be a productive avenue for future study.

Respiration measures have received scant attention in studies of sexual psychophysiology, despite Masters and Johnson's (1966) observation of increases in respiratory rate and depth as sexual arousal proceeds. Investigations that have included breathing indices have yielded inconsistent findings, although given recent advances in assessment of respiratory psychophysiology (e.g., Porges *et al.*, 1982), this may change in the future.

Measures of muscle tension (EMG) have yielded interesting results, particularly in studies of pelvic musculature and facial EMG. As illustrated by Sullivan and Brender's (1986) recent findings, asymmetrical patterns of facial EMG during sexual arousal parallel findings in related investigations of other affective states and may be useful as an objective index of sexual interest. Studies of central (EEG) processes similarly have recently "come of age" in sexual psychophysiology, as illustrated by recent data concerning hemispheric asymmetry during sexual arousal in males. Future studies of central activation processes are likely to contribute to our understanding of brain-body relationships in the mechanisms of sexual response.

The current status of extragenital measures in the study of the sexual response indicates that continued application of these measures appears warranted, albeit with a different aim. Specifically, the use of measures of electrodermal, cardiovascular, thermal, somatic, and central arousal needs to be construed in terms of a broader framework for understanding sexual arousal, with the intention of delineating relevant cognitive, affective, and physiological contributions to sexual response. In certain respects, application of extragenital measures has only begun to yield useful and interesting data in recent years, as our conceptualization and understanding of the nature of sexual responding have evolved. Continued study of the extragenital concomitants of the arousal processes thus appears to be an area where important further research can be expected.

CHAPTER SIX

The Psychophysiology of Orgasm

> The body's involuntary movements are the essence of its life. The beat
> of the heart, the cycle of respiration, the peristaltic movements of the
> intestines—all are involuntary actions. But even on the total body
> level, these involuntary movements are the most meaningful! We con-
> vulse with laughter, cry for pain or sorrow, tremble with anger, jump
> for joy, leap with excitement and smile with pleasure. Because these
> are spontaneously, unwilled or involuntary actions, they *move* us in a
> deep, meaningful way. And most fulfilling of these involuntary re-
> sponses is the orgasm . . . in which the pelvis moves spontaneously and
> the whole body convulses with ecstasy of release—Lowen (1965, p. 244)

Throughout the brief history of modern sexology, the topic of orgasm has
served as a conceptual lightning rod for opposing viewpoints and theories
of sexual response. For instance, no aspect of Freudian theory has elicited
more heated controversy than the vaginal–clitoral orgasm doctrine and its
supposed relationship to women's psychosexual development. Likewise,
Wilhelm Reich's explorations of "orgastic potency" as the cure for neurosis
and ultimate path to psychological health shook the psychoanalytic establishment to its core (C. Wilson, 1981), and led to his ultimate denunciation.
In contrast, Van de Velde's (1926) concept of "simultaneous orgasm" was
uncritically accepted for almost half a century as the ideal goal for heterosexual intercourse.

In recent years the debate has focused increasingly on psychophysiological definitions and models of orgasm. Masters and Johnson (1966),
for example, have argued for the unitary and parallel nature of male and
female orgasmic responses, while Singer (1973), Bentler and Peeler (1979),
Ladas *et al.* (1982), and others have proposed multiple typologies and
varieties of orgasm.

Few would contest the centrality of orgasm to sexual experience and
satisfaction. There is, however, widespread disagreement about the role
of specific physiological or psychological mechanisms. Given the prominence of orgasm in both the sexual psychophysiological and the popular

literature, it is surprising that empirical research has only recently begun to appear.

Laboratory studies of orgasm have been limited by several factors. First, there are obvious social and professional restrictions on the types of sexual behavior that can be observed under laboratory conditions. Moreover, researchers face the problem of controlling the means of stimulation used for achieving orgasm in the laboratory, and the need to limit gross motor activity as a source of measurement artifact. In general, empirical research on orgasm requires considerable comfort on the part of subjects, researchers, and the institutional setting with direct observation of overt sexual activity. As a result, we find that much of the scientific literature on orgasm has been based on interview or survey findings (e.g., Kinsey *et al.*, 1953; Fisher, 1973; Hite, 1976), clinical reports (e.g., Kegel, 1952; Graber & Kline-Graber, 1979), or the largely qualitative laboratory observations of Masters and Johnson (1966).

Despite the relative paucity of experimental data on the topic, theories of orgasm have continued to flourish in the past few years. Among the theoretical issues that have received particular attention are the similarities and differences in male and female patterns of orgasm, and the capacity of each sex for single versus multiple orgasms. Whereas some authors have emphasized the importance of peripheral physiological processes in orgasm, others have focused on CNS and/or subjective dimensions of the response. The issue of "triggering" mechanisms, or the psychophysiological events that precede the occurrence of orgasm, has also been widely discussed, as has the relationship among orgasm, ejaculation, and the so-called "refractory period."

In recent years, sex therapists have highlighted the prevalence of orgasmic disorders in both sexes (e.g., Kaplan, 1974; Leiblum & Pervin, 1980), thereby adding a significant clinical dimension to basic theory and research. Although much has been written on each of these topics, we focus in this chapter on psychophysiological models of orgasm and empirical observations of orgasmic responses elicited in the laboratory. Overall, it is clear that limited progress has been made to date in developing a comprehensive or generally accepted account of orgasm. Indeed, this fundamental aspect of human behavior remains an elusive, largely mysterious, and poorly understood phenomenon.

CENTRAL VERSUS PERIPHERAL MODELS OF ORGASM

Sexual orgasm constitutes one of the most amazing aspects of human behavior. There is only one other phenomenon, namely sneezing, which is physiologically close in its summation and explosive discharge of tension. Sneezing is, however, a localized event, while sexual orgasm involves the whole of the reacting body—Kinsey *et al.* (1953, p. 631)

Given that orgasm is a distinctive, intense, and uniquely pleasurable response, which may typically be experienced thousands of times over the course of an individual's lifetime (Gagnon, 1977), there is surprisingly little agreement about what an orgasm really is. In part, this may be due to the common association of orgasm with the highest levels of sexual arousal. At such times individuals typically experience a loss of contact with reality, which Levin (1981) describes as a "clouding of consciousness" that "makes it impossible for a person experiencing it to describe it until restoration of normal consciousness occurs" (p. 121). Other authors, such as Bancroft (1983), have similarly suggested that orgasm may be difficult to describe, "because it is such a subjective experience occurring often at a time when one's powers of observation are impaired, if not suspended" (p. 54).

In contrast, peripheral physiological accounts of orgasm have tended to focus on the sudden, involuntary release of vasocongestive and myotonic tension, primarily in the pelvic area, but also in other parts of the body. This approach dates back to Ellis's original two-stage model of "tumescence–detumescence," and clearly influenced Kinsey *et al.*'s (1953) description of orgasm as an "explosive discharge of neuromuscular tension" (p. 635). Although viewing orgasm as a brief, reflexive phenomenon of tension release, Kinsey *et al.* took pains in their description of orgasm to emphasize the discharge of sexual tension at *all* physiological levels, including the CNS. Later authors such as Masters and Johnson (1966), Kaplan (1979), Graber (1981), and others have restricted the focus to specific somatic and vascular concomitants. To complicate matters further, there appears to be considerable variation in physiological patterns of orgasm from one person to another (individual response stereotypy), as well as important gender differences.

From a psychophysiological perspective, orgasm appears to consist of a highly synchronized, distinctive combination of somatic, autonomic, and subjective responses, which may nevertheless vary considerably from one individual to another. Thus, Komisaruk (1982) has defined orgasm as an "efferent excitation peak" (p. 22), which is said to occur as the culmination of a process of synchronous afferent discharge throughout the autonomic and somatic systems. Along similar lines, Davidson (1980) has emphasized the importance of "patterning forces" in orgasm that produce marked alterations in ergotropic–trophotropic (autonomic) dominance, somatic muscle activity, and cortical arousal. This model is described more fully in a later section. More recently, Bancroft (1983) has defined orgasm as a complex psychophysiological response, involving multiple interactive changes in the genital, skeletomuscular, cardiovascular, and respiratory systems, as well as somatic sensory experiences and alterations in consciousness.

Clearly, the emphasis in each of these approaches is on the complex interaction between peripheral and central processes in orgasm, with particular recognition of the role of subjective phenomena. Davidson (1980) and Komisaruk (1982), in particular, have postulated specific mechanisms to account for the unique afferent and sensory dimensions of the experience. Although certainly more speculative than the peripheral, physiologically based models of tension release offered by Masters and Johnson (1966), Kaplan (1979), and others, these "whole-body" accounts are better able to accommodate the existing data on orgasm, as well as providing useful heuristics for future research.

Finally, it has recently been suggested that orgasm is fundamentally a CNS event, with a variable pattern of peripheral concomitants. For example, Alzate (1985) has argued that *only* CNS changes are essential to the experience of orgasm, and that somatic or peripheral events should be viewed as secondary or incidental concomitants. According to this author, "Orgasm, then, basically is a *psychic* phenomenon, a sensation (or more neurophysiologically, a cerebral neuronal discharge)" (p. 276). Indeed, we review a limited body of laboratory research on EEG changes during orgasm that has supported this claim (e.g., Mosovich & Tallafero, 1954; Cohen *et al.*, 1976; Sarrel *et al.*, 1977).

MALE–FEMALE PATTERNS OF ORGASM

If the sum of love's pleasure adds up to ten,
Nine parts go to women, only one to men.
—Tiresias

Perhaps as a result of the lack of agreement concerning a definition of orgasm, investigators appear to be equally divided concerning the similarities and differences in patterns of orgasm between men and women. Masters and Johnson (1966), for example, in keeping with their general approach of emphasizing the similarities in male and female reactions to sexual stimulation, have generally described orgasm as the essential culmination or climax of sexual arousal for both sexes. However, these authors have also acknowledged significant gender differences in the typical experience of orgasm—notably, the longer duration of orgasm in women; the occurrence of emission and ejaculation in men versus the formation of the "orgasmic platform" in the outer third of the vagina in women; and the capacity for multiple orgasms in women. Most importantly, Masters and Johnson have disavowed earlier distinctions among orgasms resulting from clitoral, vaginal, or other sources of stimulation, while strongly asserting their position that, from both a male and a female perspective, "an orgasm is an orgasm."

In arguing further for the underlying similarity between male and female orgasms, Masters and Johnson have noted that a feeling of "orgasmic inevitability" typically occurs 2–4 seconds prior to orgasm in both sexes. This experience is identified with the initial spasms of the orgasmic platform in the female, which, they suggest, may parallel the early contractions of the male internal organs just before ejaculation. Another significant similarity is the timing of clonic pelvic muscle contractions during orgasm, which have been recorded at exactly 0.8-second intervals in both sexes. Although this latter finding has been widely cited as evidence for a common neurophysiological basis for orgasm in men and women (e.g., Kaplan, 1979; Mould, 1980), research has yet to demonstrate its significance to the experience of orgasm. Commenting on Masters and Johnson's failure to account for the similarity in timing of the muscle contractions, Robinson (1976) has observed: "The true significance of Masters and Johnson's finding is not practical but symbolic. It suggests that at the supreme sexual moment men and women are in perfect harmony. They march to the same drummer" (p. 169).

Indeed, it is their general tendency toward minimizing gender differences in sexual response that has led Masters and Johnson to gloss over key differences in male and female patterns of orgasm, such as differences in duration or the capacity for multiple orgasms in women. Thus, one can just as easily view their findings as evidence for a fundamental difference in the patterns of orgasm between men and women. Unlike later investigators, for example, Masters and Johnson have identified ejaculation solely with the male orgasm, whereas they view multiple orgasms as possible only in women. Duration of orgasm is noticeably longer in women, including the uniquely female "status orgasmus" response. These essential differences, it might be argued, overshadow the similarities in preorgasmic sensations and timing of pelvic contractions that these authors observed.

Another common assumption is that patterns of orgasm are more variable in women than men. For example, several authors have argued that female orgasm is particularly susceptible to inhibition or interruption effects (Fisher, 1973; Jayne, 1981); that learning factors appear to be more important in the development of female orgasm (Levin, 1981); and that complaints of anorgasmia are far more prevalent in women than men (Kaplan, 1974). On the other hand, it is also frequently stated that women have the capacity to experience longer-lasting or more frequent orgasms than men. According to Bancroft (1983), an essential paradox exists: "Women, we have reason to believe, have greater orgasmic potential than men and yet a much higher proportion of women never experience orgasm" (p. 59). The "refractory period," or period after orgasm, also appears to be different in males and females, as women do not necessarily experience disengorgement of the pelvic vasculature within a short period of time following orgasm (Fisher et al., 1983; Amberson & Hoon, 1985). Finally, while numerous variations and typologies of female orgasm have been proposed, male orgasm is generally viewed as a unitary pattern of response.

TYPES OF FEMALE ORGASM

Despite Masters and Johnson's (1966) efforts to establish the physiological equivalence of clitoral and vaginal orgasms, the notion of a typology of female orgasm has continued to attract attention in both the popular and the scientific literature. Some investigators have acknowledged the presence of a uniform pattern of physiological responses, as proposed by Masters and Johnson, but have reported major differences in women's subjective experience of orgasm, depending upon the site or circumstances of stimulation (e.g., Bentler & Peeler, 1979; Newcomb & Bentler, 1983). Others have argued for distinct patterns of physiological response in association with different "types" of female orgasm (e.g., Fox & Fox, 1969; Singer, 1973; Ladas et al., 1982). The ability of some women to experience repeated orgasms in response to continuous sexual stimulation has led to further distinctions among single, multiple, and sequential orgasms (e.g., Sherfey, 1966; Hite, 1976), or the "status orgasmus" pattern described by Masters and Johnson (1966). Unfortunately, most typologies of female orgasm to date have been based primarily on anecdotal or introspective data from highly selected samples of women. While attesting to the considerable variation in patterns of female orgasm, these reports cannot be viewed as adequate empirical validation of the proposed typologies.

The first study attempting to replicate Masters and Johnson's findings regarding female orgasm (Fox & Fox, 1969) was reported by a husband-and-wife team of physiologists, whose data for this study were collected "in the habitual environment of their own bedroom" (p. 407). On the basis of a variety of subjective and physiological measures, including heart rate, blood pressure, and respiration, the authors distinguished between "preejaculatory" or "nonterminative" orgasms and a "postejaculatory" or "terminative" orgasm. The nonterminative (i.e., clitoral) orgasms were experienced as pleasurable, but briefer and not deeply satisfying, whereas the terminative orgasm was accompanied by powerful contractions in the vagina and uterus, and provided "complete satisfaction." Although this finding has frequently been cited as providing experimental evidence for two distinct types of orgasm in women, the use of single-case methodology and the involvement of the researchers as subjects for the study severely limit the generalizability of the results.

Building upon the initial physiological observations of Fox and Fox (1969), Singer (1973) has proposed that female orgasms can be further differentiated into at least three separate types:

1. A "vulval" orgasm, which consists primarily of spastic contractions of the outer third of the vagina, as well as other physiological concomitants described by Masters and Johnson (1966).
2. A "uterine" orgasm, which is caused by deep intravaginal stimu-

lation, and the "pleasurable effects of uterine and visceral buffeting by the thrusting penis" (p. 72). Although not necessarily associated with contractions of the vaginal platform, the uterine orgasm is said to initiate reflexive autonomic changes—most notably, a brief period of inspiratory apnea due to laryngeal displacement. This type of orgasm is analogous to Fox and Fox's "postejaculatory" orgasm and is followed by feelings of satiation and fulfillment, as well as a subsequent loss of sexual arousal.

3. A "blended" orgasm, which is described as including both contractions of the vaginal platform and a sense of terminative satisfaction.

In support of this typology, Singer (1973) draws upon the clinical observations of Lowen (1965), Clark (1970), and Robertiello (1970) that orgasms associated with deep cervical or uterine stimulation are fundamentally different (i.e., more satisfying) than those caused by clitoral stimulation alone. Although Singer claims to have avoided the "confusing and value-laden connotations" of the terms "clitoral orgasm" and "vaginal orgasm," it is clear that the overall intention of Singer's typology is to assert the primacy of female orgasm experienced in conjunction with deep penile thrusting during intercourse. And while some of the physiological implications (e.g., the occurrence of inspiratory apnea during uterine but not vulval orgasm) are interesting and potentially testable, the psychological dimension remains highly speculative. This is especially clear in Singer's discussion of the emotional aspects of each type of orgasm: "There is reason to believe that vulval orgasms are consummations in which the sensuous predominates while uterine orgasms have a special dependency upon the passionate" (p. 79).

More recently, Ladas et al. (1982) have added the category of "ejaculatory orgasm" to the types proposed by Singer (1973). As described in Chapter 4, these authors claim to have observed the occurrence of female ejaculation, primarily in response to direct stimulation of the so-called "G spot," and to have documented a new variety of female orgasm. According to Ladas et al. (1982), the "ejaculatory orgasm" differs from the pattern of female orgasm observed by Masters and Johnson (1966) in at least two major respects. First, they report no formation of the orgasmic platform, as the vaginal musculature appears particularly relaxed during this type of orgasm. Second, in contrast to the "tenting effect," or ballooning out of the inner portion of the vagina, Ladas et al. describe an "A-frame effect," in which the upper portion of the vagina appears to be compressed and the uterus is forced downward. The two types of orgasm are also differentiated in terms of sensory innervation: The "vulval" orgasm is attributed to the effects of the pudendal nerve, while the ejaculatory orgasm is said to be innervated by the pelvic nerve and hypogastric plexus. Finally, ejaculatory orgasms are described as terminative, and as including subjective experiences similar to those of the "uterine" orgasm described by Singer (1973).

Given the recent failures to substantiate experimentally either the G spot or female ejaculation (e.g., Goldberg *et al.*, 1983; Alzate, 1985), the conclusions of Ladas *et al.* (1982) regarding the so-called "ejaculatory orgasm" need to be viewed with caution. On the other hand, there does appear to be a growing body of evidence that orgasm can be initiated for many women by pressure against either the upper anterior or lower posterior vaginal walls (Alzate & Londono, 1984; Alzate, 1985), and that contractions of the outer third of the vagina are not always present during female orgasm. Whether it is possible to differentiate orgasms achieved in this way from those produced by direct or indirect clitoral stimulation remains an open question.

Results from a number of self-report studies also have been viewed as evidence for a typology of female orgasm. For example, Fisher (1973) conducted interviews with several hundred female respondents concerning the types of orgasm experienced and the sensations associated with each. From these interview data, the author concluded that women clearly differentiate between orgasms elicited by vaginal or clitoral stimulation, and that most women have a strong preference for one type or the other. Surprisingly, a majority of women in this study (64%) indicated a preference for the masturbatory (clitoral) orgasm, which was also associated with higher levels of excitement. Clitorally stimulated women also were found to have fewer body image problems and lower levels of sexual anxiety overall. Despite the clear subjective differences observed between clitoral and vaginal orgasms in this study, Fisher (1973) concurred with Masters and Johnson's claim that vaginal orgasms result from indirect clitoral stimulation during intercourse.

As indicated above, several investigators have also distinguished between single (terminative) and multiple or sequential orgasms in women. According to Kinsey *et al.* (1953), approximately 15% of adult women interviewed reported being able to experience more than one orgasm in a single sexual encounter. Masters and Johnson (1966) similarly reported that 12% of women in their sample were multiply orgasmic, while a few subjects exhibited a pattern referred to as "status orgasmus." This pattern was described as "either a series of rapidly recurrent orgasmic experiences between which no recordable plateau-phase levels can be demonstrated, or a single, long-continued orgasmic episode" (p. 84). Women's capacity for multiple orgasms has also been strongly emphasized by Sherfey (1966), who views this potential as the basis of female "sexual insatiability." According to this author, successive orgasms are experienced as stronger and more intense. This latter pattern is termed "sequential orgasms" by Hite (1976), who argues that the term "multiple orgasms" should be reserved for a more continuous pattern of orgasmic response without pauses or interruption of stimulation. Furthermore, Hite's (1976) questionnaire findings corroborated Sherfey's claim that successive orgasms are experienced as more intense.

In contrast to the view of multiple or sequential orgasms as indicative of greater orgasmic responsivity, several authors have suggested that multiple orgasms are associated only with clitoral stimulation, and are unlikely to occur with the "deeper" uterine or terminative orgasms described by Fox and Fox (1969) and Singer (1973). From this perspective, multiple orgasms are viewed as essentially unsatisfying, and lacking in the complete "orgasmic release" of a single terminative orgasm (Lowen, 1965). It is not clear, however, that multiple orgasms indeed are limited to clitoral stimulation, as Levin (1981) notes that repeated orgasms can occur during coitus, "especially if the male partner learns to maintain coital thrusting for extended periods" (p. 126).

Few studies to date have attempted to differentiate patterns of physiological arousal during single and multiple orgasms. The only data provided by Masters and Johnson (1966) in this regard were for a single subject experiencing a 43-second "status orgasmus" response. Extreme tachycardia was noted throughout this period, with heart rate in excess of 180 beats per minute, in addition to recurrent contractions of the orgasmic platform. More recently, Levin and Wagner (1985) obtained measures of heart rate and vaginal blood flow during patterns of single and multiple ("serial") orgasms in normal female volunteers. No obvious differences were observed in the cardiovascular or hemodynamic patterns associated with each of the orgasm types. Similarly, Amberson and Hoon (1985) failed to differentiate vasocongestive reactions (measured by means of a heated oxygen electrode) during single and repeated orgasms. As shown in Figure 6.1, there was no evidence for Sherfey's (1966) claim that successive orgasms are more intense, at least according to the vasocongestive measures employed in this study. Another finding of interest was that subjects tended to remain highly engorged following orgasm, as had been previously noted by Masters and Johnson (1966) and Fisher et al. (1983).

Clearly, opinions continue to be extremely divided on the topic of female orgasm. Despite the strong convictions and persuasive theorizing of several investigators, none of the typologies proposed to date have been validated empirically. Furthermore, inconsistencies are apparent in the terminology used to differentiate types of orgasm (e.g., "multiple" vs. "serial" vs. "sequential" orgasms), as well as in the proposed mechanisms of stimulation (e.g., "cervical jostling" vs. "deep vaginal thrusting" vs. "G-spot stimulation"). Several of the current typologies can also be criticized as intrinsically evaluative or judgmental—in particular, those emphasizing the greater "satisfaction" or "fulfillment" associated with one or

142

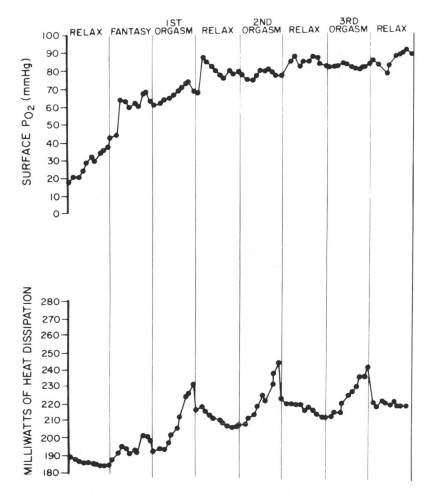

Figure 6.1. Changes in vaginal blood flow (below) and oxygen (above) during repeated orgasms in a single subject. From "Hemodynamics of Sequential Orgasm" by J. I. Amberson and P. W. Hoon, 1985, *Archives of Sexual Behavior, 14*, p. 358. Copyright 1985 by Plenum Publishing Corporation. Reprinted by permission.

another type of orgasm (e.g., Fox & Fox, 1969; Singer, 1973; Ladas *et al.*, 1982). And while most authors claim to have abandoned the traditional Freudian distinction between vaginal and clitoral orgasms, several of the typologies proposed bear striking similarities to the original Freudian distinction. Overall, one can hardly fail to be impressed with the range and variability of female orgasmic experiences, despite the current lack of consensus concerning specific orgasm types.

MALE ORGASM AND EJACULATION

The male orgasm is typically distinguished from its female counterpart in at least two major respects: (1) the experience of a "refractory period," or period of quiescence and sexual unresponsiveness following orgasm; and (2) the occurrence of ejaculation, or forceful expulsion of semen from the urethra. Perhaps due to the emphasis on these specific markers of orgasm in the male, less attention has been directed toward (and certainly much less controversy has been generated by) the topic of male orgasm. Accordingly, male orgasm tends to be viewed as a uniformly brief, reflexive, and predictable culmination to sexual stimulation. In recent years, however, some tentative challenges have been offered to this view, particularly in light of evidence that ejaculation may not be a necessary concomitant to male orgasm in all instances (Williams, 1985) and that variations in the normal pattern of male orgasm are possible (e.g, Robbins & Jensen, 1978).

Historically, male orgasm and ejaculation have frequently been viewed as one and the same phenomenon. For example, Masters and Johnson (1966) clearly view male orgasm and ejaculation as entirely synonymous: "The actual expulsion of seminal-fluid content . . . and the progression of the fluid content under pressure through the full length of the penile urethra to the urethral meatus are the physiological expression of male orgasmic experience" (p. 212). Unlike previous authors, however, Masters and Johnson (1966) divide male ejaculation into two distinct phases. During the first phase, which is frequently referred to as the "emission" phase, sperm and seminal fluids are produced by contractions of the accessory sexual glands, and transported by means of smooth muscle contractions through the genital ducts to the prostatic urethra. Contraction of the internal sphincter prevents retrograde passage of these fluids into the bladder or mixing of urine with the semen. The increasing buildup of seminal fluid in the prostatic urethra and resulting dilation of the urethral bulb are accompanied, according to Masters and Johnson, by a "sensation of ejaculatory inevitability," which occurs approximately 2–3 seconds before ejaculation proper.

The second, or "expulsion," phase begins with relaxation of the external bladder sphincter, thereby allowing passage of the fluid into the penile urethra. Forceful expulsion of semen from the penis is caused by rhythmic contractions of the striated bulbospongiosus and ischiocavernosus muscles, the urethral sphincter, and the urethral bulb. According to Masters and Johnson, the subjective response to the expulsion phase is determined both by the strength of the urethral contractions and the volume of sperm ejaculated. Sperm volume tends to be greater after periods of ejaculatory abstinence, which, they report, "may account for the male's relatively greater pleasure in an initial ejaculatory episode after a significant period of continence" (1966, p. 216). This is in sharp contrast to their observation of increasing intensity of subjective response to multiple or repeated orgasms in women.

Several authors have commented on the differential neural innervation of the two phases of the ejaculation process. For example, Kaplan (1979) considers the emission phase to be controlled entirely by sympathetic innervation—in particular, alpha-adrenergic receptor stimulation of the smooth muscles in the male accessory glands. According to Kaplan, the emission response is experienced subjectively as "ejaculatory inevitability," but is not intrinsically pleasurable. Ejaculation, on the other hand, is controlled by somatic innervation of striated muscle groups at the base of the penis, and is accompanied by "the typical pleasurable orgastic sensations" (1979, p. 20). Kaplan also postulates the existence of an "orgasm center" in the sacral spinal cord, which is said to coordinate both phases of the response.

The two-phase model of male ejaculation also has been incorporated by Davidson (1980) into a novel theory of the psychophysiology of orgasm, termed the "bipolar hypothesis." According to this theory, the sympathetic discharge associated with the emission phase invariably results in "sexual satiety," and is therefore the basis of the refractory period in males. In contrast, the synchronous contractions of the pelvic skeletal musculature associated with the expulsive phase are said to be accompanied by the central effects of "orgasmic experience without satiety." As shown in Figure 6.2, the seminal emission (sympathetic) component results in an "upward" suppression of sexual arousal, together with a "downward" ejection of semen from the accessory sexual glands. On the right side of the figure, the effects of striated (somatic) muscle contractions are seen to result in an "upward" change in consciousness, together with a "downward" ejection of semen from the penile urethra. The "organ of orgasm" shown at the center of the figure is intended to represent a hypothetical neural source, as Davidson (1980) notes: "Nothing can be said as yet about the location or nature of the putative neural 'center(s)' which triggers the bipolar reactions" (p. 303).

Although highly speculative, this model has been used to explain several important phenomena associated with male orgasm. First, there are numerous instances in which orgasm may be experienced subjectively without actual passage of semen through the urethra. Certain alpha-adrenergic antihypertensive drugs, for example, cause retrograde ejaculation due to inhibited contraction of the internal sphincter, but do not eliminate the sensation of orgasm. Similarly, orgasmic capacity has been reported following cystectomy (removal of the accessory sexual organs) for bladder cancer in men. This surgical procedure has been shown to result in a complete loss of seminal emission, while not affecting the contractions of the bulbocavernosus or levator ani muscles (Williams, 1985). According to Davidson's bipolar hypothesis, orgasmic experience is retained in each of these instances because of the continued presence of synchronous striate

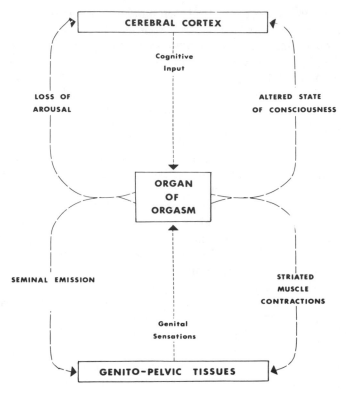

Figure 6.2. Davidson's bipolar model of orgasm. From "The Psychobiology of Sexual Experience" by J. M. Davidson, 1980, in J. M. Davidson and R. J. Davidson (Eds.), *The Psychobiology of Consciousness* (p. 294), New York: Plenum Press. Copyright 1980 by Plenum Publishing Corporation. Reprinted by permission.

muscle contractions. On the other hand, procedures that cause seminal emission without contractions of the pelvic musculature, such as the vibrating-cup technique used by Sobrero (1965) for the collection of semen samples from schizophrenic patients and others, are not associated with any subjective experience of orgasm.

The bipolar hypothesis appears to be on relatively firm ground in accounting for the suppression of sexual arousal following sympathetically innervated seminal emission. As noted by Davidson, detumescence typically follows emission, whether or not ejaculation has taken place. Furthermore, the fact that women do not experience a corresponding physiological response during orgasm may help to explain why the refractory period seems to be invariable for men but not for women.

A notable weakness of the model, however, is the direct linking of altered states of consciousness during orgasm with the pelvic muscle (somatic) contractions of ejaculation. According to Davidson (1980), major changes in consciousness are caused by the "centrifugal" effects of striated pelvic muscle contractions. This concept is highly speculative, particularly as it is unclear how or why convulsive contractions of the peripheral somatic musculature might produce such profound changes in consciousness. The model is also insufficient to account for instances in which the subjective aspects of orgasm are experienced without striate muscle contractions, such as during the "phantom orgasms" of paraplegic men and women (Money, 1960). Likewise, Williams (1985) has described a number of clinical cases of "anesthetic ejaculation" in which normal ejaculation occurs without any subjective experience of orgasm.

Although several authors have referred to the possibility of multiple or repeated orgasms in the male, only one study to date has provided empirical support for this. Specifically, Robbins and Jensen (1978) identified 13 males, ranging in age from 22 to 56, who claimed to have experienced repeated orgasms during sexual stimulation. All subjects reported the typical pattern of extragenital responses (e.g., tachycardia and hyperventilation) during each of the repeated orgasms, as well as urethral contractions without ejaculation. In each case ejaculation occurred during the final orgasm in the series, and was followed by the usual refractory period and detumescence. Most of these men reported between 3 and 10 orgasms per session, with one subject claiming to have experienced up to 30 orgasms during a 1-hour period of intercourse. Physiological recordings were obtained from one subject during intercourse, indicating three distinct periods of elevated heart rate, respiration, and anal contractions, which corresponded to subjective reports of orgasm. Unfortunately, it appears that the subject did not ejaculate during the recording period, making it impossible to determine whether the same pattern of physiological arousal occurs during ejaculatory and nonejaculatory orgasms, as suggested by the investigators.

Whether or not men are capable of multiple orgasms, it is clear that wide variations exist in the latency and duration of the male refractory period. For example, Masters and Johnson (1966) noted that many males below the age of 30 are able to ejaculate more than once during a session of lovemaking, and are "subject to only very short refractory periods during the resolution phase" (p. 213). One subject, in particular, was observed to ejaculate three times within a 10-minute period of sexual stimulation. Predictably, the volume of seminal fluid diminished markedly with each successive ejaculation. With increasing age, however, the refractory period appears to lengthen, and a considerable interval may be required before sexual stimulation is again effective.

It has also been suggested that from a reproductive perspective the male refractory period may serve a "spacing" function, thereby facilitating the replenishment of sperm between sexual episodes (Bancroft, 1983).

From this point of view, there would be no particular reason for a "spacing" mechanism to separate female orgasms, leading to the capacity for multiple orgasm in women. Although highly speculative, this argument is not without logical appeal.

Overall, it is apparent that a number of questions remain to be answered concerning the nature of male orgasm and its relationship to ejaculation and the refractory period. Although most of the evidence to date would support Masters and Johnson's two-phase model of ejaculation, there is little agreement concerning the relationship of either phase to the subjective experience of orgasm. Furthermore, while it is clear that the first phase typically begins with smooth muscle contractions of the internal organs, and the second phase begins with relaxation of the external sphincter, the processes by which each of these phases is initiated have yet to be examined. Finally, although the possibility of multiple orgasms in men is certainly intriguing, the evidence for this is largely anecdotal at present.

ORGASM "TRIGGERS" AND THE ROLE OF PELVIC MUSCLE CONTRACTIONS

An important characteristic of most psychophysiological theories of orgasm is the emphasis on one or another physiological event as a determining antecedent or "trigger" response. An orgasm "trigger" can be any physiological (or psychological) response, such as hyperventilation or pelvic muscle contractions, that elicits orgasm in a given individual. Given the prevailing view of orgasm as a sudden-onset, all-or-none, qualitative change in state, it is clearly necessary to account for the striking transition from preorgasmic to orgasmic levels of arousal. Identifying the orgasm trigger is thus an important concern for basic research on sexual response, as well as in the development of clinical procedures for treating anorgasmic individuals (e.g., Lobitz & LoPiccolo, 1972; Barbach, 1980; de Bruijn, 1982).

In keeping with the overall emphasis of the field on peripheral physiology, investigators have frequently identified specific myotonic or vascular responses as orgasm triggers. Thus, Masters and Johnson (1966) indicate that female orgasm is initiated by involuntary contractions in the orgasmic platform of the outer third of the vagina. Recognizing the need to explain further the onset of these contractions, Masters and Johnson tentatively suggest the creation of a "trigger-point" level of vasocongestive and myotonic increment" (p. 129). For the male, Masters and Johnson describe the onset of orgasm as occurring with the contractions of the internal organs, as described above. No specific explanation is offered, in turn, to account for the initiation of these contractions in the male.

Several authors have focused on the role of pelvic muscle contractions as the key eliciting event. For example, Sherfey (1966, 1974) has proposed that orgasm in both sexes is a spinal reflex that is triggered by firing of the stretch receptors in the pelvic musculature. Stretching of the pelvic muscles is said to be caused, in turn, by the progressive engorgement of the pelvic vasculature. Sherfey (1966) succinctly describes this model as follows: "When the vasocongestive distension reaches a certain point, a reflex stretch mechanism in the responding muscles is set off, causing them to contract vigorously. These contractions expel the blood trapped in the tissue and venous plexi, creating the orgasmic sensations" (p. 74).

Despite the appealing simplicity of this model, Mould (1980) has identified at least one major difficulty—that pelvic vasocongestion alone would be expected to result in activation of a *static* stretch reflex in the intrafusal fibers of the pelvic musculature, which is inconsistent with the *dynamic*, clonic contractions normally associated with orgasm. Instead, Mould (1980) proposes that the principal effect of vasocongestion is to cause *biasing* of the gamma fusimotor muscle spindles. Once the muscle spindles become highly biased, and a dynamic stretch reflex is initiated in the alpha fusimotor system via clitoral stimulation, the necessary conditions become established for orgasmic contractions to occur. The clonic nature of the contractions is attributed primarily to the effects of muscle spindle biasing, which is, in turn, progressively diminished by the dynamic contractions of orgasm: "As each contraction reduces the degree of congestion and hence the degree of bias, the contractions are of decreasing magnitude, terminating when the spindle bias is sufficiently decreased" (Mould, 1980, pp. 199–200). An obvious clinical implication of this model is that drugs that cause inhibition of gamma fusimotor activity, such as chlorpromazine, should particularly affect the onset of orgasm. This and other implications of the model have yet to be experimentally tested.

Clearly, Mould has offered the most detailed and comprehensive account of the triggering process to date. Although the primary focus of the model is on female orgasm, the author suggests that it may also be useful in explaining the initiation of orgasm in men. In regard to male orgasm, however, the model fails to account for the onset of specific responses associated with either emission or ejaculation. As Mould notes, the model is also of little value in explaining subjective or other extragenital aspects of orgasm, as well as their relationship to the neuromuscular events described. Furthermore, despite the clarity and sophistication of the approach, little or no empirical research appears to have resulted. It is interesting to note that none of the theories to date have considered the possible role of *psychological* events as orgasm triggers.

Studies of pelvic muscle contractions prior to and during orgasm have recently emphasized the importance of these responses in males as well as females (e.g., Bohlen & Held, 1979; Bohlen, Held, & Sanderson, 1980). Moreover, increasing attention has been paid to the role of the levator ani muscles of the pelvic diaphragm, and the PC muscles in particular, in eliciting orgasm. Perry and Whipple (1981), for example, reported correlations in one study between PC muscle strength (as measured by the perineometer) and orgasm latency. As described in Chapter 4, however, methodological difficulties in the use of the perineometer in this study, together with the lack of independent EMG measures, limit the generalizability of the findings.

A modified perineometer has recently been developed by Bohlen and Held (1979) for the measurement of anal contractions during orgasm in males and females. As shown in Figure 6.3, this device consists of a photoplethysmograph and pressure transducer in a closed air chamber located in the neck of the probe, and is designed to fit comfortably in the anal canal. Signals from the probe are recorded on a polygraph and digitized by means of an analog-to-digital converter. In a study of 11 normal males, Bohlen et al. (1980) observed various patterns of anal contractions associated with orgasm. The authors noted, however, that the subjective experiences of orgasm did not always correspond with the period of anal contractions, which seemed to begin before or after orgasm in several of the subjects. Nor did the contractions correlate with subjective reports of the intensity of arousal or orgasm. Recognizing that anal contractions may not be a primary focus of orgasmic response, the authors nevertheless

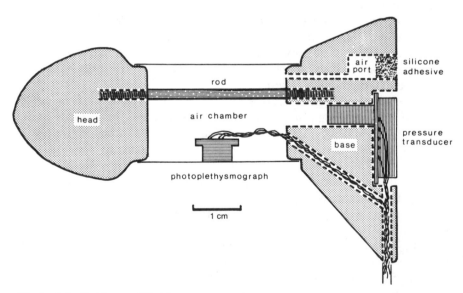

Figure 6.3. Bohlen and Held's anal probe for measurement of blood flow and anal contractions during orgasm. From "An Anal Probe for Monitoring Vascular and Muscular Events during Sexual Response" by J. G. Bohlen and J. P. Held, 1979, *Psychophysiology, 16,* 318–323. Copyright 1980 by the Society for Psychophysiological Research. Reprinted by permission.

recommend this site for ease of measurement and potential comparability of male and female response.

Only one study to date has investigated pelvic muscle changes *following* orgasm. Specifically, Gillan and Brindley (1979) obtained intravaginal EMG recordings from a small sample of women during and after orgasm induced by vibrator stimulation. Although EMG recordings during orgasm served only to confirm the typical pattern of rhythmic contractions, the authors were surprised to note sustained high levels of EMG activity for several minutes following orgasm. The significance of this finding is not explained, and it is unclear to what extent the effect is an artifact of the vibrator method used for stimulation.

CARDIOVASCULAR AND RESPIRATORY CHANGES DURING ORGASM

Among the physiological changes observed during orgasm, Masters and Johnson (1966) have reported particularly striking effects on the cardiovascular and respiratory systems. Specifically, high levels of tachycardia were observed in both sexes, with heart rates ranging from 100 to 180+ beats per minute, along with increases in systolic blood pressure of 4–100 mm Hg. Hyperventilation also was observed as a constant accompaniment to orgasm in both sexes, with respiratory rates as high as 40 breaths per minute.

Similar results were obtained in the single-case observations of Fox and Fox (1969), described above. While marked hyperventilation was observed in association with orgasm in both sexes, the authors also recorded the occurrence of bouts of inspiratory apnea, as measured by a spirometer, prior to orgasm in the female subject. Fox and Fox noted that the sharp rise and fall in systolic blood pressure observed during orgasm may have been mediated by the muscular exertion involved in sexual activity. Furthermore, in a subsequent study of the effects of a beta-blocker (propranolol) on coital physiology, Fox (1970) found that the normal systolic blood pressure rise was markedly attenuated, without any apparent effect on the subjective experience or ease of attainment of orgasm. The results of this latter study strongly suggest that the cardiovascular changes typically observed are incidental to both the physiological and subjective aspects of orgasm.

Using procedures for continuous recording of blood pressure and heart rate, Littler, Honour, and Sleight (1974) reported further effects of intercourse on cardiovascular function in seven normal male subjects. Direct arterial pressure was measured by means of an indwelling catheter attached to a transducer and perfusion pump. Maximum systolic blood pressure reported was 120 mm Hg and diastolic pressure ranged between 25 and 50 mm Hg, which the authors attributed to overriding of the baroreceptor regulation of blood pressure at the time of orgasm. Again, it was unclear to what extent these cardiovascular changes were secondary to the effects of muscular exertion. Rapid heart decelerations following orgasm have been demonstrated by Geer and Quartararo (1976) and by Gillan and Brindley (1979).

Studies of cardiovascular function during orgasm are of particular relevance, in view of current clinical concerns with the risks of sexual activity for cardiac or hypertensive patients (e.g., Hellerstein & Friedman, 1969; Stein, 1977). According to most authorities, however, stress on the cardiovascular system during orgasm is generally no greater than during routine physical exercise, such as climbing two flights of steps at a moderate pace. On the other hand, the deleterious effects of antihypertensive and other cardiovascular drugs on sexual functioning are well known; these are discussed in detail in Chapter 12.

CNS AND SUBJECTIVE CHANGES DURING ORGASM

As we have indicated throughout this chapter, research on orgasm has tended to focus primarily on peripheral somatic and autonomic concomitants in both sexes. While useful in some respects, this tendency toward "somatic reductionism" (Alzate, 1985) has largely obscured the importance of CNS and subjective phenomena during orgasm. In contrast, much has been written in the popular literature about the unique phenomenological aspects of orgasm, such as D. H. Lawrence's (1928/1959) evocative description of Lady Chatterley's orgasm as "pure deepening whirlpools of sensations swirling through her tissue and consciousness, till she was one perfect concentric fluid of feeling" (p. 128).

In reviewing the evidence for orgasm as an altered state of consciousness, Davidson (1980) has observed that orgasm involves a decreased awareness of environmental stimuli, which is generally referred to as "sensory loss." Lowen (1965) describes this as an instance of "losing consciousness of the self," and orgasm has also been discussed by psychoanalytic writers (e.g., Keiser, 1952) as involving a brief loss of contact with immediate external reality (*le petit mort*, or "the little death"). This concept has been elaborated further by Fisher (1973), who speculates that the "blurring" of consciousness during orgasm may elicit fears of object loss, and hence may be a causal factor in orgasmic difficulties for some individuals.

Indirect evidence for this hypothesis can be found in a recent study of time estimation during orgasm in normal women (Levin & Wagner, 1985). Specifically, the authors recorded several measures of orgasm duration and intensity in 28 healthy young females who masturbated to orgasm under laboratory conditions. Subjects were required to signal verbally the onset and termination of orgasm, which was also assessed by means of a heated oxygen electrode measure of vaginal blood flow (Wagner & Levin, 1978a). Approximately 2 minutes after orgasm had terminated, each subject was asked to estimate the duration (in seconds) of the orgasm. Results indicated a dramatic underestimation effect, with the mean estimated duration (12.2 seconds) being less than half of the measured duration (26 seconds). It is interesting to note that studies that have obtained only subjective estimates of orgasm (e.g., Fisher, 1973), have generally reported orgasm durations of 10 seconds or less, whereas studies employing objective measures (e.g., Geer & Quartararo, 1976) have observed much longer durations. This marked discrepancy between "real time" and estimated duration of orgasm is explained by the authors as most likely due to alterations in consciousness typically associated with orgasm.

Direct evidence for the role of cortical events in orgasm comes from a small number of studies in which continuous EEG recordings have been obtained during sexual arousal and orgasm. Mosovich and Tallafero (1954), for example, observed a striking change in the EEG of six normal male and female subjects during masturbation to orgasm in the laboratory. Although appropriate quantitative data analysis was not available at that time, visual inspection of the EEG records indicated a generalized slowing of electrical activity with concomitant voltage increases. EEGs from four of the six subjects were characterized by paroxysmal 3/sec waves.

In the first study of hemispheric laterality changes during sexual arousal (Cohen et al., 1976), left and right parietal EEG was continuously recorded while seven male and female subjects masturbated to orgasm under controlled laboratory conditions. Using an amplitude integration method developed by Goldstein (1975), the investigators computed integrated EEG amplitude ratios (right:left) for all phases of the sexual response cycle. Significant changes in cortical asymmetry were observed, due in large part to a marked increase in amplitude in the nondominant hemisphere during orgasm, as shown in Figure 6.4. These results were interpreted as indicating a dissociation between the right and left EEG, with a predominant change in the nondominant hemisphere.

Included in this study were experimental tests of two major alternative hypotheses. First, in view of the possible confounding effects of the hand used during masturbation, one subject repeated the experiment with stimulation from the nondominant (left) hand. The subject was able to achieve orgasm in this fashion, and the resulting shift in EEG laterality was consistent with that observed during masturbation with the dominant (right) hand. Second, in order to assess the effects of generalized somatic and autonomic exertion on the pattern of cortical activity, a female subject volunteered to produce a "faked" orgasm under laboratory conditions. This "faked" orgasm resulted in the respiratory and cardiovascular changes

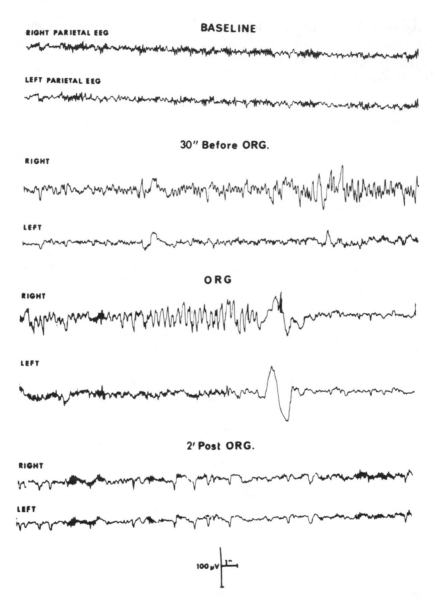

Figure 6.4. EEG tracings from the right and left parietal hemispheres in a male subject during baseline, prior to and during orgasm, and 2 minutes following orgasm. From "Electroencephalographic Laterality Changes during Human Sexual Orgasm" by H. D. Cohen, R. C. Rosen, and L. Goldstein, 1976, *Archives of Sexual Behavior, 5,* p. 195. Copyright 1976 by Plenum Publishing Corporation. Reprinted by permission.

typically found during orgasm, but without the accompanying shift in EEG laterality.

Only two additional studies of EEG changes during orgasm have been reported since. Specifically, Sarrel et al. (1977) have observed a similar pattern of slow-wave, high-amplitude EEG during masturbation to orgasm in a single female subject. An event marker was used to signal the onset and termination of orgasm, and concurrent electrocardiographic (EKG) and VBV measures were also obtained. A positive feature of this study was the use of a portable electrophysiological recorder to allow for data collection in a naturalistic environment. Unfortunately, however, EEG data were recorded from only a single channel with an unspecified electrode site, thus limiting any direct comparison with the results of Cohen et al. (1976).

In the most recent study of this type, Graber et al. (1985) failed to observe significant EEG changes in a laboratory study involving masturbation to orgasm in four young male subjects. Fourteen channels of EEG were recorded from a wide variety of sites, as well as measures of penile tumescence, anal contractions, wrist movements, EKG, and EMG. Although a slight suppression of EEG activity was observed in the alpha frequency band, this effect was much less pronounced than in the Cohen et al. (1976) or Sarrel et al. (1977) studies. In accounting for the relative lack of EEG effects in this study, it is possible that the extensive and highly invasive array of recording devices, in addition to the repeated instructions to the subjects to avoid unnecessary movements, may have sufficiently inhibited changes in consciousness normally associated with orgasm. The average duration of masturbation was less than 6 minutes, which may also have been insufficient to produce high levels of arousal. On the other hand, Graber et al. (1985) suggest that EEG changes during orgasm observed in the previous studies may have been largely an artifact of muscle movements involved in masturbation. It remains for future studies to determine whether orgasm induced by partner stimulation or some other source would produce a similar pattern of EEG changes.

It is interesting to note that the similarity in male and female patterns of EEG hemispheric asymmetry observed in the Cohen et al. (1976) study were mirrored to a large extent in the results of a study of written descriptions of orgasm (Vance & Wagner, 1976). These authors obtained written descriptions of orgasm from several hundred students of both sexes in an undergraduate introductory psychology class. Orgasm description were then rated by several panels of judges as to the likely gender of the respondent. Except for the more frequent experience of multiple orgasm in the female respondents, the reports of orgasm were so similar as to lead Vance and Wagner to conclude: "Until there is empirical evidence to the contrary, it is reasonable to assume that the experience of orgasm for males and female is essentially the same" (1976, p. 93).

Given the limited evidence of CNS changes during orgasm, how does one account for the marked alterations in consciousness frequently reported in the literature? To date, the most promising explanation of this phenomenon has been proposed by Davidson (1980), who argues that rapid shifts in autonomic balance from parasympathetic (trophotropic) to sympathetic (ergotropic) dominance may be accompanied by "major alterations in conscious experience" (p. 315). Drawing upon Gellhorn's (1957) original hypotheses on the effects of autonomic "imbalance" on central arousal states, Davidson suggests that high levels of sexual arousal result in simultaneous (i.e., "nonreciprocal") activation of both autonomic systems, and a consequent change in central arousal. Gellhorn's model would also predict a rapid "rebound" effect following strong ergotropic activation, which may account for the state of quiescence usually associated with the refractory period. Finally, Davidson notes that major changes in autonomic balance appear to be associated with a shift to right (nondominant) cerebral activation, which is consistent with the results obtained by Cohen *et al.* (1976).

SUMMARY AND CONCLUSION

Despite the emphasis on orgasm in both the popular and professional literature on sexuality, laboratory research on the topic is a relatively recent phenomenon. Over the years, however, numerous theories have been proposed, to account for the uniquely pleasurable subjective aspects of the response, and for the variety of orgasmic reactions observed in both sexes. As noted at the outset of this chapter, laboratory research on orgasm has been restricted by methodological constraints and human-subjects concerns; such research requires considerable comfort on the part of both investigators and subjects.

Psychophysiological models of orgasm have clearly evolved from an earlier focus on peripheral physiological concomitants to an increasing emphasis on central and subjective factors. While Kinsey and colleagues, Masters and Johnson, and others have emphasized the function of orgasm as tension release, Bancroft (1983) has observed that there is little agreement at present concerning the specific locus or level of sexual tension required. Disagreement also exists concerning the need to conceptualize orgasm as a "whole-body" phenomenon, as opposed to the more restrictive definitions offered by Kaplan (1979), Graber (1981), and others. In addition, models of orgasm have been proposed to account for the patterning of autonomic and central effects during orgasm, and for the special sensory experiences usually associated with the response.

How similar is the experience of orgasm for men and women? In keeping with their overall emphasis on the parallels between male and female patterns of orgasm, Masters and Johnson (1966) have tended to underplay gender differences, such as the occurrence of ejaculation in males and the capacity for more frequent and longer orgasmic responses in females. These authors have also sought to demonstrate the physiological equivalence of orgasms achieved through different means of stimulation (e.g., vaginal vs. clitoral orgasms), although subsequent investigators have resurrected the issue of orgasm typologies in recent years. In general, more attention has been given to developing typologies of orgasm for women than for men.

Accounts of male orgasm typically begin with a separation of ejaculation into two phases: emission and expulsion. Noting the major role of sympathetic smooth muscle activity in the first phase, followed by pelvic skeletal contractions in the second phase, Davidson (1980) has proposed a bipolar model of orgasm. This model has been used to explain alterations in consciousness during orgasm, as well as postejaculatory suppression effects in the male. Certain aspects of female orgasm can also be accounted for in terms of this model. More recent research on male orgasm has highlighted the possibility of multiple orgasms (without ejaculation) in men, as well as marked variations in the timing of the male refractory period.

Orgasm "triggers" have been considered in some detail, including the role of pelvic muscle contractions as a key antecedent. Anal contractions prior to and during orgasm have been recorded in several studies, although this response does not appear to correlate well with subjective reports. Other authors have suggested that marked respiratory changes, such as periods of inspiratory apnea, may be important in eliciting orgasm in both genders. Significant cardiovascular changes during orgasm have also been noted, although it is not clear to what extent these changes are secondary to the effects of muscular exertion.

Finally, we have reviewed a growing body of research on the role of CNS and subjective changes during orgasm. Recent research on EEG aspects of orgasm, in particular, has indicated a possible means for objective assessment of central phenomena. Laboratory findings in this area have not always been consistent, however, due to possible differences in experimental conditions or recording techniques. Clearly, there is a major need for further replication of these results.

CHAPTER SEVEN

Endocrine Factors in Sexual Psychophysiology

JULIAN M. DAVIDSON
LIN S. MYERS

INTRODUCTION

From the biological perspective, hormones are seen to occupy a position alongside that of the nervous system, as the "other"—and very different— global communication network of the organism. Thus it is unfortunate that studies on endocrine factors in sexual psychophysiology have been so neglected in the past, and it is exciting to see signs of a reversal of this trend.

The endocrine system impinges on sexual psychophysiology in two ways: (1) modulation of physiological responses by changes in hormone levels, and (2) endocrine change as a component of the sexual response. Both of these processes are discussed in this chapter. Because endocrine factors have not often been included in writings on sexual psychophysiology, our approach is to present general information on the role of hormones in sexuality, in addition to discussing specific psychophysiological studies.

Indisputable evidence shows that gonadal hormones are vital to the expression of sexual behavior in animals (Beach, 1948; Young, 1961). A similar role for such hormones in men has been amply established in the last 7 or so years; in women, though the issue is still controversial, the discussion is more about the nature and extent of endocrine involvement than its actual existence.

Recent decades of research have identified a bewildering array of cellular and organismic chemical modulators, of which hormones are a very important class. Thus the reader should bear in mind the strict definition of a "hormone": a chemical agent produced by specialized organs (en-

Julian M. Davidson and Lin S. Myers. Department of Physiology, Stanford University, Stanford, California.

docrine glands) and secreted or "released" into the bloodstream to act on target tissues at a distance from the site of secretion. Such a definition excludes non-blood-borne agents that affect membranes or cells by diffusion into the immediate environment of the site of production (e.g., neurotransmitters such as norepinephrine, dopamine, and serotonin, and the ubiquitous prostaglandins whose biological functions are legion). The uniqueness of hormones is that, because their transportation medium is almost invariably the bloodstream, they can act on any organ system in the body. Thus their actions do not depend on their sites of production— the pituitary, thyroid, parathyroid, gonads, adrenals, and pancreas. Most relevant to psychophysiology, is the fact that hormonal effects on behavior can be mediated via direct action on any part of the nervous system— brain, spinal cord, or peripheral nerve.

Chemically, the sex hormones are steroids or peptides. These steroids are made in three steroid-producing endocrine glands: the testis and ovary (gonads) and the adrenal cortex. These sex hormones belong in three categories—androgens, estrogens, and progestins, of which the most important are testosterone, estradiol, and progesterone, respectively.

Each class of sex steroids has major roles in reproductive function and affects nonsexual targets apart from its effects on sexual behavior. The differences in sex hormones between the two sexes are not the result of separate hormones being produced by males and females, for all three of the above-mentioned glands produce "male" and "female" sex hormones. Rather, the differences depend on the relative rates of production of different hormones in the two sexes. Thus males make much more testosterone than females, and females make much more estradiol and progesterone. The adrenal cortex produces (apart from its "own" corticosteroid hormones) quite a large amount of various androgens. These, however, are less important except in pathological situations, because of the low potency of most adrenal androgens.

The peptide (or protein) hormones relevant to sexual function are made first in the anterior pituitary gland—follicle-stimulating hormone (FSH), luteinizing hormone (LH), and prolactin. FSH and LH have the role of controlling the production of the gonadal sex steroids (and aspects of reproduction), and prolactin suppresses sexual function in pathological situations, while stimulating milk production in lactating women. A posterior pituitary peptide hormone, oxytocin, stimulates milk letdown and uterine contractions, and may have a role in sexuality (Davidson, 1980; Carmichael et al., 1987).

Pivotal questions on the agenda of a developing endocrine sexual psychophysiology are easy to pose but not to dispose. They include the following: Do the large shifts in hormone levels that women experience at several points in their menstrual cycle, and the dramatic change at menopause, result in effects on the physiological sexual response? Do normal healthy men with different androgen levels have different behavioral–psychophysiological capacities? What are the differences in the effect of hormones on male versus female sexual response? Is the hormone–psychophysiological relationship a one-way street, or can hormone release be a dependent as well as an independent variable in sexuality?

HORMONE REPLACEMENT THERAPY AS AN EXPERIMENTAL METHOD

The classic experimental approach to establishing the role of a hormone in terms of physiological or behavioral function is that of "ablation–replacement." First, the gland suspected of producing the hormone is removed surgically from animals, and the effects of this maneuver are noted. Then the gland, or extracts of it, are administered. If specific changes occur after ablation (e.g., gonadectomy, thyroidectomy, etc.), and these are reversed by administering extracts derived from the ablated gland, the hypothesis is established that these changes represent specific effects of some material secreted from the gland. These methods are exemplified by the precocious work of Berthold (1849), who removed the testes (testicles) of roosters and noted the atrophy of the masculine features, including sexual and aggressive behavior. Transplantation of testes back into the castrated animals resulted in restoration of sexual behavior and other characteristics.[1] The clarity of the effects of these procedures in male animals and humans persuades us to further discussion of them in this section, while hormone replacement therapy (HRT) of human females (which relates to much larger public health issues than does male HRT) is dealt with later.

The ablation–replacement therapy approach is still widely used in experimental endocrinology, although the sophistication of such studies has grown immensely. As to ablation of the testes in men, we can observe the loss of hormonal effects without surgical extirpation of the endocrine gland (i.e., castration), though such surgery is still practiced for testicular cancer and sometimes for other conditions. The major physical consequences are atrophy of the internal reproductive–genital structures, increases in fat at the cost of decreases in muscle, and interference with various other secondary sexual characteristics (including balding).

Most research of this type, however, has not been on castrates, but on patients (hypogonadal men) whose testes fail to produce adequate amounts

1. This study heralded the birth of endocrinology, the discipline of the scientific study of hormones. Berthold's elegant experiment remained as a solitary and neglected observation for half a century, until the work of Bayliss and Starling (1904) set endocrinology in motion as a recognized discipline. Thus Berthold's prescient observations began the study of hormones and sex behavior at the very inception of endocrinology.

of androgen by virtue of a variety of disease processes. Chemical methods are now available for suppressing hormone production in males, both animal and human. Thus, various androgen antagonists (antiandrogens) and other drugs temporarily suppress blood testosterone levels, producing "reversible castration." A notable application of these compounds is the use of the antiandrogens cyproterone acetate (Laschet, 1973) and medroxyprogesterone acetate (Money, 1970) for treatment of sexual offenders in Europe and the United States, respectively. Such drugs may inactivate effects of sex hormones by preventing their binding and entry into cells and/or by decreasing their production rates.

As to experimental HRT, the days of having to transplant hormone-producing glands, as Berthold did, are long gone. Synthetic hormones, androgen among them, are available in a variety of forms, allowing precise dosing. Moreover, chemical measurements now allow us to determine levels of hormones in the blood, and the doses can be adjusted such that the treatment provides a true replacement (i.e., normal blood levels can be reinstated).

The goal of the ablation-replacement process is further facilitated by modern methods of hormone administration. "Depot" preparations of slowly absorbed hormonal drugs enable infrequent injections under the skin (subcutaneously), lasting for several weeks. Solid subcutaneous pellets of testosterone are widely used in Europe to provide effective and reasonably stable blood levels for up to 6 months. New methods of "transdermal" treatment are being researched; these achieve their effects by absorption of externally applied "patches" of hormones through the skin to the bloodstream. Most impressive, perhaps, is the discovery that various reproductive and other hormones are secreted in pulsatile spurts. In some cases (notably the neurohormone gonadotropin-releasing hormone [GnRH]), a regular intermittent release of the hormone is essential for function (in this case, LH release). Mechanical pumps have been developed that "replace" not only the absolute amount of hormone naturally secreted, but also the normal pattern of its delivery into the bloodstream.

Hypogonadal patients available for testosterone HRT studies are rare, compared with such organically dysfunctional patients as diabetics. This is both because extremely low testosterone levels are not often found and because the condition of such patients is well controlled by treatment so that they are often not highly motivated to participate in long-term studies. The problem is confounded by the fact that well-conducted experiments of this kind generally require many months of a volunteer's time if the most effective double-blind crossover experimental design is to be used.

Ablation of the gonad, and with it the loss of most of the sex hormones, is much more common in women (oophorectomy) than in men (orchidectomy). This is in large part due to the cavalier practice of removing healthy ovaries during hysterectomy (Garcia & Cutler, 1985). Moreover, *all* women who live into their 50s become hypogonadal after menopause. A great many postmenopausal women take ovarian HRT, though mostly not for sexual complaints. Given the much greater prevalence of gonadectomy in women, one might expect that there is much greater knowledge of the effects of ovarian hormones on female sexuality. The fact that few rigorous studies are actually available is probably due in part to the relative lack of interest of the medical profession in female sexual problems, but it also reflects the real difficulties of implementing this research, as we discuss in a later section.

ACTIONS OF TESTOSTERONE ON MALE SEXUALITY

General Effects

The effect of testosterone on sexual behavior is arguably the most striking example of an essential role of a natural hormone in a natural behavior. The loss of sexual function when testosterone is removed by surgical ablation, or through seasonal regression in animals, seems to be universal among vertebrates (Beach, 1948; Hart, 1974). The concomitant failures of semen production and of sexual activity provide a dual barrier to reproduction. Throughout recorded history, conquerors and other power elitists have used castration to achieve these and other behavioral ends. Yet only very recently have we begun to obtain reliable information about the sequence of events that takes place when a human male undergoes ablation and/or HRT.

Testosterone's capacity to initiate or restore sexual activity has been established through research on males of many species, from fishes to primates (Beach, 1948). Even the details of the localization of the actions of testosterone seem to be quite similar among diverse groups. A key question for psychophysiology, in light of this remarkable evolutionary conservation of a vital hormone–behavior relationship, is whether androgen treatment mediates primarily the *physiological* manifestations of the sexual response, as opposed to the more mysterious cognitive–affective processes.

Astonishingly, no properly controlled experimental findings in humans on the sexual effects of androgen were available until 1979 (J.M. Davidson, Camargo, & Smith, 1979). At the time of this writing, about 10 HRT studies of adequate scientific worth have been published. They show that testosterone acts to stimulate/increase sexual behavior in general, and spontaneous erections in particular. In addition, it facilitates an entity referred to variously as "sexual drive," "interest," "motivation," "appetite," or more generally as "libido." This is measured by verbal reports, preferably daily records of frequency of sexual thoughts and fantasies. Despite claims to this effect (Bancroft, 1980; Salmimies, Kockott, Pirke, Vogt, & Schill, 1982; and see below), there is little if any evidence of a *direct* effect of testosterone on ejaculation/orgasm.

Some studies have also demonstrated an elevation of mood, concomitant with the recovery of sexual function, following HRT in hypogonadal men. Could this improvement of mood be responsible for the sexual effect? Bancroft's group has given the most attention to this question in recent years, with results that have tended to be too mild or inconsistent for the proposed role (O'Carroll, Shapiro, & Bancroft, 1985). Other investigators have found no effect. A reasonable interpretation for this body of data would be that the affective changes found were a secondary consequence of improved sexual expression. Nevertheless, more studies are needed that pay close attention to observations of mood, as well as to other possible extragenital components of the sexual response. This is far from a simple question, involving as it does the complex issues of response patterning, which are thoroughly discussed in Chapter 2.

Psychophysiological Effects

Two psychophysiological methods have been employed to elucidate the role of androgen in physiological sexual response: (1) laboratory measurements of responses (particularly genital) elicited, for example, by erotic film or fantasy; and (2) NPT measurements.

Both procedures generally employ the mercury-in-rubber strain gauge and use penile circumference increase as the major outcome measure. In an early study, Bancroft, Tennent, Loucas, and Cass (1974) gave an antiandrogen (cyproterone) or estrogen to sex offenders in order to effectively suppress endogenous androgen ("chemical castration"). Normal erections were obtained in response to an erotic film, although there was little or no response to fantasy. This indirect approach to the assessment of androgen's action suggested that normal levels of testosterone may not be necessary for erections, while the response to fantasy may be testosterone-dependent.

In 1983, the main conclusion of the Bancroft *et al.* 1974 study (i.e., that film-elicited erections were not androgen-dependent) was supported in two double-blind crossover studies utilizing the direct approach of testosterone administration to hypogonadal patients (Kwan, Greenleaf, Mann, Crapo, & Davidson, 1983 [see Figure 7.1]; Bancroft & Wu, 1983). The latter study included eight hypogonadal men and found no effect of testosterone on the response to film, but the response to fantasy was diminished in the absence of androgen. Bancroft (1980) and Bancroft and Wu (1983) proposed a hypothesis that testosterone deficiency decreases an attentional mechanism needed for maintenance of sexual fantasy. As sup-

163

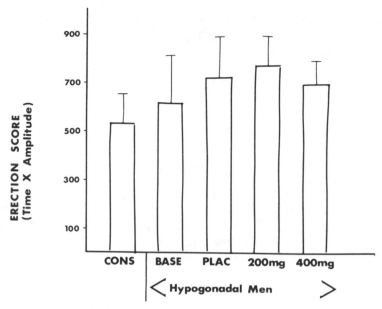

Figure 7.1. Film-elicited erection response following testosterone administration to hypogonadal men. Based on data from Kwan *et al.* (1983).

port for this idea, a reported effect of testosterone to increase "persistence of attention" in chickens was cited. Further support may be adduced from a somewhat obscure finding of Broverman, Klaiber, and Vogel (1980), which suggested that testosterone treatment increases the capacity to maintain certain repetitive cognitive tasks. Kwan *et al.* (1983), studying six hypogonadal men, also found excellent responses to film (Figure 7.1), but at least half of the subjects also responded well to fantasy. It was proposed that the discrepancy in responses to film versus fantasy had to do with the intensity of the stimulus: For most subjects, male or female, fantasy is considerably less effective in eliciting genital responses than is explicit heterosexual moving color film (Davidson, Kwan, & Greenleaf, 1982).

This study also demonstrated that NPT is severely depressed in the untreated hypogonadal man and that NPT levels are restored to normal by testosterone treatment (see Figure 7.2)—a finding since confirmed by O'Carroll *et al.* (1985). Taken in combination with the observation that spontaneous daytime erections are testosterone-dependent (J.M. Davidson *et al.*, 1979; Kwan *et al.*, 1983), and the common report from untreated hypogonadal patients that erectile difficulties with their sexual partners can be overcome, a picture emerges of two differentially regulated forms of erection: (1) those non-androgen-dependent erections elicited by sexual stimuli during sexual behavior or in response to erotic films; and (2) those occurring "spontaneously" (i.e., in response to no known stimulus) during sleep or waking, which are androgen-dependent.

Bancroft (1980) first proposed that because visual stimuli can elicit normal erections in androgen-deficient men, the primary effect of testosterone is not on erections but on sexual "interest." Accordingly, the erectile failure reported by patients should be regarded as a secondary result of decreased libido. In an attempt to clarify this much-abused term, Davidson et al. (1982) defined "libido" as the category of all "affective–cognitive processes which result in the tendency to engage in sexual behavior." It was speculated that the specific component of libido stimulated by androgen might be "pleasurable awareness of sexual response." O'Carroll et al. (1985) claimed that their finding that hypogonadal men reported no significant increase in sexual satisfaction in response to graded doses of testosterone "failed to support" the suggestion regarding pleasure.

The clearly stimulatory effects of androgen on spontaneous erections, further complicate the issue. We have to presume that the neural pathways

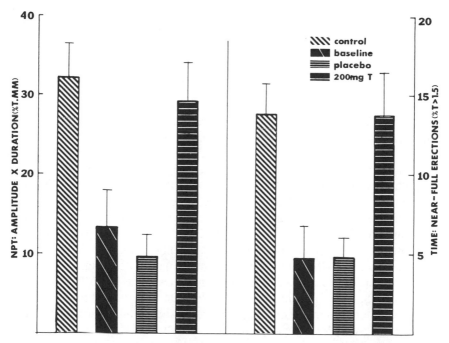

Figure 7.2. The effects of testosterone treatment on NPT levels in hypogonadal men. From "The Nature of Androgen Action on Male Sexuality: A Combined Laboratory–Self-Report Study on Hypogonadal Men" by M. Kwan, W. J. Greenleaf, J. Mann, L. Crapo, and J. M. Davidson, 1983, *Journal of Clinical Endocrinology and Metabolism, 57,* 557–562. Copyright 1983 by The Endocrine Society. Reprinted by permission.

subserving spontaneous daytime erections and NPT diverge from those involved in "sexual erections" (those elicited by film or, presumably, other effective sexual stimulation). Moreover, the former but not the latter are directly dependent on testosterone. These androgen-dependent neural pathways seem to be bypassed when the stimulus is explicitly sexual, as in laboratory presentation of erotic film stimuli and probably direct stimulation by a sexual partner.

The regulation of erection involves a complex neural system at multiple levels of the neuraxis: brain, spinal cord, and peripheral nerve. Very little is known about the cerebral level of control, though it is clear from animal research that there is overall inhibitory control by the brain of erectile reflexes (Beach, 1967). As discussed in Chapter 3, a commonly cited view of erectile mechanisms assigns "reflex" erections to the sacral parasympathetic outflow from the lower spinal cord and (with less authentication) "psychogenic" erections to the thoracic–lumbar sympathetic outflow (Bors & Comarr, 1960). Though the cerebral regulation of the two types of erection has not been clarified, common sense suggests that both are probably regulated by brain mechanisms. The psychogenic type is influenced by the brain for obvious reasons, and the reflex type because erectile responses to genital stimuli are facilitated in spinal-cord-lesioned men (and rats), if the sacral cord region is intact (Beach, 1967; Hart & Leedy, 1985).

This dichotomy of erectile mediation does not correspond to the dichotomy of androgen-dependent sexual and non-androgen-dependent spontaneous erections, discussed above. Closer to that is the following situation: Estrogen will not restore spontaneous erections in castrated male rats[2] (Gray, Smith, & Davidson, 1980; Hart, 1978), yet estrogen, administered in sufficient quantity, *will* restore mating behavior with erections adequate for intromission (O'Hanlon, Meisel, & Sachs, 1981).

The main point of this discussion is to emphasize the apparent diversity of erectile mechanisms. It is difficult to imagine how one might conduct research on humans to clarify the underlying physiological mechanisms. First must come neuroendocrine investigation of the control of erectile phenomena at various points in the neuraxis of animals, and then extensive studies of human pathology. A better alternative to the latter strategy may be the future use of advanced technology to visualize brain function noninvasively. Such a program is no mere academic exercise, for at stake is the very understanding of the physiology of sexual function and dysfunction in the male (and, by extension, in the female too).

Testosterone Level and Sexual Response

A number of studies have examined dose–response relationships between testosterone and sexual function (J.M. Davidson *et al.*, 1979; Salmimies *et*

---

2. These erections can be elicited by simply restraining the rats in a supine position.

al., 1982; de Kretser *et al.*, 1983; O'Carroll *et al.*, 1985). All agree that testosterone shows a dose-related response to behavioral measures. However, because of the lack of studies on a large enough scale and the peculiar release pattern of the widely used depot injections of testosterone enanthate, the precise form of the dose–response curve is unknown. It is generally agreed that the dramatic changes in response to androgen are found clearly below the normal range, and no study has yet demonstrated a continuation of the dose–response curve through the normal range.

How much androgen is actually needed to maintain or enhance sexual function in men? A time-honored clinical tradition (now supported by some data) has set 3 ng/ml of total testosterone as the lower range of normality, and healthy men can reach levels as high as 11–12 ng/ml. Is there any difference in behavior or physiology within this rather broad range of "normality"? Until recent years, the educated assumption would have been negative. Thus Brown, Monti, and Corriveau (1978) correlated questionnaire items concerning sexual activity and level of sexual interest with testosterone levels for 101 young adult men. There was no correlation between the variables in this healthy population.

Kraemer *et al.* (1976), strangely, found a negative relationship between self-reported frequency of orgasm and testosterone level in 20 normal men and could advance no very plausible explanation. Most recently, Knussman, Christiansen, and Couwenbergs (1986) reported positive inter- and intraindividual correlations (*r* generally below .26) between serum testosterone and orgasm frequencies. Similarly modest degrees of statistically significant correlations between testosterone or estradiol and various aspects of sexual behavior were obtained by Davidson, Chen, Crapo, Gray, Greenleaf, and Catania (1983) in a study of aging (see below). Such correlations may be due to effects of behavioral events on hormone levels (Knussman *et al.*, 1986)—an issue discussed at the end of this chapter.

Rubin, Henson, Falvo, and High (1979), in a psychophysiological experiment, attempted to correlate plasma testosterone with parameters of erectile response in six normal volunteers aged 25–44. Plasma testosterone was significantly correlated with two separate measures of tumescence (peak and mean erection) and with latency of erection to 90% of full tumescence. A much larger and more convincing psychophysiological study (Lange, Brown, Wincze, & Zwick, 1980) showed similar results. A total of 24 men aged 20–29 participated in viewing of erotic videotapes and gave two blood samples for hormone assay. Mean testosterone titers were significantly negatively correlated with latency to maximum tumescence ($r = -.51$) and positively with latency to detumescence ($r = .40$).

Clinical attempts to treat sexual dysfunction in eugonadal men with androgen have been almost invariably unsuccessful. However, a recent controlled double-blind study of testosterone treatment in men with psychogenic impotence did show a mild improvement in sexual interest (O'Carroll & Bancroft, 1984). The cumulative results of this body of research indicate that there may be a slight effect of variation in testosterone levels throughout the so-called "normal" range, but no striking or clinically relevant effects have as yet been identified. Why is this so? A simple explanation is plausible though speculative: The strong selection pressure to be expected for a function so vital to reproduction may simply have led to the evolution of a large margin of error for testosterone availability, protecting androgen levels from falling into the danger zone.

DIFFERENTIAL DIAGNOSIS OF HORMONE-RELATED CONDITIONS IN THE MALE

Decline in men's sexual function is most often associated with diabetes and aging. Indications are that diabetes-related sexual dysfunction is significantly less prevalent in women (Bancroft, 1982; Jensen, 1986), but the main reason for limiting this discussion to men is that few psychophysiological data are available on diabetic and aging women or those with any organic dysfunction. Both aging and diabetes involve significant (though very different) forms of endocrine deficiency, and in both, physiological sexual response is frequently impaired. The negative effects of aging on sexuality are no doubt universal, though they are subject to great variability and certainly do not necessarily lead to dire consequences (Kinsey *et al.*, 1948; Davidson, Gray, & Smith, 1983). As to diabetes, various estimates of the incidence of diabetic impotence usually bracket the range of 40–50% of affected men and the effects are frequently devastating (Fairburn, McCulloch, & Wu, 1982). The endocrine cause of diabetes (lack or ineffectiveness of insulin) is undoubtedly crucial in the etiology of sexual dysfunction, which is not to say that we understand the mechanisms involved. For aging men, on the other hand, endocrine factors may not be importantly involved in the ubiquitous age-related decline of sexual functioning.

One of the goals of this book is the attempt to distinguish between normal psychophysiological events associated with sexual behavior and "aberrations" of the psychophysiological response in sexual dysfunction. A prominent theme in human sex research, also emphasized in this volume (see Chapter 10), is the differential diagnosis of organic versus psychogenic impotence. If we are to understand the sexual dysfunctions of aging and diabetes and to compare them to those of hypogonadism (and hyperprolactinemia), it is necessary to delineate the physiological changes that occur under these three conditions. Again, our attempts to obtain clarity are limited by the paucity of research data, but the following is a discussion of relevant present knowledge.

Diabetes

Diabetes affects the whole body, including the brain. Insulin itself has no known direct, specific effects on the sexual system. However, its deficiency has widespread and devastating effects on body tissues, including the genitalia. Two etiologies of diabetic sexual dysfunction are generally implicated, both involving peripheral regulation of the genital–pelvic vaso-congestive response. These are (1) arterial occlusion resulting from athero-sclerotic deposits and (2) degeneration of penile autonomic nerves, presumably due to hypoinsulinemic derangement of metabolism in the nerves. The well-known peripheral neuropathy of diabetes may be the result of microvascular changes, though the sequence of events is still obscure (Niakan, Harati, & Comstock, 1986). But whatever the specific roles of neuropathy and vasculopathy may be, the net result is failure of the corpora cavernosa spaces to fill and the consequent failure to achieve penile rigidity. This view of diabetic sexual dysfunction, incomplete though it is, provides the rationale for diagnosing diabetic impotence as an organic sexual dysfunction.

Nevertheless, psychogenic causes for impotence are not absent in diabetics and are probably even more prevalent because of the exigencies of the illness (Fairburn *et al.*, 1982). As discussed in Chapter 10, NPT measurements are useful in the differential diagnosis of this organic dysfunction. Unfortunately, the designation of diabetes and aging as organic causes of dysfunction is so firmly established that physicians may pay little attention to other possibilities, and thus may fail to obtain such diagnostic evidence as NPT supplies.

A dramatic example of the risk involved in the sometimes unthinking pursuit of the organic option is the use of the penile prosthesis, a remarkable surgical replacement for the natural psychophysiological event of erection. These pliable or inflatable plastic implants are widely used, often without clear evidence that no hope remains for less stringent treatments than the irreversible implants. While this "therapy" provides a rigid structure around which the penis is tightly draped, so to speak, the genital sexual response is not reinstated—and never will be, because of the inevitable destruction of the corpora. An interesting psychophysiological question is whether and how the lack of the normal genital sexual response affects the quality of sexual experience. Existing research on implants, though becoming voluminous, does not directly address this question; the main assessment of outcome is often limited to asking whether the treatment is "satisfactory" to the patient and/or his spouse. This superficiality is unfortunate not only from the scientific point of view, but also because such poor assessment of outcome tends to obscure failures, which leaves patients without the opportunity of benefiting from future possible therapies.

As expected in organic erectile dysfunction, impotent diabetic men show deficiencies in the NPT assessment of a variety of measures, including duration, amplitude, and number of erectile episodes. A complication is illustrated by the findings of Schiavi, Fisher, Quadland, and Glover (1985) that nonimpotent diabetics had a deficiency in their NPT records (specifically, lowered circumference increase), though the effects were not as extensive as in diabetic impotence. If such a patient has psychogenic problems, he might receive a firm diagnosis of organic diabetic impotence, based on the combined evidence of his diabetes and somewhat reduced NPT. On the other hand, nonimpotent diabetics may have "an incipient and subclinical impairment in erectile capacity, although not of sufficient magnitude to interfere with penetration" (Schiavi et al., 1985). More knowledge is needed about the physiological or possibly psychological correlates of *specific* changes in the parameters of NPT. At present, the different measures tend to be regarded as equivalents, any one of which merely indicates undifferentiated organic erectile dysfunction. In this context, it is interesting to note that Schiavi et al. (1985) could eliminate the significant decrease in total tumescence *duration* in impotent diabetics versus nondysfunctional groups, if they expressed this measure as a percentage of REM sleep duration. The authors suggested that REM sleep may be disrupted by diabetes-related metabolic change. So the plot thickens, as NPT metamorphoses from a simple indicator of organic impotence (as often presented) to a highly complex phenomenon potentially sensitive to nonsexual disabilities (see Chapter 10).

A number of investigators have held out the hope that the use of waking monitoring of response to erotic stimuli, combined with NPT, would increase the discriminability of diagnosis. Zuckerman et al. (1985) compared diabetic men, sexually dysfunctional nondiabetic men, and normal controls, and found that the two dysfunctional groups showed significant decreases in erectile response to film and audiotapes. Though they did not differ in this "waking assessment," the diabetic dysfunctionals had significantly lower NPT scores than the nondiabetics. Kockott et al. (1980) had earlier reported no difference in the waking film test between impotent diabetics and subjects with secondary psychogenic erectile impotence; both groups were inhibited.

In a study with more complete diagnostic analysis of the medical and psychological condition of the subjects, Bancroft et al. (1985) found that men with psychogenic impotence had normal erectile responses to film (but not fantasy), while the responses of the impotent diabetics were markedly reduced. (The methodological details of this study are described in Chapter 3.) However, the impotent diabetic group contained a subgroup of men with a history suggesting psychogenicity and another in which organicity was indicated. The diabetics diagnosed as psychogenic, based on cardiovascular autonomic tests and a history of psychogenicity, had larger erectile responses than the organic diabetic dysfunctionals, but the difference was not significant. An additional measurement (that of penile pulse amplitude), on the other hand, did show significant differences: There were considerably higher amplitudes for the psychogenic diabetics. In addition, a smaller but still significant difference in systolic blood pressure was also found, the measurements being higher in nonpsychogenic diabetics. This novel study contained so many independent and dependent variables (including several not previously studied) that considerably more work is needed to clarify the issues it raises. Altogether, the four studies discussed in this section provide a corpus of data on which to base future research.

Sexual Aging

Aging effects on male sexuality have received surprisingly little attention from sexual psychophysiologists, except to document the decrease in peak tumescence and the much-decreased rate of erectile response to erotic films (Solnick & Birren, 1977). The sparse psychophysiological results do little to explain the etiology of age-related impotence. Certainly the aging individual is susceptible to psychogenic dysfunction, be it from depression, illness, or psychosocial problems; however, most cases of age-related impotence cannot be ascribed to psychogenic factors. A decrease in NPT is well documented (Karacan, Hursch, & Williams, 1972; Kahn & Fisher, 1969b), though the relationship of age-related changes to those related to geriatric sexual dysfunction has not been clarified.

CNS changes in neurotransmitter function have been repeatedly implicated in the general disabilities of aging. Damage to the central libido function could conceivably result in secondary impotence, but the decline of libido is less extensive than that of potency (Kinsey *et al.*, 1948; Davidson, Chen, *et al.*, 1983). However, the brain and spinal cord are involved in the regulation of erectile and ejaculatory responses as well as libido functions. In rats, it has been demonstrated that the failure of sexual behavior in aging is associated with decreases in content of the endogenous opiate beta-endorphin and of another sex-related peptide, GnRH, in specific nuclei of the hypothalamic–limbic system (Dorsa, Smith, & Davidson, 1984). The changes were significantly greater in old rats that had ceased copulating by 27 months of age than in those that continued to mate.

While many studies have investigated endocrine changes in aging of men and many others have studied the changes in sexuality, very little investigative effort has been devoted to relating the two functions. Though androgen has such a crucial role in males, the hypothesis that the decline in testosterone could be responsible for sexual decline was not investigated directly until the 1980s. In a study of 220 men aged from 41 to 93 years, blood samples were obtained and a simple sexual questionnaire was administered in order to examine correlations between the two measures (Davidson, Chen, *et al.*, 1983). As was previously known, both total and free testosterone showed significant progressive decreases over the decades, with the greatest changes occurring after the 60s. The trajectory of declining testosterone was expectedly mirrored by increased LH and FSH, responding to the well-known negative feedback regulation. However, no significant correlations were found between total testosterone levels and any of the sexual measures. Free testosterone[3] and LH were significantly correlated with a number of sexual function measures, but the correlation coefficients were only on the order of .14 to .29. This indicated that only a small amount of the variance in sexual behavior during aging could be accounted for by the change in reproductive hormone levels. Similar conclusions were reached in research on rats (Gray, Smith, Dorsa, & Davidson, 1981) and in rhesus monkeys (Chambers, Hess, & Phoenix, 1981). Tsitouras, Martin, and Harman (1984) studied a highly selected group of medically and educationally advantaged men in their 60s and 70s who showed no overall decline in testosterone with age. Nevertheless, the group reporting the lowest frequency of sexual activity had a small but significant decrement in testosterone compared to the others. As mentioned before, this does not necessarily indicate a *causal* hormone–behavior relationship.

Thus, the etiology of the decline in sexual function in aging men is almost as mysterious as many other behavioral and physiological geriatric changes. Aging differs from hypogonadism in the relatively small role of hormones, but the nature of the aging dysfunction is also quite different. Much more prominent in aging is the loss of erectile responses to such sexual stimuli as erotic films; moreover, the decline in libido is much less than in hypogonadism. Though all three dysfunctions often show up in the clinic with the major presenting complaint of erectile impotence, the causes can be quite different in origin.

Although they belong strictly to psychophysics rather than to psychophysiology, recent data on sensory changes in aging and diabetes are worth mentioning, if only because they point to a little-studied set of changes of probable biological origin in these two conditions. Rowland, Greenleaf, Mas, and Davidson (1987) examined thresholds of sensation in response to vibrotactile and electric stimulation in (1) normal young men, (2) impotent diabetic men, and (3) aging men, using the method of forced choice. (This method, which requires the subject to decide whether or not the stimuli is felt, avoids bias in the rigorous assessment of thresholds.) Mean ages were (1) 30, (2) 45, and (3) 67 years. Sexual dysfunction is not prevalent until the 60s (Kinsey *et al.*, 1948; Davidson, Chen, *et al.*, 1983).

As shown in Figure 7.3, there was a marked *increase* in the threshold (decrease in sensitivity) in both aging and diabetic men, compared to the group of normal young men, when either mild electric or vibrotactile stimuli were administered to the penis. The sensory deficit for vibrotactile stimuli was greater than for electric. Smaller aging effects were found when the

3. "Free testosterone" is the fraction (less than 5% of the total testosterone) that is protein-bound and presumably unavailable to cells.

index finger was examined. There was, however, no significant change of threshold in the diabetic finger. Thus, although the aging effect was consistent across forms of stimulation and different tissues (albeit with considerable quantitative differences), the diabetic subjects showed a more specific vibrotactile effect, limited to the penis. Penile vibratory thresholds were significantly negatively correlated with sexual activity and positively correlated with erectile capacity.

The differences between the vibrotactile and electric stimulation results can be explained in part by the fact that electric stimuli affect sensory neurons directly, whereas vibrotactile stimuli activate the sensory receptors. The psychophysical measurement of sensory function may be a useful future diagnostic and investigative tool for the understanding of different forms of sexual dysfunction.

One other well-known hormone-related dysfunction occurs in men with high levels of the hormone prolactin. When certain pituitary tumors, drugs, or other factors cause such hyperprolactinemia, sexual dysfunction is a well-known sequela. NPT studies provide some evidence of the organic nature of this condition (Cunningham, Karacan, Ware, Lantz, & Thornby, 1982; Murray, Cameron, & Ketchum, 1984). In many cases, testosterone levels are severely reduced as a result of the suppressive effect of high prolactin on the hypothalamus–pituitary–testis axis. However, cases have been reported where the testosterone deficiency has been reversed without change in the patient's sexual status. Moreover, many of these patients have normal testosterone levels (e.g., Carter *et al.*, 1978). Thus this dysfunction is not thought to be hypoandrogenic in origin.

While we do not yet know the pathophysiology of hyperprolactinemic

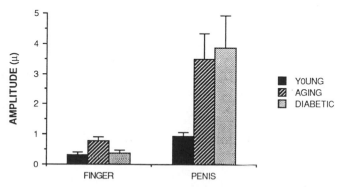

Figure 7.3. Thresholds of sensation in response to vibrotactile and electric stimulation in normal young men, aging men, and impotent diabetic men. From *Penile and Finger Sensory Thresholds in Aging and Diabetes* by D. L. Rowland, W. J. Greenleaf, M. Mas, and J. M. Davidson, 1987, manuscript submitted for publication. Reprinted by permission of the authors.

sexual dysfunction, the following facts provide some understanding. First, the levels of prolactin in the blood are generally extremely high, sometimes astronomically elevated over the normal range. Thus it is quite likely that prolactin is not importantly involved in the normal regulation of sexuality. Second, it is known that high prolactin can increase the turnover (i.e., production rate) of dopamine in the brain (Hokfelt & Fuxe, 1972). Dopamine is a neurotransmitter often implicated in changes in sexual function; bromocryptine, the usual treatment for reducing prolactin levels, is a powerful dopamine agonist. This being so, it is not clear whether hyperprolactinemic dysfunction is due to a direct effect of prolactin or to a change in dopaminergic transmission in the nervous system. Animal studies, particularly in rats, have demonstrated a negative effect on male sexual behavior of the elevation of prolactin levels by tumor or pituitary transplants (Svare *et al.*, 1979). The effects on the pattern of sexual behavior tend to be marginal, but there is a quite consistent effect of suppression of spontaneous erections (Doherty, Baum, & Todd, 1987; Smith & Davidson, 1987).

In an interesting "$n = 1$" study by Bancroft, O'Carroll, McNeilly, and Shaw (1984), hyperprolactinemia was discovered after the patient was treated for a presumed psychogenic erectile problem, coexistent with lack of sexual interest. The former problem was responsive to counseling, and the latter was corrected by bromocryptine in a twice-repeated double-blind experiment. The picture that emerges is that hyperprolactinemic sexual dysfunction resembles that of hypogonadism, although the physiological etiology of hyperprolactinemia is obscure.

ROLE OF HORMONES IN FEMALE SEXUAL PSYCHOPHYSIOLOGY

Given the consistency of the sexual roles of *male* animals and humans, and the essential role of hormones in the control of *female* animal sex behavior (Beach, 1948), the search for endocrine factors in the sexual psychophysiology of women is imperative. We have previously hinted that this extension is problematic. In this section, we attempt to clarify the extent to which hormones may be or are involved in women's sexuality, and point to the issues that need to be settled by future research.

Menstrual Cycle

Studies examining hormonal factors in female sexual behavior have frequently focused on the menstrual cycle as a natural source of major hormonal fluctuations, enabling noninvasive investigation. Menstrual cycle hormones of major importance are estrogens, progestins, androgens, LH, and FSH. First, a brief discussion of these hormones, their major functions, and their normal levels during the menstrual cycle is presented; this is followed by a discussion of psychophysiological assessment of the menstrual cycle fluctuations.

Three major estrogens—estradiol (E_2), estrone (E_1), and estriol (E_3),[4] in decreasing order of biological activity—are produced almost entirely from the ovarian follicles. Estrogens are responsible for maturation of female sexual organs, proliferation and growth of the endometrium, and breast development, as well as osteoblastic (bone development) activity, regulation of aspects of protein and fat metabolism, and other effects unrelated to sexual function.

Progesterone, the major progestin, is secreted primarily from the ovarian corpus luteum, prepares the endometrium for implantation of an ovum, and reduces uterine contractility.

Androgens, although probably not significant participants in the reproductive cycle, also appear to have a role in female sexuality. Testosterone, androstenedione, and dehydroepiandrosterone [DHEA], in decreasing order of biological potency, are the major androgens. DHEA is weakly androgenic and is a precursor for estrogen secreted by the ovary and adrenal gland. Approximately two-thirds of the circulating level of androgens in the female are due to adrenal secretion (Gray & Gorzalka, 1980). The ovarian contribution causes peak levels of androgens during the late follicular and early luteal phases (Vermeulen & Verdonck, 1976), but the peaks are low and inconsistent.

Cyclic variations of estrogens and progestins are completely dependent upon the release of two anterior pituitary hormones, FSH and LH. The cycle is usually divided into menstrual, follicular, ovulatory, luteal, and premenstrual phases, reflecting ovarian and pituitary changes. During the menstrual phase of the prototypic 28- or 29-day cycle (days 1–5), blood levels of the gonadotropins and sex steroids are low. E_2 rapidly increases during the late follicular phase, peaks around day 12, then rapidly declines. FSH (and, to a greater extent, LH) exhibits a large peak around day 13, approximately 18 hours prior to ovulation. Days 13–15 represent the ovulatory phase, with FSH, LH, and E_2 rapidly declining and reaching preovulatory levels by day 16. The progesterone level (and, to a lesser extent, E_2) increases during the next (luteal) phase, days 16–25. Progesterone levels peak and, if pregnancy does not occur, gradually decline. The few days prior to the onset of menses constitute the premenstrual phase (days 26–28).

---

4. The subscripts in the abbreviations used for estrogens denote the number of hydroxyl groups in the molecule of each estrogen type.

The majority of studies assessing the relationship between menstrual-cycle-stage-related hormone levels and sexuality have utilized retrospective self-reports of sexual arousal or of behavioral activity, primarily intercourse and orgasm frequency. Relying on such self-reported sexual arousal, some investigators have identified a peak in sexual desire and activity near mid-cycle, or during the ovulatory phase, when estrogen is high (Udry & Morris, 1968; Adams, Gold, & Burt, 1978; Englander-Golden, Chang, Whitmore, & Dienstbier, 1980); however, others have found no relationship between estrogen level and sexual response (Apblanalp, Rose, Donnelly & Livingston-Vaughan, 1979; Persky, Lief, Strauss, Miller, & O'Brien, 1978). An additional problem in many of these studies has been the convention of relying on standardization of cycle lengths to 28 days and backward counting to determine cycle phase. These procedures have been shown to bias results. By reanalyzing the data of Adams *et al.* (1978) to reflect ovulation times more accurately, Tessman (1979) showed that sexual response and activity in their study were not significantly changed throughout the entire cycle. James (1971) also reanalyzed several studies reporting peaks of sexual arousal, intercourse, and orgasm rates around midcycle, including that of Udry and Morris (1968), and found peaks in these behaviors immediately after menstruation. In sum, this literature has failed to show consistent relationships between cycle stage and sexual behavior.

When only self-report is used, response bias is a major methodological problem, particularly in women. In addition, the definitions of "sexual response" and "arousal" vary from study to study. The development of the vaginal photoplethysmograph has enabled a critical assessment of sexual arousal, although, as previously discussed (see Chapter 4), this is only a first step in measurement of genital–sexual response. More sensitive and readily available methods of measuring steroid levels have made feasible a proper assessment of actual hormonal status and menstrual cycle phase. Thus, in order to determine the relationship of sex steroids to sexual arousal as accurately as possible, it is necessary to use (1) a physiological measure of sexual arousal (rather than simple self-report), and (2) an accurate determination of cycle phase (through hormonal assessment or at least careful readings of basal body temperature).

Schreiner-Engel, Schiavi, Smith, and White (1981) reported the first study using psychophysiological measures of sexual arousal during the menstrual cycle. Significant peaks in physiological sexual arousal were found during the early follicular and late luteal phases, but self-assessment of arousal varied widely, with no relation to the cycle phase. A measure of the adjusted maximum response of VPA (see Chapter 4) was significantly lower during the ovulatory phase, a time when testosterone levels were found to be higher than in the other two phases studied. While correlations between testosterone levels and all measures of sexual arousal were non-significant, these correlations were positive during the ovulatory phase and primarily negative during the follicular and luteal phases. Due to the wide range of testosterone levels found in these subjects, the relationship of endogenous testosterone levels and sexual arousal was further examined by breaking the subject groups into average high-testosterone (>0.54 ng; $n = 9$), medium-testosterone ($0.36–0.54$ ng; $n = 14$), and low-testosterone (<0.36 ng; $n = 7$) groups. The high-testosterone group showed significantly greater VPA than the other two groups. The low-testosterone group showed less physiological responsiveness and consistently lower reports of subjective sexual arousal to erotic stimuli than the other two groups, but these differences were not statistically significant.

Correlations between the other hormones (E_2 and progesterone) and physiological sexual arousal were not significant. Thus, while this study provided evidence of lower physiological arousal during the ovulatory phase, it did not identify any one hormone as responsible for the effect.

A second examination of menstrual cycle and sexual arousal (Hoon et al., 1982) included psychophysiological measures of VBV and VPA, labial temperature, and self-reports of sexual arousal. Five phases of the menstrual cycle were assessed (menstrual, days 1–5; follicular, days 6–12; ovulatory, days 13–15; luteal, days 16–21; and premenstrual, days 22–28). Phase was determined by basal body temperature. An analysis of covariance revealed no significant difference in labial temperature, VBV, or VPA as a function of menstrual cycle phase; nor were self-report measures found to differ across the menstrual cycle. While not statistically significant, due to a large variance, maximum VPA and VBV responses were seen during the luteal phase. Thus, in contrast to the findings of Schreiner-Engel et al. (1981), fluctuations of hormones during the menstrual cycle appeared to have little effect on vasocongestive sexual response.

Finally, Morrell, Dixen, Carter, and Davidson (1984) examined VPA and subjective sexual arousal during the follicular, midcycle, and luteal phases. Hormone levels validated phase assessment. No significant differences in VPA or subjective sexual arousal between cycle phases were found. In this sample, testosterone levels did not show midcycle peaks.

Thus, two of three studies failed to identify menstrual-cycle-related fluctuations in subjective or physiological arousal. However, the comparisons among these three studies are complicated by the differing methods of data analysis used. Schreiner-Engel et al. (1981) used mean adjusted VPA of only those pulse changes within a 10-second period of the maximum response. The significance of maximum arousal has yet to be established, especially since the range of VPA change possible is not even known. Morrell et al. (1984) used three erotic stimulus presentations, but only the middle 10 pulses for each 3-minute stimulus were used. The data were further reduced by obtaining a mean for each segment, a ratio of the mean divided by the preceding neutral segment, and finally one percentage change score for the erotic presentations per session. More detailed analysis might have revealed more subtle differences. Hoon *et al.* (1982) used robust data analysis, including a repeated-measures analysis of covariance.

Thus, the preponderance of evidence (albeit limited) points to a lack of correspondence between endogenous hormone levels associated with the menstrual cycle and greater or lesser psychophysiologically measured sexual arousal. Yet two sets of negative findings out of three are not definitive, especially given the different types of analyses used. Additional studies are obviously needed before the final verdict is in. Several nonpsychophysiological studies have found no links between E_2 level and sexual behaviors (e.g., Persky, Charney, Lief, O'Brien, Miller, & Strauss, 1978), while midcycle levels of testosterone have been significantly positively correlated with masturbation frequency (Bancroft, Sanders, Davidson, & Warner, 1983) and intercourse frequency of a couple (Persky, Lief, *et al.*, 1978).

Menopause

As women age and approach menopause, cycles vary in length—often becoming longer, due to an extended follicular phase (Abe, Yamaya, Wada, & Suzuki, 1983)—and menstrual flow may diminish or increase. FSH levels rise, and LH levels less so at first, while estrogen levels remain within the normal range or slightly lower than normal (Adamopoulos, Loraine, & Dove, 1971; Abe *et al.*, 1983). Unfortunately for prospective studies, there is great individual variation in age at menopause, the normal range being between 45 and 55 years. In several studies, E_2 blood levels have been found to correlate positively with sexual activity in the perimenopause (e.g., McCoy & Davidson, 1985). Yet the impact of these major hormone changes in perimenopausal women, and the ways in which they affect sexuality, have not yet received adequate psychophysiological assessment.

A widely used criterion to define the postmenopausal state is the absence of vaginal bleeding for 1 year. After this time a 60–90% decrease in E_2 level is found, and FSH and LH levels rise 8- to 14-fold (Greenblatt, Ottinger, & Boehler, 1976; Nordin, Crilly, Marshall & Barkworth, 1981). Vermeulen (1980) has shown that up to 4 years after natural menopause the ovaries still secrete E_2 and testosterone, but that after 4 years essentially no E_2 is secreted. A result of the dramatic decrease of E_2 is a marked decrease in vaginal lubrication, thinning of the vaginal mucosa, and possible shortening in length of the vagina. Masters and Johnson (1966), in their clinical studies, noted a difference in latency to arousal between pre- and postmenopausal women when genital color change (which indicates vasocongestion) and vaginal lubrication were observed. The major postmenopausal estrogen becomes E_1, principally derived from peripheral conversion of androstenedione (Grodin, Siiteri, & McDonald, 1973). Since the conversion occurs in adipose tissues, obesity has been found to be significantly correlated with circulating E_1 level (Vermeulen, 1980). Thus, in investigations of endocrine relationships to sexual factors, age, weight, years since menopause, natural or surgical menopause, and actual hormone values should be assessed.

As discussed in Chapter 4, the earliest VPA measurement in postmenopausal women was reported by Palti and Bercovici (1967). A marked decreased in VPA was found, compared to premenopausal women; however, actual data were not presented. Semmens and Wagner (1982), and later Semmens, Tsai, Semmens, and Loadholt (1985), assessed vaginal blood flow in postmenopausal women in a pilot study using a heated thermistor that measured oxygen changes transcutaneously. In the latter study, decreased vasocongestion in the basal (unstimulated) state of the vaginal wall was found to increase gradually over a 24-month period of oral estrogen therapy. These studies provided physiological evidence of an estrogenic contribution to levels of vaginal vasocongestion.

Two recent studies have assessed sexual arousal psychophysiologically and subjectively in postmenopausal women. In the previously mentioned study of Morrell *et al.* (1984), which showed no psychophysiological changes related to the menstrual cycle phase, vaginal changes of young cycling women (mean age = 31), older cycling women (mean age = 51), and postmenopausal women (mean age = 57) were assessed and compared (see Figure 7.4). Estrogen levels of the postmenopause group were 20%

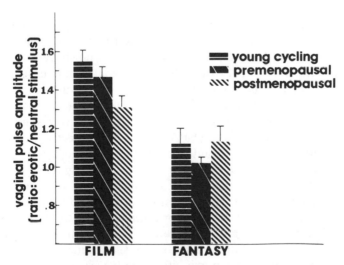

Figure 7.4. VPA levels of young cycling women, older cycling women, and postmenopausal women. From "The Influence of Age and Cycling Status on Sexual Arousability in Women" by M. J. Morrell, J. M. Dixen, C. S. Carter, and J. M. Davidson, 1984, *American Journal of Obstetrics and Gynecology, 148,* 66–71. Copyright 1984 by the C. V. Mosby Company. Reprinted by permission.

of those of the premenopausal women. Using an erotic film and fantasy as stimuli, the investigators found no significant differences in VPA between the young and older cycling women. However, the postmenopausal women showed significantly lower mean VPA (16% less) for the erotic film. Subjective response did not vary significantly between groups.

The absence of demonstrable change throughout 20 years of aging, together with a significant psychophysiological decline over the mean 6.8-year time span between the ages of the pre- and postmenopausal women, suggests that the effect may have been due to the loss of E_2 at menopause and not to aging. Nevertheless, there is the remote possibility that the small difference in age could have had an effect on peripheral vascular response or on central arousal, independent of hormonal changes due to menopause. The point is also made in this report that the clinical significance of the 16% lower VPA in the postmenopausal women is unclear; the postmenopausal subjects did not rate themselves as dysfunctional and did not differ from the premenopausal women on the Sexual Arousal Inventory (E. F. Hoon, Hoon, & Wincze, 1976) or a Likert-type scale of menopausal symptoms.

Considerably more research is obviously needed. Unfortunately, the study of Morrell et al. (1984) has been the only one of its kind to assess older and younger premenopausal women. Ideally, definitive conclusions on the influence of hormones at menopause would be better obtained with a different approach. Given the complex set of interacting psychosocial and medical variables bearing on the outcome of menopause, only controlled HRT studies can solve the question of which hormone does what in female sexuality. At the time of writing, only one psychophysiological study including women taking HRT has been published, and it involved women receiving HRT treatment prior to the actual study.

Myers and Morokoff (1986) studied physiological and subjective sexual arousal in premenopausal women (mean age = 37), untreated postmenopausal women (mean age = 58), and postmenopausal women taking replacement hormones (mean age = 59). The three groups did not differ in physiological sexual arousal (VPA), although subjective reports of vaginal lubrication were significantly lower in postmenopausal women not taking estrogen than in the other two groups (see Figure 7.5). Premenopausal subjects did have significantly higher levels of E_2 than the nonreplacement group. Latency of sexual arousal was also assessed. The percentage of maximum VPA achieved by 2 minutes into the 10-minute erotic film revealed no statistically significant differences between groups, although there was a trend in the direction of significance, with nonreplacement postmenopausal women exhibiting the lowest percentage achieved. The study did not find statistically significant differences in sexual response between pre- and postmenopausal women, in contrast to the findings of Morrell et al. (1984).

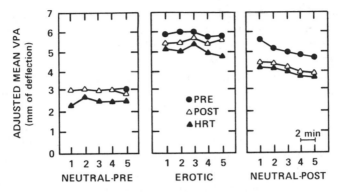

Figure 7.5. Adjusted mean VPA levels during a neutral pretest, an erotic film, and a neutral posttest for premenopausal women, untreated postmenopausal women, and postmenopausal women receiving HRT. From "Physiological and Subjective Sexual Arousal in Pre- and Postmenopausal Women and Postmenopausal Women Taking Replacement Therapy" by L. S. Myers and P. J. Morokoff, 1986, *Psychophysiology, 23,* 283–292. Copyright 1986 by the Society for Psychophysiological Research. Reprinted by permission.

Of interest were the relationships of hormone levels to some measures of subjective sexual arousal. Testosterone, for all subjects, was significantly positively related to two of three measures of physical arousal (vaginal lubrication and breast sensation), with genital sensations being marginally significant. E_2 was also significantly positively related to self-report of vaginal lubrication across groups. Since testosterone is converted to estrogen in a variety of tissues, it is difficult to distinguish between the influence of the two hormones here. Additional problems in this study were the measurement at only one time point and the non-double-blind and non-homogenous HRT in this clinical population.

The sparsity of psychophysiological HRT research contrasts starkly with the plethora of HRT studies without psychophysiology but including measures of sexual function. Unfortunately, very few of these have been directed primarily at sexual behavior. The two best-designed and most focused studies in this literature present self-report data that provide an interesting backdrop for future psychophysiological research, since their results are rather different. Both had double-blind crossover designs, and, notably, both utilized subjects who had undergone so-called "surgical menopause" (i.e., combined oophorectomy and hysterectomy). First, Dennerstein, Burrows, Wood, and Hyman (1980) studied the effects of two synthetic agents (ethinyl E_2 and the progestin Norgestrel). The latter hormonal drug showed no significant effect, either alone or in addition to the estrogen. Estrogen did not significantly affect intercourse frequency or subjective sexual response, but monthly interviews revealed a significant

181

stimulatory effect on sexual desire, enjoyment, and orgasmic frequency, while vaginal dryness was decreased. The differences associated with hormonal treatments were not great, and daily visual analogue testing on various sexual parameters showed no significant effect of the drugs.

Sherwin, Gelfand, and Brender (1985) compared groups receiving injections of E_2, testosterone, E_2 plus testosterone, and a placebo group. No significant effect of estrogen was observed, but the two androgen-containing preparations increased intensity of sexual desire and fantasies and of subjective arousal during sexual activity. Of considerable interest is the finding that specific libido-type effects—desire, fantasy, and so on—were selectively stimulated by testosterone. This result is in line with the previously discussed effects of testosterone on the male. In a follow-up study of the same women after 2 years of treatment (Sherwin, 1986), the results remained as before, with the testosterone groups still showing significant differences from those treated with E_2 alone. However, at this time coitus and orgasm were also more frequent in subjects treated with testosterone.

In the studies on women, by far the greatest effects were those resulting from the Sherwin *et al.* (1985) testosterone treatment. Careful observation of their data suggest that a somewhat supraphysiological dose of testosterone was used, however. Thus it remains to be seen whether testosterone replacement with a somewhat lower dose, mimicking more natural levels, would have similar results.

The question of dose regimen is particularly important in comparing the outcomes of different studies. At present, the relevant studies all used different hormonal preparations and/or dose regimens. In addition, four other important issues deserve close attention if future psychophysiological studies are to be of value. The first is obvious but bears repeating: the need for adequate prospective, behavioral, and experiential self-report methods to complement the physiological findings. The other three points are subject selection; so-called "domino effects" (Green, 1984)—that is, the possibility that nonsexual symptoms, particularly hot flashes, could interfere with sexual behavior; and the possibly confounding factor of oophorectomy.

Selecting subjects for this kind of research is a major problem. Obviously, the use of clinical populations may tell us little or nothing about the prevalence within the population of specific effects. If women not taking HRT are compared to those who are, there is a distinct possibility that the two groups will differ in hormonal requirements (i.e., those who have not taken HRT in the past will have lower requirements and accordingly may show less response). This consideration makes it more surprising that Myers and Morokoff (1986) could find no significant differences in VPA; it strengthens the psychophysiological findings in this study, but weakens the positive effects found on subjective response. A solution to the self-selection dilemma in this kind of study would be to include both women who have used HRT and women who have not, and compare the results of treatment in each.

As to the domino effect, it can be dealt with by comparing HRT results in menopausal women showing different configurations of symptoms. Using this approach, Studd, Chakravarti, and Oram (1977) noted that 20 women not complaining of hot flashes showed some improvement in sexual function following HRT, suggesting that the improvement was not due merely to the relief from hot flashes. Another method of "assessing" the putative domino effect was used by Dennerstein *et al.* (1980)—namely, statistical procedures such as covariance analysis, which separate vasomotor from sexual functions. Finally, one can differentiate effects on different menopausal symptoms. Thus, Sherwin and Gelfand (1984) demonstrated that testosterone did not ameliorate hot flashes in women, though sexual functioning was improved (Sherwin *et al.*, 1985). These three items of evidence certainly weaken the argument for the hot flash–domino effect, or at the very least place the burden of proof on the proponents of this idea.

An interesting issue is the possibility that "surgical" menopause has a different impact from that of "natural" menopause, such that the HRT experiment would have different effects in each case. Removal of the ovaries entails a much greater and more rapid removal of gonadal steroids, since naturally postmenopausal women retain a significant level of ovarian estrogen for years, and of androgen more permanently. Moreover, most studies have not included very old women. It may not be merely the absolute difference in the hormone levels between oophorectomized or ovary-intact women that is relevant; the rate of decline may be an important factor. Thus, withdrawal effects of ovarian steroids could be important quite apart from the level of the nadir reached (Brincat *et al.*, 1984). Follicular estrogen levels decline somewhat gradually in the perimenopause. Though luteal estrogen secretion disappears when cycling stops, ovulation may occur sporadically over a prolonged period of time.

If this view is correct, it can explain the discrepancy between the psychophysiologically negative conclusion of the Myers and Morokoff (1986) study on naturally menopausal women and the other three studies of surgical menopause, which showed clearly positive responses to HRT. Hence, there is a need to compare effects of HRT on oophorectomized and naturally menopausal women of about the same age and under similar experimental conditions.

THE HORMONAL SEXUAL RESPONSE

So far, we have considered the hormonal factor as a variable influencing the neural regulation of sexual response, in a "tonic" role. Psychophysiologists customarily measure neuronal responses to behavior—either directly, or, more usually, indirectly by peripheral nerve-mediated muscular or vascular changes. But does the endocrine system play a direct, "clonic" role as part of the sexual response itself? Are hormones released in response to sexual stimuli, and, moreover, do they contribute to subsequent events during sexual activity? If blood hormone levels change during sexual response, such endocrine events certainly qualify as psychophysiological phenomena, and it behooves us to consider their role in the implementation of sexual goals.

An evolutionary perspective on this question is easy to find. Females of many animal species are "induced ovulators" (e.g., cats, rabbits, and various avian species) and only ovulate (thereby becoming immediately capable of conception) after mating-induced hormone release. Pituitary gonadotropins are released first, followed by steroids from the ovaries; the former cause ovulation and the latter prepares the reproductive tract for fertilization and implantation. However, in spontaneous ovulators (humans and most mammalian species), if ovulation is blocked for whatever reason, the normally latent reflex of copulation-induced ovulation may be substituted. This may be thought of as a fail-safe procedure.

What about humans? Most of the evidence that sex hormones may induce pituitary gonadotropin and gonadal hormone release originated in Germany during the 1940s. A variety of more or less anecdotal reports from that period proposed that copulation could induce ovulation, especially in traumatic conditions such as alleged rape of German women by the conquering Russian troops (see references in Jochle, 1973).

Heterodox kinds of evidence continued to appear into the early 1970s. They included an anonymous report in a prestigious journal on (presumably testosterone-mediated) stimulation of beard growth by a scientist living on an island, just before and during his days of periodic sexual activity on visits to the mainland (Anonymous, 1970). Many months of records of a couple's sexual activity were correlated with daily blood testosterone measurements, which showed increased levels on the days of coitus (Fox, Ismail, Love, Kirkham, & Loraine, 1972).

Shortly afterward, more comprehensive studies failed to find effects of coitus or masturbation on FSH and LH in both sexes, E_2 and progesterone in women, and testosterone in men (Stearns, Winter, & Faiman, 1973; Lee, Jaffe, & Midgley, 1974; Shirai, Matsuda, Mitsukawa, Nakamura, & Yonezawa, 1974; Davidson & Trupin, 1975).

More positive results on LH or testosterone were obtained using erotic visual stimulation in men (Pirke, Kockott, & Dittmar, 1974; LaFerla, Anderson, & Schalch, 1978). Lincoln (1974) reported negative results. Purvis, Landgren, Cekan, and Diczfalusy (1976) found a rise in androgens after masturbation. Recently, salivary testosterone was found to rise significantly when 20 men were exposed to each of two erotic films for 15 minutes

(Hellhammer, Hubert, & Schurmeyer, 1985). An erotic film may be a more potent stimulus to hormone release than coitus, at least under the experimental conditions of these studies, just as it seems to be a more potent stimulus to erection in hypogonadal men complaining of erectile difficulties with their partners (see above).

The results described above are consistent with a rather fragile phenomenon of sexual-stimulation-induced pituitary–gonadal hormone release. Unfortunately, no investigator seems to have persevered long enough to determine the parameters of success or failure for demonstrating these effects. Even more mysterious is the possible functional utility of such sexually stimulated hormone release. The possibility of LH-induced ovulation has not been satisfactorily demonstrated in women. As to men, we know of no behavioral effect of testosterone on sexual function that has a latency of less than several days (in rats, 12–24 hours; Gray et al., 1980). Of course, there may be some more rapid fertility-promoting effects of LH or FSH, or a behavioral effect of GnRH release (Moss, Dudley, Foreman, & McCann, 1975; Dorsa, Smith, & Davidson, 1981).

For many years, the neuropeptide of hypothalamic–posterior pituitary origin, oxytocin, has been suspected to be a sexually released hormone. This hormone ejects milk in lactating women by contraction of the smooth-muscle-like myoepithelial cells in the breast, in response to the suckling stimulus. It also contracts the uterine smooth muscle during the final stages of labor. The relationship to sexual activity was based on anecdotal evidence of milk release from lactating women during coitus (Harris & Pickles, 1953), and a very few early observations by Fox and Knaggs (1969) of coitus-induced oxytocin release, using a crude bioassay method of measurement.

Only recently did radioimmunoassays sensitive enough to pick up the minute concentrations of oxytocin in blood become available. Using such an assay to examine the response of oxytocin to sexual behavior, samples were obtained before, during, and after self-stimulation to orgasm in males and females (Carmichael et al., 1987). Orgasm was objectively assessed by psychophysiological measurement of anal muscle contractions and anal pulse amplitude, using a probe bearing both EMG electrodes and a photoplethysmograph. Oxytocin was found to rise significantly during sexual stimulation, reaching a peak during orgasm for both males and females. Although baseline levels of oxytocin were significantly higher during the luteal phase, no significant differences in oxytocin response to self-stimulation or latency to orgasm were found between the follicular and luteal phases.

Oxytocin release may facilitate reproductive smooth muscle contraction in one or both sexes, such as to assist transportation of the gametes and thereby increase the likelihood of reproductive success. It has also been hypothesized that oxytocin release may stimulate uterine contraction during orgasm, which could contribute to the subjective and/or physiological events of orgasm—specifically, those involved in sexual satiation (Davidson, 1980).

SUMMARY AND CONCLUSION

Though still in the early stages of development, the study of endocrine factors in sexual psychophysiology promises to become a fruitful area of investigation. Endocrinology contributes to psychophysiology by providing new measures—changes in hormone levels—to add to the sexual psychophysiological menu. On the other hand, psychophysiology contributes to behavioral endocrinology by providing data on the effects of hormones in modifying physiological sexual response, thereby helping to elucidate the mechanism of action of hormones on behavior.

Among major findings in the male are the observations that spontaneous daytime erections and NPT responses are dependent on adequate testosterone levels. Yet erectile responses to strong sexual stimuli appear to be independent of male hormones. In women, it is still controversial whether the major changes in hormone levels occurring during the normal menstrual cycle are reflected in alteration of physiological sexual response. Likewise, the role of endocrine factors in sexual response at the menopause has not yet been established. However, an initial report yielded no significant difference in vaginal photoplethysmographic response to an erotic videotape, though subjective response was reduced.

As to the role of hormonal effects as dependent variables in sexual activity, evidence exists that coitus, self-stimulation, or erotic films can release gonadotropin—specifically, LH and testosterone (in men) and oxytocin (in women and men). The functions of such endocrine responses to sexual arousal remain to be elucidated.

ACKNOWLEDGMENTS

Original work was supported by National Institutes of Health Grant Nos. NIA 1437 and MH 21178. We are grateful to Merry Weeks for help in preparation of the manuscript.

Current Applications of Sexual Psychophysiology

Since its inception, the field of sex research has been characterized by a major emphasis on clinical or applied concerns. As Masters and Johnson (1970) rapidly extended their basic research findings to the classification and treatment of sexual dysfunction, other investigators have similarly made extensive use of laboratory methods and findings in the study of a wide variety of applied issues. In some instances, the need for an effective clinical tool has spurred the development of specialized measurement approaches, such as occurred in the area of sexual deviation. In other instances, existing laboratory research on a particular topic has assumed greater social significance, as evidenced by the current controversy over the effects of pornography. In fact, given the widespread use of explicit erotica in society at large, as well as in psychophysiological studies of sexual arousal, we have chosen to begin this section on current applications of sexual psychophysiology with a critical review of research on laboratory responses to erotica and pornography.

Among the earliest areas of application for laboratory sex research was the assessment and treatment of individuals with anomolous sexual preferences, or "paraphilias" as they are now referred to. In Chapter 9 we consider several key conceptual and methodological issues in psychophysiological studies of sexual deviation, such as the use of concurrent measures of physiological and subjective arousal, and the possible use of "faking" strategies by certain subjects. Clearly, laboratory studies in this area are complicated by legal, ethical, and professional concerns, which are also addressed in this chapter.

With the growth of sex therapy in recent years, increasing attention has been focused on problems of sexual dysfunction in both sexes. Chapters 10 and 11 are devoted to a detailed discussion of laboratory methods used in the evaluation and treatment of such sexual problems as anorgasmia in women or erectile dysfunction in men. This latter problem is especially susceptible to laboratory assessment procedures, such as the nocturnal penile tumescence (NPT) test. In Chapter 10 we review the theoretical and empirical evidence for this and other psychophysiological assessment approaches.

The section concludes with an in-depth presentation of research on alcohol and other drug effects on sexual response. Given that the search for a "perfect aphrodisiac" has been a recurrent theme throughout human history, it is likely that pharmacological remedies for sexual disorders will always play an important role. In addition to reviewing the effects of a wide variety of prescription and nonprescription drugs on sexual function, Chapter 12 addresses several key methodological issues, such as the effects of set and setting, in evaluating specific drug effects.

CHAPTER EIGHT

Laboratory Responses to Erotica and Pornography

Descriptions of sex are as old as sex itself. There can be little doubt that talking about sex has been around as long as talking, that writing about sex has been around as long as writing, and that pictures of sex have been around as long as pictures.—Attorney General's Commission on Pornography (1986, p. 233)

Erotic stimuli are a pervasive part of modern life. As noted by the Attorney General's Commission on Pornography (1986), explicitly sexual materials have been used by most societies throughout history for purposes of entertainment or sexual stimulation. Among the ancient Greeks and Romans, for example, erotic painting, sculpture, and poetry were commonplace. Eastern cultures were no less interested in explicit erotica, as evidenced by such works as the *Kama Sutra* and *The Thousand and One Nights*. Even at the height of the sexually repressive Victorian era in England, the sale and distribution of pornography (e.g., *The Pearl*, Frank Harris's *My Life and Loves*) continued to flourish. It is also clear, however, that no other culture or time period in history can match the present for the range, diversity, and sheer volume of erotic materials available for popular consumption. At the same time, societal concern about the potential consequences of exposure to pornography is at an all-time high.

In this context, it is not surprising to note that laboratory studies involving the presentation of sexually explicit, erotic stimuli—usually in the form of visual, audiotaped, or written materials—have come to play an increasingly important role in sexual psychophysiology. Several reasons for this are apparent. First, by presenting such stimuli to specific subject groups (e.g., sex offenders, sexually dysfunctional males and females), or under particular conditions (e.g., alcohol or drug ingestion, enhanced expectancy instructions), it is possible to investigate experimentally a number of socially sensitive and clinically relevant topics. In fact, this approach has emerged as the standard laboratory paradigm for the study of applied issues in the field. Thus, psychophysiological studies of sexual deviance and paraphilias, male and female dysfunctions, drug and alcohol effects, and, of course, pornography have all been conducted within this framework.

Additional reasons for the popularity of this paradigm are its usefulness in testing basic assumptions concerning sexual arousal in the laboratory. For example, the effects of different stimulus modalities (e.g., visual vs. auditory) and types of erotic content (e.g., explicit vs. romantic) on sexual responding have been examined with this approach. Also, assumptions concerning male versus female patterns of arousal, the influence of sexual experience and personality factors, and the role of expectations and social setting on responses to laboratory stimulation have all been investigated in this way. Theoretical models of sexual arousal, such as Byrne's (1983) model of the sexual behavior sequence, have guided several studies in the area, just as findings from laboratory research on erotica have in turn served to generate new concepts of sexual arousal. Finally, given the intense societal concern with the effects of pornography in recent years, it is hardly surprising that results from laboratory studies of this type have played an increasingly prominent role in the current debate over pornography and sexual violence (Attorney General's Commission on Pornography, 1986).

Despite the growing interest in experimental research in these areas, it is also important to consider the weaknesses and limitations of the paradigm. For example, the question of generalizability of results beyond the laboratory setting (i.e., external validity) is a major concern that has not been sufficiently addressed in the literature. Also, the issue of discordance or discrepancy between alternative response measures, which we have already considered in regard to measurement of male and female arousal patterns, is especially problematic here. Moreover, results from different studies have not always been consistent, as investigators have frequently failed to replicate findings from other laboratories. Finally, unbiased interpretation of disparate research findings is increasingly difficult, given the highly charged nature of this research. In a prophetic statement regarding the limitations of laboratory research in affecting public policy on pornography, Amoroso and Brown (1973) noted, "We are not optimistic regarding the influence of research on changing opinions and entrenched attitudes in this area" (p. 187). Judging by the intense political and social controversy that has surrounded the topic of pornography in recent years, this prediction appears to have been more than justified.

LABORATORY STUDIES OF EROTICA

Early studies of sexual arousal in response to erotic stimulation tended to focus either on subjective reports of arousal (e.g., Byrne, 1961; Jakobovits,

1965; Schmidt & Sigusch, 1970) or on nonspecific measures of somatic and autonomic activation (e.g., Davis & Buchwald, 1957; Wenger *et al.*, 1968; Colson, 1974). These studies generally were oriented toward investigating the short-term effects of erotica on physiological activation or self-reported arousal in normal subjects. In particular, comparisons were made of the effects of different stimulus materials and different modalities of presentation, and of male–female differences in response to laboratory presentations of erotica. In contrast, the first studies to make use of specific genital measures of arousal were aimed at differentiating response patterns in deviant and normal males to erotic stimulation (e.g., Freund, 1965, 1967a, 1967b; McConaghy, 1967). In view of the exclusive focus of these latter studies on deviant arousal, and comparisons between subject groups of varying sexual orientation, they are reviewed in detail in Chapter 9.

The first study to investigate patterns of physiological arousal to laboratory erotica (Davis & Buchwald, 1957) assessed peripheral physiological responses in college males and females to a range of visual stimuli, including photographs of classical nudes. Although one of the nude stimuli (Goya's *Unclothed Maja*) was associated with increased galvanic skin response (GSR) and finger pulse volume responses in male subjects, no clear pattern of responses was found overall for males or females. As described in Chapter 2, the study by Wenger *et al.* (1968) investigated cardiovascular, respiratory, and electrodermal responses in normal male subjects as they read erotic or neutral passages. In this study, the pattern of autonomic arousal to the erotic stimuli was significantly different from that to the nonerotic (travelogue) materials. It should be noted that the sexual stimuli in both of these studies were minimally erotic by contemporary standards, and that little or no attention was paid to the subjective dimensions of responding.

In contrast, Colson (1974) evaluated both subjective arousal and heart rate responses in college males to written passages containing descriptions of adult heterosexual or pedophiliac sexual activities. Scores on a variety of semantic differential scales distinguished between subjects' responses to the two types of stimuli, indicating greater arousal and interest in the adult heterosexual stimuli, whereas heart rate changes did not. An interesting additional component of this study was the inclusion of a false-feedback condition, in which subjects were led to believe that they had achieved either high or low levels of GSR during presentation of the stimulus. This false-feedback procedure had been used previously by Bramel (1963) and Valins (1966) to investigate attributional processes in self-ratings of sexual arousal, but without concomitant measurement of actual physiological responding. In the Colson study, the attributional manipulation significantly influenced subjective evaluations of the stimulus materials (i.e., the pedophiliac stimuli were rated as more "obscene" with feedback of high arousal), whereas actual physiological (heart rate) responses were not affected.

In a further study of the role of attributional processes in male subjects' arousal to erotica, Cantor *et al.* (1975) manipulated to the degree of non-specific physiological arousal prior to presentation of an erotic film. Initially, subjects were instructed to ride on an exercise bicycle for several minutes, following which physiological (heart rate, blood pressure) and self-report measures of arousal were obtained at successive 2-minute intervals. Having determined that physiological excitation tended to persist for several minutes beyond the subjective perception of arousal, the experimenters further demonstrated that erotic films were experienced as maximally arousing when presented approximately 5 minutes after the exercise task, at which time subjects were least aware of residual physiological effects. In contrast, the prior physiological excitation had the least effect on erotic arousal when the film was presented immediately after the exercise task, when physiological arousal closely matched subjective awareness. In interpreting this complex series of findings, Cantor *et al.* (1975) state, "Residual arousal which is properly recognized as such not only does not intensify ongoing responses, but may actually impair them" (p. 74).

Although these studies are provocative in suggesting that attributional processes may play a major role in determining perceived arousal to erotica, and in providing further support for the "cognitive arousal" model of sexual response presented in Chapter 2, the findings need to be interpreted cautiously. In particular, in the absence of specific measures of genital response, it is unclear to what extent the subjects' perceptions of increased arousal were accompanied by changes in physiological arousal. The experimental conditions were also highly contrived, and the effects that were obtained may not generalize outside the laboratory. Finally, each of these studies was conducted on young male subjects only, and it may be questioned whether similar results would be obtained with females, more experienced subjects, or subjects exposed to more intense levels of stimulation.

MALE–FEMALE PATTERNS OF AROUSAL TO EROTICA

Self-report studies of responses to erotica have frequently focused on the issue of male–female differences in arousal. In fact, according to Kinsey *et al.* (1953), this is one of the few areas in which men and women have fundamentally dissimilar reactions to sexual stimulation. On the basis of their interview findings concerning responses to a wide variety of "psychosexual stimuli," such as observing the opposite sex, reactions to nude photographs and pictures, viewing erotic fine art, and so on, Kinsey and his colleagues concluded:

The sexual responses and behavior of the average male are, on the whole, more often determined by the male's previous experience, by his association with objects that were connected with his previous sexual experience, and by his sympathetic reactions to the sexual responses of other individuals. The average female is less often affected by such psychologic factors. (1953, p. 650)

While emphasizing the greater "conditionability" of males to erotic stimuli in general, Kinsey *et al.* nevertheless acknowledged the wide range of individual reactions in both sexes, especially in women: "[I]t should be constantly borne in mind that there are many individuals, and particularly many females, who widely depart from these averages" (1953, p. 650). Kinsey and his colleagues believed that such sex differences in conditionability to erotica were probably innate, and they cited Ford and Beach's (1951) conclusions that among infrahuman species, learning and conditioning play a much greater role in shaping male than female sexual behavior.

In the intervening years, this assumption was first challenged by Jakobovits (1965), in a study of subjective responses of males and females to written narratives described as either "erotic realism" or "hard-core obscenity." The "erotic realism" passages contained the same sexual content as the "hard-core obscenity," but included additional nonsexual details, such as the nature of the relationship between the characters. The "hard-core" material, on the other hand, minimized nonsexual details and presented the sexual interactions in an exaggerated and unrealistic manner. Using a series of semantic differential scales, the author found that both sexes responded with sexual interest and arousal to both types of erotic stimuli. Contrary to expectation, however, the female subjects reported significantly greater arousal to the "hard-core" passages, whereas males were slightly more aroused by the "erotic realism." It is interesting to note that even though the female subjects rated the "hard-core obscene" materials as "dirty and unrefined," they still considered them to be sexually stimulating.

In direct contradiction to the Kinsey *et al.* (1953) interview findings, a series of studies conducted by Schmidt and his colleagues in West Germany (Schmidt & Sigusch, 1970; Sigusch, Schmidt, Reinfeld, & Wiedemann-Sutor, 1970; Schmidt, Sigusch, & Schafer, 1973) found strong evidence of male–female similarities in self-reported arousal to erotic stimuli. Using young, sexually experienced German college students as subjects, these studies evaluated subjective responses to a wide range of visual stimuli, including erotic films and slide materials (Schmidt & Sigusch, 1970), in addition to written stories containing both romantic and nonromantic erotic elements (Schmidt *et al.*, 1973). That males and females would use equivalent scale responses in their evaluations of pornography was, unfortunately, an untested assumption in each of these studies.

The major finding was that men and women reported approximately equivalent degrees of physiological arousal to all types of stimulus mate-

193

rials. Furthermore, the authors noted that while a small increase in sexual activity occurred in both sexes during the 24 hours following stimulus presentation, this effect was more marked in females. Despite the absence of direct physiological data, the authors nevertheless concluded that these results indicate a dramatic shift in gender roles since Kinsey's times. Alternatively, it could be argued that the equal responsivity of males and females may have been due in large part to the very young and sexually experienced subjects in the study. Gebhard (1973) has also noted that the Kinsey *et al.* data were based on retrospective reports and made use of more global ratings of responsivity, whereas the subjective ratings in the Schmidt studies were very detailed and specific, and were obtained immediately after stimulus presentation.

Other self-report studies have produced mixed results. For example, Steele and Walker (1974) exposed students at a private, church-affiliated university to explicit erotic slides depicting a wide range of sexual activities. Using Likert-type scales to assess sexual interest and arousal, the authors were able to demonstrate significantly greater arousal in the male subjects to most of the stimulus slides. Positive correlations also were found between scores on a measure of sex drive and interest, and subjects' ratings of arousal to the erotic stimuli. Similarly, Byrne, Fisher, Lamberth, and Mitchell (1974) found that females tended to experience predominantly negative affective responses to erotica, such as disapproval and disgust, whereas males were more likely to experience a combination of positive and negative affective reactions.

Griffitt (1975), in a study of college undergraduates' responses to erotic photographs, found that sexual arousal to the stimuli was mediated in both males and females by the extent of previous sexual experiences, including both masturbation and heterosexual activities. Other studies (e.g., Herrell, 1975; Hatfield, Sprecher, & Traupman, 1978) found no overall differences in the responses of male and female subjects to erotic literature and films. An additional finding of note in the Hatfield *et al.* (1978) study, however, was that male subjects appeared to be considerably more aroused than females to films of lesbian sexual activity. Given the major differences in subject groups, types of stimulus materials, and measures of sexual arousal employed from one study to another, it is not surprising that such inconsistent findings have been reported.

In the first psychophysiological study to compare both genital and subjective measures of sexual arousal in males and females, Heiman (1977) found further evidence of male–female similarities in response to erotic stimulation. This study was noteworthy in a number of respects. First, an impressive battery of dependent measures was employed, ranging from physiological assessments of genital blood flow, heart rate, and finger pulse amplitude to a series of scaled self-report measures of arousal. Although the stimulus materials were limited to erotic and control audiotapes, an attempt was made to vary the degree of romantic content in the erotic tapes, as well as the gender-role dimensions of the script (e.g., male-initiated vs. female-initiated activity). The effects of sexual fantasy on arousal to erotica were also evaluated, as 2-minute periods of subject-generated fantasy were included prior to and following each tape sequence. Subjects for the study were 119 male and female college undergraduates, each of whom was presented with one of four combinations of erotic, romantic or neutral stimulus tapes.

As shown in Figure 8.1, results indicated a high degree of overlap in the patterns of response for male and female subjects to erotic stimulation. Specifically, both males and females were significantly more aroused by the erotic than by the romantic tapes. Nontraditional sex-role content was also more arousing for both sexes, although this effect was stronger for the female subjects. Similar correlations between genital and subjective measures of arousal (ranging from .40 to .68) were obtained for both sexes, with the most reliable measure of arousal being genital pulse amplitude. In contrast, no significant differences were found on the measures of heart rate and finger pulse amplitude. As for the effects of fantasy on sexual arousal, it appeared that both sexes were able to produce significant arousal to fantasy alone, but that exposure to erotica did not appear to facilitate this response. Finally, the amount of prior sexual experience was not significantly correlated with genital arousal in either sex.

In addition to demonstrating similarities in male and female patterns of arousal to erotica, the results of this study also raise several interesting hypotheses concerning the effects of specific types of content materials. Contrary to popular misconception, it appeared that women in the study were no more responsive to romantic script elements than were men, and that erotic content alone was responsible for arousal in both sexes. Furthermore, the fact that female-initiated scripts were found to be more arousing for both sexes appears to contradict conventional sex-role expectations in this society. This finding is interpreted by Heiman (1977) as suggesting that a certain degree of unconventionality may enhance the erotic value of the stimuli: "Perhaps erotica must be socially unacceptable or norm breaking, in order to be maximally arousing" (p. 272).

Similar results were obtained in a subsequent study of female responses to written erotica (Osborn & Pollack, 1977). In an attempt to replicate the earlier findings of Jakobovits (1965), these authors presented the same two series of stories ("hard-core obscenity" and "erotic realism") to a group of female graduate students, while measuring genital blood flow (VPA) and subjective arousal. Results indicated that while both sets of stories were associated with significant arousal, the "hard-core" material produced significantly greater arousal on both the VPA and self-report measures. As in the Heiman (1977) study, it appeared that the explicitness of the sexual material far outweighed the romantic content in creating sexual

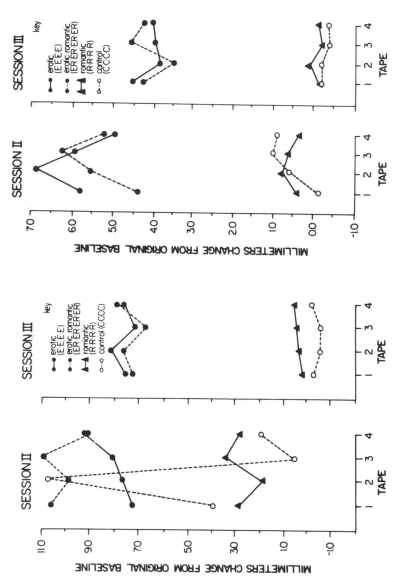

Figure 8.1. Penile and vaginal pulse amplitude responses to erotic and nonerotic tapes over two sessions of testing. Both males and females showed considerable arousal to erotic, but not romantic, audiotaped depictions. From "A Psychophysiological Exploration of Sexual Arousal Patterns in Females and Males" by J. R. Heiman, 1977, *Psychophysiology, 14,* p. 269. Copyright 1977 by the Society for Psychophysiological Research. Reprinted by permission.

arousal in these young female subjects. Taken together, the results of the two studies also suggest that these effects are independent of the stimulus modality employed (i.e., erotic audiotapes vs. written stories).

Female arousal patterns to laboratory erotica have also been investigated in recent studies by Stock and Geer (1982) and Korff and Geer (1983). In the first study, it was shown that young female subjects with greater experience in sexual fantasy during masturbation were more responsive to both erotic tape recordings and instructions to fantasize in the laboratory. Although VPA responses were more pronounced in the audiotaped stimulus condition, a high degree of intersubject consistency in the overall pattern of responses to the audiotaped and fantasy stimuli was observed.

Similarly, Korff and Geer (1983) demonstrated increased arousal to visual erotica by varying the experimental set of young female subjects viewing a series of erotic slides. Specifically, experimental subjects were instructed to attend to either genital or nongenital bodily responses during erotic presentations, while the control subjects were given no specific instructions. Results indicated markedly increased correlations between self-report and physiological arousal under conditions of enhanced bodily attention, as described in Chapter 4. This finding suggests that female subjects may have the capacity both to respond to and to fully experience sexual arousal to these stimuli, at least under conditions of enhanced bodily awareness.

In contrast to the findings reported by Heiman (1977), Osborn and Pollack (1977), and others, at least one study to date (Steinman, Wincze, Sakheim, Barlow, & Mavissakalian, 1981) has reported significant gender differences in physiological–subjective response patterns to both heterosexual and homosexual erotic videotapes. As can be seen in Figure 8.2, male subjects in this study tended to downplay their subjective ratings of arousal to heterosexual videotapes, as compared to genital arousal responses, whereas females reported higher levels of subjective arousal relative to vasocongestion. Again, however, we need to point out the assumption of equivalent scaling between male and female subjects, as noted above in regard to the studies by Schmidt and colleagues.

Overall, it appears that a significant change has taken place in female arousal patterns to erotica in the three decades since the Kinsey *et al.* studies. On the basis of the psychophysiological evidence reviewed, it seems that female subjects in many of these studies have attained capacities for arousal to erotica that are similar to those of their male counterparts. However, this conclusion should be viewed cautiously, in light of possible volunteer bias for participants in laboratory sex research and the availability of increasingly explicit erotica in certain segments of society (Attorney General's Commission on Pornography, 1986). Other investigations of male–female differences in arousal to erotica have focused increasingly on re-

197

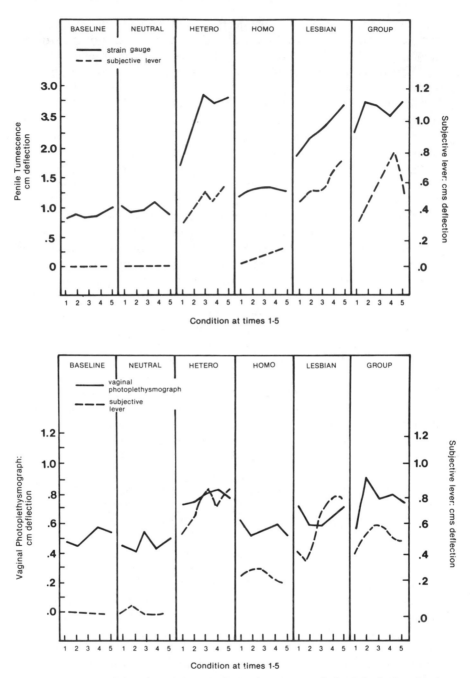

Figure 8.2. Male (above) and female (below) patterns of physiological and subjective arousal to erotic videotapes of varying content. Adapted from Steinman *et al.* (1981).

actions to violent pornography (e.g., Malamuth, Heim, & Feshbach, 1980; Malamuth & Check, 1983) and comparisons of arousal patterns to violent and nonviolent erotic materials (Sapolsky, 1984; Malamuth, Check, & Briere, 1986). Given the particular emphasis of these studies on sexual violence and aggression, rather than patterns of arousal to erotica per se, they are reviewed in a later section.

PERSONALITY FACTORS AND INDIVIDUAL DIFFERENCES IN RESPONSE TO EROTICA

Cultural background and personality factors are frequently viewed as a filter through which erotic stimuli are experienced (Sapolsky, 1984). Due to wide variations in early socialization, in particular, individual differences are apparent in the extent of previous exposure to erotica and in the degree of approval–disapproval previously experienced in this regard. In an early formulation of the "erotophobia–erotophilia" construct, for example, Byrne (1977) proposed that an individual's prior learning history with regard to reinforcements or punishments generally associated with sexual stimuli will determine, via a classical conditioning process, which stimuli will be associated with positive or negative affective consequences. These conditioned affective responses (i.e., erotophobia or erotophilia) are then viewed as the basis for subsequent evaluative reactions to particular stimulus materials.

Some support for this hypothesis comes from an early study by Byrne *et al.* (1974), in which married couples were exposed to either explicit slides or written erotica, and were required to complete a self-rating scale of feelings and of subjective arousal during the erotic presentations, as well as several personality inventories. Results for both husbands and wives indicated that negative affective responses to the erotic stimuli were correlated with judgments of how "pornographic" the materials appeared. Negative evaluative responses to erotica were also shown to be associated with the degree of authoritarism, religious preference, and church attendance in both sexes.

Regarding the role of previous sexual experience in determining responses to erotica, it has been reported that negative affective reactions are more often elicited in sexually inexperienced subjects (Brady & Levitt, 1965; Griffitt, 1975; Baron, 1979). In this regard, Kinsey *et al.* (1953) first proposed that the total frequency of heterosexual experience would reflect male sexual interest levels, whereas frequency of masturbation would be more reflective of this dimension in women. The direct opposite was found in the study by Griffitt (1975), however, as self-report ratings of sexual arousal to erotica were found to be more strongly associated with masturbation experience in men, but with overall heterosexual experience in

199

women. Finally, we have noted above that in the Heiman (1977) study, genital measures of arousal failed to discriminate between the responses of experienced and inexperienced subjects of either sex. Thus, it appears that evaluative or self-report arousal measures may be more strongly associated with subjects' ratings of prior sexual experience, whereas genital changes appear to be a more sensitive indicator of arousal to specific stimulus characteristics.

Studies also have been conducted on the relationship between responses to erotica and personality traits such as "sex guilt" (Mosher, 1971), or the "erotophobia–erotophilia" dimension of personality proposed by Byrne (1977, 1983). One recent study (Becker & Byrne, 1985) demonstrated that erotophilic subjects spent more time than erotophobic subjects in viewing laboratory erotica. Of interest in this study was the additional finding that among Type A coronary-prone individuals, time urgency factors overrode the normal positive effects of erotophilic interest in the stimuli. In another study including psychophysiological measures, Morokoff (1985a) noted that women who were high in sex guilt reported lower levels of arousal to erotic videotapes, despite the presence of significantly greater physiological arousal. Finally, it has also been shown (Eysenck & Nias, 1978) that more positive responses to erotica are experienced by extraverts than by introverts.

In summary, while studies have pointed to a number of individual differences and personality factors that need to be considered, the findings to date should be cautiously interpreted, in view of the reliance on self-report, lack of replication, and limited sampling in most of these studies. Certainly, the extent of previous sexual experience or exposure to pornography is an important variable that warrants further investigation. In the next section, we consider studies that have specifically controlled for repeated exposure in an experimental setting.

EFFECTS OF REPEATED EXPOSURE TO EROTICA

From a theoretical perspective, it is unclear whether one would expect repeated exposure to erotica to produce increased or decreased arousal. Some authors (e.g., Byrne, 1977; Zillmann & Bryant, 1984) have argued that repeated exposure is likely to cause disinhibition of negative associations, in addition to enhancing familiarity and comfort with the stimuli, and thereby is likely to lead to increased interest in and arousal to erotica. In particular, Byrne (1977) has proposed a three-stage model to account for increasing responsivity with repeated exposure to erotic stimuli. According to this model, the subject first experiences a change in attitudinal and evaluative responses, akin to systematic desensitization, in which the subjective reaction typically progresses from negative to neutral to mildly positive. The next stage of the process involves increasing attitudinal tolerance to the activities portrayed (e.g., fellatio, group sex, anal intercourse) and the beginning of positive imaginative rehearsal. Finally, the subject may initiate changes in overt behavior, as was shown in the Schmidt *et al.* studies; this serves to reinforce further the arousal value of the stimuli. Commenting on the overall impact of this process, Byrne suggests: "In this way, the erotic images prevalent in the culture become transferred to private erotic images which are later translated into overt behavior" (1977, p. 346).

To date, there is limited experimental evidence in support of this conceptualization. For example, in the Jakobovits (1965) study described above, subjects were required to read and evaluate 20 erotic stories, half of which were described as "erotic realism" and half as "hard-core obscenity." Results indicated cumulative positive effects on arousal across both sexes and types of erotic materials, despite adequate counterbalancing for order of stimulus presentations. Similarly, in a study of sexually inexperienced and anxious college females, Wishnoff (1978) found that exposure to explicit erotic videotapes reduced sexual anxiety and increased subjects' interest in engaging in a greater variety of sexual behaviors. Similar findings were also reported by McMullen and Rosen (1979) in a study of videotaped therapy in the treatment of anorgasmic women. Finally, it has also been noted by Zillmann and Bryant (1984) and others that the enormous growth of the pornography industry in the past decade would seem to suggest that increased interest in erotica has occurred along with the increased availability of these materials.

In contrast to the limited evidence of positive effects of repeated exposure, there is a growing body of literature suggesting that habituation, boredom, or fatigue are likely effects in many instances. As noted in Chapter 2, early psychophysiological studies of habituation effects in sexual arousal (e.g., Reifler, Howard, Lipton, Liptzin, & Widmann, 1971) demonstrated that repeated exposure to visual and written pornography for 90 minutes a day over a 3-week period produced significant decrements in physiological and self-reported arousal in young male subjects. Measures of arousal included penile circumference and changes in urinary acid phosphatase in this study. Although subjects continued to show moderate levels of arousal on both measures at the end of the 3-week period, the authors suggest that complete satiation would have occurred had the study been continued for a longer period of time. On the other hand, it should also be noted that this study involved unusually intensive and protracted exposure to the erotic materials, as noted by Reifler *et al.*: "By the end of the experiment our subjects' experience with pornography had been considerably greater than that which most people would have in their entire lifetimes" (1971, p. 581).

In a more "naturalistic" study of repeated exposure effects, Mann,

Sidman, and Starr (1971) presented erotic movies once weekly for a month to 68 happily married and sexually active couples. Based upon daily self-report measures throughout the study, it appeared that the level of sexual activity was significantly increased on nights immediately following movie viewing. The authors found no evidence of disinhibition to novel sexual activities, however, as only those behaviors already present in the subjects' repertoires were increased. Overall, these results are consistent with the findings of Schmidt *et al.* (1973) that transient increase occurred only in currently practiced sexual activities following exposure to erotica. More-over, in a subsequent reanalysis of their results, Mann, Berkowitz, Sidman, Starr, and West (1974) demonstrated that the activating effects of the erotic movies had declined significantly over the course of the study; this decline provides evidence of habituation or satiation effects with repeated expo-sure, even in the face of initial increases in sexual activity.

Arguing that the reduction in arousal observed in the Reifler *et al.* (1971) study could be attributed to the effects of unreinforced exposure to the experimental stimuli (extinction) rather than habituation, Schaefer and Colgan (1977) attempted to control for the effects of sexual gratification following exposure. Specifically, young male subjects were presented with six trials of reading pornographic material from a book by Henry Miller, following which half of the subjects were permitted to masturbate to ejac-ulation. In addition to the repeated ("standard") passages, each trial in-cluded presentation of an additional page of novel material. As indicated in Figure 8.3, penile circumference measures clearly differentiated the responses of experimental and control subjects; this finding indicates that sexual gratification following exposure, or the opportunity to masturbate to orgasm in the experimental situation, can dramatically affect the results. Whereas a typical extinction curve can be seen following repeated exposure without ejaculation (controls/standard material), an increase in responding was observed for the experimental subjects, particularly during trials in which the novel stimulus was presented. Overall, the results of this study indicate that the effects of repeated exposure to erotica may be mediated by other factors, such as the opportunity for sexual gratification following exposure.

Fatigue effects may also account for the decline in arousal following repeated laboratory presentations of erotica. In order to control for this possibility, O'Donohue and Geer (1985) compared the responses of young male subjects to repeated presentations of constant and varied sequences of erotic slides. Inclusion of the varied-stimulus condition in this study permitted an independent assessment of the effects of physiological fatigue, which would be expected to be about equal in responses to the varied and the constant stimuli. As discussed in Chapter 2, repeated presentation of the constant stimuli was associated with a significantly greater decline in both physiological and subjective responses; this suggests that fatigue ef-

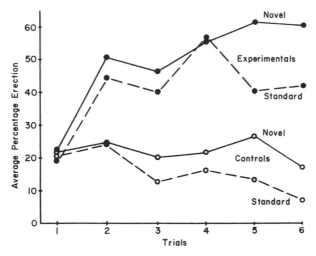

Figure 8.3. Mean erection responses (as a percentage of maximum erection) to repeated ("standard") versus novel presentation of erotica. Experimental subjects were permitted to masturbate to orgasm following presentation, whereas controls were not. From "The Effect of Pornography on Penile Tumescence as a Function of Reinforcement and Novelty" by H. H. Schaefer and A. H. Colgan, 1977, *Behavior Therapy, 8,* p. 943. Copyright 1977 by the Association for Advancement of Behavior Therapy. Reprinted by permission of the publisher and author.

fects alone are not a sufficient explanation of the results. Although this study also attempted to assess the effects of stimulus intensity on the rate of habituation, the results on this dimension were less conclusive, perhaps due to the fact that none of the stimuli were sufficiently arousing.

Habituation has not always been demonstrated in studies of this type. In particular, Julien and Over (1984) exposed 24 young males to erotic materials presented in one of five different formats: movies, slides, audiotapes, written stories, or self-generated fantasies. Each of these stimulus modalities was presented to subjects over five sessions of repeated testing in a Latin-square design. As we have noted, the failure to observe habituation in this study was most likely a function of variations in the stimulus modality from session to session. Similarly, Rosen (1973) found no evidence of habituation with repeated presentation of audiotaped erotica, perhaps because of variations in the stimulus content of each of the tapes. The results of these studies, when taken together with the findings of Schaefer and Colgan (1977), raise concerns that habituation effects may be markedly modulated in the natural environment by control of stimulus factors (e.g., novelty) or reinforcement contingencies (e.g., orgasm) by the subject.

Studies of repeated exposure to erotica have raised a number of key conceptual and methodological issues. In particular, as noted by O'Donohue and Geer (1985), it is essential for laboratory psychophysiological studies that include the use of repeated stimulus presentations to control for potential habituation effects. On the other hand, factors such as stimulus intensity, variability, and content can markedly affect the course of habituation, as shown in a number of studies to date. Schaefer and Colgan (1977) have also drawn attention to the importance of postexposure contingencies in determining the outcome of repeated stimulation. Under some circumstances it appears that repeated exposure can lead to enhanced tolerance of the activities portrayed (Byrne, 1977), and we consider this issue further in our discussion of exposure to violent pornography in the next section. Finally, as noted by Sapolsky (1984), the response of the pornography industry to habituation effects has been to provide consumers with erotic materials that are increasingly intense and unusual, often involving themes of aggression and violence.

EXPOSURE TO VIOLENT PORNOGRAPHY

It is clear that the conclusion of "no negative effects" advanced by the 1970 Commission is no longer tenable. — Attorney General's Commission on Pornography (1986, p. 1031)

Noting that commercially available pornography has tended increasingly to bring together themes of sex and violence in recent years, the Attorney General's Commission on Pornography (1986) placed particular emphasis on studies of sexually violent material. Included in this category are sadomasochistic portrayals, scenes of forced sexual activity, and "slasher" films, as well as material that is "more 'mainstream' in its availability, that portrays sexual activity or sexually suggestive nudity coupled with extreme violence, such as disfigurement or murder" (1986, p. 324). It was also noted that the earlier President's Commission on Obscenity and Pornography (1970) had paid scant attention to these kinds of stimuli, possibly biasing the report's conclusions against harmful effects. By contrast, the Attorney General's Commission on Pornography (1986) particularly chose to emphasize studies demonstrating changes in patterns of aggression or sexual arousal in response to violent erotica. This hypothesized relationship between pornography and sexual violence has also become a rallying point for certain social activist and feminist groups, as expressed in Robin Morgan's (1978) widely cited aphorism: "Pornography is the theory, and rape is the practice" (p. 142).

Perhaps fueled by societal concerns, laboratory studies on the effects of violent pornography have proliferated in the past decade. In addition to investigating patterns of sexual arousal to these stimuli, much of this research has been conducted in the context of the laboratory aggression paradigm, first described by Buss (1961) and widely used since in experimental studies of hostility and aggression. This paradigm typically involves at least two key elements: a procedure for eliciting frustration or aggressive feelings in the subjects, followed by a bogus experimental task in which the subject is required to administer electric shocks or other aversive stimuli to an experimental confederate. Among the research questions that have been addressed to date are a comparison of male and female arousal patterns to violent erotica; delineation of the role of cognitive, affective, and physiological reactions to sexual violence; and evaluation of the effects of both violent and nonviolent erotica on laboratory aggression. Complete reviews of recent research in these areas are provided by Donnerstein (1980, 1984) and Malamuth (1984).

Early experimental studies in this area examined the effects of exposure to nonaggressive pornography on subsequent aggressive behavior in college males and females. For example, Mosher and Katz (1971) presented 10-minute erotic or control films to young male subjects, followed by instructions to express verbal hostility toward a female confederate. Although presentation of the erotic film per se did not lead to an increase in aggression, subjects increased their level of hostility when told that they would be permitted to view a more "exciting" film if they could be more aggressive. In contrast, Jaffe, Malamuth, Feingold, and Feshbach (1974) reported that exposure to written pornography directly increased laboratory aggression in both male and female subjects. Specifically, sexually aroused subjects were found to deliver more intense shocks than unaroused subjects to either a male or a female confederate. This latter finding has been presented by the authors as evidence for the link between sexual arousal and aggressive behavior in general, rather than as a specific effect of pornography on aggression toward women.

In addition to reports of no effect or increased aggression following exposure, at least one study (Baron & Bell, 1977) found that presentation of "mild" erotic stimuli, such as seminude and nude female pictures, appeared to *inhibit* subsequent aggression in college males. In explaining these disparate findings, Sapolsky (1984) has postulated that stimulus characteristics, such as modality and intensity, may mediate the effects of erotica on aggression. According to this author, aggression may be most likely to occur following exposure to erotica that are associated with high levels of sexual arousal, but also with negative affective reactions, such as guilt or disgust. Evidence for this hypothesis comes from a study by Zillmann, Bryant, Comisky, and Medoff (1981), in which male subjects were exposed to highly explicit films portraying either conventional heterosexual activities or scenes of bestiality and sadomasochism. Consistent with the hypothesis, the films that were rated as sexually arousing but also unpleasant to watch (e.g., sadomasochism) were associated with the greatest increase in subsequent aggression.

The context of stimulus presentation may also be important in determining experimental effects. For example, Leonard and Taylor (1983) presented erotic or neutral slides to college males in the company of a female accomplice who made sexually permissive comments, nonpermissive comments, or no comments during the presentation. It was demonstrated, using the Buss (1961) procedure again, that exposure to the erotic slides in the presence of a permissive female was associated both with higher levels of arousal and with increased aggression against the female confederate. In explaining these results, Leonard and Taylor (1983) suggest that subjects may have inferred from the confederate's permissive comments during the slide presentation that "normally inappropriate behaviors would be tolerated" (p. 298). This may have served, in turn, to disinhibit responses in the shock tolerance situation, leading to higher levels of aggression.

While the effects of nonviolent erotica on laboratory aggression remain equivocal, a growing body of research has supported the view that exposure to violent pornography profoundly affects male attitudes toward rape, the use of aggressive themes in sexual fantasy, and the likelihood of direct aggression toward women. For example, one of the first studies of this type (Malamuth, Haber, & Feshbach, 1980) reported that males who had been exposed to a written description of sadomasochistic activities were more likely to respond favorably on attitude measures to a subsequent depiction of rape. In a related study, Malamuth, Heim, and Feshbach (1980) investigated specific dimensions of violent pornography that appeared to be associated with sexual arousal in male or female viewers. Specifically, it was found that portrayal of the victim in the script as experiencing involuntary sexual arousal (orgasm) and no pain was associated with maximal arousal in the female subjects, whereas males responded most to depictions involving both pain *and* sexual gratification for the victim. It should be noted, however, that neither of these studies employed direct genital measures of sexual arousal.

The importance of victim responses in determining arousal to violent pornography was also demonstrated by Malamuth and Check (1980) in a study that included penile tumescence measures of arousal in college males. Portrayal of the victim as experiencing involuntary sexual arousal, as opposed to pain or abhorrence, was associated with significantly greater tumescence responses in the viewers. It was also reported that arousal to violent pornography was subsequently associated with more callous attitudes toward rape, including perception of the victim's experience as less traumatic. In a second study of this type, Malamuth (1981) exposed college males to slide–audio presentations involving rape or mutually consenting sexual activities. In addition to demonstrating increased tumescence and self-reported arousal to both violent and nonviolent stimuli, subjects were found to have significantly more violent sexual fantasies following exposure to the rape depictions.

More recently, Malamuth and Check (1983) have extended this design to include assessment of individual difference factors, such as personality type, prior sexual experience, and attitudes toward sexual aggression in general. For purposes of this study, the content of audiotaped erotic depictions was manipulated in order to portray either consenting or nonconsenting sexual activity, presence or absence of pain, and perceived sexual arousal or disgust in the victim. As in the previous studies, both penile tumescence and subjective arousal were diminished when the victim in a nonconsenting script was portrayed as experiencing disgust. When the victim was perceived as becoming aroused, however, marked differences in the responses of individual subjects appeared.

As illustrated in Figure 8.4, subjects who had previously rated themselves as likely to commit rape if they were certain of not being caught or punished (high likelihood of raping, or LR) were found to have significantly greater arousal to the nonconsenting stimuli than those subjects who rated themselves as unlikely to commit rape under any circumstances (low LR). In addition, reported sexual arousal to rape depictions was positively correlated with scores on personality measures reflecting aggressive tendencies, such as psychoticism and power motivation, and negatively correlated with previous sexual experience. In explaining this latter finding, the authors state, "The association between sexual experience and arousal to rape may be due to the existence of a third variable, such as hostility toward women, that causes both less sexual experience and increased arousal to rape depiction" (Malamuth & Check, 1983, p. 65).

In a further replication of these findings, Malamuth et al. (1986) investigated the responses of males and females to written stories, the content of which was varied systematically along the dimensions of aggression and sexual explicitness. Thus, the aggressive sexual stimulus involved a graphic description of rape, whereas the aggressive nonsexual stimulus portrayed a brutal assault and stabbing of a female victim. While both men and women reported increased sexual arousal to nonaggressive as opposed to aggressive sexual stories, the opposite pattern occurred for the nonsexual depictions. In a second part to the study, male subjects were classified according to their responses on a questionnaire item assessing how sexually arousing they would find "forcing a female to do something she didn't want to." When subsequently exposed to the same stimulus depictions, it was found that males who scored low on this measure were more likely to be aroused by nonaggressive than aggressive scenes, whereas the opposite was true for males who were high on the arousal-from-force classification. These subjects also were found to be more accepting of the use of aggression in nonsexual situations, and to more likely to endorse a value system that justified male aggression and dominance over women.

Other investigators have used the paradigm of elicited aggression to

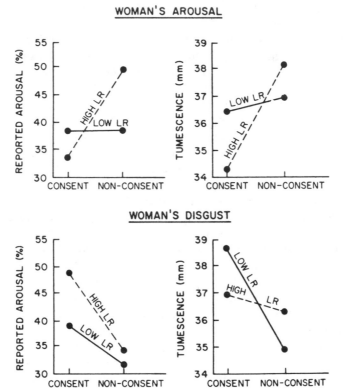

WOMAN'S AROUSAL

WOMAN'S DISGUST

Figure 8.4. Penile tumescence and subjects' self-reported arousal when the victim was portrayed as showing arousal or disgust. The likelihood of raping (LR) classification refers to scores on a self-report instrument measuring attitudes toward rape. From "Sexual Arousal to Rape Depictions: Individual Differences" by N. M. Malamuth and J. V. P. Check, 1983, *Journal of Abnormal Psychology, 92,* p. 61. Copyright 1983 by the American Psychological Association. Reprinted by permission.

evaluate the effects of violent pornography on interpersonal aggression. For example, Donnerstein (1980) first had an experimental accomplice of either sex provoke male subjects to anger or treat them in a neutral manner. Subjects then were exposed to one of three stimuli: a sexually violent film involving rape at gunpoint; a film of mutually consenting intercourse; or a neutral, nonsexual film. Penile tumescence responses indicated approximately equal levels of arousal to the two erotic films. However, when subjects were subsequently provided with an opportunity to aggress against the accomplice, it was found that exposure to the rape film only increased aggression against the female as opposed to the male confederate. The results of this study suggest that exposure to violent pornography of this type leads to a specific increase in female-directed aggression, rather than an increase in aggressive behavior generally. Similarly, Donnerstein and Berkowitz (1981) found that exposure to sexually aggressive materials, regardless of the outcomes portrayed, were associated with an increased level of aggression toward female targets.

One additional study with female subjects (Stock, 1983) has been reported in which college women were exposed to audiotaped depictions of various rape scenarios. The sexual aggression stimuli for this study consisted of a realistic rape depiction, an eroticized or "pornographic" rape scene, and a comparison tape describing consenting heterosexual intercourse. Overall, subjects responded with the least physiological and subjective arousal to the realistic rape depiction, but were about equally aroused by the tapes depicting eroticized rape and consenting intercourse. On the other hand, Stock found that subjects exposed to the realistic rape depiction reported the highest levels of anger during the experiment.

Few studies to date have investigated the effects of repeated or long-term exposure to sexually violent pornography. One recent study (Linz, 1985) exposed college males to a series of "slasher" films, involving high levels of explicit sex and violence, for 5 consecutive days. When reactions of subjects were subsequently evaluated in a bogus study of jury procedures, which was presented as unrelated to the previous pornography experience, it appeared that massive exposure to violent pornography was associated with perception of the films as significantly less violent or degrading to women, with fewer negative emotional reactions to the films, and with more punitive attitudes toward victims of rape generally. These results are consistent with the hypotheses proposed by Byrne (1977), at least concerning the desensitizing effects of repeated exposure to violent pornography. Moreover, it appeared that desensitization effects (as measured by emotional reactivity to the films) could be detected after the first 3 hours of exposure.

In evaluating the generalizability of findings from the studies described above, a number of issues need to be addressed. First, none of the laboratory studies to date have provided an opportunity for immediate reinforcement (i.e., sexual gratification) following exposure to sexually violent materials. From the results of Schaefer and Colgan (1977) with nonviolent pornography, it might be anticipated that masturbation to orgasm following exposure (as might be expected to occur frequently in the natural environment) could affect the strength or direction of responses to violent erotica. Certainly, this is an important variable to be examined in future studies. Second, all of the studies reviewed in this section have been conducted on college-aged male and female volunteer samples, and it is unclear to what extent the age and volunteer status of the subjects may have influenced the pattern of results obtained. In recent years, an increasing number of studies have been conducted on the responses of sex offenders and aggressive criminals to these materials, as discussed in the next chapter. Finally, the contrived nature of the dependent measures in many of these studies raises concerns about the external validity of the findings.

SUMMARY

There is no doubt that laboratory studies of erotica and pornography have come to occupy a central role in applied sexual psychophysiological research. Beginning with early studies of self-report and nongenital physiological arousal to explicit erotica, researchers have increasingly employed a wide variety of stimulus modalities and types, experimental conditions, and dependent measures in recent studies of these effects. In fact, this approach has emerged as the leading paradigm for much of the current psychophysiological research on the role of pornography, sexual preference and orientation, deviance and dysfunction, and drug and alcohol effects on sexual response. Despite the obvious advantages in terms of experimental control and efficiency of this paradigm, we have also sought to emphasize important limitations in this chapter.

One of the earliest questions to be addressed in this research was the issue of male–female differences in arousal to erotica. The position of Kinsey and his colleagues on this issue was quite clear: Women were said to be less conditionable, and consequently less responsive to the effects of explicit erotica. However, based upon more recent questionnaire studies in both West Germany and the United States, it has begun to appear that a notable convergence has occurred between the responses of males and females—at least, between the responses of the young, relatively well-educated, and sexually experienced males and females studied. Furthermore, laboratory studies by Heiman (1977), Osborn and Pollack (1977), and others have demonstrated substantial overlap in male and female psychophysiological patterns of arousal to such stimuli. Male–female differences in responses to violent pornography have also begun to be investigated.

A major topic of investigation in this area has been the effects of repeated exposure to various types of erotic stimuli. According to the model proposed by Byrne (1977), long-term or repeated exposure is likely to lead to increased attitudinal tolerance of the activities portrayed, and to enhanced arousal via imaginal rehearsal. Increased arousal to repeated presentations may also result when subjects are provided with the opportunity for sexual reinforcement (i.e., masturbation to orgasm) following exposure (Schaefer & Colgan, 1977).

In contrast, a number of studies have been reviewed that indicate the role of habituation factors in causing a decline in arousal levels following repeated presentation. At least one study to date (O'Donohue & Geer,

1985), however, has shown that stimulus constancy or variability can markedly affect the rate of habituation. Similarly, in the study by Julien and Over (1984), variations in the modality of stimulus presentation were associated with an absence of habituation over five sessions of repeated testing. Habituation effects have recently been offered as an explanation for the increasingly unusual and violent themes portrayed in commercial pornography.

Perhaps most controversial have been the results of laboratory studies on the effects of exposure to violent pornography in young volunteer subjects. In particular, it has been shown that exposure may lead to increased tolerance for sexual coercive or aggressive behavior, to greater acceptance of "rape myths," and to increased hostility toward a female accomplice in laboratory analogues of aggression. Male–female differences and stimulus characteristics, such as the responses of victims portrayed in rape scenes, have also been shown to be important in these studies. In addition, the effects of massed exposure to violent pornography have recently been addressed in this research. On the other hand, insufficient attention has been paid to important methodological issues, such as response consistency and external validity.

In conclusion, we should note that the current societal backlash against pornography has led some commentators to question whether it is even possible to conduct objective and unbiased research in such a highly charged area of investigation. And, while it is also apparent from the recommendations of the Attorney General's Commission on Pornography (1986) that legal, ethical, and social considerations have largely tended to overshadow empirical research findings in determining public policy on pornography, it remains clear that a new impetus has been given to laboratory psychophysiological studies of erotica.

211

CHAPTER NINE

Assessment and Treatment of Sexual Deviation (Paraphilias)

Why were we crucified into sex?
Why were we not left rounded off, and finished in ourselves.
As we began . . . so perfectly alone?
 —D. H. Lawrence, "Tortoise Shout" (1923)

BACKGROUND

Few topics in the fields of psychology and psychiatry have generated as much controversy as the diagnosis and treatment of sexual deviation. With some notable exceptions (e.g., Socarides, 1974), health professionals have generally adopted a more tolerant stance toward alternative sexual behavior. These attitudinal shifts have been associated with major revisions in the classification, terminology, and definitions of sexual deviation. For example, the American Psychiatric Association, after a lengthy and vociferous debate, voted in 1974 to remove homosexuality from the then-current psychiatric diagnostic nomenclature (DSM-II; American Psychiatric Association, 1968). This decision followed an earlier landmark stance by the Association for Advancement of Behavior Therapy to treat homosexuality as a viable and alternative expression of normal sexuality (see Davidson, 1977).

As this controversy continued to attract attention, DSM-III (American Psychiatric Association, 1980) adopted a compromise nomenclature, distinguishing Ego-syntonic Homosexuality and Ego-dystonic Homosexuality, with the latter retained as a diagnosis subsumed under the category of Psychosexual Disorders. The prevailing view of most mental health professionals today appears to uphold this decision, reflecting the practical realities of contemporary social norms, as aptly noted by one recent commentator (Silverstein, 1984): "Homosexuality no longer seems so abnormal because it is increasingly common, not in the sense of there being more homosexuals, but in that it is more feasible to live one's life as a homosexual in today's society" (p. 31).

However, despite evidence of increasing social acceptance of homosexuality between consenting adult partners and a greater degree of tolerance of the more innocuous deviations, such as fetishism and transvestism, these attitudes are far less prevalent in current responses to the sexually aggressive offenses or child molestation. In fact, the growing public concern with the prevalence and potential harmfulness of sexually aggressive behavior has highlighted the need for more intensive clinical and research programs in this area (cf. Greer & Stuart, 1983). Thus, laboratory studies of the assessment and treatment of rapists, child molesters, exhibitionists, and other deviant offenders have received growing attention in the last decade. Much of this research has focused on the development of psychophysiological measures of deviant arousal to identify causal factors in sexual deviation, and to isolate relevant variables for clinical intervention.

It is the intent of this chapter to review the major theoretical and methodological issues involved in psychophysiological approaches to sexual deviation. In light of the issues raised in this brief review of the field's background, the application of psychophysiological methods to assessment and treatment illustrates the full range of sociocultural concerns discussed in Chapter I, and provides a dramatic example of the interplay among advances in measurement technology, therapeutic innovations, and the cultural context of applied research. The majority of studies to be reviewed in this chapter have involved applications to the "sexual deviations" or "paraphilias" (e.g., rape, pedophilia, exhibitionism), and with some exceptions, have not focused on the "sexual variations" (e.g., homosexuality).

In addition, this chapter focuses on a number of key methodological issues, such as the relative advantages and disadvantages of using erection measures as an index of deviant arousal, as well as the potential role of nongenital measures of deviant arousal as alternatives to erection measures. An important question to be discussed in this regard is the relationship between changes in psychophysiological measures in the laboratory and related changes in behavior in the "outside world." Finally, specific methodological problems, such as the discrepancy between physiological and self-report measures, the potential for "faking" of penile erection responses by certain subjects, the effects of alcohol on deviant sexual arousal, and the medical–legal implications of psychophysiological laboratory studies in clinical decision making, are considered.

DEFINING SEXUAL DEVIANCE

Historical Approaches

"Sexual deviance" has historically been defined as immoral, sinful, illegal, or disturbed behavior. In defining sexual deviance, however, one needs to be aware that while standards for acceptability of sexual conduct are present in all cultures, the actual content of these standards has varied greatly from one culture to another (Ford & Beach, 1951; Bullough, 1976). In our own society, non-normative sexual behaviors have increasingly been viewed as variant life styles rather than as deviant behavior. Thus, the term "normal deviance" has been used by sociologists Gagnon and Simon (1967) to describe sexual behaviors such as premarital intercourse or anal sex. Although not officially sanctioned, these widely practiced forms of sexual behavior have clearly become an integral part of conventional sexual scripts of our society and are generally not regarded as deviant by those engaged in such behaviors (e.g., Hunt, 1974; Hite, 1976).

Bancroft (1974) has distinguished further between "individual" and "subcultural" forms of sexual deviance. "Individual deviance," according to this author, refers to those sexual behaviors that are generally perceived by both the perpetrator and the society at large as socially unacceptable. Most rapists, exhibitionists, and child molesters would be classified as "individual deviants," while many homosexuals and transvestites could be viewed as "subcultural deviants." The latter generally seek out others engaged in similar behavior, and regard their membership in a subcultural group as an important aspect of their psychological and social identity.

Nosological Issues

The term "sexual deviation" has generally been replaced by the term "paraphilia," and DSM-III lists nine major diagnostic subcategories under the heading of Paraphilias: (1) Fetishism; (2) Transvestism; (3) Zoophilia; (4) Pedophilia; (5) Exhibitionism; (6) Voyeurism; (7) Sexual Masochism; (8) Sexual Sadism; and (9) Atypical Paraphilia (including paraphiliac or compulsive rape). It is noteworthy that in DSM-II and other previous classification systems, these syndromes were presented as a subdivision of the so-called Sociopathic Personality Type. The current diagnosis of Paraphilia, in contrast, makes no such assumptions regarding the underlying character structure of the patient. DSM-III, for example, emphasizes the critical role of deviant sexual preferences as the defining characteristic of the Paraphilias: "The Paraphilias are characterized by arousal in response to sexual objects or situations that are not part of normative arousal–activity patterns and that in varying degrees may interfere with the capacity for reciprocal affectionate sexual activity" (p. 261). Clearly, this emphasis on deviant sexual arousal patterns as the core element in paraphilias has highlighted the potential value of psychophysiological approaches to the assessment of these disorders.

While this change in the definition of paraphilias has been largely accepted by most professionals, criticisms of this conceptualization have also been raised. For example, Money (1984) has commented that the first eight categories of Paraphilia in DSM-III represent the minority of paraphilias found in actual practice, and that these subcategories were selected because of their forensic history rather than the degree of pathology involved. Money further emphasizes that the subcategory of Atypical Paraphilia includes the largest number of deviant sexual behaviors, which he divides into approximately 30 separate diagnostic entities in six major categories. Other authors (e.g., Suppe, 1984) have noted the significant omission of relatively prevalent and serious offenses such as incest and acquaintance rape from the classification system. In addition, the emphasis in the DSM-III definition on interference with the capacity for normal sexual relationships has been criticized, as many paraphiliacs are able to maintain conventional relationships that are concurrent with their deviant interests.

Presently, only one generalization can be made about the paraphilias with relative certainty: They are predominantly, and indeed almost exclusively, male disorders. Explanatory theories for this sex difference have ranged from the supposed biological vulnerability of males during the process of masculine differentiation (e.g., Money & Ehrhardt, 1972) to the demands of masculine socialization processes (Gagnon & Simon, 1973). Paraphilias have often been viewed as excesses of male libido, or hypersexuality (Money, 1984), although the emphasis in recent years has generally been on the inappropriate *direction* rather than the *strength* of the sexual drive (Berlin, 1983). Some theorists have also interpreted the paraphilias as disorders of courtship behavior, in which the patient is only able to engage in limited or distorted aspects of the normal courtship script (Freund, Scher, & Hucker, 1984).

Deviant Arousal and the Mediation of Paraphiliac Behavior

Laboratory studies of sexual deviance have generally been based on the underlying assumption that paraphiliac behavior is motivated, in large part, by sexual arousal to deviant stimuli (e.g., male or female children, the use of sexual coercion, etc.). Central to the laboratory assessment of sexual deviance is the concept of a *chain* of sexual response components, leading up to and including genital arousal and overt behavior. This concept was first detailed by Barlow (1974, 1977), and has formed the basis for much of the experimental and clinical work to date. Briefly, this model postulates three major components of sexual deviation: (1) deviant sexual arousal, (2) heterosocial skills deficits, and (3) deviations in gender role. Barlow has emphasized the need to assess all *three* components in each case, and a few recent studies have attempted to evaluate both gender role and sexual arousal patterns in the investigation of pedophilia (Freund, Scher, Chan,

& Ben-Aron, 1982) and exhibitionism (Langevin *et al.*, 1979). By and large, however, laboratory studies of deviant sexual behavior have tended to focus almost exclusively on the evaluation of deviant arousal, and in particular on erectile responses to visual or auditory stimuli.

The practical and theoretical advantages of this focus on deviant arousal as the key mediating factor in paraphiliac behavior are clear. First, existing technology for measuring male sexual arousal is easily adapted to assessing responses to deviant stimuli and can readily be used to compare response patterns of different groups of deviant and nondeviant subjects. Second, a wide range of intervention techniques has been developed for modifying deviant arousal, and the effectiveness of these techniques can be determined by laboratory evaluations.

Along with the assessment of deviant arousal, most studies have monitored concurrent arousal patterns to a range of nondeviant stimuli, thereby permitting evaluation of other aspects of treatment designed to facilitate appropriate sexual interests. In addition, laboratory assessments have been used in some studies in conjunction with clinical follow-up to evaluate the long-term outcome and maintenance of treatment effects (Quinsey & Marshall, 1983). In this regard, sexual arousal measures are certainly preferable to the more traditional, "static" measures of personality or psychometric performance, upon which the prediction of dangerousness has frequently been based in the past (Abel, Becker, Murphy, & Flanagan, 1981; Laws, 1984).

Despite considerable benefits, the Barlow model with its focus on deviant sexual arousal is not without potential difficulties. Most critical, perhaps, is the assumed relationship between deviant arousal in the laboratory and the probability that sexually inappropriate behavior will occur outside the laboratory. It would certainly be naive to assume a one-to-one relationship between laboratory arousal and the proclivity to act on such feelings in the external environment. According to Laws (1984), deviant arousal patterns are predictive in a qualitative rather than a quantitative manner: "The measures [of deviant arousal] will *not* reliably and validly predict the probability of future offending, although . . . they *will* rather accurately describe the quality of the offending" (p. 129). The assessment of *specificity* of arousal patterns is thus a critical issue, and is discussed further below.

Another drawback of the Barlow model is the assumption that deviant arousal is equally important in the mediation of all forms of paraphiliac behavior. However, clinical studies have indicated that this is not the case; for example, exhibitionists appear to be less strongly motivated by deviant arousal per se than are child molesters or rapists (Langevin *et al.*, 1979; Abel, Blanchard, & Barlow, 1981). Furthermore, a number of recent studies have shown that many normal male subjects, who appear to have no known history of paraphiliac behavior, can show significant arousal to deviant stimuli in the laboratory (e.g., Malamuth & Check, 1983; Quinsey, Chaplin, & Upfold, 1984). Although other studies have attempted to differentiate the quality of arousal patterns between offenders and normals (e.g., Abel, Barlow, *et al.*, 1977), the extent of deviant arousal in some normal subjects should be viewed as an additional caveat against equating deviant arousal with the proclivity for deviant behavior.

CAUSAL FACTORS IN THE ETIOLOGY OF SEXUAL DEVIATION

Conditioning

Assuming that deviant arousal typically functions as a necessary precursor to deviant sexual behavior, several studies have examined the role of learning and conditioning factors in the development of deviant arousal. In the first systematic investigation of the conditioning hypothesis, McGuire *et al.* (1965) reviewed the case records from 45 mixed paraphiliac patients, and concluded that fantasy rehearsal during masturbation played a key role in conditioning deviant arousal in virtually every instance. The authors noted that early traumatic experiences, such as sexual molestation, were also reported in many cases, but that the effects of these early experiences appeared to be strongly mediated and maintained by fantasy rehearsal during masturbation. While noting that most of the patients also had negative early experiences with conventional heterosexual relationships, McGuire *et al.* postulated that the experience of repeated masturbation with deviant fantasies outweighed the importance of other negative sexual experiences. The masturbatory conditioning hypothesis has similarly been invoked to explain the observation that sexual deviations are uncommon in women, as women typically begin masturbation at a later age and are less reliant on fantasy stimulation.

In order to demonstrate further the specific role of classical conditioning factors in the development of deviant sexual arousal (specifically fetishism), Rachman (1966) conducted a laboratory analogue study with three normal male subjects. Utilizing an early version of the mercury-in-rubber strain gauge, the author measured penile tumescence in response to the pairing of slides of women's black leather boots (CSs) with slides of attractive nude women (UCSs). Conditioning trials were continued until each of the subjects attained the conditioning criterion (five successive tumescence responses to the CS). Stimulus generalization was assessed by presenting a variety of slides of female footwear. The results indicated that all three subjects acquired arousal CRs to the CS, although one of the subjects showed a particularly weak and unstable response, which extinguished after only three trials. The author noted that the choice of the CS for this study (women's boots) may have enhanced the effects of conditioning as being an intrinsically "sensitive" stimulus.

In a second study, Rachman and Hodgson (1968) attempted to replicate these results with an additional control for pseudoconditioning or sensitization, by means of a backward conditioning procedure. Specifically, in the forward conditioning procedure, the CS (a photograph of women's boots) was always followed immediately by the UCS (a slide of a nude woman), and produced a CR of approximately the same magnitude as was found in the first study. On the other hand, when the UCS was presented before the CS (backward conditioning), little or no conditioning was observed on test trials. Stimulus generalization and extinction were again demonstrated in the forward conditioning procedure. These results were interpreted by the authors as indicating that the development of sexual arousal responses to the CS (women's boots) was accomplished by means of a genuine conditioning process, as opposed to response faking or sensitization of the subjects. Although conditioning processes are seldom viewed as a sufficient explanation for the acquisition of paraphiliac arousal, both classical and instrumental conditioning procedures have been widely used in the application of behavioral approaches to treatment (e.g., Abel, Blanchard, & Becker, 1977; Quinsey, Chaplin, & Carrigan, 1980); these are reviewed in a later section.

Biological Factors

Several studies have implicated the possible role of biological determinants in the development of sexual deviation. For example, Rada, Laws, and Kellner (1976) obtained plasma testosterone samples from a large sample of rapists and child molesters. After classifying the rapists according to the degree of violence involved in the offense, the investigators found that the plasma testosterone levels discriminated significantly between the violent rapists and the less aggressive rapists and child molesters. Considering that the mean testosterone level was approximately 200 ng/100 ml higher in the group of violent rapists, this finding certainly warrants further attention. It is also noteworthy that approximately 40% of the subjects in this study were intoxicated at the time of the offense, and a large percentage were found to have a history of alcohol abuse.

More recently, Berlin (1983) has reviewed extensive medical data from the Johns Hopkins Biosocial Hormonal Clinic evaluation of a sample of 34 deviants, primarily pedophiles. Some evidence of biological abnormality was found in almost every case, although the extent of the abnormalities ranged from relatively minor problems such as dyslexia to rather severe chromosomal disorders (7 cases) and major cortical atrophy (4 cases). Hormonal abnormalities (e.g., elevated testosterone and LH levels) were present in approximately 50% of the patients studied. Despite the absence of an appropriate matched control group, and the likelihood of subject selection bias, these data are useful for documenting the potential role of biological factors in the etiology of paraphilias.

Not all studies, however, have found significant biological differences between paraphiliacs and normals. For example, Karacan *et al.* (1974) conducted a study of NPT and sleep patterns in institutionalized rapists, individuals institutionalized for nonsexual offenses, and normal controls. After examining a wide variety of sleep and NPT parameters, the authors concluded that there were no significant differences in NPT patterns between the groups, and only minimal differences in other sleep parameters (e.g., percentage of Stage 2 sleep).

Drug use and alcohol consumption have also been shown to be important contributing factors in sexually deviant behavior. In particular, several authors have emphasized the role of alcohol consumption in potentiating deviant arousal in normals (Briddell *et al.*, 1978; G. T. Wilson, 1981) and in sex offenders (Berlin, 1983). Furthermore, the role of alcohol has been well established as a contributing factor to rape or other sexually violent behaviors (e.g., Amir, 1967; Rada, Kellner, Laws, & Winslow, 1978). It is unclear from these studies, however, what specific mechanisms are involved in alcohol's potentiation of deviant arousal—whether the effects are due to an increased salience of deviant cues under conditions of intoxication, or to a disinhibition of the normal physiological or psychological control mechanisms (G. T. Wilson, 1981; Wydra, Marshall, Earls, & Barbaree, 1983).

Psychological Factors

Much has been written about the personality types and developmental histories associated with each of the paraphilias. For example, on the basis of extensive clinical experience with rapists and child molesters, Groth (1983) has identified six key "personality deficits" that are characteristic of these disorders: (1) a sense of worthlessness and low self-esteem; (2) a pervasive feeling of vulnerability and helplessness; (3) impaired social relationships; (4) dysphoric mood state; (5) mismanagement of aggression; and (6) tenuous masculine identity. Other authors (e.g., Rosen & Fracher, 1983) have emphasized the inability of many paraphiliacs to cope with stress, and the vicious cycle of inappropriate tension reduction that appears in many instances to follow and maintain deviant behavior or masturbation to deviant fantasy (see Figure 9.1).

On the other hand, it should be emphasized that such factors cannot be reliably or objectively assessed at present. As Quinsey (1977) has noted in regard to the assessment of psychological factors in pedophilia, "It is

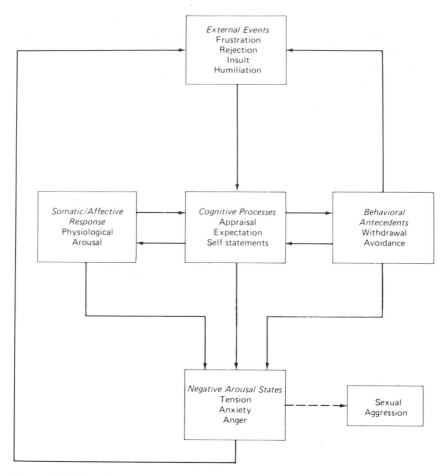

Figure 9.1. Negative arousal states in the mediation of sexual aggression. From "Tension-Reduction Training in the Treatment of Compulsive Sex Offenders" by R. C. Rosen and J. C. Fracher, 1983, in J. G. Greer and I. R. Stuart (Eds.), *The Sexual Aggressor: Current Perspectives on Treatment* (p. 149), New York: Van Nostrand Reinhold. Copyright 1983 by Van Nostrand Reinhold, Inc. Reprinted by permission.

unclear as to what extent the expression of these traits are due to the child molesters' personalities, and to what extent they are a result of the child molesters' attempts to convince institutional staff and supervisory personnel of their nondeviance" (p. 213). In fact, the unreliability of both self-report data and traditional personality testing in this context is one of the main arguments in favor of laboratory psychophysiological assessment. In addition to providing a more objective means for evaluating deviant arousal, psychophysiological assessment has important clinical advantages, as is demonstrated in a recent study by Abel, Cunningham-Rathner, Becker, and McHugh (1983). Specifically, these authors contrasted the results of clinical interviews with a mixed group of paraphiliac patients before and after laboratory psychophysiological assessment (penile tumescence measures). Results indicated that after confrontation with the results of their laboratory testing, and further reiteration of the confidentiality of their records, more than half of the subjects admitted to a large number of additional deviant behaviors. This finding suggests that the use of objective laboratory measures can serve to increase the reliability of patients' self-report as well as providing an important source of external validation of these reports.

LABORATORY METHODS IN THE ASSESSMENT OF DEVIANT AROUSAL

Erection Measures

The primary focus in laboratory psychophysiological studies of sexual deviance in the past two decades has been on the measurement of penile tumescence in order to assess patterns of deviant sexual arousal in both clinical and nonclinical subjects. The typical reasons given for choosing erection measures over other physiological or self-report indices of deviant arousal are the accessibility of measurement technology, the objectivity of the measure, and the relative reliability of erection measurement as an index of sexual arousal, as discussed in Chapter 3. Perhaps of greatest importance, however, is the potential offered by laboratory tumescence measures as a kind of "sexological lie detector," or a way of determining with relative precision the extent and direction of deviant arousal in given individuals, regardless of their willingness to admit to or wish to conceal such proclivities. Much of the research in this area has been conducted in the context of assessment of sex offenders with serious criminal records (e.g., Abel, Barlow, *et al.*, 1977; Abel, Becker, *et al.*, 1981; Barbaree, Marshall, & Lanthier, 1979; Quinsey & Chaplin, 1984), and the hope remains that laboratory tumescence measures will provide key information for the evaluation, treatment, and follow-up of such cases (Laws, 1984).

Despite the considerable promise and growing body of experimental work in this area, major differences in methodology from one study to another severely limit the generalizations that can be drawn from this research. In particular, the use of different methods of measuring tumescence, different modalities and duration of stimulus presentation, and the comparison of different type of offenders and nonoffenders from one study to another need to be taken into account. In addition, few studies have paid sufficient attention to the assessment of reliability and validity of tumescence measurement in this context; in particular, the crucial issue of predictive validity has only recently been addressed (Quinsey & Chaplin, 1982).

TYPES OF MEASURES AND STIMULUS MODALITIES

The first systematic studies on the use of erection measures for differentiating deviant from nondeviant patterns of arousal were carried out by Freund (1963). Making use of the volumetric plethysmograph described in Chapter 2, Freund attempted to differentiate homosexual and heterosexual response patterns in a heterogeneous group of male subjects. The laboratory procedure involved brief presentations of slides of nude males and females of different ages, and subsequent computation of the relative response amplitudes to each slide category. Despite the somewhat crude experimental methodology employed in these early studies, Freund did consider and specifically addressed the important issue of the potential "faking" of tumescence responses by certain subjects. In order to evaluate the role of faking in the context, heterosexual subjects were instructed to imagine an aversive image while viewing the female slides, and a positive sexual image while viewing the male slides; converse instructions were given to the homosexual subjects. From this and other studies of faking (e.g., Freund, 1967a), it was concluded that most subjects have only limited ability to fake a response, and that inhibition of sexual responses to the preferred stimulus is easier to accomplish than voluntary arousal to a nonpreferred stimulus.

Another noteworthy feature of Freund's studies was the inclusion of pharmacological "priming" of the subjects by means of intramuscular injections of testosterone on the day before testing, and administration of alcohol and caffeine immediately prior to the test sessions. This procedure was designed to maximize sexual responsivity during the testing sessions, although no independent evaluation of drug priming was conducted. Penile volume assessment has also been used by Freund and others to study response patterns of pedophiles (Freund, 1967a; 1967b; Freund & Langevin, 1976; Freund, Chan, & Coulthard, 1979) and exhibitionists (Kolarsky & Medlafousek, 1972; Langevin et al., 1979; Freund et al., 1984). While cumbersome and potentially invasive, the method does provide a highly sensitive and reliable measure of arousal to deviant stimuli.

A similar use of volumetric plethysmography for the assessment of sexual orientation in homosexual patients was reported by McConaghy (1967). In this study, a simplified version of the Freund transducer was used to assess penile responses to brief movie presentations of male and female nudes. Although the method was largely successful in differentiating the responses of the clinical group from those of heterosexual controls, about a third of the homosexual patients showed an absence of arousal to the male stimuli. The device has also been successfully employed for differentiating the arousal patterns of transvestites from fetishistic transsexuals (Buhrich & McConaghy, 1979).

Most subsequent studies have utilized penile circumference measures—either the mercury-in-rubber strain gauge, or the Barlow resistance gauge for the assessment of deviant arousal. Abel, Barlow, et al. (1977), for example, used the Barlow gauge to assess deviant arousal in rapists and in nonrapist sex offenders. In addition to measuring patterns of arousal in the two groups, this widely cited study is noteworthy in two other respects. First, the authors compared tumescence responses to individually tailored 2-minute audiotapes, containing descriptions of forced and mutual sexual interactions. Individualized erotic stimulus materials had been described in a previous study with a mixed group of deviants (Abel, Blanchard, et al., 1975), in which the experimenters developed a method for constructing stimulus audiotapes based upon the content of subjects' own erotic fantasies. With repeated presentations of an audiotaped script, specific content elements are added or removed according to the extent of a subject's polygraph responses to each phase of the tape presentation. Although this method is effective in producing stimulus materials that are maximally arousing for deviant subjects, it has the disadvantage of making between-group comparisons of idiosyncratic stimulus materials difficult if not impossible (Barbaree et al., 1979).

Second, the authors developed an index of relative erection response to the deviant stimuli, which they termed the "rape index," and which was obtained by dividing the average percentage of erection to rape cues by the average percentage of erection to cues of mutually enjoyable intercourse. Comparison of rape index scores with the previous histories of the individual subjects indicated a strong correlation with the frequency of previous rapes. Moreover, rape index scores were found to differentiate the more violent rapists in the group, as well as those who had sexually abused children. Although this study has been criticized on several grounds, including the failure to include nonoffender controls and the absence of controls for faking, the development of the rape index as a measure of relative erotic preference has clearly had a major impact on all subsequent research in the area. Furthermore, Abel and his colleagues have extended the use of their method to a comparison of patterns of deviant arousal in child molesters (Abel, Becker, et al., 1981) and other paraphiliacs (Abel, Blanchard, & Barlow, 1981).

Several studies have subsequently replicated the findings of Abel, Barlow, et al. (1977) by means of mercury-in-rubber strain gauge assessments of deviant arousal patterns in various offender and nonoffender groups (e.g., Barbaree et al., 1979; Hinton, O'Neill, & Webster, 1980; Quinsey, Chaplin, & Verney, 1981; Quinsey et al., 1984). In the Barbaree et al. (1979) study, erection responses of incarcerated rapists were compared with responses of male graduate students to standardized audiotapes of mutually consenting sex, rape, and violent nonsexual assault. Results of the study are shown in Figure 9.2, which indicates that rapists and controls responded about equally to descriptions of mutually consenting intercourse, but that rapists showed significantly more arousal to rape and assault stimuli than normals. By varying the degree of consent given by the female partner in the audio descriptions, the authors were further able to demonstrate that the nonrapists appeared to be specifically inhibited in their responses by the absence of consent. For reasons unknown, this did not apply to the rapists.

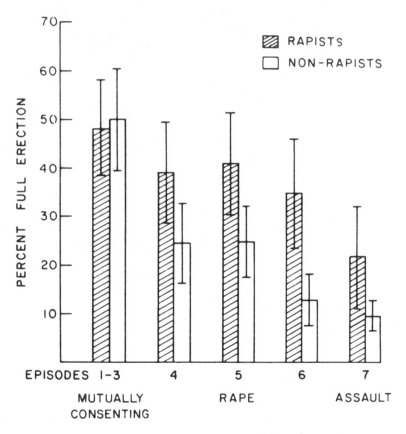

Figure 9.2. Mean sexual arousal in rapists and nonrapists, in response to 2-minute verbal descriptions of mutually consenting sex (1–3), three varieties of rape (4, 5, and 6), and nonsexual assault (7). From "Deviant Sexual Arousal in Rapists" by H. E. Barbaree, W. L. Marshall, and R. Lanthier, 1979, *Behaviour Research and Therapy, 17,* 215–222. Copyright 1979 by Pergamon Journals, Ltd. Reprinted by permission.

Quinsey *et al.* (1981) similarly attempted to replicate the Abel, Barlow, *et al.* (1977) study, but with several noteworthy additions. First, these authors compared penile responses (assessed via the mercury-in-rubber strain gauge) of incarcerated rapists to those of institutionalized controls (individuals incarcerated for nonsexual offenses in the same maximum-security institution) and to those of matched normal controls from the same socioeconomic backgrounds as the rapists. Audiotaped descriptions of sexual and nonsexual violence were again included in the study. Another novel feature of this study, however, was an attempt to facilitate arousal to rape cues in the normal controls by manipulation of instructional set. Specifically, one group of normals was told prior to stimulus presentation: "Most men will become aroused to sexual situations they have never even imagined in their fantasies. Do not be surprised if you become sexually aroused. . . ." (p. 130). While the instruction was moderately effective in increasing overall responsiveness in this group, it did not produce differential responsivity to the rape stimuli, as predicted. Quinsey *et al.* computed rape indices for all subjects in the same way as Abel, Barlow, *et al.* (1977) had done; they, too, found that rapists could clearly be differentiated from both institutional and normal controls on the basis of these scores. Similar findings were reported by Hinton *et al.* (1980), using a different index of responsiveness; this was computed by dividing the increase in diameter for a specific stimulus $(d_x - d_{min})$ by the maximum range $(d_{max} - d_{min})$ for all stimuli.

Three additional studies by Quinsey and his colleagues further investigated the effects of subject selection and stimulus dimensions for this experimental paradigm (Quinsey & Chaplin, 1982; 1984; Quinsey *et al.*, 1984). Specifically, Quinsey and Chaplin (1982) examined in greater detail the relationship between penile circumference responses of 44 convicted rapists to the degree of injury inflicted on the rapists' victims as described by the police reports. A nonsexual violence ratio, consisting of a subject's mean response to the nonsexual violence descriptions divided by the mean response to the consenting sex episodes, was found to be significantly correlated with the degree of physical abuse involved in the actual rapes.

In the second study, Quinsey and Chaplin (1984) compared penile circumference responses of rapists and individuals institutionalized for non-sexual offenses to audiotaped rape narratives in which the responses of the victim were shown as assertive or unassertive, and in which the victim was depicted as experiencing varying degrees of pleasure or pain from the assault. The results were consistent with previous studies in showing high levels of responsiveness in the rapist group to all categories of stimulus presentation, but proportionately less responding in the controls, depending on the degree of victim suffering described. Finally, Quinsey *et al.* (1984) compared the responses of rapists, institutionalized controls, and community controls to audiotaped descriptions of consenting sex, rape, nonsexual violence, and both consenting and nonconsenting sadomaso-chistic presentations. The gender of the victim was also varied across all content themes. Results showed that rapists were again responsive to all heterosexual erotic stimuli, regardless of the degree of violence contained in the narratives. On the other hand, it appeared that the rapists were relatively unresponsive to rape depictions involving male victims, nor were they more responsive than normal controls to depictions of sadomasochistic activities (bondage and spanking).

As is evident from this discussion, most recent laboratory studies have relied upon audiotaped stimuli for the comparison of deviant arousal between different offender groups and controls. Two major reasons are typically offered for this choice. First, maximum flexibility is offered by the audiotapes, which can be targeted to any sexual or nonsexual content themes imaginable. Furthermore, audiotapes can be specifically tailored to the idiosyncrasies of an individual offender's fantasies (Abel, Blanchard, et al., 1975). Laws (1984) has also noted that audiotapes are preferable for portraying erotic interests not readily shown in visual form (e.g., exhibitionism), and for controlling subjects' attention to specific aspects of the stimulus content.

Second, it has been suggested by several authors that voluntary suppression of penile responses may be more difficult in the presence of audiotapes than in response to visual stimuli (e.g., Rosen, 1973; Quinsey & Carrigan, 1978). This may be due to the fact that subjects can more easily avoid visual stimuli by a simple shifting of the gaze, whereas auditory stimuli are typically presented through headphones, thus requiring more complex strategies for inattention. While audiotaped stimuli have generally been preferred for these reasons, at least one study with male homosexuals (Abel, Barlow, Blanchard, & Mavissakalian, 1975) and another with a mixed group of offenders (Abel, Blanchard, & Barlow, 1981) have shown that both videotapes and slides elicit considerably greater penile circumference responses than audiotapes. In the latter study, it was also found that subjects could suppress arousal to audiotape stimuli as effectively as to visual stimuli, thus calling into question the assumption of less suppression with audio stimuli. It should be noted, however, that the audiotapes in these studies were not individually tailored, and thus may they not have matched the degree of erotic intensity of the visual stimuli.

OFFENDER TYPES

Laboratory erection measures have also varied considerably, depending upon the types of offenders studied. Overall, it appears that these measures have been most effective in differentiating the responses of child molesters and violent rapists, but somewhat less effective in distinguishing exhibitionists. For example, Abel, Blanchard, and Barlow (1981) found significantly less responsivity to deviant cues among the exhibitionists in their sample than among the other offender types; the authors attributed this finding to the difficulty in recreating exhibitionistic cues in a laboratory stimulus.

The most extensive study to date of sexual arousal patterns in exhibitionists was conducted by Langevin *et al.* (1979), who used volumetric plethysmography to investigate responses to a wide range of deviant cues in 96 exhibitionists. In most respects, the erection responses of the clinical subjects could not be differentiated from those of normal controls, with the exception of the exhibitionists' responses to descriptions of peeping and outdoor masturbation. Another interesting finding from this study was that almost half of the subjects reported an absence of sexual arousal or orgasm during typical exposure *in vivo*, bringing into question the role of sexual arousal in the "chain" of deviant behavior, as proposed by Barlow (1974, 1977) and others. Possibly genital arousal is less critical in the mediation of exhibitionism than of other paraphiliac behaviors. Thus, Freund *et al.* (1983) have proposed that the motivation for exposure may arise from distortions of the normal courtship pattern, rather than the effects of the deviant arousal per se.

On the other hand, the degree to which laboratory erection measures have succeeded in differentiating specific components of arousal in child molesters and rapists has been impressive. For example, Quinsey, Chaplin, and Carrigan (1979) found that nonincestuous child molesters could be differentiated from a comparable group of incestuous offenders in terms of the nonincestuous group's greater responsivity to age-inappropriate partners (i.e., the incest offenders were less strongly aroused by pedophiliac stimuli). Freund and Langevin (1976) and Freund *et al.* (1982) have similarly shown that bisexual arousal patterns are far more common in pedophiliac, as opposed to androphilia (preference for postpubescent children) or hebephilia (preference for pubescent children), suggesting that offenders against young children might be more likely to choose victims of either sex.

In their studies comparing the rape index responses of different groups of rapists and child molesters, Abel, Becker, *et al.* (1981) have demonstrated that scores on this measure correlate strongly with the frequency and brutality of subjects' previous offenses. The authors emphasize that the differentiation of offenders with more frequent and violent histories is relevant to the prediction of future offenses, as it has been repeatedly shown that past behavior is generally the best predictor of future criminal or sexually deviant behavior (Megargee, 1976).

Finally, it has recently been reported that laboratory tumescence measures can be used to assess deviant arousal in adolescent sex offenders (Murphy, Haynes, & Stailgate, 1985)—a subject group of particular concern. In this study, audiotaped pedophile cues were presented to 20 adolescent males referred for evaluation following instances of child sexual abuse. Although the assessment failed to differentiate responses to pedophiliac and nondeviant stimuli, the subjects with significant histories of delinquency were significantly more aroused by the more aggressive pedophilic cues.

ISSUES OF VALIDITY ("RESPONSE FAKING")
OF ERECTION MEASURES

Despite the impressive evidence that laboratory erection measures of deviant arousal in certain subject groups are specific and reliable, numerous authors have questioned the validity of these measures when applied to subjects who are willing or able to voluntarily control arousal (i.e., to "fake"). The issue was originally raised by Freund (1963, 1967a), in the context of the earliest laboratory studies of deviant arousal in homosexuals and pedophiles. Noting that some subjects have the capacity either to simulate or to dissimulate erectile responses to visual erotic stimuli, Freund (1963) first attempted to address this issue by varying the instructional set provided to the subjects, and thereby manipulating independently the degree of voluntary control. Other procedures used for dealing with faking were the presentation of slides for brief time periods only, and the alternation of target slides with "priming" or nondeviant stimuli. Freund also developed a method for classifying individual subjects as "admitters" or "nonadmitters," based upon evidence of response inhibition to the preferred stimuli. From these and other studies, it appears that most paraphiliacs have greater facility in suppressing responses to preferred stimuli than in producing voluntary arousal to nonpreferred stimuli; this indicates a potentially greater risk of false negatives in psychophysiological assessments of this type.

While most subsequent studies of voluntary control have relied on the manipulation of instructional sets to the subject as the primary means for assessing faking (e.g., Quinsey & Carrigan, 1978; Abel, Barlow, et al., 1975; Abel, Blanchard, & Barlow, 1981), this approach is clearly not sufficient in all instances. For example, Laws and Holmen (1978) report on a case of a particularly ingenious child molester who successfully employed a wide variety of faking strategies. Having serendipitously discovered this individual's ability to fake, the authors engaged the subject in a systematic study of faking strategies, which ranged from manual manipulation of the strain gauge to various cognitive and imagery techniques for producing voluntary suppression of arousal. On the basis of the findings from this case study, the authors recommend careful inspection of the polygraph records (see Figure 9.3), or video surveillance of the subject to guard against direct interference with the functioning of the transducer. Cognitive faking techniques are clearly more difficult to prevent, although the authors recommend the use of simultaneous detection tasks (e.g., requiring the subject to verbally describe the stimulus), as utilized by Laws and Rubin

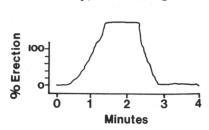

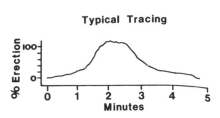

Figure 9.3. Two samples of polygraph (tumescence) record from deviant subjects. The record at left indicates a genuine tumescence response, with gradual onset of response and slow detumescence. The record at right indicates a "faked" response, as latency is too short, the pen pegs at maximum, and the detumescence is too sudden. From "Sexual Response Faking by Pedophiles" by D. R. Laws and M. L. Holmen, 1978, *Criminal Justice and Behavior, 5,* 343–356. Copyright 1978 by Sage Publications, Inc. Reprinted by permission.

(1969) and Henson and Rubin (1971). The problem remains a serious one, as Laws and Holmen note: "We are continually astonished at the creativity in circumventing our procedures shown by supposedly uncreative, under-educated, and undersocialized sex offenders" (1978, p. 344).

In a study of Scottish sex offenders, Hinton *et al.* (1980) attempted to address the faking issue in several innovative ways. First, each subject's overt behavior was monitored by means of a concealed video camera, which was used in conjunction with an infrared illumination system for insuring that the subject's gaze was directed to the stimulus presentation throughout. Second, subjects were required to indicate their degree of subjective arousal to each stimulus presentation by means of a button-press response, and the degree of inconsistency across trials between the subjective and physiological responses was viewed as another potential index of faking. Finally, a blind review of each patient's case records and previous psychological test reports was conducted in order to obtain an independent determination of "defensiveness." When the offender group was broken down into those subjects who could be suspected of faking according to one or more of these three criteria (13 out of 24 patients), it was found that the correlations between erection measures and self-report were significantly higher in the nonfakers than the fakers. While response faking represents a serious threat to the reliability of laboratory measures of sexual arousal, this study suggests several useful means for circumventing response faking.

The threat to validity posed by response faking is further underscored by a recent study of incarcerated rapists and nonrapist offenders (Murphy, Krisak, Stalgaitis, & Anderson, 1984). These authors point out that in previous research by Abel *et al.*, Quinsey *et al.*, and others, the majority of offenders studied had admitted to committing sexual offenses and were motivated to participate in return for treatment. In contrast, Murphy *et al.* selected a group of 18 sex offenders who had been convicted of rape or attempted rape, only 3 of whom admitted to either past or present interest in rape, and all of whom were being evaluated as a condition of parole. The rape index scores of this group were compared to those of a matched group of incarcerated offenders with no history of sex offenses in either prison or police records. Unlike the earlier results of Abel, Barlow, *et al.* (1977), the rape index scores were relatively ineffective in differentiating the responses of the rapists and nonrapists, even when the instructional set of the subjects was manipulated. While noting that the results have been confounded by other group differences, the authors suggested that the conditions of testing (i.e., the motivation to appear "normal") were the main reason for the invalid physiological assessment data in this group.

There is no doubt that response faking represents the major threat to both external and predictive validity of laboratory erection measures when used in this context (Farkas, 1978). Although there appears to be relative agreement concerning the importance of the issue, no standard method has emerged as yet for assessing or controlling faking from one study to another. Some of the procedures outlined in the studies described above, such as requiring the subject to verbally describe the stimulus, can be viewed as a promising first step toward dealing with this critical problem. However, researchers need to be careful not to underestimate the skill and ingenuity of subjects in "beating the system" (Laws & Holmen, 1978; Laws, 1984).

Nongenital Measures of Deviant Arousal

As is clear from the preceding discussion, laboratory studies of deviant arousal have been largely dominated by the investigation of tumescence measures in response to a variety of stimulus modalities and types. Despite the major advantages of penile erection as a measure of sexual interest or preference, a number of studies have examined the use of nongenital psychophysiological measures in this context. Some reasons offered for investigating alternative measures are briefly as follows. First, while penile erection measures provide information specific to sexual arousal, it may be of value to assess other dimensions of the subjects' emotional response (e.g., anxiety or anger) to certain stimuli given current conceptualizations of the etiology of sexual deviation. Second, there are some subjects who typically show little or no tumescence in the standard laboratory situation. In some instances this is due to self-consciousness or embarrassment, and in other cases it may be indicative of an elevated threshold for erectile response to visual or auditory stimuli.

In either event, the use of alternative psychophysiological measures offers some possibility of assessing deviant sexual interest in the absence of erections. Moreover, the inclusion of related autonomic measures may provide a solution to the problem of response faking, as these measures may differentiate between simple lack of interest and intentional dissimulation on the part of a subject. Two types of measures have been particularly investigated: GSRs and pupillometry.

GSR RESPONSES IN THE ASSESSMENT OF DEVIANT AROUSAL

The first study to systematically compare the GSRs of paraphiliac and nonparaphiliac subjects was reported by Kercher and Walker (1973). These authors presented heterosexual slides to convicted rapists and a control group of individuals incarcerated for nonsexual offenses, while measuring tumescence, palmar skin resistance, and attitudinal responses on a series of semantic differential scales. The results were surprising in several respects. First, the penile tumescence measure failed to discriminate between the rapists and controls, in contrast to the studies reported above. In fact, several of the subjects in both groups showed penile circumference decreases during presentation of the erotic slides, which the authors interpreted as possibly reflecting a "startle" response to the explicit sexual stimuli. On the other hand, significant group differences were found on both the GSR measures and semantic differential ratings of the sexual stimuli, with the rapists showing greater skin resistance responses and more negative attitudinal reactions to the erotic slides. Two alternative explanations for this pattern of results were offered: Either the rapists found the erotic stimuli more unpleasant than did the controls, or the circumstances of testing could have produced greater anxiety for the rapists.

GSR responses were also found to differentiate the reactions of three groups—transsexuals, homosexuals, and heterosexual controls—to brief film sequences of male and female nudes (Barr & Blaszczynski, 1976). In this study, palmar skin resistance was compared to penile volume responses, as measured by the McConaghy volumetric plethysmograph (described in Chapter 3). Whereas both the homosexual and heterosexual subjects showed increased GSR responding to the preferred sexual stimulus the transsexuals tended to show greater GSR responses to the female (nonpreferred) films. Of the three groups, the transsexuals showed the highest sexual preference scores (degree of relative tumescence) to the male stimuli, followed by the homosexual group. Heterosexual controls showed much greater tumescence in response to the female stimuli, as predicted. This apparent inconsistency between GSR and tumescence measures has been interpreted by the authors as indicating the considerable nonsexual interest of the transsexuals in the female bodies and clothing shown in the stimuli, despite the relatively greater erotic appeal of the males.

Before concluding that the measurement of GSR can serve as a useful adjunct in the assessment of deviant arousal patterns, we should note that at least one study has failed to support its use in this context. Specifically, Quinsey, Steinman, Bergersen, and Holmes (1975) compared penile circumference and skin conductance responses to a variety of stimuli in three groups: incarcerated child molesters, inmates of the same institution incarcerated for nonsexual offenses, and normal controls. While the penile circumference measure clearly differentiated the responses of the child molesters to slides of young children, the skin conductance measure did not. Furthermore, while this study confirmed the greater reliability of tumescence measures of sexual preference in comparison with the subjects' self-ratings of arousal, the skin conductance measure again failed to discriminate responses among or within the groups.

PUPILLOMETRIC RESPONSES

As described in Chapter 5, studies by Hess and his colleagues (Hess & Polt, 1960; Hess et al., 1965) have suggested that changes in pupil size can be related to the degree of sexual interest in a specific stimulus. Positive results for the role of pupillometry in assessing deviant sexual arousal have similarly been reported by Atwood and Howell (1971). In this study, pedophiles were found to show pupillary constriction in response to pictures of adult females, whereas other types of offenders showed the more typical dilation pattern to age-appropriate erotic stimuli.

O'Neill and Hinton (1977) assessed both tumescence responses and pupil dilation in a group of heterosexual sex offenders (rapists and exhibitionists). A noteworthy aspect of this study was the use of an unobtrusive infrared video technique for monitoring pupil size. Results indicated significant pupil dilation in response to both heterosexual and homosexual slides, again suggesting a lack of specificity with this measure. Finally, the most recent study of this type (Lucas et al., 1983) compared pupillary responses in heterosexual and homosexual pedophiles; it was found that the pupil dilation responses in the homosexual group differentiated their preference for slides of male versus female children. However, for reasons unexplained, the heterosexual pedophile group showed equally large dilation responses to prepubescent and adolescent, as well as male and female, slides.

COMMENT

Overall, it appears that neither GSR nor pupillary responses are sufficiently robust to be of value in the differential diagnosis of paraphiliac sexual interest. With the exception of the results reported by Kercher and Walker (1973), penile tumescence measures have consistently proven to be more reliable than other autonomic measures in delineating deviant sexual preferences. On the other hand, several studies have indicated that other aspects of the subjects' emotional response to the stimulus may be reflected in concurrent measures of GSR or pupil dilation. Further studies are required to determine whether these aspects of the subjects' response are related to behavior outside the laboratory, and whether these measures have any role in differentiating the responses of subjects who attempt to fake.

PSYCHOPHYSIOLOGICAL MEASURES IN THE TREATMENT OF SEXUAL DEVIATION

As would be expected, the questions surrounding the choice and mode of treatment for paraphiliacs are equally controversial. Particularly in the case of sex offenders who have been arrested or convicted of crimes such as rape and child sexual abuse, there is currently intense disagreement concerning the desirability of criminal incarceration versus medical or psychiatric treatment for the offenders. Arguing in favor of a treatment approach, Abel, Mittelman, and Becker (1985) point to two important facts: first, that incarceration has generally not been an effective deterrent to the commission of these offenses; and, second, that a large percentage of sex crimes are committed by repeat offenders, among whom the recidivism rates after serving prison terms have traditionally been extremely high. The treatment program described by Abel and colleagues (Abel, Blanchard, & Becker, 1977; Abel, Becker, et al., 1981) is aimed specifically at those offenders with the highest frequency and longest duration of deviant behavior, many of whom have committed several hundred offenses over 10 years or more (Abel et al., 1985). By reducing the probability of such individuals' reoffending, Abel and his colleagues have provided important justification for the further use of psychiatric treatment in this context.

Concerning the choice of treatment modalities for specific offenders, key questions include the relative efficacy of strategies to suppress deviant arousal versus attempts to develop more appropriate sexual outlets; the efficacy and desirability of various forms of aversive conditioning; the value of pharmacological interventions, either alone or in combination with other forms of therapy; and the use of psychophysiological measures of arousal as an integral part of treatment. Despite the considerable controversy surrounding these issues, researchers generally agree that some form of directive intervention, usually multifaceted behavior therapy, is preferable to nondirective or psychoanalytic therapy; that clients' self-reports should not be relied on as the sole source of data; and that systematic maintenance and follow-up strategies are of prime importance (e.g., Quinsey & Marshall, 1983). Although it is beyond the scope of this chapter to review completely the recent literature on treatment of sex offenders, those studies that have incorporated laboratory psychophysiological methods in some aspect of the treatment warrant discussion here.

Aversive Conditioning in the Treatment of Sexual Deviations

Early case reports of aversive conditioning for homosexuality (Max, 1935) and fetishism (Raymond, 1956) indicated the possibility of modifying sexual interest in motivated individuals through systematic pairing of undesired stimuli with aversive consequences. However, it was not until the late 1960s that the first systematic research was conducted at the Maudsley Hospital in London to evaluate the effects of aversive conditioning on various components of deviant arousal and behavior (Marks & Gelder, 1967; Marks, Gelder, & Bancroft, 1970). Despite the relative crudity of the treatment approach employed and the confounding of patient selection factors, the Maudsley studies remain a model of scientific care and precision, and set the stage for much of the future treatment outcome research in the area.

The subjects for this research were a mixed group of transsexuals, transvestites, sadomasochists, and fetishists, all of whom were admitted as inpatients to the Maudsley Hospital for approximately 3 weeks of treatment. Aversive conditioning sessions were conducted twice daily, with electric shocks being administered to each patient's forearm or leg at an intensity selected as "unpleasant but not unduly painful." Two types of conditioning trials were employed: "practice" trials, in which the patients were required to cross-dress or fondle fetishist items in the laboratory, and "fantasy" trials, in which patients imagined various deviant activities. Shocks were administered at random intervals during both conditions, and were continued until the patient terminated all deviant behavior or fantasies (escape conditioning). Over the course of treatment, conditioning progressed from the most critical aspects of deviant behavior (e.g., cross-dressing) to the less disturbing aspects (e.g., attraction to female undergarments). Assessments were conducted throughout the conditioning trials of the frequency of deviant behavior and fantasies, as well as of penile tumescence responses to deviant and nondeviant stimuli; attitudinal reactions were monitored by means of semantic differential scales. Follow-up assessment were continued for approximately 2 years after treatment, and included evaluations of the patients' sexual and marital adjustment.

A number of interesting findings were reported. First, of the different patient groups included in the study, the transsexuals proved to be the most resistant to treatment and showed virtually no change overall, while the transvestites and fetishists showed the best response to treatment. The specificity of treatment effects was also demonstrated, as erection latencies and magnitude to a particular stimulus were shown to be affected only when conditioning was introduced for that stimulus. Changes in fantasy and attitudes usually preceded changes in tumescence, and were in the same direction. Suppression of deviant arousal did not appear to influence the development of nondeviant arousal patterns, as those patients with histories of dysfunctional or absent heterosexual relationships continued to have social and sexual adjustment difficulties following treatment. Finally, treatment effects for the successful patients were generally maintained for 2 years or more, despite minor relapses (Marks *et al.*, 1970).

Several early studies also attempted to modify homosexual preferences by means of aversive conditioning procedures (Feldman & MacCullough, 1965; McConaghy, 1971; Tanner, 1973). There are numerous problems in interpreting the results of this research, however: The response contingencies used varied from one study to another, as did the criteria for patient selection and therapeutic outcome. Feldman and MacCullough (1965), for example, developed an aversive conditioning procedure for the treatment of homosexuality that was based on the laboratory paradigm of animal avoidance learning. This treatment was judged to be only moderately effective in modifying sexual orientation in those homosexuals with previous heterosexual experience. No objective erection measures were used in this study. A subsequent comparison of the effects of avoidance learning, classical conditioning, and backward conditioning (McConaghy, 1971) showed no difference among treatments, as assessed by both volumetric plethysmography and clinical outcome. Furthermore, Tanner (1973) showed that avoidance conditioning for homosexuals was most effective with relatively high levels of shock intensity, despite the fact that Feldman and MacCullough and others have argued for the use of low-intensity shocks. Finally, it is noteworthy that very few studies have been conducted on aversion therapy for homosexuals since 1975, in view of the changing attitudes in the past decade toward the diagnosis of homosexuality.

Signaled punishment procedures have also been used in several treatment studies with mixed subject groups. Callahan and Leitenberg (1973), using a within-subject crossover design, compared the effects of contingent shock for erections to deviant slides with "covert sensitization," an imagery-based aversive conditioning procedure (see below). The subjects for this study included two exhibitionists, one transvestite, two homosexuals, and one pedophile. Despite the heterogeneity of the subject group, results indicated that the two treatments produced similar levels of erectile suppression to the deviant stimuli, although the covert sensitization procedure appeared to produce somewhat greater suppression of deviant urges. Similarly, Quinsey *et al.* (1980) compared the effects of signaled punishment of deviant arousal with biofeedback in the treatment of child molesters. The signaled punishment procedure again proved to be moderately effective, as assessed by both erectile response and clinical outcome. In this study, however, a combination of signaled punishment and tumescence biofeedback proved to be optimally effective.

Covert Sensitization

Although classical conditioning approaches to the modification of deviant arousal have generally produced disappointing results (e.g., Marshall, 1974; Quinsey, Bergersen, & Steinman, 1976), covert sensitization has been found to be moderately effective in a number of studies. Covert sensitization is viewed as a form of classical conditioning, in which aversive imagery is systematically paired with imaginal presentations of the deviant stimuli. The technique was first used in a case study by Gold and Neufeld (1965), although the term "covert sensitization" was subsequently coined by Cautela (1967), who used the technique for reducing homosexual urges in three patients. Further case study reports attested to the clinical utility of this procedure with sadistic, pedophiliac, and homosexual patients (Davison, 1968; Barlow *et al.*, 1969; Barlow, Agras, Leitenberg, Callahan, & Moore, 1972). In addition, as described above, Callahan and Leitenberg (1973) found covert sensitization to be about as effective as signaled punishment on both objective and subjective measures of deviant arousal. More recently, McConaghy *et al.* (1981) compared covert sensitization with a classical conditioning procedure for reducing homosexual urges, and found both treatments to be equally effective.

The most compelling evidence to date of the effectiveness of covert sensitization comes from a study by Brownell, Hayes, and Barlow (1977). Using a single-subject, multiple-baseline methodology to evaluate the treatment of five patients with mixed paraphilias, these authors found that covert sensitization produced marked suppression of deviant arousal in all but one of the cases, and that these effects were specific to the arousal patterns being treated. Changes in erectile response were highly correlated with self-report for all patients. An important additional finding was that reductions in deviant arousal were not associated with any significant increase in nondeviant, heterosexual arousal, which required additional treatment by means of orgasmic reconditioning. The clinical outcome with these patients was highly satisfactory, as there were no reports of a return to deviant behavior during treatment or at a 6-month follow-up.

Maletzky (1980) has described a variation of this procedure, termed "assisted covert sensitization," in which the usual pairing of deviant and aversive imagery is augmented by presentation of a foul odor such as valeric acid. Assisted covert sensitization has been used extensively in the treatment of exhibitionism, and the author has described one study in which 20 exhibitionists provided both penile tumescence and self-report data at regular intervals throughout treatment and follow-up. Although the results indicated an overall reduction in frequency of deviant behavior and tumescence response to exhibitionist fantasies, there were several individual cases in which patients continued to expose themselves, despite the absence of tumescence in the laboratory. Furthermore, there was no apparent relationship between the strength of erection at baseline and the response to treatment or probability of remission.

Masturbatory Satiation

A relative newcomer to the field of aversive conditioning approaches, "masturbatory satiation" has rapidly gained acceptance as a powerful and cost-effective technique for the treatment of most paraphilias (Abel et al., 1985). The procedure was initially developed by Marshall (Marshall & Barbaree, 1978; Marshall, 1979), and was designed to associate boredom and "satiation" effects with a patient's preferred deviant fantasies. Following the usual psychophysiological assessment, the patient is seated in a darkened laboratory and instructed to commence masturbating while verbalizing aloud every imaginable variation of the deviant fantasy themes. The verbalized fantasies are monitored throughout via an intercom system to assess thematic content and to insure compliance. Treatment sessions are continued for at least 1 hour at a time, and include continued masturbation and verbalization: "Even if he ejaculated he was to continue, stopping only to wipe himself clean if he found this necessary" (Marshall, 1979, p. 308).

The findings from a series of case studies evaluating this technique in the treatment of patients with multiple deviations indicate that the procedure was associated with rapid and complete suppression of the deviant arousal patterns, and that the suppression effects were specific to the targeted deviant fantasies. In one instance masturbatory satiation was associated with a concomitant increase in arousal to appropriate stimuli, while in another case it was not. In general, the author recommends using the technique in conjunction with other interventions designed to facilitate positive behavior changes, such as assertiveness training (Marshall, 1979).

Biofeedback Control of Erection

Since it has been demonstrated that feedback and reward procedures can be an effective means for developing voluntary control of erection in normal males (Rosen, 1973; Rosen et al., 1975), several studies have investigated the use of biofeedback for control of tumescence in the treatment of paraphilias. Two early studies with homosexual patients (Quinn et al., 1970;

Barlow, Agras, Abel, Blanchard, & Young, 1975) attempted to increase erections to heterosexual stimuli by means of feedback and reward procedures. Although the results of the first study suggested that the operant conditioning technique could produce some degree of heterosexual arousal in two patients, the lack of experimental controls and confounding of biofeedback with other treatment interventions prohibit strong conclusions about treatment efficacy. In the series of case studies described by Barlow *et al.* (1975), biofeedback and reinforcement procedures were found to be largely ineffective for increasing heterosexual arousal.

Rosen and Kopel (1977) attempted to develop voluntary suppression of arousal in a transvestite–exhibitionist by means of contingent feedback procedures. The stimulus training materials included a videotape of the patient's complete cross-dressing script and two brief films of explicit heterosexual and homosexual intercourse. Analogue feedback in the form of a tape-recorded alarm clock bell was provided during presentation of the transvestite stimulus. The patient was instructed to minimize the sound of the bell, while paying close attention to the videotape at all times. Twelve sessions of treatment resulted in complete suppression of tumescence, as well as markedly diminished subjective arousal. After 2 years of apparently successful follow-up, however, the patient's wife disclosed that he had resumed cross-dressing and exposure, and had deliberately deceived the therapists during the greater part of the follow-up period. In addition to illustrating the potential limitations of biofeedback treatment for the paraphilias, this case study presents a dramatic example of the unreliability of self-report as a treatment outcome measure.

A more successful outcome was reported by Laws (1980), who used visual analogue feedback for training self-control of arousal in a bisexual pedophile. A multiple-baseline case study approach was used to target specific changes in tumescence to deviant stimuli during an intensive training period lasting over 88 days. In the course of this lengthy treatment period, the patient appeared to have improvised a form of self-administered covert sensitization; this may have been the critical therapeutic element, with the biofeedback procedure adding only confirmation of treatment effectiveness.

Only one study to date has evaluated the effectiveness of biofeedback in a controlled outcome design (Quinsey *et al.*, 1980). The patients for this study were hospitalized child molesters, who were treated by means of biofeedback alone or biofeedback in combination with signaled punishment aversion therapy. Feedback was provided by means of light signals of different colors, and signaled punishment was presented in the form of mild electric shocks to a patient's forearm whenever tumescence exceeded a preset criterion. Results indicated that biofeedback alone was relatively ineffective in modifying deviant arousal, but that the combination of biofeedback and signaled punishment appeared to produce optimal results.

238

Techniques for Increasing Nondeviant Arousal

Following the model of sexual deviance proposed by Barlow (1974, 1977), treatment of the paraphilias has generally focused on the suppression of deviant arousal by one or more of the techniques described above. It has frequently been observed, however, that reductions in deviant arousal per se do not necessarily lead to increased nondeviant arousal (Brownell et al., 1977; Abel et al., 1985). Several approaches have therefore been developed to facilitate positive arousal patterns in paraphiliacs.

On the basis of the early observations by Rachman (1966) and Rachman and Hodgson (1968) on conditioning of fetishistic arousal in a laboratory study with normal males, Beech, Watts, and Poole (1971) used a classical conditioning paradigm for developing sexual arousal to nondeviant stimuli in a pedophilic patient. Using nude pictures of adult females as the CSs, and photographs of young girls as the UCSs, the authors were able to demonstrate increases in tumescence to the adult stimulus after 3 weeks of treatment. This more adaptive arousal pattern was found to generalize to behavior outside the laboratory, as the patient experienced heterosexual intercourse for the first time shortly after treatment. Unfortunately, subsequent attempts to replicate this procedure with larger clinical samples have been generally unsuccessful (Marshall, 1974; Herman, Barlow, & Agras, 1974).

"Stimulus fading," a procedure derived from basic research on errorless discrimination training, has been effectively used for increasing heterosexual arousal in homosexuals (Barlow & Agras, 1973). The key element in this procedure is the gradual introduction ("fading") of a heterosexual stimulus while the patient maintains arousal to a homosexual stimulus (see Figure 9.4). This is accomplished by systematically altering the light intensity of two slide projectors, one of which is used for projecting the homosexual slide and the other for projecting the heterosexual slide. The patient's tumescence response is monitored throughout and is used as the criterion for advancing the light intensity of the heterosexual stimulus. The authors reported the use of this innovative procedure in the treatment of three homosexuals, two of whom appeared to develop some degree of heterosexual responsivity following treatment.

The most widely used technique at present for increasing nondeviant arousal is "masturbatory conditioning." This technique was introduced by Marquis (1970), who instructed his patients at first to shift their masturbatory fantasies from a deviant to a nondeviant theme at the moment of orgasmic inevitability. Over the course of therapy, the patients were instructed to introduce the nondeviant stimulus at progressively earlier intervals, until they were able to masturbate with nondeviant fantasies alone. The first controlled study of this procedure was reported by Conrad and Wincze (1976), who applied masturbatory conditioning in the treatment

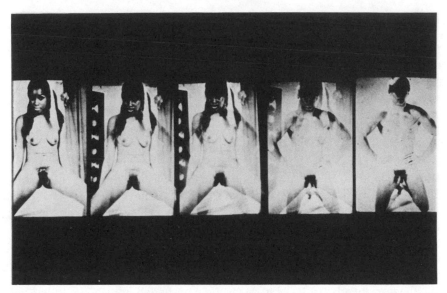

Figure 9.4. Stimuli for fading. The series of slides depicts gradual transformation of a nude female to a nude male figure. Courtesy David H. Barlow.

of four male homosexuals. Despite reports of improved sexual adjustment in three cases, laboratory erection measures failed to show any significant changes. Perhaps because of its use in the context of changing sexual preference in homosexual patients, the authors concluded that the technique is relatively ineffectual and of little clinical value.

More positive results have been obtained by Laws and his colleagues (Laws & O'Neil, 1981; Laws, 1985), using a variation of masturbatory conditioning for the development of nondeviant arousal in pedophiles and rapists. The Laws variation, described as "sexual fantasy alternation," consists of controlled trials of masturbation to orgasm, in which weekly blocks of five trials with a deviant theme are alternated with similar blocks of trials with nondeviant fantasy themes. Psychophysiological assessments of deviant and nondeviant arousal are conducted after each treatment session. Laws and O'Neil have presented the results of controlled cross studies on the use of this procedure with six hospitalized offenders, all of whom showed both marked reductions of deviant arousal and increased response to nondeviant themes. Based on the results reported by Laws and others, Abel *et al.* (1985) have recommended this procedure as the treatment of choice for increasing nondeviant arousal in paraphiliac patients.

In addition to treatment techniques for decreasing deviant arousal or increasing nondeviant arousal, a wide range of adjunctive therapy proce-

240

dures have been recommended, including social skills training (Becker, Abel, Blanchard, Murphy, & Coleman, 1978; Whitman & Quinsey, 1981), assertiveness training (Abel, Blanchard, & Becker, 1977), tension reduction management (Rosen & Fracher, 1983), and cognitive restructuring (Pithers, Marques, Gibat, & Marlatt, 1983). In addition, it has frequently been noted that alcohol and drug abuse contribute significantly to relapse (e.g., Abel *et al.*, 1985), and referral for concurrent treatment of these problems is strongly recommended.

THE USE OF ANTIANDROGENS IN THE TREATMENT OF SEXUAL DEVIATION

Over the years, a number of biological therapies have been employed in the treatment of sexual deviations, such as castration, brain surgery, and various forms of pharmacological intervention (see Freund, 1980, and Berlin, 1983, for recent reviews of these treatments). Of the various pharmacological approaches, medroxyprogesterone acetate (MPA), an antiandrogenic drug, has been used with increasing frequency in the United States, while a similar drug, cyproterone acetate (CPA), is widely used in Europe. MPA is a synthetic progestinic steroid that was first reported by Money (1968) to be effective in the treatment of male sex offenders. According to Money and Bennett (1981), the drug produces a temporary cessation of libido (and erectile dysfunction in some cases), during which psychotherapy can be instituted. Although it is clear that both MPA and CPA have significant testosterone-lowering effects, the mechanisms of their action require further explanation. Freund (1980) has proposed that both drugs reduce the production of testosterone from its precursors, but that MPA appears to affect LH output by the pituitary, while CPA seems to have a greater effect on the output of FSH.

Berlin and Meinecke (1981) have reported on the effects of administering large doses (200–500 mg/week) of MPA for periods of up to 5 years to 20 chronic paraphiliacs. Most of the patients in this study were child molesters with very high frequencies of offenses prior to treatment. Although the administration of MPA was largely successful, as 17 of the 20 patients showed no recurrences of deviant behavior while on the drug, most of the patients in the study were reported to have relapsed shortly after discontinuation of the drug. The authors interpret this finding as consistent with the notion that MPA functions as a "sexual appetite suppressant," whose effects appear to be temporary and almost completely reversible. Berlin (1983) also notes that no large-scale double-blind studies of the effects of MPA have been conducted to date, and that the effects of subject or therapist expectations may have confounded the results obtained thus far.

241

Regarding the psychophysiological effects of MPA treatment, Wincze, Bansal, and Malamud (1986) have conducted a preliminary study of NPT and waking responses to erotic stimuli in male sex offenders. The subjects for this study were three chronic child molesters who ranged in age from 36 to 60, and who were admitted to an open psychiatric ward for the duration of the study. MPA was administered in oral form (160 mg/day) over approximately 30 days of treatment. A single-subject, multiple-baseline methodology was employed, and measures were obtained of pedophiliac urges, subjective and physiological responses to deviant films and slides, and NPT for two of the subjects. The results indicated that erectile responses to the erotic stimuli were maintained, despite a significant decrease in subjective reports of arousal. The authors interpret this latter change as most likely due to expectation effects. On the other hand, a striking decrease in the amplitude of the NPT response was observed in both patients on whom this measure was taken; this decrease was found to be correlated with diminished testosterone levels in both cases. It thus appears that while MPA has the effect of altering physiological responsivity at a neurohormonal level, it is possible that erectile capacity is maintained in the face of strong psychological stimulation. This intriguing pattern of results awaits further replication.

Overall, the clinical use of antiandrogenic agents appears to hold considerable promise for future research and treatment of the more dangerous and socially disapproved of the paraphilias. Berlin (1983) has noted that the potential side effects of MPA (e.g., weight gain, infertility, increased diabetes risk) raise serious ethical problems for long-term use of the drug in many cases. Nevertheless, in view of the questionable efficacy of and negative social attitudes toward conditioning techniques, it is likely that greater attention will be paid to such pharmacological treatments. For this reason, it is important that well-controlled psychophysiological studies of the effects of these drugs be conducted, and that such studies be used to evaluate both the mechanisms of action and outcome of treatment.

SUMMARY AND CONCLUSION

This chapter has considered the application of concepts and methods of sexual psychophysiology to paraphiliac behaviors, such as rape, child molestation, and exhibitionism. In view of the change in professional attitudes toward viewing homosexuality as a viable alternative of normal sexuality, studies of sexual deviance in the past decade have rarely focused on subjects with age-appropriate homosexual preferences alone. On the other hand, increasing social concern with the prevalence and potential harmfulness of rape and child molestation has highlighted the value of psychophysiological methods in defining, assessing, and treating the aggressive and socially unacceptable paraphilias.

Much of the research in this area has been guided by the model of sexual deviance proposed by Barlow (1974, 1977). A key assumption in this model is that paraphiliac behavior is primarily mediated by genital arousal to deviant stimuli. Although this assumption has been useful in guiding research on the assessment of deviant arousal patterns, and appears to be well founded in the case of pedophiliac and aggressive sexual deviations, it is less applicable to exhibitionism, transsexualism, and other paraphilias. Research has also indicated that the conditions of assessment— in particular, stimulus modality and instructional set of the subject—may have a major effect on tumescence responses to deviant stimuli. In addition, several studies have suggested that response faking can present a major threat to the validity of genital arousal measures.

Unfortunately, little research has been conducted to date on other (nongenital) measures of deviant arousal. Specifically, GSR and pupil dilation have been shown to have limited value as concurrent measures of deviant arousal. Both of these measures, however, tend to reflect generalized autonomic arousal and do not adequately differentiate deviant sexual interest from other affective responses to the stimulus materials.

Treatment approaches for sexual deviation have also been greatly influenced by concepts and methods of sexual psychophysiology. Beginning with the early studies on aversive conditioning for suppression of deviant arousal, a number of innovative treatment techniques have been developed, such as covert sensitization and masturbatory satiation. In addition, procedures for enhancing nondeviant arousal, such as stimulus fading and orgasmic reconditioning, have assumed increasing importance in the overall approach to treatment. Laboratory erection measures have proven valuable in objective assessment of both the short-term and long-term impact of treatment, and have been found to have a degree of prognostic utility in a number of recent treatment studies.

Finally, the rationale and evidence for antiandrogenic therapy have been briefly discussed. Overall, it appears that most paraphiliac patients experience a temporary cessation of deviant sexual interest when given large doses of MPA or CPA. However, relapse usually occurs soon after the drug is withdrawn, and potentially serious side effects limit the clinical use of these drugs. One recent study of the effects of MPA on both waking and sleep (NPT) measures of arousal suggests that the effects of the drug are subtle and complex; this may lead to a re-examination of certain basic questions concerning the psychohormonal mediation of sexual arousal.

CHAPTER TEN

Male Sexual Dysfunction

The erection is considered by almost all men as the star performer in the drama of sex and we all know what happens to a show when the star performer doesn't make an appearance.—Zilbergeld (1978, p. 53)

References to erectile dysfunction and other forms of male sexual disorders can be traced to the time of the Old Testament and the writings of Hippocrates (Gee, 1975); however, direct and detailed discussions of these disorders did not appear until publication of Kinsey *et al.*'s interview findings in 1948. Since that time, the reported prevalence of male sexual dysfunction has increased— a rise that is attributable, perhaps, to heightened public awareness of and interest in sexuality. The application of psychophysiological methods in the evaluation and treatment of male sexual dysfunction represents a clear example of the success of this approach in practice, while also illustrating a number of important methodological issues.

In contrast with other areas of application, the use of sexual psychophysiology for assessing disorders of erectile functioning has gained considerable professional acceptance. Sexual psychophysiological methods are used in classification and differential diagnosis of etiological factors in dysfunction; in analysis of laboratory analogues of etiological factors in dysfunction; in treatment evaluation; and in direct therapeutic intervention. These advances have occurred in conjunction with developments in measurement technology and only recently have begun to receive recognition in related medical specialties, such as urology. A review of these applications highlights the uneven pace of growth across relevant aspects of the field and includes discussion of emerging themes for practice and research.

CLASSIFICATION, NOSOLOGY, AND DIAGNOSIS

Definitions of Dysfunction

Sophistication in formal classification and nosology for the full range of sexual disorders is a relatively new development. Based in part on the work of Kaplan (1979) and Masters and Johnson (1966, 1970), DSM-III (American Psychiatric Association, 1980) divides the Psychosexual Dysfunctions into disorders of appetite, excitement, orgasm, and ejaculation; this is certainly an advance over the single, general diagnosis of Psychophysiologic Genito-urinary Disorder provided by DSM-II (American Psychiatric Association, 1968). While the DSM-III classification represents considerable progress in specifying disorders according to the point of the sexual response cycle at which impaired functioning occurs, further information is needed to specify the unique physiological and psychological features of each form of sexual dysfunction. The most widely studied of these disorders is erectile dysfunction; this attention is a direct result of applications of sexual psychophysiology to diagnostic assessment.

In presenting issues concerning the current classification system, the first consideration is the definition of "dysfunction"—specifically, the need to distinguish between "usual" and "persistent" sexual problems. Frank *et al.* (1978), for example, surveyed 100 predominantly white, well-educated, "happily married" couples; in this survey, 36% of the men reported difficulties in ejaculating too quickly, and 16% reported problems in achieving and/or maintaining erections. Thirty years earlier, Kinsey and colleagues had reported that 35% of a general community sample reported "incidental" erectile failure, 7.1% reported "more than incidental" erectile failure, and 1.6% of males in this sample experienced chronic impotence (Gebhard & Johnson, 1979; Kinsey *et al.*, 1948).

Given that male sexual disorders are apparently quite prevalent in the population at large, diagnostic criteria need to specify the parameters that distinguish clinical from nonclinical forms of dysfunction. It is conceivable that with further refinements of the classification system, a diagnosis of dysfunction may come to depend on qualitative factors in sexual interaction (e.g., inhibited desire or sexual dissatisfaction) in the context of reduced genital responsivity under specific circumstances (e.g., during sexual encounters with a partner). The careful use of sexual psychophysiology in exploring both qualitative and quantitative differences in "usual" and "persistent" sexual problems may be fruitful in this respect.

Erectile Dysfunction

DEFINITION

Erectile failure, or inhibited sexual excitement in the male, has received the most intensive empirical scrutiny from a psychobiological perspective. By definition, "erectile dysfunction" can be subdivided into two forms. The diagnosis of "primary erectile dysfunction" is generally reserved for cases where no history of adequate responding has been noted, whereas prior intervals of erectile adequacy are typically present in cases of "secondary dysfunction" (Masters & Johnson, 1970). Other authors, such as

Rosen and Hall (1984), distinguish between "global impotence," indicating the complete absence of adequate functioning, and "secondary dysfunction," or the loss of tumescence in at least 25% of attempts at intercourse.

To date, one direct comparison of autonomic responding in these two groups has been reported. Kockott *et al.* (1980) presented a full range of physiological measures for five patient groups (men with primary and secondary erectile failure, men with premature ejaculation during all sexual encounters and during intercourse only and men with diabetes-related erectile failure), plus two age-matched control groups of sexually functional men. Results of this study indicated that the sample with primary erectile dysfunction was indistinguishable from sexually functional controls on several tumescence parameters. In contrast, the sample with secondary dysfunction had reduced circumference changes, longer latencies to erection, and shorter duration of erectile response, relative to the normal males. Comparison of the erection patterns of this group with those of the diabetic men did not reveal significant differences in penile responding.

Thus, a striking difference emerged between the men with primary and secondary dysfunction: The former showed relatively normal levels of arousal, and the latter, surprisingly, appeared more similar to organically impaired men. Kockott *et al.* interpreted these differences as suggesting different emotional reactions accompanying primary and secondary erectile dysfunction, although the exact nature of these differences was not specified. This report suggests the need for exploration of factors such as cognitive distractions, specific attitudes toward sexuality, and other processes that influence tumescence, with specific reference to the various forms of erectile dysfunction.

Given that males with primary dysfunction are treated less successfully by conventional sex therapy techniques than are men with secondary dysfunction (Cooper, 1981), this type of psychophysiological comparison could conceivably assist in refining therapeutic approaches by more directly addressing individual treatment needs. For example, clinical observations suggest that men with primary dysfunction more easily habituate to sexual cues and have lower expectations for arousal than those with secondary erectile dysfunction (Kaplan, 1979); this indicates, perhaps, that newer techniques designed to diminish sensitivity response thresholds may be important in effectively addressing primary dysfunction. Future experimental studies addressing sensitization and habituation effects in both forms of erectile dysfunction would be useful in the development of newer forms of sex therapy.

A related examination of psychophysiological response patterns associated with erectile dysfunction has involved monitoring EEG asymmetry during sexual arousal in men with secondary erectile dysfunction and in sexually responsive and unresponsive normal controls (Cohen *et al.*, 1985). As discussed in Chapter 6, a pattern of right temporal activation was observed to accompany maximum tumescence in responsive normal subjects during visual stimuli in this study. In contrast, the dysfunctional sample showed significant activation in right temporal and occipital sites during erotic audiotapes, but not during video presentations. The authors suggest that these patterns of asymmetry may be indicative of increased cognitive activity, concurrent with negative affective responses in dysfunctional subjects. The interplay of central and autonomic determinants of sexual arousal is particularly interesting in this study and potentially can expand our understanding of cognitive–affective patterning in erectile dysfunction.

DIAGNOSIS

NPT Assessment. A key clinical issue in the assessment of erectile dysfunction is the differential diagnosis of psychogenic and organic etiologies (e.g., Wagner & Green, 1981). For example, Figure 10.1 outlines a flow chart model for the evaluation of impotency, highlighting the multifocus assessment that is necessary (Fracher *et al.*, 1981). An important component of this process is the evaluation of NPT, which is based on the occurrence of periodic nocturnal tumescence associated with REM sleep, as first described by Ohlmeyer *et al.* in 1944.

Nocturnal assessment of tumescence has been used to investigate the etiological determinants of erectile disorder (e.g., Fisher *et al.*, 1965; Karacan, 1978; Marshall *et al.*, 1981). The rationale for this procedure is that for psychogenically impotent men, the interpersonal, attitudinal, and emotional factors that might impair arousal during waking states generally will be inoperative during sleep, and normal patterns of nocturnal tumescence can occur. In contrast, for men with an organic basis for erectile failure, a diminished or absent sleep erection response is expected (Karacan, 1970).

In one of the earliest systematic reports, Jovanovic (1972) found diminished NPT in a sample of impotent patients; this trend was more marked in cases with known organic causes than in psychogenic cases, although the diagnostic significance of this difference was not established in this report because patients were not assigned to diagnostic groups. This study also demonstrated that as sleep progresses, the duration of NPT increases, with tumescence during the final uninterrupted REM cycle lasting an average of 45 minutes. The largest increase in NPT was correlated with the interval of slowest heart rate, usually occurring during the final complete REM cycle.

Common practice for an NPT evaluation is to schedule two or three consecutive nights of sleep laboratory assessment using EEG, electro-oculographic (EOG), EMG, and other physiological measures while simultaneously monitoring NPT (Fisher *et al.*, 1979; Hursch, Karacan, & Williams, 1972; Karacan, Hursch, Williams, & Thornby, 1972; Wasserman, Pollack, Spielman, & Weitzman, 1980b). Two or three nights are generally

247

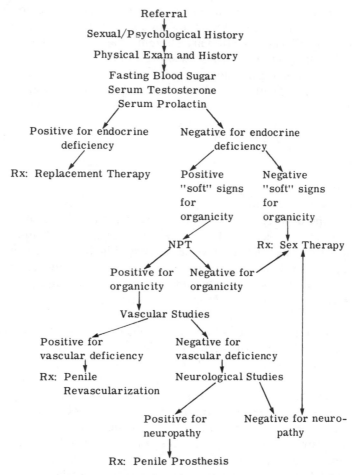

Figure 10.1. A flow chart model for comprehensive assessment of erectile dysfunction. Adapted from Fracher *et al.* (1981).

required to complete the assessment because of the "first-night effect," which may cause artifactual suppression of the tumescence response (Karacan *et al.,* 1978; Coble, McPartland, Silva, & Kupfer, 1974). This procedural detail minimizes the false-positive misidentification rate for organically based impotency, although by some estimates, up to 20% of patients may still be misclassified even with the addition of this procedure (e.g., Wasserman, Pollack, Spielman, & Weitzman, 1980a; Wasserman *et al.,* 1980b; Schmidt & Wise, 1981). For example, Kahn and Fisher (1969a) present case reports of two men with grossly impaired NPT responses who did not experience waking erectile failure. Other authors have similarly noted diminished NPT recordings in sexually functional men (e.g., Hursch *et al.*, 1972; Tulloch *et al.*, 1982).

Overall, the process of validating the NPT procedure has helped to refine the diagnostic significance of nocturnal tumescence in discriminating between forms of organic and psychogenic impotence. Fisher *et al.* (1975) and Karacan, Williams, Thornby, and Salis (1975) provided the first attempts to use NPT for this purpose. In each of these studies, patients were assessed for two or three nights in a sleep laboratory, and both reports indicated that the two groups could be distinguished on the basis of duration, frequency, and pattern of NPT response, which were then used to establish a diagnosis. Until recently, this type of correlational demonstration has provided the only evidence of the utility of NPT evaluation, and this has created some uncertainty about the external validity of the procedure.

Marshall *et al.* (1981) addressed this issue in a recent study, employing evaluations of etiological factors in erectile dysfunction by independent medical and psychiatric practitioners for group assignment. Organic causes included Peyronie disease, peripheral neuropathy resulting from advanced diabetes mellitus, and neurological dysfunction following aorta–femoral bypass surgery. Examples of identifiable psychogenic factors included chronic marital discord, depressive illness, and performance anxiety. In addition to patients from these two well-defined groups, the authors included a sample of patients with mixed etiology and a sample with an uncertain basis for their erectile dysfunction.

A series of decision rules was formulated to provide optimal discrimination between the known organic and psychogenic groups, using findings from NPT evaluations. First, a penile circumference change of less than 11.5 mm was coded as "organic," whereas tumescence responses exceeding this criterion were coded as "psychogenic." On this basis, 9 of 10 organic and 7 of 10 psychogenic patients were correctly classified. A second decision rule considerably improved diagnostic accuracy: Fewer than two NPT episodes per night classified a patient as "organic," while a "psychogenic" classification was made if three or more NPT episodes were observed. With this additional criterion, misclassification resulted for one psychogenic patient only. This study established the first stage in validation of NPT testing as a diagnostic tool. Further studies need to be conducted to investigate changes in NPT over time, in addition to the delineation of guidelines for its utility with patients with mixed and uncertain etiology.

Although the validation of NPT testing is in its early stages, concerns have been raised regarding the assumptions on which the NPT evaluation is based (e.g., Bancroft, 1983). Specifically, the procedure assumes a neurophysiological equivalence between nocturnal and waking erections. While it is recognized that NPT occurs independently of bladder distension (Karacan, 1970), questions have been raised concerning the relative contributions of central and autonomic innervation. Some authors have suggested that NPT may be regulated by an independent hypothalamic–limbic mechanism, and thus may be minimally related to erotic responding at the cortical level (e.g., Fisher *et al.*, 1979). Evidence for this hypothesis comes from the fact that extreme differences in erectile potential during waking and sleep states have been noted in some organically impaired patients (Sakheim, 1985). In addition, REM-related tumescence appears to have different topographical features from waking responses; the circumference changes in NPT are usually larger, and NPT is shorter in duration (Allen, 1981). Finally, for certain forms of neuropathy, patients are able to achieve adequate erectile responding while lying supine, but not while sitting, standing, or moving the legs and pelvis (Nath *et al.*, 1981). These data suggest that the assumption of equivalence between waking and nocturnal tumescence may need to be reconsidered. Further exploration of the basic physiological mechanisms involved in both states of tumescence appears warranted.

In evaluating the role of NPT in determining the treatment of choice for erectile failure, it is important to note that considerable individual variation exists in the form of the nocturnal erectile response. As illustrated by Karacan (1976, Karacan, 1978), the nocturnal procedure relies on the use of concurrent measures of penile circumference—specifically, two mercury strain gauges placed at the base and the tip of the penis. The use of two gauges allows for determination of structural deficits or disease states that may result in differential vasocongestion of the cavernous bodies. For example, localized fibrosis or a Peyronie obstruction may restrict vasocongestion in part of the corporus cavernosum and may not influence tumescence of the remainder of the erectile tissue (Wagner, 1981b). A sample polygraph record from a patient with organically based erectile dysfunction is included in Figure 10.2.

However, in diagnosis, additional information may be needed to augment circumferential measures. For example, it is common for significant circumference change to be noted, without adequate rigidity. A report by Wein *et al.* (1981) indicated that 17% of a sample of 134 patients with organically based impotence demonstrated significant penile expansion without rigidity adequate for vaginal penetration during NPT assessment. Conceivably, this type of diagnostic inaccuracy could result in misapplication of sex therapy and create continued frustration for the patient, whose impotence would thus be incorrectly diagnosed as psychogenic in origin.

Karacan (1978) has described the use of three additional strategies to address this concern. When the patient achieves a full erection on the third night of testing, he is awakened and asked to estimate the fullness of his erection. In addition, the buckling pressure test, described in Chapter 3, is used to determine the rigidity of the erection. Finally, the patient's erection is photographed to provide a permanent record of penile dimen-

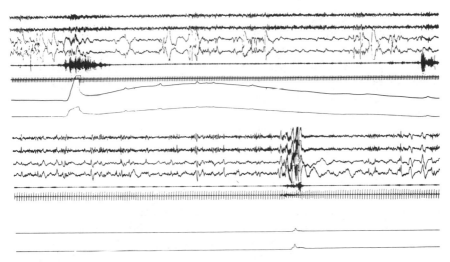

Figure 10.2. Representative sample of a polygraph record of NPT with simultaneous recording from two clinical patients. Upper eight channels: A portion of the record from one patient. The first two channels are EEG tracings from central (cortical) placements; channels 3 and 4 are EOG tracings from the outer canthi of the left and right eyes; channel 5 shows EMG tracings from a submentalis recording site; channel 6 shows EKG tracings from a modified V_4 placement; channel 7 is a DC tracing of penile circumference from the tip of the penis; and channel 8 shows circumference changes at the base of the penis. This portion of the record clearly illustrates REM sleep, associated in this case with a maximum penile tumescence response of about 15-mm circumference change, as well as with rapid detumescence. Lower eight channels: Record from another patient, illustrating a period of Stage 2 sleep, without concomitant changes in penile circumference.

sions. The addition of these strategies allows for the collection of important additional assessment information, although they increase the invasiveness of the procedure.

As noted by Wasserman *et al.* (1980a), approximately 20% of patients with impaired NPT are not subsequently diagnosed with organic disease. These results suggest that for about 80% of patients assessed, the NPT evaluation, with the inclusion of rigidity measures and other additional procedures, can be valuable in the process of differential diagnosis. The estimate of a 20% misidentification rate, however, suggests that exclusive reliance on this technique may be premature at present.

The question of clinical base rates for psychogenic and organic impotence also needs to be considered in evaluating the role of NPT in differential diagnosis. For example, one may question whether the NPT procedure improves the accuracy of prediction based simply on statistical base rates (e.g., Magee, 1980; Slag *et al.*, 1983; Legros, Mormont, &

Servais, 1978). As discussed by Meehl (1954) in regard to psychometric assessment, any clinically based diagnostic procedure needs to demonstrate sensitivity beyond that achievable with statistically based prediction methods. Given that organic causes of erectile dysfunction can be difficult to diagnose, especially those resulting from endocrine and neurological factors, an examination of the relative costs and benefits of NPT assessment appears warranted.

Since sleep laboratories are not equally accessible to all patients, the applicability of this procedure has been limited until recently. In the past several years, portable NPT monitors have become available commercially. For example, American Medical Systems and Event Systems, Inc., both manufacture portable NPT systems. These devices consist of two circumferential gauges, placed at the tip and the base of the penis; these are attached to a chart recorder, as in laboratory-based NPT studies. A major weakness of this approach, however, is the absence of EEG data to verify sleep staging. Thus, portable NPT assessments suffer inherently from being less definitive and more susceptible to false-positive findings than the laboratory-based procedure. Preliminary investigations of these portable devices have helped delimit their utility. Procci, Moss, Boyd, and Baron (1983), for example, examined consecutive-night reliability of measurement in a clinical sample of organically impaired patients and in sexually functional controls. For each of several aspects of the NPT response, consecutive-night correlations were high, suggesting that this procedure yields consistent results with repeated measurements.

A follow-up study (Procci & Martin, 1984) compared the findings from sexual history interviews with the results of NPT testing using a portable device. Unfortunately, 19% of one patient group had abnormal NPT findings in the face of reports of adequate sexual functioning, although the inaccuracy rates varied considerably across diagnostic categories. To date, no investigations of this type have included men with verified psychogenic impotence. This suggests that while portable NPT recording can serve as a first stage in screening, the clinician needs to exercise extreme caution in interpreting the findings from this procedure. Given the question raised above in regard to representative base rates for organic and psychogenic impotence, the possibility for false-positive identification appears to be a major risk of portable NPT systems.

To date, only one investigation has systematically compared laboratory and portable NPT findings—a necessary step for establishing the diagnostic potential of this alternative method. Marshall, McGrath, and Schillinger (1983) compared the results of laboratory and home NPT monitoring with 13 patients; home monitoring resulted in overestimation of NPT magnitude at the tip of the penis. The authors suggest that this was most likely due to the lack of EMG recording to distinguish between true NPT increases and movement artifact. NPT measured at the base of the penis was not affected by this confound and resulted in equally accurate classification with home and laboratory procedures. Related studies of this type are needed in order to examine the limits and utility of home monitoring systems.

Several recent reports have highlighted the importance of assessing related autonomic parameters in the differential diagnosis of erectile dysfunction. Schmidt and Wise (1981) detail sleep-associated events during NPT assessment of patients with secondary impotence; included in their measures were EOG, masseter EMG, EEG, air exchange, and an index of blood oxygen saturation. Of their patient sample, 46% showed diminished NPT, in conjunction with one or more of the following sleep parameters: frequent apnea and hypoventilation; decreased oxygen saturation; myoclonus; and a slow, stable heart rate. The authors suggest that in the absence of clear signs of organicity, CNS factors may be implicated in the etiology of erectile dysfunction.

A related study by Ware et al. (1984) reported an unusual pattern of skin conductance during sleep in a subgroup of organically impaired men. Unlike normal patterns, where electrodermal activity during Stage 2 sleep is elevated relative to activity during REM sleep, these patients showed fewer spontaneous electrodermal responses during Stage 2. There was no obvious relation between this pattern and various hormonal levels, disease state, penile blood pressure, or psychological factors, again suggesting the potential importance of CNS processes. These reports highlight the importance of including a full range of polysomnographic measures during NPT assessment—an inclusion that practically necessitates the use of a sleep laboratory.

As these advances in measurement technology illustrate, the NPT procedure has brought sexual psychophysiology into new stature in the medical and psychological fields (e.g., Geer & Messé, 1982). With this change has come a variety of simplified assessment techniques, such as the snap gauge to measure penile rigidity and circumference changes (Ek, Bradley, & Krane, 1983) (see Figure 10.3), a similar device termed an "erectometer" (Morales, Marshall, Surridge, & Fenemore; 1983), and even the use of a ring of stamps that encircles the penis during sleep (Barry et al., 1980; Marshall, et al., 1983). The key methodological issue with each of these devices is potential inaccuracy, resulting from movement artifacts, improper placement of the gauge, or the possibility of repositioning of the gauge. Moreover, none of these devices permits the assessment of relevant sleep parameters, thus adding an additional source of error in measurement.

Given that the patient with a chronic history of erectile failure is often considered a candidate for penile implant surgery (cf. Bennett, 1982), the importance and irreversibility of this decision should warrant a comprehensive evaluation, using procedures that are maximally sensitive for de-

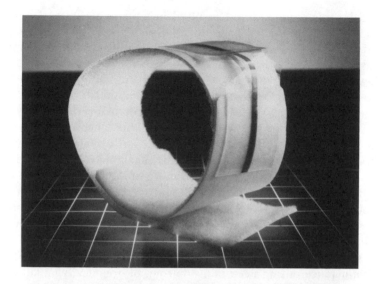

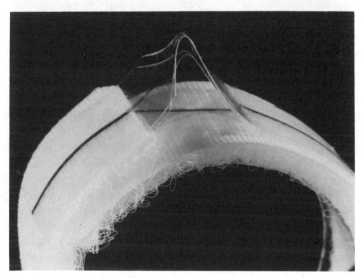

Figure 10.3. A snap gauge to measure penile circumference changes, as described in Ek *et al.* (1983).

tecting erectile potential. Ideally, all aspects relevant to the patient's sexual functioning, including the status of his primary relationship, sexual attitudes, communication skills, and perceptions of subjective sexual sensations, need to be assessed. The ease with which current additions to NPT technology allow practitioners to make differential diagnoses is deceptive and should not imply a secondary role for clinical interviews, careful reviews of a patient's history, and other forms of psychosocial assessment.

Waking Assessment Procedures. Recently, several authors have begun to examine the possibility of assessment procedures during the waking state for differential diagnosis of erectile potential. Graber and Kline-Graber (1981), for example, have reported that the majority of men with psychogenic erectile failure often experience erectile difficulty during sexual interactions, but not during masturbation. On the basis of this observation, Sakheim, Barlow, and Beck (1985) assessed the utility of a diurnal procedure for determining erectile potential. A combination of explicit erotic films and self-stimulation was utilized, and both sexually functional subjects and men with psychogenic erectile dysfunction were assessed. The results indicated that dysfunctional men could achieve significant tumescence under these conditions (in some cases, tumescence was equal to responding seen in sexually functional control subjects), and the authors suggested that this approach may be a useful adjunct to conventional assessment. A follow-up to this report (Sakheim, 1985) involved a sample of organically impaired men, a group of men with psychogenically based erectile failure, and an age-matched control group of sexually functional men. The results indicated that this procedure was as accurate as typical NPT results; that is, an 80% accuracy rate was observed in correctly identifying patients in each of the three groups. However, both false negatives and false positives were noted, and some men with verified organic pathology demonstrated significant erectile responsivity, while others with psychogenic dysfunction showed minimal tumescence.

A similar investigation has been reported by Wincze, Bansal, Balko, and Malhotra (1984). These authors compared genital responding to erotic stimuli and NPT in men with psychogenic and organic erectile dysfunction. In addition, a sample of men with erectile dysfunction of mixed etiology and a normal control sample were included. The results indicated that the psychogenic sample was the only group with differential tumescence responses during daytime and nocturnal assessment; NPT response was unimpaired in this sample, as would be expected. Interestingly, the sample with organic etiology showed normal levels of subjective arousal, indicating that the impact of dysfunction did not appear to influence stated desire to a significant extent. These reports suggest that waking assessment may prove useful in diagnosis, as an alternative to the more extensive NPT evaluation.

Throughout the literature on the assessment of erectile failure, frequent references have been made to observed discrepancies between subjective arousal and physiological responsivity in organic and psychogenic erectile dysfunction. For example, Sakheim (1985) and Wincze *et al.* (1984) have both noted that these two groups appear to construe subjective arousal in different fashions. In Sakheim's report, men with psychogenic problems showed less concordance between subjective and objective arousal measures during waking assessment than did the organic sample. Wincze *et al.*'s investigation, however, indicated that subjective arousal appeared to correspond more closely with NPT responding for psychogenically impaired men, but that this sample was less able to track tumescence during waking states. Men with vascular disease in this study showed the greatest discrepancies between subjective and tumescence measures during both the waking and sleep phases of the assessment.

The question of patterning of specific response parameters appears to be important in understanding the cognitive–affective processes operative in erectile dysfunction. Since it is clear that psychological factors can influence tumescence, irrespective of the etiology of dysfunction, the inclusion of some measure of subjective arousal in future studies of waking assessment appears to be a necessary element. This may advance our understanding of the experiential aspects of sexual arousal as well.

A related issue concerns potential psychological factors that may influence NPT, given that the NPT technique rests on the assumption that sleep bypasses the influence of psychological impediments to adequate responding. For example, it has been shown recently that various psychiatric states, such as depression, can result in diminished NPT responses, which can be reversed once the affective problem is treated (e.g., Roose, Glassman, Walsh, & Cullen, 1982; C. Fisher *et al.*, 1979; Wasserman *et al.*, 1980b). The conclusions to which these studies point, as echoed in previous reviews of the NPT procedure (e.g., Wagner, Hilsted, & Jensen, 1981; Wasserman *et al.*, 1980b), are the uncertain validity of this procedure when used in isolation and the need to integrate multiple sources of laboratory and clinical information.

Furthermore, there is growing recognition that the differential diagnosis of organic and psychogenic erectile dysfunction is not an either–or decision. Rather, for patients with verified disease states, psychological factors often appear highly relevant, and in certain cases they may be primary in creating reduced arousal. For example, Zuckerman *et al.* (1985) compared diabetic and nondiabetic men with sexual dysfunction, and contrasted their responding to that of sexually functional volunteers. Both NPT and waking assessments were included in this study. The dysfunctional subjects showed less erectile response to erotic films and audiotapes than did sexually functional controls. However, it was not possible to differentiate diabetic from nondiabetic dysfunctionals during the waking film and audiotape assessment. In contrast, during sleep assessment, diabetic subjects had significantly weaker NPT responses than did nondiabetics. A significant relationship was noted between nocturnal and waking responses; this was most pronounced for the diabetic dysfunctionals and the control subjects. This study provides an excellent example of the use of sexual psychophysiology in differentiating organic from psychogenic features in a dysfunctional population.

Disorders of Ejaculation

PREMATURE EJACULATION

Undesired rapid ejaculation is a relatively common sexual dysfunction in males (Frank *et al.*, 1978), although an adequate definition of it has yet to emerge, owing to the difficulty of defining the problem in relation to the female partner's arousal cycle. Various diagnostic definitions have included assessing the inability of the male to inhibit ejaculation long enough to satisfy his partner in at least 50% of sexual contacts (Masters & Johnson, 1970); the inability of the male to exert voluntary control over the ejaculatory reflex (Kaplan, 1979); and mutual agreement by both the male and female partner that ejaculation too frequently is too rapid (LoPiccolo, 1977).

To date, little systematic empirical work has been conducted in this area, although clinical observations of relevant psychophysiological processes abound. Semans (1956) stated that this disorder is due to an abnormally rapid ejaculation reflex, and located the cause for premature ejaculation at the level of the CNS. Kaplan (1979) has further theorized that short ejaculatory latencies may be due to heightened tactile sensitivity to erotic stimulation. In addition, she observes that premature ejaculators do not experience or perceive the sensations that normally precede orgasm and ejaculation.

In the face of such clinically relevant speculations, the dearth of laboratory psychophysiological data on premature ejaculation is somewhat surprising. One exception to this is a recent research report by Spiess, Geer, and O'Donohue (1984). These authors explored a series of hypotheses concerning differences in arousal parameters between premature ejaculators and sexually functional men. The experimental procedure included the presentation of an erotic audiotape and slides, as well as sexual fantasy; measures of tumescence and subjective sexual arousal were included. Premature ejaculators were expected to show faster arousal, higher amplitudes of tumescence, arousal to a wider range of sexual cues, and less accurate judgment of their physiological arousal than sexually functional men.

Group differences did emerge on three self-report questions in this study: Rapid ejaculators reported that they achieved lower levels of arousal at ejaculation; that the shorter their latency to ejaculation was, the longer their period of abstinence from intercourse had been; and that they experienced longer intervals of abstinence from masturbation and intercourse. The other results, however, indicated no significant differences between groups, suggesting that the type of laboratory analogues employed in this study may not have been appropriate for the assessment of premature ejaculation. The authors note that the lack of physiological differences also may have resulted from the small sample size. The results of a second study, however, support Speiss *et al.*'s findings. Kockott *et al.* (1980) included 16 men with premature ejaculation and contrasted their physiological responding to erotic films with that of patients with primary and secondary erectile dysfunction, patients with diabetes-related impotence, and normal controls. No differences between the premature ejaculators and the sexually functional men were noted in autonomic arousal (e.g., skin resistance, blood pressure) or in sexual responsivity, suggesting that relevant etiological factors may involve other aspects of sexual behavior. Similar results have been reported recently by Strassberg, Kelly, Carroll, and Kircher (1985) as well.

Alternative experimental approaches that systematically vary psychological factors, such as sexual expectations for particular forms of sexual activity or a partner's emotional response to rapid ejaculation, might provide a clearer understanding of relevant psychophysiological determinants of premature ejaculation. Given that premature ejaculation can often be a precursor to erectile failure (e.g., Kaplan, 1979; Masters & Johnson, 1970), particular attention needs to be paid to the relevant emotional sequelae of the disorder, such as distraction or worry, as well as influences from sexual activity patterns.

In addressing this issue, it should be noted that aging affects the ejaculation response. In general, young males are likely to ejaculate quickly, especially if a period of sexual abstinence has preceded sexual intercourse. As the male ages and accumulates greater sexual experience, this pattern becomes less common (Kinsey *et al.*, 1948). An area that would be well suited for psychophysiological exploration would be an evaluation of individual variation across the life cycle in the ability to detect sensations that are premonitory to ejaculation. It is conceivable that aging effects in ejaculatory control are the result of reduced physiological reactivity, as opposed to the learning of cognitive control skills. Furthermore, an experimental paradigm of the type employed by Korff and Geer (1983), which used careful definitions of anchor points for ratings of subjective arousal and signal detection methodology, might be helpful in examining clinical speculations concerning the development of ejaculatory control. Clearly, further investigations of this topic could contribute to our understanding of the interaction between physiological processes and affective and cognitive factors in defining sexual arousal.

RETARDED EJACULATION

"Ejaculatory incompetence," or the inability to ejaculate intravaginally (Masters & Johnson, 1970), is a less common disorder than premature ejaculation, although some authors report that its incidence appears to be increasing in recent years (Rosen & Hall, 1984). While no experimental psychophysiological studies of retarded ejaculation have appeared in the literature to date, several authors have speculated about relevant maintaining factors for retarded ejaculation. Apfelbaum (1980), for example, has suggested that retarded ejaculators experience minimal or no subjective sexual arousal, yet feel obligated to satisfy a sexual partner. Furthermore, he asserts that men with this problem are physiologically capable of full erections (termed "automatic erections") in the absence of significant subjective arousal. The combination of these factors results in experiencing intercourse as an undesirable, potentially aversive demand.

A variety of medical and pharmacological factors may also account for retarded ejaculation; for example, phenothiazines and certain antihypertensives may impair the ejaculatory reflex by blocking the adreneregic innervation involved in the control of ejaculation (Kaplan, 1979; Mitchell & Popkin, 1983). Usually, however, the primary causes are viewed as psychogenic, and this suggests the need to develop guidelines for differential diagnosis in this disorder. A review by Munjack and Kanno (1979) concludes that since the original report of this disorder (Ovesey & Meyers, 1968), substantial attention has been paid to retarded ejaculation. Detailed information, however, is lacking on etiology, treatment, and outcome, as well as on relevant patient characteristics and patterns of physiological response.

COMMENT

Overall, a key assumption on which the present classification system for male sexual disorders is based is that ejaculation and orgasm are synonymous and occur simultaneously in all instances. This assumption does not necessarily follow from our current understanding of sexual physiology as discussed in Chapters 3 and 6. Ejaculation is initiated by a sudden discharge of the sympathetic nervous system, accompanied by a release of norepinephrine. This is followed by a parasympathetic rebound and a surge of acetylcholine, which creates the sensations of warmth and relaxation associated with orgasm. It is unclear what role each of these aspects of autonomic functioning plays in male disorders of sexual functioning, although the assumed equivalence of ejaculation and orgasm appears oversimplified. This is especially true for patients with spinal cord injuries and neurological lesions of the sympathetic nervous system (e.g., Higgins, 1979). It would appear that considerable advantage could be gained in future studies by separating subjective and physiological aspects of ejaculation—a task for which the methods of sexual psychophysiology are ideally suited.

Inhibited Sexual Desire

The appearance of DSM-III introduced a major conceptual advance in classifying disorders of sexual function through the inclusion of Inhibited

Sexual Desire as a diagnosis for both males and females. Based on the work of Kaplan (1977, 1979), the present classification system defines the disorder as a persistent and distressing absence of sexual desire, often presenting clinically as a statement of one partner's lack of interest or overinterest in sexual interaction. While the inclusion of Inhibited Sexual Desire into the existing diagnostic schema is generally recognized as a valuable and necessary clinical addition (e.g., Rosen & Leiblum, 1987), to date little experimental work has resulted from this nosological addition. Perhaps this dearth of research results from the difficulties in defining the concept operationally, as well as from the absence of appropriate methodology for investigations of a motivational factor such as sexual desire.

Further studies in this area could help to define the concept of sexual desire, especially in the context of other forms of sexual dysfunction. Certainly, the notion of sexual desire is poorly understood at present and could benefit from a careful examination of relevant physiological and cognitive processes.

LABORATORY ANALOGUE STUDIES OF MALE SEXUAL DYSFUNCTION

The application of psychophysiological measurement approaches has begun to gain wide acceptance in the classification and assessment of etiological factors in certain forms of male sexual dysfunction. A separate but related application of this approach involves laboratory analogue studies of factors identified as potentially important in maintaining sexual disorders. As in classification studies, most investigations have examined affective, cognitive, and physiological states relevant to erectile failure, although some investigators have generalized their findings to related problems, such as premature ejaculation.

The appearance of Masters and Johnson's *Human Sexual Inadequacy* in 1970 introduced a new perspective on etiological factors in male and female sexual problems. According to Masters and Johnson's formulation, one important factor in accounting for sexual dysfunction is the experience of distraction during the process of sexual interactions. This distraction is said to be accompanied by performance anxiety, especially for males, and often leads individuals to focus on their sexual performance in an emotionally distanced fashion (termed "spectatoring"). In laboratory analogue studies of these factors, both clinical and control samples have been included, indicating dimensions of differences in sexual responding during experimental conditions in clinical and nonclinical samples (e.g., Cooper, Furst, & Bridger, 1969; Bernstein & Paul, 1971).

As the present review of these studies indicates, the use of analogue studies allows for the isolation of theoretically relevant factors, and insures adequate experimental control of psychophysiological determinants during sexual responding. However, the question of external validity of findings from these studies needs to be raised, especially given the artificial nature of the laboratory setting, the potentially obtrusive nature of psychophysiological measures, and the fact that this approach ignores the relational context of most "real-life" sexual interactions. As discussed by Berkowitz and Donnerstein (1982), the ways in which subjects construe the laboratory experience determines, in certain respects, the extent to which external and ecological validity have been achieved. Unfortunately, most studies fail to include assessment of the participants' perceptions of the research setting, and thus make ecological validity uncertain.

To date, much of the research in this area has focused on the influences of distraction and anxiety on concurrent states of sexual arousal. A range of experimental approaches has evolved to examine these concepts in the context of laboratory paradigms using sexual psychophysiology.

Distraction

The notion of distraction as a factor in male sexual responding has been explored by three studies to date—two using sexually functional men as subjects, and the third comparing men with secondary erectile failure to age-matched normal controls.

In the first study of this type, Geer and Fuhr (1976) examined four levels of increasingly complex arithmetic operations with healthy, college-aged males. The cognitive distractors were presented simultaneously with matched erotic audiotapes, using a dichotic listening paradigm, so that the subjects heard both the erotic and distracting stimuli through earphones. In the control condition, subjects were asked to listen to the erotic tape without distraction. In a low-distraction condition, the subjects listened to numbers being read simultaneously with the erotic tape and were asked simply to copy these numbers. The third condition was moderately distracting, as the subjects were asked to add successive pairs of digits and to write down the results. A final, maximum-distraction condition required all or most of the subjects' attention, as they were asked to classify pairs of digits according to a complex scheme.

The results revealed that as the distracting cognitive task became more complex, erectile responding decreased proportionately (see Figure 10.4). Several subjects reported on postexperimental interviews that at the most complex level of distraction, they failed to hear the erotic message; this suggested a complete absence of attention to sexual cues during high levels of distraction. Geer and Fuhr have aptly noted that in order for the results of this study to be applied to clinical samples, more detailed exploration of the content of distracting thoughts is necessary.

A subsequent study by Farkas *et al.* (1979) examined distraction in

261

Figure 10.4. Mean amplitude of penile changes in conditions involving different levels of distraction. From "Cognitive Factors in Sexual Arousal: The Role of Distraction" by J. H. Geer and R. Fuhr, 1976, *Journal of Consulting and Clinical Psychology, 44,* p. 241. Copyright 1976 by the American Psychological Association. Reprinted by permission.

the presence and absence of performance demand, using sexually functional males as subjects. In this report, "distraction" was defined as listening to two types of tones and keeping separate tallies of each. Performance demand was manipulated through instructions to the subjects that most men had found the erotic stimulus either highly arousing or unarousing, and that they could expect this particular outcome in their own responding. Tumescence and subjective arousal were monitored continuously throughout the experiment; erotic videotapes were used as stimuli, and the degree of stimulus explicitness was manipulated as a third experimental factor. The results indicate that distraction significantly reduced tumescence, especially in conjunction with low levels of performance demand. On the continuous measure of subjective arousal, however, no distraction effects were seen. Correlations between tumescence and subjective arousal were lower during distraction than during full attention. The authors interpreted their results in light of methodological differences with the previous study of Geer and Fuhr (1976), suggesting that potential differences in visual versus auditory processing of sexual stimuli may have accounted for the observed differences.

The most recent examination of the influence of distraction involved a comparison of men experiencing secondary erectile dysfunction with an age-matched group of sexually functional controls (Abrahamson, Barlow, Sakheim, Beck, & Athanasiou, 1985). This study used an auditory distractor (a neutral story) heard during erotic videotapes that were either high or low in explicitness. The results indicated that sexually functional men showed less tumescence during distraction than during no distraction, while, surprisingly, the men with erectile dysfunction were not influenced by the diverting audiotapes. No marked differences were seen in reports of subjective arousal between distraction and full-attention states for either group.

These findings are interpreted in the context of the specific nature of distraction in erectile dysfunction. It is hypothesized that a particular type of cognitive interference—specifically, thoughts concerning sexual performance—is highly salient for the dysfunctional male, and is responsible for reductions in arousal during actual sexual situations. In contrast, the sexually functional male may not spontaneously report this type of mental distraction (e.g., thoughts about performance), although he may show a sensitivity to more neutral interruptions, such as a telephone ringing. These findings suggest that greater attention needs to be paid to specific types of distractors for both sexually functional and dysfunctional men. It is possible that the normal male is distracted more easily by cognitive tasks that draw his attention away from sexual responding, as demonstrated in the studies by Geer and Fuhr (1976) and Farkas et al. (1979). The dysfunctional male appears to be more influenced by factors that orient his attention toward his sexual responding, and thus appears to be relatively unaffected by more neutral distractors, as demonstrated by Abrahamson, Barlow, Sakheim, et al. (1985).

Anxiety

The concept of anxiety has maintained a central role in most recent conceptualizations of male sexual dysfunction, and generally has been specified as fear of failure (Kaplan, 1979), performance anxiety (Masters & Johnson, 1970), and fear of displeasing one's partner (Zilbergeld, 1978). In fact, much of the early research on sex therapy was focused on techniques designed to reduce excessive anxiety concerning sexual performance, such as systematic densensitization and nongenital pleasuring, with the stated rationale that these direct interventions would address the major maintaining factor in sexual dysfunction. Current conceptualizations of dysfunction are considerably more complex (e.g., Beck & Barlow, 1984; Everaerd, 1983), and are based in part upon psychophysiological investigations of the influence of anxiety on tumescence.

One of the first studies to examine the influence of anxiety on sexual arousal in males was conducted by Wolchik *et al.* (1980). This study was a partial replication of an earlier investigation with women (Hoon, Wincze, & Hoon, 1977b), employing a pre-exposure paradigm: Subjects were first shown either a neutral or an anxiety-producing film (scenes of automobile accidents), followed by explicit erotic films, while tumescence and subjective arousal were continuously monitored. The results indicated that anxiety pre-exposure heightened subsequent responding for sexually functional college-aged males. This finding suggests that anxiety may not always operate to diminish tumescence, as originally stated, although Wolpe (1978) has cogently argued that this effect may be the result of an anxiety relief phenomena. That is, increases in sexual arousal following an anxiety-producing event may demonstrate a positive-contrast effect, rather than confirming the facilitatory effect of anxiety on sexual arousal.

To address this concern, Barlow *et al.* (1983) examined the effect of anxiety induced simultaneously with sexual arousal, using a threat of electrical shock to produce anxiety. Two forms of anxiety manipulations were employed: a threat of shock that was stated as contingent on subjects' not achieving adequate arousal, and a threat of shock that was to be delivered independently of any subject response. No shocks were actually delivered during the erotic films, although the credibility of the deception was maintained throughout the procedure with the use of a prestimulus shock tolerance procedure and relatively brief erotic stimuli. The results of this study indicated that both forms of shock threat created significantly higher levels of tumescence than did the neutral control condition. Interestingly, no significant differences among the three conditions were noted in levels of subjective arousal.

A follow-up report has recently focused on potential mechanisms through which anxiety may influence tumescence. Beck, Barlow, Sakheim, and Abrahamson (1987) employed a sentence recognition task in order to assess stimulus-focused attention during simultaneous states of anxiety and sexual arousal in college-aged, sexually functional males. Erotic audiotapes were used as stimuli, and four levels of shock threat were examined: half tolerance, tolerance, twice tolerance, and a no-shock control condition. Results were interesting in a number of respects. First, anxiety appeared to produce effects according to an inverted U-shaped curve, with moderate levels of threat diminishing arousal. No significant change in tumescence occurred during the twice-tolerance shock threat, relative to the neutral control condition. This pattern of results corresponds to clinical predictions, although it differs from previous findings, as no facilitatory effect of shock threat was noted.

The findings from this study can be viewed from the perspective of cognitive responding: Stimulus-directed attention was most accurate during moderate levels of anxiety, when the lowest levels of tumescence were seen. During the twice-tolerance shock threat, subjects were most inaccurate at stimulus recognition, even though no decrement in tumescence was noted. Interestingly, during the extreme level of threat, subjects reported the widest range of emotional states and the greatest occurrence of sexual fantasies and erotic thoughts. This study suggests that moderate levels of anxiety may diminish sexual responding by drawing the male's attention exclusively toward environmental stimuli; this appears to diminish his awareness of affective and cognitive processes such as fantasies, which play a critical role in facilitating arousal. If this explanation is accurate, it would suggest that a complex interaction of cognitive and emotional influences is important in mediating arousal and may comprise the salient aspects of "anxiety" as discussed in the clinical literature (cf. Beck & Barlow, 1984).

A related study has approached this issue from a different perspective. Lange, Wincze, Zwick, Feldman, and Hughes (1981) injected normal volunteers with epinephrine hydrochloride prior to showing them erotic films. The study used a single-blind design, and subjects were informed that the injections would have no predictable effects on their physical and emotional states. While no differences between the epinephrine and placebo conditions were observed in erectile responses to the erotic films, subjects who had received epinephrine showed a faster latency to detumescence following termination of the stimulus. While the results of this study are difficult to reconcile with the results of the previous studies because of paradigmatic differences, it would appear that heightened autonomic arousal does not necessarily interfere with sexual responding, at least for sexually functional subjects.

This issue has been examined in a more naturalistic setting as well. Morokoff (1985b) has explored the effects of generalized life stress on sexual arousal. Specifically, a group of men experiencing chronically high levels of stress (defined by unemployment and an elevated score on the Daily Hassles Questionnaire) was contrasted with a low-stress group. Each subject was exposed in a counterbalanced design to an erotic film that had been preceded by an acute stressor, as well as an erotic film without this pre-exposure. The results indicated that the men with elevated life stresses achieved less tumescence when stressed prior to erotic stimulation than did the low-stress group. No group differences were noted when erotic stimulation preceded the acute stressor; this suggests that sexual arousal may be relatively robust in the context of mild, transient anxiety.

Focus of Attention

According to most clinical accounts, an important consequence of sexual performance anxiety is a disruption of attention to sexual sensations and an increased focus on sexual performance as if from a third-party perspective; this process has been termed "spectatoring" by Masters and Johnson (1970) and is postulated as distracting and thus disruptive of the normal process of arousal. Several investigations have explored directional attention, contrasting sexually functional and dysfunctional men in some instances. Beck, Barlow, and Sakheim (1983b) examined the effects of self- and partner-directed attention, combined with varying levels of perceived partner arousal (high, low, and ambiguous), in these two subject groups. The instructions were delivered during presentation of erotic videotapes and validated with self-report credibility measures. When the stimulus partner was perceived as highly aroused, and when subjects were under instructions to attend to her response, dysfunctional subjects demonstrated lower levels of tumescence, while functional subjects showed increased arousal (see Figure 10.5). Postexperimental interviews indicated that in actual sexual situations, the sexually functional subjects reported that high partner arousal facilitated their own responding, while dysfunctional subjects indicated that high partner arousal created pressures to perform and diminished their responding. A partial replication of this study has been conducted by Abrahamson, Barlow, Beck, Sakheim, and Kelly (1985), with similar results.

A similar study was conducted by Heiman and Rowland (1983). In this investigation, the subjects were sexually functional men and men with a history of erectile failure; they were given prestimulus instructions to mirror conditions of sensate focus or performance demand. The normal controls showed increased tumescence to an erotic audiotape if it was preceded by demand instructions, while the dysfunctional men showed greater arousal to the tape if it was preceded by sensate focus instructions. In addition, the dysfunctional sample reported greater awareness of a range of physiological responses (e.g., heart rate, respiration) and reported more negative emotional states during the experimental session. Thus, it would appear that specific attentional instructions differentially influence these two groups, perhaps owing to specific attributions concerning their erectile potential and other perceptions of sexual interactions.

Recently, these hypotheses have received some further experimental support. In a study involving men with secondary erectile dysfunction and age-matched controls, Beck and Barlow (1986a, 1986b) examined the interaction of performance anxiety and two forms of attentional instructions. Subjects were instructed either to focus on their degree of tumescence (spectator focus) or to attend to private thoughts, sensations, and feelings of arousal (sensate focus). The results indicated that performance demand lowered responding for sexually functional men (unlike Heiman and Rowland's [1983] findings), while no significant effects were noted for sexually dysfunctional subjects. The discrepancy in the findings of these two studies may have been due to the use of different forms of demand manipulations. Whereas Beck and Barlow used a threat of electrical shock, Heiman and

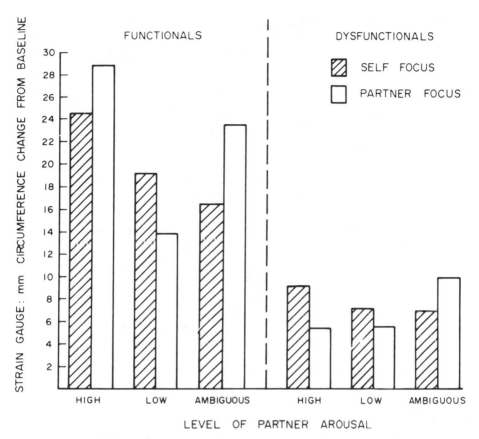

Figure 10.5. Mean penile circumference change from baseline for sexually func-
tional and dysfunctional men under conditions of high, low, or ambiguous perceived
partner arousal. From "The Effects of Attentional Focus and Partner Arousal on
Sexual Responding in Functional and Dysfunctional Men" by J. G. Beck, D. H.
Barlow, and D. K. Sakheim, 1983, *Behaviour Research and Therapy, 21*, p. 4.
Copyright 1983 by Pergamon Journals, Ltd. Reprinted by permission.

Rowland employed verbal demands for their subjects to become "as aroused
as possible." However, one condition (demand/spectator focus) in the Beck
and Barlow study appeared to result in heightened tumescence for the
dysfunctional males. Examination of cognitive and affective measures suggested that the dysfunctional men had difficulty in attending to their degree
of tumescence in the presence of demand, and reported a greater allocation
of attention to the stimulus film. In contrast, the sexually functional sample
reported more attention to the erotic stimuli across all conditions. The
dysfunctional sample reported more thoughts concerning their degree of

tumescence, made fewer mentions of affective states, and held perceptions that physiological and subjective measures of arousal would be poorly correlated, in spite of the lack of actual differences in correlations between groups.

Overall, these findings suggest that specific cognitive and emotional differences distinguish sexually functional and dysfunctional men. Continued exploration of cognitive and emotional processes associated with physiological arousal states will help to further refine our understanding of these perceptual and attentional processes, and perhaps will lead to more sophisticated, individualized treatment approaches to male dysfunction.

A related study provides additional insight into specific attentional mechanisms and their role in influencing tumescence in sexually functional males. Dekker, Everaerd, and Verhelst (1985) examined the effect of instructions to attend to the stimulus descriptors of an erotic audiotape, relative to instructions to attend to both the stimulus and the subject's own responses, following the distinction made in Lang's (1979) theory of emotional imagery. Reports of subjective sexual arousal were higher for sexually functional men during the stimulus/responses instructional condition; this suggests the importance of attentional focus on one's own sexual responding in facilitating arousal. Unfortunately, this study did not employ a measure of tumescence, nor did it include a group of dysfunctional subjects.

A second study, however, complements these results. Sakheim *et al.* (1984) examined the effect of availability of genital response feedback on subjective arousal and tumescence. In two experimental sessions, normal volunteers were shown erotic films of varying degrees of explicitness. In one session, the subjects were prevented from viewing their genital responding (a sheet covered the genital area), while in the second session, the subjects were given visual access for feedback of tumescence. At low and moderate levels of arousal, subjects displayed less arousal when visual cues were visually available; during higher levels of arousal, visual feedback resulted in increased tumescence. These data suggest that a positive feedback process may be operative for sexually functional men, wherein adequate responding facilitates arousal through validation of sexual self-perceptions. A replication of this study with males experiencing erectile failure would be valuable.

Comment

While laboratory studies have begun to explore important differences between clinical and nonclinical samples in their responses to experimental distraction, anxiety, and manipulations of attentional focus, the emerging data are inconsistent and somewhat incomplete in explaining relevant etiological factors. Available studies that directly contrast age-matched groups of men with erectile failure with sexually functional controls have generally reported significant effects of these conditions for the control samples, but not the clinical subjects. For example, dysfunctional men do not appear to be significantly affected by a neutral distractor during an erotic presentation (Abrahamson, Barlow, Sakheim, et al., 1985), or by an anxiety-producing performance demand (Beck et al., 1984). In contrast, sexually functional subjects show substantial changes in response to these laboratory manipulations, demonstrating reduced arousal in the first case and, most often, heightened responding in the second. Adding to the difficulties in interpretation is the fact that when college-aged males are employed as subjects, the pattern of findings takes a different form from that obtained for older men, thus raising questions of the relevance of analogue samples in researching these issues.

One type of investigation that seems to hold particular promise is the study of attentional states during sexual responding. Available studies have shown consistent differences in clinical and nonclinical patterns of responding to attentional instructions. An interesting corollary to these research reports would be studies that assessed focused attention during the course of ongoing erotic stimulation—a needed addition in light of questions concerning the external validity of attentional-focus instructions.

TREATMENT CONCERNS: PSYCHOPHYSIOLOGY IN APPLICATION

Based in part on early observations of voluntary control of tumescence, along with recent attempts at empirical investigation of the effectiveness of sex therapy, sexual psychophysiology has been recommended for two aspects of treatment application. First, given that a number of studies have demonstrated facilitation of tumescence through biofeedback and monetary reward (e.g., Rosen, 1973, 1976; Rosen et al., 1975; Herman & Prewett, 1974), the potential for using these procedures in a clinical context seems clear, and several attempts have been made to develop the use of biofeedback for the treatment of erectile dysfunction. Second, psychophysiological measures have been recommended for outcome evaluation of sex therapy programs. In reviewing these areas of application, clinical issues also need to be considered.

Despite the interest generated by laboratory demonstration of voluntary control of erectile responding, a consensus has evolved in recent years that biofeedback for arousal disorders may not be an appropriate or effective treatment procedure (e.g., Geer, 1979; Rosen, 1976; Reynolds, 1980). Prior to this, however, several reports of biofeedback applications to erectile dysfunction appeared in the literature (e.g., Csillag, 1976; Herman & Prewett, 1974; Quinn et al., 1970). Overall, the results of these investigations indicate that while biofeedback may temporarily improve erectile responding in dysfunctional men, these incremental changes tend not to endure over time and in some cases are not clinically significant. In addition, Rosen (1976) has commented that biofeedback programs typically downplay interpersonal factors that are often critical in cases of erectile dysfunction. The issue of transfer of training from the laboratory to "real life" is also salient, although no empirical data exist to date on this issue.

Geer (1979) has suggested a particularly creative application—namely, that biofeedback might be useful in identifying fantasy material, which could then be incorporated into more conventional sex therapy approaches. This application would capitalize on the fact that sexual dysfunction, particularly erectile failure, can be viewed among the psychophysiological disorders that have a strong learning component (e.g., Shapiro & Schwartz, 1972). Moreover, by drawing on the unique role that fantasies and cognitions play in sexual arousal, this unusual type of biofeedback application has the potential to integrate one of the strengths of sexual psychophysiology (i.e., assessing specificity of the genital response) with current treatment approaches.

A second example of the application of sexual psychophysiology to current approaches to treatment is reported by Davis and Davis (1980). These authors describe the use of a home NPT conditioning procedure to address a case of secondary erectile dysfunction. In this procedure, nocturnal tumescence as monitored by the female partner served as a cue for the introduction of sensate focus and genital pleasuring exercises, which eventually culminated in intercourse. Over time, the partners were able to perform these exercises in a waking state, and at a 2-year follow-up they were functioning well sexually. While atypical in its approach, this application represents one method of circumventing emotional and cognitive processes that may interfere with compliance to sex therapy techniques. Naturally, to the extent that resistance is due to chronic marital distress or psychological disturbance, this approach may easily be sabotaged.

Sexual psychophysiology has also been recommended for evaluating treatment outcome for male sexual dysfunction. Many reviews of treatment efficacy have highlighted the need for direct, objective measures of therapeutic change (e.g., Bancroft, 1971a; Levine, 1980; Kuriansky & Sharpe, 1976; Mills & Kilmann, 1982; LoPiccolo, 1985), although the inclusion of physiological measures for outcome assessment in sex therapy programs is rare at present. Hartman and Fithian (1974), for example, have reported on the use of direct genital assessment prior to initiation of a course of sex therapy, although no systematic outcome data are available for their program.

Certainly, in light of recent concerns regarding the effectiveness of traditional sex therapy programs (Zilbergeld & Evans, 1980) and the increased realization that the criteria for successful outcome in sex therapy frequently include change across a number of dimensions, greater emphasis on psychophysiological evaluation of sex therapy appears warranted. Given our increased awareness of the potential for discordance between physiological and cognitive–motivational processes in disorders of sexual responding (e.g., as noted in cases of inhibited desire), this type of treatment analysis would benefit from examination of treatment effects on specific aspects of the arousal response, as well as of patterns of change between these response components. It is possible that a lack of covariation in measures of the arousal response may be predictive of poorer treatment outcome, and that outcome may also be influenced by client expectations for sexual performance or by other, as yet unidentified processes.

SUMMARY

In this review of the various applications of sexual psychophysiology to male sexual dysfunction, it is apparent that substantial progress in understanding these disorders has resulted from use of this approach. The pace of these advances has been uneven, focusing principally on the diagnosis of erectile dysfunction and experimental analysis of its presumed etiological factors. Given the available methodology for measuring male sexual responding, as reviewed in Chapter 3, this state of affairs reflects the current context of laboratory psychophysiology; sophisticated technology has yet to be developed for assessing disorders of ejaculation and sexual desire.

To date, laboratory studies of erectile dysfunction have begun to delimit psychophysiological patterns in primary and secondary dysfunction, as well as to examine EEG responding during arousal states. These studies have suggested the potential utility of experimental paradigms that explore sensitization and habituation processes in erectile disorders, especially given the need to expand available treatment strategies for cases resistant to traditional sex therapy.

Applications of the psychophysiological method have made the greatest impact in the differential diagnosis of organic and psychogenic impotence, with the introduction of NPT monitoring. At present, this procedure has been adopted by many urologists and has been adapted for home use with the development of portable NPT monitors. Despite its popularity, the NPT procedure only recently has received experimental validation with the work of Marshall and colleagues; this suggests that caution should be exercised in relying on this procedure alone for diagnosis. In particular, the issues of diagnostic accuracy, the relative costs and benefits of this approach compared with those of psychosocial assessments, and the relationship of tumescence responding during sleep and waking states appear salient.

Applications of sexual psychophysiology to disorders of ejaculation and sexual interest have begun to make progress, although these are limited by the available methodology and by the more recent introduction of these dysfunctions into classification schemes for sexual dysfunction. In particular, the contributions of aging, specific interactional patterns in the sexual relationship, and cognitive–emotional processes to the etiology of sexual disorders of ejaculation and desire deserve to be explored. Advances in understanding the physiology of the ejaculatory reflex and the development of conceptual frameworks of sexual interest may help to clarify relevant dimensions for psychophysiological study of these disorders.

Laboratory analogue studies of male dysfunction constitute a related application of the psychophysiological approach, revolving around Masters and Johnson's (1970) conceptualization of etiological factors in sexual problems. The typical study of this type involves creating an experimental condition designed as an analogue to performance demand, distraction, spectator focus, or other relevant states, while monitoring tumescence. While the importance of the contribution made by this type of investigation is clear, greater attention to the ecological validity of these paradigms appears warranted. To date, studies examining the influence of distraction on tumescence have indicated that for sexually functional men, neutral cognitive tasks diminish penile responding, but that this effect is not noted for sexually dysfunctional men; these findings suggest the possibility that dysfunctional men are better able to screen external distractions. However, dysfunctional males do appear to be more distracted by thoughts concerning sexual performance.

The role of anxiety in sexual performance disorders has been examined within this context as well, often with surprising results. Several studies with college-aged volunteers have indicated that performance demand heightens tumescence, while not influencing subjective reports of sexual arousal. The effect of this type of experimental condition appears to influence dysfunctional subjects' responding somewhat differently, with the available data showing little if any effect on penile responding of these patients. These patterns may be mediated through selective attention to erotic cues and sexual feeling states, as indicated by preliminary studies, although further investigations utilizing the methods of cognitive psychology appear warranted. A related type of inquiry has explored the effects of specific attentional states, such as spectator and sensate focus, on arousal. This type of investigation appears promising for expanding our conceptual understanding of sexual response patterning in sexual dysfunction.

The final area of application, treatment of male sexual disorders, has yielded interesting findings as well. To date, several trials of biofeedback have illustrated that this intervention is not the treatment of choice for erectile dysfunction, although creative suggestions have been offered by Geer (1979) to expand the relevance of sexual psychophysiology for enhancing erectile potential. The need for objective indices of treatment outcome represents another salient issue for the future of treatment applications.

In sum, applications of sexual psychophysiology have made clear and distinctive progress in the study of male sexual dysfunction. One reason for this appears to be the utility of psychophysiological methods and measures for related medical specialties and the availability of laboratory settings for clinical assessment. Throughout this recent history of application, however, many impediments to laboratory psychophysiology have arisen, including unfounded objections of community groups and skepticism from professional colleagues. In spite of these obstacles, considerable progress in understanding male sexual dysfunction has been made in the past two decades. Among the salient issues that emerge for future research is the need for collaborative investigations of physiological and psychological factors, particularly in disorders of ejaculation and sexual desire. With a focus on these areas, continued progress in understanding and treating male sexual dysfunction appears probable and, most likely, fruitful.

CHAPTER ELEVEN

Female Sexual Dysfunction

Yesterday's cherished virgin could easily become today's [sex therapy] patient.—Leiblum & Pervin (1980, p. 19)

Definitions of female sexuality and expectations for the sexual behavior of women have changed radically during the last century, reflecting a gradual loosening of Victorian mores and the development of greater equality between the sexes in both social and sexual roles. This cultural transition has created a new set of sexual dilemmas and performance myths for women, including expectations that a woman should have more than one orgasm during any given sexual encounter, that a woman should be aggressive in sexual activities, and (assuming a good relationship exists) that sex will be equally satisfying to both partners (e.g., Barbach, 1975; Heiman, LoPiccolo, & LoPiccolo, 1976). Thus, within the span of less than 100 years, the topic of female sexuality has gone from a highly restricted, virtually unacknowledged status to its current state, characterized according to some commentators by an emphasis on "hypersexuality" (LoPiccolo & Heiman, 1978).

One result of these shifts in cultural definitions of female sexuality has been a changing view of the nature and prevalence of sexual dysfunction in women. For example, Kinsey and his colleagues (1953) were the first to document changes across the life span in women's ability to reach orgasm. In this sample, approximately half of the subjects in their late teens had not yet experienced orgasm, whereas among women in their mid-30s, only about 10% reported failure to achieve orgasm. Twenty years later, Hunt (1974) reported a prevalence rate of 15% for anorgasmia in adult women, a figure that has been substantiated further by Gebhard's (1978) findings. Given that the importance of the female orgasm has acquired near-epic proportions in the popular press, it is possible that a small rise in the percentage of women experiencing anorgasmia has taken place, due to changing cultural expectations.

The epidemiological picture becomes even more clouded when one considers the findings of Frank *et al.*'s (1978) study assessing sexual difficulties and dysfunction in normal, "happily married" couples who had not sought treatment for any reason. Approximately 65% of the women in this study reported having experienced sexual dysfunctions, most frequently anorgasmia, and 77% reported occasional sexual difficulties, which included an inability to relax and diminishing sexual interest. Thus, in considering issues in the diagnosis and treatment of sexual dysfunction in women, a major question appears to be the *definition* of these disorders. Clearly, nosological descriptions cannot be based solely on the frequency of a given complaint in the population at large, since the prevalence of sexual problems appears to be fairly common and the reporting of these is changing slowly over time.

Let us consider the example of secondary orgasmic dysfunction. By some accounts (e.g., Hite, 1976; Kaplan, 1979), lack of orgasm during intercourse may be a normal variation in female sexuality, since the majority of women who have been surveyed report experiencing orgasm only through manual and oral stimulation. This highlights the need for a more detailed account of factors differentiating sexually functional and dysfunctional women; of disorders occurring during all aspects of the arousal process; and of the qualitative dimensions of sexual functioning, such as satisfaction and interest. The first steps toward a psychophysiological mapping of patterns of female arousal have been made, as we review here, and several key issues have been identified as a result of empirical progress to date.

CLASSIFICATION, DEFINITIONS, AND DIAGNOSIS

Current Conceptualizations: Advantages and Problems

Prior to 1970 and the publication of Masters and Johnson's *Human Sexual Inadequacy*, most forms of female sexual dysfunction were referred to as "frigidity." Because this term is vague and nonspecific and has pejorative connotations, it has been abandoned by most practitioners in the field. In its place, a number of specific female dysfunctions have been identified, based in large part on the Masters and Johnson classification system. This approach has been particularly valuable in differentiating specific forms of female dysfunction according to which phase of the four-stage arousal sequence is most affected. In addition, Masters and Johnson highlighted the importance of differential diagnosis based on key elements of the patient's sexual history, and illustrated the use of this information in assessment and treatment of specific case studies. Thus, by distinguishing between primary and secondary or situational forms of orgasmic dysfunction, this classification approach has led to refinements in our understanding both of treatment mechanisms and of the limits of sex therapy in approaching complex sexual and marital problems (e.g., Kinder & Blakeney, 1977; Kilmann, 1978).

To date, the most systematic classification scheme for female sexual dysfunction can be found in DSM-III (American Psychiatric Association, 1980), which includes diagnoses of Inhibited Sexual Desire, Inhibited Sexual Excitement, and Inhibited Female Orgasm, as well as diagnoses relating to penetration, such as Functional Dyspareunia and Functional Vaginismus. The first three categories of female dysfunction closely parallel sexual problems in males, and share diagnostic criteria.

The inclusion of a separate category for sexual desire problems has improved diagnostic accuracy by providing a formal notation for coding absent or inhibited sexual motivation. Unfortunately, the use of the same diagnostic descriptors for male and female disorders of sexual desire may mask potential differences in these syndromes. For example, Kaplan (1979) recommends that the diagnosis of Inhibited Sexual Desire be based in part on a comparison of the patient's sexual history with "the norm." However, in outlining developmental patterns of normal sexual behavior, Kaplan describes two gender-specific courses of maturation. For males, the intensity of sexual interest appears to peak around late adolescence, whereas females more typically reach maximum levels of desire at about age 40. Specific guidelines for comparing an individual patient's behavior to age-appropriate norms would clearly be a valuable asset in diagnosis, although this suggestion may be premature, given the current status of empirical knowledge.

To complicate matters further, recent cultural shifts in expectations for female sexual development have resulted in earlier acquisition of key sexual behaviors, such as masturbation and sexual fantasy elaboration (Rosen & Hall, 1984; Gagnon, Rosen, & Leiblum, 1982). What effects these changing patterns of adolescent sexual development will have on subsequent sexual interest in adulthood is currently unknown, although the use of the same diagnostic criteria for assessment of male and female desire problems may not be adequate to account for this difference and may obscure changing trends over time.

Unlike studies in the area of male dysfunction, the issue of organic versus psychogenic factors in the etiology of female dysfunction has been addressed only rarely in either laboratory or clinical studies. Instead, prevailing conceptualizations of female dysfunction have revolved principally around psychological concepts, such as fear of loss of control (Barbach, 1975), negative sexual sanctions learned in childhood (Kaplan, 1981), religious inhibition, and fears of pregnancy (Masters & Johnson, 1970). As discussed in Chapter 4, the physiology of the female arousal response has yet to be thoroughly delineated, and thus a clearer understanding of relevant organic influences is precluded. In the absence of this knowledge, a principally psychological account of female sexual dysfunction risks becoming overly simplified and maintaining too narrow a focus.

Fortunately, recent psychophysiological studies have begun to address the relative contributions of physiological and psychological factors. For example, Myers and Morokoff (1986) examined physiological and subjective indices of sexual arousal in pre- and postmenopausal women. The latter group was divided into women receiving replacement estrogen and women who were not currently receiving any medication. Results indicated that VPA did not differentiate the three groups during presentation of an erotic film, unlike an earlier finding reported by Morrell et al. (1984). However, group differences were found for subjective arousal in the Myers and Morokoff study. In particular, premenopausal women and women taking estrogen reported significantly higher ratings of vaginal lubrication during the erotic film than did postmenopausal women who were not maintained on hormones. Endocrine assays provided interesting ancillary data in this respect: The authors reported that testosterone levels were correlated significantly with subjective ratings of physical genital sensations, vaginal lubrication, and breast sensations for all three groups.

A related investigation has been reported by Semmens and Wagner (1982), using the Levin–Wagner heat probe to measure vaginal blood flow. In this report, postmenopausal women showed lower levels of engorgement, diminished vaginal blood flow, and reduced vaginal blood oxygenation. Administration of estrogen reversed these effects, resulting in levels of vasocongestion, vaginal blood flow, and oxygenation that were comparable with levels for a sample of premenopausal women. Clinically, following HRT, these postmenopausal patients reported normal lubrication and the absence of pain during intercourse.

Notwithstanding the absence of an objective measure of vaginal lubrication, these data suggest that organic processes such as the thinning of the vaginal epithelium and associated decrements in lubrication may interact with attributional states to influence the process of sexual arousal. It is possible, for example, that expectancies of diminished sexual responsivity due to menopause set the stage for discomfort during intercourse, by heightening a woman's awareness of reduced lubrication. This may create performance anxiety, similar to what is noted clinically in men with erectile dysfunction; the anxiety may exacerbate this pattern and ultimately confirm the woman's belief that she is not capable of sexual activity without pain or discomfort. Other organic factors, such as medical conditions that interfere with the nerve supply to the pelvis (e.g., multiple sclerosis, spinal cord tumors, nutritional deficiencies, or diabetic neuropathy) and conditions that influence the vascular integrity of the pelvic blood supply (e.g., arteriosclerosis, arthritis), deserve greater attention for their influence on sexual arousal. The need for measures of genital responsivity other than vasocongestion is highlighted by the Semmens and Wagner (1982) report.

Clearly, studies of this type play an important role in sexual psychophysiology and potentially offer new understanding of the interaction of organic and psychological processes in female dysfunction, an area much in need of further study.

A related issue concerns the use of physiological measurement techniques for recording arousal during sleep states with women. While NPT assessment has played a central role in the diagnosis of male erectile dysfunction, similar clinical investigations have yet to be conducted with women. The beginning stages of this application have been undertaken, however: Fisher et al. (1983) have described the use of a thermoconductive vaginal flow meter to evaluate sleep cycles in ten sexually functional women. The results of this study indicated a cyclical pattern of blood flow changes during sleep. Unlike the NPT response, however, vaginal engorgement appeared less closely related to REM sleep and of shorter duration. A similar finding has been reported by Abel, Murphy, Becker, and Bitar (1979) using the vaginal photoplethysmograph. In an attempt to explore the clinical application of nocturnal monitoring of vasocongestion, Hayashi et al. (1983) report that with four consecutive nights of monitoring, sufficient reliability can be achieved with this approach to be of value in differential diagnosis. An additional case study describing the utility of this approach has been described by Cunningham-Rathner and Abel (1984). Without more extensive research in this area, however, the potential diagnostic utility of sleep assessment with women remains unknown.

Beyond Current Classifications

The current diagnostic and classification system for female sexual dysfunctions can be described as incomplete and, at best, tentative. Specifically, the system is incomplete with respect to relevant etiological and maintaining factors; specific physiological, cognitive, and affective processes interrupting arousal; and the influence of functioning in related areas, such as marital happiness and sexual communication. Several key omissions from the present nosological system deserve comment here, as they constitute important dimensions of sexual function and dysfunction for women.

One such omission from the existing nosological system that has received considerable public recognition of late is the topic of rape and sexual assault. Increased public awareness of this issue has been motivated by dramatic increases in the rates of reported rapes and data indicating that the ratio of unreported to reported rapes can range from 2:1 to 3.5:1 (Chappell, 1976; Kilpatrick, 1979). Part of the syndrome experienced by survivors of sexual assault can include sexual dysfunction (e.g., Becker, Skinner, Abel, & Tracy, 1982; Burgess & Holmstrom, 1979; Ellis, Calhoun, & Atkeson, 1980), which sometimes manifests itself as orgasmic difficulties, low sexual desire, or fearful avoidance of sexual encounters (e.g., Kilpatrick, Veronen, & Resick, 1979). For example, Becker, Skinner, Abel, and Cichon (1984) report that 65% of the sexual assault survivors included in their treatment study experienced arousal dysfunctions, 51.5% experienced inhibited sexual desire, and 43% reported elevated anxiety and fear of sex. These authors report that with a time-limited therapy program focusing on restructuring fear-related cognitions and modifying anxious avoidance, over 96% of the participants reported a return of sexual function to pretrauma levels. Further research on the patterns of dysfunction that are aftermaths to rape and sexual assault would be a valuable addition and would help to augment existing classification schemes.

A related area that has been overlooked in existing classification approaches to female dysfunction is the topic of incest or other sexual trauma in childhood as this influences adult sexual adjustment (e.g., Meiselman, 1978; Finkelhor, 1979; Browne & Finkelhor, 1986). Preliminary reports suggest that differences in adult sexuality may emerge, depending on how an incest experience was responded to during childhood (e.g., McGuire & Wagner, 1978), although there is a paucity of data concerning the exact nature of this process.

Thus, in considering relevant domains of sexual disorders in adult women, assessment of sexual trauma appears to be an important feature, because such trauma may affect physiological responsivity in an unpredictable fashion. Preliminary reports, for example, suggest that substantial autonomic arousal, resembling an exaggerated anxiety response, often occurs immediately after a sexual trauma, and this pattern gradually generalizes to other stimuli as the interval following the rape increases (Kilpatrick et al., 1979). The inclusion of sexual trauma occurring during either adulthood or childhood in our current classification of female sexual disorders may prove to be an important key for understanding relevant anxiety processes in sexual functioning.

A related factor that is not adequately covered by the current diagnostic system is the role of partner interactions in precipitating and maintaining female sexual dysfunction. It is not unusual for case reports to describe the husband or male partner's role as an important factor in female dysfunction, including sexual difficulties resulting from a lack of sexual skill and difficulty in communication. For example, Caird and Wincze (1977) have described several cases in which specific partner-related problems were the primary cause of the females' sexual disorders. For example, in one case, the husband was impervious to his wife's feelings and moods; consequently, intercourse frequently occurred at times that were far from ideal for her, with a resulting lack of enthusiasm on her part. This type of process has also been observed in cases of erectile dysfunction, where the female initiates sexual activity without attention to her partner's wishes. Clinically, the distinction between a sexual problem that is the result of poor marital and sexual skills and one that stems from more individual factors, such as negative attitudes about sex, appears important (Kaplan, 1981). However, the present classification system offers few guidelines for determining what role the partner plays in a given case of sexual dysfunction, and how to determine the implications of this interaction for treatment.

Greater attention to this issue and to the development of multidimensional conceptualizations of sexual dysfunction that include the relational context thus appears warranted (e.g., Beck, 1985; Schover, Friedman, Weiler, Heiman, & LoPiccolo, 1982), given the relative lack of information concerning many forms of female dysfunction. It is possible, for example, that when marital factors complicate the presenting picture, physiological aspects of the problem may be less striking or even nonexistent. For example, a woman who presents with arousal difficulties and a troubled marriage may not show diminished vasocongestion, indicating that the presenting problems reflect the interaction of individual and dyadic difficulties. In cases without marital strife, there may be clear evidence of disrupted physiological responsivity, perhaps relating to affective responses to sexual activity. This type of distinction appears to have relevance for treatment and could benefit our understanding of the interplay between psychosocial and physiological processes.

Orgasmic Dysfunction

Difficulties with reaching orgasm can be conceptualized as varying along a continuum ranging from occasional problems in achieving climax to complete inability to reach orgasm through any means. While occasional orgasmic difficulties are fairly common, the term "primary orgasmic dysfunction" is reserved to describe the latter group. By most estimates, 1 woman in 10 can fit the criteria for primary orgasmic dysfunction (Hite, 1976; de Bruijn, 1982). The term "preorgasmic" has also been applied to this group (Barbach, 1975), indicating the belief that while these women are capable of learning the orgasmic response, they have yet to do so.

A recent survey from the Netherlands contributes some insight into this diagnostic distinction (de Bruijn, 1982). This study polled a large number of female readers of a popular magazine; the results indicated that those women who were orgasmic during sexual interactions with a partner achieved this by using the same types of manual and tactile stimulation employed during masturbation. In fact, this poll suggested that only 20% of women felt that orgasm was the most important source of sexual pleasure. These results indicate that the criteria for orgasmic disorders in women may need to be re-evaluated, with greater attention to normative data concerning the frequency, stated importance, and function of orgasm in female sexuality.

"Secondary orgasmic dysfunction" or "situational orgasmic dysfunction" is an even more common form of sexual problem and is one of the more pervasive complaints in sex therapy. This category involves a full spectrum of orgasmic problems, including women who are only orgasmic in certain sexual positions or with specific partners; women who were once orgasmic but are no longer responsive; and women who are not responsive in the presence of a partner but can reach orgasm through self-stimulation (Kaplan, 1981; Masters & Johnson, 1970).

To date, several studies have compared autonomic responsivity in samples of anorgasmic and sexually functional women, although the findings from these investigations have presented a somewhat contradictory picture. In one of the earliest reports, Fisher (1973) examined the full spectrum of autonomic measures in women with varying degrees of orgasm consistency, using readings taken during a gynecological examination, while listening to an erotic audiotape, and while observing a film of a live birth. This study indicated that orgasmic capacity was not related to physiological responsivity during any of these tasks, nor were there any particular body sites that appeared to discriminate differing degrees of orgasm consistency.

Somewhat later, Heiman (1975), in a preliminary report, compared 6 women presenting with primary and secondary orgasmic dysfunction to 16 normal volunteers on physiological and subjective indices of arousal during erotic films, audiotapes, and self-generated sexual fantasies. The clinical sample evidenced less vaginal engorgement (measured via VPA) than did the normal controls, although parametric analyses were lacking, owing to the preliminary nature of this study.

In a subsequent paper that presented a larger sample of anorgasmic women (Morokoff & Heiman, 1980), a different response pattern was noted, using the same stimulus presentations. In this second report, 11 women experiencing low arousal were compared with 11 community volunteers, matched for age and duration of marriage. Both groups were presented with an erotic film and a sexually explicit audiotape, and were also instructed to engage in sexual fantasy during the assessment procedure; both VPA and subjective ratings of arousal were included in this assessment. Clinical subjects were assessed prior to participating in conjoint sex therapy, following a Masters-and-Johnson-style format. No differences were noted on VPA between the clinical and control samples. Sexually functional and dysfunctional women differed on subjective measures of arousal, however, with the clinical sample reporting significantly less arousal during all types of erotic stimuli. The pattern of correlations between VPA and various emotional states was not consistent. For clinical subjects, ratings of anxious affect correlated positively with VPA; for nonclinical subjects, a significant positive relationship was observed between VPA and ratings of sexual arousal, and, conversely, between VPA and ratings of offensiveness and boredom.

A second investigation failed to replicate these findings and, in certain respects, provided contradictory results to the pattern of autonomic responding observed by Morokoff and Heiman. Wincze *et al.* (1976) compared the psychological and physiological responses to an erotic film of six sexually functional women and six women presenting with complaints of orgasmic dysfunction. The functional sample displayed higher levels of VBV and diastolic blood pressure during presentation of the stimuli than did the clinical sample (see Figure 11.1). Unlike Morokoff and Heiman's findings, no between-group differences were noted for subjective arousal.

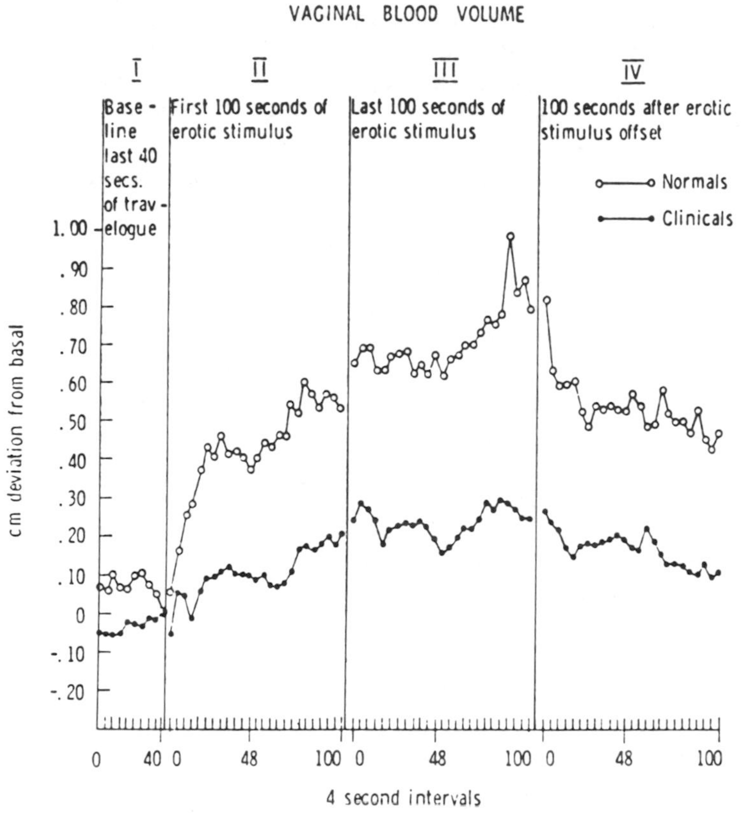

Figure 11.1. Mean polygraph pen deviations in centimeters during travelogue and before, during, and after erotic stimulus exposure for normal and sexually dysfunctional (clinical) women. From "Physiological Responsivity of Normal and Sexually Dysfunctional Women during Erotic Stimulus Exposure" by J. P. Wincze, E. F. Hoon, and P. W. Hoon, 1976, *Journal of Psychosomatic Research, 20,* p. 450. Copyright 1976 by Pergamon Journals, Ltd. Reprinted by permission.

Significant correlations were observed between VBV and several self-report measures, such as frequency of intercourse, attitudes toward sexuality, and attention to physiological arousal; these results led the authors to suggest that the frequency and variety of a woman's sexual repertoire may be influential in affecting her physiological responsivity to laboratory stimuli.

Thus, the only two studies to date that have systematically compared psychophysiological responding in sexually functional and dysfunctional women have produced very different patterns of results. In one report, differences in vasocongestion were noted, while indices of subjective arousal were relatively constant across groups (Wincze et al.); the other report yielded exactly the opposite pattern of results, with group differences noted on a measure of subjective arousal, but not on VPA (Morokoff & Heiman). Several possible explanations exist for this discrepancy of results. First, these two reports employed differing measures of vasocongestion (VBV as opposed to VPA); in light of the uncertainty over the vasocongestive processes measured by each of these signals, direct comparison of the measures is unwise. Second, there may have been differences between these two studies in the level of arousal produced by the stimulus presentations. For example, in both Heiman's earlier study and the later one with Morokoff, a wider range of stimuli was employed, which included sexual fantasy material; by contrast, Wincze et al. exposed subjects to erotic films that only included scenes of heterosexual foreplay and may have resulted in lower levels of arousal for both groups.

A key question in this type of investigation is the relationship between varying levels of arousal and physiological–subjective interactions in the patterning of sexual arousal. More specifically, the possibility that patterns of physiological–subjective correlation are dependent on the level of sexual arousal achieved appears relevant for reconciling this apparent discrepancy. In addition, given that anorgasmia specifically involves the orgasmic response and may or may not be related to arousal difficulties in individual cases, one can question what meaning to attribute to differences in low to moderate levels of the vasocongestion response in women experiencing this problem. Alternative experimental approaches that examine specific factors related to achieving orgasm, such as the ability to screen out external distraction, a lack of fear over loss of control, and positive attitudes toward sexuality, may be equally important in exploring relevant features of this disorder.

A preliminary report has recently appeared that begins to address these issues. Hoon, Coleman, Amberson, and Ling (1981) presented three case studies in which the Levin–Wagner heat probe was used to measure vaginal blood flow. Two of the subjects did not report sexual difficulties, while the third had sought treatment for low arousal and anorgasmia. All subjects were assessed during fantasy and masturbation conditions. Few differences were noted between the clinical subject and the functional women during low levels of arousal; however, marked differences appeared during the latter phases of the arousal process. The clinical subject showed a pattern of stabilizing vasocongestion midway through self-stimulation, in contrast with both control subjects, who demonstrated increasing vaso-congestion during stimulation, culminating in orgasm. The authors hypothesize that the physiological markers for sexual dysfunction may not appear before the second half of the arousal process. Based on this initial finding, larger-scale explorations of this hypothesis appear warranted.

As a final point, anorgasmia often presents clinically as part of a general pattern of low or inhibited arousal. In these cases, diminished vasocongestion may be expected early in the arousal process, reflecting lowered responsivity. In other cases, the lack of orgasm is quite specific, and may only be associated with certain situations or partners. In these cases, in which arousal disorders are an infrequent complaint, physiological indicators of dysfunction may not appear until the latter part of the arousal response. Future studies that differentiate between these subtypes of orgasmic dysfunctions would be valuable in unraveling the psychophysiological interplay among vasocongestion, subjective arousal, and the clinical manifestations of the disorder.

Penetration Problems

Two separate and less common forms of female sexual dysfunction are vaginismus and dyspareunia. Vaginismus involves spasmodic, involuntary constriction of the musculature surrounding the vaginal opening and the outer third of the vagina. In its most severe form, vaginismus may present as an unconsummated marriage (e.g., Leiblum *et al.*, 1980), as penetration of the vagina by any object, including a penis, may be impossible. In less extreme cases, penetration may be possible, albeit painful. Most commonly, women with vaginismus have little difficulty with sexual arousal; lubrication may occur naturally, the woman may report that noncoital sex is satisfying and arousing, and orgasmic responsiveness is often unimpaired (Kolodny, Masters, & Johnson, 1979). Clinical data suggest that women who are orgasmic are more likely to have positive treatment outcomes than are nonorgasmic women presenting with vaginismus (Ellison, 1972). No epidemiological studies exist to date concerning the incidence or prevalence of this disorder.

Another female dysfunction involving difficulty with penetration is dyspareunia, a condition characterized by pain or discomfort during intercourse. This pain is often described as tearing, burning, aching, or excessive pressure occurring during or immediately after intercourse, in contrast with the pain accompanying vaginismus, which is often attributed to constriction or muscle tension. A salient feature distinguishing these two disorders is their probable etiology: Most cases of vaginismus are psychologically based, while dyspareunia is more frequently associated with organic factors, such as endometriosis, recurrent urinary tract infections, tumors, and/or damage to the uterine or vaginal structures caused by surgery or childbirth. Kolodny, Masters, and Johnson (1979) have summarized specific causes of pain that accompany particular conditions, among which they aptly include a lack of lubrication, a frequent concomitant in cases of dyspareunia.

An issue for investigation in this disorder is whether low arousal precedes painful intercourse or is a conditioned reflex resulting from organically based discomfort and repeated painful sexual intercourse. Based on clinical experience, it appears that a complex interaction of psychological and physiological factors is operative in dyspareunia, although at this writing no systematic studies have attempted to unravel these two processes. Thus, the penetration disorders offer a potentially important opportunity for the differentiation of psychological and organic contributions to female sexual dysfunction.

Other Disorders of Female Sexual Function

Several other forms of sexual disorders are described by the current classification system and deserve note. Disorders of inhibited excitement, or failure to achieve and maintain lubrication and vasocongestion, are often diagnosed in conjunction with orgasmic dysfunction. In fact, until the advent of DSM-III, these two disorders were not separated in most clinical studies and case reports. While this distinction is logically derived from the Masters and Johnson model of the sexual response cycle, as discussed in Chapter 2, this model is problematic in certain respects; the distinction among the various phases of the arousal process is particularly problematic (Robinson, 1976). Given the frequent overlap in the presenting clinical constellations of inhibited excitement and anorgasmia, the need appears strong for studies aimed at differentiating presenting features and psychophysiological parameters in these two disorders. To date, there is virtually no experimental knowledge of disorders of sexual excitement that is separate from knowledge of orgasmic dysfunction.

Inhibited sexual desire is another sexual disorder that has only recently received diagnostic mention. In her recent review of male and female disorders of sexual desire, Kaplan (1979) discusses specific etiological factors relevant in inhibited desire, among which are included an involuntary but active psychological suppression mechanism, usually motivated by anger or anxiety. In fact, in related studies of sexual behavior in animals, it is commonly held that sexual interest in organisms higher on the phylogenetic scale is controlled by neural processes rather than by hormonal or peripheral processes, as is seen in animals lower on the phylogenetic scale (e.g., Hampson & Hampson, 1961; Hart, 1969, 1970; Bancroft, 1983). This would appear to be an important area for future psychophysiological research, with the aim of providing empirical data to augment existing conceptualizations of sexual desire and interest. The inclusion of measures of CNS activity, such as the EEG, could be valuable in establishing an empirical understanding of disorders of sexual desire.

LABORATORY ANALOGUE STUDIES OF FEMALE SEXUAL DYSFUNCTION

A related application of sexual psychophysiology has involved the experimental analysis of factors relevant in female dysfunction. The majority of these reports examine the influence of anxiety and distraction on sexual responding. This emphasis reflects Masters and Johnson's stress on the central role of psychological factors, such as fear and distraction, in maintaining the male and female sexual dysfunctions.

Another factor frequently cited as an important contributing influence to inhibited sexual responding in adulthood is that of specific sexual attitudes and values learned in childhood—a surprisingly neglected area in research to date. For example, as Masters and Johnson (1970) note,

[I]t is obvious that man has had society's blessing to building his sexual value system in an appropriate, naturally occurring context and woman has not. . . . during her formative years, the female dissembles much of her developing functional sexuality in response to societal requirements for a "good girl" facade. (p. 207)

This distinction suggests a range of specific attitudes that might be relevant in diminishing arousal, inhibiting orgasm, and reducing sexual desire. This area would appear to be ideally suited for psychophysiological study and could provide greater sophistication in our understanding of the interrelationships between social and psychological influences to female sexual disorders. To date, the roles of anxiety, distraction, and specific attentional processes in the etiology of female sexual dysfunction have received specific investigation, as we describe below.

Anxiety

Among the first experimental investigations of the effects of anxiety on sexual arousal was a study by Hoon *et al.* (1977b). These authors showed a series of film sequences that were either neutral (scenes from a travelogue) or anxiety-producing (scenes of automobile accidents) to sexually

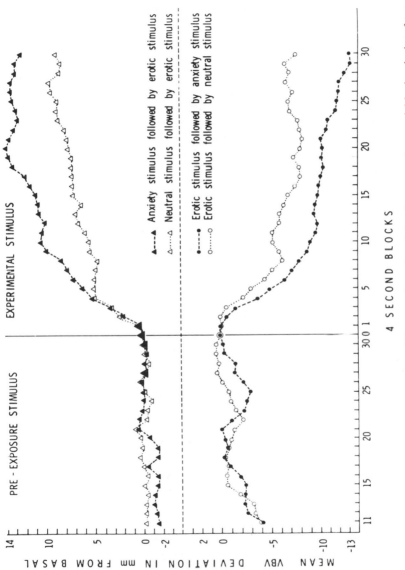

Figure 11.2. Mean VBV deviation in millimeters from basal levels across 4-second blocks during four sequences of stimulus exposure. From "A Test of Reciprocal Inhibition: Are Anxiety and Sexual Arousal in Women Mutually Inhibitory?" by P. W. Hoon, J. P. Wincze, and E. F. Hoon, 1977, *Journal of Abnormal Psychology*, 86, p. 70. Copyright 1977 by the American Psychological Association. Reprinted by permission.

functional women. Immediately following these pre-exposures, subjects were shown additional films containing heterosexual foreplay scenarios. In this study, anxiety pre-exposure resulted in significant increases in vaginal engorgement during the erotic film, relative to neutral pre-exposure. Reversing the order of presentation of the films (erotic film preceding the anxiety or neutral film) resulted in significantly greater decrements of arousal during the anxiety film, relative to the neutral film (see Figure 11.2).

While this study suggests that the initial experience of anxiety may not inhibit sexual arousal, as is suggested by the conceptualizations of Masters and Johnson, Kaplan, and others, Wolpe (1978) has suggested that the results of this study may have been due to a phenomenon of anxiety relief. That is, the heightened arousal following anxiety pre-exposure may have been indicative of a positive-contrast effect. To date, all other investigations of the influence of anxiety on sexual responding have been conducted with male subjects, thus leaving open the experimental question of the influence of anxiety on women's sexual responding.

Distraction

The notion of distraction has also been examined in this context. Lifshitz and Adams (1980) conducted a study exploring the influence of a brief distractor (the ringing of a telephone) on VPA during erotic audiotapes in orgasmic and nonorgasmic women. The results revealed that distraction had differential effects on vasocongestion, depending on group membership. Sexually functional women demonstrated increased VPA during the telephone distraction, while anorgasmic women showed a decrease in VPA in this condition.

Postsession interviews suggested that the sexually functional sample reported attending to their own physical response and to their partner's reactions during actual sexual encounters. The dysfunctional women reported a similar pattern of attending to their own sexual responsivity at first, but this shifted at the point of advanced foreplay to excessive rumination over their inability to achieve orgasm. At very high levels of arousal, the anorgasmic women reported an increased awareness of their external surroundings, while women in the normal control group reported feeling "absorbed" by the sexual situation and thus were relatively unaware of the environment. These different cognitive processing styles reported during sexual interaction by functional and dysfunctional women constitute one of the more intriguing aspects of this investigation. The increase in VPA noted during distraction in the sexually functional women is somewhat curious, however, especially in light of the second investigation of this type.

Adams, Haynes, and Brayer (1985) conducted a similar study, using an erotic audiotape of longer duration and an arithmetic addition task as the distractor. Their results showed significant decreases in VPA and subjective arousal in both groups during distraction. In this report, measures of vasocongestion and subjective arousal were poorly correlated for the anorgasmic women, while significant positive correlations were noted for the control sample. Unlike the earlier report, little support was shown here for the notion that distractibility from erotic stimuli is a salient feature distinguishing orgasmic from anorgasmic women.

In considering the conflicting results of these two studies, several possible explanations deserve consideration, including the potential unreliability of the vaginal photoplethysmograph (cf. Hatch, 1979; Beck, Sakheim, & Barlow, 1983). These two studies also employed distracting stimuli that differed in intensity: The arithmetic addition task would seem to be a more salient and involving distractor than a ringing telephone, which may have been easier for subjects to ignore in the Lifshitz and Adams study.

A recent study of the effects of distraction in a more naturalistic setting has been reported by Geer (1984). This author examined sexual arousal both during and subsequent to distraction, reflecting the more usual reports of interrupted erotic responding. Sexually functional women were presented with a dichotic listening task, much like the procedure used in an earlier report with male subjects (Geer & Fuhr, 1976; see Chapter 10). The arithmetic task was introduced in the context of an ongoing erotic stimulus, in order to explore the effect of distraction on pre-existing arousal. In this design, distraction rapidly reduced arousal—in some cases, below resting baseline. On the second presentation, however, the distractor had a lessened effect on arousal, suggesting that individuals can learn to efficiently screen out or habituate to external sounds and tasks. Clearly, the significance of this finding for the treatment of sexual dysfunction deserves continued attention, particularly with respect to creating resistance to distraction as a strategy for facilitating arousal.

It thus appears that external distraction may not necessarily influence sexual arousal in a direct or linear fashion; rather, disruption of vasocongestion appears to depend on a woman's prior experience with interruption during sexual responding, and possibly on her level of arousal at the time that the distractor occurs (Lifshitz & Adams, 1980). Future studies in this area might investigate clinical applications of these results, given the implications of Geer's (1984) report for constructing strategies to assist dysfunctional women in filtering out irrelevant stimuli during ongoing sexual responding.

Focus of Attention

A related area of inquiry involves the effects of focus of attention during sexual responding. While the notion of "spectatoring" has been applied principally to male dysfunctions, several authors have suggested that a similar process may be involved in disorders of female arousal: The woman may not be attending to her physical sensations, and hence may be unaware of pleasing sensations or specific activities that heighten arousal. To date, two studies have examined directional attention in women without complaints of sexual dysfunction.

In the first study of this type, Smith (1980) instructed college-aged women volunteers to focus either on the erotic stimulus or on their physical sensations, or to imagine that they were observing themselves. A mirror was placed in front of the subjects in this last condition, in order to facilitate self-observation. Following these instructions, an erotic audiotape was presented. The results indicated that substantially higher arousal was seen during instructions to attend to the stimulus, while the remaining two conditions were not significantly different from each other. Contrary to clinical speculations, instructions to focus on genital sensations did not facilitate responding.

A second study explored a similar question, although from a somewhat different theoretical perspective. Dekker *et al.* (1985) examined the relative effects of instructions to college-aged women to attend to specific aspects of the erotic stimulus, compared to attention to both stimulus and response components, following Lang's (1979) theory of emotional imagery. Subjects were asked to "attend to the description of situations and events in the story" (stimulus instructions), to "attend to images of sexual feelings" (stimulus/response instructions), or to "bring about sexual arousal by imagery" (a separate condition, to assess vividness of imagery as an unrelated predictor). These instructions were delivered simultaneously with the presentation of erotic audiotapes, and subjective sexual arousal, genital sensations, and specific mood states were assessed. Self-reported arousal was higher during the stimulus/response condition for these normal volunteers, although, unfortunately, no measure of vasocongestion was included in this report. These instruction effects did appear on several dimensions of subjective sexual arousal (e.g., detection of genital sensations, assessment of specific sensual states) and mood states. Further studies of this type with dysfunctional women appear necessary before greater understanding of the role of attentional focus in female disorders can be gained.

Related Studies

As noted above, information concerning the influence of sexual attitudes and beliefs (cognitive factors) on physiological and subjective arousal is beginning to accumulate, although this type of research is in its infancy. An exception to this can be found in a recent report by Morokoff (1985a), examining the effects of sex guilt, repression, sexual arousability, and sexual experience on patterns of arousal in women. Subjects were assigned randomly to view either an erotic or a nonerotic film, after completion of a number of scales to assess relevant sexual attitudes. Women scoring high on the Mosher scale of sex guilt reported less subjective arousal, but actually showed significantly greater vasocongestion (measured via VPA) than did women low in sex guilt. For the high-guilt group, the initial presentation of an erotic videotape facilitated vasocongestion during subsequent sexual fantasy instructions. A similar pattern was noted for women with little or no sexual experience and for women low in sexual arousability. The author suggests that a pattern of behavioral inhibition may actually facilitate sexual responding through a sensitization effect; that is, infrequent exposure to erotica may elicit a stronger reaction, based on its stronger stimulus quality, than it does from women with more frequent exposure to erotica.

The lack of correspondence in this study between physiological and subjective arousal (e.g., $r = .42$ during the erotic film) suggests that some amount of desynchrony is an outcome of this avoidant pattern; this may imply that women high in sex guilt do not learn to experience their genital sensations fully, and instead conform to what they perceive to be societal standards. A replication of this study with women experiencing sexual difficulties would be valuable, especially given the lack of related research in this area.

A similar study examined the physiological, affective, and cognitive patterns of sexual arousal in sexually functional women aged 21–58 (Heiman, 1980). Physiological and subjective arousal were measured during erotic audiotapes and films, as well as during sexual fantasy. The experimental procedure was repeated twice, to assess reliability of responding over time. In this report, subjective sexual arousal was correlated with a range of positive mood states, including ratings of liking, enjoying, and being interested. In contrast, negative affect was significantly associated with vaginal engorgement but not with subjective ratings of sexual arousal; this suggests that these two processes may operate somewhat independently, and may be influenced by separate emotional factors. VPA responses of these subjects, subdivided into married and unmarried groups, are shown in Figure 11.3. Generally, negative correlations were found between vaginal response in the laboratory and reported sexual responsiveness at home, thus raising the issue of the external validity of the laboratory paradigm. Given the correlational nature of these results, the conclusions concerning the patterning of the affective-physiological relationships should be viewed as tentative and await more specific hypothesis testing.

A separate but related issue involves the influence of prior sexual behaviors to current genital responsivity. Many authors have noted, for example, the importance of masturbation and fantasy in the acquisition of healthy sexual functioning, stressing that until recently these behaviors

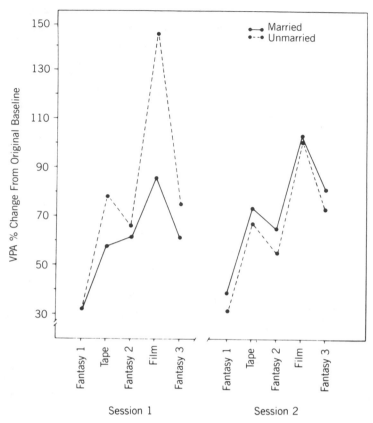

Figure 11.3. VPA response for married and unmarried women during erotic conditions, sessions 1 and 2. From "Female Sexual Response Patterns: Interactions of Physiological, Affective, and Contextual Cues" by J. R. Heiman, 1980, *Archives of General Psychiatry, 37,* p. 1313. Copyright 1980 by the American Medical Association. Reprinted by permission.

have been socially proscribed for most women (e.g., Gagnon *et al.*, 1982; Kaplan, 1981; Kinsey *et al.*, 1953). Stock and Geer (1982) have examined this issue experimentally, using both erotic audiotapes and fantasy during VPA measurement with undergraduate volunteers. Subjects were given several measures to assess imagery ability (e.g., the Betts Q.M.I. Vividness of Imagery Scale), as well as a scale to determine the frequency of sexual fantasy during a typical day. Sexually functional women who reported more frequent use of fantasy during masturbation in their natural sexual repertoires showed greater vasocongestion to both erotic audiotapes and sexual fantasy in the laboratory, as shown in Table 11.1. In addition, a significant relationship was noted between responses to one of the imagery questionnaires and the magnitude of VPA during the fantasy condition ($r = .26$). This study is one of the first examples of integrating extralaboratory sexual experiences with arousal patterns in the laboratory, and thus provides an important illustration of a potentially fruitful application of sexual psychophysiology. This type of investigation also begins to address certain reservations concerning the external validity of the laboratory paradigm in sexual psychophysiology, and suggests that particular sexual behavior patterns can be accurately measured in the experimental setting.

Unfortunately, experimental approaches to relevant factors in sexual dysfunction in women have not progressed as rapidly as similar work with the male disorders has. Among the possible causes of this delay are the difficulties with available measures of genital blood flow in women, combined with biases about research on female sexuality. In addition, current conceptualizations of factors relevant to impairment of the arousal response have not been as clearly delineated for women as for men, and this has resulted in more retrospective or correlational studies of women. One important direction for future research in this area would be to investigate the effects of specific affective states, such as anger or disgust, on sexual responding. Moreover, the inclusion of dysfunctional samples in studies of this type is much needed to expand our available knowledge concerning specific processes that influence sexual arousal in clinical samples.

APPLICATIONS OF PSYCHOPHYSIOLOGY TO SEX THERAPY

In sharp contrast to the available literature on maintaining factors in female dysfunction, a relatively large body of research exists on the use of sexual psychophysiology in the treatment of these disorders. Two types of studies have been reported: those that have investigated biofeedback as a primary

Table 11.1. Mean Size of Vaginal Response to Erotic Stimulation by Report of Fantasy Use during Masturbation

Questionnaire response	Mean change (mm) in pressure pulse amplitude	
	Fantasy period	Tape period
Always use fantasy	0.93	1.08
Use fantasy 75% of time	0.72	1.02
Use fantasy 25–75% of time	0.44	0.87
Use fantasy 25% of time	0.15	0.26
Never use fantasy	0.12	0.02

Note. From "A Study of Fantasy-Based Sexual Arousal in Women" by W. S. Stock and J. H. Geer, 1982, *Archives of Sexual Behavior, 11*, p. 41. Copyright 1982 by Plenum Publishing Corporation. Reprinted by permission.

form of treatment, and those that have utilized psychophysiological assessment methods to evaluate the efficacy of more traditional forms of sex therapy. Each of these approaches has included a focus on individualized factors in treatment response—a feature that lends increased sophistication to psychophysiological explorations of sex therapy.

The use of biofeedback as a treatment approach for inhibited sexual excitement has been based on the rationale that vasocongestive responses can be shaped or acquired, given an adequate number of trials and the use of a clear feedback signal. Several early studies explored this possibility with sexually functional women, because of an initial concern about the feasibility of the approach for dysfunctional women, who were presumed to have a poor subjective awareness of genital arousal (e.g., Heiman, 1975). This supposition was based on weak correlations between physiological and subjective measures of arousal in other studies; these could, however, have been due to factors other than poor perception of vasocongestion. Nonetheless, the initial studies were conducted with sexually functional volunteers, and often had interesting outcomes.

In one of the first reports of this type, Hoon et al. (1972) reported a time-series analysis of data from two subjects during biofeedback. Their results suggested that this approach could enhance sexual arousal above levels noted during erotic fantasy, and that other autonomic indices (e.g., heart rate, blood pressure, and skin conductance) did not show simultaneous changes with biofeedback, suggesting specificity of conditioning.

A related study, reported by Cerny (1978), examined the administration of feedback to sexually functional women, with instructions either to increase vasocongestion or to decrease vaginal responding. In addition, both veridical and false feedback were examined in this report, although, interestingly, no differences were noted between these two conditions. The results suggested that with feedback, subjects were able to lower their level of vasocongestion, but were not able to enhance arousal. Cerny's findings thus raise questions concerning the appropriateness of biofeedback applications for female arousal disorders; this report includes anecdotal evidence that several subjects found the auditory feedback signal to be distracting. Other investigations of biofeedback have shown some degree of instructional control of the vasocongestive response in normal women (e.g., Hoon, 1980; Zingheim & Sandman, 1978), although in each of these cases, the observed changes were small and did not appear to affect the overall pattern of arousal significantly.

To date, several applications have been reported with dysfunctional samples, most usually anorgasmic women. In one report, Amberson, Hoon, Coleman, Hoon, and Ling (1980) treated women presenting with inhibited sexual desire, low arousal, and infrequent occurrence of orgasms with a program of fantasy training and biofeedback. This approach was contrasted with a standard sex therapy program, in order to determine whether differential effects on the women's ability to discriminate sexual arousal from nonaroused states would emerge. No significant treatment effects were noted on multiple measures of vasocongestion for the fantasy–biofeedback program. Individual patient data were examined, to assess whether subtle changes might have resulted from this treatment approach; surprisingly, neither vaginal blood flow nor subjective arousal revealed posttreatment changes, and none of these women reported an increase in orgasmic consistency. The results of this study are somewhat disheartening, especially in the context of earlier findings with normal volunteers.

A second report by the same investigators (Hoon, Hoon, Amberson, Coleman, & Ling, 1983) detailed the pattern of changes during fantasy retraining and biofeedback with a single case of orgasmic dysfunction; this time, there was a positive outcome. The case involved a 26-year-old married woman who presented with complaints of an inability to reach orgasm, accompanied by low sexual arousal and moderate levels of anxiety concerning sexual interactions. Treatment involved five sessions of sexual fantasy training, followed by six sessions of visual biofeedback training. Despite verbal reports of satisfaction with therapy from both the patient and her husband, and the fact that she became orgasmic during the course of the 11 treatment sessions, the only objective indicators of improvement were increased VBV and the patient's ability to use imagery and to fantasize. The authors speculate that since related changes were not noted on any dimension of VPA, biofeedback may result in highly specific changes in vaginal engorgement, thus potentially limiting its utility in clinical settings.

In considering the existing data on biofeedback, it would appear that there is little to support its use at present as a specific treatment modality for sexual disorders in women. As physiological assessment procedures for female genital arousal continue to be refined, repeated trials of this treatment approach that utilize more sensitive measures of vasocongestion appear warranted.

Sexual psychophysiology has also been applied to the evaluation of outcome of more conventional forms of sex therapy. In earlier discussions of this application (e.g., Heiman, 1976; Bancroft, 1971a), considerable enthusiasm was expressed for the possibility of evaluating existing treatment approaches for sexual dysfunction by means of clinical trials and the inclusion of physiological measures of vasocongestion. However, with increased awareness of the limits of sexual psychophysiology has come a realization that a sole reliance on vasocongestion as an indicator of change is overly simplistic, and may compromise a more complete understanding both of therapeutic mechanisms of sex therapy and of female sexuality.

To date, two investigations have examined the efficacy of traditional sex therapy, both with women experiencing inhibited sexual arousal. In the first, Wincze *et al.* (1978) contrasted pre- and posttreatment measures of vasocongestion, subjective arousal, and behavioral indicators of sexual activity. While all patients expressed positive feelings about the sex therapy program and increased satisfaction with their sexual relationships, there were no posttherapy differences on any of the physiological or behavioral measures relevant to sexual arousal. Wincze *et al.* have discussed the potential impact of social demands and expectations for therapeutic effects in explaining their pattern of results.

The second study of this type has been reported by Morokoff and Heiman (1980). In testing prior to conjoint sex therapy, women with a lack of arousal or low frequency of arousal in their sexual relationships reported lower levels of subjective arousal than did sexually functional volunteers, although equivalent levels of vasocongestion were observed in the two samples. Following 15 sessions of sex therapy modeled after the Masters and Johnson format, no differences in subjective arousal or vasocongestion were noted between the two groups (see Figure 11.4). The authors have suggested that sexually functional and dysfunctional women may differ in their interpretation of genital changes and that sex therapy may operate to change this physiological labeling process. Given the conflicting evidence concerning patterns of vasocongestion and subjective arousal in clinical and nonclinical samples, as reviewed earlier in this chapter, it is difficult to reach a conclusion about the impact of sex therapy on physiological responding. An accumulation of studies examining autonomic parameters in sexual dysfunction would appear to be a necessary step before sexual psychophysiology is employed as an index of treatment efficacy.

A related use of sexual psychophysiology has focused on the effects of Kegel exercises—a specific set of interventions designed to exercise the vaginal musculature (Kegel, 1951, 1952) and, as a consequence, to increase awareness of vaginal sensations and orgasmic ability. Until very recently, the only empirical support for the Kegel exercises came from *ex post facto* correlational studies that examined differences between orgasmic and anorgasmic women in the strength of the PC muscle (e.g., Graber & Kline-Graber, 1979). The first prospective study (Chambless *et al.*, 1982) failed to find the predicted relationship between PC strength and orgasmic responsivity in a sample of women experiencing varying types of orgasmic dysfunctions. A follow-up report (Chambless *et al.*, 1984) failed to find a significant influence of increased PC strength on orgasmic ability in a large sample of women with low orgasmic frequency.

Recently, one psychophysiological study has been reported (Messé & Geer, 1985) examining the effects of training in the Kegel exercises on VPA and subjective arousal in sexually functional volunteers. Subjects were assigned to a condition that taught Kegel exercises and emphasized practice, to a condition that merely taught the exercises but did not include practice, or to an attention control group. The results indicated that vaginal

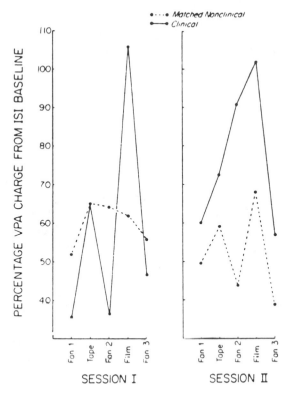

Figure 11.4. VPA responses for clinical and nonclinical samples during erotic conditions, sessions I and II. Mean VPA responses were derived from a repeated-measures ANOVA on percentage change from interstimulus interval baseline scores. From "Effects of Erotic Stimuli on Sexually Functional and Dysfunctional Women: Multiple Measures before and after Sex Therapy" by P. J. Morokoff and J. R. Heiman, 1980, *Behaviour Research and Therapy, 18,* p. 131. Copyright 1980 by Pergamon Journals, Ltd. Reprinted by permission.

contractions both enhanced subjective ratings and increased VPA, although this technique did not increase the concordance between these two measures, as indicated by correlational analyses. This type of study appears to represent the future for treatment applications of sexual psychophysiology. Compared to investigations that have sought to examine multifaceted treatment programs, this type of application is considerably more focused and offers more sophisticated knowledge concerning the therapeutic effects of specific interventions. Greater use of sexual psychophysiology in this fashion appears promising, especially for use in the evaluation of specific techniques that have been developed to treat female sexual dysfunction.

SUMMARY

As reviewed in this chapter, advances in the psychophysiological assessment of sexual dysfunction in women have occurred over the past decade, although the pace of this progress appears somewhat slower than comparable advances in regard to male dysfunction have been. Several possible reasons for this discrepancy have been enumerated throughout this chapter, including both public and professional sensitivity to the study of female sexuality, a relative lack of knowledge about the physiology of the female sexual response, and difficulties in genital assessment. To these, Hoon (1984) has added the field's overemphasis on vasocongestion as the sole measure of physiological responding in women; certainly, given the range of sexual disorders occurring in women, measures of lubrication, genital muscle tone, and specific features of the orgasmic response (e.g., the formation of the "orgasmic platform") are needed in this context.

One outstanding characteristic of many of the studies reviewed in this chapter is the inclusion of data on individual subjects—a feature that allows for exploration of individual stereotypy, or stable patterns of autonomic response to particular stimuli. As noted at points above, certain important facts have emerged through this approach, such as the observation that dysfunctional women show disruptions in sexual responding beginning at medium to high levels of arousal, relative to sexually functional women (e.g., Hoon et al., 1981; Lifshitz & Adams, 1980). In contrast, the area is most in need of studies exploring response stereotypy—a gap that is especially notable, given the correlational analyses often used in these studies, the considerable variance observed between measures of subjective arousal and vasocongestion, and the difficulty in determining the source of these patterns. With the continuing support of a culture that only recently has acknowledged the importance of female sexuality, investigations in this area are likely to provide a more complete understanding of sexual function and dysfunction in women.

Thus, the current state of psychophysiological information on female sexuality and sexual dysfunction reflects in certain respects specific measurement issues outlined in Chapter 4, as well as shifting cultural trends in perceptions of women and the role of sexuality in definitions of femininity. As in any field, one sign of maturity is the ability to adapt a measurement methodology for the study of clinical and applied issues in related areas. This type of synthesis with related areas of inquiry is beginning to occur for female sexual psychophysiology—a development that highlights the promise of work that has been conducted to date. With continued application, the state of knowledge concerning female sexual dysfunction will advance and ultimately will contribute to diagnosis, treatment, and the understanding of the role of individual factors in determining the outcome of sex therapy.

CHAPTER TWELVE

Alcohol and Other Drug Effects on Sexual Response

Compared with sex under LSD, the way you've been making love—no matter how ecstatic the pleasure you think you get from it—is like making love to a department store window-dummy—Timothy Leary (1968, p. 84)

Myths and folklore about the effect of drugs on sexuality pervade almost every culture. In fact, the search for the perfect aphrodisiac—a drug that will heighten sexual desire, pleasure, or performance—has been a continuing cultural quest from ancient to modern times. Natural substances such as datura, belladonna, and henbane were key ingredients in the sexual orgies of ancient fertility cults. Similarly, yohimbine has long been used by the natives of Africa to enhance their sexual prowess, and the mandrake plant was used in medieval Europe for the same purpose. Oysters, ginseng, and Vitamin E have similarly been recommended at various times as possessing aphrodisiacal qualities (Rosen & Hall, 1984). Despite cultural lore, the results of contemporary research seem to indicate that this search has largely been in vain. There are few, if any, drug substances that have a direct and positive effect on any aspect of sexual response. In fact, much of the research in recent years has focused on the effects of "anaphrodisiacs," or substances that have the capacity to diminish or inhibit sexual arousal, desire, and satisfaction.

Experimental research on the topic is a relatively recent phenomenon, as the bulk of existing literature on drug effects on sexual function is based upon anecdotal or clinical reports. This is particularly true of the literature on side effects of prescription drugs, where references to associated sexual difficulties are common, despite the relative absence of controlled studies. In addition, Buffum (1982) has noted that clinical reports of sexual side effects of prescription drugs are generally based on the treatment of individuals with pre-existing medical or psychological disorders, and thus the observed sexual difficulties could be attributed either to the underlying

299

disorder or to the treatment drug. Clinical reports and case studies are also highly susceptible to biases on the part of both patients and clinicians. For example, it is well known that the sexual attitudes and values of physicians play a major role in determining the likelihood that patients will report sexual problems generally, including the sexual side effects of drugs (Burnap & Golden, 1967).

Evaluation of drug effects on sexual function is further complicated by the effects of dosage level and duration of use, the individual characteristics of the user, and the context in which the drug is taken. The effects of set and setting, in particular, are important in determining the sexual effects of alcohol and recreational drugs. Generally, if a drug is expected to heighten sexual arousal, it will, and vice versa. A striking example is found in the report of the Indian Hemp Drugs Commission (1893–1894/1969); by this account, marihuana was used in 19th-century houses of prostitution as a sexual stimulant, as well as by religious ascetics to destroy sexual appetite.

Other important factors to be considered are the dosage and duration of use. For example, several studies have demonstrated a dose–response curve for the effects of alcohol on sexual arousal in both men and women (Farkas & Rosen, 1976; Rubin & Henson, 1976; Wilson & Lawson, 1978). Likewise, whether drug use is acute or chronic can be a major factor in determining the effect on the user. Whereas short-term users may be responsive to the novelty and positive expectation effects associated with initial use of the drug, chronic users tend to suffer adverse effects on physical and psychological health. Furthermore, the chronic user is likely to develop either physical or psychological tolerance, and hence to use increasingly high dosages, which are more likely to have a detrimental effect on sexual function.

Despite the prevalence of adverse effects, alcohol and recreational drugs continue to be widely used in association with sexual behavior. Among the explanations offered for this frequent association is the notion that both sexual arousal and drug or alcohol consumption involve the most easily available means in our society for achieving altered states of consciousness. Thus, R. E. L. Masters (1967) has suggested that erotic imagery may be greatly enhanced by consciousness-altering substances such as cocaine, marijuana, and alcohol. It has frequently also been noted that alcohol and drug use, like sexual behavior, are highly controversial and value-laden social activities (Abel, 1985). For the individual with high levels of sexual guilt, drug or alcohol consumption may serve an important disinhibition role in facilitating subsequent sexual behavior. As noted in Chapter 9, drug and alcohol use are also commonly associated with the commission of sexual offenses, such as rape and child molestation, as well as of most other criminal offenses.

ALCOHOL EFFECTS ON SEXUAL FUNCTION

Acute Effects on Male Sexual Arousal

Until the mid-1970s, research on alcohol effects on sexual response was limited to a few studies of copulatory behavior in laboratory animals (Gantt, 1952; Hart, 1968) and projective measures of sexual interest in humans (Clark, 1952). In the past decade, however, an impressive collection of studies has appeared in which laboratory psychophysiological methods have been applied to the complex question of alcohol's effects on sexual arousal. It is noteworthy that the first laboratory studies on alcohol and sex were conducted primarily with prototypical male college students. The use of male subjects reflected in part the earlier availability of measurement technology for males (i.e., penile tumescence measures), as well as the predominant bias of viewing males as the primary users and abusers of alcohol (Carpenter & Armenti, 1971). Nonetheless, in the past 5 years a number of studies involving female subjects have appeared, and reflect our increased understanding of patterns of alcohol use in the population at large.

The first study to assess directly the acute effects of alcohol consumption on male sexual response was reported by Farkas and Rosen (1976). These investigators administered four controlled combinations of ethanol and orange juice in a crossover design to 16 healthy male college students. When subjects reached a series of predetermined dosage levels (0, 0.025, 0.050, and 0.075% blood alcohol concentration [BAC]), measures of penile tumescence and heart rate were obtained in response to the presentation of an erotic film. The design for the study was a repeated-measures, Latin-square design, in which each of the subjects was exposed to each of the alcohol dosages in counterbalanced order.

The results of this study are shown in Figure 12.1. A slight increase in arousal at the lowest BAC (0.025%) was followed by a significant and relatively greater decrease in arousal at the higher dosage levels. Similarly, tonic heart rate reflected a strong, incremental trend associated with greater dosage levels. Subjects' self-report corresponded closely with the physiological results: The greatest subjective estimates of arousal occurred at the lowest alcohol dosage level.

Similar results were obtained in a study by Rubin and Henson (1976) using comparable alcohol dosages (0.5, 1.0, and 1.5 ml/kg). In this study, again, 16 volunteer male subjects viewed erotic stimuli in the laboratory while their penile tumescence responses were recorded at each of the three different blood alcohol levels. A repeated-measures design was used, and subjects' ability to voluntarily control tumescence under both alcohol and placebo conditions was also examined. As in the earlier Farkas and Rosen (1976) study, these authors found that moderate amounts of alcohol were

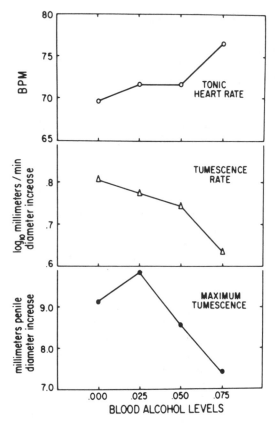

Figure 12.1. Effects of BAC (%) on male tumescence and heart rate. From "Effect of Alcohol on Elicited Male Sexual Response" by G. M. Farkas and R. C. Rosen, 1976, *Journal of Studies on Alcohol, 37,* p. 269. Copyright 1976 by Alcohol Research Documentation, Inc., Rutgers Center of Alcohol Studies, New Brunswick, New Jersey. Reprinted by permission.

associated with some impairment of erectile response, whereas at the highest alcohol dose, significant inhibition of tumescence occurred. There was little evidence for alcohol's effects on voluntary control of erection, despite cultural predictions. In addition, most of these subjects believed that alcohol enhanced sexual performance, and this belief was unaffected by the subjects' disconfirming experience in the laboratory.

A third study published in the same year (Briddell & Wilson, 1976) used a somewhat different methodology for assessing the acute effects of alcohol on male sexual arousal. A total of 48 male student volunteers were randomly assigned to one of eight groups. Half of the groups were told that alcohol would facilitate their sexual arousal, while the other groups were told to expect a negative effect. In addition, each of the groups received one of four alcohol dosages (0.08, 0.5, 0.8, and 1.2 g/kg). Sexual arousal was assessed by direct measurement of penile tumescence in response to erotic videotapes. Results showed that tumescence was inversely proportional to the amount of alcohol consumed, and that this effect was uninfluenced by the subjects' expectations. In a subsequent study, however, Wilson and Lawson (1976b) manipulated subjects' beliefs concerning whether they had consumed either alcohol or placebo (a "balanced-placebo" design); they found that those subjects who believed they had ingested alcohol showed increased tumescence, compared to those who believed they had drunk only tonic water. Interestingly, no main effect of alcohol was found in this study, apparently due to the fact that only modest amounts of alcohol were administered (0.5–0.6 g/kg).

In the most recent study of alcohol and expectation effects on male sexual arousal, Wilson, Niaura, and Adler (1985) investigated the effects of alcohol intoxication, and the expectation that alcohol had been consumed, on the cognitive processing of sexual stimuli. This study was designed to serve as a laboratory analogue for alcohol's effects on performance anxiety and the consequent effects on penile tumescence in male social drinkers. In a balanced-placebo design, as in the earlier study (Wilson & Lawson, 1976b), subjects received either alcohol or placebo, and were required to perform either a simple or a complex cognitive task while listening to erotic tapes in a dichotic listening paradigm. The cognitive tasks for this study consisted of copying a list of random digits (simple task) or organizing a list of random digits according to specific classification rules (complex task). It may be recalled that a similar procedure was employed by Geer and Fuhr (1976) to investigate the effects of attention on sexual arousal.

A number of interesting results were obtained in this study. First, during the simple cognitive task, the belief that the subjects had consumed alcohol enhanced arousal, as in Geer and Fuhr's study. While the subjects were sober, however, there appeared to be no differences in arousal between the simple and complex cognitive tasks, in contrast to the findings of Geer and Fuhr. Of particular interest, however, was the finding that the pharmacological effect of alcohol was manifested most clearly in the condition of the complex cognitive task, where alcohol ingestion produced significantly decreased arousal compared to placebo when subjects were required to process complex stimuli (see Figure 12.2). These findings can perhaps be attributed to the varying attentional demands of the two cognitive tasks, and the differential impact of alcohol on each. The applied implication of these findings is that alcohol's effects on sexual performance are likely to vary, depending upon the degree of comfort the male feels in the sexual situation. Under conditions of low cognitive demand, sexual arousal may be enhanced by the expectancy of alcohol. In contrast, during

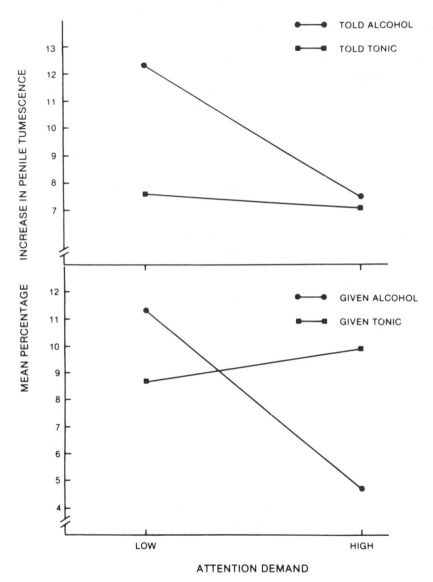

Figure 12.2. Effects of alcohol and task complexity on penile tumescence. From "Alcohol, Selective Attention and Sexual Arousal in Men" by G. T. Wilson, R. S. Niaura, and J. L. Adler, 1985, *Journal of Studies on Alcohol, 46,* p. 113. Copyright 1985 by Alcohol Research Documentation, Inc., Rutgers Center of Alcohol Studies, New Brunswick, New Jersey. Reprinted by permission.

conditions of high cognitive demand, performance is likely to be diminished by the pharmacological effects of alcohol.

It is important to note that the inhibiting effects of alcohol on sexual response have not been replicated in all of the studies conducted to date. For example, Langevin *et al.* (1985) studied the effects of three different alcohol dosage levels (0,0.05, and 0.10% BAC) on tumescence responses to erotic slides of varying content, including both conventional and unconventional stimulus materials. A total of 48 paid male volunteers with no history of alcohol abuse served as subjects for this study. Unlike other investigators to date, these researchers found that alcohol, even at the highest dosage level, did not significantly reduce the overall level of erection responses achieved. This apparently inconsistent result may have been due to a number of key methodological differences in this study. For example, a volumetric method of penile measurement was used instead of the more typical circumference technique; erotic slides instead of films or videotapes were used as stimulus materials; and subjects were tested early in the morning, as opposed to the more usual afternoon or evening times. Finally, as Langevin *et al.* point out, none of the studies described above have controlled carefully for the prior drinking histories or other potentially confounding characteristics of the subjects, and this also may account for some of the discrepancies reported.

Thus far only one study to date has examined the acute effects of alcohol on the male orgasmic/ejaculatory response (Malatesta, Pollack, Wilbanks, & Adams, 1979). In this study, 24 male social drinkers were observed during masturbation to orgasm in the laboratory. Alcohol was administered to one of four blood alcohol levels (0, 0.03, 0.06, and 0.09% BAC) as latency to ejaculation was measured. Results clearly indicated a marked impairment of ejaculation at the higher alcohol dosage levels, as 10 of the subjects were completely unable to ejaculate at the 0.09% level. Also significant were the subjective responses of the subjects, which similarly showed decreased pleasurability and diminished intensity of orgasm at the higher alcohol dosage levels. The authors also note that the moderate increase in latency of ejaculation at the lower alcohol dosage levels may serve a useful function for males experiencing difficulties with premature ejaculation. This finding remains to be replicated, however.

Overall, the studies described here indicate the role of independent and interactive effects of pharmacological and psychosocial factors in mediating the influence of alcohol on sexual response. Pharmacologically, alcohol appears to impair male sexual arousal and orgasm at the higher blood alcohol levels, although this finding has not been replicated in all studies (Langevin *et al.*, 1985). However, self-reports of sexual arousal, and the likelihood of initiation of sexual behavior, appear to be influenced greatly by the setting and circumstances under which alcohol is consumed. In a cogent review of the literature in this area, G. T. Wilson (1981) has observed: "Sexual responsiveness is often attributed to the influence of alcohol, but the evidence suggests that the circumstances under which it is consumed is [sic] the more important determinant of sexual behavior" (p. 35).

Acute Effects on Female Sexual Arousal

Throughout history, drinking in women has been associated with sexual permissiveness, and even promiscuity. For example, Abel (1985) quotes the rabbis of the Jewish Talmud as follows: "One glass of wine is becoming to a woman, two are somewhat degrading, and if she has three glasses she solicits coitus, but if she has four, she solicits even an ass in the streets and forgets all decency" (Ketuboth, 65a). Abel also quotes Geoffrey Chaucer's *The Canterbury Tales*: "Women have no defense against wine / As lechers know from experience."

The laboratory investigation of acute alcohol effects in women was initiated with the development of the vaginal photoplethysmograph (Sintchak & Geer, 1975), as described in Chapter 4. Making use of this instrument to measure VPA as an index of sexual arousal, Wilson and Lawson (1976a) tested the effects of four alcohol doses (0.005, 0.025, 0.050, and 0.075% BAC) on 16 female social drinkers. All subjects were shown an erotic film, and vasocongestive responses as well as subjective reports of arousal at each dosage level were recorded. While the pharmacological effects of alcohol on VPA appeared to mirror the decremental effects found with males (see Figure 12.3), the measure of subjective arousal in female subjects produced some unexpected findings. Surprisingly, women predicted that they would experience more arousal at higher alcohol levels. Indeed, despite impaired VPA responses observed with increasing intoxication, the women reported feeling more aroused. The authors have interpreted this finding as perhaps due to the difficulties some women experience in accurately identifying and labeling physiological cues of sexual arousal, particularly in the face of the nonspecific physiological action of alcohol.

This finding was replicated in a second study (Wilson & Lawson, 1978), in which the same balanced-placebo design previously used with male subjects was employed with female social drinkers. Again, the authors found that even a moderate alcohol dose (0.4 g/kg) depressed VPA significantly. On the other hand, subjective reports of arousal increased under both conditions of alcohol intake, as well as the belief that alcohol was consumed.

Malatesta, Pollack, Crotty, and Leacock (1982) evaluated the effects of four alcohol doses (0, 0.025, 0.050, and 0.075% BAC) on latency and intensity of orgasm during masturbation with 18 university women. As in

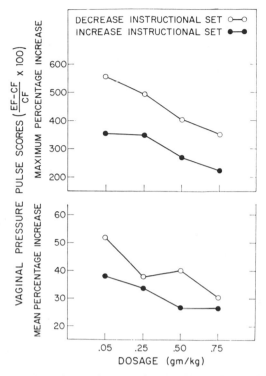

Figure 12.3. Effects of alcohol and instructions on VPA. From "Effects of Alcohol on Sexual Arousal in Women" by G. T. Wilson and D. M. Lawson, 1976, *Journal of Abnormal Psychology, 85,* p. 494. Copyright 1976 by the American Psychological Association. Reprinted by permission.

the Wilson and Lawson studies, the results of vaginal photoplethymography indicated a progressive impairment of physiological responding with increased intoxication. Orgasmic latency clearly increased, while the intensity of orgasm appeared to be diminished. Paradoxically, subjects reported higher levels of subjective arousal and orgasmic pleasure at the moderate and high alcohol dosage levels, despite the evidence of diminished physiological arousal.

Taken together, these three studies suggest that alcohol seems to depress physiological arousal in women, while nevertheless permitting the belief that it facilitates sexual enjoyment. Overall, there appear to be marked similarities in the acute effects of alcohol on sexual response in male and female social drinkers, with the exception of the findings of Wilson and Lawson discussed above. It appears that attributions of sexual arousal under conditions of alcohol intoxication (real or imagined) are maintained for women, despite physiological evidence to the contrary.

Males, on the other hand, appear more likely to modify their attribution of arousal, depending upon their awareness of physiological response. It should be emphasized, however, that the external validity of these findings is unclear, particularly given the contrived nature of the laboratory situation in each of the studies.

Chronic Effects of Alcohol on Sexual Function in Males and Females

Evaluating the long-term effects of alcohol abuse on sexual function raises additional problems beyond those identified in the preceding sections. Specifically, the extent and chronicity of abuse are quite variable from one individual to another and are not always adequately controlled for in clinical studies. In addition, the prealcoholic sexual competency of the individual is typically not assessed, and hence there may be significant confounding between pre-existing sexual function (or dysfunction) and long-term alcohol effects. In fact, the impact of alcohol on sexual function may vary considerably, depending upon the particular stage of alcoholic progression. For example, Forrest (1983) notes that early in a male alcoholic's career, a few drinks may serve to disinhibit the individual and facilitate greater sexual initiative, especially if he is sexually inept or anxious. Similarly, Forrest also notes that female drinkers may initially experience more confidence in their femininity and sexual attractiveness when drinking. These effects may be reversed in the later stages of the illness, particularly as physical health deteriorates.

Other problems also exist in identifying the causal mechanisms involved in sexual impairment of the chronic alcoholic. Explanations to date have focused on underlying endocrine, neurological, psychological, and interpersonal disturbances that may all result from long-term alcohol abuse. Wilsnack (1980) summarizes six possible physiological mechanisms that may account for the disruptive effects of chronic alcoholism on sexual function. These include (1) the acute depressant effects of alcohol on sexual response; (2) the disruption of gonadal hormone metabolism as a result of liver damage; (3) reduced sexual sensation due to alcohol-induced neuropathy; (4) organic brain damage causing impairment of both interpersonal and sexual interest; (5) various systemic health disorders associated with alcoholism (e.g., diabetes, hypertension) that may in turn lead to sexual problems; and (6) in the most severe cases of alcohol abuse, major disruption in all aspects of the biopsychosocial system. This variety of deterioration effects makes it difficult, if not impossible, to parcel out specific etiological mechanisms. With these limitations in mind, we review a number of recent studies of chronic alcohol effects on male and female sexual response.

All aspects of the male sexual response cycle may be negatively affected by chronic alcohol abuse (Mandell & Miller, 1983; Forrest, 1983). However, there appears to be accumulating evidence that the mechanisms of arousal, and the capacity for erection in particular, are most dramatically impaired. Past studies of the incidence of erectile dysfunction associated with alcoholism have ranged from 8% (Lemere & Smith, 1973) to 54% (Whalley, 1978). More recently, Mandell and Miller (1983) have reported findings from interviews of 44 male alcoholics, in which the authors observed that frequency, duration, and quantity of drinking were related proportionately to sexual impairment.

More detailed studies have refined our understanding of the relationship between alcohol abuse and sexual dysfunction. For example, Jensen (1979) reported that erectile dysfunction in alcoholic men was related significantly to both age and marital status. In this study, men over 40 and single alcoholic men were more likely to report erectile difficulties, although the duration of the alcoholism was not significant in this relationship. Another finding of this study was that 80% of the alcoholics reported that their partners were sexually uninterested when they (the alcoholics) were drunk. Thus, the social rejection and lack of arousability of the male alcoholic's partner may mediate some aspects of his resulting dysfunction.

An obvious methodological criticism of the above-described studies is the reliance on the self-reports of the respondents and the absence of psychophysiological assessment of sexual dysfunction. A notable exception is the recent study by Snyder and Karacan (1981), which assessed NPT responses in a sample of 26 chronic male alcoholics in the process of detoxification. Results of this study indicated a number of significant differences between the chronic alcoholic group and an age-matched nonalcoholic control group in erectile function. Specifically, the alcoholic subjects displayed longer latency to tumescence, less frequent and less rigid erections, and a greater number of partial erections than did the controls. These findings indicate that the sexual difficulties associated with chronic alcohol abuse are due in part to organic factors, probably of neurological origin. Although the subjects in this study were only 3 weeks into the detoxification program, the magnitude and extent of the erectile impairment suggest the likelihood of irreversible damage.

Like the male alcoholic, the female alcoholic typically progresses through a series of stages of physical and psychological deterioration that have a negative impact on sexual function. For example, Covington (1983) compared 35 women in an alcohol recovery program to appropriate controls and found a significantly higher rate of sexual dysfunction in the alcoholic women. Specifically, 64% of the alcoholic women indicated a lack of sexual interest, 61% reported a lack of sexual arousal, and 64% complained of the absence of orgasm. This author also reported a high association between drinking and sexual activity prior to sobriety. She notes, "The major love relationship in an alcoholic's life is with the liquor bottle." The same paradoxical finding that was noted earlier in regard to the acute effects of alcohol on female sexual response is also evident in Covington's findings on chronic female abusers: The alcoholic women believed that alcohol contributes positively to sexual experience, while their own clinical histories indicated the reverse.

Alcohol and Sexual Aggression

In our discussion of the etiology of sexual paraphilias (Chapter 9), we have noted the frequently reported association between alcohol consumption and sexually aggressive behavior (Amir, 1967; Rada et al., 1978). For example, in one study of a large sample of committed rapists (Rada, 1973), 50% reported being intoxicated at the time of the assault, and 35% were diagnosed as chronic alcoholics according to standardized psychiatric criteria. While this prevalence rate is typical of a number of studies showing strong correlations between alcoholism and sexual misconduct, the causal relationships involved are unclear. In particular, the degree of alcohol consumption at the time of the offense—a key factor in the presumed chain of mediation—may be highly variable and typically is only inferred from the retrospective self-reports of the offenders. In this regard, G. T. Wilson (1981) has suggested that offenders may exaggerate their degree of intoxication as a form of legal defense, further biasing the self-report data on which this association is based.

One of the more provocative questions in this area has been raised by Langevin et al. (1985). Specifically, Langevin et al. pose the question of how it is that alcohol is believed both to suppress sexual function at high dosages *and* to permit some men to perform sexually deviant acts. After reviewing the available literature on this topic, the authors raise a number of hypotheses as follows. First, it is possible that the studies reviewed above on the acute effects of alcohol intoxication on sexual arousal may have unduly emphasized the inhibitory effects, particularly if one assumes that certain individuals may develop tolerance to prolonged drinking. Also, several studies have indicated elevated plasma testosterone levels in some violent offenders, and have shown that high testosterone levels may be positively correlated with both aggressiveness and enhanced sexual arousability. Therefore, the use of alcohol by such individuals may not dampen sexual arousal sufficiently, in view of the overriding impact of higher androgen levels.

Clearly, the relationship between alcohol and sexual aggression is much in need of further study. One recent line of research that complicates the issue even further concerns the effects of alcohol, or the expectation of alcohol consumption, on elicitation of arousal to deviant stimuli in non-offender, nonalcoholic subjects. For example, Briddell *et al.* (1978) used a balanced-placebo design to assess tumescence responses to coercive and noncoercive sexual stimuli in male social drinkers. Results indicated that subjects who believed that they had consumed alcohol showed greater tumescence responses to the deviant stimuli than did subjects who believed that they had received the placebo dose. On the other hand, the pharmacological effect of alcohol on either the physiological or subjective measures was not significant in this study.

More recently, Langevin *et al.* (1985) have found that in male social drinkers, alcohol consumption led to more indiscriminate arousal to a wide range of erotic stimuli. Specifically, the findings indicated that at moderate or high alcohol dosages, subjects were more easily aroused by both mild and atypical sexual stimuli. The implication from both of these studies is that alcohol may act, even in nonoffender males, as a cue for arousal to sexually deviant stimuli. However, it is unclear at present whether this effect is primarily due to pharmacological factors or to the social disinhibition effects of alcohol.

Comment

A number of issues have been highlighted in the preceding sections. First, the effects of alcohol on sexual function need to be considered from the perspectives of both acute and chronic consumption. Short-term alcohol effects, which have been investigated primarily in young social drinkers, have been shown to be influenced by both pharmacological and attitudinal factors. Male–female differences in this regard are especially interesting, and suggest that ratings of subjective arousal in women may be more positively affected by the belief that alcohol has been consumed. On the other hand, studies of chronic alcohol abuse have yielded a consistent picture of sexual and interpersonal deterioration in most cases. The possible causative factors in this regard are multiple and overlapping. Unfortunately, much of the clinical literature on sexual dysfunction associated with alcoholism has been based on retrospective and self-report data. Studies of alcoholic subjects are typically conducted during the early stages of the recovery period, and it is unclear to what extent this has affected the findings reported. Clearly, there is a major need for long-term prospective studies if the relationship between chronic alcohol abuse and sexual function is to be addressed adequately.

MARIHUANA EFFECTS ON SEXUAL FUNCTION

In different cultures, marihuana has been used as an antidote for fatigue, as a medication for diseases such as glaucoma, and as a key element in religious rituals. In contexts such as these, the drug appears to have few sexual side effects. In most Western societies, however, marihuana has acquired a reputation as a potent aphrodisiac. Although its physiological effects on the user tend to be subtle, at least at the dosages usually consumed, the strong expectation of increased sexual pleasure is often borne out in the experience of marihuana smokers. Moreover, cultural mythology about the relationship between sex and marihuana has produced lurid tales of sexual orgies, perversion and debauchery, as marihuana has been described as a "killer weed" that destroys will power and the ability to discriminate right from wrong. As early as 1944, however, the LaGuardia Commission on Marihuana reported that there was no evidence that the drug was a direct causal factor in stimulating prostitution, hypersexuality, or debauchery.

Research data concerning the effects of marihuana on sexual response come from several sources, including laboratory experiments on animal sexual behavior, questionnaire and interview studies with volunteer subjects, and a few recent investigations of endocrine effects associated with acute marihuana use in human males. Regrettably, there is a complete absence of direct psychophysiological research comparable to that reported above for the effects of alcohol on male and female sexual response. Since the major difficulties encountered by H. B. Rubin and his colleagues in attempting to conduct research of this type (Holden, 1976), there have been no further attempts to date to fill this critical void.

Effects on Subjective Reports

Most of the current literature on marihuana and sexual arousal is based upon survey or interview studies. Although the results of these studies are generally suggestive of positive or arousal-enhancing effects of the drug, these findings need to be cautiously interpreted, in view of a number of major methodological difficulties. First, the sampling for such studies tends to be highly selective, typically including a disproportionate number of individuals who have experienced positive effects with the drug. Second, the criteria for drug use or sexual satisfaction are rarely specified. Finally, the frequent marihuana user is also likely to be using alcohol or other drugs, making it difficult if not impossible to attribute sexual effects to marihuana use alone.

With these reservations in mind, it appears that most users describe the association between marihuana and sexual experience in positive terms

312

(Goode, 1972). For example, an early questionnaire study (Tart, 1971) reported the responses of 150 male and female college students on the side effects of marihuana. The results indicated that marihuana generally increased sexual desire, but only when the user was in the company of a likely sexual partner. In such a situation, desire was intensified and sexual sensations were enhanced. Users often experienced greater contact, responsiveness, sharing, and empathy with a sexual partner. Most users in this study reported that marihuana was the ideal aphrodisiac, and that the level of intoxication was related directly to feelings of sexual pleasure. However, with very high levels of intoxication, some users reported that their involvement with their own fantasies and inner experiences detracted from their sexual interaction with a partner.

Similar findings have been reported by Koff (1974) in a survey of sex and marihuana use in 345 college undergraduates. Approximately half of the respondents reported increased sexual desire in association with the drug, and most of the subjects also reported increased sexual enjoyment. Again, high doses of the drug were said to be associated with lessened desire and satisfaction. An interesting difference was found in this study between the experiences of male and female respondents: Females were more likely to report increases in sexual desire, while males were more likely to note increased sexual pleasure in association with marihuana. This overall pattern of results has been confirmed in several other studies (e.g., Goode, 1969; Halikas, Goodwin, & Guze, 1971).

In addition to the typical studies of college student samples, Gay and Sheppard (1973) reported on the experiences of 50 long-term drug users interviewed at the Haight-Ashbury Free Medical Clinic in San Francisco. Marihuana was mentioned by 80% of this group as the drug that most enhanced sexual pleasure. Summarizing the findings from a number of early studies, Goode (1972) concluded, "The most obvious and dominant impression is that users overwhelmingly describe their marihuana experience in favorable and pleasurable terms" (p. 51). Furthermore, it should be noted that the majority of subjects who do not report increases in sexual desire or pleasure report that marihuana causes little or no change in their sexual response.

Despite the apparent consistency in reports of increased sexual appetite and pleasure associated with marihuana, explanations of this association have varied considerably. For example, some authors have suggested that expectations, set, and setting are more important determinants of increased sexual pleasure than are the physiological effects of the drug. Respondents in the Gay and Sheppard (1973) study also mentioned release of inhibitions as an important effect of the drug. Tart (1971) has discussed the possible role of enhanced tactile sensitivity and alteration of time perception as contributing to the sexual enhancement effects of the drug. Finally, it has also been noted (e.g., Abel, 1985) that marihuana use and heightened sexual interest may both be concomitants of a life style oriented toward physical pleasure and sensation seeking.

Endocrine Effects of Marihuana

In contrast to the generally positive reports of marihuana's effects on sexual desire and satisfaction, there is considerable controversy at present concerning the effects of the drug on sex steroid production. In the first study of this type, Kolodny, Masters, Kolodner, and Toro (1974) compared the early-morning plasma testosterone levels of male marihuana users with those of a matched control group of nonusers. The marihuana users were aged 18 to 28, and had all taken the drug at least four times per week for a minimum of 6 months. The results indicated that the users had significantly lower testosterone levels than nonusers, and also that heavy users had lower levels than light users. After discontinuation of the drug for a 2-week period, a significant increase in testosterone levels among the users was noted. It is noteworthy, however, that little or no change in sexual behavior was observed during the course of the experiment, despite the marked changes in level of marihuana use.

Other investigators have failed to replicate the negative effects of this study. For example, Mendelson, Kuehnle, Ellingboe, and Babor (1974) found no evidence of a relationship between the extent of marihuana use and testosterone levels in male subjects. In this study, casual and heavy users were confined to a research ward for 1 month, where they were permitted to smoke marihuana on a daily basis. Comparison of early-morning plasma testosterone samples, as in the Kolodny *et al.* (1974) study, indicated no significant changes in the testosterone levels for either the light or heavy users. The only apparent differences in the design of the two studies was in regard to the use of a within-subjects design (Mendelson *et al.*) versus a between-subjects design (Kolodny *et al.*), as well as stricter environmental controls in the Mendelson *et al.* study through the confinement of subjects to a research ward. In other studies the use of the between-subjects design has failed to show significant differences between users and nonusers (Cushman, 1975).

The effects of marihuana on sperm production have also been examined in a number of studies. For example, approximately one-third of the marihuana users in the Kolodny *et al.* (1974) study were found to have abnormally low sperm counts. Similar reductions in sperm count also have been reported by Hembree, Zeidenberg, and Nahas (1976) following a period of very heavy marihuana use (more than 10 "joints" per day). Similarly, studies of marihuana effects on mice (Zimmerman & Zimmerman, 1979) have shown a dose-related increase in abnormal sperm production. On the basis of its evaluation of the major studies in this area, the National Academy of Sciences, Institute of Medicine (1982) reported that marihuana indeed suppressed testosterone production, decreased the size and weight of the prostate and testes, and reduced sperm production, but that the results were reversed rapidly after discontinuation of use. The report concluded that there was no evidence that marihuana may cause sterility.

In regard to the effects of marihuana on endocrine functioning in women, Abel (1985) has observed that cannabis has historically been used to treat dysmenorrhea and menstrual cramps, and as a folk remedy to facilitate childbirth. To date, however, only one study has directly examined the effects of the drug on female hormone function (Kolodny, Webster, Tullman, & Dornbush, 1979). Findings from this study indicated that female marihuana users had shorter menstrual cycles than nonusers, as well as a greater number of anovulatory cycles. In contrast to their findings in the male studies, Kolodny, Webster et al. (1979) reported that female marihuana users showed higher testosterone levels than nonusers. No differences were found in estrogen, progesterone, LH, or FSH levels between the two groups. As noted by the authors, the results of this study should be cautiously considered, however, in view of the confounding factor of alcohol use; the marihuana group consumed about twice as much alcohol as the controls.

EFFECTS OF COCAINE AND OTHER ILLICIT DRUGS ON SEXUAL FUNCTION

A shot of cocaine feels more like an orgasm than anything in the world except an orgasm.—Selden (1979, p. 163)

Like alcohol and marihuana, a variety of illicit drugs have acquired reputations as aphrodisiacs in recent years. Among the drugs to be most widely cited in this regard are cocaine, amphetamines, barbiturates, methaqualone (Quaalude), amyl nitrite, LSD, and other hallucinogens. In contrast, the narcotic and opiate drugs, particularly heroin, are generally viewed as sexual depressants (Gay & Sheppard, 1973). Among the difficulties in evaluating the sexual effects of these drugs is the phenomenon of "polydrug use"—that is, the fact that users of any one of these drugs are likely to have experimented with several others, often at the same time. Another problem is the great variability in the quality and composition of the drugs and in the dosages consumed. Finally, the influence of set and setting are as important as, if not more important than, the pharmacological effects of the drugs. None of the studies conducted to date has controlled adequately for these factors.

Contributing to the belief that illicit drug use stimulates sexual behavior is the finding from numerous survey studies that drug users tend to have greater sexual experience than nonusers. For example, Goode (1972) found that the number of types of drugs used by members of his college student sample was related to the number of sexual partners reported. Drug use also was significantly correlated with an increased frequency of intercourse, and with an earlier age at first intercourse. The author cautions, however, against concluding that drug use causes increased sexual activity; he suggests instead that the student drug user becomes socialized into a sexually permissive milieu and adopts the attitudes of this peer group toward both drug use and sexuality.

Much of the current information on illicit drug use and sexual function is derived from a series of interview studies conducted at the Haight-Ashbury Free Medical Clinic (Gay & Sheppard, 1973; Gay, Newmeyer, Elion, & Wieder, 1977; Gay, Newmeyer, Perry, Johnson, & Kurland, 1982). Having observed the changing preferences among interview subjects over a 10-year period both for types of drugs consumed and for sexual practices engaged in, or the "ebb and flow of sex–drug practices and preferences of those eras" (Gay et al., 1982), the authors concluded that cocaine has emerged as the drug of choice for sexual enhancement by the mid-1970s. Cocaine was preferred over all other drugs in terms of its positive effects on sexual desire, sensuality, the ability to control orgasm, and the ability to act out sexual fantasies. The authors' comment on these findings is as follows: "This survey strongly suggested that were cocaine as cheap and as readily available as marihuana, it might well supplant grass and almost every other pharmacological adjunct now used to boost sensual eroticism" (Gay et al., 1982, pp. 115–116). It has also been noted, however, that the use of large quantities of cocaine, or chronic use of the drug, may be associated in some users with loss of sexual interest or impotence.

Other stimulant drugs, most notably amphetamines, have been associated with increased sexual desire and improved control of orgasm for some users, although the effects have varied widely from one user to another (Cox & Smart, 1972). Some of the variability may be due to differences in dosage, method of administration, and drug experience of the user. Methamphetamine appears to have its most powerful effect when taken intravenously. According to Gay and Sheppard (1973), "With intravenous injection an overwhelming total body orgasmic 'flash' or 'rush' was repeatedly described" (p. 154). Male users have reported erection simultaneously with injection of the drug, and users frequently note both an increased desire for sexual activity and an increased aggressiveness in intercourse. However, while subjects report that sexual activity is often prolonged, orgasm may become difficult or impossible, perhaps due to the sympathomimetic effects of the drug.

Illicit drugs that have received particular attention for their supposed enhancing effects on sexuality are amyl nitrite ("poppers") and methaqualone (Quaalude). Amyl nitrite, which is a potent vasodilator and smooth muscle relaxant used in the treatment of angina pectoris, was also used with increasing frequency in the 1970s as a sexual stimulant. In the past the drug has been particularly favored by male homosexuals (Everett, 1975; Gay et al., 1982), but recent evidence linking its use to the development of acquired immunity deficiency syndrome (AIDS) may have decreased its popularity in this group. The vasodilation effects of the drug appear to intensify the experience of orgasm greatly, as one user reports: "It's like being shot through the stars in a rocket. The orgasm is truly awesome. I can feel my whole body accelerate; my climax keeps building up and building up; all the rest of the world just disappears and it seems to go on forever" (quoted in Lowry, 1979, p. 19).

Methaqualone is a sedative–hypnotic drug that is chemically unrelated to the barbiturates, but that has been prescribed to facilitate sleep or relaxation in agitated patients. Soon after the drug became available in the United States in the mid-1960s, it acquired a reputation among both heterosexual and homosexual drug users as a potent aphrodisiac, becoming known as the "love drug" or "heroin for lovers" (Abel, 1985). However, to judge by the experience of the Haight-Ashbury sample (Gay et al., 1982), it appears that methaqualone, like alcohol and other CNS depressants, is more effective as a means of overcoming inhibitions than as a direct sexual stimulant. In this regard, it is interesting to note that several surveys have reported greater preference for the drug among female than among male users. At higher doses it is also associated with performance difficulties, including loss of erection and anorgasmia.

In contrast to the drugs described above, the opiate narcotics, including morphine, heroin, and methadone, have long been associated with decreased sexual interest and ability. Interview data from a number of studies indicate that both male and female addicts experience reduced desire and delayed orgasm in association with drug use. In addition, DeLeon and Wexler (1973) found in their study of recovering heroin addicts that all subjects reported a decrease in the frequency of intercourse, masturbation, and nocturnal emissions. Time to ejaculation also increased markedly for all male heroin users. Decreased testosterone levels have also been associated with both heroin and methadone use (Mendelson & Mello, 1975; Mendelson, Mendelson, & Patch, 1975).

A curious phenomenon during detoxification from heroin is the appearance of spontaneous erection and orgasm. The recovery of sexual interest and potency is usually very rapid, and may occur in such unlikely environments as hospitals and prisons (Cushman, 1972). As with other drugs, a distinction can be made between the effects of chronic and acute use, as initial experimentation with heroin often produces desirable sexual effects, such as delayed ejaculation. Brecher (1972) has reported that opium was often used in India during the 19th century for this purpose.

EFFECTS OF PRESCRIPTION DRUGS ON SEXUAL RESPONSE

Among the more positive effects of the so-called "sexual revolution" of the past two decades has been a growing sensitivity in medicine to the impact on sexual functioning of various disease states, and the associated drugs used in treatment. This trend is evidenced in the considerable attention currently devoted to the potential sexual side effects of prescription drugs (e.g., *Physicians' Desk Reference*, 1986), as well as in the growth of clinical and laboratory research on the sexual effects of these drugs. Given the increasing use in our society of antihypertensive, psychotropic, and other classes of prescription drugs, the findings of studies in this area have considerable relevance to both clinical practice and basic research on sexual psychophysiology.

Before reviewing the effects of specific drugs, it is important to note that research in this area is limited by a number of methodological constraints. First, the reported side effects of any prescription drug will depend in part on the length of use and the dosage taken; on possible interactions with other drugs; and on the age, sex, and general health of the patient (Kolodny, Masters, & Johnson, 1979). One may expect that a drug that successfully treats an incapacitating medical condition will indirectly improve sexual functioning. Similarly, psychotropic medications that reduce anxiety or alleviate depression may well improve sexual abilities in an indirect fashion. If the effect of these drugs is to improve interpersonal relationships, they are likely to facilitate better sexual performance as a function of improved social adjustment. Most of the research has been conducted on male subjects, and generalizations to female sexuality are questionable. Finally, as we have noted repeatedly in regard to the effects of nonprescription drugs on sexual function, the attitudes and expectations of the user play a major role in determining the ultimate effect.

Antihypertensive Drugs

Antihypertensive drugs are presently the most commonly prescribed medications in our society, and concerns about their potential sexual side effects have increased greatly in recent years (e.g., Poloniecki & Hamilton, 1985; Wartman, 1983; Moss & Procci, 1982). Estimates of the incidence of sexual dysfunction have varied widely, ranging from a low of less than 10% for patients on hydrophilic beta-blockers (Heel, Brogden, Speight, & Avery, 1979) to a high of more than 30% for patients on alpha-agonist drugs (Reichgott, 1979) and lipophilic beta-blockers (Mann, Abbott, Gray, Thiebaux, & Belzer, 1982).

Several authors have observed that the percentage of sexual problems reported depends largely on the way in which this information is obtained.

Thus, clinical trials that have not specifically assessed sexual function, beyond recording spontaneous patient complaints, have generally reported sexual problems in 10% or less of patients (e.g., Veterans Administration Cooperative Study Group on Antihypertensive Agents, 1982). On the other hand, studies that have used a structured interview or questionnaire evaluation of sexual function (e.g., Lazar, Eisold, Gadson, & Tesch, 1984; Medical Research Council Working Party on Mild to Moderate Hypertension, 1981) have reported incidence rates of 20% or more, depending on the type of drug and dosage levels. Few studies have included assessment of the incidence of sexual dysfunction in untreated hypertensive controls, which may range from 10% to 20% (Bulpitt, Dollery, & Carne, 1976).

The two major classes of antihypertensive drugs that have been associated with changes in sexual function are the sympatholytic or adrenergic-inhibiting drugs (e.g., reserpine, alpha-agonists, beta-blockers) and the diuretics (e.g., thiazides, spironolactone). For example, one recent study (Hogan, Wallin, & Baer, 1980) made use of a standardized questionnaire for assessing sexual dysfunction in 861 male patients being treated in a hypertension clinic. A number of drugs were evaluated in this study, and results indicated that sexual dysfunction was most common with a combination of propranolol and diuretics (23%), followed by clonidine (15%) and methyldopa (13%). In contrast, these authors found a very low rate of dysfunction in untreated controls (4%).

Similarly, Mann et al. (1982) administered anonymous sexual function questionnaires to a large group of male and female patients on various antihypertensives. Sexual problems were found in a high percentage of male patients on beta-blockers, 36% of whom reported major difficulties with erection while on the drug. Both male and female patients reported decreased libido in association with beta-blocker therapy, although female orgasmic ability appeared unaffected by treatment. Of particular interest was the finding that the effects on libido were related to perceived changes in mood and decreased energy; this suggests that sexual problems may be indirectly mediated by other CNS effects of the drugs (Rosen & Kostis, 1985).

One of the earliest studies to evaluate specific sexual side effects of antihypertensive drugs was reported by Money and Yankowitz (1967). These authors investigated the effects of guanethidine, a potent peripheral antiadrenergic agent, on the sexual performance of six hypertensive male patients. All six patients complained of erectile impairment during the course of treatment, and retrograde ejaculation was also reported by five of the six. This latter effect could have been due to the fact that guanethidine inhibits the action of norepinephrine on the sympathetic fibers responsible for closure of the bladder neck during ejaculation, thereby leading to inhibition of bladder neck closure and subsequent retrograde ejaculation. Horowitz and Goble (1979) have suggested that impotence

319

may be a secondary effect of the anxiety engendered by the patient's sudden awareness of having "gone dry." Kolodny (1978) has also noted delayed or retarded ejaculation in men receiving alpha-methyldopa (aldomet), many of whom also reported erectile dysfunction.

Among the sympatholytic drugs currently used in the treatment of hypertension, the alpha-agonists (methyldopa, clonidine) and the beta-blockers (e.g., propranolol, metoprolol, atenolol) are the most widely prescribed. Evaluation of the sexual side effects of these drugs is complicated by the wide variety of neurophysiological and endocrine changes associated with their use. However, based upon a comprehensive review of research in this area, Moss and Procci (1982) drew a number of conclusions. Surprisingly, these authors found much stronger evidence of impairment of sexual function with propranolol than with the alpha-adrenergic drugs. Moreover, sexual dysfunction with propranolol was concluded to be strongly related to dosage levels, as Moss and Procci found consistent evidence of impairment of erection at the higher doses (120 mg/day or more). In addition, a number of major methodological problems were noted, such as the failure to assess pretreatment sexual functioning, the lack of appropriate control groups, and the absence of physiological measures of erectile capacity.

Only one study to date has evaluated both physiological (NPT) and subjective measures of sexual function in response to acute effects of antihypertensive drugs (Rosen, Kostis, & Jekelis, in press). Specifically, 30 healthy male subjects were randomly assigned to a double-blind, placebo-controlled study of the effects of four common beta-blockers: propranolol, a nonselective lipophilic beta-blocker; metoprolol, a selective lipophilic beta-blocker; atenolol, a selective hydrophilic beta-blocker; and pindolol, a nonselective beta-blocker with intrinsic sympathomimetic activity. Each drug was administered for a 1-week period, following which laboratory evaluations were conducted; these consisted of NPT monitoring and completion of a battery of questionnaires for assessment of mood and sexual function. In addition, early-morning blood samples were drawn at each visit for determining plasma and free testosterone levels.

As shown in Figure 12.4, the results indicated a significant decrease in both plasma and free testosterone for all four drugs, particularly propranolol. Although the differences in NPT between drugs and placebo failed to reach significance, the trend observed in the NPT scores was toward impaired tumescence with each of the drugs, particularly the lipophilic beta-blockers. Analysis of the subjective data indicated that subjects complained more often of sexual difficulties on propranolol; one subject, in particular, experienced erection difficulties in association with propranolol on 4 successive days. Within each drug condition, testosterone levels were also significantly correlated with the frequency of intercourse and the subjects' ratings of desire for sex.

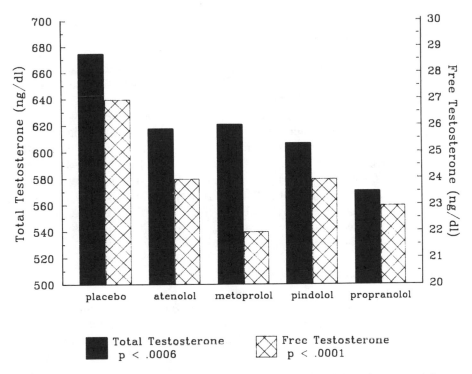

Figure 12.4. Effect of placebo, atenolol, metoprolol, pindolol, and propranolol on total and free testosterone. From "Beta-Blocker Effects on Sexual Function in Normal Males" by R. C. Rosen, J. B. Kostis, and A. Jekelis, *Archives of Sexual Behavior,* in press.

To turn to the effects of diuretics on sexual function, clinical reports have indicated that sexual difficulties may be at least as common with these drugs as with the other antihypertensives. For example, the Medical Research Council Working Party on Mild to Moderate Hypertension (1981), which has conducted the largest and best-controlled clinical hypertension trial to date, found that sexual dysfunction was more prevalent with diuretic than with beta-blocker therapy. Specifically, after 2 years of treatment, 23% of men receiving bendrofluazide (a thiazide diuretic) complained of erection difficulties, as compared with 13% of those receiving propranolol and 10% of those receiving a placebo control. Other studies (e.g., Poloniecki & Hamilton, 1985; Hogan *et al.*, 1980) have found that a combination of beta-blockers and diuretics is the most likely to be associated with sexual dysfunction. Although these effects have generally been reported in male hypertensives, Poloniecki and Hamilton (1985) recently found that about one-fourth of the female hypertensives studied (total $n = 64$) reported sexual difficulties associated with treatment. The mechanisms responsible for sexual dysfunction associated with diuretics are unknown at present.

One additional drug worth noting in this regard is spironolactone, an aldosterone antagonist that acts as a potassium-sparing diuretic. An early report suggested that increased erectile dysfunction was associated with spironolactone therapy (Spark & Melby, 1968), and subsequent studies have demonstrated that the drug has potent endocrine effects, causing decreased sexual desire, erectile dysfunction, and gynecomastia (breast enlargement) in men (Loriaux, Menard, Taylor, Pita, & Santen, 1976) and menstrual irregularities in women (Levitt, 1970). According to Kolodny, Masters, and Johnson (1979), the depressed libido and potency seen in men, as well as the menstrual difficulties in women, are typically reversed promptly on cessation of spironolactone treatment. The gynecomastia effects in men, however, are not always reversible.

Antipsychotics and Antidepressants

Despite the widespread use of antipsychotic and antidepressant drugs in the treatment of psychiatric disorders, there are few systematic data available concerning the effects of these drugs on sexual response. In part, this may be due to the difficulties involved in obtaining reliable sex histories from psychiatrically disturbed individuals. In addition, severely depressed or psychotic individuals typically have poor interpersonal relationships, a premorbid history of sexual inadequacy, and a variety of related emotional difficulties. Thus it is difficult, if not impossible, in most instances to separate the effects on sexual function of the illness itself from possible sexual complications of the drugs used in treatment. With these reservations in mind, we briefly discuss the existing literature on antipsychotic and antidepressant effects on sexual response.

Among the antipsychotic drugs currently in use, the two most preferred types are the phenothiazines (e.g., chlorpromazine, thioridazine) and the butyrophenones (e.g., haloperidol). The former class of drugs inhibits the action of alpha-adrenergic receptors in the autonomic nervous system, and possibly blocks adrenergic pathways in the reticular activating system as well (Abel, 1985). In contrast, the butyrophenones achieve the desired antipsychotic effects primarily by means of blockade of dopamine receptors. Both the phenothiazines and the butyrophenones are endocrinologically active, and have been associated with elevations in prolactin and depression of gonadotopin secretion in both sexes (Meltzer & Fang, 1976; Rubin, Poland, O'Connor, Gouin, & Tower, 1976).

Early clinical reports suggested a high prevalence of sexual difficulties in association with the use of phenothiazines generally, and thioridazine (Mellaril) in particular. For example, Shader (1964) described a pattern of sexual dysfunction, including an absence of ejaculation, in a series of patients treated with thioridazine. Similarly, Blair and Simpson (1966) reported that about 30% of patients receiving thioridazine complained of an inability to ejaculate. Other authors (e.g., Haider, 1966; Kotin, Wilbert, Verburg, & Soldinger, 1976) have found that erectile dysfunction occurs in 40–60% of male patients on this drug. Almost half of the subjects in the Kotin *et al.* (1976) study reported changes in ejaculation, and two patients also reported pain at orgasm. Although similar effects have been reported for the other phenothiazines, the incidence of sexual dysfunction does not appear to be as high (Abel, 1985).

Of the butyrophenones, haloperidol (Haldol) has been associated with marked changes in endocrine function, and occasional erectile problems in men (Kolodny, Masters, & Johnson, 1979). In particular, studies by Rubin and his colleagues (Rubin, Poland, & Tower, 1976; Rubin, Poland, O'Connor, *et al.*, 1976) showed that acute doses of haloperidol given to normal male subjects resulted in significant increases in plasma prolactin levels, which lasted up to 4 hours following drug administration. The authors suggest that the increased prolactin observed could have been a function of the dopamine-inhibiting action of the drug. It is unclear, however, whether these changes in circulating prolactin would be related to complaints of erectile dysfunction in male patients.

The two main categories of antidepressant drugs to be considered here are the tricyclic antidepressants (e.g., imipramine, amitriptyline, clomipramine) and the monoamine oxidase inhibitors (MAOIs). In evaluating the effects of these drugs on sexual responses, it should be borne in mind that depressed patients, for whom these drugs are typically prescribed, frequently show a marked reduction in sexual desire or arousal associated with the disorder. In addition to the usual reports of anhedonia and diminished libido, Howell *et al.* (1987) recently demonstrated significant impairment in NPT in 10 male depressed patients who were free of medication. It is noteworthy that 2 of the men who had depression-related sexual dysfunction and abnormal NPTs in this study experienced improvements of sexual function and NPT studies upon recovery.

Sexual difficulties in response to antidepressant drugs were first reported by Simpson, Blair, and Amuso (1965). Based upon reports from both clinical patients and normal volunteers, these authors found that administration of tricyclic antidepressants, particularly imipramine, was associated with either erectile or ejaculatory problems in about one-third of the cases studied. Similarly, reports of decreased sexual arousal and inhibited ejaculation in male patients being treated with imipramine have been noted by Couper-Smartt and Rodham (1973). Although few studies have considered the effects of these drugs on female sexuality, a recent case study of anorgasmia has been reported in a female patient being treated with imipramine (Sovner, 1983). It is noteworthy that the orgasmic difficulties in this case were completely resolved when desipramine, a tricyclic with minimal effects on serotonin uptake, was substituted. Female anorgasmia has also been associated with the effects of amoxapine (Shen, 1982) and the MAOI antidepressants (Lesko, Stotland, & Segraves, 1982).

It should be noted that sexual difficulties have not always been reported in association with these drugs. For example, Beaumont (1973) found that sexual arousal was increased in more than half of both male and female patients receiving clomipramine. As noted above, Howell *et al.* (1987) observed positive changes in subjective and NPT measures of sexual function in depressed patients following antidepressant therapy. Finally, a recent study of bupropion, a nontricyclic antidepressant (Gardner & Johnston, 1985), found that few if any sexual side effects could be attributed to the drug. According to the authors, the lack of anticholinergic and antiadrenergic effects makes this drug particularly appropriate for the treatment of depression in patients with a previous history of sexual dysfunction.

Other Prescription Drugs

Although there are a wide variety of prescription drugs that can affect sexual response, specific classes of drugs that have received increasing attention in this regard are the antiepileptics (e.g., phenobarbital, primidone), the antiulcer drugs (e.g., cimetidine, ranitidine), and the antiparkinsonian agent L-dopa. Again, clinical reports on the sexual effects of these drugs are typically confounded by the potential influence of the underlying diseases, as well as by the nonspecific effects of the drugs on both physical and psychological health. In view of the fact that these three classes of drugs are also among those most commonly prescribed in our society, there is clearly a major need for controlled research on their sexual side effects.

Epilepsy and the drugs used in its treatment have long been associated with sexual disorders. In fact, because of the early belief that the disease was caused by excessive sexuality, epilepsy was treated in the 19th century by means of bromide salts. More recently, clinical studies have generally found evidence of marked hyposexuality in both male and female epileptics (e.g., Pritchard, 1980; Toone, Wheeler, & Fenwick, 1980); this may be due to neurological disturbances in the limbic structures, or to interference with the functions of the hypothalamic–pituitary–gonadal axis (Mattson & Cramer, 1985). Among the drugs currently used in the treatment of epilepsy, those most likely to be associated with further impairment of sexual desire and arousal are phenobarbital and primidone. For example, in the Veterans Administration Cooperative Study of Antiepileptic Drugs, it was found that 16% of patients receiving phenobarbital and 22% of patients on primidone reported impotence or decreased libido as a side effect of the drug (Mattson *et al.*, 1985). Kolodny, Masters, and Johnson (1979) have also reported a loss of orgasmic ability in some patients being treated with barbiturates.

Cimetidine, a histamine antagonist which is widely used in the treatment of peptic ulcer disease, has also been shown to be a potent antiandrogenic agent with potentially disruptive effects on male erectile function. Following early case reports of impotence in association with cimetidine therapy (e.g., Wolfe, 1979), a controlled study was performed on seven male patients of the effects of the drug on the hypothalamic–pituitary–gonadal axis (Van Thiel, Gavaler, Smith, & Paul, 1979). Significant effects of cimetidine were observed on the response of LH to LH-releasing factor (LHRF), as well as on sperm count, which was reduced by approximately 50%.

More recently, Jensen *et al.* (1984) have compared the effects of cimetidine with ranitidine, a newer and more potent histamine antagonist, on male endocrine and sexual function. The results of this study confirmed the previous reports of sexual dysfunction, as 60% of the subjects developed erectile dysfunction or breast enlargement in association with cimetidine. Three subjects who had developed complete erectile dysfunction were further studied by means of NPT (see Figure 12.5), which confirmed the fact that a drug-specific, organic impotence had been caused by cimetidine treatment. In all cases, the sexual dysfunction effects were reversed when cimetidine was replaced by ranitidine.

L-Dopa, which is a highly effective drug in the treatment of Parkinson disease, has also been associated with marked changes in sexual function. Unlike other prescription drugs considered in this chapter, however, L-dopa has enjoyed a reputation for some time as a possible sexual stimulant. Soon after the drug became available for the treatment of Parkinson disease, a number of clinical studies reported instances of increased sexual arousal and desire in association with L-dopa treatment (e.g., Hyyppa, Rinne, & Sonninen, 1970; Bowers, Van Woert, & Davis, 1971). In the latter study (Bowers *et al.*, 1971), two specific patterns of improved sexual function were observed. Some of the patients treated with L-dopa showed major improvements in their overall level of psychosocial functioning, and appeared to experience some improvement in their sexual relationships as a result. On the other hand, for three of the patients in this study, increased sexual drive that appeared unrelated to more general changes in mood or interpersonal functioning was reported. "In one instance, an 80-year-old man reported that following L-dopa therapy he began to have regular nocturnal emissions and erotic dreams" (Bowers *et al.*, 1971, p. 693).

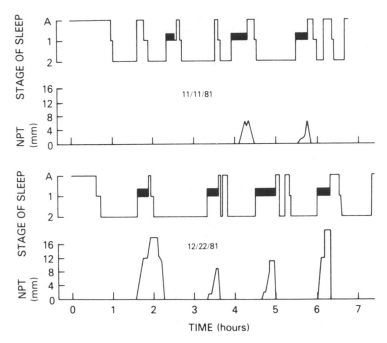

Figure 12.5. Recording of NPT and stages of sleep in one patient. Recordings were made while the patient was taking cimetidine and was totally impotent) top two tracings (and later when the patient was taking ranitidine and his sexual function was normal (bottom two tracings). Periods of REM sleep are indicated by the black bars. NPT was expressed as millimeters of increase in penile circumference. From "Cimetidine-Induced Impotence and Breast Changes in Patients with Gastric Hypersecretory States" by R. T. Jensen *et al.*, 1983, *New England Journal of Medicine, 308,* p. 886. Reprinted by permission of the *New England Journal of Medicine.*

Subsequent studies have not confirmed a specific aphrodisiac effect for L-dopa. Hyyppa, Falck, and Rinne (1975), for example, evaluated the effects of L-dopa therapy on sexual function in 11 male and female patients. Although this study confirmed the nonspecific improvements in physical and psychological health seen in the earlier investigations, there was no evidence of additional benefits in sexual arousal or performance. When L-dopa was given to a group of psychiatric patients (Angrist & Gershon, 1976), about half reported increased sexual interest. However, it appeared that only those patients who were relatively "hypersexual" prior to the administration of the drug experienced this effect. On the basis of this finding, the authors suggest that the possible sexual stimulation effects of the drug are likely to have the least influence on those patients who might benefit from such effects.

SUMMARY

Given the recent emphasis on sexual aspects of medical practice generally (e.g., Kolodny, Masters, & Johnson, 1979; Green, 1984), one might anticipate that studies of drug and alcohol effects on sexual function will receive increasing attention in the years to come. As is clear from the findings discussed in this chapter, this area of investigation is of considerable importance to both basic research and clinical practice. Studies of drug and alcohol effects contribute to our understanding of the basic neurophysiological and psychophysiological mechanisms in sexual arousal; they are also of considerable relevance for the practicing clinician concerned with the sexual well-being of his or her patients. Furthermore, given that the search for the perfect aphrodisiac has been a continuing theme throughout the history of our society, it is likely that research in this area will provide important information to a concerned public.

It is also apparent that research in this area has been quite uneven, with considerable attention being devoted to the sexual effects of alcohol and certain prescription drugs (e.g., antihypertensives), while relatively little research has been reported on the effects of nonprescription drugs such as marijuana and cocaine. It is equally apparent that the effects of drugs and alcohol on male sexual response have been far more widely studied than the corresponding effects on women. On a more positive note, however, it appears that recent studies in this area have paid increasing attention to female sexuality, and that research in this area is showing less of a sexist bias than it did earlier.

Although much of the information on drug effects continues to be based on clinical or anecdotal reports, there is evidence of an increasing trend toward the use of laboratory psychophysiological methods in this regard. Beginning with the alcohol studies in the mid-1970s (e.g., Farkas & Rosen, 1976; Rubin & Henson, 1976; Briddell & Wilson, 1976), there appears to be increasing recognition of the potential value of psychophysiological assessment methods in the evaluation of drug effects on sexual response. Of particular interest are the recent studies reporting on the use of NPT recording for assessing the effects of chronic alcohol use (Snyder & Karacan, 1983), beta-blocker effects in normals (Rosen et al., in press), antidepressant effects in depressed patients (Howell et al., 1987), and the effects of chronic cimetidine therapy on patients with peptic ulcer disease (Jensen et al., 1984).

The research conducted to date makes it abundantly clear that the search for the perfect aphrodisiac, while destined to continue, has thus far been in vain. Although the effects of set and setting appear to interact at times with the pharmacological effects of alcohol or drugs to produce an enhancement of sexual arousal (e.g., Wilson & Lawson, 1978), none of the drugs studied to date appears to have a direct stimulatory effect on sexual response. Rather, a number of the drug substances that have been reviewed appear to have considerable anaphrodisiac properties, particularly when taken in large quantities on a chronic basis.

Conclusion

In considering the future of sexual psychophysiology, a number of issues surface that will shape new directions of the field. Given the synergistic interaction of basic and applied research on sexual response, future laboratory studies of these questions can, it is hoped, provide greater understanding of the delicate and complex patterns and processes involved in sexual arousal. From a historical perspective, the future of sexual psychophysiology ideally will build upon earlier models, as presented by Masters and Johnson and others, while continuing to apply our knowledge of assessment strategies to a range of important applied issues.

In Section III we summarize several of the major themes of the book, illustrating, where possible, the implications for further research. Included in this review (in Chapter 13) is a discussion of patterning of sexual arousal responses, highlighting the interplay between clinical models of the sexual response cycle and basic research. Measurement issues and questions of applied and clinical concern are considered as well. Finally, the Appendix, containing detailed information on ethical safeguards for conducting laboratory research on sexual behavior, discusses such issues as the protection of human subjects, selection of research participants, procedural concerns, debriefing, informed consent, ecological validity, and the potential misuse of research findings. Throughout Section III our emphasis remains focused on the future role of sexual psychophysiology in contributing to the science of human behavior, and the careful conduct of this endeavor.

CHAPTER THIRTEEN

Future Directions in Sexual Psychophysiology

Can that facet of our lives, affecting more people in more ways than any other physiologic response other than those necessary to our very existence, be allowed to continue without benefit of objective, scientific analysis?—Masters and Johnson (1966, p. vii)

Case 1. Mr. R was a 46-year-old married male referred for evaluation of erectile dysfunction. The patient had a history of hypertension, which was first diagnosed at age 40 and had since been controlled through medication (diuretics and beta-blockers). He was referred by his family physician after complaining for some time of lack of sexual interest and erectile difficulties. In addition to hypertension, Mr. R's medical history included an extended period of alcohol abuse between the ages of 24 and 38, culminating in his entry into an alcohol treatment program in 1980. He had been abstinent for the past 6 years.

The patient's pattern of sexual interaction in recent years had been characterized by declining sexual frequency (i.e., intercourse less than once per month) and frequent episodes of erectile failure either prior to or immediately following penetration. All sexual encounters at this time were initiated by his wife, who expressed increasing frustration and resentment at his lack of sexual interest. Despite the diminishing occurrence of marital intercourse, Mr. R stated that he continued to masturbate occasionally (i.e., once or twice per month), albeit with less than full erection on most occasions.

Following the initial evaluation, a recommendation was made for NPT and hormonal evaluation, as well as a change in the patient's medication regimen. NPT findings indicated a pattern of "borderline" erectile impairment, with inconsistent and partial tumescence responses over two nights of testing. Hormonal assessment was similarly inconclusive, as test results indicated a low-normal level of plasma testosterone (320 ng/dl), along with normal-range levels of prolactin, FSH, and LH. Changing the patient's medication resulted in a gradual improvement in his mood and energy level, but little change was noted in his sexual interest or performance.

Case 2. John B was a 28-year-old single male referred for treatment following his arrest for stealing items of female underwear in a well-known department store. He reported that he had been actively engaging in transvestite behavior for the past 7 years, and that he made frequent use of female underwear, shoes, and wigs for this purpose. The patient's transvestite script consisted primarily of cross-dressing in private, with active fantasy and masturbation throughout. He denied any homosexual or transsexual inclinations, and claimed to have had limited heterosexual experience with two previous partners.

Psychophysiological evaluation in this case was focused on assessing the range and extent of John's arousal to sexually deviant stimuli. For this purpose, a hierarchy of erotic stimuli was constructed, ranging from slides of conventional heterosexual activities to depictions of sexual situations involving young children, coercive sex, adult homosexual interactions, and cross-dressing. Penile tumescence was found to be consistently greater to the cross-dressing stimuli, although significant arousal was also noted in association with adult homosexual stimuli. The remaining stimuli produced inconsistent and generally lower levels of response. When asked to attempt voluntary suppression of his arousal to these stimuli, the patient became anxious, claiming to have "no control over my reactions."

On the basis of the findings from this evaluation, John was referred for masturbatory satiation treatment, in order to gain greater control over his transvestite urges. Additional supportive therapy was recommended for exploring his homosexual feelings. A re-evaluation following 6 months of therapy indicated a significant reduction in arousal to transvestite stimuli, with little change in adult sexual orientation. Based upon the test results and the patient's expressed commitment to continuing therapy, a recommendation was made for early termination of his probation.

These brief case vignettes serve to illustrate several issues and concerns that typically arise in the "real-world" application of sexual psychophysiological techniques. All too often, the problems to be evaluated are complex and multidetermined, with a variety of potential etiological factors in each case. Clinicians are frequently hard pressed to unravel an intricate sequence of determining or causal events. Furthermore, the urgent demands of clinical decision making may foster overreliance on "objective" or laboratory-based testing procedures, such as NPT, hormone assays, and psychophysiological studies of deviant arousal. Increasingly, the findings from laboratory testing are viewed as the *sine qua non* for determining treatment objectives and evaluating clinical outcome. A major goal of this book has been to critically evaluate the rationale and empirical status of these methods in the study of sexual function and dysfunction.

Aside from the traditional concerns with reliability, validity, and clinical utility that are associated with these procedures, the case illustrations above raise additional questions regarding the ethical status and cost-effectiveness of these methods. For example, Mr. R's evaluation for erectile dysfunction involved a time-consuming and costly series of tests, which ultimately appeared to contribute little to the patient's long-term treatment plan. When are the inconvenience and expense of such tests justified, and when not? In the case of John B, important treatment decisions and the ultimate clinical disposition were based largely on the laboratory assessment. In this instance, was too much reliance being placed on psychophysiological testing? How certain can we be that laboratory arousal patterns indeed predict future behavior? Are there overt or subtle forms of coercion that may have influenced the outcome of the testing? What if the patient had refused to participate? In each instance, the use and interpretation of laboratory findings are clearly influenced by a complex set of social and ethical constraints.

Historically, theory and research on human sexuality have originated from a variety of loosely related interdisciplinary sources. Furthermore, the focus of the field has been increasingly divided between basic and applied topics, with a tendency to emphasize clinical application at the expense of more fundamental empirical investigations. For example, as discussed in Chapter 10, the NPT procedure currently enjoys widespread clinical use, despite limited research concerning the underlying psychophysiological mechanisms involved. Similarly, penile tumescence measures have frequently been employed in the assessment and treatment of male sex offenders, as discussed in Chapter 9, despite the relative lack of understanding at present concerning the mechanisms involved in the control of deviant sexual behavior. A clear danger here is that the demands of applied settings tend to push the limits of our measurement technology beyond basic knowledge.

At times we have noted a synergistic interaction between basic and applied research, as, for example, is evident in the recent laboratory studies of pornography or of drug and alcohol effects on sexual arousal. In addition to addressing important applied issues, research in these areas has furthered our understanding of basic phenomena in sexual psychophysiology. Laboratory analogue studies of sexual dysfunction in males and females have similarly contributed both to clinical application and to understanding of the role of cognitive and affective determinants of sexual arousal. Given the current constraints on research funding and the high priority accorded to socially relevant research, we would anticipate that most, if not all, laboratory research on sexual arousal will be conducted in this framework in the coming years.

In this concluding chapter, we have chosen to briefly review several of the major themes of the book, illustrating, where possible, the implications for further research. As we have been primarily concerned with the origins and scope of sexual psychophysiology to date, it is appropriate in closing to consider a number of important directions for the future. Finally, in view of the intricate link between basic and applied research in this field, we attempt to raise additional questions concerning future applications of methodology and findings from basic research.

RESPONSE PATTERNS IN SEXUAL AROUSAL

Issues in Research to Date

Involvement in the response to sexual tensions, although physiologically
well-defined, is experienced subjectively on the basis of individual
reaction patterns.—Masters and Johnson (1966, p. 6)

A central issue in the laboratory study of sexual arousal has been the specification of essential elements or dimensions of sexual responding. Many investigators have emphasized the physiological dimensions of arousal, often at the expense of subjective or cognitive factors. Others, such as Bancroft (1983), have attempted to accord equal weighting to central, somatic, and autonomic components of arousal. As described in Chapter 2, theory and research in sexual psychophysiology have increasingly emphasized the role of *cognitive* factors in sexual arousal, leading to our current focus on the "cognitive arousal" model of sexual response (Reisenzein, 1983). Despite the increasing attention directed at the interplay of cognitive, affective, and physiological patterns of response, however, investigators have yet to reach a consensus concerning the number or type of response components involved, or the chain of antecedent events that typically culminate in sexual response. Thus, for example, while recent models of sexual arousal (e.g., Byrne, 1986; Barlow, 1986) have described complex interactions between subjective and physiological dimensions of arousal, marked differences are apparent in the nature of the components included in each model, and in the hypothesized role of interactive mechanisms.

Notwithstanding these theoretical advances, we have noted a general tendency for laboratory studies to be based upon physiological indices of arousal, particularly peripheral autonomic changes. In contrast, more recent research has underscored the necessity for placing *subjective experience* in a central position in our definition of the sexual response. Although the physiological substrate is clearly more amenable to empirical definition and measurement than are the subjective components of arousal, it is clear that genital engorgement (or other autonomic changes) should not be viewed as necessary or sufficient in defining the sexual response. Numerous instances have been presented in which sexual arousal may be experienced without genital responding, and vice versa. Despite a growing awareness of the importance of including cognitive and affective components in the definition of sexual arousal, however, there continues to be little consensus in the field concerning the choice of specific cognitive–subjective factors to be studied.

Wherever possible, we have highlighted the value of traditional psychophysiological constructs in understanding patterns of interaction observed between response components. In particular, we have applied the concepts of SSR patterning and ISR patterning (see Chapter 2) to understanding the variability observed in sexual response patterns from one situation or individual to another. These complementary approaches to the study of response patterning provide a useful framework for deciphering the relative influences of situational determinants (SSR) and individual factors (ISR) in sexual arousal. For example, research on the effects of pornography on normal subjects has highlighted specific stimulus effects, and is generally viewed within the framework of SSR patterning. On the other hand, clinical studies of psychological and personality factors in sexual dysfunction have typically focused on individual differences in the arousal process (particularly variables that differentiate sexually functional from dysfunctional individuals), and thus follow clearly in the tradition of ISR research.

A related issue in the study of response patterning is the assessment of response concordance or association between dimensions of sexual arousal, particularly physiological and self-report measures. Delineating patterns of response clearly is facilitated when a high degree of concordance exists between these response dimensions. In reality, most studies have demonstrated varying degrees of *dissociation* between response components from one individual or situation to another. We should note, however, that this concern is not unique to sexual psychophysiology, but has emerged as a central theme in the laboratory study of emotion generally, as noted by Schwartz (1986): "A major problem and challenge for research on the psychophysiology of emotion involves individual differences in degree of association within psychological and physiological levels and between psychological and physiological levels" (p. 371).

Numerous examples have been discussed in which the dissociation between physiological and subjective dimensions of sexual arousal is particularly problematic. For example, treatment outcome studies employing psychophysiological assessment frequently have shown improvement in subjective measures of sexual satisfaction, without accompanying changes in genital vasocongestion (Wincze et al., 1978). Similarly, studies with normal subjects have frequently demonstrated wide variations in response concordance, depending upon the level of arousal of subjects (Hall et al., 1985) and the availability of visual feedback of response (Sakheim et al., 1984). Studies of alcohol effects on female sexual arousal have also reported marked dissociation between physiological and subjective indices of arousal (Wilson & Lawson, 1978).

A final issue to be considered in the laboratory study of response patterning is the choice of research design and approaches to be used for statistical analysis. To date, much of the research in the area has been constrained by the use of ANOVA and simple correlation–regression approaches to data analysis. A central problem in this regard is the application of univariate statistical models to the study of multiple, interactive response dimensions. Although the pattern-analytic approach to psychophysiological research recently developed by Fahrenberg (1986) and others (as described in Chapter 2) has yet to be incorporated into studies of sexual arousal, this approach offers considerable promise to future studies of response patterning in sexual arousal.

Future Research Questions on Response Patterning

To date, a relatively neglected area of research is the development of sexual response patterns over the course of the life span. While studies in developmental psychophysiology have begun to show changes in electrodermal, cardiovascular, and electrocortical activity associated with the processes of development and aging (Porges & Fox, 1986), this approach has yet to be systematically applied to issues in sexual psychophysiology. Examples of specific questions to be addressed are as follows:

- To what extent do sexual response patterns change or evolve over the life cycle? Conversely, what is the impact of life cycle events on patterns of sexual arousal? For example, considering the case of an individual woman who typically experiences copious lubrication early in the response cycle, how would the physiological changes of menopause impact on her pattern of sexual arousal?
- Is there evidence for a "critical period" effect in the development of sexual arousal patterns? Are deviant arousal patterns, in particular, more likely to emerge during specific developmental periods?
- What influence do sexual arousal patterns have on the processes of attraction and mate selection? To what extent might synchrony or congruence in sexual arousal patterns between partners contribute to emotional bonding?

Another key area for future investigation is the occurrence of stable ISR patterns in sexual arousal and the potential behavioral correlates of such individual patterns. Specific questions to be addressed include the following:

- Can ISR patterns be identified that would place individuals at risk for the development of sexual dysfunction? Would these patterns be different for men and women? What impact would effective treatment for sexual dysfunction have on ISR patterns?

- Are there specific ISR patterns that could function prognostically in predicting the likelihood of successful treatment outcome? Might specific sexual arousal patterns be predictive of relapse following treatment for sexual deviation?
- Can studies of drug and alcohol effects on sexual response be refined through the assessment of ISR patterns at baseline and during drug administration? Might such ISR patterns be used to predict which individuals will show greater susceptibility to drug or alcohol effects?

MODELS OF THE SEXUAL RESPONSE CYCLE

Issues in Research to Date

Nowhere is the chasm between basic research and clinical conceptualizations of sexual response more striking than in current approaches to the sexual response cycle. Whereas clinical nosology and diagnosis have been based largely on Masters and Johnson's (1966) four-stage model, and more recently on Kaplan's (1977) three-stage model of the sexual response cycle, these models have had negligible impact on laboratory psychophysiological research to date. Instead, most laboratory studies have focused predominantly on sexual excitement phenomena, with a few recent studies on orgasm, as described in Chapter 6. Furthermore, despite the emphasis of the current DSM-III diagnostic system on disorders of sexual desire, laboratory investigators have generally made little or no attempt to develop a specific methodology for the assessment of sexual desire. This disparity between basic and applied approaches to the sexual response cycle clearly limits the applicability of laboratory research concepts and methodology to the study of sexual dysfunctions.

Several reasons why current clinical models of the sexual response cycle have not had a greater impact on basic research have been considered. Among these are the lack of empirical support for the separation of specific phases of arousal, such as excitement and plateau in the four-stage model, or desire and arousal in the three-stage model. In fact, both the Masters and Johnson model and the Kaplan model can be viewed as arbitrary abstractions, lacking in both conceptual clarity and empirical validation. Commenting further on this problem, Robinson (1976) has observed: "Ellis's doctrine of tumescence and detumescence, though more general, turns out to be a more appropriate and far less pretentious abstraction, since it allows for both those phenomena that are cumulative and those that are sudden and evanescent, rather than imposing boxlike categories (e.g., excitement, plateau) that correspond to neither" (p. 130). Other authors have questioned the assumption of a unitary sequence of sexual arousal, in which a consistent pattern of changes is assumed to occur concurrently

337

across response dimensions (Bancroft, 1983). Thus, even though genital vasocongestive changes appear at times to conform to the four-stage response cycle sequence described by Masters and Johnson (1966), this pattern is seldom observed in cardiovascular, respiratory, or subjective concomitants of sexual response. In general, this fundamental assumption of response synchronization over time has not been systematically studied to date, despite its importance to existing models of the response cycle.

Another problematic issue is the presumed parallel between male and female sexual response cycles. In this regard, Masters and Johnson have repeatedly emphasized that "Aside from obvious anatomic variants, men and women are homogeneous in their physiologic responses to sexual stimuli" (1966, p. 285). Similarly, Kaplan's three-stage model equates the sequencing of desire, excitement, and orgasm phase changes for both men and women, despite her acknowledgment of significant gender differences in the processes and stages of sexual development. This assumption has similarly had a major impact on clinical theory and practice; for example, DSM-III currently subsumes male and female dysfunctions within the same generic categories, such as Inhibited Sexual Desire and Inhibited Sexual Excitement.

Clearly, a major challenge for future research in sexual psychophysiology is the integration of clinical and laboratory models of the sexual response cycle. For example, a few investigators have recently attempted to develop standardized self-report instruments for the assessment of sexual desire in men and women (e.g., LoPiccolo & Stock, 1986; Howell *et al.*, 1987). Ideally, these measures are to be used in conjunction with traditional measures of excitement and orgasm in further studies of the sexual response cycle. In addition to bridging the gap between laboratory and clinical concerns, empirical research on the sexual response cycle should lead to further theoretical development of existing models of the response cycle and to improved clinical application of these models.

Future Research Questions on the Sexual Response Cycle

Given the dearth of empirical research on the sexual response cycle, as well as the desirability of reconciling laboratory and clinical approaches to the study of sexual response, several research issues in this area are urgently in need of attention. Clearly, a major goal is the development of a research-based and empirically grounded conceptualization of the sexual response cycle, which we may hope will serve as both a clinical heuristic and a guide to further laboratory studies. Specific research questions in this regard are as follows:

- Can current laboratory assessment techniques be used to measure psychophysiological changes at increasing levels of arousal during the response cycle? Considering that most laboratory studies to date have been limited to the measurement of changes during the initial stages of sexual excitement, what additional findings would emerge if such investigations were extended to include higher levels of arousal? For example, in reviewing studies of anxiety and distraction effects on sexual arousal (Chapters 10 and 11), it can be questioned whether similar results would have been obtained if the experimental paradigm had included more extended periods of erotic stimulation and subjects had experienced higher levels of arousal prior to the introduction of the anxiety or distraction stimulus.

- Is there a discrete pattern of psychophysiological changes that accompanies the experience of sexual desire in men and women? What are the relative contributions of central versus peripheral physiological processes to this phase of sexual response? Can individuals with inhibited desire be differentiated from normals on the basis of laboratory measures of response patterning?

- Can psychophysiological changes be identified that reliably signal the initiation of orgasm in men or women? In particular, is there a specific sequence of central or peripheral activation that serves to trigger orgasm in both sexes? Are there ISR patterns in this regard, and what clinical implications might such patterning have?

- Can the phenomenon of the postorgasmic "refractory period" be adequately explained by means of traditional psychophysiological concepts, such as autonomic balance and parasympathetic rebound? To what extent do ISR patterns influence the characteristics of the refractory period?

MEASUREMENT ISSUES IN SEXUAL PSYCHOPHYSIOLOGY

The State of Research to Date

Like most areas of psychophysiology, laboratory research on human sexuality has been greatly influenced by the availability and effectiveness of specific measurement techniques. Particularly with the advent of quantitative methods for assessment of genital arousal in males and females, as discussed in Chapters 3 and 4, laboratory sex research has come to achieve a reasonable degree of scientific precision. Measurement devices such as the penile strain gauge and the vaginal photoplethysmograph are also relatively easily adapted for the study of a wide variety of applied issues, as illustrated by the numerous examples in Section II of the book. Considering that virtually all of these studies have been conducted in the two decades since the advent of the present measurement techniques, the impact of these techniques on the scope and content of laboratory sex research can hardly be overestimated.

Notwithstanding the impressive accomplishments and obvious benefits of the existing measurement technology, a number of critical issues and concerns have also emerged. First, we have noted that several of these devices originated from historically unrelated or serendipitous sources, such as the prevention of masturbation in stallions (Mountjoy, 1974) or the detection of ovulation in ewes during estrus (Abrams & Stolwijk, 1976). Despite continuing efforts to adapt these devices for experimental research with humans, it is apparent that current measurement approaches in laboratory sex research are based more upon the availability and ease of use of particular transducers than upon a sound understanding of the underlying processes of sexual arousal.

In this regard, we have especially emphasized a growing body of evidence on the neurovascular basis of penile tumescence that suggests that current measures may provide an inaccurate or distorted view of the process. Specifically, recent studies on the hemodynamics of erection have indicated that differences in penile circumference, as measured by the mercury-in-rubber or electromechanical strain gauges, do not appear to provide an adequate index of relevant vascular changes. Arterial inflow and venous closure, for instance, have been shown to be important dimensions of the process that are not assessed adequately by circumferential measures (Bancroft & Bell, 1985; Wagner, 1981a). Similarly, clinical research on the measurement of NPT has focused increasingly on the need for independent assessment of penile rigidity, in addition to conventional measures of engorgement (Karacan et al., 1978; Metz & Wagner, 1981). Finally, recent studies on the physiological basis of sexual arousal in women have highlighted serious limitations in the vaginal photoplethysmograph as an adequate measure of genital engorgement (Wagner & Ottesen, 1980).

In addition to concerns about underlying physiology, recent studies of the measurement characteristics of these devices have begun to raise serious questions concerning their validity and reliability. For example, Earls and Marshall (1982) have shown that current penile tumescence measures may fail to record changes at both the high and the low end of the normal range of responses. Reliability issues are a major concern in the use of the vaginal probe, as studies utilizing repeated-measures analyses have indicated that test–retest reliability may be less than desirable (D. E. Henson et al., 1979). Also, several authors have noted the lack of an absolute scale of measurement for the vaginal probe (Beck, Sakheim, & Barlow, 1983; Hatch, 1979). In recent years, these and other psychometric issues have been raised with increasing frequency, leading to present efforts to modify and improve existing measurement strategies.

Future Research Questions on the Measurement of Sexual Arousal

Given the central role of measurement techniques in all laboratory research, future research on the measurement of sexual arousal no doubt will contribute in a significant fashion to the development of psychophysiology in general. Two specific implications of the current review are particularly salient. First, further psychometric studies are needed to determine the range of arousal values for which each device can be reliably used. Second, additional research is clearly needed on alternative measures of genital arousal in both sexes. In particular, new approaches are needed that will more adequately represent the underlying physiological processes. Additional specific questions are as follows:

- To what extent might the sensitivity and reliability of current genital measures be improved with greater attention to instrumentation design and construction? Would further advances contribute to the limited improvements that have thus far been made on these devices? For example, could the reliability of the vaginal probe be increased by design changes to ensure more constant intravaginal positioning?
- Can alternative laboratory assessment approaches be developed to provide measures of arousal that are comparable or superior to existing approaches? In light of the recent emphasis on multiple vascular components of arousal, can devices be introduced for measuring both male and female arousal that will more adequately reflect the influence of these underlying processes? Finally, can measures of genital vasocongestion be developed that are less invasive than existing approaches?

APPLIED AND CLINICAL ISSUES IN SEXUAL PSYCHOPHYSIOLOGY

The State of Research to Date

The past decade has witnessed a veritable mushrooming of clinical and applied research in sexual psychophysiology. Throughout Section II of this book, numerous examples are described of the application of laboratory research to issues of current concern, such as the effects of erotica and pornography, alcohol and drug effects on sexual response, sexual aggression, and the etiology and treatment of a wide range of sexual disorders. Unlike other areas of psychophysiological research, laboratory investigation of these topics has generated considerable scientific interest and controversy. This trend can be viewed as positive in several respects. First, an impressive body of practical information has accumulated concerning the effects of drugs and disease on the capacity for sexual arousal, on innovative techniques for the diagnosis and treatment of sexual dysfunction, and on laboratory methods for the assessment and treatment of sex offenders. Recent laboratory studies have also increased awareness of the potential consequences of exposure to pornography and sexual abuse. Conversely, the application of laboratory psychophysiological techniques to issues of widespread social concern has provided increased impetus for basic research. Finally, greater public and professional acceptance of the potential significance of laboratory sex research has resulted from the publication of research findings in these areas.

Applied research is not without certain limitations and drawbacks, however. In particular, we have frequently noted a tendency toward premature acceptance of laboratory findings by practitioners and the lay public alike, as well as inappropriate extrapolation from available research data. Obvious examples of these problems include an overreliance on laboratory assessment in the evaluation and treatment of sex offenders, uncritical acceptance of diagnostic techniques such as NPT testing, and the use of unvalidated laboratory procedures (e.g., genital biofeedback and PC muscle training) in the treatment of sexual dysfunction.

Future Applied and Clinical Research Questions

Given the current emphasis on clinical relevance in biobehavioral research generally, it is safe to predict that sex researchers will continue to search for new and challenging areas of application for some time to come. Specific areas of application that have received little attention to date include the effects of sexually transmitted diseases, of sexual victimization, and of chronic illness and injury. Examples of future research questions in these areas are as follows:

- Aside from the well-documented effects of sexually transmitted diseases on physical and emotional health in general, are there specific sexual sequelae of diseases such as herpes and AIDS? Can laboratory psychophysiological methods be used to further our understanding of these effects?
- What are the long-term effects of childhood sexual abuse on adult arousal patterns? Do these effects differ for men and women who were victimized at various ages? How might laboratory assessment methods contribute to the clinical evaluation and treatment of such individuals?
- Clinical studies have increasingly highlighted the sexual concerns and difficulties of disabled and chronically ill individuals (Bullard &

Knight, 1981). Are there distinctive patterns of sexual arousal associated with these conditions, and might laboratory assessment of arousal patterns in these individuals be used for diagnostic or rehabilitative purposes?

SOCIAL AND ETHICAL CONCERNS IN SEXUAL PSYCHOPHYSIOLOGY

Sexuality must not be described as a stubborn drive. . . . [It] is not the most intractable element in power relations, but rather one of those endowed with the greatest instrumentality: useful for the greatest number of maneuvers and capable of serving as a point of support, as a linchpin, for the most varied strategies.—Foucault (1978, p. 103)

The conduct of sex research in Western society is fraught with potential social and ethical pitfalls. Irrespective of the particular issue under investigation, the study of sexuality inevitably raises concerns and problems that are not encountered in other fields of research. Sex research continues to maintain, in Gagnon's phrase, its "exemplary status as the observable margin between the sacred and the profane" (1978, p. 225). Thus, researchers need to be cognizant at all times of the social impact of both methods and findings of research in these areas, whether they are investigating contraceptive practices among college students, assessing the emotional trauma of rape victims, or studying sexual practices among AIDS victims. These concerns are heightened when investigators make use of techniques for laboratory observation and recording of sexual responses.

First among these concerns are the possible risks to the subject. As in other areas of laboratory psychophysiology, physical safety is a primary concern, such as prevention of accidental electric shock. In addition, several authors have warned against the possibility of transmission of sexually transmitted diseases through improper sterilization of genital devices (Rosen & Keefe, 1978; Geer, 1976). Other potential risks to the subject include the experience of psychological discomfort, such as embarrassment associated with arousal to unconventional stimuli. In view of the increasing concern with the protection of human subjects in experimental research, we have included a detailed appendix on strategies for safeguarding subjects' rights in laboratory sex research. Readers who are currently engaged in research in any area of sexual psychophysiology are strongly urged to consider the guidelines included in the Appendix.

Investigators, as well as subjects, may find themselves at risk in the conduct of sex research. As discussed in Chapter 1, several early pioneers in the field of sex research, including John B. Watson, Havelock Ellis, and Alfred Kinsey, paid a considerable personal price for the "prurience" of their research interests. Although the social context of sex research has

343

changed over time, giving investigators greater freedom to enter this once-tabooed field of study, the enterprise is not without continuing risks. For example, sex researchers frequently encounter resistance in obtaining institutional approval for specific projects and in acquiring grant support for these projects from federal and other sources. Moreover, a number of instances of considerable intolerance from academic and community groups have been documented (Holden, 1976).

At a broader societal level, we have repeatedly emphasized that the findings from laboratory sex research can have profound effects on moral and legal decision making. Nowhere is this more apparent than in the recent debate over the effects of pornography. According to the Attorney General's report, "The Commission has examined social and behavioral science research in recognition of the role it plays in determining legal standards and social policy" (Attorney General's Commission on Pornography, 1986, p. 901). Noting the potential problems that this presents, however, the report provides this caution: "Some might argue that given the controversy and heated debate that inevitably surrounds any discussion about pornography, we might be better off relying on studies initiated, funded, and presented outside the context of such a milieu" (1986, p. 901). Another area of application with considerable potential for influencing social policy is the use of sexual psychophysiology in the assessment and treatment of sexual deviation, as indicated in Chapter 9.

Caveats aside, research in sexual psychophysiology has played an important role in lifting the veil of secrecy and ignorance that has too long obscured our understanding of human sexuality. The work is far from complete, however, and we have attempted in this final chapter to point the way for future studies in the field. We believe that in meeting the challenges to further research, a unique opportunity exists for adding to our knowledge of sexual response in men and women, as well as to the broader investigation of human behavior.

Concerns Involving Human Subjects in Sexual Psychophysiology

Given the inherent risks involved in the study of the human sexual response (as illustrated by the experiences of John B. Watson, Alfred Kinsey, and, most recently, Harris Rubin), careful attention to laboratory construction, protection of subjects' rights, and procedural safeguards are important concerns in the conduct of sexual psychophysiology. While attention to these issues will not necessarily assure the investigator freedom from public or professional censure, this appendix is intended to outline specific laboratory procedures for safeguarding both research participants and investigators, and, ultimately, to create a climate in which sex research is no longer viewed as "fraught with danger" (Watson, 1929; cf. Chapter 1) (Figure A.1).

While each particular investigation will involve unique human-subjects considerations, depending on location (e.g., university campus, medical center), type of subjects selected for study (e.g., males or females, subjects with dysfunctional or deviant arousal patterns), and the choice of specific experimental procedures, a number of common issues arise in the conduct of laboratory sex research. In considering these concerns, the reader may note that sexual psychophysiology necessitates precautions beyond those required in other, less sensitive areas of research. This is attributable to greater public scrutiny of laboratory explorations of human sexuality (Kolodny, 1977) and to the need to safeguard all involved in the research process, subjects and investigators alike. The following discussion describes key issues in the protection of human subjects in sex research, including laboratory construction, subject safety, procedural concerns, and broader issues (e.g., volunteer bias and the design of experimental manipulations that balance human-subjects concerns and ecological validity).

LABORATORY CONSTRUCTION

In designing and constructing a psychophysiology laboratory, the sex researcher is immediately confronted with an array of complex technical considerations. In general, it is advisable to seek consultation concerning these issues from a specialist,

345

Figure A.1. Copyright 1978 by Gahan Wilson. Reprinted by permission.

such as a qualified biomedical engineer, as mastery of all aspects of laboratory design and construction is difficult.

The first step in laboratory construction involves choosing an appropriate site. The investigator needs to be mindful of noise and activity levels in the surrounding environment; if at all possible, he or she should find a location that is quiet and secluded. The investigator will also need to consider temperature and ventilation control of the setting where equipment is housed and subjects are studied. This is particularly important with the use of transducers that are reactive to ambient climate changes, such as thermistors and electrodermal measures. Lighting is a factor in laboratory construction as well, as the investigator may wish to vary levels of illumination in which subjects are assessed. Furthermore, incandescent lights must be used, as fluorescent lighting generates 60-Hz electrical noise that confounds physiological signals.

Optimally, a psychophysiological laboratory should include two adjacent, electrically shielded rooms. Given that the cost involved in shielding is often prohibitive, alternatives are available. Several companies (e.g., Solo, Inc.) manufacture devices that screen radio-frequency oscillation from wall current, as well as indicate the presence of excessive amounts of leakage current to the equipment. This is a particularly useful approach if power surges are noted in the building where the laboratory is housed. The use of a surge protector is recommended as well, to safeguard computer equipment and prevent damage resulting from uncontrolled variations in wall current, such as those that occur during electrical storms. All equipment must be grounded and checked for electrical safety on a regular basis, using a device such as the RCA Leakage Current tester.

In configuring leads for assessment devices, it is particularly important for the investigator to consider placement of the subject in relation to other electrical equipment (e.g., a video monitor), to assure that the subject cannot accidentally shock himself or herself through inadvertent differentials in grounding. In addition, the subject must be isolated from electrical outlets and water sources, such as a sink.

While a number of other design and engineering issues are involved in laboratory construction, the reader is referred to Stern, Ray, and Davis (1980) and Coles, Gratton, Kramer, and Miller (1986) for more detailed discussions. Overall, it is clear that careful attention to laboratory design and construction can circumvent many future problems in signal analysis, subject safety, and experimental control.

PROTECTION OF SUBJECTS

In addition to providing a laboratory environment that is physically safe and comfortable, the investigator needs to consider a number of additional human-subjects issues in order to provide adequate protection of participants' rights. Foremost among these are the orientation of subjects to laboratory procedures, informed consent, assurance of confidentiality, and sterilization of genital devices. While a recent review of the reporting of subject orientation procedures indicated infrequent mention of specific precautions taken to protect subjects' rights, safety, and welfare (Bohlen, 1980), most investigators are well aware of the need to provide adequate protection of human subjects, particularly given the role of institutional review boards in the research process. Specific safeguards are outlined below.

Protection of subjects begins with orientation to the research protocol. This involves introducing a prospective subject to all research procedures, including interviews, questionnaires, and the laboratory assessment. Currently, there are several approaches to insuring adequate orientation, such as providing the subject with a tour of the laboratory and a demonstration of genital devices. Each step in the procedure is described thoroughly, particularly the provision of privacy during undressing and data collection. It is of note that most laboratory settings assure visual privacy during data collection, although audio privacy cannot be granted if an intercom is used for communication between the subject chamber and the experimenter. In orienting the subject, precautions designed to protect the subject from potential physical, psychological, and social hazards should be outlined, and the subject should be informed that he or she can discontinue participation at any point in the procedure without consequences. Steps to protect anonymity should also be reviewed in the initial orientation process. Subjects should be encouraged to raise doubts and questions throughout this orientation.

347

Most investigators allow the prospective participant a 1- to 2-day interval to decide whether to pursue research involvement. As outlined by Bohlen (1980), this procedure permits the subject to consider the information provided during the laboratory tour and to raise additional questions prior to making a commitment to participate. At the return appointment, the subject is provided with the informed consent statement, which details the procedures involved, describes potential risks and benefits of participation, delineates whether medical or psychological services will be provided to the subject in the event of a negative outcome, and assures the subject that all data will be kept confidential. The wording of an informed consent statement is a critical component of subject protection, and requires careful attention to detail. A sample consent statement is given in Figure A.2. This sample

---

Title: Psychological factors in inhibited sexual desire: A test of Kaplan's model

Principal investigator: _____

I acknowledge that I have been given a full description of the following research project, conducted with the University of Houston, Department of Psychology. I will be asked to complete a structured interview involving questions about my sexual and personal behavior. I understand that this structured interview will include questions about the frequency of my sexual encounters, the nature of my sexual encounters, my sexual preference, and other questions that concern my sexual behavior. I am fully aware that I may refuse to answer any questions and that I may discontinue participation at any time without penalty or prejudice. Following this I will have small bodily recording devices attached to my hands and my forehead. These measure sweating and muscle tension. The devices are attached by sterile tape or soft plastic strips and present little discomfort. Furthermore, I will be asked to place a small bodily recording device on my penis, which causes no discomfort. This device is known as the strain gauge and is designed to measure penile tumescence (erection). I understand that I will be given *complete privacy* to attach this device. While wearing these devices I will be seated in a comfortable chair and asked to listen to three audiotapes, each containing an explicit description of a heterosexual encounter. I understand that these tapes will contain frank language and detailed descriptions of sexual activity. Immediately after each tape, I will be asked to fill out a brief questionnaire describing my experiences. The entire procedure will take no more than 2 hours.

The purpose of this project is to examine psychological aspects of sexual response. I understand that this work is experimental. I have been fully informed of the following risks and benefits of this project. The risks include experiencing temporary emotional arousal. The benefits include (1) a deeper understanding of how my state of mind may affect my sexual responsiveness, and (2) payment of $10.00.

I understand that *complete confidentiality* will be maintained, that my records will be coded with an identification number and will not contain my name, and that this information will be released to no one without my consent. I understand that monetary compensation for physical or psychological injury or illness is not available.

I understand that my participation is completely voluntary and that I may withdraw from this project at any time, without penalty or prejudice. This project has been reviewed by the University of Houston Committee for the Protection of Human Subjects.

Signature _____ Age ___ Date _____

Figure A.2. Sample informed consent statement.

statement assumes that the subject has been oriented to the laboratory and has had his or her questions answered prior to signing the statement. Depending upon the invasiveness of the experimental procedures to be used, the signature of a witness may need to be included. This precaution is typically used only when subjects are exposed to procedures that may produce physically harmful effects, such as electrical shock.

Of interest in this regard is Bohlen's (1980) observation that authors reporting sexual psychophysiological studies with female subjects tend to provide a more comprehensive description of subject orientation procedures, and to discuss the use of same-sex experimenters in conducting laboratory procedures. It is our experience that matching experimenter and subject gender can make for greater subject comfort for both males and females. Matching may also eliminate a source of experimental variance during data collection, particularly with male subjects.

It is essential that subjects be provided with complete anonymity and confidentiality for all responses made during laboratory assessment. The use of numerical codes as a means of data identification, rather than subjects' names or initials, is one method of guaranteeing anonymity. In keeping with this goal, documents that a subject has signed, such as the informed consent statement, should be stored in a separate location from research data. The investigator may not release the subject's results to any individual or agency without a signed release statement, and specific steps should be taken to protect further the confidentiality of the data. This includes training research assistants in the handling of sensitive information, including questionnaire responses and polygraph records.

Equally important in the protection of subjects are the procedures used for sterilization of genital devices (e.g., Geer, 1980). In addition to screening out those subjects with sexually transmitted diseases, the investigator needs to establish procedures to sanitize equipment. Currently, most investigators rely on dialdehyde (commonly known as Cidex-7), a sterilizing solution that can be used to soak genital instruments such as thermistors, photoplethysmographs, and strain gauges. A potential shortcoming of this approach is the acidity of the solution, which tends to erode the protective surface of the device with prolonged use. While other sterilization techniques (e.g., gas sterilization and heat methods) have been used, these approaches do not currently appear suitable for use with genital devices, as they may damage the equipment. Irrespective of the strategy chosen, the investigator must be certain that genital devices are sterilized properly prior to use with each research participant.

PROCEDURAL CONCERNS

In addition to strategies designed to orient subjects, receive informed consent, and sterilize equipment, a number of procedural concerns are also involved in sexual psychophysiology. Such issues as subject selection, use of deception and debriefing, potential risks and benefits of experimental procedures, and ecological validity concerns are integral parts of research design and often influence the nature of results obtained in the laboratory.

Subject Selection

An important issue in subject selection is the method used to recruit potential participants. Most often, investigators rely on volunteer subjects, particularly for basic research on sexual response, evaluation of measurement devices, and examination of the effects of psychological processes (e.g., distraction and anxiety) on sexual arousal. Volunteer bias has been documented in all areas of psychological research; volunteers tend to have higher educational levels, higher occupational status, higher need for approval, and lower authoritarianism scores than nonvolunteers (Rosenthal & Rosnow, 1969). In particular, empirical studies of human sexuality are susceptible to subject selection bias, given the unconventional nature of the research.

In several studies of self-selection patterns in human sexuality research, it has been reported that males tend to volunteer more frequently for participation than do females. Male volunteers are more sex-role-stereotyped than nonvolunteers, while women volunteers are less sex-role-stereotyped than female nonparticipants (e.g., Wolchik, Braver, & Jensen, 1985; Diamant, 1970). Volunteers also tend to differ from nonvolunteers in attitudes toward sexuality and experience with specific sexual activities. For example, volunteers have been shown to be more sexually liberal and permissive, to have greater curiosity about sexuality, and to value sex research to a greater extent (e.g., Wolchik *et al.*, 1985). Volunteers also tend to be more sexually experienced (Diamant, 1970; Farkas, Sine, & Evans, 1978), to have a greater frequency of masturbation (Wolchik, Spencer, & Lisi, 1983), and to have had a greater number of sexual partners (Wolchik *et al.*, 1985).

Selection bias appears to be more extreme in studies involving sexual psychophysiology than in investigations requiring self-report of sexual behavior, attitudes, and fantasies (Farkas *et al.*, 1978; Wolchik *et al.*, 1983, 1985; Morokoff, 1986). The influence of these subject biases on psychophysiological data is unknown, given constraints in examining this issue directly. What these findings reveal, however, is that the subject samples that have been used in much of the laboratory research on sexual response are not representative of the general population.

Other methods of subject selection used in sexual psychophysiological research raise somewhat different issues. Applied studies, such as investigations of NPT assessment and examination of deviant arousal patterns, tend to rely on clinical referrals for subject recruitment. If an individual is referred for a laboratory evaluation and is subsequently offered involvement in a research protocol, the investigator needs to take special precautions to insure "true" consent from the subject. Implicit coercion, in the form of a reduction or elimination of evaluation fees or an offer of free treatment, needs to be considered with this approach to subject selection. If subjects are referred from an institutional setting (e.g., sex offenders), special care needs to be taken to insure that institutional duress or coercion is not applied for participation (or failure to participate) in the research. Regardless of the approach used for selection of subjects, the sex researcher needs to be aware that important human-subjects issues are involved in subject selection and that the results of his or her investigation may be influenced by a host of factors that are neither assessed nor controlled experimentally.

Use of Deception and Debriefing

While the use of deception in psychological research has generally declined in recent years, owing to increased concern about protection of human subjects, certain paradigms within sexual psychophysiology require that subjects be unaware of the true nature of the experiment. For example, the series of studies conducted by Barlow and colleagues reviewed in Chapter 10 (Barlow et al., 1983; Beck & Barlow, 1986a, 1986b) utilized a threat of electrical shock to the forearm as a means of invoking anxiety simultaneously with the presentation of erotic films. Subjects were informed that there was a 60% chance of receiving shock if their level of arousal was less than the average research subject at any given point during the film, although, in actuality, the shock device was disconnected during the procedure. Similarly, investigations conducted by Malamuth (1984) and Donnerstein (1980), reviewed in Chapter 8, involved presentation of pornographic rape portrayals, following which subjects were debriefed. Several days later, subjects were assessed covertly for their attitudes toward pornography and rape. In each of these paradigms, the use of deception was justified by the nature of the experimental design; yet it raises important issues involving the possibility of harmful short- and long-term effects.

In studies of this type, the use of postexperimental debriefing is essential for assurance that subjects have not experienced unforeseen effects. While it is common for investigators to assume that their debriefing procedures are adequate, Sherif (1980) has highlighted the need for evaluation of the effectiveness of current practices. In response to this issue, several reports have appeared recently that document the short-term effects of experimentation on pornography. For example, Malamuth and Check (1984) and Check and Malamuth (1984) presented 150 male and female undergraduates with pornographic stories, some of which depicted a rape and some of which described mutually consenting intercourse. Following the presentation, the subjects in the rape condition were debriefed with explanations of the horror of rape and the existence of rape myths.

Ten days later, a "public survey" was given to students during their classes, ostensibly conducted by a local citizens' group. Included in this survey were several accounts of recent rapes, as well as articles concerning other current legal and political issues. Students were polled about each of these events, and postexperimental surveys indicated that subjects were unaware of the connection between the two phases of the research. Results showed that those subjects who were exposed to the rape story, followed by the debriefing, were less likely to endorse certain rape myths (e.g., "Women secretly desire to be raped"). Subjects in the rape/debriefing condition gave rapists a longer prison sentence, saw the victim as less responsible, and tended to perceive pornography as a cause of rape to a greater extent than subjects in the control condition. Similar findings have been reported by Donnerstein and Berkowitz (1981).

These findings support the effectiveness of debriefing practices in studies on the effect of pornography on subjects' attitudes and beliefs about sexual victimization and rape. However, since these investigations have relied on self-report alone, and have assessed rather limited influences of exposure to pornography, further study of the influence of deception in laboratory sexual psychophysiology is warranted. Related procedures (e.g., NPT evaluation, assessment of vaginal vasocongestion, and determination of deviant arousal patterns) deserve closer scrutiny, as their short- and long-term effects are currently unknown.

Potential Risks and Benefits of Participation in Sexual Psychophysiology Research

While experimental paradigms that involve deception clearly pose the risk of negative effects for subjects, other assessment and treatment procedures involving sexual psychophysiology can produce unintended outcomes. For example, it is common for subjects, particularly those who are young and relatively sexually inexperienced, to experience anxiety if they do not achieve significant levels of genital vasocongestion in the laboratory. The manner in which these concerns are handled by the experimenter can be important in determining the effect on the subjects' "sexual self-efficacy" and subsequent responding. Similarly, the presentation of homosexual or deviant stimuli can evoke a range of negative emotional reactions in subjects, which need to be discussed following the experimental procedure. In each of these examples, provision of accurate information concerning the full range of responses that are observed across subjects is a necessary part of allaying a subject's fears, as well as mitigating the possibility of undesired long-term effects of participation. For this reason, debriefing is recommended for all forms of sexual psychophysiology.

Beneficial outcomes are noted for some participants in sex research, as well. In the assessment of sexually dysfunctional individuals, for example, it is not uncommon for subjects to express pleasant surprise at their ability to respond to erotic presentations. The laboratory paradigm offers the opportunity for subjects to gain feedback concerning their sexual responsivity in a situation that makes no demands for partner gratification. In this instance, the assessment procedure can offer an incentive for dysfunctional individuals to pursue sex or marital therapy. Furthermore, in rare instances, an individual will disclose the existence of deviant sexual urges to the experimenter, often with the intent of seeking accurate information concerning treatment options. In these cases, despite the risk that disclosure might contain sensitive information, such as sexual arousal to children or adolescents, the experimenter can play an important role in providing a prompt clinical referral. Similarly, psychophysiological assessment occasionally yields information concerning an untreated medical condition in a subject (e.g., hypertension), which, once detected, can be referred to an appropriate physician.

In consideration of the risks and benefits of sexual psychophysiological research, questions are often raised concerning the possible effects of investigating sexual responding on subjects' attitudes and sexual behavior in the natural environment. To date, several reports have examined the consequences of involvement in sex research. Abramson (1977), for example, assessed 80 male and female undergraduate volunteers using the presentation of an erotic story, assessment of information on reproductive biology, and responses to *double entendre* words. During debriefing, subjects were polled for their views concerning participation in sex research. All of the male subjects and 96% of the females indicated that their participation had been informative and felt that the provisions to safeguard their rights were adequate. Subjects were particularly positive about the utility of the debriefing procedure as a means to gain feedback concerning participation. These results suggest that current practices designed to protect human subjects may be effective in studies such as this and may produce positive experiences for participants.

A related question concerns unintended effects of participation in sex research on sexual behavior. Persky, Strauss, Lief, Miller, and O'Brien (1981) followed two cohorts of married couples over a 6-month interval, during which time subjects completed a variety of measures assessing sexual behavior. Of 29 separate measures of sexual behavior, only 1 (a self-rating of male sexual gratification) showed a small, albeit significant, change over time. Given the possibility that this result may have been a chance finding, the authors conclude that research methodology employed to study sexual behavior is not reactive. Replication of these findings with participants in research involving sexual psychophysiology is needed, as presentations of erotic stimuli may produce greater reactivity than self-report instruments. Overall, these findings suggest that if adequate attention is paid to human-subjects concerns in sexual psychophysiology, the risks will be minimal. The training of experimenters in research conduct and debriefing procedures, the use of carefully worded informed consent statements, and the like can clearly facilitate a subject's positive experience with laboratory studies in sexual psychophysiology.

Ecological Validity

A final procedural concern that has implications for experimental design and interpretation of results involves the extent to which laboratory assessment mirrors "real life." For example, in most experimental protocols, subjects are presented with relatively brief erotic stimuli (ranging from 1 to 15 minutes). During this interval, only the early stages of the arousal response can be observed and quantified, and this leaves unanswered many questions concerning relevant processes during higher levels of sexual arousal. However, to examine the complete process of the sexual response, from early arousal through orgasm and resolution, would necessitate an experimental design that few human-subjects committees would approve. Although Masters and Johnson made direct observations of couples engaging in intercourse, this type of investigation is highly invasive and may violate subjects' privacy to such an extent that the risks of negative psychological effects from participation outweigh the scientific benefits that would result. Thus, current experimental procedures do not include actual sexual encounters or analogues for such encounters, and, as such, represent a possible threat to ecological validity.

A clear example of this issue can be found in the available research on the effects of pornography, as reviewed in Chapter 8. Common practice in this type of experimentation is to present various types of pornography, following which sexual attitudes are assessed. As noted by Schaefer and Colgan (1977), this procedure is at variance with naturalistic uses of pornography, as individuals are not permitted to achieve orgasm following the presentation of erotic material. When the laboratory procedure is altered to create a closer analogue, significant differences in the effects of pornography are observed, as discussed in Chapter 8.

Examples of the need to balance ecological validity and human-subjects concerns can be found in other areas of sexual psychophysiology research. For example, studies of relevant factors in sexual dysfunction have typically presented subjects with experimental instructions designed to create analogues of distraction, anxiety, attentional states, and efforts to voluntarily control sexual responding. While each of these paradigms includes a check of the manipulation employed, the relevance of these instructions for understanding operative factors in individuals with low sexual arousal remains unknown. Ultimately, subjects' perceptions of the particular experimental manipulation determine the extent to which ecological validity has been established (Berkowitz & Donnerstein, 1982). Human-subjects concerns and ecological validity are both central issues in designing experimental manipulations and deserve careful consideration by the investigator.

A FINAL NOTE

In all types of research on human sexual responding, the concerned investigator needs to be aware of the many clinical and social implications of empirical findings. In clinical applications, the use of psychophysiology for decision making poses an array of questions. For example, in the evaluation of sexual deviation, penile tumescence measurement is frequently integral to the assessment of deviant arousal, the formulation of treatment interventions, and the evaluation of therapeutic outcome (e.g., Abel, Barlow, *et al.*, 1977; Laws & Osborn, 1983). While this research has provided a much-needed objective and quantitative approach for clinical assessment, a central issue is the concern with "response faking" in individuals being assessed for treatment or legal decisions. As discussed in Chapter 9, considerable disagreement exists concerning the extent to which faking occurs, what types of sexual offenders may attempt to modify their response, and the implications of voluntary control for treatment outcome. Quinsey and Marshall (1983), for example, propose that the problem is limited to a select subgroup of offenders. These authors further suggest that "patients who can 'fake' improvement are demonstrating that they have acquired the ability to control their arousal and are therefore good risks" (p. 283). Unfortunately, no empirical evidence is provided to support this controversial claim. Overall, this issue is of major social importance, as decisions regarding disposition are based increasingly upon laboratory assessment.

Other concerns also have been noted in regard to the use of psychophysiological assessment of deviant arousal. First, the relationship between deviant arousal and the actual commission of deviant sexual acts needs to be considered. Groth and Birnbaum (1979), for example, have described numerous case histories of violent sex offenders who appear to be motivated entirely by nonsexual forms of gratification. Conversely, the work of Malamuth and his associates has indicated that sexual arousal to deviant stimuli is common among normal males, most of whom are unlikely to act on their arousal. Second, the problem of the external validity of laboratory assessment of offenders has been raised by a number of authors (e.g., Farkas, 1978; Laws & Osborn, 1983). It is unclear at present to what extent deviant arousal in the laboratory is predictive of arousal patterns in a naturalistic setting. This type of concern has subtle implications for clinical decision making involving all aspects of laboratory psychophysiology.

A related area of concern is the potential misuse of laboratory research results as a basis for the setting of sexual performance standards. Concerns about sexual "normality" are so pervasive in our society that individuals are extremely susceptible to the findings of sex research in general. The unfortunate result is that research on topics such as masturbation, sexual fantasy, multiple orgasms, and female ejaculation frequently serve as the basis for prescriptive notions of sexual function. Sex manuals and self-help guides, in particular, all too often oversimplify the results of laboratory research and encourage conformity to ever-changing sexual standards. Our experience as sex therapists has also confirmed that popular coverage of research findings commonly evokes concern in the larger community about "normal" sexual functioning.

The most recent example of this phenomenon is the attention devoted to the "G spot" and female ejaculation as new "discoveries" about female sexuality (Ladas et al., 1982). Although individual differences in sexual response patterns in women clearly constitute a legitimate research topic, most reports of investigations in this area have unfortunately been colored by a prescriptive tone. The novelty of these "discoveries," along with the persuasive rhetoric of the reports, has resulted in pressure on many women (and their partners) to achieve new forms of sexual response.

Despite these potential areas of misuse, the laboratory study of sexual responding holds considerable promise for understanding many facets of male and female sexuality. With careful attention to the conduct of sexual psychophysiology and the context in which this type of investigation is conducted, continued progress is likely in this field.

References

Abe, T., Yamaya, Y., Wada, Y., & Suzuki, M. (1983). Pituitary–ovarian relationships in women approaching the menopause. *Maturitas, 5,* 31–37.

Abel, E. L. (1985). *Psychoactive drugs and sex.* New York: Plenum Press.

Abel, G. G., Barlow, D. H., Blanchard, E. B., & Guild, D. (1977). The components of rapists' sexual arousal. *Archives of General Psychiatry, 34,* 895–903.

Abel, G. G., Barlow, D. H., Blanchard, E. B., & Mavissakalian, M. (1975). Measurement of sexual arousal in male homosexuals: The effects of instructions and stimulus modality. *Archives of Sexual Behavior, 4,* 623–629.

Abel, G. G., Becker, J. V., Murphy, W. D., & Flanagan, B. (1981). Identifying dangerous child molesters. In R. Stuart (Ed.) *Violent behavior: Social learning approaches to prediction, management, and treatment* (pp. 117–137). New York: Brunner/Mazel.

Abel, G. G., Blanchard, E. B., & Barlow, D. H. (1981). Measurement of sexual arousal in several paraphilias: The effects of stimulus modality, instructional set and stimulus content. *Behaviour Research and Therapy. 19,* 25–33.

Abel, G. G., Blanchard, E. B., Barlow, D. H., & Mavissakalian M. (1975). Identifying specific erotic cues in sexual deviations by audio-taped descriptions. *Journal of Applied Behavior Analysis, 8,* 247–260.

Abel, G. G., Blanchard, E. B., & Becker, J. V. (1977). An integrated treatment program for rapists. In R. T. Rada (Ed.), *Clinical aspects of the rapist* (pp. 161–214). New York: Grune & Stratton.

Abel, G. G., Blanchard, E. B., Murphy, W. D., Becker, J. F., & Djenderedjian, A. (1981). Two methods of measuring penile response. *Behavior Therapy, 12,* 320–328.

Abel, G. G., Cunningham-Rathner, J., Becker, J. V., & McHugh, J. (1983). *Motivating sex offenders for treatment with feedback of their psychophysiologic assessment.* Paper presented at the World Congress of Behavior Therapy, Washington, DC.

Abel, G. G., Mittelman, M. S., & Becker, J. V. (1985). Sexual offenders: Results of assessment and recommendations for treatment. In M. H. Ben-Aron, S. J. Hucker, & C. D. Webster (Eds.), *Clinical criminology: The assessment and treatment of criminal behavior* (pp. 191–205). Toronto: M & M Graphics.

Abel, G. G., Murphy, W., Becker, J., & Bitar, A. (1979). Women's vaginal responses during REM sleep. *Journal of Sex and Marital Therapy, 5,* 5–14.

Abplanalp, J., Rose, R., Donnelly, A., & Livingston-Vaughan, L. (1979). Psychoendocrinology of the menstrual cycle: II. The relationship between enjoyment of activities, moods and reproductive hormones. *Psychosomatic Medicine, 78,* 605–615.

Abrahamson, D. J., Barlow, D. H., Beck, J. G., Sakheim, D. K., & Kelly, J. P. (1985). The effects of attentional focus and partner responsiveness on sexual responding: Replication and extension. *Archives of Sexual Behavior, 14,* 361–371.

Abrahamson, D. J., Barlow, D. H., Sakheim, D. K., Beck, J. G., & Athanasiou, R. (1985). Effects of distraction on sexual responding in functional and dysfunctional men. *Behavior Therapy, 16,* 503–515.

REFERENCES

Abrams, R., Kalna, O., & Wilcox, C. (1978). Vaginal blood flow during the menstrual cycle. *American Journal of Obstetrics and Gynecology, 132,* 396–400.

Abrams, R., & Stolwijk, J. (1972). Heat flow device for vaginal blood flow studies. *Journal of Applied Physiology, 23,* 143–146.

Abramson, P. R. (1977). Ethical requirements for research on human behavior: From the perspective of participating subjects. *Journal of Social Issues, 33,* 184–192.

Abramson, P. R., & Pearsall, E. H. (1983). Pectoral changes during the sexual response cycle: A thermographic analysis. *Archives of Sexual Behavior, 12,* 357–368.

Abramson, P. R., Perry, L. B., Seeley, T. T., Seeley, D. M., & Rothblatt, A. B. (1981). Thermographic measurement of sexual arousal: A discriminant validity analysis. *Archives of Sexual Behavior, 10,* 171–176.

Adamopoulos, D. A., Loraine, J. A., & Dove, G. A. (1971). Endocrinological studies in women approaching the menopause. *British Journal of Obstetrics and Gynaecology, 78,* 62–79.

Adams, A. E., III, Haynes, S. N., & Brayer, M. A. (1985). Cognitive distraction in female sexual arousal. *Psychophysiology, 22,* 689–696.

Adams, D. B., Gold, A. R., & Burt, A. D. (1978). Rise in female-initiated sexual activity at ovulation and its suppression by oral contraceptives. *New England Journal of Medicine, 229,* 1145–1150.

Addiego, F., Belzer, E. G., Comolli, J., Moger, W., Perry, J. D., & Whipple, B. (1981). Female ejaculation: A case study. *Journal of Sex Research, 17,* 13–21.

Allen, R. (1981). Erectile impotence: Objective diagnosis from sleep related erections (nocturnal penile tumescence). *Journal of Urology, 126,* 353.

Alzate, H. (1985). Vaginal eroticism and female orgasm: A current appraisal. *Journal of Sex and Marital Therapy, 11,* 271–284.

Alzate, H., & Londono, M. L. (1984). Vaginal erotic sensitivity. *Journal of Sex and Marital Therapy, 10,* 49–56.

Amberson, J. I., Hoon, E. F., Coleman, E., Hoon, P. W., & Ling, F. (1980). *Failure of biofeedback for low sexual arousal.* Paper presented at the annual convention of the American Psychological Association, Los Angeles.

Amberson, J. I., & Hoon, P. W. (1985). Hemodynamics of sequential orgasm. *Archives of Sexual Behavior, 14,* 351–360.

American Psychiatric Association. (1968). *Diagnostic and statistical manual of mental disorders* (2nd ed.). Washington, DC: Author.

American Psychiatric Association. (1980). *Diagnostic and statistical manual of mental disorders* (3rd ed.). Washington, DC: Author.

Amir, M. (1967). Alcohol and forcible rape. *British Journal of Addiction, 62,* 219–232.

Amoroso, D. M., & Brown, M. (1973). Problems in studying the effects of erotic material. *Journal of Sex Research, 9,* 187–195.

Angrist, B., & Gershon, B. (1976). Clinical effects of amphetamine and L-dopa on sexuality and aggression. *Comprehensive Psychiatry, 17,* 715–722.

Anonymous. (1970). Effects of sexual activity on beard growth in man. *Nature* (London), *226,* 869–870.

Apfelbaum, B. (1980). The diagnosis and treatment of retarded ejaculation. In S. R. Leiblum & L. A. Pervin (Eds.), *Principles and practice of sex therapy* (pp. 263–298). New York: Guilford Press.

Attorney General's Commission on Pornography. (1986). *Final report.* Washington, DC: U.S. Department of Justice.

Atwood, R.W., & Howell, R. J. (1971). Pupillometric and personality test score differences of female aggressing pedophiliacs and normals. *Psychonomic Science, 22,* 115–116.

Ax, A. F. (1953). The physiological differentiation between anger and fear in humans. *Psychosomatic Medicine, 15,* 433–442.

Ax, A. F. (1964). Goals and methods of psychophysiology. *Psychophysiology, 1,* 8–25.

Bacon, M. (1976). Thermography—explanation and description. *Thermography Quarterly*, *1*, 8.

Bancroft, J. H. (1971a). The application of psychophysiological measures to the assessment and modification of sexual behavior. *Behaviour Research and Therapy, 9,* 119–130.

Bancroft, J. H. (1977b). Autonomic correlates of penile erection. *Journal of Psychosomatic Research, 15,* 159–166.

Bancroft, J. H. (1974). *Deviant sexual behaviour.* London: Oxford University Press.

Bancroft, J. H. (1978). Psychological and physiological responses to sexual stimuli in men and women. In L. Levi (Ed.), *Society, stress, and disease: Vol. 3. The productive and reproductive age* (pp. 214–232). London: Oxford University Press.

Bancroft, J. H. (1980). Endocrinology of sexual function. *Clinics in Obstetrics and Gynaecology, 7,* 253–281.

Bancroft, J. H. (1982). Sexuality of diabetic women. *Clinics in Endocrinology and Metabolism, 11,* 785–789.

Bancroft, J. H. (1983). *Human sexuality and its problems.* New York: Churchill Livingstone.

Bancroft, J. H., & Bell, C. (1985). Simultaneous recording of penile diameter and penile arterial pulse during laboratory-based erotic stimulation in normal subjects. *Journal of Psychosomatic Research, 29,* 303–313.

Bancroft, J. H., Bell, C., Ewing, D. J., McCulloch, D. K., Warner, P., & Clarke, B. F. (1985). Assessment of erectile function in diabetic and nondiabetic impotence by simultaneous recording of penile diameter and penile arterial pulse. *Journal of Psychosomatic Research, 29,* 315–324.

Bancroft, J. H., Gwynne Jones, H. E., & Pullan, B. P. (1966). A simple transducer for measuring penile erection with comments on its use in the treatment of sexual disorder. *Behaviour Research and Therapy, 4,* 239–241.

Bancroft, J. H., O'Carroll, R., McNeilly, A., & Shaw, R. W. (1984). The effects of bromocryptine on the sexual behavior of hyperprolactinemic men: A controlled case study. *Clinical Endocrinology, 21,* 131–137.

Bancroft, J. H., Sanders, D., Davidson, D., & Warner, P. (1983). Mood, sexuality, hormones and the menstrual cycle: III. Sexuality and the role of androgens. *Psychosomatic Medicine, 45,* 509–516.

Bancroft, J. H., Tennent, T. G., Loucas, K, & Cass, J. (1974). Control of deviant sexual behavior by drugs: Behavioural effects of oestrogens and anti-androgens. *British Journal of Psychiatry, 125,* 310–315.

Bancroft, J. H., & Wu, F. C. W. (1983). Changes in erectile responsiveness during androgen replacement therapy. *Archives of Sexual Behavior, 12,* 59–66.

Barbach, L. G. (1975). *For yourself: The fulfillment of female sexuality.* Garden City, NY: Doubleday.

Barbach, L. G. (1980). Group treatment of anorgasmic women. In S. R. Leiblum & L. A. Pervin (Eds.), *Principles and practice of sex therapy* (pp. 107–146). New York: Guilford Press.

Barbaree, H. E., Marshall, W. L., & Lanthier, R. (1979). Deviant sexual arousal in rapists. *Behaviour Research and Therapy, 17,* 215–222.

Bardwick, J. M., & Behrman, S. J. (1967). Investigation into the effects of anxiety, sexual arousal, and menstrual cycle phase on uterine contractions. *Psychosomatic Medicine, 29,* 468–482.

Barlow, D. H. (1974). The treatment of sexual deviation: Towards a comprehensive behavioral approach. In K. S. Calhoun, H. E. Adams, & K. M. Mitchell (Eds.), *Innovative treatment methods in psychopathology* (pp. 121–148). New York: Wiley.

Barlow, D. H. (1977). Assessment of sexual behavior. In R. A. Ciminero, K. S. Calhoun, & H. E. Adams (Eds.), *Handbook of behavioral assessment* (pp. 461–508). New York: Wiley.

Barlow, D. H. (1986). Causes of sexual dysfunction: The role of anxiety and cognitive interference. *Journal of Consulting and Clinical Psychology, 54,* 140–157.

Barlow, D. H., & Agras, W. S. (1973). Fading to increase heterosexual responsiveness in homosexuals. *Journal of Applied Behavior Analysis, 6,* 355–366.

Barlow, D. H., Agras, W. S., Abel, G. G., Blanchard, E. B., & Young, L. D. (1975). Biofeedback and reinforcement to increase heterosexual arousal in homosexuals. *Behaviour Research and Therapy, 13,* 45–50.

Barlow, D. H., Agras, W. S., Leitenberg, H., Callahan, E. I., & Moore, R. C. (1972). The contribution of therapeutic instruction to convert sensitization. *Behaviour Research and Therapy, 10,* 411–416.

Barlow, D. H., Becker, R., Leitenberg, H., & Agras, W. S. (1970). A mechanical strain gauge for recording penile circumference change. *Journal of Applied Behavior Analysis, 3,* 73–76.

Barlow, D. H., Leitenberg, H., & Agras, S. (1969). The experimental control of sexual deviation through manipulation of the noxious scene in covert sensitization. *Journal of Abnormal Psychology, 74,* 596–601.

Barlow, D. H., Sakheim, D. K., & Beck, J. G. (1983). Anxiety increases sexual arousal. *Journal of Abnormal Psychology, 92,* 49–54.

Baron, R. A. (1979). Heightened sexual arousal and physical aggression: An extension to females. *Journal of Research in Personality, 13,* 91–102.

Baron, R. A., & Bell, P. A. (1977). Sexual arousal and aggression by males: Effects of type of erotic stimuli and prior provocation. *Journal of Personality and Social Psychology, 35,* 79–87.

Barr, R. F., & Blaszczynski, A. (1976). Autonomic responses of transsexual and homosexual males to erotic film sequences. *Archives of Sexual Behavior, 5,* 211–222.

Barr, R. F., & McConaghy, N. (1971). Penile volume responses to appetitive and aversive stimuli in relation to sexual orientation and conditioning performance. *British Journal of Psychiatry, 119,* 377–383.

Barry, J. M., Blank, B., & Boileau, M. (1980). Nocturnal penile tumescent monitoring with stamps. *Urology, 15,* 171–173.

Bartlett, R. G., Jr. (1956). Physiologic responses during coitus. *Journal of Applied Physiology, 9,* 469–472.

Baumberger, J. P., & Goodfriend, E. B. (1951). Determination of arterial oxygen tension in man by equilibration through intact skin. *Federation Proceedings, 10,* 10–14.

Bayliss, W. M., & Starling, E. H. (1904). The chemical regulation of the secretory process. *Proceedings of the Royal Society B, 73,* 310–322.

Beach, F. A. (1948). *Hormones and behavior.* New York: Hoeber.

Beach, F. A. (1956). Characteristics of masculine sex drive. In *Nebraska Symposium on Motivation* (Vol. 4, pp. 1–32). Lincoln: University of Nebraska Press.

Beach, F. A. (1967). Cerebral and hormonal control of reflexive mechanisms involved in copulatory behavior. *Physiology Review, 47,* 289–316.

Beatty, J. (1982). Task-evoked pupillary responses, processing load, and the structure of processing resources. *Psychological Bulletin, 91,* 276–292.

Beaumont, G. (1973). Sexual side effects of clomipramine (Anafranil). *Journal of Internal Medicine and Research, 1,* 469–473.

Beck, J. G. (1985). Secondary orgasmic dysfunction: Modifying sexual and marital scripts. In M. Hersen & C. G. Last (Eds.), *Behavior therapy casebook* (pp. 185–199). New York: Springer.

Beck, J. G., & Barlow, D. H. (1984). Current conceptualizations of sexual dysfunction: A review and an alternative perspective. *Clinical Psychology Review, 4,* 363–378.

Beck, J. G., & Barlow, D. H. (1986a). The effects of anxiety and attentional focus on sexual responding: I. Physiological patterns in erectile dysfunction. *Behaviour Research and Therapy, 24,* 9–17.

Beck, J. G., & Barlow, D. H. (1986b). The effects of anxiety and attentional focus on sexual responding: II. Cognitive and effective patterns in erectile dysfunction. *Behaviour Research and Therapy, 24,* 19–26.

Beck, J. G., Barlow, D. H., & Sakheim, D. K. (1983a). Abdominal temperature changes during male sexual arousal. *Psychophysiology, 20,* 715–717.

Beck, J. G., Barlow, D. H., & Sakheim, D. K. (1983b). The effects of attentional focus and partner arousal on sexual responding in functional and dysfunctional men. *Behaviour Research and Therapy, 21,* 1–8.

Beck, J. G., Barlow, D. H., Sakheim, D. K., & Abrahamson, D. J. (1984). *Sexual responding during anxiety: Clincial and nonclinical patterns.* Paper presented at the annual meeting of the Association for Advancement of Behavior Therapy, Philadelphia.

Beck, J. G., Barlow, D. H., Sakheim, D. K., & Abrahamson, D. J. (1987). Shock treatment and sexual arousal: The role of selective attention, thought content, and effective states. *Psychophysiology, 24,* 165–172.

Beck, J. G., Sakheim, D. K., & Barlow, D. H. (1983). Operating characteristics of the vaginal photoplethysmograph: Some implications for its use. *Archives of Sexual Behavior, 12,* 43–58.

Becker, J. V., Abel, G. G., Blanchard, E. B., Murphy, W. D., & Coleman, E. (1978). Evaluating social skills of sexual aggressives. *Criminal Justice and Behavior, 5,* 357–367.

Becker, J. V., Skinner, L. J., Abel, G. G., & Cichon, J. (1984). Time limited therapy with sexually dysfunctional, sexually assaulted women. *Journal of Social Work and Human Sexuality, 3,* 97–115.

Becker, J. V., Skinner, L. J., Abel, G. G., & Tracy, E. C. (1982). Incidences and types of sexual dysfunctions in rape and incest victims. *Journal of Sex and Marital Therapy, 8,* 65–74.

Becker, M. A., & Byrne, D. (1985). Self-regulated exposure to erotica, recall errors, and subjective reactions as a function of erotophobia and Type A coronary-prone behavior. *Journal of Personality and Social Psychology, 48,* 760–767.

Beech, H. R., Watts, F., & Poole, A. D. (1971). Classical conditioning of sexual deviation: A preliminary note. *Behavior Therapy, 2,* 400–402.

Bell, A. P., & Weinberg, M. S. (1978). *Homosexualities: A study of diversity among men and women.* New York: Simon & Schuster.

Bell, A. P., Weinberg, M. S., & Hammersmith, S. K. (1981). *Sexual preferences: Its development in men and women.* Bloomington: Indiana University Press.

Belzer, E. G. (1981). Orgasmic expulsions of women: A review and heuristic inquiry. *Journal of Sex Research, 17,* 1–12.

Bennett, A. (1982). *Management of male impotence.* Baltimore: Williams & Wilkins.

Benson, G. S. (1981). Mechanisms of penile erection. *Investigative Urology, 19,* 65–69.

Benson, G. S., McConnell, J. A., & Schmidt, W. A. (1981). Penile polsters: Functional structures or atherosclerotic changes? *Journal of Urology, 125,* 800–803.

Bentler, P. M., & Peeler, W. H. (1979). Models of female orgasm. *Archives of Sexual Behavior, 8,* 405–423.

Berkowitz, L., & Donnerstein, E. (1982). External validity is more than skin deep: Some answers to criticisms of laboratory experiments. *American Psychologist, 27,* 245–257.

Berlin, F. S. (1983). Sex offenders: A biomedical perspective and a status report on biomedical treatment. In J. G. Greer & I. R. Stuart (Eds.), *The sexual aggressor: Current perspectives on treatment* (pp. 83–125). New York: Van Nostrand Reinhold.

Berlin, F. S., & Meinecke, C. F. (1981). Treatment of sex offenders with antiandrogenic medication: Conceptualization, review of treatment modalities, and preliminary finding. *American Journal of Psychiatry, 138,* 601–607.

Bermant, G. (1976). Sexual behavior: Hard time with the Coolidge effect. In M. H. Siegel

& H. P. Zeigler (Eds.), *Psychological research: The inside story* (pp. 214–237). New York: Harper & Row.

Bernstein, D. A., & Paul, G. L. (1971). Some comments on therapy analogue research with small animal "phobias." *Journal of Behavior Therapy and Experimental Psychiatry, 2*, 225–237.

Berthold, A. A. (1849). Transplantation der hoden. *Archives of Anatomy and Physiology, 1*, 42–46.

Blair, J. H., & Simpson, G. M. (1966). Effect of antipsychotic drugs on reproductive functions. *Diseases of the Nervous System, 27*, 645–647.

Blumstein, P., & Schwartz, P. (1983). *American couples: Money, work, and sex.* New York: William Morrow.

Boas, E. P., & Goldschmidt, E. F. (1932). *The heart rate.* Springfield, IL: Charles C Thomas.

Bohlen, J. G. (1980). A review of subject orientation in articles on sexual physiology research. *Journal of Sex Research, 16*, 43–58.

Bohlen, J. G. (1982). "Female ejaculation" and urniary stress incontinence. *Journal of Sex Research, 18*, 360–368.

Bohlen, J. G., & Held, J. P. (1979). An anal probe for monitoring vascular and muscular events during sexual response. *Psychophysiology, 16*, 318–323.

Bohlen, J. G., Held, J. P., & Sanderson, M. D. (1980). The male orgasm: Pelvic contractions measured by anal probe. *Archives of Sexual Behavior, 9*, 503–521.

Boring, E. G. (1950). *A history of experimental psychology* (2nd ed.). New York: Appleton-Century-Crofts.

Bors, E., & Comarr, A. E. (1960). Neurological disturbances of sexual function with special reference to 529 patients with spinal cord injury. *Urology Survey, 10*, 191.

Bowers, M. B., Van Woert, M., & Davis, L. (1971). Sexual behavior during L-dopa treatment for parkinsonism. *American Journal of Psychiatry, 127*, 1691–1693.

Brady, J. P., & Levitt, E. E. (1965). The relation of sexual preferences to sexual experiences. *Psychological Record, 15*, 377–384.

Bramel, D. (1963). Selection of a target for defensive projection. *Journal of Abnormal and Social Psychology, 66*, 318–324.

Brecher, E. (1969). *The sex researchers.* Boston: Little, Brown.

Brecher, E. (1972). *Licit and illicit drugs.* Boston: Little, Brown.

Briddell, D. W., Rimm, D. C., Caddy, G. R., Krawitz, G., Sholis, D., & Wunderlin, R. J. (1978). Effects of alcohol and cognitive set on sexual arousal to deviant stimuli. *Journal of Abnormal Psychology, 87*, 418–430.

Briddell, D. W., & Wilson, G. T. (1976). Effects of alcohol and expectancy set on male sexual arousal. *Journal of Abnormal Psychology, 85*, 225–234.

Brincat, M., Studd, J. W. W., O'Dowd, T., Magos, A., Cardoza, L. D.,Cooper, D. (1984). Subcutaneous hormone implants for the control of climateric symptoms. *Lancet, i*, 16–18.

Brindley, G. S. (1983). Cavernosal alpha-blockade: A new technique for investigating and treating erectile impotence. *British Journal of Psychiatry, 143*, 332–337.

Broverman, D. M., Klaiber, E. L., & Vogel, W. (1980). Gonadal hormones and cognitive functioning. In E. Parsons (Ed.), *The psychobiology of sex differences and sex roles* (pp. 57–80). Washington, DC: Hemisphere.

Brown, C. (1972). Instruments in psychophysiology. In N. Greenfield & R. Sternbach (Eds.), *A handbook of psychophysiology* (pp. 159–196). New York: Holt, Rinehart & Winston.

Brown, E. A., Monti, P. M., & Corriveau, D. P. (1978). Serum testosterone and sexual activity and interest in men. *Archives of Sexual Behavior, 7*, 97–103.

Browne, A., & Finkelhor, D. (1986). Impact of child sexual abuse: A review of the literature. *Psychological Bulletin, 99*, 66–77.

Brownell, K. D., Hayes, S. C., & Barlow, D. H. (1977). Patterns of appropriate and deviant sexual arousal: The behavioral treatment of multiple sexual deviations. *Journal of Consulting and Clincial Psychology, 45,* 1144–1155.

Buffum, J. (1982). Pharmacosexology: The effects of drugs on sexual function. *Journal of Psychoactive Drugs, 14,* 5–44.

Buhrich, N., & McConaghy, N. (1979). Three clinically discrete categories of fetishistic transvestism. *Archives of Sexual Behavior, 8,* 151–157.

Bullard, D. G., & Knight, S.E. (1981). *Sexuality and physical disability.* St. Louis: C. V. Mosby.

Bullough, V. L. (1976). *Sexual variance in society and history.* New York: Wiley.

Bulpitt, C. J., Dollery, C. T., & Carne, S. (1976). Changes in symptoms of hypertensive patients after referral to hospital clinic. *British Health Journal, 38,* 121–128.

Burgess, A. W., & Holmstrom, L. L. (1979). Rape: Sexual disruption and recovery. *American Journal of Orthopsychiatry, 49,* 648–657.

Burnap, D. W., & Golden, J. S. (1967). Sexual problems in medical practice. *Journal of Medical Education, 42,* 673–686.

Buss, A. (1961). *The psychology of aggression.* New York: Wiley.

Byrne, D. (1961). Some inconsistencies in the effect of motivation arousal on humor preferences. *Journal of Abnormal and Social Psychology, 62,* 158–160.

Byrne, D. (1977). The imagery of sex. In J. Money & H. Musaph (Eds.), *Handbook of sexology* (pp. 327–350). Amsterdam: Elsevier.

Byrne, D. (1983). The antecedents, correlates, and consequents of erotophobia–erotophilia. In C. Davis (Ed.), *Challenges in sexual science* (pp. 53–75). Lake Mills, IA: Graphic.

Byrne, D. (1986). The study of sexual behavior as a multidisciplinary venture. In D. Byrne & K. Kelley (Eds.), *Alternative approaches to the study of sexual behavior* (pp. 1–12). Hillsdale, NJ: Erlbaum.

Byrne, D., Fisher, J. D., Lamberth, J., & Mitchell, H. E. (1974). Evaluations of erotica: Facts or feelings? *Journal of Personality and Social Psychology, 29,* 111–116.

Byrne, D., Jazwinski, C., DeNinno, J. A., & Fisher, W. A. (1977). Negative sexual attitudes and contraception. In D. Byrne & L. A. Byrne (Eds.), *Exploring human sexuality* (pp. 246–261). New York: Harper & Row.

Byrne, D., & Kelley, L. (Eds.). (1986). *Alternative approaches to the study of sexual behavior.* Hillsdale, NJ: Erlbaum.

Cacioppo, J. T., & Petty, R. E. (1981). Electromyograms as measures of extent and affectivity of information processing. *American Psychologist, 36,* 441–456.

Cacioppo, J. T., Petty, R. E., Losch, M. E., & Kim, H. S. (1986). Electromyographic activity over facial muscle regions can differentiate the valence and intensity of affective reactions. *Journal of Personality and Social Psychology, 50,* 260–268.

Caird, W., & Wincze, J. P. (1977). *Sex therapy: A behavioral approach.* New York: Harper & Row.

Callahan, E. J., & Leitenberg, H. (1973). Aversion therapy for sexual deviation: Contingent shock and covert sensitization. *Journal of Abnormal Psychology, 81,* 60–73.

Cannon, W. B. (1927). The James–Lange theory of emotions: A critical examination and an alternative theory. *American Journal of Psychology, 39,* 106–124.

Cannon, W. B. (1939). *The wisdom of the body* (2nd ed.). New York: Norton.

Cantor, J. R., Zillmann, D., & Bryant, J. (1975). Enhancement of experienced sexual arousal in response to erotic stimuli through misattribution of unrelated residual excitation. *Journal of Personality and Social Psychology, 32,* 69–75.

Carmichael, M. S., Humbert, R., Dixen, J., Palmisano, G., Greenleaf, W., & Davidson, J. M. (1987). Oxytocin increase in human sexual response. *Journal of Clinical Endocrinology and Metabolism, 64,* 27–31.

Carpenter, J. A., & Armenti, N. P. (1971). Some effects of ethanol on human sexual and aggressive behavior. In B. Kissin & H. Begleiter (Eds.), *The biology of alcoholism: Vol. 2. Physiology and behavior* (pp. 308–324). New York: Plenum Press.

REFERENCES

Carter, J. N., Tyson, J. E., Tolis, G., van Vliet, S., Faiman, C., & Friesen, H. G. (1978). Prolactin-secreting tumors and hypogonadism in 22 men. *New England Journal of Medicine, 299,* 847–852.

Cautela, J. R. (1967). Covert sensitization. *Psychological Record, 20,* 459–468.

Cerny, J. A. (1978). Biofeedback and the voluntary control of sexual arousal in women. *Behavior Therapy, 9,* 847–855.

Chambers, K. C., Hess, D. L., & Phoenix, C. H. (1981). Relationship of free and bound testosterone to sexual behavior in old rhesus males. *Physiology and Behavior, 27,* 615–620.

Chambless, D. L., Stern, T., Sultan, F. E., Williams, A. J., Goldstein, A. J., Hazzard-Lineberger, M., Lifshitz, J., & Kelly, L. (1982). The pubococcygens and female orgasm: a correlational study with normal subjects. *Archives of Sexual Behavior, 11,* 479–490.

Chambless, D. L., Sultan, F. E., Stern, T. E., O'Neill, C., Garrison, S., & Jackson, A. (1984). Effects of pubococcygeal exercise on coital orgasm in women. *Journal of Consulting and Clinical Psychology, 52,* 114–118.

Chappell, D. (1978). Forcible rape and the criminal justice system: Surveying present practices and projecting future trends. In M. J. Walker & S. L. Brodsky (Eds.), *Sexual assault: The victim and the rapist.* Lexington, MA: D. C. Heath.

Check, J. V. P., & Malamuth, N. M. (1984). Can there be positive effects of participation in pornography experiments? *Journal of Sex Research, 20,* 14–31.

Christenson, C. V. (1971). *Kinsey: A biography.* Bloomington: Indiana University Press.

Clark, L. (1970). Is there a difference between a clitoral and a vaginal orgasm? *Journal of Sex Research, 6,* 25–28.

Clark, R. (1952). The projective measurement of experimentally induced levels of sexual motivation. *Journal of Experimental Psychology, 44,* 391–399.

Coble, P., McPartland, R., Silva, W., & Kupfer, D. (1974). Is there a first night effect (a revisit). *Biological Psychiatry, 9,* 215–219.

Cohen, A. S., Rosen, R. C., & Goldstein, L. (1985). EEG hemispheric asymmetry during sexual arousal: Psychophysiological patterns in responding, unresponsive, and dysfunctional males. *Journal of Abnormal Psychology, 94,* 580–590.

Cohen, B. H., & Thayer, J. F. (1982). Emotional responses to music as measured by facial electromyography. *Psychophysiology, 19,* 555. (Abstract)

Cohen, H. D., Rosen, R. C., & Goldstein, L. (1976). Electroencephalographic laterality changes during the human sexual orgasm. *Archives of Sexual Behavior, 5,* 189–199.

Cohen, H. D., & Shapiro, A. (1970). A method of measuring sexual arousal in the female. *Psychophysiology, 8,* 251. (Abstract)

Coles, M. G. H., Gratton, G., Kramer, A. K., & Miller, G. A. (1986). Principles of signal acquisition and analysis. In M. G. H. Coles, E. Donchin, & S. W. Porges (Eds.), *Psychophysiology: Systems, processes, and applications* (pp. 183–226). New York: Guilford Press.

Colson, C. E. (1974). The evaluation of pornography: Effects of attitude and perceived physiological reaction. *Archives of Sexual Behavior, 3,* 307–323.

Conrad, S. R., & Wincze, J. P. (1976). Orgasmic reconditioning: A controlled study of its effects upon sexual arousal and behavior of adult male homosexuals. *Behavior Therapy, 7,* 155–166.

Conti, G. L. (1952). L'érection du penis humain et ses bases morphologiques et vasculaires. *Acta Anatomie* (Basel), *14,* 217–225.

Cook, M. R. (1974). Psychophysiology of peripheral vascular changes. In P. A. Obrist, A. Black, J. Brener, & L. V. DiCara (Eds.), *Cardiovascular psychophysiology: Current issues in response mechanisms, biofeedback, and methodology* (pp. 60–84). Chicago: Aldine.

Cooper, A., Furst, J. B., & Bridger, W. H. (1969). A brief commentary on the usefulness of studying fears of snakes. *Journal of Abnormal Psychology, 79,* 413–414.

Cooper, A. J. (1981). Short-term treatment in sexual dysfunction: A review. *Comprehensive Psychiatry, 22,* 206–217.

Corman, C. (1968). *Physiological response to a sexual stimulus.* Unpublished bachelor's thesis, University of Manitoba, 1968.

Costell, R. M., Lunde, D. J., Kopell, B. S., & Wittner, W. K. (1972). Contingent negative variation as an indicator of sexual object preference. *Science, 177,* 718–720.

Couper-Smartt, J. D., & Rodham, R. (1973). A technique for surveying side effects of tricyclic drugs with reference to reported sexual effects. *Journal of Internal Medicine and Research, 1,* 473–476.

Covington, S. (1983, May). *Sex and alcohol: What do women tell us?* Paper presented at the 6th World Congress of Sexology, Washington, DC.

Cox, C., & Smart, R. G. (1972). Social and psychological aspects of speed use. *International Journal of the Addictions, 7,* 201–217.

Csillag, E. R. (1976). Modification of penile erectile response. *Journal of Behavior Therapy and Experimental Psychiatry, 7,* 27–29.

Cunningham, G. R., Karacan, I., Ware, J. C., Lantz, D. C., & Thornby, J. J. (1982). The relationship between serum testosterone and prolactin levels and nocturnal penile tumescence (NPT) in impotent men. *Journal of Andrology, 3,* 241–247.

Cunningham-Rathner, J., & Abel, G. G. (1984). Psychophysiologic measurement of sexual arousal in females. In M. Fisher (Ed.), *Sexual arousal* (pp. 70–87). Springfield, IL: Charles C Thomas.

Cushman, P. (1972). Sexual behavior in heroin addiction and methadone maintenance. *New York State Journal of Medicine, 3,* 1261–1265.

Cushman, P. (1975). Plasma testosterone levels in healthy male marijuana smokers. *American Journal of Drug and Alcohol Abuse, 2,* 269–274.

Dana, C. L. (1921). The anatomic seat of the emotions: A discussion of the James–Lange theory. *Archives of Neurology and Psychiatry, 6,* 634–640.

Danesino, V., & Martella, E. (1976). Modern conceptions of corpora cavernosa functions in the vagina and clitoris. In T. P. Lowry & T. S. Lowry (Eds.), *The clitoris* (pp. 75–86). St. Louis: Warren P. Green.

Davidson, J. M. (1980). The psychobiology of sexual experience. In J. M. Davidson & R. J. Davidson (Eds.), *The psychobiology of consciousness* (pp. 271–332). New York: Plenum Press.

Davidson, J. M., Camargo, C., & Smith, E. R. (1979). Effects of endrogen on sexual behavior in hypogonadal men. *Journal of Clinical Endocrinology and Metabolism, 48,* 955–958.

Davidson, J. M., Chen, J. J., Crapo, L., Gray, G. D., Greenleaf, W. J., & Catania, J. A. (1983). Hormonal changes and sexual function in aging men. *Journal of Clinical Endocrinology and Metabolism, 57,* 71–77.

Davidson, J. M., Gray, G. D., & Smith, E. R. (1983). The sexual psychoendocrinology of aging. In J. Meites (Ed.), *Neuroendocrinology of aging* (pp. 221–258). New York: Plenum Press.

Davidson, J. M., Kwan, M., & Greenleaf, W. (1982). Hormonal replacement and sexuality in men. *Clinics in Endocrinology and Metabolism, 11,* 599–624.

Davidson, J. M., & Trupin, S. (1975). Neural mediation of steroid-induced sexual behavior in rats. In M. Sandler & G. L. Gessa (Eds.), *Sexual behavior: Pharmacology and biochemistry* (pp. 13–20). New York: Raven Press.

Davidson, P., Malcolm, P. B., Lanthier, R. D., Barbaree, H. E., & Ho, T. P. (1981). Penile response management: Operating characteristics of a Parks plethysmograph. *Behavioral Assessment, 3,* 137–143.

Davidson, R. J., Schwartz, G. E., Saron, C., Bennett, J., & Goleman, D. J. (1979). Frontal versus parietal EEG symmetry during positive and negative affect. *Psychophysiology, 16*, 202–203.

Davis, R., & Davis, T. (1980). Treatment of erectile impotence using a nocturnal penile tumescence conditioning procedure. *Journal of Behavior Therapy and Experimental Psychiatry, 11*, 63–65.

Davis, R. C. (1957). Response patterns. *Annals of the New York Academy of Sciences, 19*, 731–739.

Davis, R. C. (1958). The domain of homeostasis. *Psychological Review, 65*, 8–13.

Davis, R. C., & Buchwald, A. M. (1957). An exploration of somatic response patterns: Stimulus and sex differences. *Journal of Comparative and Physiological Psychology, 50*, 44–52.

Davison, G. C. (1968). Elimination of a sadistic fantasy by a client-controlled counter-conditioning technique: A case study. *Journal of Abnormal Psychology, 73*, 84–90.

Davison, G. C. (1977). Homosexuality, the ethical challenge. *Journal of Homosexuality, 2*, 79–81.

DeAmicis, L. A., Goldberg, D. C., LoPiccolo, J., Friedman, J., & Davies, L. (1985). Clinical follow-up of couples treated for sexual dysfunction. *Archives of Sexual Behavior, 14*, 467–489.

de Beauvoir, S. (1961). *The second sex* (H. M. Parshley, Trans.). New York: Bantam Books. (Original work published 1949)

de Bruijn, G. (1982). From masturbation to orgasm with a partner: How some women bridge the gap—and why others don't. *Journal of Sex and Marital Therapy, 8*, 151–167.

Dekker, J., Everaerd, W., & Verhelst, N. (1985). Attending to stimuli or to images of sexual feelings: Effects on sexual arousal. *Behaviour Research and Therapy, 23*, 139–149.

de Kretser, D. M., Simpson, R. W., Wilson, J. D., Rennie, G. C., Hudson, B., & Burger, H. G. (1983). Androgens and sexual behavior. In G. Burrows, L. Dennerstein, & I. Fraser (Eds.), *Obstetrics, gynaecology and psychiatry* (pp. 49–53). Melbourne: Australian Society of Psychosomatic Obstetrics and Gynaecology.

DeLeon, G., & Wexler, H. K. (1973). Heroin addiction: Its relation to sexual behavior and sexual experience. *Journal of Abnormal Psychology, 81*, 36–38.

Dennerstein, L., Burrows, G. D., Wood, C., & Hyman, G. (1980). Hormones and sexuality: Effect of estrogen and progestogen. *Obstetrics and Gynecology, 56*, 316–322.

Dhabuwala, C. B., Ghayad, P., Smith, J. B., & Pierce, J. M. (1983). Penile calibration for nocturnal penile tumescence studies. *Urology, 22*, 614–616.

Diamant, L. (1970). Attitude, personality, and behavior in volunteers and nonvolunteers for sexual research. *Proceedings of the 78th Annual Convention of the American Psychological Association, 5*, 423–424.

Dickinson, R. L. (1925). The average sex life of American women. *Journal of the American Medical Association, 85*, 1113–1117.

Dickinson, R. L. (1933). *Human sex anatomy*. Baltimore: Williams & Wilkins.

Doherty, P. C., Baum, M. J., & Todd, R. B. (1987). Effects of chronic hyperprolactinemia on sexual arousal and erectile function in male rats. *Neuroendocrinology, 42*, 368–375.

Donnerstein, E. (1980). Aggressive erotica and violence against women. *Journal of Personality and Social Psychology, 39*, 269–277.

Donnerstein, E. (1984). Pornography: Its effect on violence against women. In N. M. Malamuth & E. Donnerstein (Eds.), *Pornography and sexual aggression* (pp. 53–82). New York: Academic Press.

Donnerstein, E., & Berkowitz, L. (1981). Victim reactions in aggressive erotic films as a factor in violence against women. *Journal of Personality and Social Psychology, 41*, 710–724.

Dorsa, D. M., Smith, E. R., & Davidson, J. M. (1981). Endocrine and behavioral effects of continuous exposure of male rats to a potent LHRH agonist: Evidence for CNS actions of LHRH. *Endocrinology, 109,* 729–735.

Dorsa, D. M., Smith, E. R., & Davidson, J. M. (1984). Immunoreactive-beta-endorphin and LHRH levels in the brains of aged male rats with impaired sex behavior. *Neurobiology of Aging, 5,* 115–120.

Earls, C. M., & Jackson, D. R. (1981). The effects of temperature on the mercury-in-rubber strain gauge. *Behavior Assessment, 3,* 145–149.

Earls, C. M., & Marshall, W. L. (1982). The simultaneous and independent measurement of penile circumference and length. *Behavior Research Methods and Instrumentation, 14,* 447–450.

Edelberg, R. (1972). The electrodermal system. In N. S. Greenfield & R. A. Sternbach (Eds.), *Handbook of psychophysiology* (pp. 367–418). New York: Holt, Rinehart & Winston.

Ek, A., Bradley, W. E., & Krane, R. J. (1983). Nocturnal penile rigidity measured by the snap-gauge band. *Journal of Urology, 129,* 964–966.

Ekman, P., Hager, J. C., & Friesen, W. V. (1981). The symmetry of emotional and deliberate facial actions. *Psychophysiology, 18,* 101–106.

Ellis, E. M., Calhoun, K. S., & Atkeson, B. M. (1980). Sexual dysfunction in victims of rape: Victims may experience a loss of sexual arousal and frightening flashbacks even one year after assault. *Women and Health, 5,* 39–47.

Ellis, H. (1906). *Studies in the psychology of sex* (7 vols.) New York: Random House.

Ellison, C. (1972). Vaginismus. *Medical Aspects of Human Sexuality, 8,* 34–54.

Engel, B. T. (1960). Stimulus–response and indvidual response specificity. *Archives of General Psychiatry, 2,* 305–313.

Engel, B. T., & Bickford, A. F. (1961). Response specificity. *Archives of General Psychiatry, 5,* 478–498.

Englander-Golden, P., Chang, H. S., Whitmore, M. R., & Dienstbier, R. A. (1980). Female sexual arousal and the menstrual cycle. *Journal of Human Stress, 6,* 42–48.

Everaerd, W. (1983). Failure in treating sexual dysfunctions. In E. B. Foa & P. M. G. Emmelkamp (Eds.), *Failure in behavior therapy* (pp. 392–405). New York: Wiley.

Everett, E. M. (1975). Amyl nitrite ("poppers") as an aphrodisiac. In M. Sandler & G. L. Gessa (Eds.), *Sexual behavior: Pharmacology and biochemistry* (pp. 97–99). New York: Raven Press.

Eysenck, H. J., & Nias, D. K. B. (1978). *Sex, violence, and the media.* New York: Harper & Row.

Eyzaguirre, C., & Fidone, S. (1975). *Physiology of the nervous system* (2nd ed.). Chicago: Year Book Medical.

Fahrenberg, J. (1986). Psychophysiological individuality: A pattern analytic approach to personality research and psychosomatic medicine. *Advances in Behaviour Research and Therapy, 8,* 43–100.

Fairburn, C. G., McCulloch, D. K., & Wu, F. C. (1982). The effects of diabetes on male sexual function. *Clinics in Endocrinology and Metabolism, 11,* 749–767.

Farkas, G. M. (1978). Comments on Levin *et al.* and Rosen and Kopel: Internal and external validity issues. *Journal of Consulting and Clinical Psychology, 46,* 1515–1516.

Farkas, G. M., & Rosen, R. C. (1976). The effects of ethanol on male sexual arousal. *Journal of Studies on Alcohol, 37,* 265–272.

Farkas, G. M., Sine, L. F., & Evans, I. M. (1978). Personality, sexuality, and demographic differences between volunteers and nonvolunteers for a laboratory study of male sexual behavior. *Archives of Sexual Behavior, 7,* 513–520.

Farkas, G. M., Sine, L. F., & Evans, I. M. (1979). The effects of distraction, performance demand, stimulus explicitness, and personality on objective and subjective measures of male sexual arousal. *Behaviour Research and Therapy, 17,* 25–32.

REFERENCES

Feldman, M. P., & MacCullough, M. J. (1965). The application of anticipatory avoidance learning to the treatment of homosexuality. *Behaviour Research and Therapy, 2,* 165–183.

Finkelhor, D. (1979). *Sexually victimized children.* New York: Free Press.

Fisher, C., Cohen, H. D., Schiavi, R. C., Davis, D., Furman, B., Ward, K., Edwards, A., & Cunningham, J. (1983). Patterns of female sexual arousal during sleep and waking: Vaginal thermo-conductance studies. *Archives of Sexual Behavior, 12,* 97–122.

Fisher, C., Gross, J., & Zuch, J. (1965). Cycle of penile erection synchronous with dreaming (REM) sleep: Preliminary report. *Archives of General Psychiatry, 12,* 29–45.

Fisher, C., Schiavi, R., Edwards, A., Davis, D., Reitman, M., & Fine, J. (1979). Evaluation of nocturnal penile tumescence in the differential diagnosis of sexual impotence: A quantitative study. *Archives of General Psychiatry, 36,* 431–437.

Fisher, C., Schiavi, R., Lear, H., Edwards, A., Davis, D. M., & Witkin, A. P. (1975). The assessment of nocturnal REM erection in the differential diagnosis of sexual impotence. *Journal of Sex and Marital Therapy, 1,* 277–289.

Fisher, S. (1973). *The female orgasm.* New York: Basic Books.

Flor-Henry, P. (1978, October). *Cerebral aspects of the orgasmic response.* Paper presented at the International Congress of Medical Sexology, Rome.

Ford, C. S., & Beach, F. A. (1951). *Patterns of sexual behavior.* New York: Harper & Row.

Forrest, G. G. (1983). *Alcoholism and human sexuality.* Springfield, IL: Charles C Thomas.

Foucault, M. (1978). *The history of sexuality: Vol. 1. An introduction.* New York: Random House.

Fowles, D. C. (1974). Mechanisms of electrodermal activity. In R. F. Thompson & M. M. Patterson (Eds.), *Methods of physiological psychology: Vol. 1. Bioelectric recording techniques* (pp. 232–271). New York: Academic Press.

Fowles, D. C. (1986). The eccrine system and electrodermal activity. In M. G. H. Coles, E. Donchin, & S. W. Porges (Eds.), *Psychophysiology: Systems, processes, and applications* (pp. 51–96). New York: Guilford Press.

Fox, C. A. (1970). Reduction in the rise of systolic blood pressure during coitus by the B-adrenergic blocking agent propranolol. *Journal of Reproduction and Fertility, 22,* 587–590.

Fox, C. A., & Fox, B. A. (1969). Blood pressure and respiratory patterns during human coitus. *Journal of Reproduction and Fertility, 19,* 405–415.

Fox, C. A., & Fox, B. A. (1971). A comparative study of coital physiology, with special reference to the sexual climax. *Journal of Reproduction and Fertility, 24,* 319–336.

Fox, C. A., Ismail, A. A. A., Love, D. M., Kirkham, K. E., & Loraine, J. A. (1972). Studies on the relationship between plasma testosterone levels and human sexual activity. *Journal of Endocrinology, 52,* 51–58.

Fox, C. A., & Knaggs, G. S. (1969). Milk-ejection activity (oxytocin) in peripheral venous blood in man during lactation and in association with coitus. *Journal of Endocrinology, 45,* 145–146.

Fox, C. A., Meldrum, S. J., & Watson, B. W. (1973). Continous measurement by radio-telemetry of vagina pH during human coitus. *Journal of Reproduction and Fertility, 33,* 69–74.

Fox, C. A., Wolff, H. S., & Baker, J. A. (1970). Measurement of intravaginal and intrauterine pressures during human coitus by radio-telemetry. *Journal of Reproduction and Fertility, 22,* 243–251.

Fracher, J. C., Leiblum, S. R., & Rosen, R. C. (1981). Recent advances in the comprehensive evaluation of erectile dysfunction. *International Journal of Mental Health, 10,* 110–121.

Frank, E., Anderson, C., & Rubinstein, D. (1978). Frequency of sexual dysfunction in "normal" couples. *New England Journal of Medicine, 299,* 111–115.

368

Freese, M. P., & Levitt, E. E. (1984). Relationships among intravaginal pressure, orgasmic function, parity factors, and urinary leakage. *Archives of Sexual Behavior, 13*, 261–268.

Freud, S. (1959). Female sexuality. In J. Riviere (Ed. and Trans.), *Collected papers* (Vol. 5, pp. 128–141). New York: Basic Books. (Original work published 1931)

Freud, S. (1963). *Dora: An analysis of a case of hysteria.* New York: Collier Books. (Original work published 1905)

Freund, K. (1960). Problems in the treatment of homosexuality. In H. J. Eysenck (Ed.), *Behaviour therapy and the neuroses* (pp. 312–326). Oxford: Pergamon Press.

Freund, K. (1963). A laboratory method for diagnosing predominance of homo- or hetero-erotic interest in the male. *Behaviour Research and Therapy, 1*, 85–93.

Freund, K. (1965). Diagnosing heterosexual paedophilia by means of a test for sexual interest. *Behaviour Research and Therapy, 3*, 229–234.

Freund, K. (1967a). Diagnosing homo- or hetrosexuality and erotic age-preference by means of a psychophysiological test. *Behaviour Research and Therapy, 5*, 209–228.

Freund, K. (1967b). Erotic preference in paedophilia. *Behaviour Research and Therapy, 5*, 339–348.

Freund, K. (1980). Therapeutic sex drive reduction. *Acta Psychiatrica Scandinavica, 62*, 5–38.

Freund, K., Chan, S., & Coulthard R. (1979). Phallometric diagnosis with 'nonadmitters.' *Behaviour Research and Therapy, 17*, 451–457.

Freund, K., & Langevin, R. (1976). Bisexuality in homosexual pedophilia. *Archives of Sexual Behavior, 5*, 415–423.

Freund, K., Langevin, R., & Barlow, D. H. (1974). A comparison of two penile measures of erotic arousal. *Behaviour Research and Therapy, 12*, 355–359.

Freund, K., Scher, H., Chan, S., & Ben-Aron, M. (1982). Experimental analysis of paedophilia. *Behaviour Research and Therapy, 20*, 105–112.

Freund, K., Scher, H., & Hucker, S. (1983). The courtship disorders. *Archives of Sexual Behavior, 12*, 369–379.

Freund, K., Scher, H., & Hucker, S. (1984). The courtship disorders: A further investigation. *Archives of Sexual Behavior, 13*, 133–139.

Freund, K., Sedlacek, F., & Knob, K. (1965). A simple transducer for mechanical plethysmography of the male genital. *Journal of the Experimental Analysis of Behavior, 8*, 169–170.

Frisinger, J. E., Abrams, R. M., Graichen, A. H., & Cassin, S. (1981). New thermal method for evaluating vaginal blood flow. *Gynecology and Obstetrical Investigations, 12*, 71–80.

Fugl-Meyer, A. R., Sjogren, K., & Johansson, K. (1984). A vaginal temperature registration system. *Archives of Sexual Behavior, 13*, 247–260.

Gagnon, J. H. (1977). *Human sexualities.* Glenview, IL: Scott, Foresman.

Gagnon, J. H. (1978). Reconsiderations. *Human Nature, 2*, 92–95.

Gagnon, J. H., Rosen, R. C., & Leiblum, S. R. (1982). Cognitive and social aspects of sexual dysfunction: Sexual scripts in sex therapy. *Journal of Sex and Marital Therapy, 8*, 44–56.

Gagnon, J. H., & Simon, W. (1967). *Sexual deviance.* New York: Harper & Row.

Gagnon, J. H., & Simon, W. E. (1973). *Sexual conduct: The social sources of human sexuality.* Chicago: Aldine.

Gantt, W. H. (1952). Effect of alcohol on the sexual reflexes of normal and neurotic male dogs. *Psychosomatic Medicine, 14*, 174–181.

Garcia, C. R., & Cutler, W. (1985). Preservation of the ovary: A reevaluation. *Fertility and Sterility, 42*, 510–514.

Garde, K., & Lunde, I. (1980). Female sexual behavior: A study in a random sample of 40 year old women. *Maturitas, 2*, 225–240.

Gardner, E. A., & Johnston, J. A. (1985). Bupropion—an antidepressant without sexual pathophysiological action. *Journal of Clinical Psychopharmacology, 5,* 24–29.

Gardner, W. U. (1950). Reproduction in the female. In J. F. Fulton (Ed.), *Textbook of physiology* (pp. 412–426). Philadelphia: W. B. Saunders.

Gay, G. R., Newmeyer, J. A., Elion, R. A., & Wieder, S. (1977). The sensuous hippie: Drug/sex practices in the Haight-Ashbury. *Drug Forum, 6,* 27–47.

Gay, G. R., Newmeyer, J. A., Perry, M., Johnson, G., & Kurland, M. (1982). Love and Haight: The sensuous hippie revisited. *Journal of Psychoactive Drugs, 14,* 111–123.

Gay, E. R., & Sheppard, C. W. (1973). Sex-crazed dope fiends—myth or reality? *Drug Forum, 2,* 125–140.

Gebhard, P. H. (1973). Sex differences in sexual response. *Archives of Sexual Behavior, 2,* 201–205.

Gebhard, P. H. (1978). Marital stress. In L. Levi (Ed.), *Society, stress, & disease: Vol. 3. The productive and reproductive age* (pp. 100–112). London: Oxford University Press.

Gebhard, P. H., Gagnon, J. H., Pomeroy, W. B., & Christenson, C. V. (1965). *Sex offenders: An analysis of types.* New York: Harper & Row.

Gebhard, P. H., & Johnson, A. B. (1979). *The Kinsey data: Marginal tabulations of the 1938–1963 interviews conducted by the Institute for Sex Research.* Philadelphia: W. B. Saunders.

Gee, W. F. (1975). A history of surgical treatment of impotence. *Urology, 5,* 401–405.

Geer, J. H. (1976). Genital measures: Comments on their role in understanding human sexuality. *Journal of Sex and Marital Therapy, 2,* 165–172.

Geer, J. H. (1979). Biofeedback and the modification of sexual dysfunction. In R. J. Gatchel & K. P. Price (Eds.), *Clinical applications of biofeedback: Appraisal and status* (pp. 228–244). New York: Pergamon Press.

Geer, J. H. (1980). Measurement of genital arousal in human males and females. In I. Martin & P. H. Venables (Eds.), *Techniques in psychophysiology* (pp. 431–459). New York: Wiley.

Geer, J. H. (1984). *Distraction affects female sexual arousal: Repeated exposure and possible recovery.* Paper presented at the annual convention of the American Psychological Association, Toronto.

Geer, J. H., & Fuhr, R. (1976). Cognitive factors in sexual arousal: The role of distraction. *Journal of Consulting and Clinical Psychology, 44,* 238–243.

Geer, J. H., & Messé, M. (1982). Sexual dysfunctions. In R. J. Gatchel, A. Baum, & J. E. Singer (Eds.), *Handbook of psychology and health: Vol. 1. Clinical psychology and behavioral medicine: Overlapping disciplines* (pp. 329–370). Hillsdale NJ: Erlbaum.

Geer, J. H., Morokoff, P., & Greenwood, P. (1974). Sexual arousal in women: The development of a measurement device for vaginal blood volume. *Archives of Sexual Behavior, 3,* 559–564.

Geer, J. H., & Quartararo, J. (1976). Vaginal blood volume responses during masturbation. *Archives of Sexual Behavior, 5,* 403–413.

Gellhorn, E. (1957). *Autonomic imbalance and the hypothalamus.* Minneapolis: University of Minnesota Press.

Gillan, P. (1976). Objective measures of female sexual arousal. *Journal of Physiology, 260,* 64–65.

Gillan, P., & Brindley, G. S. (1979). Vaginal and pelvic floor responses to sexual stimulation. *Psychophysiology, 16,* 471–481.

Gold, S. A., & Neufeld, I. L. (1965). A learning approach to the treatment of homosexuality. *Behaviour Research and Therapy, 3,* 201–204.

Goldberg, D. C., Whipple, B., Fishkin, R. E., Waxman, H., Fink, P. J., & Weisberg, M. (1983). The Grafenberg spot and female ejaculation: A review of initial hypotheses. *Journal of Sex and Marital Therapy, 9,* 27–37.

Goldstein, L. (1975). Time domain analysis of the EEG: The integrative method. In G.

Dolce & H. Kunkel (Eds.), *C.E.A.N—Computerized EEG analysis* (pp. 251–270). Stuttgart: Gustav Fisher.

Goode, E. (1969). Drug use and sexual activity on a college campus. *American Journal of Psychiatry, 128,* 92–96.

Goode, E. (1972). *Drugs in American society.* New York: Knopf.

Graber, B. (1981). Circumvaginal musculature and female sexual function: The past, present, and future. *Journal of Sex and Marital Therapy, 7,* 31–36.

Graber, B., & Kline-Graber, G. (1979). Female orgasm: Role of pubococcygeus muscle. *Journal of Clinical Psychiatry, 40,* 33–39.

Graber, B., & Kline-Graber, G. (1981). Research criteria for male erectile failure. *Journal of Sex and Marital Therapy, 7,* 37–48.

Graber, B., Rohrbaugh, J. W., Newlin, D. B., Varner, J. L., & Ellingson, R. J. (1985). EEG during masturbation and ejaculation. *Archives of Sexual Behavior, 14,* 491–503.

Gray, D. S., & Gorzalka, B. B. (1980). Adrenal steroid interaction in female sexual behavior. A review. *Psychoneuroendocrinology, 5,* 157–175.

Gray, G. D., Smith, E. R., & Davidson, J. M. (1980). Hormonal regulation of penile erection in castrated male rats. *Physiology and Behavior, 24,* 463–468.

Gray, G. D., Smith, E. R., Dorsa, D. M., & Davidson, J. M. (1981). Sexual behavior and testosterone in middle-aged male rats. *Endocrinology, 109,* 1597–1604.

Green, J. G. (1984). *Social and psychologic origins of the climacteric.* Brookfield, VT: Gower.

Greenblatt, R. B., Oettinger, M., & Bohler, C. S. S. (1976). Estrogen–androgen levels in aging men and women: Therapeutic considerations. *Journal of the American Geriatric Society, 24,* 173–178.

Greer, J. R., & Stuart, I. R. (Eds.). (1983). *The sexual aggressor: Current perspectives on treatment.* New York: Van Nostrand Reinhold.

Griffitt, W. (1975). Sexual experience and sexual responsiveness: Sex differences. *Archives of Sexual Behavior, 4,* 529–540.

Grodin, J. M., Siiteri, P. K., & MacDonald, P. (1973). Source of estrogen production in postmenopausal women. *Journal of Clincial Endocrinology and Metabolism, 36,* 207–214.

Groth, A. N. (1983). Treatment of the sexual offender in a correctional institution. In J. G. Greer & I. R. Stuart (Eds.), *The sexual aggressor: Current perspectives on treatment* (pp. 160–176). New York: Van Nostrand Reinhold.

Groth, A. N., & Birnbaum, H. J. (1979). *Men who rape: The psychology of the offender.* New York: Plenum.

Hahn, P.M., & Leder, R. (1980). Quantification of penile "buckling" force. *Sleep, 3,* 95–97.

Haider, I. (1966). Thioridazine and sexual dysfunctions. *International Journal of Neuropsychiatry, 2,* 255–257.

Halikas, J. A., Goodwin, D. W., & Guze, S. B. (1971). Marihuana effects—a survey of regular users. *Journal of the American Medical Association, 217,* 692.

Hall, K. S., Binik, Y., & Di Tomasso, E. (1985). Concordance between physiological and subjective measures of sexual arousal. *Behaviour Research and Therapy, 23,* 297–303.

Hampson, J. L., & Hampson, J. G. (1961). The ontogenesis of sexual behavior in man. In W. C. Young (Ed.), *Sex and internal secretions* (Vol. 2, pp. 1401–1432). Baltimore: Williams & Wilkins.

Hardonk, H. J., & Beumer, H. M. (1979). Hyperventilation syndrome. In P. J. Vinken & G. W. Bruyn (Eds.), *Handbook of clinical neurology* (Vol. 38, pp. 309–360). Amsterdam: North-Holland.

Harris, G. W., & Pickles, V. P. (1953). Reflex stimulation of the neural hypophysis and the nature of posterior pituitary hormone(s). *Nature, 172,* 1049.

Hart, B. L. (1968). Effects of alcohol on sexual reflexes and mating behavior in the male dog. *Quarterly Journal of Studies on Alcohol, 29,* 839–844.

REFERENCES

Hart, B. L. (1969). Gonadal hormones and sexual reflexes in the female rat. *Hormones and Behavior, 1*, 65–71.

Hart, B. L. (1970). Mating behavior in the female dog and the effects of estrogen on sexual reflexes. *Hormones and Behavior, 1*, 93–104.

Hart, B. L. (1974). Gonadal androgen and sociosexual behavior of male mammals: A comparative analysis. *Psychological Bulletin, 81*, 383–400.

Hart, B. L. (1978). Activation of sexual reflexes of male rats by dihydrotestosterone but not by estrogen. *Physiology and Behavior, 23*, 107–109.

Hart, B. L., & Leedy, M. G. (1985). Neurological bases of male sexual behavior. In N. Adler, D. W. Pfaff, & R. W. Goy (Eds.), *Handbook of behavioral neurobiology* (Vol. 7, pp. 373–422). New York: Plenum Press.

Hartman, W. E., & Fithian, M. A. (1974). *Treatment of sexual dysfunction* (2nd ed.). New York: Jason Aronson.

Hatch, J. P. (1979). Vaginal photoplethysmography: Methodological considerations. *Archives of Sexual Behavior, 8*, 357–374.

Hatch, J. P. (1981). Voluntary control of sexual responding in men and women: Implications for etiology and treatment of sexual dysfunctions. *Biofeedback and Self-Regulation, 6*, 191–205.

Hatfield, E., Sprecher, S., & Traupman, J. (1978). Men's and women's reactions to sexually explicit films: A serendipitous finding. *Archives of Sexual Behavior, 7*, 583–593.

Hayashi, J., Hoon, P. W., & Amberson, J. (1983). *Reliability of nocturnal vaginal bloodflow measures*. Paper presented at the annual meeting of the International Academy of Sex Research, Harriman, NY.

Heel, R. C., Brogden, R. N., Speight, T. M., & Avery, G. S. (1979). Atenolol: A review of its pharmacological properties and therapeutic efficacy in angina pectoris and hypertension. *Drugs, 17*, 425–460.

Heiman, J. R. (1975). *The use of the vaginal photoplethysmograph as a diagnostic and treatment aid in female sexual dysfunction*. Paper presented at the annual convention of the American Psychological Association, Chicago.

Heiman, J. R. (1976). Issues in the use of psychophysiology to assess female sexual dysfunction. *Journal of Sex and Marital Therapy, 2*, 197–204.

Heiman, J. R. (1977). A psychophysiological exploration of sexual arousal patterns in female and males. *Psychophysiology, 14*, 266–274.

Heiman, J. R. (1980). Female sexual response patterns: Interactions of physiological, affective, and contextual cues. *Archives of General Psychiatry, 37*, 1311–1316.

Heiman, J. R., & LoPiccolo, J. (1983). Clincal outcome of sex therapy: Effects of daily versus weekly treatment. *Archives of General Psychiatry, 40*, 443–449.

Heiman, J. R., LoPiccolo, L., & LoPiccolo, J. (1976). *Becoming orgasmic: A sexual growth program for women*. Englewood Cliffs, NJ: Prentice-Hall.

Heiman, J. R., & Rowland, D. L. (1981). Sexual dysfunction from a psychophysiological perspective. *International Journal of Mental Health, 10*, 3–8.

Heiman, J. R., & Rowland, D. L. (1983). Affective and physiological sexual response patterns: The effects of instructions on sexually functional and dysfunctional men. *Journal of Psychosomatic Research, 27*, 105–116.

Hellerstein, H. A., & Friedman, E. H. (1969). Sexual activity and the post coronary patient. *Medical Aspects of Human Sexuality, 3*, 70–96.

Hellhammer, D. H., Hubert, W., & Schurmeyer, J. S. (1985). Changes in saliva testosterone after psychological stimulation in men. *Psychoneuroendocrinology, 10*, 77–87.

Hembree, W. C., Zeidenberg, P., & Nahas, G. G. (1976). Marihuana effects upon human gonadal function. In G. G. Nahas (Eds.), *Marihuana: Chemistry, biochemistry, and cellular effects* (pp. 112–131). New York: Springer-Verlag.

Henson, C., Rubin, H. B., & Henson, D. E. (1979). Women's sexual arousal concurrently assessed by three genital measures. *Archives of Sexual Behavior, 8*, 459–469.

Henson, D. E., & Rubin, H. B. (1971). Voluntary control of eroticism. *Journal of Applied Behavior Analysis, 4,* 37–44.

Henson, D. E., & Rubin, H. B. (1978). A comparison of two objective measures of sexual arousal of women. *Behaviour Research and Therapy, 16,* 143–151.

Henson, D. E., Rubin, H. B., & Henson, C. (1979). Analysis of the consistency of objective measures of sexual arousal in women. *Journal of Applied Behavior Analysis, 12,* 701–711.

Henson, D. E., Rubin, H. B., & Henson, C. (1982). Labial and vaginal blood volume responses to visual and tactile stimuli. *Archives of Sexual Behavior, 11,* 23–31.

Henson, D. E., Rubin, H. B., Henson, C., & Williams, J. (1977). Temperature changes of the labia minora as an objective measure of human female eroticism. *Journal of Behavior Therapy and Experimental Psychiatry, 8,* 401–410.

Herman, S. H., Barlow, D.H., & Agras, W. S. (1974). An experimental analysis of classical conditioning as a method of increasing heterosexual arousal in homosexuals. *Behavior Therapy, 5,* 33–47.

Herman, S. H., & Prewett, M. (1974). An experimental analysis of feedback to increase sexual arousal in a case of homo- and hetero-sexual impotence: A preliminary report. *Journal of Behavior Therapy and Experimental Psychiatry, 5,* 271–274.

Herrell, J. M. (1975). Sex differences in emotional responses to "erotic literature." *Journal of Consulting and Clinical Psychology, 43,* 921.

Hess, E. H. (1968). Pupillometric assessment. *Research in Psychotherapy, 3,* 573–583.

Hess, E. H., & Polt, J. M. (1960). Pupil size as related to interest value of visual stimuli. *Science, 132,* 349–350.

Hess, E. H., Seltzer, A. L., & Shlien, J. M. (1965). Pupil response of hetero- and homosexual males to pictures of men and women: A pilot study. *Journal of Abnormal Psychology, 70,* 165–168.

Higgins, G. E. (1979). Sexual response in spinal cord injured adults: A review. *Archives of Sexual Behavior, 8,* 173–196.

Hinton, J. W., O'Neill, M. T., & Webster, S. (1980). Psychophysiological asessment of sex offenders in a security hospital. *Archives of Sexual Behavior, 9,* 205–216.

Hirshkowitz, M., Ware, J. C., Turner, D., & Karacan, I. (1979). EEG amplitude asymmetry during sleep. *Sleep Research, 8,* 25.

Hite, S. (1976). *The Hite report.* New York: Macmillan.

Hogan, M. J., Wallin, J. D., & Baer, R. M. (1980). Antihypertensive therapy and male sexual dysfunction. *Psychosomatics, 21,* 235–237.

Hokfelt, T., & Fuxe, K. (1972). Effects of prolactin and ergot alkaloids on the tuberoinfundibular dopamine neurons. *Neuroendocrinolgy, 9,* 100–122.

Holden, C. (1976). House chops sex–pot probe. *Science, 192,* 450.

Hoon, E. F. (1980). Biofeedback-assisted sexual arousal in females: A comparison of visual and auditory modalities. *Biofeedback and Self-Regulation, 5,* 175–191.

Hoon, E. F., Hoon, P. W., Amberson, J. I., Coleman, E. M., & Ling, F. W. (1983). Low female sexual arousal: Negative results using biofeedback and sex therapy. *Behavior Modification, 7,* 197–210.

Hoon, E. F., Hoon, P. W., & Wincze, J. P. (1976). An inventory of female sexual arousability: The SAI. *Psychophysiology, 19,* 21–27.

Hoon, P. W. (1984). Physiologic assessment of sexual response in women: The unfulfilled promise. *Clincial Obstetrics and Gynecology, 27,* 767–780.

Hoon, P. W., Bruce, K., & Kinchloe, B. (1982). Does the menstrual cycle play a role in sexual arousal? *Psychophysiology, 19,* 21–26.

Hoon, P. W., Coleman, E., Amberson, J. J., & Ling, S. (1981). A possible physiological marker for female sexual dysfunction. *Biological Psychiatry, 16,* 1101–1106.

Hoon, P. W., Murphy, W. D., Laughter, J. S., & Abel, G. G. (1984). Infrared vaginal photoplethysmography: Construction, calibration, and sources of artifact. *Behavioral Assessment, 6,* 141–152.

Hoon, P. W., Wincze, J. P., & Hoon, E. F. (1976). Physiological assessment of sexual arousal in women. *Psychophysiology, 13,* 196–204.

Hoon, P. W., Wincze, J. P., & Hoon, E. (1977a). The effects of biofeedback and cognitive mediation upon vaginal blood volume. *Behavior Therapy, 8,* 694–702.

Hoon, P. W., Wincze, J. P., & Hoon, E. (1977b). A test of reciprocal inhibition: Are anxiety and sexual arousal in women mutually inhibitory? *Journal of Abnormal Psychology, 86,* 65–74.

Horowitz, J. D., & Goble, A. J. (1979). Drugs and impaired male sexual function. *Drugs, 18,* 206–217.

Howard, J. L., Reifler, C. B., & Liptzin, M. G. (1971). Effects of exposure to pornography. In *Technical report of the Commission on Obscenity and Pornography* (Vol. 8, pp. 382–403). Washington, DC: U. S. Government Printing Office.

Howell, J., Reynolds, C. F., III, Thase, M., Frank, E., Jennings, J. R., Hauck, P. R., Berman, S., Jacobs, E., & Kupfer, D. J. (1987). Assessment of sexual interest and activity in depressed men. *Journal of Affective Disorders, 13,* 61–66.

Huffman, J. (1947). The detailed anatomy of the paraurethial ducts in the adult human female. *American Journal of Obstetrics and Gynecology, 55,* 80–100.

Huggins, G. R., & Preti, G. (1976). Volatile constituents of human vaginal secretions. *American Journal of Obstetrics and Gynecology, 126,* 129–138.

Hunt, M. (1974). *Sexual behavior in the 1970's.* New York: Dell.

Hursch, C. J., Karacan, I., & Williams, R. L. (1972). Some characteristics of nocturnal penile tumescence in early middle-aged males. *Comprehensive Psychiatry, 13,* 539–548.

Hyman, C., & Winsor, T. (1961). History of plethysmography. *Journal of Cardiovascular Surgery, 2,* 506–510.

Hyyppa, M. T., Falck, S. C., & Rinne, U. K. (1975). Is L-dopa an aphrodisiac in patients with Parkinson's disease? In M. Sandler & G. L. Gessa (Eds.), *Sexual behavior: Pharmacology and biochemistry* (pp. 315–328). New York: Raven Press.

Hyyppa, M., Rinne, U. K., & Sonninen, V. (1970). The activating effect of L-dopa treatment on sexual functions and its experimental background. *Acta Neurologica Scandinavica, 46* (Suppl. 43), 223–224.

Indian Hemp Drugs Commission. (1969). *Report of the Indian Hemp Drugs Commission.* Silver Springs, MD: Thomas Jefferson Publishing. (Original work published 1893–1894)

Jaffe, Y., Malamuth, N. M., Feingold, J., & Feshbach, S. (1974). Sexual arousal and behavioral aggression. *Journal of Personailty and Social Psychology, 30,* 759–764.

Jakobovits, L. A. (1965). Evaluational reactions to erotic literature. *Psychological Reports, 16,* 985–994.

James, W. (1884). What is an emotion? *Mind, 9,* 188–205.

James, W. H. (1971). The distribution of coitus within the human intermenstruum. *Journal of Biosocial Science, 3,* 159–171.

Jayne, C. (1981). A two-dimensional model of female sexual response. *Journal of Sex and Marital Therapy, 7,* 3–31.

Jensen, R. T., Collen, M. J., McArthur, K. E., Howard, J. M., Maton, P. N., Cherner, J. A., & Gardner, J. D. (1984). Comparison of the effectiveness of ranitidine and cimetidine in inhibiting acid secretion in patients with gastric hypersecretory states. *American Journal of Medicine, 77,* 90–105.

Jenson, R. T., Collen, M. J., Pandol, S. J., Allende, H. D., Raufman, J. P., Bissonnette, B. M., Duncan, W. C., Gillin, J. C., & Gardner, J. D. (1983). Cimetidine-induced impotence and breast changes in patients with gastric hypersecretory states. *New England Journal of Medicine, 308,* 883–887.

Jensen, S. B. (1979). Sexual customs and sexual dysfunction in alcoholics. *British Journal of Sexual Medicine, 54,* 30–34.

374

Jensen, S. B. (1986). Sexual dysfunction in insulin-treated diabetics: A six year follow-up of 101 patients. *Archives of Sexual Behavior, 15,* 271–284.

Jochle, W. (1973). Coitus-induced ovulation. *Contraception, 7,* 523–564.

Johnson, L. C., & Lubin, A. (1966). Spontaneous electrodermal activity during waking and sleeping. *Psychophysiology, 3,* 8–17.

Jong, E. (1985). *Parachutes and kisses.* New York: Signet.

Jovanovic, U. J. (1967). A new method of phallography. *Confinator Neurologie, 29,* 299–312.

Jovanovic, U. J. (1971). The recording of physiological evidence of genital arousal in human males and females. *Archives of Sexual Behavior, 1,* 309–320.

Jovanovic, U. J. (1972). *Sexuelle reaktionen and schlafperiodik bei menschen: Ergebnisse experimenteller untersuchungen.* Stuttgart: Ferdinand Ente Verlag.

Julien, E., & Over, R. (1984). Male sexual arousal with repeated exposure to erotic stimuli. *Archives of Sexual Behavior, 13,* 211–222.

Kahn, E., & Fisher, C. (1969a). REM sleep and sexuality in the aged. *Journal of Geriatric Psychiatry, 2,* 181–199.

Kahn, E., & Fisher, C. (1969b). The sleep characteristics of the normal aged male. *Journal of Nervous and Mental Disease, 148,* 477–494.

Kaplan, H. S. (1974). *The new sex therapy.* New York: Brunner/Mazel.

Kaplan, H. S. (1977). Hypoactive sexual desire. *Journal of Sex and Marital Therapy, 3,* 3–9.

Kaplan, H. S. (1979). *Disorders of sexual desire.* New York: Brunner/Mazel

Karacan, I. (1970). Clinical value of nocturnal erection in the prognosis and diagnosis of impotence. *Medical Aspects of Human Sexuality, 4,* 27–34.

Karacan, I. (1976). Impotence: Psyche versus soma. *Medical World News, 17,* 28.

Karacan, I. (1978). Advances in the psychophysiological evaluation of male erectile impotence. In J. LoPiccolo & L. LoPiccolo (Eds.), *Handbook of sex therapy* (pp. 137–146). New York: Plenum.

Karacan, I., Aslan, C., & Hirshkowitz, M. (1983). Erectile mechanisms in man. *Science, 220,* 1080–1082.

Karacan, I., Hursch, C. J., & Williams, R. L. (1972). Some characteristics of nocturnal penile tumescence in elderly males. *Journal of Gerontology, 27,* 39–45.

Karacan, I., Hursch, C. J., Williams, R. L., & Thornby, J. I. (1972). Some characteristics of nocturnal penile tumescence in young adults. *Archives of General Psychiatry, 26,* 351–356.

Karacan, I., Rosenbloom, A., & Williams, R. L. (1970). The clitoral erection cycle during sleep. *Psychophysiology, 7,* 338. (Abstract)

Karacan I., Salis, P. J., & Williams, R. L. (1978). The role of the sleep laboratory in diagnosis and treatment of impotence. In R. L. Williams & I. Karacan (Eds.), *Sleep disorders: Diagnosis and treatment* (pp. 353–382). New York: Wiley.

Karacan, I., Williams, R. L., Guerrero, M. W., Salis, P. J., Thornby, J. I., & Hursch, C. J. (1974). Nocturnal penile tumescence and sleep of convicted rapists and other prisoners. *Archives of Sexual Behavior, 3,* 19–26.

Karacan, I., Williams, R. L., Thornby, J. I., & Salis, P. J. (1975). Sleep related penile tumescence as a function of age. *American Journal of Psychiatry, 132,* 932–937.

Kegel, A. (1948a). The non-surgical treatment of genital relaxation. *Annals of Western Medical Surgery, 2,* 213–216.

Kegel, A. (1948b). Progressive resistance exercise in the functional restoration of the perineal muscles. *American Journal of Obstetrics and Gynecology, 56,* 238–248.

Kegel, A. H. (1950). Active exercise of the pubococcygeus muscle. In J. V. Meigs & S. H. Sturgis (Eds.), *Progress in gynecology* (Vol. 2). New York: Grune & Stratton.

Kegel, A. (1951). Physiologic therapy for urinary stress incontinence. *Journal of the American Medical Association, 146,* 915–917.

REFERENCES

Kegel, A. (1952). Sexual functions of the pubococcygeus muscle. *Western Journal of Surgery, Obstetrics, and Gynecology, 60,* 521–524.

Keiser, S. (1952). Body ego during orgasm. *Psychoanalytic Quarterly, 21,* 153–166.

Kercher, G. A., & Walker, E. (1973). Reactions of convicted rapists to sexually explicit stimuli. *Journal of Abnormal Psychology, 81,* 46–50.

Kilmann, P. R. (1978). The treatment of primary and secondary orgasmic dysfunction: A methodological review of the literature since 1970. *Journal of Sex and Marital Therapy, 4,* 155–176.

Kilpatrick, D. G. (1979). The scientific study of rape: A clinical research perspective. In R. Green & J. Weiner (Eds.), *Methodology in sex research* (pp. 179–191). Washington, DC: U.S. Government Printing Office.

Kilpatrick, D. G., Veronen, L. J., & Resick, P. A. (1979). Assessment of the aftermath of rape: Changing patterns of fear. *Journal of Behavioral Assessment, 1,* 133–148.

Kinder, B. N., & Blakeney, P. (1977). Treatment of sexual dysfunction: A review of outcome studies. *Journal of Clinical Psychology, 33,* 523–530.

Kinsey, A. C., Pomeroy, W. B., & Martin, C. E. (1948). *Sexual behavior in the human male.* Philadelphia: W. B. Saunders.

Kinsey, A. C., Pomeroy, W. B., Martin, C. E., & Gebhard, P. H. (1953). *Sexual behavior in the human female.* Philadelphia: W. B. Saunders.

Kline-Graber, G., & Graber, B. (1978). Diagnosis and treatment procedures of pubococcygeus deficiencies in women. In J. LoPiccolo & L. LoPiccolo (Eds.), *Handbook of sex therapy* (pp. 227–240). New York: Plenum.

Klumbies, G., & Klensorge, H. (1950). Das herz in orgasmus. *Medizinische Klink, 45,* 952–958.

Kluver, H., & Bucy, P. (1939). Preliminary analysis of functions of the temporal lobes of monkeys. *Archives of Neurology and Psychiatry, 42,* 979–1000.

Knussman, R., Christiansen, K., & Couwenbergs, C. (1986). Relations between sex hormone levels and sexual behavior in men. *Archives of Sexual Behavior, 15,* 429–445.

Kockott, G., Feil, W., Ferstl, R., Aldenhoff, J., & Besinger, V. (1980). Psychophysiological aspects of male sexual inadequacy: Results of an experimental study. *Archives of Sexual Behavior, 9,* 477–493.

Koegler, R. R., & Kline, L. Y. (1965). Psychotherapy research: An approach utilizing autonomic response measurement. *American Journal of Psychotherapy, 19,* 268–279.

Koff, W. C. (1974). Marihuana and sexual activity. *Journal of Sex Research, 10,* 194–204.

Kolarsky, A., & Madlafousek, J. (1972). Female behavior and sexual arousal in heterosexual male deviant offenders. *Journal of Nervous and Mental Disease, 155,* 110–118.

Kolodny, R. C. (1977). Ethical requirements for sex research in humans: Informed consent and general principles. In W. H. Masters, V. E. Johnson, & R. C. Kolodny (Eds.), *Ethical issues in sex therapy and research* (pp. 52–68). Boston: Little, Brown.

Kolodny, R. C. (1978). Effects of alpha-methyldopa on male sexual function. *Sexuality and Disability, 1,* 223–228.

Kolodny, R. C., Masters, W. H., & Johnson, V. E. (1979). *Textbook of sexual medicine.* Boston: Little, Brown.

Kolodny, R. C., Masters, W. H., Kolodner, R. M., & Toro, G. (1974). Depression of plasma testosterone levels after chronic intensive marihuana use. *New England Journal of Medicine, 290,* 872–874.

Kolodny, R. C., Webster, S. K., Tullman, G. D., & Dornbush, R. I. (1979, June 28–29). *Chronic marihuana use by women: Menstrual cycle and endocrine findings.* Paper presented at the 2nd Annual Conference on Marijuana, New York University Postgraduate Medical School, New York.

Komisaruk, B. R. (1982). Visceral–somatic integration in behavior, cognition, and psychosomatic disease. In *Advances in the study of behavior* (Vol. 12, pp. 1–26). New York: Academic Press.

Korff, J., & Geer, J. H. (1983). The relationship between sexual arousal experience and genital response. *Psychophysiology, 20,* 121–127.

Korenchevsky, V. (1937). The female prostatic gland and its reaction to male sexual compounds. *Journal of Physiology, 90,* 371–376.

Korner, A. (1968). REM organization in neonates. *Archives of General Psychiatry, 19,* 330–340.

Kotin, J., Wilbert, D. E., Verburg, D., & Soldinger, S. M. (1976). Thioridazine and sexual dysfunction. *American Journal of Psychiatry, 133,* 82–85.

Kraemer, H. C., Becker, H. B., Brodie, H. K. H., Doering, C. H., Moos, R. H., & Hamburg, D. A. (1976). Orgastic frequency and plasma testosterone levels in normal human males. *Archives of Sexual Behavior, 5,* 125–132.

Krafft-Ebing, R. von. (1965). *Psychopathia sexualis.* New York, Putnam. (Original work published 1886)

Krane, R. J., & Siroky, M. B. (1981). Neurophysiology of erection. *Urologic Clinics of North America, 8,* 91–102.

Kuriansky, J. B., & Sharpe, L. (1976). Guidelines for evaluating sex therapy. *Journal of Sex and Marital Therapy, 2,* 303–308.

Kwan, M., Greenleaf, W. J., Mann, J., Crapo, L., & Davidson, J. M. (1983). The nature of androgen action on male sexuality: A combined laboratory–self-report study on hypogonadal men. *Journal of Clinical Endocrinology and Metabolism, 57,* 557–562.

Lacey, J. I., Kagan, J., Lacey, B. C., & Moss, H. A. (1963). The visceral level: Situational determinants and behavioral correlates of autonomic response patterns. In P. H. Knapp (Ed.), *Expression of the emotions in man* (pp. 147–165). New York: International Universities Press.

Ladas, A. K., Whipple, B., & Perry, J. D. (1982). *The G spot and other recent discoveries about human sexuality.* New York: Holt, Rinehart and Winston.

LaFerla, J. J., Anderson, D. L., & Schalch, D. S. (1978). Psychoendocrine response to sexual arousal in human males. *Psychosomatic Medicine, 40,* 166–172.

Lang, P. J. (1979). A bio-informational theory of emotional imagery. *Psychophysiology, 16,* 495–512.

Lang, W. R. (1955). Vaginal acidity and pH: A review. *Obstetrics and Gynecology Survey, 10,* 546–562.

Lange, C. (1885). *Om Sindsbevägelser.* Copenhagen: Vergeiser.

Lange, J. D., Brown, W. A., Wincze, J. P., & Swick, W. (1980). Serum testosterone concentration and penile tumescence changes in men. *Hormones and Behavior, 14,* 267–270.

Lange, J. D., Wincze, J. P., Zwick, W., Feldman, S., & Hughes, K. (1981). Effect of demand for performance, self-monitoring of arousal, and increased sympathetic nervous system activity on male erectile response. *Archives of Sexual Behavior, 10,* 443–464.

Langevin, R., Ben-Aron, M., Coulthard, R., Day, D., Hucke, S. J., Purins, J. E., Roper, V., Russon, A. E., & Webster, C. D. (1985). The effect of alcohol on penile erection. In R. Langevin (Ed.), *Erotic preference, gender identity, and aggression in men* (pp. 101–111). Hillsdale, NJ: Erlbaum.

Langevin, R., & Martin, M. (1975). Can erotic responses be classically conditioned? *Behavior Therapy, 6,* 330–335.

Langevin, R., Paitich, D., Ramsay, G., Anderson, C., Kamrad, J., Pope, S., Geller, G., Pearl, L., & Newman, S. (1979). Experimental studies of the etiology of genital exhibitionism. *Archive of Sexual Behavior, 8,* 307–331.

Larsen, P. B., Schneiderman, N., & Pasin, R. D. (1986). Psychological bases of cardiovascular psychophysiology. In M. G. H. Coles, E. Donchin, & S. W. Porges (Eds.), *Psychophysiology: Systems, processes, and applications* (pp. 122–165). New York: Guilford Press.

Laschet, U. (1973). Antiandrogen in the treatment of sex offenders: Mode of action and

377

therapeutic outcome. In J. Zubin & J. Money (Eds.), *Contemporary sexual behavior: Critical issues in the 1970's* (pp. 311–319). Baltimore: Johns Hopkins University Press.

Lawrence, D. H. (1923). Tortoise shout. In *Aaron's rod* (p. 87). New York: Viking Press.

Lawrence, D. H. (1959). *Lady Chatterley's lover.* New York: Grove Press. (Original work published 1928)

Laws, D. R. (1977). A comparison of the two circumferential penile transducers. *Archives of Sexual Behavior, 6,* 45–51.

Laws, D. R. (1980). Treatment of bisexual paedophilia by a biofeedback-assisted self-control procedure. *Behaviour Research and Therapy, 18,* 207–211.

Laws, D. R. (1984). The assessment of dangerous sexual behavior in males. *Medicine and Law, 3,* 127–140.

Laws, D. R. (1985). Sexual fantasy alternation: Procedural considerations. *Journal of Behavior Therapy and Experimental Psychiatry, 16,* 39–44.

Laws, D. R., & Bow, R. A. (1976). An improved mechanical strain gauge for recording penile circumference change. *Psychophysiology, 13,* 596–599.

Laws, D. R., & Holmen, M. L. (1978). Sexual response faking by pedophiles. *Criminal Justice and Behavior, 5,* 343–356.

Laws, D. R., & O'Neil, J. A. (1981). Variations on masturbatory conditioning. *Behavioural Psychotherapy, 9,* 111–136.

Laws, D. R., & Osborn, C. A. (1983). How to build and operate a behavioral laboratory to evaluate and treat sexual deviance. In J. G. Greer & I. R. Stuart (Eds.), *The sexual aggressor: Current perspectives on treatment* (pp. 293–335). New York: Van Nostrand Reinhold.

Laws, D. R., & Rubin, H. B. (1969). Instructional control of an autonomic sexual response. *Journal of Applied Behavior Analysis, 2,* 93–99.

Lazar, J., Eisold, J., Gadson, I., & Tesch, D. (1984). Recognition and management of antihypertensive drug side effects. *Clinical Pharmacology and Therapeutics, 35,* 254–255.

Lazarus, A. A. (1964). The treatment of a sexually inadequate man. In L. P. Ullmann & L. Krasner (Eds.), *Case studies in behavior modification* (pp. 243–245). New York: Holt, Rinehart & Winston.

Leary, T. (1968). *The politics of ecstacy.* New York: Putnam.

Lee, P. A., Jaffe, R. B., & Midgley, A. R. (1974). Lack of alteration of serum gonadotropins in men and women following sexual intercourse. *American Journal of Obstetrics and Gynecology, 120,* 985–987.

Legros, J. J., Mormont, C., & Servais, J. (1978). A psychoneuroendocrinological study of erectile psychogenic impotence: A comparsion between normal patients and patients with abnormal reactions to glucose tolerance test. In L. Carenza, P. Panchori, & L. Zichella (Eds.), *Psychoneuroendocrinology in reproduction* (pp. 310–319). New York: Academic Press.

Leiblum, S. R. & Pervin, L. A. (Eds.). (1980). *Principles and practices of sex therapy.* New York: Guilford Press.

Leiblum, S. R., Pervin, L. A., & Campbell, E. H. (1980). The treatment of vaginismus: Success and failure. In S. R. Leiblum & L. A. Pervin (Eds.), *Principles and practice of sex therapy* (pp. 167–194). New York: Guilford Press.

Leiblum, S. R., & Rosen, R. C. (Eds.). (in press). *Sexual desire disorders.* New York: Guilford Press.

Lemere, F., & Smith, J. W. (1973). Alcohol-induced sexual impotence. *American Journal of Psychiatry, 130,* 212–213.

Leonard, K. E., & Taylor, S. P. (1983). Exposure to pornography, permissive and non-permissive cues, and male aggression toward females. *Motivation and Emotion, 7,* 291–299.

Lesko, L. M., Stotland, N. L., & Segraves, R. T. (1982). Three cases of female anorgasmia associated with MAOIs. *American Journal of Psychiatry, 139,* 1353–1354.

Leventhal, H. (1980). Toward a comprehensive theory of emotion. In L. Berkowitz (Ed.), *Advances in experimental social psychology* (Vol. 13, pp. 62–91). New York: Academic Press.

Levin, R. J. (1981). The female orgasm—current appraisal. *Journal of Psychosomatic Research, 25,* 119–133.

Levin, R. J., & Wagner, G. (1976). *Human vaginal fluid, pH, urea, potassium, and potential difference during sexual excitement.* Paper presented at the International Congress of Sexology, Montreal.

Levin, R. J., & Wagner, G. (1977). Haemodynamic changes of the human vagina during sexual arousal assessed by a heated oxygen electrode. *Journal of Physiology, 275,* 23P–24P.

Levin, R. J., & Wagner, G. (1985). Orgasm in women in the laboratory—quantitative studies on duration, latency, and vaginal blood flow. *Archives of Sexual Behavior, 14,* 439–449.

Levin, R. M., & Wein, A. J. (1980). Adrenergic alpha receptors outnumber beta receptors in human penile corpus cavernosum. *Investigative Urology, 18,* 225–226.

Levine, S. B. (1980). Conceptual suggestions for outcome research in sex therapy. *Journal of Sex and Marital Therapy, 6,* 102–108.

Levine, S. B., & Agle, D. (1978). The effectiveness of sex therapy for chronic secondary psychological impotence. *Journal of Sex and Marital Therapy, 4,* 235–258.

Levitt, E. E., Konovsky, M., Freese, M. P., & Thompson, J. F. (1979). Intravaginal pressure assessed by the Kegel perineometer. *Archives of Sexual Behavior, 8,* 425–430.

Levitt, J. I. (1970). Spironolactone therapy and amenorrhea. *Journal of the American Medical Associaton, 211,* 2014–2015.

Leyson, J. F., & Powell, R. B. (1982). Comparative study of two nocturnal penile tumescence monitors. *Journal of the Medical Society of New Jersey, 79,* 647–650.

Lifshitz, K. (1966). The average evoked cortical response to complex visual stimuli. *Psychophysiology, 3,* 55–68.

Lifshitz, J. L., & Adams, H. E. (1980). *Female sexual arousal: Distraction and attention in orgasmic and nonorgasmic women.* Paper presented at the annual meeting of the Association for Advancement of Behavior Therapy, New York.

Lincoln, G. A. (1974). Luteinising hormone and testosterone in man. *Nature, 252,* 232–233.

Linz, D. (1985). *Sexual violence in the mass media: Effects on male viewers and implications for society.* Unpublished doctoral dissertation, University of Wisconsin–Madison.

Littler, W. A., Honour, A. J., & Sleight, P. (1974). Direct arterial pressure, heart rate and electrocardiogram during human coitus. *Journal of Reproduction and Fertility, 40,* 321–331.

Lobitz, W. C., & LoPiccolo, J. (1972). The role of masturbation in the treatment of orgasmic dysfunction. *Archives of Sexual Behavior, 2,* 163–171.

Logan, T. G. (1975). The vaginal clasp: A method of comparing contractions across subjects. *Journal of Sex Research, 11,* 353–358.

Loisselle, R. H., & Mollenauer, S. (1965). Galvanic skin responses to sexual stimuli in a female population. *Journal of Genetic Psychology, 73,* 273–278.

LoPiccolo, J. (1977). Direct treatment of sexual dysfunction in the couple. In J. Money & H. Musaph (Eds.), *Handbook of sexology* (pp. 1227–1244). New York: Elsevier/North-Holland.

LoPiccolo, J. (1985). *Diagnosis and treatment of male sexual dysfunction.* Paper presented at the Banff International Conference on Behavior Sciences, Banff, Alberta, Canada.

LoPiccolo, J., & Heiman, J. (1978). The role of cultural values in the prevention and treatment of sexual problems. In C. B. Qualls, J. P. Wincze, & D. H. Barlow (Eds.), *The prevention of sexual disorders* (pp. 43–74). New York: Plenum.

379

LoPiccolo, J., & Stock, W. E. (1986). Treatment of sexual dysfunction. *Journal of Consulting and Clinical Psychology, 54,* 158–167.

Loriaux, D. C., Menard, R., Taylor, A., Pita, J. C., & Santen, R. (1976). Spironolactone and endocrine dysfunction. *Annals of Internal Medicine, 85,* 630–636.

Lowen, A. (1965). *Love and orgasm.* New York: Macmillan.

Lowry, T. P. (1979). Amyl nitrite: An old high comes back to visit. *Behavioral Medicine, 6,* 19–21.

Lucas, L., Abel, G. G., Mittelman, M. S., & Becker, J. V. (1983, December). *Pupillometry to determine the sexual preference of paraphiliacs.* Paper presented at the World Congress of Behavior Therapy, Washington, DC.

MacLean, P. D. (1965). New findings relevant to the evolution of psychosexual functions in the brain. In J. Money (Ed.), *Sex research: New developments* (pp. 192–212). New York: Holt, Rinehart & Winston.

Magee, M. (1980). Psychogenic impotence: A critical review. *Urology, 15,* 435–442.

Magoun, H. W. (1981). John B. Watson and the study of human sexual behavior. *Journal of Sex Research, 17,* 368–378.

Malamuth, N. M. (1981). Rape fantasies as a function of exposure to violent sexual stimuli. *Archives of Sexual Behavior, 10,* 33–47.

Malamuth, N. M. (1984). Aggression against women: cultural and individual causes. In N. M. Malamuth & E. Donnerstein (Eds.), *Pornography and sexual aggression* (pp. 19–52). New York: Academic Press.

Malamuth, N. M., & Check, J. V. P. (1980). Penile tumescence and perceptual responses to rape as a function of victim's perceived reactions. *Journal of Applied Social Psychology, 10,* 528–547.

Malamuth, N. M., & Check, J. V. P. (1983). Sexual arousal to rape depictions: Individual differences. *Journal of Abnormal Psychology, 92,* 55–67.

Malamuth, N. M., & Check, J. V. P. (1984). Debriefing effectiveness following exposure to pornographic rape depictions. *Journal of Sex Research, 20,* 1–13.

Malmuth, N. M., Check, J. V. P., & Briere, J. (1986). Sexual arousal in response to aggression: Ideological, aggressive and sexual correlates. *Journal of Personality and Social Psychology, 50,* 330–340.

Malamuth, N. M., Haber, S., & Feshbach, S. (1980). Testing hypotheses regarding rape: Exposure to sexual violence, sex differences, and the "normality" of rapists. *Journal of Research in Personality, 14,* 121–137.

Malamuth, N. M., Heim, M., & Feshbach, S. (1980). Sexual responsiveness of college students to rape depictions: Inhibitory and disinhibitory effects. *Journal of Personality and Social Psychology, 38,* 399–408.

Malatesta, V. J., Pollack, R. H., Crotty, T. D., & Peacock, L. J. (1982). Acute alcohol intoxication and female orgasmic response. *Journal of Sex Research, 18,* 1–17.

Malatesta, V. J., Pollack, R. H., Wilbanks, W. A., & Adams, H. E. (1979). Alcohol effects on the orgasmic–ejaculatory response in human males. *Journal of Sex Research, 15,* 101–107.

Maletzky, B. M. (1980). Assisted covert sensitization. In D. J. Cox & A. J. Daitzman (Eds.), *Exhibitionism: Description, assessment, and treatment.* New York: Garland Press.

Mandell, W., & Miller, C. M. (1983). Male sexual dysfunction as related to alcohol consumption: A pilot study. *Alcoholism: Clinical and Experimental Research, 7,* 65–69.

Mann, J., Berkowitz, L., Sidman, J., Starr, S., & West, S. (1974). Satiation of the transient stimulating effect of erotic films. *Journal of Personality and Social Psychology, 30,* 729–735.

Mann, J., Sidman, J., & Starr, S. (1971). Effects of erotic films on sexual behavior of married couples. In *Technical report of the Commission on Obscenity and Pornography* (Vol. 8, pp. 170–254). Washington, DC: U. S. Government Printing Office.

Mann, K. V., Abbott, E. C., Gray, J. D., Thiebaux, H. J., & Belzer, E. G. (1982). Sexual dysfunction with beta-blocker therapy: More common than we think? *Sexuality and Disability, 5,* 67–77.

Marks, I. M., & Gelder, M. G. (1967). Transvestism and fetishism: Clinical and psychological changes during faradic aversion. *British Journal of Psychiatry, 113,* 711–730.

Marks, I. M., Gelder, M. G., & Bancroft, J. H. (1970). Sexual deviants two years after electric aversion therapy. *British Journal of Psychiatry, 117,* 173–185.

Marquis, J. (1970). Orgasmic reconditioning: Changing sexual object choice through controlling masturbation fantasies. *Journal of Behavior Therapy and Experimental Psychiatry, 1,* 263–271.

Marshall, G. D., & Zimbardo, P. G. (1979). Affective consequences of inadequately explained physiological arousal. *Journal of Personality and Social Psychology, 37,* 970–988.

Marshall, P. G., McGrath, P., & Schillinger, J. (1983). Importance of electromyographic data in interpreting nocturnal penile tumescence. *Urology, 22,* 153–156.

Marshall, P. G., Morales, A., Phillips, P., & Fenemore, J. (1983). Nocturnal penile tumescence with stamps: A comparative study under sleep laboratory conditions. *Journal of Urology, 130,* 88–89.

Marshall, P. G., Surridge, D., & Delva, N. (1981). The role of nocturnal penile tumescence in differentiating between organic and psychogenic impotence: The first stage of validation. *Archives of Sexual Behavior, 10,* 1–10.

Marshall, W. L. (1974). The classical conditioning of sexual attractiveness: A report of four therapeutic failures. *Behavior Therapy, 5,* 298–299.

Marshall, W. L. (1979). Satiation therapy: A procedure for reducing deviant sexual arousal. *Journal of Applied Behavior Analysis, 12,* 10–22.

Marshall, W. L., & Barbaree, H. E. (1978). The reduction of deviant arousal. *Criminal Justice and Behavior, 5,* 294–303.

Martin, B. (1964). Expression and inhibition of sex motive arousal in college males. *Journal of Abnormal and Social Psychology, 68,* 307–312.

Marx, M. H. (1969). Learning process. In M. H. Marx (Ed.), *Learning: Processes* (pp. 3–34). Toronto: Macmillan.

Maslach, C. (1979). Negative emotional biasing of unexplained arousal. *Journal of Personality and Social Psychology, 37,* 953–969.

Masson, J. M. (1984). *The assault on truth: Freud's suppression of the seduction theory.* New York: Farrar, Strauss & Giroux.

Masters, R. E. L. (1967). Sexual self-stimulation and altered states of consciousness. In R. E. L. Masters (Ed.), *Sexual self-stimulation* (pp. 232–247). Los Angeles: Sherbourne Press.

Masters, W. H. (1959). The sexual response cycle of the human female: Vaginal lubrication. *Annals of the New York Academy of Sciences, 83,* 30–43.

Masters, W. H., & Johnson, V. E. (1966). *Human sexual response.* Boston: Little, Brown.

Masters, W. H., & Johnson, V. E. (1970). *Human sexual inadequacy.* Boston: Little Brown.

Masters, W. H., Johnson, V. E., & Kolodny, R. C. (Eds.). (1977). *Ethical issues in sex therapy and research.* Boston: Little, Brown.

Masters, W. H., Johnson, V. E., & Kolodny, R. C. (1982). *Human sexuality.* Boston: Little, Brown.

Mattson, R. H., & Cramer, J. A. (1985). Epilepsy, sex hormones, and antiepileptic drugs. *Epilepsia, 26,* 540–551.

Mattson, R. H., Cramer, J. A., Collins, J. F., Smith, D. B., *et al.* (1985). Comparison of carbamazepine, phenobarbitol, phenytoin, and primidone in partial and secondarily generalized tonic–clonic seizures. *New England Journal of Medicine, 313,* 145–151.

Mavissakalian, M., Blanchard, E. B., Abel, G. G., & Barlow, D. H. (1975). Responses to complex erotic stimuli in homosexual and heterosexual males. *British Journal of Psychiatry, 126,* 252–257.

381

REFERENCES

Max, L. W. (1935). Breaking up a homosexual fixation by the conditioned reaction technique. *Psychological Bulletin, 32,* 734.

McCauley, E., & Ehrhardt, A. A. (1976). Female sexual response: Hormonal and behavioral interactions. *Primary Care, 3,* 455–476.

McConaghy, N. (1967). Penile volume change to moving pictures of male and female nudes in heterosexual and homosexual males. *Behavior Therapy, 5,* 43–48.

McConaghy, N. (1971). Aversive therapy of homosexuality: Measures of efficacy. *American Journal of Psychiatry, 127,* 1221–1224.

McConaghy, N. (1974). Measurements of change in penile dimensions. *Archives of Sexual Behavior, 4,* 381–388.

McConaghy, N. Armstrong, M. S., & Blaszczynski, A. (1981). A controlled comparison of aversive therapy and covert sensitization in compulsive homosexualtiy. *Behaviour Research and Therapy, 19,* 425–434.

McConnel, J. A., Benson, G. S., & Wood, J. (1979). Autonomic innervation of the mammalian penis: A histochemical and physiological study. *Journal of Neural Transmission, 45,* 227–238.

McCoy, N., & Davidson, J. M. (1985). A longitudinal study of effects of menopause on sexuality. *Maturitas, 7,* 203–210.

McDonald D. G., Shallenberger, H. D., Keosko, R. K., & Kinney, B. G. (1976). Studies of spontaneous electrodermal responses in sleep. *Psychophysiology.* 128–134.

McGuire, L. S., & Wagner, N. N. (1978). Sexual dysfunction in women who were molested as children: One response pattern and suggestions for treatment. *Journal of Sex and Marital Therapy, 4,* 11–15.

McGuire, R. J., Carlisle, J. M., & Young, B. G. (1965). Sexual deviations as conditioned behaviour: A hypothesis. *Behaviour Research and Therapy, 2,* 185–190.

McMullen, S., & Rosen, R. C. (1979). The use of self-administered masturbation training in the treatment of primary orgasmic dysfunction. *Journal of Consulting and Clinical Psychology, 47,* 912–918.

Medical Research Council Working Party on Mild to Moderate Hypertension. (1981). Adverse reactions to bendrofluazide and propranolol for the treatment of mild hypertension. *Lancet, ii,* 539–543.

Meehl, P. E. (1954). *Clinical versus statistical prediction.* Minneapolis: University of Minnesota Press.

Megargee, E. J. (1976). The prediction of dangerous behavior. *Criminal Justice and Behavior, 3,* 3–21.

Meiselman, K. (1978). *Incest: A psychological study of causes and effects with treatment recommendations.* San Francisco: Jossey-Bass.

Meltzer, H. Y., & Fang, V. S. (1976). The effect of neuroleptics on serum prolactin in schizophrenic patients. *Archives of General Psychiatry, 33,* 279–286.

Mendelson, J. H., Kuehnle, J., Ellingboe, J., & Babor, T. F. (1974). Plasma testosterone levels before, during, and after chronic marihuana smoking. *New England Journal of Medicine, 290,* 1051–1055.

Mendelson, J. H., & Mello, N. K. (1975). Plasma testosterone levels during chronic heroin use and protracted abstinence. *Clinical Pharmacology and Therapeutics, 17,* 529–533.

Mendelson, J. H., Mendelson, J. E., & Patch, V. D. (1975). Plasma testosterone levels in heroin addiction and during methadone maintenance. *Journal of Pharmacology and Experimental Therapuutics, 192,* 211–217.

Messé, M. R., & Geer, J. H. (1985). Voluntary vaginal musculature contractions as an enhancer of sexual arousal. *Archives of Sexual Behavior, 14,* 13–28.

Metz, P., & Wagner, G. (1981). Penile circumference and erection. *Urology, 18,* 268–270.

Mills, K. H., & Kilmann, P. R. (1982). Group treatment of sexual dysfunctions: A methodological review of the outcome literature. *Journal of Sex and Marital Therapy, 8,* 259–296.

Mitchell, J., & Popkin, M. (1983). The pathophysiology of sexual dysfunction associated with antipsychotic drug therapy in males: A review. *Archives of Sexual Behavior, 12,* 173–183.

Money, J. (1960). Phantom orgasm in the dreams of paraplegic men and women. *Archives of General Psychiatry, 3,* 373–382.

Money, J. (1968). Discussion on hormonal inhibition of libido in male sex offenders. In R. P. Michael (Ed.), *Endocrinology and human behavior* (pp. 247–261). London: Oxford University Press.

Money, J. (1970). Use of androgen-depleting hormone in the treatment of male sex offenders. *Journal of Sex Research, 6,* 165–172.

Money, J. (1980). *Love and love sickness: The science of sex, gender difference, and pair-bonding.* Baltimore: The Johns Hopkins University Press.

Money, J. (1984). Paraphilias: Phenomenology and classification. *American Journal of Psychotherapy, 38,* 164–179.

Money, J., & Bennett, R. G. (1981). Postadolescent paraphilic sex offenders: Antiandrogenic and counseling therapy follow-up. *International Journal of Mental Health, 10,* 122–133.

Money, J., & Ehrhardt, A. (1972). *Man and woman, boy and girl.* Baltimore: Johns Hopkins University Press.

Money, J., & Musaph, H. (Eds.). (1977). *Handbook of sexology.* Amsterdam: Elsevier/North-Holland.

Money, J., & Yankowitz, R. (1967). The sympathetic inhibiting effects of the drug Ismelin on human male eroticism, with a note on Mellaril. *Journal of Sex Research, 3,* 69–82.

Morales, A., Marshall, P. G., Surridge, D. H., & Fenemore, J. (1983). A new device for diagnostic screening of nocturnal penile tumescence. *Journal of Urology, 129,* 288–290.

Moreault, D., & Follingstad, D. R. (1978). Sexual fantasies of females as a function of sex guilt and experimental response cues. *Journal of Consulting and Clinical Psychology, 46,* 1385–1393.

Morgan, R. (1978). *Going too far.* New York: Random House.

Morokoff, P. J. (1985a). Effects of sex guilt, repression, sexual "arousability," and sexual experience on female sexual arousal during erotica and fantasy. *Journal of Personality and Social Psychology, 49,* 177–187.

Morokoff, P. J. (1985b). *The stress of unemployment: Effects on male sexual arousal.* Paper presented at the annual convention of the American Psychological Association, Los Angeles.

Morokoff, P. J. (1986). Volunteer bias in the psychophysiological study of female sexuality. *Journal of Sex Research, 22,* 35–51.

Morokoff, P. J., & Heiman, J. R. (1980). Effects of erotic stimuli on sexually functional and dysfunctional women: Multiple measures before and after sex therapy. *Behaviour Research and Therapy, 18,* 127–137.

Morrell, M. J., Dixen, J. M., Carter, C. S., & Davidson, J. M. (1984). The influence of age and cycling status on sexual arousability in women. *American Journal of Obstetrics and Gynecology, 148,* 66–71.

Mosher, D. L. (1971). Psychological reactions to pornographic films. In *Technical report of the Commission on Obscenity and Pornography* (Vol. 8, pp. 255–312). Washington, DC: U. S. Government Printing Office.

Mosher, D. L. (1980). Three dimensions of depth of involvement in human sexual response. *Journal of Sex Research, 16,* 1–42.

Mosher, D. L. & Katz, H. (1971). Pornographic films, male verbal aggression against women, and guilt. In *Technical report of the Commission on Obscenity and Pornography* (Vol. 8, pp. 357–379). Washington, DC: U. S. Government Printing Office.

383

REFERENCES

Mosher, D. L., & O'Grady, K. E. (1979). Sex guilt, trait anxiety, and females' subjective sexual arousal to erotica. *Motivation and Emotion, 3,* 235–249.

Mosovich, A., & Tallafero, A. (1954). Studies of EEG and sex function at orgasm. *Diseases of the Nervous System, 15,* 218–220.

Moss, H. B., & Procci, N. R. (1982). Sexual dysfunction associated with oral antihypertensive medication: A critical survey of the literature. *General Hospital Psychiatry, 4,* 121–129.

Moss, R. L., Dudley, C. A., Foreman, M. M., & McCann, S. M. (1975). Synthetic LRF: Potentiator of sexual behavior in the rat. In M. Motta, P. G. Crosignani, & L. Martini (Eds.), *Hypothalamic hormones* (pp. 269–278). New York: Academic Press.

Mould, D. E. (1980). Neuromuscular aspects of women's orgasms. *Journal of Sex Research, 16,* 193–201.

Mountjoy, P. T. (1974). Some early attempts to modify penile erection in horse and human: An historical analysis. *Psychological Record, 24,* 291–308.

Munjack, D. J., & Kanno, P. H. (1979). Retarded ejaculation: A review. *Archives of Sexual Behavior, 8,* 139–150.

Munro, D., Horne, H. W., & Paul, D. P. (1948). The effect of injury to the spinal cord and cauda equina on the sexual potency of man. *New England Journal of Medicine, 239,* 903–911.

Murphy, W. D., Krisak, J., Stalgaitis, S., & Anderson, K. (1984). The use of penile tumescence measures with incarcerated rapists: Further validity issues. *Archives of Sexual Behavior, 13,* 545–554.

Murray, F. T., Cameron, D., & Ketchum, C. (1984). Return of gonadal function in men with prolactin-secreting pituitary tumors. *Journal of Clinical Endocrinology and Metabolism, 59,* 79–85.

Myers, L. S., & Morokoff, P. J. (1986). Physiological and subjective sexual arousal in pre- and postmenopausal women taking replacement therapy. *Psychophysiology, 23,* 283–292.

Nalbandov, A. V. (1976). *Reproductive physiology of mammals and birds* (3rd ed.). San Francisco: W. H. Freeman.

Nath, R., Menzoian, J., Kaplan, K., Millian, M., Siroky, T., & Krane, R. (1981). The multidisciplinary approach to vasculogenic impotence. *Surgery, 89,* 124–133.

National Academy of Sciences, Institute of Medicine. (1982). *Marijuana and health.* Washington, DC: National Academy Press.

Newcomb, M. D., & Bentler, P. M. (1983). Dimensions of subjective female orgasmic responsiveness. *Journal of Personality and Social Psychology, 44,* 862–873.

Newman, H. F., & Northup, J. D. (1981). Mechanism of human penile erection: An overview. *Urology, 17,* 399–408.

Newman, H. F. & Tchertkoff, V. (1980). Penile vascular cushions and erection. *Investigative Urology, 18,* 43–45.

Niakan, E., Harati, Y., & Comstock, J. P. (1986). Diabetic autonomic neuropathy. *Metabolism, 35,* 224–234.

Nordin, B. E., Crilly, R. G., Marshall, D. H., & Barkworth, S. A. (1981). Oestrogens the menopause and the adrenopause. *Journal of Endocrinology, 89,* 131–141.

Nowinski, J. (1980). *Becoming satisfied: A man's guide to sexual fulfillment.* Englewood Cliffs, NJ: Prentice-Hall.

Obrist, P. A. (1981). *Cardiovascular psychophysiology: A perspective.* New York: Plenum Press.

O'Carroll, R., & Bancroft, J. (1984). Testosterone for low sexual interest and erectile dysfunction in men: A controlled study. *British Journal of Psychiatry, 145,* 146–151.

O'Carroll, R., Shapiro, C., & Bancroft, J. (1985). Androgens, behaviour and nocturnal erection in hypogonadal men: The effects of varying the replacement dose. *Clinical Endocrinology, 23,* 527–538.

O'Donohue, W. T., & Geer, J. H. (1985). The habituation of sexual arousal. *Archives of Sexual Behavior, 14,* 233–246.

O'Hanlon, J. K., Meisel, R. L., & Sachs, B. D. (1981). Estradiol maintains castrated male rats' sexual reflexes *in copula* but not *ex copula. Behavioral and Neural Biology, 32,* 269–273.

Ohlmeyer, P., & Brilmayer, H. (1947). Periodische Vorgange im Schlaf II. *Pfluegers Archiv fuer Die Gesamte Physiologie, 251,* 110–114.

Ohlmeyer, P., Brilmayer, H., & Hullstrung, H. (1944). Periodische vorgange im schlaf. *Pfluegers Archiv fuer Die Gesamte Physiologie, 249,* 50–55.

O'Neill, M. T., & Hinto, J. W., (1977). Pupillographic assessment of sexual interest and sexual arousal. *Perceptual and Motor Skills, 44,* 1278.

Osborn, C. A., & Pollack, R. H. (1977). The effects of two types of erotic literature on physiological and verbal measures of female sexual arousal. *Journal of Sex Research, 13,* 250–256.

Oswald, P. J., & Cleary, P. J. (1986). Effects of pelvic muscle tension and expectancy on general and specific indicators of sexual arousal. *Archives of Sexual Behavior, 15,* 247–260.

Ottesen, B., Wagner, G., Virag, R., & Fahrenkrug, J. (1984). Penile erection: Possible role for vasoactive intestinal polypeptide as a neurotransmitter. *British Medical Journal, 288,* 9–11.

Ovesey, L., & Meyers, H. (1968). Retarded ejaculation: Psychodynamics and psychotherapy. *American Journal of Psychotherapy, 22,* 185–201.

Palti, Y., & Bercovici, B. (1967). Photoplethysmographic study of the vaginal blood pulse. *American Journal of Obstetrics and Gynecology, 97,* 143–153.

Patel, C., Marmot, M. G., & Terry, D. J. (1981). Controlled trial of biofeedback aided behavioral methods in reducing mild hypertension. *British Medical Journal, 282,* 2005–2008.

Perry, J. D. (1980). *Two devices for the physiological measurement of sexual activity.* Paper presented at the meeting of the Society for the Scientific Study of Sex, Philadelphia.

Perry, J. D., & Whipple, B. (1981). Pelvic muscle strength of female ejaculators: Evidence in support of a new theory of orgasm. *Journal of Sex Research, 17,* 22–39.

Persky, H., Charney, N., Lief, H. I., O'Brien, C. P., Miller, W. R., & Strauss, D. (1978). The relationship of plasma estradiol level to sexual behavior in young women. *Psychosomatic Medicine, 40,* 523–535.

Persky, H., Leif, H. I., Strauss, D., Miller, W. R., & O'Brien, C. P. (1978). Plasma testosterone level and sexual behavior of couples. *Archives of Sexual Behavior, 7,* 157–173.

Persky, H., Strauss, D., Lief, H. I., Miller, W. R., & O'Brien, C. P. (1981). Effect of the research process on human sexual behavior. *Journal of Psychiatric Research, 16,* 41–52.

Physicians' Desk Reference (40th ed.). (1986). Oradell, NJ: Medical Economics.

Pirke, K. H., Kockott, G., & Dittmar, F. (1974). Psychosexual stimulation and plasma testosterone in man. *Archives of Sexual Behavior, 3,* 577–584.

Pithers, W. D., Marques, J. K., Gibat, C. E., & Marlatt, G. A. (1983). Relapse prevention with sexual aggressives: A self-control model of treatment and maintenance of change. In J. E. Greer & I. R. Stuart (Eds.), *The sexual aggressor: Current perspectives on treatment* (pp. 214–239). New York: Van Nostrand Reinhold.

Polak, J. M., & Bloom, S. R. (1984). Localisation and measurement of VIP in the genitourinary system of man and animals. *Peptides, 5,* 225–230.

Poloniecki, J., & Hamilton, M. (1985). Subjective costs of antihypertensive treatment. *Human Toxicology, 4,* 287–291.

Porges, S. W., & Fox, N. A. (1986). Developmental psychophysiology. In M. G. H. Coles,

385

REFERENCES

E. Donchin, & S. W. Porges (Eds.), *Psychophysiology: Systems, processes, and applications* (pp. 611–625). New York: Guilford Press.

Porges, S. W., McCabe, P. M., & Yongue, B. G. (1982). Respiratory–heart rate interactions: Psychophysiological implications for pathophysiology and behavior. In J. T. Cacioppo & R. E. Petty (Eds.), *Perspectives in cardiovascular psychophysiology* (pp. 223–264). New York: Guilford Press.

President's Commission on Obscenity and Pornography. (1970). *Report of the Commission on Obscenity and Pornography*. New York: Random House.

Prince, W. T. (1977). Fluid secretion in exocrine glands. In B. L. Gupta, R. B. Moreton, J. L. Oschman, & B. J. Wall (Eds.), *Transport of ions and water in animals* (pp. 382–391). New York: Academic Press.

Pritchard, P. B. (1980). Hyposexuality: A complication of complex partial epilepsy. *Transactions of the American Neurological Association, 105*, 193–195.

Procci, W. R., & Martin, D. J. (1984). Preliminary observations of the utility of portable NPT. *Archives of Sexual Behavior, 13*, 569–580.

Procci, W. R., Moss, H. B., Boyd, J. L., & Baron, D. A. (1983). Consecutive-night reliability of portable nocturnal penile tumescence monitor. *Archives of Sexual Behavior, 12*, 307–316.

Purvis, K., Landgren, B. M., Cekan, Z., & Diczfalusy, E. (1976). Endocrine effects of masturbation in men. *Journal of Endocrinology, 70*, 439–444.

Quinn, J. T., Harbison, J. J., & McAllister, H. (1970). An attempt to shape human penile responses. *Behaviour Research and Therapy, 8*, 213–216.

Quinsey, V. L. (1977). The assessment and treatment of child molesters: A review. *Canadian Psychological Review, 18*, 204–220.

Quinsey, V. L., Bergersen, S. G., & Steinman, C. M. (1976). Changes in physiological and verbal responses of child molesters during aversion therapy. *Canadian Journal of Behavioural Science, 8*, 202–212.

Quinsey, V. L, & Carrigan, W. F. (1978). Penile responses to visual stimuli: Instructional control with and without auditory and sexual fantasy correlates. *Criminal Justice and Behavior, 5*, 333–342.

Quinsey, V. L., & Chaplin, T. C. (1982). Penile responses to nonsexual violence among rapists. *Criminal Justice and Behavior, 9*, 372–384.

Quinsey, V. L., & Chaplin, T. C. (1984). Stimulus control of rapists' and non-sex offenders' sexual arousal. *Behavioral Assessment, 6*, 169–176.

Quinsey, V. L., Chaplin, T. C., & Carrigan, W. F. (1979). Sexual preferences among incestuous and non-incestuous child molesters. *Behavior Therapy, 10*, 562–565.

Quinsey, V. L., Chaplin, T. C., & Carrigan, W. F. (1980). Biofeedback and signaled punishment in the modification of inappropriate sexual age preferences. *Behavior Therapy, 11*, 567–576.

Quinsey, V. L., Chaplin, T. C., & Upfold, D. (1984). Sexual arousal to nonsexual violence and sadomasochistic themes among rapists and non-sex-offenders. *Journal of Counsulting and Clinical Psychology, 52*, 651–657.

Quinsey, V. L., Chaplin, T. C., & Varney, G. (1981). A comparison of rapists' and non-sex offenders' sexual preferences for mutually consenting sex, rape, and physical abuse of women. *Behavioral Assessment, 3*, 127–135.

Quinsey, V. L., & Marshall, W. L. (1983). Procedures for reducing inappropriate sexual arousal: An evaluation review. In J. G. Greer & I. R. Stuart (Eds.), *The sexual aggressor: Current perspectives on treatment* (pp. 267–292). New York: Van Nostrand Reinhold.

Quinsey, V. L., Steinman, C. M., Bergersen, S. G., & Holmes, T. F. (1975). Penile circumference, skin conductance, and ranking responses of child molesters and "normals" to sexual and non-sexual stimuli. *Behavior Therapy, 6*, 213–219.

386

Rachman, S. (1966). Sexual fetishism: An experimental analogue. *Psychological Record, 16*, 293–296.

Rachman, S., & Hodgson, R. J. (1968). Experimentally-induced "sexual fetishism": Replication and development. *Psychological Record, 18*, 25–27.

Rada, R. T. (1973). Alcoholism and forcible rape. *American Journal of Psychiatry, 132*, 444–446.

Rada, R. T., Kellner, R., Laws, D. R., & Winslow, W. W. (1978). Drinking, alchoholism, and the mentally disordered sex offender. *Bulletin of the American Academy of Psychiatry and the Law, 6*, 296–300.

Rada, R. T., Laws, D. R., & Kellner, R. (1976). Plasma testosterone levels in the rapist. *Psychosomatic Medicine, 38*, 257–268.

Ramsey, G. (1943). The sexual development of boys. *American Journal of Psychology, 56*, 217.

Raymond, M. J. (1956). A case of fetishism treated by aversion therapy. *British Medical Journal, ii*, 854–856.

Redmond, D. E., Kosten, T. B., & Reiser, M. F. (1982). Spontaneous ejaculation associated with anxiety: Psychophysiologic considerations. *American Journal of Psychiatry, 140*, 1163–1166.

Reich, W. (1967). Experimentelle Ergebnisse uber die elektris: Funktion von sexualitat und und angst (Institut für valokonomische forschung klinishe und experimentale, Report No. 4). *Journal of Orgonomics, 3*, 4–29. (Translation: Original work published 1937)

Reichgott, M. J. (1979). Problems of sexual function in patients with hypertension. *Cardiovascular Medicine, 4*, 149–156.

Reifler, C. B., Howard, J., Lipton, M. A., Liptzin, M. B., & Widmann, P. (1971). Pornography: An experimental study of effects. *American Journal of Psychiatry, 128*, 575–582.

Reinisch, J. M., & Rosen, R. C. (1981). The growth and diversity of sex research in the past decade: An introduction to selected topics. *International Journal of Mental Health, 10*, 3–9.

Reisenzein, R. (1983). The Schachter theory of emotion: Two decades later. *Psychological Bulletin, 94*, 239–264.

Reynolds, B. S. (1980). Biofeedback and facilitation of erection in men with erectile dysfunction. *Archives of Sexual Behavior, 9*, 101–113.

Rinn, P. (1984). The neurophysiology of the face. *Psychological Bulletin, 39*, 234–245.

Robbins, M. R., & Jensen, G. D. (1978). Multiple orgasm in males. *Journal of Sex Research, 14*, 21–26.

Robertiello, R. C. (1970). The "clitoral versus vaginal orgasm" controversy and some of its ramifications. *Journal of Sex Research, 6*, 307–311.

Robinson, P. (1976). *The modernization of sex*. New York: Harper & Row.

Rogers, G. S., Van de Castle, R. L., Evans, W. S., & Critelli, J. W. (1985). Vaginal pulse amplitude response patterns during erotic conditions and sleep. *Archives of Sexual Behavior, 14*, 327–342.

Roose, S. P., Glassman, A. H., Walsh, B. T., & Cullen, K. (1982). Reversible loss of nocturnal penile tumescence during depression: A preliminary report. *Neuropsychobiology, 8*, 284–288.

Rooth, G., Sjöstedt, T. S., & Caligara, F. (1957). Bloodless determination of arterial oxygen tension by polarography. *L. K. W. Instrument Journal, 4*, 37–45.

Rosen, R. C. (1973). Suppression of penile tumescence by instrumental conditioning. *Psychosomatic Medicine, 35*, 509–514.

Rosen, R. C. (1976). Genital blood flow measurement: Feedback applications in sexual therapy. *Journal of Sex and Marital Therapy, 2*, 184–196.

Rosen, R. C., & Fracher, J. C. (1983). Tension-reduction training in the treatment of compulsive sex offenders. In J. G. Greer & I. R. Stuart (Eds.), *The sexual aggressor: Current perspectives on treatment* (pp. 144–159). New York: Van Nostrand Reinhold.

Rosen, R. C., Goldstein, L., Scoles, V., & Lazarus, C. (1986). Psychophysiological correlates of nocturnal penile tumescence in normal males. *Psychosomatic Medicine, 48,* 423–429.

Rosen, R. C., & Hall, E. (1984). *Sexuality.* New York: Random House.

Rosen, R. C., & Keefe, F. J. (1978). The measurement of human penile tumescence. *Psychophysiology, 15,* 366–376.

Rosen, R. C., & Kopel, S. A. (1977). Penile plethysmography and biofeedback in the treatment of a transvestite–exhibitionist. *Journal of Consulting and Clinical Psychology, 45,* 908–916.

Rosen, R. C., & Kostis, J. B. (1985). Biobehavioral sequelae associated with adrenergic-inhibiting antihypertensive agents: A critical review. *Health Psychology, 4,* 579–604.

Rosen, R. C., Kostis, J. B., & Jekelis, A. (in press). Beta-blocker effects on sexual function in normal males. *Archives of Sexual Behavior.*

Rosen, R. C., & Leiblum, S. R. (1987). Current approaches to the evaluation of sexual desire disorders. *Journal of Sex Research, 23,* 141–162.

Rosen, R. C., Shapiro, D., & Schwartz, G. (1975). Voluntary control of penile tumescence. *Psychosomatic Medicine, 37,* 479–483.

Rosenthal, R., & Rosnow, R. L. (1969). The volunteer subject. In R. Rosenthal & R. L. Rosnow (Eds.), *Artifact in behavioral research* (pp. 59–118). New York: Academic Press.

Rowland, D. L., Greenleaf, W. J., Mas, M., & Davidson, J. M. (1987). *Penile and finger sensory thresholds in aging and diabetes.* Manuscript submitted for publication.

Rubin, H. B., & Henson, D. E. (1976). Effects of alcohol on male sexual responding. *Psychopharmacology, 47,* 123–124.

Rubin, H. B., Henson, D. E., Falvo, R. E., & High, R. W. (1979). The relationship between men's endogenous levels of testosterone and their penile responses to erotic stimuli. *Behaviour Research and Therapy, 17,* 305–312.

Rubin, R. T., Poland, R. E., O'Connor, D., Gouin, P. R., & Tower, B. B. (1976). Selective neuroendocrine effects of low dose haloperidol in normal adult men. *Psychopharmacology, 47,* 135–140.

Rubin, R. T., Poland, R. E., & Tower, B. B. (1976). Prolactin-related testosterone secretion in normal adult men. *Journal of Clinical Endocrinology and Metabolism, 42,* 112–116.

Rubinsky, H. J., Hoon, P. W., Eckerman, D. A., & Amberson, J. I. (1985). Groin skin temperature: Testing the validity of a relatively unobtrusive physiological measure of psychosexual arousal. *Psychophysiology, 22,* 488–492.

Ruzbarsky, V., & Michal, V. (1977). Morphologic changes in the arterial bed of the penis with aging: Relationship to the pathogenesis of impotence. *Investigative Urology, 15,* 194–198.

Sackeim, H. A., Gur, R. C., & Saucy, M. C. (1978). Emotions are expressed more intensely on the left side of the face. *Science, 202,* 434–435.

Sakheim, D. K. (1985). *Waking assessment of erectile potential: The validation of a laboratory procedure to aid in the differential diagnosis of psychogenic and organic impotence.* Unpublished doctoral dissertation, State University of New York at Albany.

Sakheim, D. K., Barlow, D. H., & Beck, J. G. (1985). Diurnal penile tumescence: A pilot study of waking erectile potential in sexual functional and dysfunctional men. *Sexuality and Disability, 4,* 68–97.

Sakheim, D. K., Barlow, D. H., Beck, J. G., & Abrahamson, D. J. (1984). The effect of an increased awareness of erectile cues on sexual arousal. *Behaviour Research and Therapy, 22,* 151–158.

Salmimies, P., Kockott, G., Pirke, K. M., Vogt, H. J., & Schill, W. B. (1982). Effects of testosterone replacement on sexual behavior in hypogonadal men. *Archives of Sexual Behavior, 11,* 345–354.

Sapolsky, B. S. (1984). Arousal, affect, and the aggression-moderating effect of erotica. In N. M. Malamuth & E. Donnerstein (Eds.), *Pornography and sexual aggression* (pp. 85–114). New York: Academic Press.

Sarrel, P. M., Foddy, J., & McKinnon, J. B. (1977). Investigation of human sexual response using a cassette recorder. *Archives of Sexual Behavior, 6,* 341–348.

Schachter, S., & Singer, J. (1962). Cognitive, social, and physiological determinants of emotional state. *Psychological Review, 69,* 379–397.

Schaefer, H. H., & Colgan, A. H. (1977). The effect of pornography on penile tumescence as a function of reinforcement and novelty. *Behavior Therapy, 8,* 938–946.

Schiavi, R. C., Fisher, C., Quadland, M., & Glover, A. (1985). Nocturnal penile tumescent evaluation of penile function in insulin-dependent diabetic men. *Diabetologia, 28,* 90–94.

Schmidt, G., & Sigusch, V. (1970). Sex differences in response to psychosexual stimulation by films and slides. *Journal of Sex Research, 6,* 268–283.

Schmidt, G., Sigusch, V., & Schaefer, S. (1973). Responses to reading erotic stories: Male–female differences. *Archives of Sexual Behavior, 2,* 181–199.

Schmidt, H., & Wise, H. (1981). Significance of impaired penile tumescence and associated polysomnographic abnormalities in the impotent patient. *Journal of Urology, 126,* 348–352.

Schover, L. R., Friedman, J. M., Weiler, S. J., Heiman, J. R., & LoPiccolo, J. (1982). Multiaxial problem-oriented system for sexual dysfunctions. *Archives of General Psychiatry, 39,* 614–619.

Schover, L. R., & Jensen, S. B. (in press). *Sexuality and chronic illness.* New York: Guilford Press.

Schreiner-Engel, P., Schiavi, R. C., Smith, H., & White, D. (1981). Sexual arousability and the menstrual cycle. *Psychosomatic Medicine, 43,* 199–214.

Schwartz, G. E. (1978). Psychobiological foundations of psychotherapy and behavior change. In S. L. Garfield & A. E. Bergin (Eds.), *Handbook of psychotherapy and behavior change: An empirical analysis* (2nd ed., pp. 63–99). New York: Wiley.

Schwartz, G. E. (1986). Emotion and psychophysiological organization: A system approach. In M. G. H. Coles, E. Donchin, & S. W. Porges (Eds.), *Psychophysiology: Systems, processes, and applications* (pp. 354–377). New York: Guilford Press.

Schwartz, G. E., Ahern, G. L., & Brown, S. (1979). Lateralized facial muscle response to positive and negative emotional stimuli. *Psychophysiology, 16,* 561–571.

Scott, T. R., Wells, W. H., Wood, D. Z., & Morgan, D. I. (1967). Pupillary response and sexual interest reexamined. *Journal of Clinical Psychology, 23,* 433–438.

Seeley, T. T., Abramson, P. R., Perry, L. B., Rothblatt, A. B., & Seeley, D. M. (1980). Thermographic measurement of sexual arousal: A methodological note. *Archives of Sexual Behavior, 9,* 77–85.

Selden, G. (1979). *Aphrodisia.* New York: E. P. Dutton.

Semans, J. H. (1956). Premature ejaculations: A new approach. *Southern Medical Journal, 49,* 353–357.

Semans, J. H., & Langworth, O. R. (1938). Observations on the neurophysiology of sexual function in the male cat. *Journal of Urology, 40,* 836–846.

Semmens, J. P., Tsai, C. C., Semmens, E. C., & Loadholt, C. B. (1985). Effects of estrogen therapy on vaginal physiology during menopause. *Obstetrics and Gynecology, 66,* 15–18.

Semmens, J. P., & Wagner, G. (1982). Estrogen deprivation and vaginal function in postmenopausal women. *Journal of the American Medical Association, 248,* 445–448.

Semmlow, J. L., & Lubowsky, J. (1983). Sexual instrumentation. *IEEE Transactions on Biomedical Engineering, 30,* 309–319.

REFERENCES

Sevely, J. L, & Bennett, J. W. (1978). Concerning female ejaculation and the female prostate. *Journal of Sex Research, 14,* 1–20.

Shader, R. I. (1964). Sexual dysfunction associated with thioridazine hydrochloride. *Journal of the American Medical Association, 188,* 1007–1009.

Shapiro, A., & Cohen, H. D. (1965). The use of mercury capillary length gauges for the measurement of the volume of thoracic and diaphragmatic components of human respiration. *Annals of the New York Academy of Sciences, 26,* 634–649.

Shapiro, A., Cohen, H. D., DiBianco, P., & Rosen, G. (1968). Vaginal blood flow changes during sleep and sexual arousal. *Psychophysiology, 4,* 394. (Abstract)

Shapiro, D., & Schwartz, G. E. (1972). Biofeedback and visceral learning: Clinical applications. *Seminars in Psychiatry, 4,* 171–184.

Shen, W. W. (1982). Female orgasmic inhibition by amoxapine. *American Journal of Psychiatry, 139,* 1220.

Sherfey, M. J. (1966). *The nature and evolution of female sexuality.* New York: Random House.

Sherfey, M. J. (1974). Some biology of sexuality. *Journal of Sex and Marital Therapy, 1,* 97–109.

Sherif, C. (1980). Comment on ethical issues in Malamuth, Heim, and Feshbach's "Sexual responsiveness of college students to rape depictions: Inhibitory and disinhibitory effects." *Journal of Personality and Social Psychology, 38,* 409–412.

Sherwin, B. B. (1986). *Effects on sexual behavior of the chronic administration of estrogen and/or androgen to postmenopausal women.* Paper presented at the 12th Annual Meeting of the International Academy of Sex Research, Amsterdam.

Sherwin, B. B., & Gelfand, M. M. (1984). Effects of parenteral administration of estrogen and androgen on plasma hormone levels and hot flushes in the surgical menopause. *American Journal of Obstetrics and Gynecology, 148,* 552–557.

Sherwin, B. B, Gelfand, M. M., & Brender, W. (1985). Androgen enhances sexual motivation of females: A prospective cross-over study of sex steroid adminstration in the surgical menopause. *Psychosomatic Medicine, 47,* 339–351.

Shirai, M., & Ishii, N. (1981). Hemodynamics of erection in man. *Archives of Andrology, 6,* 27–32.

Shirai, M., Matsuda, S., Mitsukawa, S., Nakamura, M., & Yonezawa, K. (1974). Effects of ejaculation induced by manual stimulation on plasma gonadotropin and testosterone levels in infertile man. *Tohoku Journal of Experimental Medicine, 114,* 91–92.

Sigusch, V., Schmidt, G., Reinfeld, A., & Wiedemann-Sutor, I. (1970). Psychosexual stimulation: Sex differences. *Journal of Sex Research, 6,* 10–24.

Silverstein, C. (1984). The ethical and moral implications of sexual classification: A commentary. *Journal of Homosexuality, 9,* 29–38.

Simpson, G. M., Blair, J. H., & Amuso, D. (1965). Effects of antidepressants on genitourinary function. *Diseases of the Nervous System, 26,* 787–789.

Singer, I. (1973). *The goals of human sexuality.* New York: Norton.

Singer, J., & Singer, I. (1978). Types of female orgasm. In J. LoPiccolo & L. LoPiccolo (Eds.), *Handbook of sex therapy* (pp. 175–186). New York: Plenum Press.

Sintchak, G., & Geer, J. H. (1975). A vaginal plethysmograph system. *Psychophysiology, 12,* 113–115.

Sirota, A. D., & Schwartz, G. E. (1982). Facial muscle patterning and lateralization during elation and depression imagery. *Journal of Abnormal Psychology, 91,* 25–34.

Skene, A. (1880). Two important glands of the urethra. *American Journal of Obstetrics, 265,* 265–270.

Skene, A. (1898). *Treatise on the diseases of women.* New York: Appleton.

Slag, M. F., Morley, J. E., Elson, M. K., Trence, D. L., Nelson, C. J., Nelson, A. E., Kinlaw, W. B., Beyer, H. S., Nultall, F. Q., & Shafer, R. B. (1983). Impotence in medical clinic outpatients. *Journal of the American Medical Association, 249,* 1736–1746.

Smith, A. D. (1980). Effect of focus of attention on female sexual arousal. *Dissertation Abstracts International, 40,* 5421B.

Smith, E. R., & Davidson, J. M. (1987). Unpublished data.

Snyder, S., & Karacan, I. (1981). Effects of chronic alcoholism on nocturnal penile tumescence. *Psychosomatic Medicine, 43,* 423–429.

Sobrero, A. J. (1965). Technic for the induction of ejaculation in humans. *Fertility and Sterility, 16,* 765–767.

Socarides, C. W. (1974). Homosexuality. In S. Arieti & E. B. Brody (Eds.), *American handbook of psychiatry* (2nd ed., Vol. 3, pp. 291–315). New York: Basic Books.

Solnick, R. L., & Birren, J. E. (1977). Age and male erectile responsiveness. *Archives of Sexual Behavior, 6,* 1–9.

Solomon, R. L., & Corbit, J. D. (1974). An opponent process theory of motivation. *Psychological Review, 81,* 119–145.

Solyom, L., & Beck, P. R. (1967). GSR assessment of aberrant sexual behavior. *International Journal of Neuropsychiatry, 3,* 52–59.

Sovner, R. (1983). Anorgasmia associated with imipramine but not desipramine: Case report. *Journal of Clinical Psychiatry, 44,* 345–346.

Spark, R., & Melby, J. (1968). Aldosterone in hypertension—the spironolactone response test. *Annals of Internal Medicine, 69,* 685–691.

Spiess, W. F. J., Geer, J. H., & O'Donohue, W. T. (1984). Premature ejaculation: Investigation of factors in ejaculatory latency. *Journal of Abnormal Psychology, 93,* 242–245.

Stearns, E. L., Winter, J. S. D., & Faiman, C. (1973). Effects of coitus on gonadotropin, prolactin and sex steroid levels in man. *Journal of Clinical Endocrinology and Metabolism, 37,* 687–691.

Steele, D. G., & Walker, C. E. (1974). Male and female differences in reaction to erotic stimuli as related to sexual adjustment. *Archives of Sexual Behavior, 3,* 459–471.

Stein, R. A. (1977). The effect of exercise training on heart rate during coitus in the post myocardial infarction patient. *Circulation, 55,* 738–740.

Steinman, D. L., Wincze, J. P., Sakheim, D. K., Barlow, D. H., & Mavissakaliam, M. (1981). A comparison of male and female patterns of sexual arousal. *Archives of Sexual Behavior, 10,* 529–547.

Stern, R. M., Ray, W. J., & Davis, C. M. (1980). *Psychophysiological recording.* New York: Oxford University Press.

Stock, W. S. (1983, August). *The effects of violent pornography on women.* Paper presented at the annual convention of the American Psychological Association, Washington, DC.

Stock, W. S., & Geer, J. H. (1982). A study of fantasy-based sexual arousal in women. *Archives of Sexual Behavior, 11,* 33–47.

Strassberg, D. S., Kelley, M. P., Carroll, C., & Kircher, J. C. (1985, August). *The psychophysiological nature of premature ejaculation.* Paper present at the annual convention of the American Psychological Association, Los Angeles.

Studd, J., Chakravarti, S., & Oram, D. (1977). The climacteric. *Clinics in Obstetrics and Gynaecology, 4,* 3–29.

Sullivan, M. J. L., & Brender, W. (1986). Facial electromyography: A measure of affective processes during sexual arousal. *Psychophysiology, 23,* 182–188.

Suppe, F. (1984). Classifying sexual disorders: The *Diagnostic and Statistical Manual* of the American Psychiatric Association. *Journal of Homosexuality, 9,* 9–28.

Svare, B., Bartke, A., Doherty, P., Mason, I., Michael, S. D., & Smith, M. S. (1979). Hyperprolactinaemia suppresses copulatory behavior in male rats and mice. *Biology of Reproduction, 21,* 529–535.

Swartzman, L. A. (1986). *The impact of stress on climacteric hot flashes.* Unpublished doctoral dissertation, Rutgers University.

Szasz, T. (1980). *Sex by prescription.* Harmondsworth, England: Penguin Books.

REFERENCES

Tanner, B. A. (1973). Shock intensity and fear of shock in the modification of homosexual behaviour in males by avoidance learning. *Behaviour Research and Therapy, 11*, 213–218.

Tart, C. T. (1971). *On being stoned: A psychological study of intoxication.* Palo Alto, CA: Science & Behavior Books.

Tessman, I. (1979). [Letter to the editor]. *New England Journal of Medicine, 300,* 626.

Toone, B. K., Wheeler, M., & Fenwick, P. B. C. (1980). Sex hormone changes in male epileptics. *Clinical Endocrinology, 12,* 391–395.

Tsitouras, P. D., Martin, C. E., & Harman, S. M. (1984). Sexual activity in healthy elderly men. *Journal of Gerontology, 37,* 288–293.

Tucker, D. M. (1983). Asymmetries of coherence topography: Structural and dynamic aspects of brain lateralization. In P. Flor-Henry & J. Gruzelier (Eds.), *Laterality and psychopathology* (pp. 218–231). Amsterdam: Elsevier.

Tucker, D. M., & Dawson, S. L. (1984). Asymmetric EEG changes as Method actors generated emotions. *Biological Psychology, 19,* 63–75.

Tucker, D. M., Stenslie, C. E., Roth, R. S., & Shearer, S. C. (1981). Right frontal lobe activation and right hemisphere performance decrement during a depressed mood. *Archives of General Psychiatry, 38,* 169–174.

Tulloch, A., Keogh, E., Csillag, E., Dunn, J., Brown, D, & Morlet, A. (1982). Impotence—the team approach to investigation and surgical treatment. *British Journal of Urology, 54,* 755–758.

Turner, C. D., & Bagnara, J. T. (1971). *General endocrinology* (5th ed.). Philadelphia: W. B. Saunders.

Tyrer, P. (1976). *The role of bodily feelings in anxiety.* London: Oxford University Press.

Udry, J. R., & Morris, N. M. (1968). Distribution of coitus in the menstrual cycle. *Nature, 220,* 593–596.

Valins, S. (1966). Cognitive effects of false heart-rate feedback. *Journal of Personality and Social Psychology, 4,* 400–408.

Van Arsdalen, K. N., Malloy, T. R., & Wein, A. J. (1983). Erectile physiology dysfunction and evaluation. *Monographs in Urology, 4,* 137–156.

Vance, E. B., & Wagner, N.W. (1976). Written descriptions of orgasm: A study of sex differences. *Archives of Sexual Behavior, 5,* 87–98.

Van de Velde, T. (1926). *Ideal marriage.* New York: Random House.

Van Thiel, D. H., Gavaler, J. S., Smith, W. I., & Paul, G. (1979). Hypothalamic–pituitary–gonadal dysfunction in men using cimetidine. *New England Journal of Medicine, 300,* 1012–1015.

Venables, P. H., & Christie, M. J. (1980). Electrodermal activity. In I. Martin & P. H. Venables (Eds.), *Techniques in psychophysiology* (pp. 3–67). New York: Wiley.

Vermeulen, A. (1980). Sex hormone status of postmenopausal women. *Maturitas, 2,* 81–89.

Vermeulen, A., & Verdonck, L. (1976). Plasma androgen levels during the menstrual cycle. *American Journal of Obstetrics and Gynecology, 125,* 491–494.

Veterans Administration Cooperative Study Group on Antihypertensive Agents. (1982). Comparison of propranolol and hydrochlorthiazide for the initial treatment of hypertension. *Journal of the American Medical Assoication, 248,* 2004–2011.

Virag, R., & Virag, H. (1983). L'épreuve à la papaverine intracaverneuse dans l'étude de l'impuissance: Perspectives therapeutiques. *Journal des Maladies Vasculaires, 8,* 293–295.

Wagner, G. (1981a). Erection: Physiology and endocrinology. In G. Wagner & R. Green (Eds.), *Impotence: Physiological, psychological, surgical diagnoses and treatement* (pp. 25–36). New York: Plenum Press.

Wagner, G. (1981b). Methods for differential diagnosis of psychogenic and organic erectile failure. In G. Wagner & R. Green (Eds.), *Impotence: Physiological, psychological, surgical diagnoses and treatment* (pp. 89–130). New York: Plenum Press.

Wagner, G., & Brindley, G. (1980). The effect of atropine and blocker on human penile erection. In A. Zorguiotti (Ed.), *First International Conference on Vascular Impotence* (pp. 82–97). Springfield, IL: Charles C Thomas.

Wagner, G., Hilsted, J., & Jensen, S. B. (1981). Diabetes mellitus and erectile failure. In G. Wagner & R. Green (Eds.), *Impotence: Physiological, psychological, surgical diagnoses and treatment* (pp. 51–62). New York: Plenum Press.

Wagner, G., & Levin, R. J. (1978a). Oxygen tension of the vaginal surface during sexual stimulation in the human. *Fertility and Sterility, 30,* 50–53.

Wagner, G., & Levin, R. J. (1978b). Vaginal fluid. In E. S. E. Hafez & T. N. Evans (Eds.), *The human vagina* (pp. 121–137). Amsterdam: Elsevier/North-Holland.

Wagner, G., & Levin, R. J. (1980). Effect of atropine and methylatorpine on human vaginal blood flow, sexual arousal and climax. *Acta Pharmacologica et Toxicologica, 46,*321–325.

Wagner, G., & Ottesen, B. (1980). Vaginal blood flow during sexual stimulation. *Obstetrics and Gynecology, 56,* 621–624.

Ware, J. C., Karacan, I., Salis, P. J., Thornby, J., & Hirshkowitz, M. (1984). Sleep-related electrodermal activity patterns in impotent patients. *Sleep, 7,* 247–254.

Wartman, S. A. (1983). Sexual side effects of antihypertensive drugs: Treatment strategies and strictures. *Anthihypertensive Drugs, 73,* 133–138.

Wasserman, M. D., Pollack, C. P., Spielman, A. J., & Weitzman, E. D. (1980a). The differential diagnosis of impotence: The measurement of nocturnal penile tumescence. *Journal of the American Medical Association, 243,* 2038–2042.

Wasserman, M. D., Pollack, C. P., Speilman, A. J., & Weitzman, E. D. (1980b). Theoretical and technical problems in the measurement of nocturnal penile tumescence for the differential diagnosis of impotence. *Psychosomatic Medicine, 42,* 575–585.

Watson, J. B. (1929). Introduction. In G. V. Hamilton & K. MacGowan (Eds.), *What is wrong with marriage.* New York: Albert & Charles Boni.

Webster, J. S., & Hammer, D. (1983). Thermistor measurement of male sexual arousal. *Psychophysiology, 20,* 111–115.

Wein, A. J., Fishkin, R., Carpiniello, V. L., & Malloy, T. R. (1981). Expansion without significant rigidity during nocturnal penile tumescence testing: A potential source of misinterpretation. *Journal of Urology, 126,* 343–344.

Weinman, J. (1967). Photoplethysmography. In P. Venables & I. Martin (Eds.), *A manual of psychophysiological methods* (pp. 283–306). New York: Wiley.

Weiss, H. D. (1972). The physiology of human erection. *Annals of Internal Medicine, 76,* 793–799.

Wenger, M. A. (1966). Studies of autonomic balance: A summary. *Psychophysiology, 2,* 173–186.

Wenger, M. A. (1972). Autonomic balance. In N. S. Greenfield & R. A. Sternbach (Eds.), *Handbook of psychophysiology* (pp. 535–570). New York: Holt, Rinehart & Winston.

Wenger, M. A., Averill, J. R., & Smith, D. D. (1968). Autonomic activity during sexual arousal. *Psychophysiology, 4,* 468–478.

Whalen, R. E. (1966). Sexual motivation. *Psychological Review, 73,* 151–163.

Whalen, R. E. (1976). Brain mechanisms controlling sexual behavior. In F. A. Beach (Ed.), *Human sexuality in four perspectives* (pp. 68–87). Baltimore: Johns Hopkins University Press.

Whalley, L. J. (1978). Sexual adjustment of male alcoholics. *Acta Psychiatrica Scandinavica, 58,* 281–298.

Wheeler, D., & Rubin, H. B. (1987). A comparison of volumetric and circumferential measures of penile erection. *Archives of Sexual Behavior, 16,* 289–300.

Whitman, W. P., & Quinsey, V. L. (1981). Heterosocial skills training for institutionalized rapists and child molesters. *Canadian Journal of Behavioural Science, 13,* 105–114.

393

REFERENCES

Williams, W. (1985). Anaesthetic ejaculation. *Journal of Sex and Marital Therapy, 11,* 19–29.

Wilsnack, S. C. (1980). Alcohol, sexuality, and reproductive dysfunction in women. In E. L. Abel (Ed.), *Fetal alcohol syndrome: Vol. 2. Human studies.* Boca Raton, FL: CRC press.

Wilson, C. (1981). *The quest for Wilhelm Reich: A critical biography.* New York: Anchor Press.

Wilson, G. T. (1981). The effects of alcohol on human sexual behavior. *Advances in Substance Abuse, 2,* 1–40.

Wilson, G. T., & Lawson, D. M. (1976a). Effect of alcohol on sexual arousal in women. *Journal of Abnormal Psychology, 85,* 489–497.

Wilson, G. T., & Lawson, D. M. (1976b). Expectancies, alcohol, and sexual arousal in male social drinkers. *Journal of Abnormal Psychology, 85,* 587–594.

Wilson, G. T., & Lawson, D. M. (1978). Expectancies, alcohol, and sexual arousal in women. *Journal of Abnormal Psychology, 87,* 358–367.

Wilson, G. T., Niaura, R. S., & Adler, J. A. (1985). Alcohol, selective attention and sexual arousal in men. *Journal of Studies on Alcohol, 46,* 107–115.

Wincze, J. P., Bansal, S., Balko, A., & Malhotra, C. (1984). *The relationship between genital response to erotic stimulation and nocturnal penile tumescence in normal males, psychologically impotent males, and organically impotent males.* Paper presented at the annual meeting of the International Academy of Sex Research, Cambridge, England.

Wincze, J. P., Bansal, S., & Malamud, M. (1986). The effects of medroxyprogesterone acetate on subjective arousal, arousal to erotic stimulation and nocturnal penile tumescence in male sex offenders. *Archives of Sexual Behavior, 15,* 293–305.

Wincze, J. P., Hoon, E. F., & Hoon, P. W. (1976). Physiological responsivity of normal and sexually dysfunctional women during erotic stimulus exposure. *Journal of Psychosomatic Research, 20,* 445–451.

Wincze, J. P., Hoon, E. F., & Hoon, P. W. (1978). Multiple measure analysis of women experiencing low sexual arousal. *Behaviour Research and Therapy, 16,* 43–49.

Wincze, J. P., Hoon, P. W., & Hoon, E. F. (1977). Sexual arousal in women: A comparison of cognitive and physiological responses by continuous measurement. *Archives of Sexual Behavior, 6,* 121–133.

Wincze, J. P., Venditti, E., Barlow, D. H., & Mavissakalian, M. (1980). The effects of a subjective monitoring task in the physiological measure of genital response to erotic stimulation. *Archives of Sexual Behavior, 9,* 533–545.

Wishnoff, R. (1978). Modeling effects of explicit and nonexplicit sexual stimuli on the sexual anxiety and behavior of women. *Archives of Sexual Behavior, 7,* 455–461.

Wolchik, S. A., Beggs, V., Wincze, J. P., Sakheim, D. K., Barlow, D. H., & Mavissakalian, M. (1980). The effects of emotional arousal on subsequent sexual arousal in men. *Journal of Abnormal Psychology, 89,* 595–598.

Wolchik, S. A., Braver, S. L., & Jensen, K. (1985). Volunteer bias in erotica research: Effects of intrusiveness of measure and sexual background. *Archives of Sexual Behavior, 14,* 93–107.

Wolchik, S. A., Spencer, S. L., & Lisi, I. S. (1983). Volunteer bias in research employing vaginal measures of sexual arousal. Demographic, sexual, and personality characteristics. *Archives of Sexual Behavior, 12,* 399–408.

Wolfe, L. (1981). *The Cosmo report.* New York: Arbor House.

Wolpe, J. (1958). *Psychotherapy by reciprocal inhibition.* Stanford, CA: Stanford University Press.

Wolpe, J. (1960). Reciprocal inhibition as the main basis of psychotherapeutic effects. In H. J. Eysenck (Ed.), *Behavior therapy and the neuroses* (pp. 88–113). Oxford: Pergamon Press.

Wolpe, J. (1978). Comments on "A test of reciprocal inhibition" by Hoon, Wincze, and Hoon. *Journal of Abnormal Psychology, 87,* 452–454.

Wood, D. M., & Obrist, P. A. (1968). Minimal and maximal sensory intake and exercise as unconditioned stimuli in human heart-rate conditioning. *Journal of Experimental Psychology, 76,* 254–262.

Wydra, A., Marshall, W. L., Earls, C. M., & Barbaree, H. E. (1983). Identification of cues and control of sexual arousal by rapists. *Behaviour Research and Therapy, 21,* 469–476.

Young, W. C. (1961). The hormones and mating behavior. In W. C. Young (Ed.), *Sex and internal secretions* (Vol. 2, pp. 1173–1239). Baltimore: Williams & Wilkins.

Zilbergeld, B. (1978). *Male sexuality.* Boston: Little, Brown.

Zilbergeld, B., & Ellison, C. R. (1980). Desire discrepancies and arousal problems in sex therapy. In S. R. Leiblum & L. A. Pervin (Eds.), *Principles and practice of sex therapy* (pp. 65–101). New York: Guilford Press.

Zilbergeld, B., & Evans, M. (1980, June). The inadequacy of Masters and Johnson. *Psychology Today,* pp. 28–43.

Zillmann, D. (1978). Attribution and misattribution of excitatory reactions. In J. H. Harvey, W. J. Ickes, & R. F. Kidd (Eds.), *New directions in attribution research* (Vol. 2, pp. 335–368). Hillsdale, NJ: Erlbaum.

Zillmann, D. (1986). Coition as emotion. In D. Byrne & K. Kelley (Eds.), *Alternative approaches to the study of sexual behavior* (pp. 173–199). Hillsdale, NJ: Erlbaum.

Zillmann, D., & Bryant, J. (1984). Effects of massive exposure to pornography. In N. M. Malamuth & E. Donnerstein (Eds.), *Pornography and sexual aggression* (pp. 115–138). New York: Academic Press.

Zillmann, D., Bryant, J., Comisky, P. W., & Medoff, N. J. (1981). Excitation and hedonic valence in the effect of erotica on motivated inter-male aggression. *European Journal of Social Psychology, 11,* 233–252.

Zimmerman, P. W., & Zimmerman, S. (1979). Effects of cannabinoids on sperm morphology. *Pharmacology, 18,* 143–148.

Zingheim, P., & Sandman, C. (1978). Discriminative control of the vaginal vasomotor response. *Biofeedback and Self-Regulation, 3,* 29–41.

Zorgniotti, A. W., & Lefleur, R. S. (1985). Auto-injection of the corpus cavernosum with a vasoactive drug combination for vasculogenic impotence. *Journal of Urology, 133,* 39–41.

Zuckerman, M. (1971). Physiological measures of sexual arousal in the human. *Psychological Bulletin, 75,* 297–329.

Zuckerman, M., Neeb, M., Ficher, M., Fishkin, R. E., Goldman, A., Fink, P. J., Cohen, S. W., Jacobs, J. A., & Weisberg, M. (1985). Nocturnal penile tumescence and penile responses in the waking state in diabetic and nondiabetic sexual dysfunctionals. *Archives of Sexual Behavior, 14,* 109–129.

Index

Acetylcholine, 100, 259
Adrenal cortex, 159
Age/aging, 168, 171–174, 276
Aggressive behavior
    alcohol and, 310, 311
    pornography and, 204–206, 208, 209
AIDS, 317, 342, 343
Alcohol and paraphilias, 218, 219
Alcohol effects on sexual function, 300,
        311, 317, 327
    acute effects, 301–308
    aggression, 310, 311
    chronic effects, 308–310
    men, 301–306, 309–311
    task complexity, 304, 305
    women, 306–309
Aldosterone, 114
Alpha-adrenergic system, 145, 318–320
Alpha-methyldopa (Aldomet), 320
Altered consciousness, orgasm, 152, 153,
        156
Amphetamines, 315, 316
Amyl nitrite, 315–317
Anal contractions, orgasm, 150
Anal intercourse, 57
Anatomy. See Genital anatomy entries
Androphilia, 227
Androstenedione, 175
Anorgasmia. See Sexual dysfunction,
        female
Antiandrogens, 241, 242
Antidepressants, 322–324
Antidiuretic hormone, 114
Antihypertensives, 259, 318–322
Antipsychotics, 322–324
Anxiety, 15, 16, 36, 37, 45, 263–265, 268,
        269, 272, 286–288, 295

Aphrodisiacs, 299, 313, 327
Artificial coition machine, 14
Atenolol, 320, 321
Atropine, 59
Attention and sexual dysfunction
    female, 289–290
    male, 265–269, 272
Aversive conditioning, 234–236

Bancroft, J. H., 33, 34
Barbiturates, 315
Barlow, D. H., 36, 37, 45, 65, 66, 68, 69,
        77, 216, 223, 243
Bartholin glands, anatomy, 81, 86
Behavioral psychology, 14–17
Bendrofluazide, 321
Berthold, A. A., 160
Beta-adrenergic system, 151, 318–321, 327
Beta-endorphin, 171
Biofeedback
    paraphilias, 237, 238
    sexual dysfunction
        female, 294, 295
        male, 269, 270
Bipolar hypothesis, male orgasm, 145, 146
Blood flow measurement, penis, 53–77
    photoplethysmography, 70–72
    strain gauge (circumference) measures,
            63–72, 77
        electromechanical (Barlow), 65, 66, 68,
            69, 77
        mercury-in-rubber, 61, 63–65, 68–70,
            76, 223, 225
        and penile rigidity, 67–68, 77
    and subjective arousal, 72–75
    thermistor, 69, 70

volumetric compared with circumference measures, 68, 69
volumetric plethysmography, 61–63, 68, 76
see also Penis *entries*
Blood flow, vagina. *See* Vaginal vasocongestion, measures
Blood pressure and sexual arousal, 119, 120, 132, 151
Breast, thermal measures, 123
Bromocryptine, 174
Bupropion, 324
Butyrophenones, 322, 323
Byrne, D., 34–36

Cannon, W. B., 24
Canterbury Tales, The (Chaucer), 306
Cardiovascular changes
in arousal, 116–121, 132
orgasm, 11, 12, 151, 152, 157
Case study method, 5–7
Central nervous system
in arousal, 33, 34, 127–131, 133
brain stimulation, monkeys, 24, 25
and subjective changes, orgasm, 152–157
Cervix, anatomy, 82
Chaucer, Geoffrey, 306
Childhood sexual trauma, 279, 342
Child molesters. *See* Pedophiles/pedophilia
Chlorpromazine, 149
Cimetidine, 324, 325
Clitoris, 81, 86, 88, 89; *see also* Orgasm, female
Clomipramine, 324
Cocaine, 300, 315–317
Cognitive lever and penile blood flow measurement, 73, 74, 77
Cognitive/subjective elements
erectile dysfunction, 256
future research directions, 334, 335
sexual response patterns, 26–29
extragenital stereotypy, 110
see also Subjective *entries*
Conditioning, paraphilias, 217, 218
Confidentiality, 347, 349
Context, violent pornography, 206
Contingent negative variation, 128, 129
Coolidge, Calvin, 46
Coolidge effect, 46–48
Covert sensitization, 236, 237
Cowper glands, anatomy, 54, 57, 81
Cyproterone acetate, 161, 163, 241, 243

Deception/debriefing, ethics, 351, 352
Dehydroepiandrosterone, 175
Desipramine, 324
Detumescence. *See under* Erection, penile (tumescence)
Developmental periods, critical, future research, 336
Deviance, normal, 214; *see also* Paraphilias *entries*
Diabetes, 168–171, 173, 249, 256, 258
Dickinson, Robert Latou, 10, 11
Distraction and sexual dysfunction
female, 288, 289
male, 261–263, 268, 269, 272
Diuretics, 319, 321, 322
L-Dopa, 325, 326
Dopamine, 174
Drug effects on sexual response, 299–326
amphetamines, 315, 316
amyl nitrite, 315–317
antidepressants, 322–324
antihypertensives, 318–322
antipsychotics, 322–324
barbiturates, 315
cocaine, 300, 315–317
L-dopa, 325, 326
epilepsy drugs, 324, 325
heroin, 315, 317
historical background, 299, 300
LSD, 315
marihuana, 300, 312–316
methylqualone (Quaalude), 315–317
setting, 300
ulcer drugs, 324, 325
see also Alcohol *entries*; specific drugs
Drug use and paraphilias, 219
DSM-II, 245
DSM-III, 42, 212, 214, 215, 245, 259, 276, 285, 337, 338
Dual innervation model, penile erection, 58, 59, 76
Dyspareunia, 284, 285

Ecological validity, laboratory research, 353, 354
EEG, 12, 19, 30, 32
and arousal, 127–131, 133
contingent negative variation, 128, 129
orgasm, 153–155
penis, erectile dysfunction, 129, 130, 246, 247, 252, 253, 271
and sexual dysfunction, female, 286

Ejaculation, female, 78, 84, 140, 141, 355
Ejaculation, male
  premature, 246, 257, 258, 271
  retarded, 258, 259
  see also Orgasm, male
Ejaculatory inevitability, 137, 138, 144, 145
EKG, 155, 251
Electrodermal measures of arousal,
    111–114, 132
Electromechanical (Barlow) blood flow
    measurement, penis, 65, 66, 68, 69,
    77
Ellis, Havelock, 3, 5, 7, 8, 38, 39, 43, 343
EMG, 21, 185
  and arousal, 125–127, 133
  orgasm, 150, 151, 155
  penis, erectile dysfunction, 247, 251–253
Endocrine factors in sexual
    psychophysiology, 158–186
  FSH, 159, 172, 175, 178, 184, 185
  GnRH, 161, 171
  hormone, defined, 158, 159
  hypogonadal men, 160–165, 168, 172,
    174
  LH, 159, 161, 172, 175, 178, 184, 185
  men, differential diagnosis, 168–174
  menopause, 178–183
  menstrual cycle, 195, 174–178
  progesterone, 159, 175, 177, 184
  sexual response, hormonal, 183–186
  see also Estrogens; Hormone
    replacement therapy; Testosterone
EOG, penis erectile dysfunction, 247, 251,
    253
Epilepsy drugs, 324, 325
Erection, penile (tumescence)
  blood flow measurement, 57–61
  and detumescence, 8, 38, 60, 136
  EEG, 129, 130
  paraphilias, 221–230
  physiology of, 57–61
  reflex compared with psychogenic, 166
  see also Penis entries
Erectometer, 253
Erotica, 189–204, 210, 211
  historical background, 189, 190
  individual differences, 199, 200
  laboratory studies, 190–192
  male–female patterns of arousal,
    192–199, 210
  repeated exposure, 200–204
  see also Pornography entries

Erotophobia–erotophilia affective response
    variable (Byrne), 36, 199
Estrogens, 159, 166
  estradiol, 175, 177, 178, 180, 182, 184
  estriol, 175
  estrone, 175, 179
  in menopause, 178–183
  in menstrual cycle, 175–178
Ethics, 20, 242; see also Human subjects
    research
Evolution, hormonal response, 184
Excitation transfer, 28
Excitement (Masters and Johnson), 39–43
Exhibitionism, 213, 214, 216, 222, 226, 227,
    235–238, 243
Extragenital measures of arousal, 110–131
  asymmetry, 126, 127, 131, 133
  cardiovascular changes, 116–121, 132
  components, 108, 109
  electrodermal, 111–114, 132
  pupils, 114–116, 132, 232, 233
  respiration measures, 124, 132, 133
  statistical analysis, 131
  thermal measures, 121–123, 131, 132
  see also EEG; EMG
Extragenital response patterning,
    stereotypy role, 109, 110, 130

Faked response, 153, 213, 218, 228–230,
    243, 354, 355
Fallopian tubes, anatomy, 83
Fantasy
  blood flow measurement, penis, 75
  sexual dysfunction, female, 292, 293
  testosterone, 163, 164
  vaginal vasocongestion, 105, 106
Fantasy training, females, 294, 295
Fatigue and response to erotica, 202
Female sexuality
  Ellis, 7, 8
  Freud, 6, 102
  Kinsey, 9, 10, 12
  Masters and Johnson, 39, 41
  masturbation, role in development, 10
Feminists on violent pornography, 204
Fetishism, 213, 214, 223, 234
Follicle-stimulating hormone (FSH), 159,
    172, 175, 178, 184, 185, 315
Freud, Sigmund, 3, 6, 7, 102
"Frigidity," 275
Future research directions, 331–344
  arousal response patterns, 334–337

clinical issues, 341–343
measurement issues, 339–341
response cycle, models, 337–339
social/ethical concerns, 343, 344

Galvanic skin response (GSR), 191,
231–233
Genital anatomy
female, 79–83
male, 54–57
Glass observation tube, vagina, 10, 13
Gonadotropin-releasing hormone (GnRH),
161, 171
G (Grafenberg) spot, 83, 84, 107, 140, 141,
355
Guanethidine, 319
Guilt
and female sexual dysfunction, 290, 291
Mosher scale, 291
and vaginal vasocongestion, 105, 106
and violent pornography, 205, 206, 208

Habituation, 47–50, 201–204
Haight–Ashbury Free Medical Clinic, 313,
316, 317
Haloperidol (Haldol), 323
Heart rate 117–120, 132, 191, 192
Hebephilia, 227
Hemispheric laterality, 153, 154
Heroin, 315, 317
Herpes, 342
Hippocrates, 244
Historical background, 3–22
behavioral psychology, 14–17
case study method, 5–7
erotica, 189, 190
laboratory physiology, 10–14
measurement technology, 17–19
normative survey research, 7–10
paraphilias, 213, 214
sexual response patterns, 24, 25
social context, 19–21
vaginal vasocongestion, 88, 89
Homosexuality/homosexuals, 214, 222, 226,
231, 239, 240
amyl nitrite use, 317
aversive conditioning, 235
behavioral modification, 15
biofeedback, 237, 238
covert sensitization, 236
ego-syntonic compared with -dystonic,
212

Ellis, 8
pedophilia, 232
removal of deviant label, 212, 213
Hormone replacement therapy, 160–163,
180, 182, 183, 185, 277
Horses, 17, 18
Human Sex Anatomy (Dickinson), 10, 11
Human Sexual Inadequacy (Masters and
Johnson), 260, 275
Human Sexual Response (Masters and
Johnson), 13
Human subjects research, 20, 345–355
deception/debriefing, 351, 352
ethics, 20
laboratory construction, 345–347
procedural concerns, 349–354
protection, 347–349
response faking, 354, 355
subject selection/bias, 350, 351
Hyperprolactinemia, male, 168, 173, 174
Hypogonadal men, 160–165, 168, 172, 174

Ideal Marriage (Van de Velde), 11
Imipramine, 323
Impotence, 16
Incest, 227, 279
Individual-specific response (ISR), 32, 51,
111, 119, 335–337, 339
Informed consent, 347–349
Inhibited sexual desire
female, 285, 286
male, 259, 260, 272
Instrumental conditioning, 48, 50
Insulin, 168, 169

James, William, 24, 25
Johnson, Virginia, 13, 14, 25, 50; see also
Masters and Johnson
Jong, Erica, 29

Kama Sutra, 189
Kaplan, Helen Singer, 6, 7, 337, 338
Kegel exercises, 296
Kinsey, Alfred, 8, 9, 12, 13, 19, 25, 343,
345
on erotica, 192–194, 197, 210
Krafft-Ebing, Richard von, 3, 5, 6, 7

Labia, anatomy, 79
Laboratory studies
erectile dysfunction, 262–269
erotica, responses to, 190–192

Laboratory studies (*Continued*)
  historical background, 10–14
  limitations in, orgasm, 135
  sexual dysfunction, female, 286–293
  sexual response cycle, future research, 338, 339
  see also Human subjects research
Lady Chatterley's Lover (Lawrence), 54, 152
Lange, C., 24
Lawrence, D. H., 54, 152
Levin–Wagner heat probe, 277, 283
Libido, Kaplan on, 42
LSD, 315
Luteinizing hormone, 159, 161, 172, 175, 178, 184, 185, 315, 325
  releasing hormone (LHRH), 325

Marihuana, 300, 312–316
Married compared with unmarried women, sexual dysfunction, 292
Masochism, 214, 234
Masters, William, 13, 14, 25, 50; *see also* Masters and Johnson
Masters and Johnson, 13, 260, 275, 337, 338
  artificial coition machine, 14
  extragenital response patterning, stereotypy role, 109
  female sexuality, 39, 41, 275, 286
  orgasm, 137, 138, 144, 148, 156, 157
Masturbation, 5, 7
  experience, and response to erotica, 200
  women, 8, 10, 11, 280, 281
Masturbatory conditioning, 239
Masturbatory satiation, 237
Measurement technology
  future research directions, 339–341
  historical background, 17–19
Medroxyprogesterone acetate, 161, 241–243
Men
  alcohol effects on sexual function, 301–306, 309–311
  hormone-related conditions, diagnosis, 168–174
  paraphilias as male disorders, 215
  see also Orgasm, male; Penis *entries*; Sexual dysfunction, male
Menopause, 178–183
Menstrual cycle, 94, 174–178, 195, 315
Mercury-in-rubber strain gauge. *See* Blood flow measurement, penis

Methylatropine, 100
Methylqualone (Quaalude), 315–317
Miller, Henry, 202
Monoamine oxidase inhibitors, 323, 324
Mons veneris, anatomy, 79
Morgan, Robin, 204
Mosher scale, sex guilt, 291
Motivation-specific response (MSR), 30, 111
Multiple orgasm
  female, 137, 139, 141, 142, 145, 148
  male, 147
Muscle tension in arousal, 125–127, 133;
    see also EMG
My Life and Loves (Harris), 189

Negative arousal states, 220
Nocturnal penile tumescence (NPT), 45, 46, 64, 67, 68, 97, 126, 130
  alcohol effects, 309
  antiandrogens, 242, 243
  and antihypertensives, 320
  diabetes, 169, 170
  erectile dysfunction, 247–256, 270, 271
  institutionalized rapists, 219
  ranitidine, 325, 326
  testosterone, 163–166
Norepinephrine, 259
Normal deviance, 214
Normative survey research, 7–10
Novelty and erotica, 203, 204

Orgasm, 27, 134–157, 317
  cardiovascular/respiratory changes, 11, 12, 151, 152, 157
  central versus peripheral models, 135–137
  CNS/subjective changes, 152–157
  hyperventilation, 124
  laboratory studies, limitations in, 135
  male–female patterns, 137, 138, 156, 157
    Masters and Johnson, 137, 138, 156, 157
    orgasmic inevitability, 137, 138
    pelvic muscle contractions, 128
    refractory period, 138, 144, 147, 148
  Masters and Johnson model, 39–43
  phantom, paraplegics, 110, 147
  simultaneous, 134
  triggers, 148–151, 157
Orgasm, female, 139–143, 157
  alcohol effects, 307
  dysfunction, 280–284, 294, 295

ejaculation, 78, 84, 140, 141, 355
  multiple/sequential, 100, 101, 137, 139, 141, 142, 145, 148
  pelvic muscles, 84, 86, 87, 101, 102
  photoplethysmography, vaginal vasocongestion, 92, 93, 96
  pre-ejaculatory (nonterminative) compared with postejaculatory (terminative), 139
  vaginal–clitoral distinction, 6, 41
  vulval compared with uterine and blended, 101, 102, 139–141
Orgasmic inevitability, 137, 138, 144, 145
Orgasm, male, 144–148, 157
  alcohol effects, 305
  alpha-adrenergic system, 145
  bipolar hypothesis, 145, 146
  ejaculatory inevitability, 144, 145
  Masters and Johnson, 144, 148
  multiple, 147
  pelvic muscle contractions, 146, 147
  refractory pattern, 144, 147, 148
Ovaries, 83, 159, 161, 162
Oxytocin, 159, 185

Paraphilias (sexual deviation), 212–221
  defining, 213–217
  etiology/causal factors, 217–221
  nosology, 214, 215
  rape, 213, 214, 216, 218, 219, 233, 240, 242
  compared with sexual variation, 213
  treatment
    antiandrogens, 241, 242
    psychophysiologic, 233–241
  see also specific types
Paraphilias, laboratory assessment, 221–233
  erection, 221–230
  exhibitionists, 222, 226, 227
  incest, 227
  nongenital measures, 230–233
  pedophiles, 222, 223, 227–229, 232
  rape, 223–226, 229–231
Paraplegics, phantom orgasm, 110, 147
Parkinson disease, 325, 326
Pearl, The, 189
Pedophiles/pedophilia, 213–216, 218–220, 222, 223, 227–229, 232, 233, 235, 238–242
Pelvic (PC) muscles
  contractions and orgasm, 128, 148–150
  EMG, 125, 126

Kegel exercises, 296
  male, 146, 147
Penis, anatomy, 54–56; see also Blood flow measurement, penis; Erection, penile (tumescence); Nocturnal penile tumescence (NPT)
Penis, erectile dysfunction, 245–257, 262–269
  cognitive–affective assessment, 256
  definition, 245–247
  incidence, 245
  laboratory studies, 262–269
  NPT, 247–256, 270, 271
  primary compared with secondary, 245, 246
  psychogenic compared with organic, 247–252, 255
  treatment, 269–271
  waking assessment, 255–257
  see also Sexual dysfunction, male
Perineal muscles, penile erection, 58
Perineum, anatomy, 81
Peripheral arousal, 33, 34
Perspiration and sexual arousal, 111
Peyronie disease, 249, 250
Phantom orgasm, paraplegics, 110, 147
Phenobarbital, 324, 325
Phenothiazines, 259, 322, 323
Photoplethysmography
  penis, 70–72; see also Plethysmography, volumetric, penis
  vagina, 71, 89–95, 103
    AC versus DC signal, 90, 92, 94–96
pH shift, female arousal, 85, 88
Pindolol, 320, 321
Pituitary, anterior, 159, 175
Plateau (Masters and Johnson), 39–42
Plethysmography, volumetric, penis, 61–63, 68, 76, 222; see also Photoplethysmography
Polsters (von Ebner pads), 57, 58, 60, 86
Pornography, 344, 354; see also Erotica
Pornography, violent, 190, 204–211
  aggressive behavior following, 204–206, 208, 209
  context, 206
  feminist view of, 204
  guilt and disgust, 205, 206, 208
  rape, 204, 206–209
  victim response and arousal, 206
Preorgasmic women, 280
Priapism, 60
Primodone, 325

Progesterone, 159, 175, 177, 184
Progestin, 175, 177
Prolactin, 322, 323; *see also*
 Hyperprolactinemia, male
Propranolol, 151, 320, 321
Prostate, anatomy, 54, 57
Prostatic acid phosphatase, 84
Psychopathia Sexualis (Krafft-Ebing), 3
Pupillary response, 114–116, 132
 paraphilias, 232, 233

Ranitidine, 324–326
Rape, 213, 214, 216, 218, 219, 233, 240,
 242, 343
 compulsive, 214
 female sexual dysfunction, 278, 279
 laboratory assessment, 223–226, 229–231
 in pornography, 204, 206–209
 social and ethical concerns, 343
Reflex, stretch, orgasm, 149
Refractory period, 138, 144, 147, 148
Reich, Wilhelm, 134
Research. *See* Future research directions
Reserpine, 319
Resolution (Masters and Johnson), 39, 40
Respiration in arousal, 124, 132, 133
 and orgasm, 151, 152, 157
Response faking, 153, 213, 218, 228–230,
 243, 354, 355
Response patterning. *See* Sexual response
 patterns
Rubin, Harris, 20, 345

Sadism, sexual, 214, 234
Scrotum, anatomy, 54, 56, 57
Seduction theory, 6
Seminal vesicles, anatomy, 54, 57
Sensory loss and orgasm, 152, 153, 156
Sex flush, 121
Sexual abuse, future research, 342
Sexual aging, male, 168, 171–174
Sexual appetite/drive, 33
Sexual arousal, 109
 and anxiety. *See* Anxiety
 deviant, 215–217
 Barlow model, 216, 243
 extragenital components, 108, 109; *see
  also* Extragenital *entries*
 future research directions, 334–337
 in menopause, 179–182
 in menstrual cycle, 176–178

and orgasmic dysfunction, 283, 284
paraphilias, increasing nondeviant
 arousal, 239–241
SAM–IEM (Beach's two-stage model),
 38, 39
Sexual deviation. *See* Paraphilias *entries*
Sexual dualism, 109
Sexual dysfunction
 anxiety, Barlow's model, 36, 37, 45
 and sexual response patterns, 36, 37,
  44–46
Sexual dysfunction, female, 274–298
 age differences, compared with men,
  276
 changing expectations, 274, 291, 292
 childhood trauma, 279
 current concepts, 275–278
 definition, 275
 inhibited sexual desire, 285, 286
 laboratory analogue studies, 286–293
  anxiety, 286–288, 295
  distraction, 288, 289
  fantasy, 292, 293
  focus of attention, 289, 290
  guilt/repression, 290, 291
  married compared with unmarried
   women, 292
 Masters and Johnson, 275, 286
 organic compared with psychogenic, 276
 orgasmic dysfunction/anorgasmia, 46,
  280–284, 294, 295
 partner's role, 279, 280
 penetration problems, 284, 285
 rape, 278, 279
 sex therapy with applied
  psychophysiology, 293–298
 vaginal lubrication, 277
 vasocongestion, pelvic, 277, 278
Sexual dysfunction, male, 244–273
 age differences, compared with women,
  276
 biofeedback, 269, 270
 definitions, 244, 245
 ejaculation
  premature, 246, 257, 258, 271
  retarded, 258, 259
 inhibited desire, 259, 260, 272
 laboratory studies, 260–269
  anxiety, 263–265, 268, 269, 272
  attention, 265–269, 272
  distraction, 261–263, 268, 269, 272
  visual feedback, 74, 268

treatment, 269–273
usual compared with persistent problems, 245
see also Penis, erectile dysfunction
Sexual experience and erotica, 199, 200
Sexual response, hormonal, 166–168, 183–186
Sexual response patterns, 23–52, 318–321, 327
  autonomic variables, 30, 31
  cognitive labeling/subjective experience, 26–29
  components of, and interactive mechanisms, 33–37
  defining, 24–26
  extragenital, 109, 110, 130
  future research directions, 337–339
  habituation, 47–50
  historical background, 24, 25
  individual-specific response (ISR), 32, 51, 111, 119, 335–337, 339
  instrumental conditioning, 48, 50
  models, 38–44, 51
    four-stage (Masters and Johnson), 39–41, 44
    three-stage (Kaplan), 41–44
    two-stage (Ellis), 38, 39, 43, 51
  motivation-specific response (MSR), 30, 111
  sexually dysfunctional individuals, 36, 37, 44–46
  stimulus-specific response (SSR), 29, 30, 32, 51, 110, 111, 114, 130, 132, 135
  voluntary control, 50
  women, physiology, 84–87
Simultaneous orgasm, 134
Singer, I., 139–141
Skin potential responses (SPRs), 112, 114, 132; see also Galvanic skin response (GSR)
Sleep
  apnea and NPT, 253
  non-REM, sexual arousal, 114
  REM, 23, 64, 69, 88, 97, 114, 130, 170, 247, 250, 253
Spironolactone, 322
Statistical analysis, 131, 336
Status orgasmus, 138, 139, 141
Stimulus fading, 239, 240
Stimulus-specific response (SSR)
  patterning, 29, 30, 32, 51, 110, 111, 114, 130, 132, 335

Strain gauge. See under Blood flow measurement, penis
Stretch reflex, 149
Studies in the Psychology of Sex (Ellis), 3, 7
Subjective arousal
  and penile blood flow, 72–75
  and vaginal vasocongestion, 103–106
Subjective changes, orgasm, 152–157
Subjective experience/cognitive labeling, sexual response patterns, 26–29
Subjective reports, response to erotica, 190–192
Subject selection/bias, 350, 351; see also Human subjects research

Temperature
  extragenital, 121–123, 131, 132
  vaginal, 98–101, 107
Testes, 54, 56, 57, 159, 160
Testosterone, 159, 161–168, 171–173, 175, 177, 178, 181, 182, 184
  antihypertensives and, 320, 321
  heroin and, 317
  marihuana and, 314
  in menopause, 181–183
  NPT, 163–166
  paraphilias, 218
  psychophysiology, 163–166
  and sexual response, 166–168
Thermistor
  clitoral, 95
  labial, 95–97
  penile, 69, 70
  vaginal, 97, 98
Thiazide diuretics, 321
Thioridazine (Mellaril), 322, 323
Thousand and One Nights, The, 189
Tonometer, buckling, 68
Transsexuals, 231, 234
Transvestitism, 213, 214, 223, 234, 235, 238, 243
Tricyclic antidepressants, 323, 324
Triggers, orgasm, 148–151, 157
Tumescence. See Erection, penile (tumescence)
Type A personality and erotica, 200

Ulcer drugs, 324, 325
Uterus, 83
  contractions, 89
  orgasm, 101, 102, 139–141

Vagina, 82
  blood flow, compared with penis, 71
  glass observation tube (Dickinson), 10,
    13
Vaginal blood volume (VBV), 123
  in menstrual cycle, 177
  photoplethysmography, 89–92, 96, 103,
    104, 106
  and sexual dysfunction, 283, 295
Vaginal compared with clitoral orgasm, 6,
  41
Vaginal lubrication, 85, 100, 277
Vaginal probe amplitude (VPA)
  alcohol effects, 306, 307
  erotica, responses to, 195, 197
  in menopause, 179–182
  in menstrual cycle, 176, 177
  photoplethysmography, 89, 90, 94, 96,
    102–106
  and sexual dysfunction, 281–283,
    289–293, 295–297
Vaginal vasocongestion, measures, 85–107,
    122, 277, 278
  clitoral enlargement, 88, 89
  historical background, 88, 89
  orgasm, sequential, 100, 101
  compared with other measures, 101, 102
  oxygenation measures, 98–101, 107
  photoplethysmography, 89–95, 103
  and subjective arousal, 103–106
  thermistors, 95–98

Vaginismus, 284, 285
Van de Velde, Theodoor, 11, 134
Vas deferens, anatomy, 54, 57
Vasoactive intestinal peptide (VIP), 60
Vasocongestion. *See* Vaginal
    vasocongestion, measures
Vestibule, anatomy, 79, 80
Victim response, pornography, 206
Violence, paraphilias, 225, 226; *see also*
    Pornography, violent
Visual feedback, erection, 74, 268
von Ebner pads, 57, 58, 60, 86
Voyeurism, 214

Watson, John B., 14, 15, 19, 343, 345
Wolpe, J., 15, 16
Women
  alcohol effects on sexual function,
    306–309
  ejaculation, 78, 84, 140, 141
  genital anatomy, overview, 79–83
  masturbation, 8, 10, 11
  postmenopausal, hormone replacement
    therapy, 277
  response to pornography, 209
  sexual response, physiology, 84–87; *see
    also* Vaginal *entries*
  see also Female sexuality; Orgasm,
    female; Sexual dysfunction, female;
    Vagina *entries*

DATE DUE